ADOLESCENT PSYCHIATRY

DEVELOPMENTAL AND CLINICAL STUDIES

VOLUME 19

ADOLESCENT PSYCHIATRY

DEVELOPMENTAL AND CLINICAL STUDIES

VOLUME 19

Edited by
SHERMAN C. FEINSTEIN
Editor in Chief

RICHARD C. MAROHN
Coeditor

Senior Editors
AARON H. ESMAN
HARVEY A. HOROWITZ
JOHN G. LOONEY
GEORGE H. ORVIN
ALLAN Z. SCHWARTZBERG
ARTHUR D. SOROSKY
MAX SUGAR

The University of Chicago Press
Chicago and London

The University of Chicago Press, Chicago 60637
The University of Chicago Press, Ltd., London

International Standard Book Number: 0-226-24065-7
Library of Congress Catalog Card Number: 70-147017

The paper used in this publication meets the minimum requirements of American National Standard for Information Sciences—Permanence of Paper for Printed Library Materials, ANSI Z39.48-1984. ♾ ™

CONTENTS

PART III. DEVELOPMENTAL ISSUES IN ADOLESCENT PSYCHIATRY

PART IV. PSYCHOPATHOLOGY IN ADOLESCENT EMOTIONAL DISORDERS

PRESIDENT'S PREFACE

It is my pleasant duty as current ASAP President to write a brief introduction for this nineteenth volume of *Adolescent Psychiatry*. The *Adolescent Psychiatry* volumes are distributed worldwide, and it was a delight on a recent visit to the shrine of Pinel to find a complete set in the library of the Adolescent Psychiatry Department at Salpetriere. I am indebted to Professors Michel Basquin and Philippe Jeammet for their courtesy and hospitality in Paris and to my good friend Dr. Hervé Benhamou.

Nothing endures but change and challenge. At this volume goes to press, a general insecurity is in the air amid promised plans for a changing medical delivery system in the United States. Our published store of psychiatric knowledge in these volumes has the power to dispel the myths and fallacies that exist about the practice of our profession and in particular in defining quality psychiatric care for adolescents. It is crucial that we integrate all our knowledge and experience in dynamic psychiatry with our greater insight into biological processes, being careful that we achieve this in a properly balanced form. At times one senses a developing imbalance with more focus on biological issues, provoking, for example, the question of whether the increasing use of pharmacotherapy at the expense of psychotherapy in the treatment of adolescents reflects improved biotechnology or economic factors in a changing health care delivery system with so-called managed care. Procedural rather than cognitive processes are at a premium, while dynamic psychiatry may be devalued or overwhelmed with ignorance. Our current diagnostic and statistical manual, DSM-III-R, seems increasingly used by some as a diagnostic cookbook with recipes lacking the zest of the psychoanalytic tradition. Some departments of psychiatry are referring to themselves as departments of be-havior medicine with the appearance of interest in motor rather than sensory phenomena, long on brain chemistry and scientific measure-ment and short on mind, soul, and common sense, the latter described by Amherst in 1726: "There is not a more uncommon thing in the world than common sense—the faculty to discern one thing from another and the ordinary ability to keep ourselves from being imposed upon by gross contradictions, palpable inconsistencies, and unmasked im-posture."

Thankfully, we can face the challenges ahead with optimism, know-ing that an experienced psychiatric clinician with a background of pro-fessional knowledge, as illustrated in these volumes, is a vastly more humane, accurate, and cost effective instrument for diagnosis and treatment of the adolescent than all the questionnaires, computer-administered inventories, or dexamethasone suppression procedures.

CHARLES MCCAFFERTY

IN MEMORIAM

This volume of *Adolescent Psychiatry* is dedicated to the memory of Roy R. Grinker, Sr., who died on May 9, 1993, at the age of ninety-two. A psychiatric educator, researcher, and clinician of wide renown, Professor Grinker was most interested in the emotional problems of children and adolescents. In a forward manner, he suggested that an adolescent treatment program be developed in the Psychosomatic and Psychiatric Institute, Michael Reese Hospital, Chicago, of which he was Director in 1956. Subsequently, he encouraged the development of *Adolescent Psychiatry,* to which he contributed a number of papers and served as a consultant to the editor in chief over the years. Under his leadership, a number of adolescent research programs were stimulated at Michael Reese: normal adolescent development, adolescent affective disorders, eating disorders, day treatments, and, with the Illinois State Psychiatric Institute, a study of violence and juvenile delinquency.

Professor Grinker had great disdain for imprecision and fuzzy thinking and believed that much metapsychology was unscientific and counterproductive. He maintained an active, lifelong participation in clinical research and confronted issues that were controversial, sometimes with lacerating perspective. Roy Grinker never left the questions to be answered in doubt and made a deep impact that was never forgotten by those privileged to study and work under his tutelage.

SHERMAN C. FEINSTEIN AND RICHARD C. MAROHN

PART I

ADOLESCENCE: GENERAL CONSIDERATIONS

EDITORS' INTRODUCTION

A career in adolescent psychiatry involves the consideration of many interesting and challenging issues, a number of which are presented in this opening section of our nineteenth volume. The chapters by this group of pioneers present a panoply that illustrates again why adolescent psychiatry has become such an interest area that it is currently considered a specific developmental phase.

Aaron H. Esman describes how, felicitously, Sigmund Freud and adolescent psychiatry arrived on these shores at about the same time. G. Stanley Hall, president of Clark University and professor of psychology, had organized an international scientific conference and invited Freud as a speaker in 1909. Five years earlier, in 1904, Hall had published his massive work on adolescence and proposed the "Sturm und Drang" theory of adolescence. In this version of development, the normal adolescent was seen as tempestuous, passionate, impulsive, rebellious, and affectively dominated. Relations with parents were conflictual, and the adult world was avoided and misunderstood. This led behavioral scientists to insist on the presence of a "generation gap," and the goal of education was to raise the adolescent to the level of civilized versus primitive thinking. Hall saw adolescence as a magical period, a growth spurt inducted by puberty, a recapitulation of early development.

Ghislaine D. Godenne describes how education plays a role in all aspects of an adolescent's life. She recalls her early professional life and the influence of her family on community service. She illustrates how a leader's reaction is introjected and becomes part of a young person's value system. She sees adolescents who are involved with a worthwhile project as "tireless, energetic, generous, and self-

3

sacrificing.'' Godenne writes that, before dealing with the formal aspects of education, the education received from one's parents is crucial. Parents must be consistent, sensitive, but at the same time open. Identity development is critical and focuses on three areas: ego identity; self-identity; and the establishment of a meaning in life. Sexual education is fundamentally a parental responsibility and should result in a comfortable ability to communicate about sexual issues. Godenne concludes that the bases of education have remained stable over the centuries while the acquisition of knowledge fluctuates. Social reality, however, changes through education.

Max Sugar discusses the need for a formal education as part of the acquisition of self-sufficiency and equilibrium and the changes in society that make this increasingly difficult to achieve. A century ago, many careers did not require much education but benefited from apprenticeship opportunities; more recently, the problems of poverty and education involve alcohol and drug abuse, dropouts, dangerousness of attending school, crime, low test scores, and excess television and sexuality. In this chapter, Sugar focuses on perinatal factors: the family, the children, the government, schools, emotional issues, protective factors, and outcome. He considers the risks for respiratory distress syndrome, prematurity, and learning disability from lead poisoning, maternal malnutrition, and infections of importance but points out that fetal alcohol syndrome is the simple largest preventable cause of mental retardation. Sugar concludes that major problems exist in the challenge of raising healthy children and sees poverty, family dysfunction, governmental ambivalence, educational incompetence, and emotional disorder in young people as critical factors. On the other hand, he outlines areas and programs that present hope for the future.

Vivian M. Rakoff discusses the development of new capacities in adolescents that were foreshadowed in childhood. These new-found talents arrive with amazing intensity, particularly in the areas of mathematical and poetic creativity, and it is the sense of newness and freshness that is characteristic of the adolescent. Rakoff, however, questions the truth of the creative impulse and warns that few adolescent productions are truly original or memorable. Using the biographies of two productive adolescents (Thomas Chatterton and Arthur Rimbaud), Rakoff shows how the young person, armed with talent, sees the world as though for the first time.

Marshall Korenblum writes that adolescents pose particular problems for clinicians trying to diagnose psychopathology. The reasons for this are numerous but can be understood as relating to two factors—the data-gathering (assessment) process itself and the classification system (DSM-III/DSM-III-R). The former involves four different sources of unreliability: patient variables; interviewer variables; family variables; and sociocultural variables. The latter can be critiqued for lacking a developmental perspective. Through a literature review and the inclusion of recent empirical research data, Korenblum examines issues of state versus trait, longitudinal studies of personality development, structured interviews, assessment alliance, parent-child diagnostic disagreements, countertransference in the assessor, family dynamics, and typical resistances as they relate to diagnosis in adolescence. Recommendations for future improvements are made in the areas of residency training and history taking, and some novel modifications to the nosology are suggested in relation to preparing for DSM-IV.

1 G. STANLEY HALL
AND THE INVENTION
OF ADOLESCENCE

AARON H. ESMAN

In 1904, G. Stanley Hall (fig. 1), president of and professor of psychology at Clark University, published a massive two-volume tome under the imposing title of *Adolescence: Its Psychology and Its Relations to Physiology, Anthropology, Sociology, Sex, Crime, Religion, and Education* (fig. 2). Hall's encyclopedic study, the first of its kind, became the established source for conceptualization and description of adolescent behavior for generations to come. In particular, Hall's model of adolescent "Sturm und Drang," along with European Romantic fiction as typified by Goethe's *Sorrows of Young Werther,* became the prototype for later psychiatric and psychoanalytic representations of pubertal and postpubertal development. Hall spoke of the adolescent's "alternation between inertia and excitement, pleasure and pain, self-confidence and humility, selfishness and altruism, society and solitude, sensitiveness and dullness, knowing and doing, conservatism and iconoclasm, sense and intellect" (1904, 1:40). The normal adolescent was conceived of as tempest tossed, torn by unmanageable passions, impulsive, rebellious, and given to florid swings of mood. Adolescents' relations with parents and the adult world in general were seen as antagonistic and conflict ridden—a pattern later to be designated as "the generation gap." As Friedenberg later put it, "Adolescence *is* conflict—protracted conflict—between the individual and society" (1959, p. 32).

The force of Hall's authority determined the dominance of this view-

FIG. 1.—G. Stanley Hall, Ph.D.

point for several decades. It is worthy of note, incidentally, that the words "adolescence" and "adolescent" appeared only late in the psychoanalytic literature. In the "Three Essays" of 1905, Freud spoke about the "transformations of puberty." August Aichhorn, who has come to be regarded as the pioneer in the psychoanalytic study of adolescence, spoke of "the child," "the boy," "the girl," "the delinquent"; he spoke, of course, of "puberty." But the word "adolescent" does not appear in his *Wayward Youth,* published in 1925. In *The Ego and the Mechanisms of Defense* (1936), Anna Freud uses the terms "puberty" and "adolescence" more or less interchangeably. Not until Siegfried Bernfeld's essay of 1938—"Types of Adolescence"—did the term begin to occupy a defined place in the psychoanalytic lexicon.

ADOLESCENCE

ITS

PSYCHOLOGY

AND ITS RELATIONS TO

PHYSIOLOGY, ANTHROPOLOGY, SOCIOLOGY
SEX, CRIME, RELIGION

AND

EDUCATION

BY

G. STANLEY HALL, Ph.D., LL.D.

PRESIDENT OF CLARK UNIVERSITY AND PROFESSOR OF
PSYCHOLOGY AND PEDAGOGY

VOLUME I

NEW YORK AND LONDON
D. APPLETON AND COMPANY
1928

FIG. 2.—Title page of Hall's *Adolescence* (1904)

Hall's picture of "normal adolescent turmoil" was sustained a half century after his writing by Anna Freud, who, in a series of papers (A. Freud 1958, 1969), spoke of adolescence as a "developmental disturbance" and declared that it was frequently impossible to distinguish aspects of normal adolescent behavior from severe psychopathology of the neurotic, borderline, or even psychotic type. "I take it," she said, "that it is normal for an adolescent to behave for a considerable length of time in an inconsistent and unpredictable manner; to fight his impulses and to accept them; to ward them off successfully and to be overrun by them; to love his parents and to hate them; to revolt against them and to be dependent on them; to be deeply ashamed to acknowledge his mother before others and, unexpectedly, to desire heart to heart talks with her; to thrive on imitation of and identification with others while searching unceasingly for his own identity; to be more idealistic, artistic, generous, and unselfish than he will ever be again, and also the opposite: self-centered, egoistic, calculating" (1958, p. 275).

Note here Miss Freud's emulation, doubtless unconscious, of Hall's dualistic style, characterizing the adolescent in paired opposites, suggesting a dialectical mode of thought that, as we shall see, grew directly out of critical elements of Hall's educational experience.

It was not until the 1960s that Hall's (and Miss Freud's) characterization was subjected to the serious challenge of systematic studies of normal populations; these, by such as Adelson, Offer, and others, have led to a major reassessment of the concept of "normal adolescent turmoil" and a more balanced view of the developmental course of young people observed in nonclinical settings. It has become clear that most adolescents manage to weather this developmental transition without major disruption and with little of the turbulence that Hall described.

Who then was G. Stanley Hall? How to account for the enormous and persistent influence of his pioneering work and for the content of his ideas both about adolescent development and about the proper education and training of the young? To most people today, Hall is remembered primarily as the man responsible for bringing Sigmund Freud, along with Jung and Ferenczi, to Clark University in Worcester, Massachusetts, where Freud delivered his now famous 1909 lectures on psychoanalysis (fig. 3). Hall was in fact one of Freud's earliest and most ardent adherents in the United States and was president of the American Psychoanalytic Association in 1917 and 1918. By that time, however, his devotion had begun to waver, and he soon parted company with Freud, as had many others, over the issues of sexual symbolism and infantile sexuality, preferring Adlerian ideas that fit more comfortably into his own psychological system.

But Hall's importance, and his role in defining or inventing adolescence as a discrete stage of development, far transcended his relationship to psychoanalysis. Hall was, along with William James, the founder of psychology as a scientific discipline in the United States. He was responsible for the foundation of the child study movement, organized the American Psychological Association, and was the founding editor of the *American Journal of Psychology*. Ultimately, he became the first president and guiding spirit of Clark University, which continues to this day to bear his imprint as a major center for education in psychology.

9

Fig. 3.—Freud and his colleagues at Clark University, 1909. Front row: Sigmund Freud, G. Stanley Hall, Carl Jung. Back row: A. A. Brill, Ernest Jones, Sandor Ferenczi.

Hall was, in fact, a prototypical figure in the transition from the nineteenth century to the twentieth in America, from the Victorian era to the modern in critical aspects of moral and educational philosophy. G. (for Granville) Stanley Hall was born in Ashfield in northwestern Massachusetts in 1844, of old but economically straitened Puritan stock. His father was a farmer and sometime preacher, an austere, demanding, moralistic man with whom Stanley never achieved a gratifying relationship and toward whom he felt both inferior and guiltily hostile. His mother was typically gentler, nurturing, and supportive of his intellectual and artistic interests. All this was a perfect breeding ground for a powerful oedipal conflict that colored Hall's early years, at least, and that powerfully shaped his emotional and intellectual development.

Obviously bright and driven by intense, oedipally charged ambition, Hall went off to nearby Williams College with a formal intention to fulfill his mother's hopes that he become a theologian and preacher. In the context of his first anxious separation from his family, and under the influence of the prevailing doctrinal ethos, he underwent a religious conversion or "rebirth" experience in his freshman year. This experience, although short lived, seems to have served as a prototype for one of his later views of normative expectations; in his book, he devotes a great deal of attention to the notion that such conversion experience (Christian, of course) is to be expected and fostered in all normal adolescents.

In the intellectual spheres, however, Hall got caught up in the study of philosophy, as personified by Mark Hopkins, then the president of Williams and a noted educator and spokesman for traditional Protestant values. At that time, the capstone course for all Williams seniors was a course in moral and intellectual philosophy taught by Hopkins (Frederick Rudolph, personal communication, March 18, 1992). Graduating, then, with a special interest in philosophy, Hall had no place to go in the United States to pursue his intellectual goals; submitting to this reality, to financial need, and to his family's wishes, he moved to New York to study at the Union Theological Seminary. Drawn to the rich cultural opportunities New York offered him and to the courses in philosophy available both at Union and nearby Columbia, Hall became increasingly fixed in his aim to become a professor of philosophy and succeeded in obtaining a grant that enabled him to fulfill the dream of every aspiring philosopher of that day—a year of study in Germany. In June 1869, off he went.

And there his future was determined. Within the discipline of philosophy, the new science of psychology was beginning to take shape in Germany. The fathers of this burgeoning infant were such now-legendary figures as Herbart, Wundt, and Helmholtz, all of whom professed an antispeculative, empirical approach to problems of mind and whose work infused in Hall a profound conviction that the real issues in philosophy were psychological rather than metaphysical. Two major threads came to dominate the fabric of his thought: (1) Wundt's devotion to the experimental method and (2) Haeckel's "recapitulationist" concept of development—"ontogeny recapitulates phylogeny."

Recapitulation in this context was meant not only in the embryological sense but also in that of psychological and social development as well—that is, the individual progresses through all the earlier or more "primitive" stages of mental and social development. Thus, Hall espoused the often-encountered equation of the child's mind with that of the "savage." Indeed, in Hall's "anthropology," "most savages in most respects are children, or, because of sexual maturity, adolescents of adult size"; patronizingly, "to know a typical savage is to love him" (Hall 1904, 2:649). He was a profound believer in the "white man's burden" of care and protection of the "adolescent races." The notion that correlates with this is, of course, that the task of Western education is to civilize the child and to raise him to the higher levels of mental functioning associated with "civilized" as opposed to "primitive" life. This, in essence, became the keystone to the arch of Hall's professional career as pedagogue and educational theoretician.

I will not trace out all the further peregrinations of Hall's complex life story. Suffice it to say that, after fifteen months in Germany, he returned to Union Theological, got his degree, did a lot of job hunting, went off to Antioch College, and then obtained various appointments at Harvard, where, under the tutelage of William James, he obtained his Ph.D. in 1879. According to Ross (1969), this was the first such degree awarded by Harvard's philosophy department and the first in the field of psychology to be given in this country anywhere. That summer, Hall returned to Germany for his second period of study and immersion in the new German theories that were to cement his identity as a scientific psychologist.

Equally fateful was his encounter—or reencounter—with a young woman he had met in his Antioch period. He had been a late bloomer in relations with women, but, like many repressed young Americans, he found in the freer air of Europe the possibility of expanding this side of his life, and in September 1879, at age thirty-five, he married a Miss Fisher, before returning to the United States and the beginnings of his career as psychologist and pedagogue. Between 1880 and 1890, he succeeded in becoming one of the major figures in the intellectual life of the United States, stimulating new aims and directions in education and in the empirical study of child development. Thus, by 1904, when at age sixty his book on adolescence appeared, when he was already president of Clark and the preeminent figure in American psychology, his authority was tremendous, and the reverberations of his powerfully and volubly argued ideas were heard in Europe as well. It was as though Hall had discovered a new continent, laden with gold and spices; others rushed in to explore it, to mine its riches, and to help in civilizing the natives. Typical was the little book published in London in 1911 by one J. W. Slaughter (1911), a psychologist trained, apparently, by Hall but working in London. The book is admittedly an attempt to distill Hall's massive opus into a 100-page handbook for those for whom "Dr. Hall's work is somewhat inaccessible." It was reprinted at least twice, so it evidently had respectable sales among educators and others charged with the care of young people. (It might be of interest that my copy of Hall's book was obtained in London and had previously belonged to a distinguished British psychiatrist of the preceding generation.)

What then were Hall's ideas about adolescence? For Hall, adolescence was an almost magical period, idealized as the peak epoch of human development, ushered in by the "spurt of growth in body, mind, and feelings" induced by puberty. To quote him (and to give a sense of his dithyrambic language), "The flood gates of heredity seem opened and we hear from our remote forebears, and receive our life dower of energy. . . . Passions and desires spring into vigorous life" (Hall 1904, 1:308). In this, one can hear the reverberations of his recapitulationist concept of development.

As Ross (1969) points out, the dichotomies that characterize the description of adolescence that I cited earlier reflect the influence of the Hegelian dialectic Hall had learned in his German period. It was these antitheses that accounted for the constant stress, the Sturm und Drang he saw as inherent in adolescence as it struggled toward the

13

mature synthesis that would conclude the dialectic process of development as he conceived it: "The dawn of puberty . . . is soon followed by a stormy period of great agitation, when the very best and very worst impulses in the human soul struggle against each other for its possession, and where there is peculiar proneness to be very good or very bad" (Hall 1904, 2:407). As Isaiah Berlin (1991) puts it, "Without conflict, struggle, strife (so Hegel tells us), progress ceases, stagnation sets in" (p. 198). Since struggle was the key to full realization of developmental potential, however, Hall advocated its prolongation as far as was possible. True to his dialectic persuasion, he advocated, on the one hand, a degree of "freedom that leans a little toward license" (Hall 1904, 2:91) but, on the other, a substantial degree of control, inhibition, and suppression. With respect to sexuality, which at times he could wax rhapsodically about, he nonetheless urged its rigorous control, which would lead to its "irradiation" to higher endeavors—much in the vein of Freud's concept of sublimation.

About one aspect of sexuality Hall was clear and categorical, and that was masturbation. For all his efforts at modernity, Hall was firmly aligned with prevailing authoritative views on this subject, and they were uniformly negative. Thus, Hall refers to masturbation consistently as "unnatural," "scourge of the human race," a "disease," "this perversion," "evil," and "the vice" of which the majority of adolescents are, unfortunately, "guilty." Masturbation stunts the growth, impairs the heredity, lowers self-esteem, and induces depression, epilepsy, "sluggishness of heart action and circulation," cowardice, egotism, and innumerable other ills to which, unfortunately, the flesh is heir. He devotes pages to methods for preventing and curing this "vice."

About sex, Hall could, as noted, express himself ecstatically: "In [the sexual organs] and their function, life reaches its maximal intensity and performs its supreme function. The *vita sexualis* is normally a magnificent symphony, the rich and varied orchestration of which brings the individual into the closest rapport with the great Biologos" (Hall 1904, 2:413). Nonetheless, despite this effusive rhetoric, Hall was firm in his insistence that sexual intercourse should, like all other aspects of adult life, be postponed as long as possible: "The most rigid chastity of fancy, heart and body is physiologically and psychologically, as well as ethically imperative until maturity is complete on into the twenties" (Hall 1904, 2:120–121). The usual prescriptions—cold baths, hard work, athletics, etc.—were recommended to ensure the chastity he demanded.

For Hall, the ultimate aim of this rechanneling of sexual energies, the highest achievement of adolescent "irradiation," was religious conversion—the experience, that is, of an ecstatic spiritual epiphany that would set the adolescent definitively on the road of higher morality and religious consciousness. As noted, it need hardly be said that this was to be a Christian rebirth, although Hall's version of Christianity was closer to pantheism than to a traditional belief in a personified deity. He was strongly opposed to religious dogmatism: "Where the clay of dogma is stamped down too hard about the roots of the growing soul either the latter is arrested or else doctrines are ruptured" (Hall 1904, 2:317). He understood and sympathized with the natural skepticism of youth, seeing it as an aspect of the "rapid expansion of the mental horizon" that was characteristic of adolescence.

Still, the "irradiation" or sublimation of adolescent sexuality into religious experience was, for Hall, the guarantee of attaining "full ethical maturity," an altruistic concern for the future of the race, the ultimate achievement of civilization. For Hall, life after adolescence, although open for sexual experience, was clearly a downhill course; adolescence was the "golden stage when life glisters and crepitates," "the apical stage of human development before the decline of the highest powers in maturity and old age" (Hall 1904, 2:131, 361). As Ross (1969) puts it, "Maturity might be acceptable for most people, Hall implied, but for the elite, it was not the goal; 'the orderly, regular life of maturity involves necessarily more or less degeneration. . . . the best definition of genius is intensified and prolonged adolescence' " (p. 332).

Where did all this come from? It certainly did not come from any systematic scientific study of adolescents from either a clinical or an epidemiological perspective. Hall's book was the product of a decade's effort to integrate a multiplicity of threads into a grand conceptual design, a gesture of release from his earlier, unsuccessful efforts to develop a psychology based, after the new German model, on laboratory experiment. As I stated earlier, a major influence was the late Romantic German philosophy he had imbibed in his student years, particularly its emphasis on the centrality of conflict, struggle, and the power of the passions—the same philosophical *Weltanschauung* that shaped Freud's thought. Since for Hall adolescence was par excellence the time of growth and developmental progress, conflict and struggle were axiomatic.

But paramount among these threads was Hall's own personal experience, his own tortuous developmental history, and his personal situation as he wrote. Hall was in his fifties when he began working on *Adolescence* and sixty when it was published. He had lived through a series of personal crises in recent years—the loss of his wife and child in a fire, the near collapse of Clark University, his institutional child, and repeated disappointments in his scientific work. It seems evident that his picture of maturity as a time of degeneration and failing powers reflected his own subjective state and that the book was an effort at restoration and recuperation from a depressive response to his sea of troubles. It was as though by identifying himself with his idealized subjects he sought to recover some of the vitality, energy, and drive he ascribed to youth.

His conflicting views of sexuality similarly communicate his own conflicted experience. As Kett (1977) states, "In his boyhood home the genitals were always referred to as 'the dirty place,' and he recalled wrapping his penis in bandages at night to prevent emissions" (p. 220). This self-imposed continence was a metaphor for the course of his own sexual development: a profound struggle against his sexual impulses and masturbatory urges throughout his adolescence and a release only in the freer—and geographically remote—air of Europe, where he was finally able, as late as thirty-five, to marry and achieve the kind of ecstatic sexual gratification he so lyrically described in his writings. His own life, that is, formed the model for this prescription of adolescent chastity and continence, for deferral of sexual activity until "maturity."

Of course, Hall's recommendations were, in most respects, in tune with his times. The puritanical sex manuals that were a staple of Victorian and Edwardian literature were unanimous in their denunciations of masturbation and their dire predictions of its outcome. Hall's Williams mentor, Mark Hopkins, "lectured to the college on its evils and distributed among the students copies of Samuel Woodward's 'Hints for the Young in Relation to the Health of Body and Mind,' a handbook on the subject, its consequences and its sinfulness" (Rudolph 1956, p. 122). All these authorities were, of course, correct in contending that masturbation might adversely affect the young person's self-esteem; like them, however, Hall omitted the role of the intervening variable represented by the influence of unremitting denunciation of the practice. Even in his early views of neurosogenesis Freud attributed what he called the "actual neuroses"—anxiety neurosis, neurasthenia—to "unhealthy" sexual practices, including masturbation.

The notion of the prolongation of adolescence also reflects both Hall's personal experience and prevailing social trends. Hall's own adolescence was protracted indeed, not only as to his sexuality, but also as to his vocational and spiritual directions. He floundered for years between theology and philosophy, between traditional New England Protestantism and the "scientific," pantheistic, post-Darwinian religion he finally arrived at. Issues that most young men in his time resolved in their teens Hall continued to struggle with well into his thirties.

At the same time, however, middle-class America was becoming increasingly concerned about its youthful population. A primary cause of this concern was the growing urbanization of society, as the industrial revolution pulled more and more people away from the farm and into the factories of the old and newly growing cities of the Northeast and Midwest. By the close of the nineteenth century, adolescents were becoming more and more a visible and definable social group. Such problems as delinquency and juvenile crime were of increasing public concern, and such adolescent institutions as the public high school and boys' clubs were emerging into prominence. There was much apprehension about the corrosive effects of the city on the moral fiber of youths, about the melting away of traditional rural values in the crucible of urban seductions. In Hall's view, the prolongation of adolescence, the extension of the period of education, training, abstinence, and moral indoctrination, would help protect and insulate the vulnerable young against these siren calls and help bring them to safe harbor.

It should surprise no one that the bulk of Hall's analysis and prescription dealt with the adolescent male. In fact, he devoted just one long chapter—right before one on "primitive cultures"—to the adolescent girl and her education. In many respects, that so little of his attention is devoted to girls and their development bespeaks both his ambivalence on the subject and the transitional state of cultural attitudes at the dawn of the century. Women are "superior" creatures, "at the top of the human curve," closer to "the race" than males. Hall is silent on their sexuality but believes that they should be permitted to "lie fallow" during their menstrual periods. The bulk of his argument is given over to a conventional, if florid, exploration of the role of woman as mother, nurturer, and homemaker. At the same time, however, he is clearly conscious of and tentatively favorably disposed toward the "newer" roles of educated women as professionals. He comes out clearly in favor of coeducation (except around puberty) but regretfully cites statistics that show a lower rate of child bearing for the graduates of the new elite women's colleges. In the end, he sets forth in extensive detail a model curriculum for the education of women (obviously middle- and upper-class white women) that emphasizes a broad exposure to the humanities (excluding Greek and Latin, which would, he said, be useless for them) but that also includes formal education for motherhood and child rearing.

Thus, as Ross (1969) makes clear, "Hall's development of a concept of adolescence . . . was part of his solution—an extremely creative solution—to a set of personal conflicts which had been reinforced by the specialization of occupational roles and the rigidly differentiated sex roles of Victorian culture" (p. 339); "the storm and stress, the ambivalence, the sublimation, the prolonged effort to find a vocation which would create the broadest possible unity among his divergent impulses, all these elements of Hall's experience were related to those conditions and were echoed in his theory" (p. 338).

But what relevance does all this have for us today? Is Hall's vision still alive, ninety years later? I would suggest that it is very much so and that both the popular and the professional views of adolescence remain strongly influenced by it. Hall's view that puberty initiates revolutionary changes in character and behavior survives in the popular imagination. The stereotype of universal "storm and stress" or "normal adolescent turmoil" persists even among professionals who should know better. Thus, one still hears the question, "Is this psychopathology or just normal adolescence?" in clinical discussions of severely disturbed, even psychotic or antisocial teenagers. In the same vein, one still hears, "Well, he'll grow out of it," as though adolescence were a disease cured by time. One is reminded here of James Masterson's dictum that the burden of proof lies with anyone who says of an emotionally disturbed adolescent that "he'll grow out of it" (Masterson 1968).

But, even further, Hall's ambivalence about adolescent sexuality is reflected in persisting cultural attitudes today. One cannot, of course, blame Hall for this; powerful forces in the culture conspire to maintain these attitudes, just as they did in Hall's time. But we see every day the paradox of idealization and romanticization of sex and the stimulation of adolescent sexuality in the media side by side with the fierce denunciation of adolescent sexuality by religious and political leaders, who still seem to believe that it can be controlled by legislation or sermonizing. Thus, just as did Hall, these authorities call for abstinence and the pursuit of "higher" aims as their solutions to the problems of adolescent pregnancy and sexually transmitted diseases. They seek, that is, to reverse history, to return to the official morality of Hall's time—a morality that, as Peter Gay, Steven Marcus, and others have shown us, was a hypocritical mask that covered many of the same problems with which we struggle more openly today.

Finally, Hall's prescription for the indefinite prolongation of adolescence has been substantially realized in our time, at least in Western culture. Not as to sexuality, perhaps, but as to vocational choice, independent living, marital commitment—in general, the deferral of what have been regarded as the marks of full adult status in society. And not only here in the United States—a recent French observer (Collange 1988) noted, with some asperity, that 76 percent of eighteen-to twenty-five-year-olds in her country were living "under the parental roof." Again, the causes go far beyond Hall—economic forces, technology, and large social movements are at play here—but Hall's vision was a prophetic one. In defining and codifying adolescence, in giving it a name and a set of defining lineaments, Hall set the stage and provided the characters for the plot that history has written. To that extent, then, all of us who conceive of ourselves as specialists in the study, understanding, and care of adolescents walk in his shadow.

NOTE

Louise J. Kaplan has covered somewhat similar ground as this chapter does in her book *Adolescence* (1984).

REFERENCES

Aichhorn, A. 1925. *Wayward Youth*. New York: Viking.
Berlin, I. 1991. *The Crooked Timber of Humanity*. New York: Knopf.
Bernfeld, S. 1938. Types of adolescence. *Psychoanalytic Quarterly* 7:243–253.

Collange, C. 1988. Today's adolescents. *International Annals of Adolescent Psychiatry* 1:1–4.

Freud, A. 1936. *The Ego and the Mechanisms of Defense*. New York: International Universities Press.

Freud, A. 1958. Adolescence. *Psychoanalytic Study of the Child* 13:255–278.

Freud, A. 1969. Adolescence as a developmental disturbance. In *The Writings of Anna Freud,* vol. 7. New York: International Universities Press.

Freud, S. 1905. Three essays on the theory of sexuality. *Standard Edition* 7:136–243. London: Hogarth, 1953.

Friedenberg, E. 1959. *The Vanishing Adolescent*. Boston: Beacon.

Hall, G. S. 1904. *Adolescence*. 2 vols. New York and London: Appleton.

Kaplan, Louise J. 1984. *Adolescence: The Farewell to Childhood*. New York: Simon & Schuster.

Kett, J. 1977. *Rites of Passage*. New York: Basic.

Masterson, J. 1968. The psychiatric significance of adolescent turmoil. *American Journal of Psychiatry* 124:1549–1554.

Ross, D. 1969. *G. Stanley Hall: The Psychologist as Prophet*. Chicago: University of Chicago Press.

Rudolph, F. 1956. *Mark Hopkins and the Log*. New Haven, Conn.: Yale University Press.

Slaughter, J. 1911. *The Adolescent*. London: Allen & Unwin.

2 EDUCATION AND SOCIAL REALITY: PRESENT AND FUTURE

GHISLAINE D. GODENNE

"Education is designed to socialize children to become productive contributors to society" (Leone and Richards 1989, pp. 531–532). Education starts at home, goes on in school, and is part of all youths' supervised or nonsupervised activities. Therefore, in the broad sense of the term, education plays a role in all aspects of an adolescent's life.

Almost forty years ago, when I arrived at the Mayo Clinic in Rochester, Minnesota, to start a pediatric fellowship, I was asked to organize a Mariner Girl Scout troop. I had been very active in Girl Guiding in my native Belgium and had started several troops. I confess that I was somewhat reluctant to spend once more the little time I had free from professional duties directing a troop. My upbringing, however, which stressed community service, made it impossible for me to turn down the request. Secretly, nevertheless, I was hoping that running a troop on a European model (with very definite and strict rules) would discourage girls from joining, and thus my conscience would not nag me. Little did I know at that time about the psychology of adolescence! At the first troop meeting fourteen girls showed up. After initial introductions, I explained what I expected of each girl. I told them to think about the commitment that they would have to make to the troop and that, if it was more than what they were willing to make, they should not join. I reassured them that my feelings would not be hurt if they did not return. I invited those who remained interested, now that they knew what was involved, to return the following week at the same day and time.

The following Monday, twenty-eight girls showed up. Each had brought a friend because this was going to be an exciting troop in which a lot would be expected from each of them. I immediately closed admissions for fear of getting even more girls at the following meeting. After dividing the girls into four patrols, we started playing a competitive game. To my horror many girls cheated. I was genuinely surprised, having only recently left Belgium, where a Girl Guide's honor is the most sacred thing she owns. I conveyed my surprise, shock, and disgust, and the girls left to return the following Monday. Once more we played a competitive game, but this time only one girl cheated, and I had to protect her from the ire of the others, who, convincingly, were loudly shouting, "How can you cheat and be a Girl Scout." An immediate identification can indeed take place when the leader is respected!

Through this short vignette I have attempted to illustrate how education takes place in all facets of the adolescent's life. Indeed, parents, teachers, ministers, group leaders, and psychotherapists are all figures that adolescents might want to emulate. In this instance, the leader's reaction to the girls' cheating brought them immediately to incorporate the leader's moral standard, which, even to win, does not allow compromise. In the example cited, the setting of strict rules appealed to these adolescent girls. They relished the idea that their troop was going to be hard and challenging and that their drives were going to have an outlet through constructive channels.

Outward Bound is another example of the appeal that strenuous and difficult tasks have for young people. They might experience fright, disappointment, and excitement, but, at the end of the experience, the adolescents who succeed gain a sense of pride and a significant boost to their self-esteem.

One more anecdote about the troop is worth mentioning. At the very first meeting, I promised to go "primitive camping" in early December. I obviously did not know that, in the winter, it snowed heavily in Minnesota and that, by early December, the campgrounds might well be under twelve feet of snow! However, when I suggested postponing the camping experience until better weather, the girls refused. I had promised, and, justifiably, they expected me to keep my word. So on the appointed night I walked to the campsite in order to be there before my troop and be able to greet them with a bonfire and hot chocolate. When, in a deep snow, I started walking toward the camp, I noticed footsteps partially covered by the falling snow. I wondered who had preceded me. To my surprise, when I reached the campsite, all my troop was there. They had built a bonfire and had hot chocolate ready to offer their foreign leader, who did not know that it snowed in Minnesota. Indeed, they had been given permission by their parents to walk, in a group, the few miles that separated the camp from the road in order to surprise me with a hot drink when I arrived. When confronted with a worthwhile project, teenagers are tireless, energetic, generous, and self-sacrificing.

Is this education? I believe it gives young people the opportunity to discharge their energy and meet challenges in constructive ways. It provides them with the satisfaction of caring for others, a very different experience as they have only just emerged from their self-centered world.

Unfortunately in today's world, we adults, involved in our own work, do not offer teenagers enough of the educational experiences they so badly need. In Belgium, forty-some years ago, groups were mostly run by young adults—single, free, just out of high school, and enrolled in college or in the work force. These leaders still had lots of energy, lots of ideals, lots of ideas, and were close enough to this age group to serve as important role models. Today, the situation is drastically different. In North America, most troops are run by tired parents who, in addition to a job, children, and a home, devote to running a troop the little time they have left to recuperate. They no longer have the stamina and the sense of adventure to give the girls what they most want: challenge.

Recently, I heard on a Boston television channel a wonderful program called "City Year," in which teenage boys and girls commit themselves to work one entire year at helping the underprivileged. For instance, they might be used to renovate decrepit houses, build playgrounds, direct after-school activities, and tutor small children. When interviewed at the end of the year, they all seemed enthusiastic about the experience, despite the fact they were paid only a pittance and had to work five days a week.

They would start the day punctually with a series of physical exercises. By groups of two or more they were then sent to work on whatever project needed them. The rewards they received from all their hard work were very meaningful: they formed lasting friendships;

they got to know people from different backgrounds; they learned new skills or perfected old ones; and they became keenly aware that they too could make a difference in other people's lives.

Many gained self-esteem by sticking, for the first time in their lives, to a job. Others learned to be part of a team and that interdependence is a necessary step after acquiring the most sought after independence. Indeed, in our highly specialized society, one has to learn to rely more and more often on the expertise of others. Finally, for some, this experience serving others became the motivating force to pursue further studies by returning to school or enrolling in college or in a technical school.

Many high school students in the Baltimore area engage in community projects. Here again, I believe that such an experience plays an important role in their overall education while bolstering their self-esteem and providing much-needed service to the community.

The evolution of programs involving youths in activities that are both educational and service oriented runs parallel to the evolution of Western societies. Forty years ago, Girl Scout or Boy Scout leaders were recruited among college students. Today, most college students have to be gainfully employed while attending college, so the pool of suitable candidates has markedly decreased. But it has not completely dried up. What has dried up is the motivation to serve. The City Year project takes care of the increasing number of teenagers who have not found their niche in society and go through a period of moratorium. It also serves to help the increasing number of needy people for whom the present social welfare program is inadequate. Finally, the young adolescent program deals with the "latch-key" children who are idle and home alone until their parents return from work. It also fills a need in the community as the pool of volunteers has decreased.

Before dealing with the formal aspect of education, the classroom education, it seems fitting to look first at the education that a child or an adolescent receives at the hands of his or her parents. Parents are the first models with whom, consciously or unconsciously, adolescents identify. Indeed, they strive to be as they believe their parents are or are not. Deeds count more than words, and parents, unlike teachers or educators, have their deeds constantly scrutinized by their offspring. Parents who are eager for their children to stay away from cigarettes, alcohol, or street drugs and thus repeatedly warn them not only of the health danger of taking such drugs but also of the legal consequences of their usage are far from convincing if they indulge in substance use themselves. All the literature describing the ill effects of drugs will not make up for the poor example that a child is given by his or her mentors.

Parents have to be consistent in setting firm and reasonable limits. It is at home that adolescents have to learn that a "no" is a "no" and that maneuvers to have it reversed do not work. Sex education, which should be given in stages corresponding to the maturity of the adolescent, is primarily the parents' responsibility. At home, sex should be talked about openly (but not openly demonstrated), as should any other activity of men or women. Adolescents should learn that there is a time for sex and a time for abstinence. A clear description of the anatomy and physiology of sexual organs should be offered before the adolescent experiences a surge in sexual feelings to avoid sexually arousing the adolescent. At the same time, contraceptive methods should be discussed as well as the dangers of promiscuity. Parents who are comfortable in their role as sex educators and are not unduly shocked by hearing the sexual misadventures of today's adolescent will often become the confidant of their offspring in the event of a sexual mishap. Miller and Sneesby (1988) write that adolescents' pre-marital sexual behavior is influenced by their educational goals and performance, which in turn are influenced by their parents' educational background. However, early sexual activity may compromise educational plans.

In today's world with the threat of AIDS, sexual education should more than ever be in the mind of parents and educators. The school curriculums and even the media (television and teen magazines) should carry their fair share of this important aspect of teen education.

Identity development in late adolescence is greatly influenced by parents: "Specifically, family relationship patterns that are character-ized by both 'connectedness' and 'individuality' seem to promote iden-tity formation, as do peer relationships" (Kamptner 1988, p. 494). By identity, Kamptner refers to an identity made up of three separate components: (1) ego identity, which includes personal values; (2) self-identity, which refers to one's perception of self; and (3) the establish-ment of meaning in life. Whereas warmth and connectedness are fre-quently present in good parents, autonomy or individuality is more difficult to achieve by even the most well-meaning parents. Parents want the best for their children and want to spare them the trials and errors they themselves went through in order to achieve their own goals. Parents want to guide their children along what they see as the road toward success—success that they have attained or want their children to attain for them. Such a road map leaves very little room for autonomy or individuality. The adolescent who blindly and unquestionably follows his or her parents' directives by engaging in a career for which he or she is neither suited nor interested will live a life of dissatisfaction. Such an adolescent has committed to a career never having looked at alternatives, never having questioned his or her choice—in brief, never having had a career crisis. Such an adolescent has not attained a true identity but suffers from an identity foreclosure. It is indeed hard for parents not to try to influence their son's or daughter's career, but it is also imperative that they allow their children to set their own goals, meet their own needs, and live their own lives.

Marriages today, and probably tomorrow, no longer have the sacred bonding they had in the past. Can an adolescent who lives in the midst of parents quarreling grow up with a chance of forming a lasting relationship with a spouse and becoming a good parent? Niemi (1988) researched this question and writes, "The richness of family-centered communication and the open expression of marital conflicts together with a positive emotional atmosphere were crucial to the number and content of the adolescents' social conceptions, especially family conceptions" (p. 428). It is felt that children who are aware of marital conflicts are better prepared for the difficult periods they themselves might experience in marriage, not only because they will be able to recognize the signs of trouble earlier, but also because they will have no unrealistic notions of marriage as a haven of happiness that can only be disappointed.

In what precedes, I have presented education as an all-encompassing experience that enables adolescents to increase their skills, gain new knowledge of themselves and the world around them, and mold their character. Let us now turn our attention to the more formal education that adolescents receive in school and to the important role played, in their lives, by their teachers.

During adolescence, there is a move away from early identifications and a search for new role models. Teachers are in a prime position to serve as models and influence the future career of their students. Indeed, it is not unusual to hear from a college student that his or her choice of career was influenced by a dynamic, interesting, and bright teacher during high school. One amazing fact in today's secondary education is that, although from day to day the amount of knowledge acquired by man is increasing, the amount of time spent in school has markedly decreased in the past fifty years. I remember going to school six days a week from 8 A.M. to 4 P.M. except for Wednesday afternoon, which was devoted to sports. Students then had no free period in the middle of the day, no study hall, just classes interrupted by recreations in which the entire class participated in some physical activity in order to release some pent-up energy. In junior high and high school, we were taught one hour a day of Latin and one hour a day of Greek. We were lectured to in French but had to study Dutch and another foreign language. Each week, in addition to classes in mathematics, geometry, algebra, trigonometry, chemistry, and physics, we were given instruction in geography, history, and other subjects I can no longer remember. I am not proposing that high school students return to such a heavy schedule, but I wonder at the constant shrinkage of the number of hours that teenagers spend in school or on their homework. Leone and Richards (1989) write, "Results revealed that students spent only 15.5 hours per week engaged in school work and only 6 hours per week doing homework, with increased homework time associated with better academic achievement . . . doing homework with their parents was associated with better academic performance" (p. 531).

In the North American public schools, all too often in the last few years the main task for teachers is to keep order, and, thus, whatever energy they have left they use to teach their assigned subject. Unfortunately, learning is frequently a very passive experience for the student, who easily becomes bored, restless, and uninterested. When students are actively engaged in searching out the material they have to learn, and when they are assigned to share with their peers the results of their findings by teaching a classroom lesson themselves, the learning is fun, challenging, and easily remembered. History and geography should be learned by following the world's events. It would tie the past to the present for the students and give them a valid reason to study these subjects. Today's schools, more than ever before, are a melting pot of children from different countries, races, cultures, and religions, and thus teachers have a unique opportunity to have our young people learn about the great world they live in. Why not have an adolescent from Bangladesh, for instance, talk about her country or have a student or a group of students interview a man from Albania and present to the class what they have learned about his home life? Math, algebra, and calculus could come to life if learning about it were part of a class project. For instance, in order to help defray the cost of the yearbook and the prom at the end of high school, why not have the class invest a small amount of money in stocks or bonds and then review and discuss its portfolio during math classes? Such an activity would teach students not only about math but also about the benefits of saving and of investing wisely and give them some idea of what the financial world is all about. Having students work in a group on a particular project while allowing them some leeway on how to realize it taps into the creativity of that stage of life. Creativity, which so often is killed by the need for conformity, also teaches collaboration, interdependence, and how in a group every member has to carry his or her share of the responsibility in order for the project to succeed. To help students reason on their own, teachers could relate stories in which a judgment must be made about the behavior of some of the characters. There would be no right or wrong opinion, but students would be expected to justify the reasoning behind their answers.

Adolescents should be encouraged to do their very best in whatever they undertake. They should not, however, be expected to be "the best." Indeed, such an expectation creates unhealthy competition and repeated frustration, and it can lead to severe depression. Doing the best one can, however, brings with it a sense of self-satisfaction, fulfillment, and overall contentment.

Larson (1988) sees the high school junior theme as the adolescent rite of passage in Western civilization. He writes that, once students have turned in their junior project to the teacher, they have learned "something about their capacity to work, to extend themselves toward a distant objective" (p. 279). "Adulthood is the ability to act and think on one's own, to stick with and carry out one's ideas over an extended period of time" (p. 281). They have had to set priorities in their lives as they might have had to forgo a party or a ball game in order to work on their projects. Although students often do not see the use of homework, they consider their junior project to be worthwhile and the product meaningful.

Self-esteem starts in one's formative years, and thus it falls to parents, teachers, and educators to cultivate it from the very beginning of a child's education. Everyone has something to offer society, and it is the task of educators to discover what that something is in each adolescent entrusted to them. One should never compare people, but one can compare their various attributes. For instance, a teenager might be exceptionally bright but poorly coordinated; yet another may be sociable and kind but physically unattractive; finally, one might know how to play the guitar but have no leadership skills. What they all have in common is an area in which they can shine, gain acceptance, and acquire self-esteem. Educators should build on their assets instead of deploring their shortcomings. In other words, teachers should counteract the superficial values in vogue today by offering students alternative experiences in which they can gain self-esteem.

Psychotherapists also play an important role in the education of adolescents. Not only do they help them better understand themselves, but through different techniques they assist them in overcoming difficulties that interfere with their growing up. Reality is in the mind of the beholder, and a therapist can help change that reality to one that fits better. For instance, a teenager depressed because he was not invited to a party and thus feeling friendless could be helped to see that he did not get an invitation because he was not in school the day invitations were given out. Although all therapies have educational values, some forms of therapy, such as behavior or cognitive therapy, are more directly educational. Group therapies are also excellent educational tools.

Conclusions

The basics of education have remained essentially stable through the centuries, even though the acquisition of knowledge, which plays a small but important part in the entire education process, is constantly in a state of flux. Social reality, on the other hand, changes with the year, the continent one lives in, the town one grows up in, and even the social group one belongs to. Thus, education can be adapted to any social reality.

REFERENCES

Kamptner, L. N. 1988. Identity development in late adolescence: causal modeling of social and familial influences. *Journal of Youth and Adolescence* 17(6): 493–515.

Larson, R. 1988. The high school "junior theme" as an adolescent rite of passage. *Journal of Youth and Adolescence* 17(4): 267–285.

Leone, C. M., and Richards, M. 1989. Classwork and homework in early adolescence: the ecology of achievement. *Journal of Youth and Adolescence* 18(6): 531–549.

Miller, B. C., and Sneesby, K. 1988. Educational correlates of adolescents' sexual attitudes and behavior. *Journal of Youth and Adolescence* 17(6): 521–531.

Niemi, P. M. 1988. Family interaction patterns and the development of social conceptions in the adolescent. *Journal of Youth and Adolescence* 17(5): 429–445.

3   EDUCATION AND POVERTY: PROBLEMS AND POSSIBILITIES

MAX SUGAR

In order to attain self-sufficiency and equilibrium with society today in the United States, youngsters need a formal education. This is quite different from a century ago, when most of the population lived in rural areas, there were many careers that did not require much education, and there were more needs for, and opportunities to be gained from, apprenticeship.

Many of the problems concerning poverty and education have been heralded in the media—drugs, dropouts, the danger of attending school, crime, low SAT scores, excess television watching, excess sexual activity. This chapter will focus on current risks for, and interferences with, the attainment of education by the poor as well as some possible hopeful aspects for outcome. Major consideration will be devoted to perinatal factors, the family, the children, the government, the schools, emotional issues, protective factors, and outcome.

Causes of Poor Academic Achievement

The media have informed us that, every year in the United States, of 400,000 babies born to drug-abusing mothers, one in five are inner-city babies. These youngsters are at risk for respiratory distress syndrome, prematurity, and learning disability. Lead poisoning is common among inner-city children and contributes to learning disabilities and lowered IQ.

Prenatal and perinatal events may have long-term effects on the attainment of an education owing to insults to the fetus or the neonate's central nervous system (CNS). Among these are maternal malnutrition, maternal rubella, maternal exposure to street drugs, small for gestational age (SGA), and failure to thrive. Other conditions and various medications in pregnancy also have a devastating effect on the youngster's CNS and intellectual functioning, such as lithium, phenobarbital, inhalation anesthetics, maternal viral infections, and maternal coma. Fetal alcohol syndrome is the single largest preventable cause of mental retardation. Smoking in pregnancy leads to low birth weight and the consideration of CNS insult (Sugar 1987).

Thirty-eight percent of youngsters are of borderline or lower intelligence, while 3 percent of children are born retarded in the United States from all causes. Twenty-five percent of youngsters have emotional or social problems, 17 percent have learning disabilities, 10 percent have speech or hearing disorders, and 8 percent have developmental problems. Twenty-five percent of all school absences are due to asthma (U.S. Department of Health, Education and Welfare 1972). Other causes of poor academic performance include hereditary factors (such as sickle cell anemia), infections (such as encephalitis), metabolic abnormalities (such as phenylketonuria), endocrinological disturbances (such as cretinism), allergies, tumors, and nutritional deficiencies.

Poverty

Currently, one in three children live in poverty in the United States; there are 37 million people in poverty, and 50 percent of these are children. In the United States, there are 11.5 million youngsters who are now hungry or at risk of being so and 100,000 homeless children. In 1987, 31 percent of children living in inner cities in the United States were in poverty, and 20 percent of all children were living below the poverty level (National Center for Children in Poverty 1990).

Compared to the nonpoor, poor children are lower achievers, repeat grades once or twice, drop out of school more often, engage in more delinquent and criminal behavior, become unmarried teens more often, are more likely to be on welfare, and earn less if they are employed. They are also more likely to have been prenatally exposed to drugs or the HIV virus, preterm, and of low birth weight. Of low-birth-weight children treated in a neonatal intensive care unit, 27 percent die there, 16 percent become disabled, and 57 percent appear normal. Of that 57 percent, however, many have learning disabilities and related difficulties later on.

Poor children between the ages of three and four benefit significantly from early childhood programs (unrelated to parental employment) with strong educational programs that prepare them for school. However, these reach only a fraction of poor preschoolers. Compared to upper-income children in 1988, the poor were more likely to have poor nutrition, lead exposure, and fatal or nonfatal injuries, and they had a seven-to-one chance of being abused and neglected. They had an increased mortality rate in 1988 of 9.9 per thousand and an increased neonatal mortality rate of 6.7 per thousand in 1987 (National Center for Children in Poverty 1990).

The Children's Defense Fund (1986) provides the following details. When black children are compared to white children, there is a two-to-one ratio of the blacks being born prematurely, having low birth weight, dying in the first year, having mothers who received little or no prenatal care, and having unemployed parents. Compared to white children, black children have a three-to-one chance of their mother dying in childbirth, of being in foster care, or of dying themselves as a result of child abuse. These children also have a four-to-one chance, compared to white children, of living with neither parent, of being supervised by a child welfare agency, and of being murdered before the age of one year or in their teens. They also have a twelve-to-one chance of living with an unmarried parent.

Of children born into poverty who are under age eighteen, 15 percent now are white, 39 percent Hispanic, and 45 percent black. In female-headed homes, more than 50 percent of all children are living in poverty, with a three-to-two ratio of white to black children in this regard.

Family Issues

Families often deny their child's poor school performance until they view a report card along with teachers' comments such as "could do better," "not trying," "doesn't participate," "excess absence," or "should be retained in the grade." With an alcoholic or severely depressed mother, a child often ends up with less education. Migrant families have decreased education for their children since the families move each season, the children work in the fields part of the school year, the families may be living and working quite a distance from schools or ignorant of their location, and the children shift schools quite regularly if they attend school at all.

Among immigrant families, there are problems with new customs and a new language and an increase in tuberculosis; with survival being the major issue, education may take a secondary role in a family's priorities. Some families provide no guidance, are nonaffectional or emotionally nonsupportive, or set no limits for the children, while others provide no stimulation toward education. Chaotic families have a difficult time functioning in an organized way, including getting their children to school or seeing that they get educated.

By age eighteen, the average child in the United States has probably watched 23,000 hours of television at a rate of 7¼ hours per family per day. Are the parents using the television as a baby-sitter or as a substitute soother or transitional object? There are many children today who are latch-key children from the time they enter school until they finish or drop out of high school since both parents are frequently working and there is no extended family to look after the youngsters.

Where there is parental abuse, 52 percent of the children have below-average or failing grades; where there is parental neglect, 82 percent of the children have below-average or failing grades. These figures compare with the control-group rates of 28 percent for both abuse and neglect (Kent 1976). Physical abuse is seven times more common in poor compared to upper-income families. Physical and sexual abuse and neglect, all of which may also occur in school, may lead to psychiatric disturbances with anxiety, depression, posttraumatic stress disorder, or more severe conditions (Sugar 1991). Abused and neglected children have a sense of betrayal and marked feelings of distrust. At a minimum, twenty-five per every thousand children are physically abused or in danger of such abuse annually (*Study Findings* 1988). One in three female children is sexually abused before age fifteen; for boys, the figure is somewhat lower (Committee on Sexual Offences against Children and Youth 1984).

The Government

From time immemorial, societies have made arrangements for the poor and the handicapped with tithing, almshouses, workhouses, poorhouses, welfare checks, charity hospitals, etc. Each state has variable arrangements for the implementation of Public Law 94-142 (designed to guarantee the education of handicapped children, including those with psychiatric difficulties). There have been recent suggestions for tax money to be given to families to place children in schools of the parents' choice or that a national curriculum be developed. These suggestions raise questions about problems of turf and the rivalry between present agencies, but the result might be that a standard, basic education would be made available across the country. But this does not necessarily mean that an adequate education would be available for all, as I will point out shortly.

Currently, there is no national policy for education. There is a variable level of support for public education. Private schools infrequently or rarely have special education or vocational training. Schools, states, and regions have a variable curriculum. Schools in affluent areas have more money for equipment and amenities, usually through parental contributions and budget arrangements, but increased money and buildings are not sufficient in themselves to provide an education. Children in rural schools get fewer school days than urban youngsters owing to time off to help out with the harvest.

There are 2.6 million poor adolescents who do not receive the benefits of Medicaid. There has been an increase in sexually transmitted diseases in recent years, and there are 280 cases per year of AIDS in children and adolescents. These problems add to school absences and poorer school achievement. In 1991, 44 percent of children in poverty had federal aid, whereas, in 1980, 70 percent of such children were covered by some aid (England 1991).

School Problems

A recent PBS documentary ("Lessons Learned" 1992) highlighted the outright and clear-cut discrimination against blacks in the New Orleans public school system from Reconstruction until a few years ago. Schools serving blacks received limited funds and were staffed by few black teachers. The result was lesser educational opportunity and achievement for all blacks in the area. This New Orleans experience is unlikely to be singular. Situations of discrimination against various racial, ethnic, and religious groups must exist across the country. This has had a negative effect on the public education of the poor nationally.

Does a classroom place a child at risk for academic failure, or does it promote achievement? There are many family and social factors that may increase the vulnerability of children to school failure before entering school, as noted above.

Teaching approaches may be nonstimulating or provide poor or low standards, relying instead on social promotions. With social promotions, there is no incentive to study and learn. The question of neglect by teachers may be raised when figures show that 13–40 percent of seventeen-year-olds are functionally illiterate. There may be abuse in school (verbal, emotional, physical, and sexual) by the teachers. There may be a minimal amount of classroom materials for the youngsters to use. There may be less money and equipment for students and less outside educational stimuli for the youngsters in schools in poor neighborhoods. There are frightened teachers who risk their lives to teach in certain impoverished areas. Drugs, weapons, and violence are not uncommon in the daily lives of youngsters in poverty-area schools.

Many who attend college still need remedial courses in college in the first several years. One-quarter of all mathematics courses taught in state colleges are remedial. One-quarter of all Navy recruits currently read below the ninth-grade level, which is the minimum required to function in today's Navy. In 1991, for the first time in eleven years, average SAT math scores were down two points to 474, and verbal scores averaged 422, the weakest showing since 1969. The 1991 SAT verbal scores continued a slide that has been going on for six years ("SAT Verbal Scores Lowest Ever" 1991).

Large numbers of children drop out of school, and the single largest reason among girls is teenage pregnancy. Boys drop out of school because of a lack of interest, self-esteem, or a sense of achievement. Their families do not often encourage them to continue with school.

After youngsters leave school without marketable skills, they are often unemployed. This leads to an increased fertility rate in girls and an increased crime rate in boys compared to the employed. The road to dropping out may begin with absences due to delinquency, substance abuse, or asthma. After missing many days, the students often feel that they can never catch up. In 1988, there was a 47 percent dropout rate after age sixteen, with a rate of 10.8 percent among white youths, 12.4 percent among African-Americans, and 29.7 among Hispanics and others (U.S. Department of Commerce 1990). The dropouts became largely unemployed. The unemployment rate was highest among blacks, lower among Hispanics, and lowest among whites. Since there is a decreased availability of apprenticeships for blacks compared to whites, their further education in a vocational track is less likely (Sugar 1991).

According to Carta (1991), preschool children in the low-income group, compared with the middle-income group, participate less, use more instructional materials, engage less in activities, and are doing nothing more frequently. The teachers in low-income preschool class-rooms read more and sing more to the children and disapprove of them more. But Carta points out that training in classroom survival skills while in preschool produces positive changes in developmental growth, vocabulary, social competence, and teachers' ratings and re-sults in a greater likelihood of being placed in kindergarten the follow-ing year.

In a grade-school research study (Greenwood, Carta, Hart, Thur-ston, and Hall 1989), the quality of classroom instruction, the teachers' planning of lessons, and the teachers' orchestration of instructions varied. These factors affected the students' achievement in a negative way. The key variable here was the opportunity to respond in class. A lower level of response is equivalent to a higher risk factor, but more responsiveness enhances scholastic achievement. Responsive-ness provides the students with the opportunity to practice academic skills. Active responses, such as reading and writing aloud, promote better learning than passively attending to the teacher. Class-wide peer tutoring sessions in grade schools of ten minutes, with student tutor and student reversing roles, improve academic achievement by 100 percent in the particular subject involved, even with only thirty min-utes of tutoring a day. This leads to increased reading aloud, silent reading, and reading speed (Bennett 1986).

High Schools

Rutter, Maugham, Mortimore, and Ouston (1979) found that disad-vantaged schools vary in delinquency rates, behavioral disturbances, attendance, and academic achievement. The better high schools in disadvantaged areas have specific factors that help the youngsters have better educational achievement. The schools that foster high self-esteem promote social and scholastic success and reduce the likelihood of emotional and behavioral disturbances. This does not depend on the size of the school, the available space, the age of the school, or the graded placement of students by ability.

Rutter et al. found that better academic achievement was based on the academic emphasis of the school, the teachers' actions in the classroom (such as giving high structure), the teachers' preparation, their planning, their emphasis on exams, their emphasis on homework, and a flexible streaming system. Contributing features were the use of incentives and rewards, out-of-school activities, the use of the library, concern with academics and work-oriented goals, allowing the students to take responsibility for their actions and activities in the school (e.g., monitoring, textbooks, pens, ink), expressing appreciation for good work being done, maintenance of a prosocial atmosphere, and the presence of a substantial nucleus of children with average or higher intelligence. These had enduring effects that served as a protection and a positive influence against the area in which the family lived under adverse conditions.

Colleges

Currently, many youngsters drop out of college (especially state colleges) because they are disinterested, unprepared, feel threatened by the challenge, or have no goals. The average college completion time is now five to six years, not the scheduled four of previous generations. Some of this added time is due to having to provide remedial teaching, as mentioned above. Some is due to cutbacks, unavailable classes, and insufficient teachers to provide additional classes in necessary subjects (Jouzaitis 1991).

Psychiatric Problems

When youngsters are sexually active, their grades go down: 54 percent of those who are sexually active have below-grade-level achievement (Coles and Stokes 1985, p. 78).

There are many emotional and social family situational problems that may interfere with education and for which psychiatric treatment is needed since one-fifth of all educational difficulties involve an emotional factor. This does not mean that emotional problems are the sole cause, although they may be. More often, however, they are compounded by some of the other problems mentioned earlier. Seventeen percent of all youngsters receive a psychiatric diagnosis in their teens. Many of the 8 million children in need of psychiatric intervention receive no care, and perhaps 50 percent of those in need of treatment

38

receive inappropriate care. Only one in three with moderate or severely disabling emotional conditions receives any systematic care.

Among the problems that may interfere with education and need psychiatric treatment, the following list is not all inclusive: oppositional disorders, obsessive disorders, anxiety reactions, depressive reactions, overachievers who are never happy and constantly berate themselves, psychoses, separation anxiety with school refusal, seventh- and twelfth-grade drops (which are usually transient and do not need treatment), substance abuse, death of a loved one, and divorce of the parents (which involves 50 percent of marriages in the United States today). Students with chronic illness (which leads to a distorted body image and feeling defective) often withdraw from school after their grades go down.

Thirty years ago, there were few services available for child/adolescent psychiatric inpatients. There were then only a handful of psychiatric inpatient hospitals or wards for children or adolescents. Now they are available in all cities and most small towns throughout the country. But the youngsters are still not getting proper care for these conditions. Fifty-four percent of psychiatrists and 50 percent of pediatricians are uncomfortable seeing adolescents (Moramarco 1991).

Educational Outcome and Poverty

According to Garmezy (1991), children born into poverty begin life with increased risks, but they are not necessarily ordained to having a poor education and failure. Garmezy raised the question of whether there is a cyclical nature and intergenerational continuity to poverty.

Comer (1980) was involved in and described a project in New Haven, Connecticut, to improve the climate of relationships among those involved in the poverty-area schools that were the site of the project. By applying the principles of social and behavioral science to all aspects of the school program, it was hoped that there would be "significant academic and social growth of students." Some of its features were meetings and workshops between teacher, principal, parents (some of whom were paid aides), social workers, and psychiatrists; special programs for teachers' seminars; social workers' and psychiatrists' support for teachers; a program for behavior-disordered children; and a program for children who were behind in grade level. The students' improved academic standing was reflected in the overall improved standing of the school compared to other inner-city and suburban schools.

Longitudinal studies (Long and Vaillant 1984) show that, among inner-city males reared in chaotic families and poverty, those who were early delinquents were on the downgrade as adults while youngsters who were from the same situation but unknown to the police ended up in the middle class as adults. Long and Vaillant felt that there were cultural protective factors that helped the latter group. Among these were being in the military in World War II, receiving an education through the GI Bill, or going into the work force and having a steady job.

Festinger (1983) noted that the outcome for male and female children reared in foster care in New York City—even children with marked at-risk factors—was not a straight-line negative. In comparing a group of foster children with controls, it was found that, despite lower scholastic achievement among the foster group, for both groups as adults the employment rate was the same, although slightly lower for blacks than for whites, and that both groups were similar in health, self-evaluation about their future, and sense of happiness. According to these data from Festinger (1983) and Long and Vaillant (1984), there was no generational transmission of poverty or foster care, respectively.

Protective Factors and Resilience

In their longitudinal study (beginning in 1955) of a cohort of children born into poverty, Werner (1989) and Werner and Smith (1989) found that some children in the study group had biological stressors and family instability that those in the control group did not. In childhood and adolescence, two-thirds of the high-risk children developed such problems as delinquency, mental illness, and teenage pregnancy. Of these, however, 75 percent of males and 90 percent of females had no problems after age eighteen, particularly if they came from a two-parent family. These youngsters became competent, able, and autonomous.

Werner (1989) and Werner and Smith (1989) noted important protective factors in the parents and child. Among the parental factors were a good relationship between the youngsters and the parents or the mother alone, supportive parents who set rules and limits, parents who showed respect for the children's individuality and autonomy, and parents who maintained stability and family cohesion. Protective factors in the children consisted of good physical health; affectional ties in the family; activity, sociability, and the ability to entice an interest in them and support from the surround; involvement with others; seeking and finding positive models for identification; good peer relations; seeking help from other adults in school, church, or at work; many interests and hobbies; reading skills; reasoning skills; having a set of goals and a belief system by which to live; above-average IQ; and having an internal locus of control.

Based on this and other reviews, it appears that cumulative life stresses, in combination, may be of great significance for the psychopathological development of the adolescent, and, in these circumstances, the family is less supportive than otherwise. These factors are maternal mental health problems, low socioeconomic status (SES) or financial problems, separation from mother through the child's fostercare placement or institutional placement of mother, temporary separation from father (including jail time), marital problems of the parents, and crises and losses in adolescence (Rutter et al. 1978; Werner and Smith 1989; and Sugar 1991).

Werner (1989) and Werner and Smith (1989) felt that poverty alone was insufficient for the development of maladaptation. This highlights the features mentioned above that are protective of and conducive to growth and development, rather than those that lead to maladaptation and pathology.

The report by Caplan, Choy, and Whitmore (1992) on the academic success of the Vietnamese boat people supports the thesis that poverty does not, by itself, pose an insurmountable barrier to educational achievement. The families' commitment and support were pivotal to the youngsters' achievement, along with a number of other factors noted by Rutter et al. (1978) and Werner and Smith (1989).

Some Goals

Among our goals should be prevention, which would include inducing pregnant women to stop using street drugs, smoking, and drinking alcohol. This would decrease the number of low-birth-weight, retarded, and learning-disabled youngsters. Prevention should also involve increased support for young parents by *their* parents regularly and the government temporarily. There would need to be increased standards for teachers with a grading system to ensure that the teachers are functioning well instead of having some (although a small number of) incompetents or abusers. There would be a smaller number of students per school and a smaller number of pupils per classroom. There would be increased apprenticeships available.

There would be a three-track system of teaching starting from the ninth grade onward, such as is found in Canada, England, Japan, Russia, and Israel. Those who are college bound would go to an academic high school. Those who are heading into the business world would attend a commercial high school for bookkeeping/secretarial skills. Those interested in trade skills would attend a vocational or technical high school, where they would learn printing, bricklaying, auto mechanics, etc. Thus, the youngsters would be prepared for and have competence in the workplace, with an increase in self-esteem and meaningful grades—all this instead of social promotions.

In addition, there should be the application of the classroom research findings mentioned earlier and others for classroom instruction. There should be training in self-care with manual training in home economics and training in courtesy, manners, and job-interviewing skills beginning in the eighth grade for both boys and girls. Then, by graduation from high school, youngsters would be able to take care of themselves (hygiene, basic shopping and cooking, laundry, balancing a checkbook) and be ready for the university (without remedial courses) or the work force with competence in some vocational area. Such preparation would lead to increased self-esteem and a readiness for the world of adulthood with responsibilities for further education or the work force.

The assumption has been made that people harm themselves physically, abuse drugs, or have premature and unprotected sex because of ignorance. This is contrary to psychiatric knowledge. The basis of these behaviors is multifactorial, and education programs have been unsuccessful in their prevention. Primary prevention programs and education for suicide prevention are unsuccessful since they consider that suicide may be seen as an option by anyone facing enough stress. This is not the case and is unsupported by psychiatric research. Self-injurious acts and suicide occur when there is mental illness. Suicide-prevention programs should target children at risk, not the population of children at large (Shaffer 1991). Those targeted would be the physically or sexually abused, those with psychiatrically ill parents, or those with CNS damage.

School personnel can aid in the awareness and promotion of earlier psychiatric diagnosis and treatment. An ongoing, open dialogue between school faculty and a psychiatrist is advisable. A crisis or need for intervention of an immediate sort should not be the only reason for psychiatric consultation. Psychiatric school consultation for the personnel may also be a significant asset to help them with various issues about their own situation, teaching difficulties, or special problems with a class or student.

All these problems will not be cured simply by wishing. There is no reason for complacency, but there is a need to seek assessment of and treatment for youngsters. The schools need to handle problems on an incremental basis through the parent-teacher association, in the polling booth, and in the legislature, with petitions and letters. The adult population needs to work at speaking out as well as at supporting their children in their school endeavors.

We need to speak out for children, and we need not be daunted by the needs or try to complete the task today, but we should continue to speak out, work, do research, and try to find more and better solutions to help the youngsters and implement them. There may be local philanthropic self-help efforts that go unnoticed but that may be models for others.

Conclusions

Among the multiple aspects of the well-publicized problems of education for children in poverty considered here are perinatal factors, the family, the children, the government, the schools, and emotional factors. Despite their high at-risk condition, children in poverty are not doomed to continue in that state or to pass it on to the next generation. Some outcome features, protective factors, prevention, and goals are outlined.

REFERENCES

Bennett, W. J. 1986. *What Works: Research about Teaching and Learning*. Washington, D.C.: U.S. Department of Education.
Caplan, N.; Choy, M. H.; and Whitmore, J. K. 1992. Indochinese

refugee families and academic achievement. *Scientific American* 166(3): 36–45.

Carta, J. 1991. Education for young children in inner city classrooms. *American Behavioral Scientist* 34(4): 440–453.

Children's Defense Fund. 1986. *Maternal and Child Health Date Book: The Health of American Children*. Washington, D.C.: U.S. Government Printing Office.

Coles, R., and Stokes, Q. 1985. *Sex and the American Teenager*. New York: Harper & Row.

Comer, J. P. 1980. *School Power*. New York: Free Press.

Committee on Sexual Offences against Children and Youth. 1984. *Sexual Offences against Children: Report of the Committee on Sexual Offenses against Children*. Ottawa: Canadian Government Publishing.

England, M. J. 1991. Access to health care and health. Paper presented at the meeting of the American Psychiatric Association, New Orleans, May 13.

Festinger, T. 1983. *No One Ever Asked Us*. New York: Columbia University Press.

Garmezy, N. 1991. Resiliency and vulnerability to adverse developmental outcomes associated with poverty. *American Behavioral Scientist* 34(4): 416–430.

Greenwood, C. R.; Carta, J. J.; Hart, B.; Thurston, L.; and Hall, R. V. 1989. A behavioral approach to research on psychosocial retardation. *Education and Treatment of Children* 12:330–346.

Jouzaitis, C. 1991. Students taking longer to graduate from college. *New Orleans Times-Picayune*, May 21.

Kent, J. T. 1976. A follow-up study of abused children. *Journal of Pediatric Psychology* 1:20–26.

Lessons learned. 1992. New Orleans: WYES Channel 12, January 15.

Long, J. F. V., and Vaillant, B. E. 1984. Natural history of male psychological health. XI. escape from the underclass. *American Journal of Psychiatry* 141:341–346.

Moramarco, S. S. 1991. Child psychiatrists. *Psychiatric Times*, May 19.

National Center for Children in Poverty. 1990. *Five Million Children: A Statistical Profile of Our Poorest Young Citizens*. New York: National Center for Children.

Rutter, M.; Maugham, B.; Mortimore, P.; and Ouston, J. 1979. *Fifteen Thousand Hours*. Cambridge, Mass.: Harvard University Press.

SAT verbal scores lowest ever. 1991. *New Orleans Times-Picayune,* August 27.

Shaffer, D. 1991. School based suicide prevention programs. Paper presented at the meeting of the American College of Psychiatrists, January, Fort Lauderdale, Fla.

Study Findings: Study of National Incidence of Child Abuse and Neglect. 1988. Washington, D.C.: U.S. Department of Health and Human Services.

Sugar, M. 1987. Diagnostic aspects of underachievement in adolescents. *Adolescent Psychiatry* 14:427–440.

Sugar, M. 1991. Adolescent pregnancy in the U.S.A. I. problems. *Journal of Adolescent and Pediatric Gynecology* 4:171–182.

U.S. Department of Commerce. Bureau of the Census. 1990. *Statistical Abstract of the United States, 1990.* Washington, D.C.: U.S. Government Printing Office.

U.S. Department of Health, Education and Welfare. 1972. *Vital Statistics of the United States.* Vol. 11A. Washington, D.C.: U.S. Government Printing Office.

Werner, E. E. 1989. High-risk children in young adulthood: a longitudinal study from birth to 32 years. *American Journal of Orthopsychiatry* 59:72–81.

Werner, E. E., and Smith, R. S. 1989. *Vulnerable but Invincible.* New York: Adams, Bannister, Cox.

4 CREATIVITY AND PRODUCTIVITY IN ADOLESCENCE

VIVIAN M. RAKOFF

One of the characteristics of adolescence is the discovery of capacities that might have been foreshadowed in childhood but that are essentially new in terms of the strength and vividness with which they appear following puberty. In intellectual cognitive terms, the most startling manifestation of these new-found talents in the gifted is the extraordinary flourish of mathematical or poetic creativity. There are almost folkloric clichés around the field: "If a mathematician or poet has not made a major contribution by age twenty-five, he is not going to make it." There are of course exceptions to the rule—Wallace Stevens springs immediately to mind—and people go on being poetically and mathematically productive well beyond early adulthood, although the rate and quantity of work generally winds down, except for such towering geniuses as Goethe and Leonardo.

This generalization is much too simple for the complex phenomenology of creativity. But it seems as if the newly developed cognitive capacity of the postpubertal adolescent, while not a tabula rasa, interacts with the domain of symbols and their transformations to perceive new connections. These connections are the operational ground of metaphor through which poetry works for those gifted with one kind of ability and mathematical relations work for those gifted with a different kind of ability. It is the sense of freshness, of newness, of seeing for the first time what is the common ground, that is the particular, almost the defining characteristic of the adolescent.

The subjective sense of first discovery, however, may often be an illusion. It is real and new enough for the particular individual, but the language, when poetry is the vehicle, is, in terms of the general culture, frequently stereotyped and worn out. Objectively, it is simply the cliché rearrangement of language, imagery, and thematic material to which the individual has been exposed in some sort of preconscious bath of possible expressions.

The trouble with the creative impulse is that it is not a guarantee of quality, and many adolescents write the stereotypical poems about their twisted hearts, the uncaring and insensitive world, love, death, and all the great scenes that jump into consciousness to express the peculiar encounter with reality that constitutes the intellectual vision of adolescence. While these poems may be normative in the sense of being typical, very few are truly original or particularly memorable. They are often a kind of aesthetic acne: signs of a remarkable and complex developmental event but not in themselves valuable. But the early work of the great poets, such as Keats, Shelley, Byron, Pope, Pushkin, Lemontov, Leopardi, and Dante, is genuine and impressive. The almost pure culture of their talent and endowment has been described by Auden (1940) in his poem "Encased in Talent Like a Uniform, the Poets Have Their Ranks." Most of those I have mentioned kept their gift and exercised it beyond the elastic boundaries of adolescence. In that sense, they are not purely adolescent geniuses. Adolescence was the beginning, but not the entire framework, of their gift.

There are, however, two poets who are quintessentially adolescent. They are compelling examples of the extraordinary unfolding of capacity, a vision that seemed to look at the world for the first time with great technical capacity and energy. So gifted were they that they startled the artistic literary environment of their times. I am referring to Thomas Chatterton, who died a suicide at seventeen, and Arthur Rimbaud, who had completed his remarkable oeuvre by the age of nineteen.

Thomas Chatterton, called "the marvelous boy" by Wordsworth, became the epitome of the doomed Romantic poet. Keats dedicated his *Endymion* to him, and Coleridge eulogized him. There is a well-known painting by Henry Wallis of his death in which he is depicted elegantly and romantically sprawled in a London garret with a dismal grey-green light coming through the windows and torn papers strewn about the floor. He became a minor cult figure during the Romantic period, and Leoncavallo wrote an opera called *Chatterton*.

Chatterton was born in Bristol, England, in 1752 after his father had died. There was a long-standing family connection with the Church of St. Mary Redcliffe, and his mother "settled into a grim struggle against starvation, making her way by keeping a little day school for very young girls (a kind of forerunning kindergarten) and by toiling industriously with her needle." She was preoccupied with Thomas's education, but he had difficulty in school. He did not care much for other children, "sometimes wept for no apparent reason, and was fond of solitude and most fond of St. Mary Redcliffe" (Russel 1908, pp. 16, 17). He was preoccupied with the church and wandered about it as though it were some private domain. At school, he was obsessed with reading and wrote his first recorded poem when he was ten years old, which was published in 1763 when he was eleven (it is reprinted in Russel [1908, p. 47]). At the age of fourteen, he was apprenticed to a lawyer.

The dates of Chatterton's life are so compressed that one finds oneself rushing through the events even for a brief retelling more quickly than the facts seem to demand. He wrote journalistic pieces, reconstructions of historical events, political polemical poems, lyrical verse, and, most significantly, dramas and narrative poems. The dramas and narrative poems are the substance of the tragic controversy that surrounded Chatterton's life. In his wanderings through St. Mary Redcliffe, he found some chests of old documents. He made himself expert in the late medieval script he found on these old parchments, and after a while he could produce (to put it directly) fairly convincing fakes of ancient documents. He colored, smoked, cracked, and dirtied the parchment and could write fluently in a pseudo-Middle English of his own invention. He adopted a persona in whose name he wrote his pseudoantique works. He claimed to have found lost manuscripts written by a monk called Thomas Rowley. The tragedies and poems written under Rowley's name are pretty turgid stuff, but they are truly amazing. Unfortunately, Chatterton was a poor boy and in need of a patron's support. At the age of sixteen, he had already published many poems and had completed *Aella, a Tragical Interlude* (Chatterton 1971). He tried to obtain support from Horace Walpole, the earl of Orford, who was one of the leading literary aristocratic intellectuals of his time. Walpole, who has been probably unjustly vilified by many people following his encounter with Chatterton, delayed and, instead of being impressed by the extraordinary capacity of a young man from the provinces who could produce the range of work that Chatterton did, stuck on the fact that Chatterton had tried to pass his pseudo-medieval work off as genuine finds. Walpole labeled Chatterton a forger. Chatterton went up to London, hoping for fame and fortune. He spent his very small supply of money and, although he wrote happy hopeful letters back to Bristol, killed himself in despair in August 1770.

Apart from his literary prodigiousness, Chatterton had a worldview, and he was "one of the earliest and most outspoken friends of the American Colonies" (Russel 1908, p. 170). To this audience it will therefore be particularly interesting that, before the Boston Tea Party and before the patriots "had thought of independence," Chatterton could write (Russel 1908, p. 170):

> Alas! America, thy ruined cause
> Displays the ministry's contempt of laws.
> Unrepresented thou art tax'd, excised,
> By creatures much too vile to be despised;
> The outcasts of an ousted gang are sent
> To bless thy commerce with misgovernment.
> Whilst pity rises to behold thy fate,
> We see thee in this worst of troubles great;
> Whilst anxious for thy wavering dubious cause,
> We give thy proper spirit due applause."

Arthur Rimbaud is much better known these days. He was not a marvelous curiosity who worked tragically on the margins of literature and was only posthumously celebrated like Chatterton. Although like Chatterton he was a provincial boy, he came to the great metropolis, Paris, where he gained a species of acceptance. In spite of his foul manners, his disgusting personal habits, and his treacherous, rancorous behavior, he was recognized as a gifted writer almost immediately. Unlike Chatterton, who hoped for acceptance by adopting an anachronistic style and a false persona, Rimbaud declared himself, as himself, to be a seer and prophet who wrote in an essentially new style. Chatterton created an elaborate mask, whereas Rimbaud discarded the most ordinary masks of politeness, tact, and sexual discretion and presented himself to the literary world as a kind of gifted, eloquent beast. He created an original entry into the poetic domain by "disorganizing" the senses; he celebrated synesthesia. In both form and content, he was one of the founders of modernism, fracturing verse forms and recreating them. He lassoed prose, forcing it into visionary poetic speeds, and produced wildly scatological and erotic poems, not for secret sniggering, but almost as manifestos of a new consciousness—an alchemical transformation of the lead of daily experience into the gold of poetically transmuted epiphanies. Then, quite suddenly, it all stopped, and the blue-eyed demon/angel/seducing seer became ordinary. Even less than oridinary: pathetic, exiled, sick, inept; a failure financially, aesthetically, and as a human being.

The bare facts of his life are these. Rimbaud's father, an army captain, deserted his wife and their four children—Arthur was the second—when Arthur was three years old. Madame Rimbaud, née Vitalie Cuif, came from a well-to-do farming family. Paul Schmidt, the translator of Rimbaud's complete works, describes her as "tall, severe, and proud, forever in black, an aspiring bourgeoise, and a bigot. A perfect opponent for her son" (1976, p. 3). He was like many children who turn into rebels after puberty: a model child, well behaved, a good student whose prodromal gifts as a translator of Latin verse foreshadowed the poetic marvels that were to come. At age ten, he wrote a sentence that uncannily parallels poor Chatterton's assumed archaic identity—"I dreamed that . . . I had been born in Rheims in 1503" (Schmidt 1976, p. 5)—but by the age of fifteen he saw himself as a companion to, and an equal of, the major young poets of his time—a Parnassian among the Parnassians. He ran away for the first time to Paris in August 1870. A teacher, George Izambard, befriended him, and Rimbaud once again ran away to him shortly after he was returned home, accompanied by the police.

And so it went. The gifted, perhaps disordered young man was caught between his wish for an independent incandescent life among the literati and his resentful dependence on his tight, unimaginative mother. As Chatterton was in tune with the crumbling of his absolutist monarchic world, his awareness moved outward to politics and was not contained by his intrapsychic storms. So Rimbaud was caught up in both his subjective turmoil and the storms engulfing France.

The Prussians defeated Napoléon III at Sedan, and the ordered bourgeois world of France fell apart. The authorities in both Rimbaud's family and his country were turned upside down. The advancing Germans occupied his home town of Charleville, and Rimbaud once again ran off to Paris. He got there just before the terrible period of the Paris Commune. Records of that period, during which the defeated government was parlaying for peace at Versailles, depict the city of Paris as a phantasmagoric place of barricades, skirmishes, hangings, rebellion, and counterrebellion, a reality in almost exact parallel with Rimbaud's marvelously disorganized sensibility. All received forms and themes fell before the assault of his unleashed poetic impulse. What we like to call primary process and secondary process were publicly and privately joined.

Rimbaud was only sixteen when a prophetic anticipation of Nietzsche and Freud seized him. He elevated respect for the irrational, for the unbridled expression of the instincts, for the exploration of individual sensibility to a new form of virtue; subjectivity and passion were in his writings the primary values and guides, in place of the received forms and orderly utterance of classicism. And for the future of literature he transcended the usual stage-specific antagonisms and pains of adolescence to create that rarest of artistic entities—new forms, subject matter, and vocabulary. Of course he built on contemporary and past French poetry, but he wedged the passionate, sensual, demonic verse of Baudelaire into a new framework, freer and more audacious than any of his predecessors.

His inventiveness flowered into a unique poem using regular verse forms to describe a lush dream generated—one might say—by an unconscious restrained only by the demands of euphony and meter. "Le Bateau Ivre" (The drunken boat) became his ticket to literary acceptance. Particularly, it was a card of introduction to Verlaine, who took him—with, as it turned out, disastrous consequences—into his home. Or, to put it more accurately, Rimbaud took Verlaine out of his staid proper household, away from his wife and young son to live with him in the squalor of Left Bank lodgings. The two of them were almost certainly lovers, and they lived out Rimbaud's dissolute fantasies in a mode to which those of us who deal with rebellious adolescents have become accustomed. They turned night into day, smoked hashish, drank absinthe, and punctuated their public speech—this was 1873— with obscenities.

Verlaine returned to his family, and Rimbaud, once again, returned home to his despairing and uncomprehending mother. But the mutual attraction remained powerful, and they fled France for London, where they had a brief, poor, quarrelsome relationship that ended when Verlaine left for Brussels. The story of their subsequent entanglements is complex; they wrote one another, and Rimbaud went—with considerable ambivalence—to Brussels. Verlaine was distraught; he threatened to kill himself and Rimbaud with a pistol. Verlaine's mother had also come to Brussels to be with her errant genius, and when Rimbaud left Verlaine's lodgings, Verlaine pursued him and shot at him, wounding him in the hand. In the court case that followed, much was made of the—assumed—erotic relationship between the two poets. Neither of them was candid about the nature of their relationship. The trial effectively terminated their association, and Verlaine served two years in prison. Verlain did see Rimbaud again when he came out of prison, but it was a dreadful meeting. They got drunk, and Rimbaud attacked Verlaine. Probably their very last contact involved Rimbaud's futile attempts to blackmail his erstwhile companion/lover.

After the shooting, Rimbaud again went back to his only point of stability, Charleville, where he wrote his masterpiece, "A Season in Hell," an inspired meditation on the wild, dangerous episode through which he had just passed. It ends with an assertion of wholeness: "I will be able now to possess the truth within one body and one soul" (Schmidt 1976, p. 213).

Some remarkable poems followed, but Rimbaud's career as as extraordinary adolescent and poet was essentially finished. He devoted himself to arcane studies, but his enthusiasms did not last long, nor did they give him the knowledge and mastery he longed for. He traveled widely—in England, Germany, and Cyprus—and he spent the penultimate period of his life as an unsuccessful trader in Aden and Ethiopia. He finally returned to France, fearful of being arrested as a military observer, sick with fever and cancer of the leg. His leg was amputated, but he could not learn to walk with his artificial leg. He died in 1891 after dictating a letter to his sister about elephant tusks he was hoping to trade.

Discussion

There is an understandable temptation to construct a general psychopathology explaining the development of prodigious creativity in adolescence based on Rimbaud and Chatterton. Both grew up in essentially fatherless homes, both thought of themselves as aliens in their time and place. Chatterton retreated from his poor, constricted home and the law office where he was apprenticed to the rooms in St. Mary Redcliffe where he found the chest full of old parchments. It was a stage bare of actors. Chatterton peopled it with ghosts suggested by the history of the church, which provided a reality synchronous with his archaic fantasies. He created out of it a transitional space, between desire and reality, where he could play in a satisfying zone of safety and creativity. Rimbaud found the synchronous reality in the overthrow of Napoléon III and the Paris Commune. Reality affirmed both poets' fantasies. Both were politically aware and on the side of the forces of rebellion–even though in Chatterton's case the work was for the most part in a past-seeking (father-seeking?) mode. They may both have suffered from cyclic mood disorders. Chatterton was a shy, withdrawn boy who was able to mobilize himself in bouts of energy. After his early and perhaps manic/hypomanic episode of creativity, Rimbaud's later years were full of remorse and doubt about the time he had pursued evil and disorganization. Both may have had a touch of delusional paranoia. Perhaps Chatterton truly believed that he was a medieval monk and assumed the persona, and Rimbaud certainly came to see himself as an alchemical seer. Both pursued an entry into a secret world that they would simultaneously explore and create, Chatterton the chest of old parchments and Rimbaud (according to Starkie [1968]) the writings of medieval alchemists.

For twentieth-century psychiatrists interested in the sexual, erotic component of the psyche, Rimbaud provides a field day: his obsessive despair and distrust of the love of women; his scatological obsessions; his homoerotic attachment to Verlaine. Chatterton remains a sexual cipher. He writes loving letters to his mother and sister, but there is nothing overtly scatological or erotic—except in the most attenuated conventional literary mode—in his published writings. So this significant aspect of their lives provides little material for the construction of a theoretical communality.

Chatterton and Rimbaud share, however, the pursuit of a prosthetic father. The significance of older males in their career development is a common theme. Rimbaud used the teacher Izambard, Izambard's friends, and later Verlaine as men who would help get him away from home. Chatterton had unrealistic expectations of Walpole, as a ladder out of his well of misery into the world of respected writers. They seem to have thought that a "good father" would help and guide them to a true, fulfilled destiny.

Having for a moment succumbed to the temptation to create a common theory, one must try to find similar themes in the lives of other gifted writers. Byron's father also abandoned his wife and children, and Byron too fled a harsh and constricting reality to wander Europe. His erotic life was as polymorphous as Rimbaud's. But Shelley and Keats, also late adolescent geniuses, had very different lives. The theory quite simply does not hold: while Wordsworth's father died when he was thirteen, he spent his early years under his mentorship, his reading following his father's program. And *The Prelude* (Wordsworth 1981), his great autobiographical poem, is a record of an almost idyllic childhood. One further example of another "marvelous boy" is Giacomo Leopardi, who spend his youth reading in his father's library. The pursuit of a prosthetic father is not good enough to explain poetic creativity. Most significantly, it does not explain why countless deprived, father-deserted, rebellious young people do not become the next Chatterton, Rimbaud, or even Ogden Nash.

Similarly, other attempts to construct a uniform psychodynamic underlying creativity fail in the particular. Some creative genius or the other refuses to fit the procrustean model of a universal psychodynamic theory. Tolstoy and Proust wrote huge panoramic historical novels. Their lives could hardly have been more different. Their communality was financial, not psychological—they were both rich and free to write. But their familial, sexual, and social histories were not similar, and their narrative techniques and obsessions were also entirely dissimilar. One can go on with this list of the dissimilar, the varied, in a negative polemic against a general psychodynamic theory. However, there is a similarity that holds all these makers together: they produce and write the poems, novels, symphonies, paintings, and sculptures, works to which many others aspire. And they make their works at characteristic life stages and in certain societies and epochs rather than others.

Recent research suggests that there may be a psychopathological rather than a psychodynamic communality among artists. Andreasen (1974) found that 67 percent of the writers she interviewed at the Iowa Writers' Workshop had been treated for affective disorder, whereas only 13 percent of the controls had been. There was, in addition, an overrepresentation of alcoholism (40 percent) in her sample. Almost all the writers reported mood swings including manic or hypomanic states. Similarly, in a survey of forty-seven British artists, Jamison (1989) found that 38 percent had been treated for an affective disorder and that two-thirds of the playwrights, 20 percent of the biographers, and 13 percent of the painters had been treated for depression. Of the eighteen artists who reported mood swings, the most vulnerable were the poets and novelists. And 17 percent of the poets had been treated for mania.

In his survey of 750 patients suffering from mood disorder or schizophrenia, Akiskal thought that 9–10 percent of those with moderate bipolar II disease/cyclothymia qualified as creative artists (unpublished study cited in Akiskal [1986]). An examination of disturbed patients and their first-degree relatives by Richards, Kinney, Lunde, Benet, and Merzel (1988) supports Akiskal's thrust that mild cyclothymic disorder during the "up" phase encourages productivity and creativity. In the Richards et al. sample, the most creative group was the normal relatives of the manic depressives. Richards et al. write, "Creativity may be facilitated . . . in subjects showing milder and perhaps 'subclinical' expressions of a potential bipolar liability" (1988, p. 282).

These studies confirm the insight of probably the greatest of poets when he wrote out of his own experience and his knowledge of others, "the lunatic, the lover, and the poet." All three are plagued or blessed by a state of heightened excitement and energy, but of the three only the poet creates unitary entities (poems) that become objectified. They become detached from the idiosyncratic subjectivity of the maker to become accessible to anyone who wants to read or listen.

Conclusions

Akiskal has said that "bipolarity may have more to do with productivity than creativity per se" (unpublished study cited in Akiskal [1986, p. 725]). I think, however, that he avoids the nub of the problem. The two entities, productivity and originality, while separate capacities (I think he intends "originality" when he says "creativity"), are inextricably connected. One can have endless routine productivity without any original spark, but originality can be assessed only in a production. It is not (as we sometimes may think) a free-floating capacity unattached to anything specific. And, as far as poetry (and mathematics) is concerned, productivity and originality are characteristic of adolescence insofar as these talents reveal themselves at a particular developmental phase. That opening up of talent appears to be the product of a particular aspect of cognitive/intellectual flowering: the capacity to see new connections and relationships. The mathematician of great talent is her own instrument of discovery, free of technology, requiring only the opportunity and the tradition to exercise the talent. In the same way, the poet is the most talent bound of writers. While the poetry he produces will inevitably be governed in form and content by the fashions of his time and place, the personal voice is the voice of the poem. Unlike the novelist, who—in spite of his personal vision—creates (or recreates) an objective world and who must animate and inhabit other personalities in his characters, the poet is only himself. Kaplan (1989) has advanced the proposition that all poetry is a form of imposture, yet the paradox remains that the poet (even the bad poet) is the most "authentic" of writers, in the sense that he is bound to his subjectivity, his endowment for both good and bad. It should not be surprising that a creativity so bonded to the fluctuations of psychic energy should be seen more in poets than in novelists and more in novelists than in historians. For these three categories—poet, novelist, historian—are ranged on a continuum from the subjective to the objective, from talent, if you like, to the exercise of will and industry. While there are great verse plays, epics, and narratives in poetic form, the essential gift for the poet is the flash, the moment, the given, which manifests itself in the relatively short lyric. With the growth of capacity in adolescence, the young person armed with talent sees the world as though for the first time: connections appear and are given form by the increase in energy, cognitive ability, and the sense of newness and discovery that is such an essential characteristic of adolescence.

REFERENCES

Akiskal, H. 1986. Manic depression and creativity. *Science* 233:725.

Andreasen, N. C. 1974. The creative writer: psychiatric symptoms and family history. *Comprehensive Psychiatry* 15:123–131.

Auden, W. H. 1940. *The Novelist: Collected Poems*. New York: Random House.

Chatterton, T. 1971. *Aella: A Tragical Interlude or Discourseynge Tragedy*. In vol. 1 of D. S. Taylor and B. Hoover, eds. *The Complete Works of Thomas Chatterton*. Oxford: Clarendon.

Jamison, K. R. 1989. Mood disorder and patterns of creativity in British writers and artists. *Psychiatry* 52(2): 125–134.

Kaplan, Louise J. 1989. *The Family Romance of the Imposter Poet,*

Thomas Chatterton. Berkeley and Los Angeles: University of California Press.

Richards, R.; Kinney, D. K.; Lunde, I.; Benet, M.; and Merzel, A. P. C. 1988. Creativity in manic-depressives, cyclothymes, and their normal relatives and control subjects. *Journal of Abnormal Psychology* 97 (August): 281–288.

Russel, Charles Edward. 1908. *Thomas Chatterton: The Marvellous Boy*. New York: Moffat, Yard.

Schmidt, P., trans. 1976. *Arthur Rimbaud: Complete Works*. New York: Harper & Row.

Starkie, E. 1968. *Arthur Rimbaud*. New York: New Directions.

Wordsworth, W. 1981. *The Prelude—a Parallel Text*. Edited by J. C. Maxwell. New Haven, Conn.: Yale University Press.

5 DIAGNOSTIC DIFFICULTIES IN ADOLESCENT PSYCHIATRY: WHERE HAVE WE BEEN, AND WHERE ARE WE GOING?

MARSHALL KORENBLUM

As disciples of developmental thinking, child and adolescent psychiatrists usually have little difficulty coping with the idea that clinical presentations can change over time. Yet, in the case of adolescents, the diagnostic process—the point at which the psychiatrist asks himself, "How am I to understand this patient sitting before me?"—is complicated by a number of interrelated factors. How the patient chooses to present himself or herself at that particular moment, how the assessor elicits, perceives, and reacts to various symptoms, the interpersonal and familial context of the teenager, and the cultural milieu that envelops both parties all interact in a dynamic fashion. Having gathered the data, the rules available for ordering the observations then come into play via the *Diagnostic and Statistical Manual of Mental Disorders* (DSM-III-R; American Psychiatric Association 1987). But the most widely used system, DSM-III-R, has no section specifically oriented to this age group; as a result, clinicians who assess adolescents often feel overwhelmed when they try to describe or understand their psychopathology.

The purposes of this chapter are to elucidate the unique aspects of adolescence that contribute to diagnostic difficulties, critically to review the relevant literature, and to suggest some novel directions for future research that might facilitate more accurate and meaningful assessments. The framework for this analysis will consist of an examination of the diagnostic process itself, with reference to patients, assessors, families, and culture. The current nomenclature will then be discussed, emphasizing particular problems with its application to adolescents.

The Diagnostic Process

PATIENT VARIABLES

Adolescence is not a homogeneous process. Early, middle, and late adolescents differ from each other (Blos 1962), clinical and nonclinical adolescents differ from each other (Golombek, Marton, Stein, and Korenblum 1987), and adolescents who are assessed cross-sectionally differ from those who are assessed longitudinally (Korenblum, Marton, Golombek, and Stein 1987). As well, adolescents need to be assessed along different parameters—biological, cognitive, psychodynamic, sociocultural, and familial dimensions may or may not be in synchrony. When growth in all areas is phase appropriate, then development is harmonious. Often, however, the profile is uneven, with delays, regressions, fixations, or precocities along one or more developmental lines. When this occurs, various forms of psychopathology often ensue. Furthermore, adolescents need to be seen against a backdrop of the tasks unique to this stage. Intrapsychic separation from one's family of origin, the formation of a value and ethical system, coming to terms with sexuality and a changed body image, and the choice of vocation are all components of the supraordinate task of adolescence, which is to form a cohesive identity.

As individuals who are growing and changing, adolescents can confound clinicians because they may present different material at different times. This has been referred to as "subject variance" or "occasion variance" (Spitzer, Endicott, and Robins 1975, 1978). As a source of diagnostic unreliability in adults, patient "inconstancy" has been found to account for 5 percent of interrater disagreements (Beck, Ward, Mendelson, Mock, and Erbaugh 1962; Ward, Beck, Mendelson, Mock, and Erbaugh 1962). With adolescents, the figure would probably be higher. Does this mean that the patient is suffering from different conditions or simply different stages of the same condition at different times? Symptom overflow, in the form of comorbidity among several disorders, is related to this question, as is the issue of "state versus trait." For example, although there is a high degree of comorbidity between affective disorder and personality disorder in adolescents (Clarkin, Friedman, Hurt, Corn, and Aronoff 1982; Friedman, Clarkin, Corn, Aronoff, Hurt, and Murphy 1982; McManus, Lerner, and Robins 1984) for certain personality disorders, the symptoms decrease markedly after the depression has cleared (Korenblum, Marton, Kutcher, Kennedy, and Pakes 1988). Cross-sectional prevalence rates of personality dysfunction vary with subphases, being higher in early and late adolescence, but, when examined longitudinally, 25 percent of teens are disturbed throughout adolescence, while 40 percent fluctuate into or out of disturbance at one subphase or another (Golombek et al. 1987). When followed over time, the types of disturbance change substantially for both groups and individuals (Korenblum, Marton, et al. 1987; Korenblum, Marton, Golombek, and Stein 1990). Even in late adolescence, as many as three out of ten teens can appear to be "atypical" (Korenblum et al. 1990).

Whether adolescents are self-referred or come at the request of another can influence what they want to tell the assessor. Teenagers are often extremely sensitive to outside opinions, especially if there is a possibility of being labeled "crazy." Many of them (especially younger ones) have a relative lack of self-awareness and a tendency to deny dysphoria that is due to cognitive immaturity and fears of dependency. This can make history taking distorted or unreliable—patients are least likely to reveal those aspects of themselves that are most necessary for making a diagnosis. Some try to protect their psyche from distress and deal with internal conflict or heal deficits by externalizing. Whether to discharge tension, achieve gratification of a neurotic conflict, or utilize someone in the environment to complete and soothe the self (Marohn 1981), this feature can complicate matters. Thus, trust and resistance are extremely important components when assessing teenagers, and the particular forms that resistances can take will be described.

INTERVIEWER VARIABLES

In addition to the inconstancy of adolescents, inconsistencies between clinicians, or even in the same clinician at different times, can contribute to diagnostic difficulties. The simple act of eliciting signs and symptoms may account for 5 percent of disagreements between assessors (Beck et al. 1962; Ward et al. 1962). Psychiatrists ask different questions of different patients. Some emphasize mental status items over past history; others give attention to phenomenology over unconscious dynamic data. Even when presented with the same information, different psychiatrists notice different data and perceive their importance differently. This has been called "observer variance" (Spitzer et al. 1975, 1978) and can account for as much as 22 percent of interrrater unreliability (Beck et al. 1962; Ward et al. 1962).

When working with adolescents, the conceptual beliefs and personality of the clinician are of crucial importance (Sanchez 1986). If the assessor ascribes to the view that adolescent turmoil is universal and inevitable, then he or she may underdiagnose serious psychopathology. A survey of mental health professionals in fact found this attitude to be widespread (Offer, Ostrov, and Howard 1981). If the clinician has unresolved residual conflict from his or her own adolescence, then there may be a neurotic tendency to overidentify or counteridentify with the patient, leading to underdiagnosis or overdiagnosis, respectively. Adults tend to stereotype adolescents to defend against their own anxieties (Anthony 1969). Responses to teenagers are determined by societal images that we internalize, idiosyncrasies based on here-and-now aspects of the patient-psychiatrist relationship, and the dynamics of transference and countertransference. Unconsciously, we may hold a number of dichotomized beliefs about teens: they are dangerous and therefore need protection; they are inherently maladjusted; or they are precociously capable because of their vivacity. As a defense against envy, exaggerated oedipal conflicts and sadistic tendencies may be mobilized, or there may be a narcissistic identification with the patient, whereby his or her success becomes ours and a kind of "hero worship" ensues. Each subphase elicits specific countertransference responses—early adolescents can leave one feeling like a gas station that is being used merely to fill the adolescent up. Middle adolescents need to spar with their psychiatrist in order to differentiate themselves and feel safe about their aggressive urges. This can be difficult for the clinician who has problems with anger or activity (Golombek 1983). Unless one is used to the rapid changes of mood states and object relations, one can have feelings of resentment and frustration at the fickleness or apparant contradictions of the patient.

Adolescents, like few other patients, are masters at pointing out our flaws and imperfections. Thus, our human needs to be flattered, to be caretakers, to be sexually desirable, to have control over situations, and to be correct can all be exposed by the teenager as neurotic fears of criticism, of engulfment, of being seduced, of passivity, and of being wrong (Kroll 1988). Personal beliefs about such issues as abortion, drug use, religion, and politics can all clash with those of the adolescent. In reaction, we may be tempted to diagnose nonexisting pathology just to protect our self-esteem.

This onslaught of our narcissism has been well described with reference to borderline adults (Maltsberger and Buie 1974). Because contact with adolescents can be intense, such descriptions have relevance to assessment in this age group. Defenses of repression, hatred turned against the self, reaction formation, projection, and denial or anger need to be recognized. And, when teenagers devalue their assessors, it is well to recall the underlying dynamics of their rage: it can represent a defense against wishes for nurturance (which are particularly threatening for adolescents, who are trying to deny dependence), a defense against envy of the therapist, projection of low self-esteem, or a transference manifestation (Adler 1970). All these factors can interfere with impartial, accurate diagnosis and, therefore, need careful monitoring.

FAMILY VARIABLES

Adolescents are in a state of transition from dependence on parents to greater autonomy and involvement with peers. Furthermore, an adolescent can appear quite differently when seen within the context of his or her family. For these reasons, an assessment of the parents as a dyad and one of the family as a whole are crucial components of the diagnostic process.

The taking of a marital and developmental history is important for the content that it will yield and for the process that should be observed. Frequent disagreements between parents on even "hard data" of developmental milestones may portend larger conflicts in other areas. Where possible, the parental interview should be supplemented with a personal history of each parent. This is important because parents may misinterpret the behavior of their adolescent children in relation to the reactivation of their own unresolved adolescent conflicts. As a couple, they may be going through "middlescence." This refers to a parallel process of accomplishing the tasks of adolescence but with reference to middle age: separating from one's own parents (the teenager's grandparents) through either illness or death; adjusting to waning sexuality (the so-called menopause-menarche syndrome between mothers and daughters); and perhaps a reevaluation of ethics and value systems as well as job definition. The parents may be subtly contributing to their adolescents' problems by having "blind spots" or even unconsciously sanctioning some unacceptable behaviors (Johnson 1949).

When trying to make a diagnosis of personality disorder, for example, one often depends on a history and corroborating evidence from people other than the patient. But the closest observers, the parents, are untrained psychiatrically and may be unaware of certain phenomena because of "superego lacunae" or because their teenagers do not talk to them. Furthermore, the hallmark of personality disorder is to create disturbance in the environment. Teenagers' behavior often elicits extreme reactions from those around them, and it can then become difficult to decide how much pathology is "secondary" to the family's response. If one does not maintain an impartial stance, there are risks of underestimating or overestimating the effect of family dysfunction on the adolescent's clinical manifestations (Sanchez 1986).

Even when using structured instruments that deal only with phenomenology, parents and children can disagree. In the Ontario Child Health Study, for example, the diagnostic agreement rate between parents and teachers, or parents and their children, was abysmally low (Offord, Boyle, and Szatmari 1986). In general, it seems that parents more reliably report antisocial and conduct behaviors while children more reliably report internal feelings states such as depression and anxiety. Paradoxically, families who support a psychiatric assessment *too* zealously, out of a need to scapegoat the patient, may stimulate mistrust and resistance in the teenager. In the face of such negativism, family dynamics should be considered as a possible contributor to difficulties in the diagnostic process.

Countertransference also plays an important role in the family component of the diagnostic assessment. The clinician can easily be drawn into "siding with" the parent against the teenager, or vice versa. Depending on the psychiatrist's own echoes from the past, there can be tendencies to view the parent or the teenager as martyr, victim, or rebellious hero. One must be especially careful to avoid competing with the caretakers and trying to be "the better parent." This can lead only to alienation on the part of the family and failure to engage (Stierlin 1975).

At the end of the assessment, the task is to integrate the data from the parental, conjoint family, and individual interviews in a manner that permits the most clinically useful formulation and diagnosis.

CULTURAL VARIABLES

Adolescence is the phase of development during which the individual's field of action expands outside his or her family. As a result, teenages are unduly sensitive to forces arising within society at large. The clinician who is unaware of such forces may unwittingly commit errors of false positive or false negative diagnosis. Increased mobility, for example, between countries or within a country can result in culture shock that may masquerade as severe psychopathology. Poverty can exert a sociosyntonic effect on antisocial behavior and academic underachievement. Thus, when confronted with these symptoms, it is important to inquire about group norms of expected behavior. The effects of separation and divorce on adolescents have been well documented (Rae-Grant and Robson 1988; Wallerstein and Kelly 1974) and should be considered as a possible contextual factor in any diagnostic assessment. Substance abuse can exist as an independent entity or can color clinical presentations of other syndromes. Especially in the areas of reality testing and affect, unusual symptoms should arouse the suspicion of drug use.

Just as the family can induce negativism in the assessment process, so can peers. If a best friend has a negative view of psychiatry or feeds into the patient's worst fears (which may actually be the friend's fears), then this can inhibit the data gathering and should be explored. Members of "cults" can be extremely difficult to assess properly without a knowledge of the mores of the cult involved (Levine 1981). To a lesser extent, punkers, rockers, etc. pose similar problems. If one subscribes to industrialized Western societal norms, one should not lose sight of culture-specific syndromes.

Certain parapsychological symptoms, such as clairvoyance, telekinesis, descriptions of reincarnation, and/or communication with dead people, can raise the specter of incipient psychosis. However, a simple inquiry as to whether the teenager is "into" séances or what movie the teenager has seen lately can change the opinion to one of heightened suggestibility in the context of peer/group behavior. The media in all its forms (print, movies, radio, television, video games) has an important influence on teenagers. In addition to the simulation of exorcist-like phenomena and pseudopsychotic symptoms, it can have a very real effect on heightening the risk of such serious behavior as suicide (Gould and Shaffer 1986; Phillips and Carstensen 1986).

One does not have to know all the details of the latest rock groups or movie stars. Instead, a simple appreciation of the fluidity of an adolescent's identity and its relative vulnerability to extrafamilial influences is all that is required.

The Current Diagnostic System

The process just described is geared toward answering many questions about an individual adolescent. Only one of these questions has to do with the definition or name of the clinical syndrome with which the adolescent presents. It is to this issue that I now turn. Inadequacies of the nomenclature can account for almost two-thirds of disagreements between clinicians assessing adults (Beck et al. 1962; Ward et al. 1962). This source of disagreement has been called "criterion variance" (Spitzer et al. 1975, 1978) and refers to differences in the formal inclusion and exclusion criteria that are used to summarize patient data. Since the system used most commonly in North America is DMS-III-R, it is this nosology that will be critiqued from the viewpoint of adolescent psychopathology.

The definition of mental illness as outlined in DSM-III-R incorporates the following notions: the manifestations of the condition are psychological, and the condition is associated with subjective distress. Unfortunately, adolescents confound each aspect of this definition. Teenagers often express their conflict behaviorally or psychosomatically instead of psychologically. Teenagers tend to have high levels of denial, and at times their behavior is ego syntonic. Thus, defining adolescents as mentally ill according to DSM-III-R can be problematic.

With adults, we usually assess psychopathology on the basis of conducting a survey of symptoms. The problem with adolescents is that a behavior that is normative at one age may be abnormal at another. Also, although we have got away from notions such as "masked depression," there is still some evidence that the same condition can manifest differently at different ages (Bemporad and Wilson 1978;

65

Carlson and Kashani 1988; Mitchell, McCaulley, Burke, and Moss 1988; Ryan, Puig-Antich, Ambrosini, Rabinovich, Robinson, Nelson, Iyengar, and Twomey 1987). Attention-deficit hyperactivity disorder, for instance, may include more hyperactivity in the younger subphases and less in the older subphases of adolescence (Cantwell and Baker 1988). Even with structured interviews, the developmental appropriateness of the symptom is not necessarily taken into consideration. Associated distress is another indicator that is sometimes used in the assessment of psychopathology. Adolescents, however, suffer less than adults with some symptoms (and in fact may obtain relief of anxiety through them) but suffer more with stressors, such as delay of gratification. Hence, the correlation between pathology and suffering may not be direct.

Developmental lines are ignored. In the cognitive area, for instance, those adolescents who have not yet reached the stage of formal operations have an incomplete understanding of concepts as fundamental as depression or death. DSM-III-R says that, "because the essential features of mood disorders and schizophrenia are the same in children and adults, there are no special categories" for those under eighteen (American Psychiatric Association 1987, p. 27). Early adolescents, however, may attribute different meaning to feelings of worthlessness, guilt, and anhedonia or may be unable truly to conceptualize hopelessness, for example, and this may affect diagnosis.

In DSM-III-R, oppositional disorder has been renamed "oppositional-defiant disorder" and requires five of nine symptoms. These include losing one's temper, often arguing with adults, often defying adults' requests, often deliberately annoying people, often blaming others, often being touchy, angry, or resentful, and often swearing or using obscene language. It seems that the distinction between normality and pathology would be most difficult given the expected developmental stance of many middle adolescents. Without a definition of "often," and without a knowledge of the base rate of these "symptoms" in a nonclinical population, this disorder seems fraught with difficulty. Even in areas such as alcohol abuse and anorexia nervosa, the problem of a continuum of behaviors beginning with normal dieting and/or normal experimentation with alcohol makes the system weak indeed. Adjustment disorder and posttraumatic stress disorder also seem to ignore developmental considerations. Research has indicated that the effects of loss or trauma differ depending on one's psychological age (Breier, Kelsoe, and Kinvin 1988; Tennant 1988). Yet this is not reflected in the current system.

The personality disorders are particularly problematic. DSM-III-R is extremely contradictory in this area: "Personality disorders by definition are recognizable by adolescence" (American Psychiatric Association 1987, p. 336); "the manifestations of personality disorders are generally recognizable by adolescence or earlier" (p. 335). At the same time, it is stated that "personality disorder categories may be applied to children or adolescents in those *unusual* instances in which the particular maladaptive personality traits appear to be stable" (p. 336). If personality disorders by definition begin in childhood, it is not clear why it should be so unusual for maladaptive traits to manifest by adolescence. No definition of "stable" is given, and the implication is that one would have to wait to observe the course of the illness before being able to diagnose it. If this logic were to apply to schizophrenia or bipolar affective disorder, diagnosis would be almost impossible, and crucial treatment would be delayed.

Even more confusing, DSM-III-R suggests that some disorders of childhood and adolescence correspond to certain personality disorders (e.g., avoidant, conduct disorder, and identity disorder; American Psychiatric Association 1987, p. 335). For reasons that are not explained, other personality disorders have no childhood counterpart. This defies the rationale for separating Axis I from Axis II and implies unproved relations between syndromes and personality disorders. Also, many eighteen-year-olds are psychologically and developmentally much younger than their chronological age.

The validity of certain personality disorders may be questioned. Parents and teachers were not able to differentiate avoidant, dependent, compulsive, and passive-aggressive teenagers from adolescents who were free of disturbed personality functioning in one study (Korenblum, Golombek, Marton, and Stein 1987). Although trained clinicians could distinguish these groups, two experienced psychiatrists had difficulty distinguishing them from subjects in the histrionic-narcissistic-borderline cluster (Korenblum, Golombek, et al. 1987). If the descriptions of these personality disorders are such that they are easily missed by parents or teachers and easily confused by psychiatrists, then perhaps there are serious problems with their definition and validity. In another study of late adolescents, almost 30 percent of the subjects with disturbed personality functioning had to be categorized in an atypical or mixed cluster because nonspecific or diffuse features prevented the identification of any single predominant pattern (Korenblum et al. 1990). This may constitute further evidence that DSM-III-R is less than adequate in establishing good criteria for personality dysfunction in adolescence.

While certain personality disorders are problematic in terms of validity, it is interesting to note that DSM-III (American Psychiatric Association 1980) demonstrates no significant differences in the kappa coefficient of agreement between adolescents and adults for personality disorder globally (pp. 470–471). Thus, Axis II as a whole seems to be no less reliable in this age group. And the reliability of Axis II diagnoses in hospitalized adolescents has shown a respectable kappa of .64, with even higher coefficients for certain specific types (histrionic and borderline; Strober, Green, and Carlson 1981).

The V code is another Axis that has poor applicability to adolescents. DSM-III-R states that "many children who come to clinical attention have problems that do not warrant a diagnosis of mental disorder" (American Psychiatric Association 1987, p. 28). Examples include adolescent antisocial behavior, parent-child problems, and other specified family circumstances. In these cases, it is suggested that the category of "conditions not attributable to a mental disorder" be used. In fact, child abuse, participating in or witnessing violence, the sequelae of divorce, and other similar situations are among the most important that a child or adolescent psychiatrist is called on to assess. It seems as if the authors wished that they had retained a label such as "adolescent adjustment reaction." The V code simply relegates too many clinically significant issues to a wastebasket category, thus impeding empirical research.

In general, DSM-III-R lacks a developmental approach to psychopathology. Rutter (1988) has masterfully outlined the necessary components of such a perspective. These are age differences in prevalence; age differences in remission rates; subdivision of disorders according to age at onset; subdivision according to developmental appropriateness; temporal continuities and discontinuities between childhood, adolescent, and adult disorders; age differences in the operation of risk factors (e.g., death, divorce, brain damage); continuities and discontinuities between normality and pathology; pervasiveness versus situation specificity; and the need for taking an interpersonal context. The implications of this perspective for future classification systems are decribed below.

Future Directions

Modifications of both the process of gathering information and the classification of data so gathered are necessary to improve our understanding of adolescents. Within the diagnostic process, there is little that we can do to change teenagers themselves. However, intervention at the level of interviewer, familial, and cultural variables is possible.

Structured interviews should be used more frequently. Evidence from many research studies suggests that this is the best way to reduce bias, decrease the chance of accidental omission in history taking, and assure that the same data are used in making diagnostic decisions (Gutterman, O'Brien, and Young 1987; Sylvester, Hyde, and Reichler 1987; Young, O'Brien, Gutterman, and Cohen 1987). Nevertheless, a tension between descriptive and dynamic methodologies still exists. Symptoms need to be viewed within an interpersonal and developmental context. The less the adolescent trusts the interviewer, the more subject and occasion variance will confound the assessor, even if he or she uses a structured interview. An "assessment alliance" is as important as a therapeutic alliance for the accurate understanding of adolescent problems. Therefore, intrapsychic, familial, and sociocultural sources of resistance should be considered. Individual interviews should always be supplemented with parental and conjoint family sessions. Ancillary sources of data such as school reports should be incorporated since teenagers often appear different in different settings. The interviewer should be sensitive to (and reasonably knowledgeable about) sociocultural, community, and peer group influences that may be impinging on the adolescent. Since the patient's problems may change quickly over time or may be situation specific, and because state may exert such a strong influence over trait, it is best to conduct a number of serial assessments over a few weeks. This will help establish persistence and pervasiveness and will tease out such transient factors as substance abuse.

In the training of residents, greater attention should be paid to developmental influences on psychopathology (Freud 1965). The effect of countertransference on decision making is especially important when working with adolescents, so this should be stressed in our training programs as well (Gauron and Dickinson 1966; Katz, Cole, and Lowery 1969). These steps will improve reliability. Validity also needs to be enhanced by conducting more longitudinal prospective studies in clinical and nonclinical populations. Adolescents are sometimes difficult to diagnose because their illnesses are just beginning. It is only when we get a clearer picture of the evolution of symptoms and syndromes, with and without treatment, that we will have more confidence in our prognostications. And the area of parent-child-other (e.g., teacher) disagreements (even with structured interviews) needs further research. Different perceptions of the same behavior, different role expectations in different settings, and cross-situational instability of behavior are all hypothetical explanations that need verification.

With respect to the classifications system itself, we need to have novel approaches that go beyond DSM-III-R. One possibility is diagnostic categories that use chronology as criteria: for example, disorders beginning in childhood and ending in childhood (e.g., enuresis); disorders beginning in adolescence and continuing in adulthood (e.g., schizophrenia); disorders beginning and ending in adolescence (e.g., situational disturbances); and disorders beginning in childhood and continuing through to adulthood (e.g., pervasive developmental disorder). Other possibilities are differentiating clinical syndromes according to their presentation in early, middle, or late adolescence and a blending of classification of resistances with classification of syndromes.

Figure 1 outlines a possible method of understanding how typical adolescent resistances relate to clinical syndromes. The headings refer to the ability or desire to recognize and convey internal emotional states. The adolescents in box A are unable to recognize feeling states in the usual manner. Adolescents in box B can recognize their internal states but choose not to. Adolescents in box D are able to recognize their feelings but will not convey them because they see no need to. Their anxiety level is so low or their defenses are so effective (albeit rigid) that intervention from a mental health professional is seen as irrelevant. The adolescents in box C cannot convey their feelings because they are tremendously anxious or depressed and have erected less successful defenses that are constricting or inhibiting. They desperately want to share their inner states but are afraid to.

The importance of such a classification system is its correlation with

	"Can't"		"Won't"
Recognize	A.	Schizophrenia Mental retardation Organic mental disorders	B. Antisocial Personality disorder
Convey	C.	Avoidant disorder Overanxious disorder Obsessive-compulsive disorder Simple phobia Major depression Dysthymia	D. Oppositional defiant disorder Passive-aggressive personality disorder Narcissistic personality disorder

FIG. 1.—The relation between diagnosis, resistance, and treatability

treatability. Type C adolescents are those most suited to individual psychotherapy (psychodynamic, cognitive, or behavioral). Type D adolescents are more difficult to treat and require either paradoxical interventions, concurrent environmental manipulation, or family therapy. Their anxiety level needs to be raised rather than lowered. Type A and B adolescents are not appropriate for psychotherapy and require either no treatment (type B) or other forms of treatment, such as medication, detoxification, or vocational rehabilitation (type A).

Conclusions

Some of the major problems confronting child and adolescent psychiatrists today are the methodological, theoretical, and practical shortcomings of the available classification systems and procedures for making diagnoses. Concentrated efforts to remedy these problems are being taken in the adult field. Child psychiatry, by comparison, lags behind, and nowhere is this more evident than in the field of adolescent psychopathology (Cantwell 1980).

Ultimately, the utility of any diagnostic system is in the eye of the user. The researcher and the clinician will want different things from a diagnostic system. But the great danger of a system as elaborate as DSM-III-R is its proclivity to induce delusions of understanding. Diagnosis is not synonymous with formulation. We must keep our minds open to what empirical research tells us in terms of distinguishing normality from abnormality. It has been shown (Offer et al. 1981)

71

that the mental health professional's concept of the normal adolescent is too often more pathological than that of adolescents themselves. Particularly in the areas of mood, social relationships, family relationships, and vocational/educational goals, clinicians predict poorer self-images than adolescents actually exhibit. Such assumptions of "normative deviance" result in underdiagnosis of true psychiatric illness.

As Offer et al. have stated, "We will probably be able to help adolescents more if we think of them as persons first and (disturbed) adolescents second" (1981, p. 152). The diagnostic process is after all both a science and an art. Given that the subjects of our nosologic efforts are human beings, perhaps it should remain that way. As human beings who are rapidily changing, adolescents pose particular challenges to scientific diagnosis when they are psychiatrically ill. Rather than letting this deter us, however, and instead of avoiding these sometimes difficult patients, we should pursue both the science and the art with renewed vigor so that clinical communication can be improved and rational treatment can be given to those who need it most. In so doing, we can hope to avoid tendencies to *furor diagnosticus* that are based on a plethora of inconsistent theories and a paucity of precise definitions.

REFERENCES

Adler, G. 1970. Valuing and devaluing in the psychotherapeutic process. *Archives of General Psychiatry* 22:454–461.

American Psychiatric Association. 1980. *Diagnostic and Statistical Manual of Mental Disorders*. 3d ed. Washington, D.C.: American Psychiatric Association.

American Psychiatric Association. 1987. *Diagnostic and Statistical Manual of Mental Disorders*. 3d ed., rev. Washington, D.C.: American Psychiatric Association.

Anthony, E. J. 1969. The reactions of adults to adolescents and their behavior. In G. Caplan and S. Lebovici, eds. *Adolescence: Psychosocial Perspectives*. New York: Basic.

Beck, A.; Ward, C.; Mendelson, M.; Mock, J.; and Erbaugh, J. 1962. Reliability of psychiatric diagnosis: a study of consistency of clinical judgement and ratings. *American Journal of Psychiatry* 118:351–347.

Bemporad, J., and Wilson, A. 1978. A developmental approach to depression in childhood and adolescence. *Journal of the American Academy of Psychoanalysis* 6(3): 325–352.

Blos, P. 1962. *On Adolescence: A Psychoanalytic Interpretation.* New York: Free Press.

Breier, A.; Kelsoe, J.; and Kinvin, P. 1988. Early parental loss and development of adult psychopathology. *Archives of General Psychiatry* 45:987–993.

Cantwell, D. 1980. The diagnostic process and diagnostic classification in child psychiatry—DSM-III. *Journal of the American Academy of Child Psychiatry* 19:345–355.

Cantwell, D., and Baker, L. 1988. Issues in the classification of child and adolescent psychopathology. *Journal of the American Academy of Child and Adolescent Psychiatry* 27(5): 521–530.

Carlson, G., and Kashani, J. H. 1988. Phenomenology of major depression from childhood through adulthood: analysis of three studies. *American Journal of Psychiatry* 145(10): 1222–1225.

Clarkin, J. F.; Friedman, R. C.; Hurt, S. W.; Corn, R.; and Aronoff, M. 1982. Affective and character pathology of suicidal adolescent and young adult in-patients. *Journal of Clinical Psychiatry* 45:19–22.

Freud, A. 1965. *Normality and Pathology in Childhood.* New York: International Universities Press.

Friedman, R. C.; Clarkin, J. F.; Corn, R.; Aronoff, M.; Hurt, S. W.; and Murphy, M. C. 1982. DSM-III and affective pathology in hospitalized adolescents. *Journal of Nervous and Mental Diseases* 170(9): 511–521.

Gauron, E., and Dickinson, J. 1966. Diagnostic decision making in psychiatry. *Archives of General Psychiatry* 14:226–237.

Golombek, H. 1983. Personality development during adolescence: implications for treatment. In H. Golombek and B. Garfinkel, eds. *The Adolescent and Mood Disturbance.* New York: International Universities Press.

Golombek, H.; Marton, P.; Stein, B.; and Korenblum, M. 1987. Personality functioning status during early and middle adolescence. *Adolescent Psychiatry* 14:365–377.

Gould, M. S., and Shaffer, D. 1986. The impact of suicide in television movies. *New England Journal of Medicine* 315:690–694.

Gutterman, E.; O'Brien, J. D.; and Young, D. 1987. Structured diagnostic interviews for children and adolescents: current status and future directions. *Journal of the American Academy of Child and Adolescent Psychiatry* 26(5): 621–630.

Johnson, A. M. 1949. Sanctions for superego lacunae of adolescents. In K. R. Eissler, ed. *Searchlights on Delinquency*. New York: International Universities Press.

Katz, M.; Cole, J.; and Lowery, H. 1969. Studies of the diagnostic process: the influence of symptom perception, past experience and ethnic background on diagnostic decisions. *American Journal of Psychiatry* 125:937–947.

Korenblum, M.; Golombek, H.; Marton, P.; and Stein, B. 1987. The classification of disturbed personality functioning in early adolescence. *Canadian Journal of Psychiatry* 32:362–367.

Korenblum, M.; Marton, P.; Golombek, H.; and Stein, B. 1987. Disturbed personality functioning: patterns of change from early to middle adolescence. *Adolescent Psychiatry* 14:407–416.

Korenblum, M.; Marton, P.; Golombek, H.; and Stein, B. A. 1990. Personality status: changes through adolescence. *Psychiatric Clinics of North America* 13(3): 389–399.

Korenblum, M.; Marton, P.; Kutcher, S.; Kennedy, B.; and Pakes, J. 1988. Personality dysfunction in depressed adolescents—state or trait? Poster presentation at the meeting of the American Academy of Child and Adolescent Psychiatry, Seattle, October.

Kroll, J. 1988. *The Challenge of the Borderline Patient*. New York: Norton.

Levine, S. 1981. Cults and mental health: clinical conclusions. *Canadian Journal of Psychiatry* 26:534–539.

McManus, M.; Lerner, H.; and Robins, D. 1984. Assessment of borderline symptomatology in hospitalized adolescents. *Journal of the American Academy of Child Psychiatry* 23(6): 685–694.

Maltsberger, J., and Buie, D. 1974. Countertransference hate in the treatment of suicidal patients. *Archives of General Psychiatry* 30:625–633.

Marohn, R. 1981. Personality disorders and adolescence. In J. Lion, ed. *Personality Disorders: Diagnosis and Management*. Baltimore: Williams & Wilkins.

Mitchell, J.; McCaulley, E.; Burke, P.; and Moss, S. J. 1988. Phenomenology of depression in children and adolescents. *Journal of the American Academy of Child and Adolescent Psychiatry* 27(1): 12–20.

Offer, D.; Ostrov, E.; and Howard, K. 1981. The mental health professional's concept of the normal adolescent. *Archives of General Psychiatry* 38:149–152.

Offord, D.; Boyle, M.; and Szatmari, P. 1986. *Ontario Child Health Study: Summary of Initial Findings*. Toronto: Queen's Printer for Ontario.

Phillips, D. P., and Carstensen, L. L. 1986. Clustering of teenage suicide after television news stories about suicide. *New England Journal of Medicine* 315:685–689.

Rae-Grant, Q., and Robson, B. 1988. Moderating the morbidity of divorce. *Canadian Journal of Psychiatry* 33:443–452.

Rutter, M. 1988. Epidemiological approaches to developmental psychopathology. *Archives of General Psychiatry* 45:486–495.

Ryan, N.; Puig-Antich, J.; Ambrosini, P.; Rabinovich, H.; Robinson, D.; Nelson, B.; Iyengar, S.; and Twomey, J. 1987. The clinical picture of major depression in children and adolescents. *Archives of General Psychiatry* 44:854–861.

Sanchez, E. 1986. Factors complicating psychiatric diagnosis of adolescents. *Adolescent Psychiatry* 13:100–115.

Spitzer, R.; Endicott, J.; and Robins, E. 1975. Clinical criteria for psychiatric diagnosis and DSM-III. *American Journal of Psychiatry* 132:1187–1192.

Spitzer, R.; Endicott, J.; and Robins, E. 1978. Research diagnostic criteria: rationale and reliability. *Archives of General Psychiatry* 35:773–782.

Stierlin, H. 1975. Countertransference in family therapy with adolescents. In M. Sugar, ed. *The Adolescent in Group and Family Therapy*. New York: Brunner/Mazel.

Strober, M.; Green, J.; and Carlson, G. 1981. Reliability of psychiatric diagnosis in hospitalized adolescents. *Archives of General Psychiatry* 38:141–145.

Sylvester, C.; Hyde, T.; and Reichler, R. 1987. The diagnostic interview for children and personality inventory for children in studies of children at risk for anxiety disorders or depression. *Journal of the American Academy of Child and Adolescent Psychiatry* 26(5): 668–675.

Tennant, C. 1988. Parental loss in childhood. *Archives of General Psychiatry* 45:987–993.

Wallerstein, J. S., and Kelly, J. B. 1974. The effects of parental di-

vorce: the adolescent experience. In E. J. Anthony and C. Kouper-
nick, eds. *The Child and His Family*. New York: Wiley.

Ward, C.; Beck, A.; Mendelson, M.; Mock, J.; and Erbaugh, J. 1962.
The psychiatric nomenclature: reasons for diagnostic disgreement.
Archives of General Psychiatry 7:60–67.

Young, G.; O'Brien, J. D.; Gutterman, E.; and Cohen, P. 1987. Research on the clinical interview. *Journal of the American Academy
of Child and Adolescent Psychiatry* 26(5): 613–620.

PART II

THE RELATIONAL MATRIX: CONTEXT FOR DEVELOPMENT AND CHANGE

EDITORS' INTRODUCTION

This special section of the *Annals,* "The Relational Matrix: Context for Development and Change," contains virtually all the papers presented at the Society's annual meeting organized around the same theme and held in New Orleans in May 1991.

That meeting attempted to capture a fundamental movement within developmental psychology, developmental psychopathology, and psychoanalysis, a movement reflecting change on the order of what Kuhn (1962) has called a "paradigm shift" within the social and physical sciences. This paradigm shift describes a movement away from the mechanistic metaphor of the machine to an organic metaphor of the living system, the cell, plant, person, or biosphere. A social science grounded in this epistemology is characterized by the fundamental categories of the organic: a relational base, necessary and inherent activity, organization, and directional change. An understanding of the person from the perspective of the organic metaphor "promotes a particular metatheoretical narrative of the individual as an inherently relational and progressively organized complex system of activity, constructing its affective and cognitive understanding, and growing in the direction of personhood, through a dialectical process of regulation and transformation" (Overton 1992).

Models of development that reflect an organic vision include those of Heinz Werner (1948, 1957), Jean Piaget (1952, 1985), and John Bowlby (1969, 1973, 1980). Werner's orthogenetic principle asserts that the pattern of development moves from states of globality and relative lack of differentiation to states of increased differentiation, articulation, and hierarchic integration. Piaget's equilibration process, the matrix of assimilation/accommodation activity, describes developmental change moving from integration and self-regulation to differentiation and transformation to a reintegration at increasingly complex levels of organization.

A dynamic model of development that seeks to account for change over time in the subjective and relational experiences of the person is offered by Bowlby's attachment theory. Emerging from an intellectual matrix that included Fairbairn, Klein, and the British object relations school of psychoanalysis, the ethology of Lorenz and Hinde, and the evolutionary biology of Waddington, Bowlby's elegant synthesis provides a view of the development of the self from a dyadic system of regulation through a dyadic dialectical process of differentiation and transformation to the increased complexity of self-organization and self-regulation. Integral to the development of the self as a unique structure of individual subjectivity is Bowlby's concept of the internal working model, a concept that describes the recursive internalized structures that are constituted by the experience of self and other and constitute the experience of self and other. Thus, the internal working model reflects a relational base, an inherent activity of co-constructive meaning making that moves irreversibly toward differentiation, transformation, and the articulation of personal narratives of increasing complexity.

It must be emphasized that attachment theory, resting on an organic metaphor and relational and dialectic premises, sees development across the life span as interactive and dynamic. Thus, the person, acting from both poles of a differentiated self as subject and self as object, is always a self in context and remains within a relational matrix. As Bowlby (1980) wrote, "Intimate attachments to other human beings are the hub around which a person's life revolves, not only when s/he is an infant or a toddler, but throughout adolescence and the years of maturity as well and on into old age" (p. 422).

Empirical support for the relational model of psychological development proposed by Bowlby comes from the field of psychoanalytically informed observational and longitudinal research with infants and toddlers pioneered by Louis Sander (1973), Margaret Mahler (Mahler, Pine, and Bergman 1975), and Mary Ainsworth (1973) and extended by Stern (1985), Emde (1980; Emde and Buchsbaum 1990), and Sroufe (1989; Sroufe and Waters 1977). Their work has further defined the relational matrix and the organizational perspective as fundamental to any dynamic theory of human development. Sroufe (1989) writes,

"Self should be conceived as an inner organization of attitudes, feelings, expectations, and meanings, which arises from an organized caregiving matrix. That is, the dyadic infant-caregiver organization precedes and gives rise to the organization that is self" (p. 71).

With human development and human nature viewed as inherently relational, our theories of psychic reality, intersubjective experience, and the healing processes of psychotherapy are then informed and enlivened by this emerging and powerful paradigm. It is hoped that the chapters in this section will contribute to this emergence for those concerned with the mental health of adolescents, a population most clearly embedded in the varying contexts and complexities of the relational matrix.

The section begins with Heinz von Foerster's, "On Seeing: The Problem of the Double Blind," a paper not read in New Orleans but rather originally presented as the first Gregory Bateson Lecture in 1985 in Philadelphia, on the occasion of the establishment of an annual lecture in Bateson's honor by the Philadelphia Society for Adolescent Psychiatry. Although neither a developmentalist nor a clinician, but a neurobiologist and philosopher, von Foerster calls our attention to the paradoxes associated with the second-order concepts of circularity and recursion as well as their correlates in the psychological domain—character, psychic reality, and the repetition compulsion. By recursively constructing our lives, our selves, and our relationships, we see what we believe and desire, and we are blind to what is outside our constructions. It is the double blind, the not seeing that we do not see, "one of the fundamental second-order dysfunctions," that brings people into therapy. The solution to the problem of the double blind, for seeing those aspects of ourselves that we are unable to see, according to von Foerster, "is to see ourselves through other people's eyes." Thus, from the view of second-order cybernetics, developmental and therapeutic change in human beings is embedded in a relational matrix.

Joseph D. Lichtenberg's paper, written from the perspectives of psychoanalysis and infant research, offers a model of the development of motivation from a relational matrix. His thesis is that motivation is but conceptualized as a dynamic organization of systems designed to promote the fulfillment and regulation of basic needs. The motivational systems each develop in response to a specific need, including (1) the need for psychic regulation of physiological requirements, (2) the need for attachment to others, (3) the need for exploration and assertion of preferences, (4) the need to react aggressively to unmet needs, expectancies, and loss by responses of antagonism and/or withdrawal, and (5) the need for sensual enjoyment and later sexual excitement. Lichtenberg proposes the self as the overarching regulatory organization of these motivational systems in relational experiential contexts. Moving to implications for a theory of technique, Lichtenberg believes that the concept of relational matrix helps define the optimal therapist as attempting an empathic mode of listening, of interaction with patients on the basis of the therapist's own sensitivity to his or her own motivations as a vehicle for empathic understanding, in form much like the infant-caregiver relationship.

The following three papers are reports of empirical research based on Bowlby's attachment theory. Charles H. Zeanah's work explores the infant's subjective experience of the world, particularly the attachment experiences of infants and parents. Asserting a constructivist premise, he maintains that the internal working models organize an individual's internal experience and behaviors in relationships and, as such, are not merely passive filters of experience but also contribute to an individual's active recreation of relationship pattern, that is, transference and repetition compulsion. Reviewing investigations that have examined concordance in types of internal working models of attachment in parents and infants and the implications of this research for the intergenerational transmission of relationship patterns, he then presents his own research, addressing two questions: (1) How do parents with qualitative differences in their internal representations of attachment perceive and interpret infant distress? (2) Are different internal representations of attachment in matters associated with different patterns of interpreting and experiencing one's own infant? Zeanah concludes with a discussion of the clinical implications of this research.

Diana S. Rosenstein and Harvey A. Horowitz examine the relationships among attachment organization, personality development, and psychopathology in a population of hospitalized adolescents. Using a methodology that includes the Adult Attachment Interview to generate an attachment classification in adolescents, the authors report findings that confirm the hypothesis that adolescents with comorbid conduct disorder and substance abuse disorder, that is, with externalizing disorders, will also manifest an avoidant attachment organization and a distancing form of relatedness. In an alternative research and treatment strategy, R. Rogers Kobak begins with conversion as the vehicle for the maintenance of cooperative, goal-corrected partnerships. From this view, if conversation mediates the child's access to attachment figures, then discourse analysis and the assessment of coherence of conversation should provide vital clues to understanding attachment security and insecurity. Kobak reports his findings using this methodology and discusses the treatment implications of attention to the coherence of conversation between adolescents and their parents.

The following three papers represent an effort by the authors to explore the place of ego and self in a relational matrix model of development. Polly Young-Eisendrath begins with the premises (1) that selves are created and developed in relationships, (2) that the geography of selves is shaped by cultural contexts, and (3) that selves carry the local meanings of the folk psychologies that sponsor them. Drawing on Loevinger's nine-stage model of ego development, which she believes is exhaustive of types of subjectivity among adolescents and adults in our society, Young-Eisendrath describes impressions from her studies of the relationship of the level of ego development and her subjects' self-other narratives from psychotherapy. The attempt is to demonstrate that the patient's self as captured by level of ego development puts limits on the narratives or therapy.

Stuart T. Hauser and Hilary A. Levine address what they consider to be a bias in Western developmental theory that emphasizes themes of autonomy and separation, while neglecting those of intimacy and connectedness, and assert their support for a developmental model that holds interdependence, a balance between autonomy and connectedness, as the optimal dynamic dialectic—the life span. Operationalizing these concepts of autonomy and relatedness in a methodology that includes Loevinger's stages of ego development and model of analysis of family interaction as either constraining or enabling, the authors present findings demonstrating positive correlations in adolescents between levels of ego development and adolescent behaviors that serve to differentiate a person from others and those that seem to strengthen the relationship through positive engagement, interest, and involvement.

Continuing this exploration of the self in context, Judith V. Jordan offers a view of the psychological development of women as the development of a "relational self" that focuses on the movement of mutual initiative and responsiveness, while mutual empathy and empowerment are seen as core organizing dynamics in women's lives. Analyzing the effects of gender socialization on the development of relational competencies, she discusses the differences among adolescent boys and girls in their organization of early sexual experiences.

The section concludes with Lyman C. Wynne's paper on the epigenesis of relational systems. Building on the core hypothesis that relational processes within families and other enduring interpersonal systems follow one another in a certain developmental sequence, he addresses the question of whether distortions of sequential patterning in this development predictably lead to distress or to constrictions of growth. Presenting an epigenetic schema, he proposes a model of the four major processes in the development of enduring relational systems as well as a discussion of illustrative dysfunctional trajectories.

Taken as a whole, the chapters in this section devoted to the relational matrix are a significant contribution to what is, in the view of the sections' contributors, a paradigm shift in the social sciences, a paradigm shift from the primacy of separate self to relational self, a shift that will deepen our understanding of human experience. As the philosopher Charles Taylor (1989) has written, "One is a self only among other selves. A self can never be described without reference to those who surround it" (p. 35). Or, as Gregory Bateson was known to say, "It takes two to know one."

REFERENCES

Ainsworth, M. D. S. 1973. The development of infant-mother attachment. In B. Caldwell and H. Riciutti, eds. *Reviews of Child Development Research,* vol. 3. Chicago: University of Chicago Press.

Bowlby, J. 1969. *Attachment and Loss.* Vol. 1, *Attachment.* New York: Basic.

Bowlby, J. 1973. *Attachment and Loss.* Vol. 2, *Separation, Anxiety and Anger.* New York: Basic.

Bowlby, J. 1980. *Attachment and Loss.* Vol. 3, *Loss, Sadness and Depression.* New York: Basic.

Emde, R. N. 1980. Levels of meaning for infant emotions: a biosocial view. In W. A. Collins, ed. *Development of Cognition, Affect, and Social Relations.* Hillsdale, N.J.: Erlbaum.

Emde, R. N., and Buchsbaum, H. K. 1990. Toward a psychoanalytic theory of affect: emotional development and signaling in infancy. In S. I. Greenspan and G. H. Pollock, eds. *The Course of Life: Psychoanalytic Contributions toward Understanding Personality Development*. Washington, D.C.: U.S. Government Printing Office.

Kuhn, T. S. 1962. *The Structure of Scientific Revolutions*. Chicago: University of Chicago Press.

Mahler, M. S.; Pine, F.; and Bergman, A. 1975. *The Psychological Birth of the Human Infant: Symbiosis and Individuation*. New York: Basic.

Overton, W. F. 1992. The arrow of time and cycles of time: concepts of change, cognition, and embodiment. Paper presented at the Twelfth Advanced Course, Jean Piaget Archives Foundation, September, Geneva University, Geneva, Switzerland.

Piaget, J. 1952. *The Origins of Intelligence in Children*. New York: Norton.

Piaget, J. 1985. *The Equilibration of Cognitive Structures*. Chicago: University of Chicago Press.

Sander, L. 1975. Infant and caretaking environment: investigation and conceptualization of adaptive behavior in a system of increasing complexity. In E. J. Anthony, ed. *Explorations in Child Psychiatry*. New York: Plenum.

Sroufe, L. A. 1989. Relationships, self, and individual adaptation. In A. J. Sameroff and R. Emde, eds. *Relationship Disturbances in Early Childhood*. New York: Basic.

Sroufe, L. A., and Waters, E. 1977. Attachment as an organizational construct. *Child Development* 48:1184–1199.

Stern, D. N. 1985. *The Interpersonal World of the Infant: A View from Psychoanalysis and Developmental Psychology*. New York: Basic.

Taylor, C. 1989. *The Sources of the Self*. Cambridge, Mass.: Harvard University Press.

Werner, H. 1948. *Comparative Psychology of Mental Development*. New York: International Universities Press.

Werner, H. 1957. The concept of development from a comparative and organismic point of view. In D. B. Harris, ed. *The Concept of Development: An Issue in the Study of Human Behavior*. Minneapolis: University of Minnesota Press.

6 ON SEEING: THE PROBLEM OF THE DOUBLE BLIND

HEINZ VON FOERSTER

I would like to begin by expressing my gratitude to you for trying to see Gregory Bateson through my eyes. It seems to me that his work centers essentially on one fundamental point, namely, *making oneself understood*. Gregory wanted to *understand understanding*. I am referring to those fascinating "second-order" concepts that often come up in his work, for example, in the idea of "learning to learn" and in many other concepts that I discuss later.

What I find particularly interesting is that Bateson felt a sense of failure in his efforts at making himself understood. But I would like also to underscore that it was this very feeling that stimulated him to go on and keep trying. In other words, while he thought he failed, I really do not think that he did. On the contrary, I think that he very much succeeded. To clarify what I am saying, I would like to relate a vignette in which Bateson talks about a student who came to him after class to try to understand what he had been talking about. This episode is reported in the introduction to *Steps to an Ecology of Mind* (1972, p. xvi): "At the end of the session, one resident came up. He glanced over his shoulder to be sure that the others were leaving, and then said rather hesitantly: 'I want to ask a question.' 'Yes.' 'It's—do you want us to *learn* what you're telling us?' I hesitated a moment, but he rushed on with, 'Or is it all a sort of example, an illustration of something else?' 'Yes, indeed!'" The student left, and Gregory asked himself, "An example of what? And then there was, almost every year, vague complaints which usually came to me as a rumor. It was alleged that 'Bateson knows something which he does not tell you,' or 'There's something behind what Bateson says, but he never says what it is.' Obviously, I was not answering the question, 'An example of what?'"

If you continue to read this passage, you will see how he desperately tries to do something about it. And I believe that this is a truly ideal way to communicate something of ours, by letting such ideas be generated among students.

When I had the pleasure of being invited to a conference together with Gregory, I too had the opportunity to wonder about what was going on, what the difficulties were in understanding, and so on. He was the first speaker of the day, while my talk was planned for the following day. Gregory gave his presentation in a brilliant, clear, and effective style, and I was utterly fascinated. During his speech, people noticed that I smiled, nodded, and laughed at the right moments, so finally they asked me, "Did you really understand what he was saying?" "Sure, it was very clear." "Clear, that?" "Of course!" and so on.

Then I thought to myself, "What's going on? Aha, I think I got it!" So I developed a theory that I presented to the group the next day. Gregory was sitting in the front row, and I was glad to test my story about him in his presence. I said, "Ladies and gentlemen, there have been difficulties yesterday in understanding what Gregory Bateson was talking about, and that's because what he was saying was very clear, and that which is clear . . . cannot be seen. Therefore, I will try to make his arguments a bit more opaque, so that you will finally see what he was talking about."

I wondered how Gregory might react to this, and I was spying on him out of the corner of my eye: he was chuckling and puffing (this was his way of laughing), so I thought that I was on the right track. Since I believe that that strategy was effective, I would like to use it here as well. I will try to make some of Bateson's concepts more opaque. I would like to focus on two fundamental concepts that I believe are present, although not always explicitly, in his dialogues and in his writings. The first one is "seeing," and I mean "seeing" in William Blake's sense, when he maintained that he saw not *with* his eyes but *through* his eyes. This means that seeing must be understood as having an *insight,* as reaching the understanding of something by using everything we have by way of explanations, metaphors, parables, and so on.

The other concept is that of "ethics" in Wittgenstein's (1961) sense,

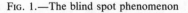

FIG. 1.—The blind spot phenomenon

when he said, "It is clear that ethics cannot be articulated in words" (p. 64). In reading Bateson, we notice a constant care to avoid having the meaning of such words as "meaning," "purpose," "control," "information," etc. somehow turned against those words.

Not Seeing That We Are Not Seeing

There is obviously a connection between these two concepts, seeing and ethics. This connection inspired the title of this chapter. You will say, "What does it mean? Surely he must have meant, with Gregory Bateson, 'double bind'; there must be a mistake."

Of course, the two are the same; it makes no difference whether the "l" is there or not. I would, however, like to explain my reason for choosing this title, and I will do so with an experiment. Examine figure 1 (the star and the circle). Close your left eye, using your left hand if necessary. Hold the figure in front of you, focusing on the star, and move it slowly forward and backward along your line of vision. Suddenly, you will notice that, in a certain position, more or less eight inches from your eye, the black circle disappears from view. This phenomenon is called the "blind spot."

Now I shall give you a physiological explanation of why this happens. While I give you this explanation, I invite you to pay attention to two things: the first, of course, is the explanation itself. The other is the effect that it produces on you while you listen to it. You have two tasks, listening to me and observing yourself while you listen. The explanation is in figure 2, where you can see a cross section of the eye, the star, and the circle and how these images project through the lens on the eye's retina.

If you look more carefully, you will see that the star is projected on the fovea, which is the part of the eye with the highest visual acuity because rods and cones have here a very high density. But, under certain conditions, the black circle is projected on the retina where the optic nerve exits the eye, and in that region there are neither rods

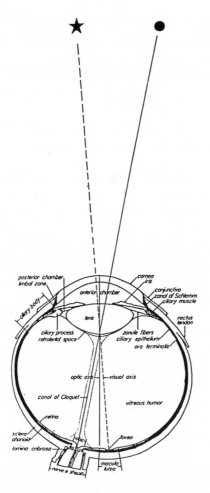

FIG. 2.—The physiological explanation of the blind spot

nor cones, no visual receptors. Therefore, of course, if something is projected on that blind spot, it cannot be seen. Is that clear? Unfortunately, it is very clear!

We can thus resume our usual occupations, forget all about it, and still feel very calm. All the wonder of the blind spot disappears as it turns into a very natural matter. So what is this explanation producing? At least two things: not only is this fascinating phenomenon swept under the carpet by it, but it has another effect that makes you blind to another observation. And this observation is the following. If you look around in the room, in all directions, with one eye, with two, left eye first, then right eye, you see an uninterrupted visual field. There are no interruptions. You do not see blind spots traveling around your visual field because, if you did, you would go to your doctor or to the ophthalmologist. There are no gaps in your visual field; that is, you are not aware of being partially blind. This means that you don't see that you don't see. This is a *second-order* dysfunction. As you see, this explanation brings the second-order dysfunction into the cognitive domain.

Actually, we are not cognitively blind to seeing such cognitive features in others. I think that you all have experienced this, for example, during political discussions with friends, when you think, "This poor fellow doesn't even realize that he does not see things as they are." This dysfunction, not seeing that you're not seeing, is one of the fundamental second-order dysfunctions on which I would like to focus this chapter, and it constitutes the crux of what I mean when I refer to the image of the double blind.

In this respect, I need to bring your attention to the fact that the logic of perception is very different from orthodox logic. In orthodox logic, a double negation produces an affirmation (if we put two negations in a proposition, it becomes affirmative), but, clearly, if we have a perceptual dysfunction such as blindness to blindness, we do not obtain sight. Thus, double negation in perceptual logic does not produce what it does in orthodox logic. It is a most fascinating issue, revisited by many a logician with an interest in second-order concepts. This field of logic concerns those concepts that can be applied to themselves. Not all concepts can be applied to themselves, but some can be, and they produce a completely different semantic depth. I could give you some common examples. Let us say that you are trying to develop a theory of the brain, of how it works, how it behaves, etc. Then one day a guy comes along and asks you, "How are you developing a theory of the brain, are you using . . . your brain?" "Of course, I am using my brain!" you reply. "Then does your theory account only for your brain or for mine as well?" "Ehm, ehm. . . ."

My point is that a theory has to account for itself. Thus, if a theory of the brain is being written, it has to account for its own being written. These are the problems that arise with concepts that have to be recursively applied to themselves. In these problems, we encounter considerable logical difficulties, of which I will give examples later on. The difficulty in grasping this kind of concept is well emphasized in Bateson's work.

In my opinion, there are two essential questions to examine in order to understand such difficulty. The first concerns the *language* that we use, while the second concerns the concept, inherited from Plato, of what is *reality*.

The Dangers of Language

I will briefly discuss two points about language. We encounter them very often, and I am sure that they will be familiar to you. The first is the confusion that leads us to think of language as mostly denotative. I say "chair" and point to a chair to denote the object. Yet Susanne Langer (1962) and other psycholinguists understood that language is essentially *connotative*. When I say "chair," I do not indicate your chair, but rather I evoke in you the concept that you have of chairs, thus counting on the fact that we rely on shared and reciprocal notions regarding that particular referent.

Margaret Mead has a very funny anecdote that illustrates this point well. During one of her studies on language among a certain tribe, she tried to learn this language by using the denotative modality. Thus, she pointed to an object, then another, waiting to be given their names, but in all cases everyone always answered, "Chemombo!" Everything was *Chemombo*. She thought to herself, "My God, what a terribly boring language! They only have one word for everything!" Finally, after some time, she managed to find out the meaning of *Chemombo*, which turned out to be "pointing with the finger"! So you see, there are remarkable difficulties in the mere interpretation of denotative language.

The second point concerns a limitation of Indo-European languages. It is the possibility of *nominalization*. This means that a verb can be transformed into a noun. And, when a verb becomes a noun, it suddenly creeps into us as if it were a thing. When we have a process that can become a thing, we really are on a bad track. Many of the difficulties that we encounter in understanding stem from the fact that we are constantly dealing with "things" that actually are processes.

Nominalization allows all functions to be localized and thus is very convenient. If you want to know something, you just have to look into the brain to discover where it is located. Figure 3 is an interesting

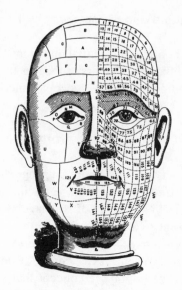

Fɪɢ. 3.—Functional localization in the phrenology of the 1920s

example of functional localization, published in the 1920s, when phrenology was very much in vogue. On the head shown, we basically have all the mental functions localized with great precision.

Figure 3 is a functional localization "gone crazy." For example, we have at 65A "Ondulatory Motion," at 149 "Republicanism," and, as its immediate neighbors, 148 "Faithful Love" and 149A "Responsibility." What is incredible is that we have not yet lost this way of thinking. It continues undaunted. If I asked you, for example, to localize the mind, there is still someone who would answer that it may be in section B, or something to that effect. Some people attempt to identify memory, to open the skull to look for the *chips,* for the magnetic tapes, etc., and they do not find them. They are not in the synapses or in the neurons. Where are these things? Where are my grandmother's glasses? They are not there.

Nominalization repeatedly creeps into our discussions. It becomes very difficult to grasp the very concept of "process" if it disappears into things. As a consequence of nominalization, for example, knowledge becomes merchandise; information too can be bought just like any merchandise, cut into pieces, elaborated, sold in bits, five dollars a pound. This is my criticism of the possibility of nominalization.

HEINZ VON FOERSTER

The Dangers of "Reality"

The other question, as I mentioned, concerns the notion of reality as we have inherited it now for over two millennia, which is actually the main obstacle to dealing with the problems such a concept carries with it. It is an incorrect interpretation, consolidated over time, of Plato's rendition of a dialogue between Socrates and Glaucon in book 7 of the *Republic*. I invite you to read it because it shows that the usual interpretation of the famous metaphor of the cave was neither in Plato's intentions nor in Socrates'. The point was quite different; let me remind you of it, retelling it my own way.

Socrates says, "Glaucon, lend me your ear, please. Listen to what I have to tell you. Imagine a great cave, with a step, a kind of platform, and at the bottom of this platform, chained to the floor, some men. They are actually chained with their necks fixed toward the wall of the place where they sit, so that they can look only straight ahead toward the cave's great wall. Behind these men, on the platform, there is a lit fire. . . . Do you follow me Glaucon? Now, between the fire and the people chained to the floor, there are other people walking back and forth carrying objects, bowls, chairs, furnishings of all sorts, and the only thing that the chained people see are the shadows reflected on the wall."

"Amazing!" says Glaucon, and Socrates continues: "Wait a minute, Glaucon, do you mean to say that the people chained to the floor would think that the shadows are reality?" "Of course," answers Glaucon, "this is the only way they can judge." "Very well! Now pay attention. Imagine for a moment that one of those men is freed from his chains and is thus allowed to see what is happening. What would he say? Of course, he would say, 'Aha! then true reality is that which is behind the things we see.'"

Unfortunately, many people stop reading Plato before getting to this point. That is, they read up to the point at which Plato speaks of reality as a shadow, so they formulate the idea that Socrates wants to say that reality is just a shadow, or something like that. Yet the story goes even further: "Well, let us now take that man *out* of the cave; let us allow him to observe the birds, the trees, the sky, the grass: what would he say now? Of course, he would say, 'Aha! this is true reality!'"

We would thus have different realities of different realities, and this of course does not make much sense if one is trying to describe reality. We thus get to the point that Socrates, or Plato, was driving at: "Well, now, let's take that man, let's lead him back to the cave, let's chain him to his place again and let him interact with the others. What would happen? Of course he would say, 'I have gone behind the scenes, and I have seen true reality; this is not reality; this is just a shadow; I have seen the other things.' . . . And what would the other men do? They would shake their heads, saying, 'This man is crazy!' "

It is thus my conviction that the famous saying "Among the blind, the one-eyed is king" is a completely wrong metaphor. Among the blind, the one-eyed will go straight to the psychiatric hospital because he sees things differently from the others. I think that this is what Socrates wanted to say, not that reality is the shadow of something else. As he actually shows us in the cave metaphor, there are levels on levels of "reality." This is one of the difficulties that we constantly have to deal with, vis-à-vis the concept of reality: our conviction that "there is something behind it."

The Invention of Reality

Language and reality are of course very closely connected. It is generally maintained that language is a representation of the world. However, I would like to suggest to you that the exact opposite is true, that is, that the world is an image of language. Language comes first, and the world is a consequence of it. And I am sure that Gregory would have said the same. You will say, "Oh, Heinz, do you really think so?" Yes, I am convinced of it, and I will prove it to you. I want to prove it by means of a wonderful story that Gregory wrote in the form of a metalogue. A metalogue is a dialogue, which some consider as fictional, between a father and a daughter. Those who knew Gregory well could say that it actually reflected his experience of dialogues with his daughter. But, real or not, the fact remains that they are very poignant accounts of dialogues. I want to read one of them to you, for two reasons. The first is that it deals with the concept of *explanation,* the effects of which are very important to know because, as I previously illustrated, explanations can be very dangerous by making you blind to something else. The second reason concerns the distinction between invention and discovery. The metalogue that I will read to you, published in *Steps to an Ecology of Mind,* is called "What Is an

Instinct?" and, like all these dialogues, it starts with a tricky question from the daughter: "Daddy, what is an instinct?"

Now, if my daughter had asked me, I would have prudently started with an explanation drawn from my knowledge of biology, maybe producing an elegant, literal explanation of what an instinct is. The father in question, however, did not fall into that trap. He immediately realizes that the word "instinct" is used within a dialogue, that it is being used for some "political" purpose, and he asks himself, "What does she want from me? What is she expecting?" So he answers as follows (see Bateson 1972, pp. 38–39):

Father. An instinct, my dear, is an explanatory principle.

Daughter. But what does it explain?

F. Anything—almost anything at all. Anything you want it to explain. [Note that, if something explains anything, it probably explains nothing.]

D. Don't be silly. It doesn't explain gravity.

F. No. But that's just because nobody wants "instinct" to explain gravity. If they did, it would explain it. We could simply say that the moon has an instinct whose strength varies inversely as the square of the distance. . . .

D. But that's nonsense, Daddy.

F. Yes, surely. But it was you who mentioned "instinct," not I.

D. All right—but then, what does explain gravity?

F. Nothing, my dear, because gravity is an explanatory principle.

D. Oh. [Brief pause.] . . . Do you mean that you cannot use one explanatory principle to explain another? Never?

F. Hmmm . . . hardly ever. That is what Newton meant when he said, "*Hypotheses non fingo.*"

D. And what does that mean? Please. [Now focus your attention on the father, while he explains what a hypothesis is. Notice how, in so doing, he remains within the linguistic domain, and within description, making reference to nothing beyond language.]

F. Well, you know what "hypotheses" are. Any statement linking together two descriptive statements is an hypothesis. If you say that there was a full moon on February 1st, and another on March 1st; and then you link these two observations together in any way, the statement that links them is an hypothesis.

    D.   Yes—and I also know what *non* means. But what's *fingo?*

    F.   Well—*fingo* is a late Latin word for "make." It forms a verbal noun *fictio,* from which we get the word "fiction."

    D.   Daddy, do you mean that Sir Isaac Newton thought that all hypotheses were just *made up* like stories?

    F.   Yes—precisely that.

    D.   But didn't he discover gravity? With the apple?

    F.   No, dear, he invented it.

If you *invent* something, then it is language that creates the world; if instead you think that you have *discovered* something, then language is just an image of the world. I hope that with this I succeeded in demonstrating to you that Gregory Bateson too would have said that it is language that generates the world, not the world that is represented in language.

A Modern Version of Plato's Cave

A couple of months ago, in Germany, I related the cave metaphor to a group of physicists. The next day, one of them left a message for me at the hotel, suggesting a continuation of the story. It read:

Suddenly, I saw the men chained to comfortable chairs. The chains were loose enough, and did not seem to bother them. I even heard them say that it was a most comfortable position. Anyway, there they sat with their arms crossed, staring at the screen in front of them. On it, the shadows danced in glittering colors, and the viewers had only one wish: being able to at least once create a shadow, or to themselves be that shadow. One of them got up, and put his chains down, I saw him do it without help. The others shook their heads, not understanding. Some, almost in anger, did not even turn their heads, not wanting to take their eyes off the screen. Settling more comfortably on their soft pillows, they thought, here's a maniac who still tries to look outside to what they once called true reality.

Three Examples

I would now like to illustrate some of my assertions with a few examples. The first of them relates to explanations and is taken from a

Carlos Castaneda story. As you will recall, Castaneda went to Sonora, Mexico, to meet a *brujo* called Don Juan, to get help in learning to see. So Don Juan goes with Carlitos in the Mexican woodland, to teach him to see what happens there. They walk for an hour or two, and suddenly Don Juan says, "Look, look there! Did you see?" Castaneda answers, "No . . . I didn't see." No problem. They resume their walk, and, after some ten minutes, Don Juan says again, "Look, look there! Did you see?" Castaneda looks and says, "I see nothing at all." "Ah." They keep walking, and the same scene happens again, two or three times, but Castaneda never sees anything. Finally, Don Juan finds the solution: "Now I understand what your problem is, Carlitos! You cannot see things you cannot explain. Try to forget about explanations, and you will start to see."

The second example is of a clinical nature. During World War I, the allied troops had helmets that did not protect them well, so many soldiers incurred damage and lesions to the brain. Many times, the skull was not completely fractured, but rather the projectile pierced the helmet from side to side. What resulted clinically were holes in the brain. In most cases, this physical problem resolved in a couple of months. The person seemed to be doing well and was discharged. There were some cases in which, a few months after discharge, the person came back presenting symptoms of motor dysfunction. He could not walk adequately or use his hands appropriately etc. Such dysfunctions were immediately looked into, but nothing abnormal was found; everything seemed to be regular. The doctors did not know what to do for these people. In one of these situations, an American doctor, who was in France at that time, offered a cigarette to one of these patients. He showed the pack, asking, "Would you like a cigarette?" The patient did not seem to understand. "What?" "I asked you if you want a cigarette!" "What?" He then took the cigarette in his hand and lifted it to the patient's eyes. "Do you want a cigarette?" "Oh, yes, I'd love to have a cigarette." So this doctor immediately realized that there was a problem with the man's vision. The patient was examined in an ophthalmology lab. In figure 4, you can see the lesion in that head, a trauma that originates in the occipital region and goes through the visual cortex. The result is an almost complete blindness, a severe peripheral scotomization that made this man virtually blind.

The man had, in other words, a blind spot almost as large as the

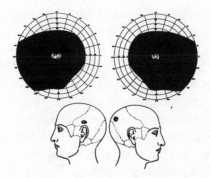

Fig. 4.—Traumatic brain lesion leading to partial blindness

whole retinal field. So this man practically did not see, and at the same time he did not see that he did not see. He did observe that at times the friends with whom he was talking had no heads but that, if they moved just a little, their heads immediately reappeared. If he paid no attention to it, he could hardly notice. So what did these doctors come up with to help this patient regain his motor functioning? They had a brilliant idea, and there are many reports about it. They blindfolded the man so that he could get no visual cues. Of course you know that, even if you are blindfolded, you know exactly the position of your body. Your proprioceptive system informs you whether your hand is stretched or your leg bent, and you know it because you listen to your body and you have no need to see your limbs move. The patient in that case could not see his limbs when he moved, and, because of that, he had lost control over them, to the point of being unable to move them. But, when he was blindfolded, the proprioceptive system regained its strength, and he was able to walk and move freely again. When they removed the blindfold, the man could finally both see and walk because he had disassociated himself from the need of controlling his movements with his sight. There were no cues available, so he could control his movements only through the proprioceptive system. I mentioned this example because, in my opinion, in many therapeutic situations such disassociation of one state from another can prove to be an extremely effective instrument, a useful strategy, when there is a specific pairing of some issues with some others that cannot be easily separated.

The third example I would like to bring you is a story that Gregory too liked very much. I had a blind student named Peter in my lab, with a form of congenital blindness. He was a very brilliant man (he was president of the association of blind students), and he worked with me, helping me translate some very difficult mathematic materials from German into English. Every week he reported to me on his work. The disposition of my office was such that, when students came in, they sat in front of me. Between us was a desk, and behind me there was a wall with a blackboard. When Peter came to talk to me about his work, he always pointed with his finger to something that I imagined to be behind me, but, when I turned to look, there were only the blackboard and the wall and nothing else, and all of this seemed silly to me. Suddenly, I realized that his desk was exactly beyond that wall and that, because he was blind, he could see through the wall while I who had sight could not. I thought that this was very interesting, so I asked him, "Peter, how do you know that your office is there?" He answered: "Oh, it's very easy; I don't walk in the building, but I move the building around me. So, to come to your office, I make the whole building do a turn, I come back a few steps, then I make the building turn again, and I get here." Because he manipulated the building while staying in the same place, he always knew exactly where he was. This is a wonderful example of perception through a sensorimotor loop, the same sensorimotor loop that we saw before in the case of the scotoma patient.

I Don't See It If I Don't Believe It

I will now give you one last example of these investigations and then draw some brief conclusions. It is an amazing example taken from an experiment run some fifteen years ago by F. G. Wordern (1959) at, I believe, Massachusetts General Hospital. He was conducting experiments with cats about auditory acuity. He registered with microelectrodes the variations within the auditory pathways from the cochlear nucleus (which is the one immediately after the cochlea) to the trapezoid nucleus, and so on, step by step all the way to the cortex. There were thus eight or ten such microelectrodes implanted in the brain of the cat, who, so prepared, was placed in a cage. In this cage, there was a small box, containing a fish. This box had a lid so that it was possible to open it to get the fish, and this lid could be opened by operating a lever. Now here is the crux of the matter: the connection

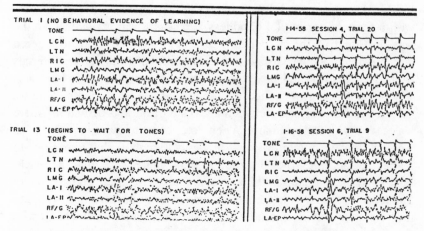

FIG. 5.—The relation between understanding and hearing in the cat

between lever and lid worked only when a brief signal was sounded, a tone of about 1,000 hertz. The cat was placed in the cage and started to hear these auditory signals. Now please examine figure 5.

The first table shows the recordings obtained from the various nuclei and, on the first line, the recording of each tone presented to the subject. The initials on the left indicate the nucleus from which the recording is taken. The tone begins to be presented, and, keeping in mind that for the cat this is the absolute first, notice the graph: there is no acoustic recording in the neuronal activity of that sense organ that we would presume should tell the cat that a tone was presented. The cat undergoes this test many times, and, on the thirteenth trial, you can see that there begins to be a minimal correlation between the acoustic signal and the activity of some nuclei. Go now to the second table, and, on session 4, trial 20, you can clearly see that, when the tone appears, it registers throughout the whole auditory pathway, all the way to the cortex, and that the response is maintained each time the tone is played. This is the moment in which the cat "knows" that the tone means "fish" and that he can finally take it from the box by correctly operating the lever. When the cat reaches full mastery of the situation, as in the last table, session 6, trial 9, as soon as the first tone appears, the whole nervous system becomes aware of it. Immediately thereafter, however, the cat can forget all about it because it knows that, even if the tones continue, it can still go on to enjoy its fish.

100

Two things I believe are important in this context. The first is that, although the tone is presented, the nervous system that we would assume should register it is in fact not hearing it because otherwise there should have been signs of it in our recording. This means that, although there has been an acoustic signal, the cat has not heard it. It starts hearing the tone when it understands what it means. Therefore, I would like to challenge another famous proverb, very popular in America, the one that says, "Seeing is believing." Well, I say, "Believing is seeing." You must understand what you see; otherwise you do not see it. In our example, this is very clear. Now of course the physiologists will jump up and down on their chairs, wondering, "How can that be?" "What happened?" "How is this possible?" etc. Fortunately, I am able to give you an answer, thanks to the work conducted in the fields of neurophysiology and neuroanatomy by two Chilean scientists, Humberto Maturana and Sammy Frenk. In their investigation of visual pathways, they demonstrated the existence of centrifugal fibers. These originate in the central portion of the brain and are directed to the retina. They distribute themselves along the whole retina, thus exercising control over what the retina sees. So the retina is subject to central control: that is why you have to believe in order to see.

In the same way, and more generally, a particular mode of *describing* what is happening can inhibit or facilitate its *perception*. What we have here is not just a sensorimotor loop; rather, we have a complete sensorisensory loop, and the closer we get to observe such loops, the more amazing the results become. I cannot give you a full report of the work done in this field, but I would like to give you an idea of the results that such recursions built into the nervous system obtain. Let us start with an example: if you take an operation and repeat it over and over, you will obtain a second-order concept; you will perform an operation on an operation.

You could also apply this to the computational process, and you could talk about computation of computation, in which the modus operandi has changed in its basic operations. You will change what is operated by operating on the operator. What are the results of these operations? They are incredible! To illustrate them, I will present a very simple case: take the square root of any arbitrary number, say sixteen, and apply it over and over to itself. After a certain number of

```
X'=SQR(X)
INITIAL X = 137
11.70469991    1.00965564    1.00003753    1.00000014
3.42121322     1.00481622    1.00001876    1.00000007
1.84965218     1.00240521    1.00000938    1.00000003
1.36001918     1.00120188    1.00000469    1.00000001
1.1661986      1.00060076    1.00000234    1
1.07990675     1.00030033    1.00000117    1
1.03918561     1.00015015    1.00000058    1
1.01940453     1.00007507    1.00000029    1
```

FIG. 6.—The recursively applied square root of an arbitrary number

operations, you will converge on the number one. In and of itself, this is nothing extraordinary. We can see what happens in figure 6.

Here in figure 6 we have a square root that observes the result of what the motor system did, taking it and computing it over and over, until it gets one as a result. If you perturb that one, moving it, say, to 1.4 or to 1.03, after one or two turns it will come back to one. Next to the figure, you will see an example of a number sequence, in which is computed the root of the root, and so on. It starts with the number 137, and you can see how, after just eighteen operations, we are very close to one. This means that we have very quickly got close to a stable operation of the system.

Now I would like to show you something similar, referring to the sensorimotor system. Let us consider the square in figure 7. The small black squares represent aggregates of immediately adjacent fibers, which project out through the motor system. What happens when you move a hand, for example, is that, through the retina, you can observe your changes, which are then immediately fed back into the system through the receptors and in this way return to the motor system. But there is a second loop, or closure, and it is of course the one affecting the synapses by means of the hormones secreted by the hypophysis. The hypophysis, which is thickly innervated, generates a certain quan-

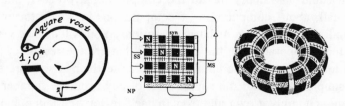

FIG. 7.—Closure in the sensorimotor system

102

tity of hormones that act on the synapses so that there is a double closure. This double loop can be represented by a figure called a torus (a doughnut). Here, the synaptic cleft between the motor and the sensory surface is represented by the striped meridian at the center of the anterior surface, while the hypophysis is represented by the dotted equator and represents the second loop.

At this point, the question naturally comes, What are the consequences of this closure? The consequences concern essentially a shifting of the notion of properties, which, from being thought of as belonging to the object, shift to being thought of as belonging to the observer. I shall give you some examples: there are no boring stories, only boring listeners; there are no old stories, only old ears; if you show a picture to somebody, ask if it is obscene, and get the answer yes, you will know a lot about who answered but very little about the picture. With regard to this, I would like to tell you one last story, about Pavlov, the famous psychologist who was also a great observer and who directed a laboratory famous for its accuracy and precision in research. As you will recall, he studied reflex responses that could be elicited in dogs after presenting a piece of meat at the sound of a bell. The dog salivated, etc. Eventually, the dog got no meat, the bell was sounded, and the dog . . . salivated. Conditioned reflex. Now, Konorski, a famous experimental psychologist, wanted to replicate Pavlov's experiment and did so very accurately because Pavlov, in his excellent book, specified all the details, how the dog had to be tied, what color clothes the experimenters wore, etc. Konorski replicated the experiment exactly: the assistant got in front of the dog, rang the bell, and presented the meat, the dog salivated, and everybody was happy—until on the last test Konorski, unbeknownst to the assistant, removed the clapper from the bell. The assistant got in front of the dog and took the bell, silence ensued, and the dog still salivated. Konorski thus concluded that *the bell sound* was the stimulus for Pavlov, not for the dog! These are things that need to be remembered.

Human Beings or Human Becomings?

I would like to conclude with a comment going back to the issue that, in many cases, it is language that, because of its denotative aspect, seduces us and makes us look for the properties of reality "out there" instead of within ourselves. In many cases, this habit generates a certain complacency: consider, for example, how, in referring to ourselves, we speak of human *beings*. Because of our being human *beings*, nothing can happen to us. We can do the worst things, and this idea of ourselves does not change. But I invite you to give up this self-indulgence of being human *beings* and enter the adventure of becoming human *becomings*. The situation changes a lot; try it on yourselves. Talk about human becomings, and observe what happens to you. The question then becomes, How do we know if we succeeded? How can we observe ourselves? The only way that I can suggest to you for seeing ourselves is to see ourselves through other people's eyes. I learned this from the psychoanalyst Victor Frankl. There was a very catastrophic situation in Austria at the end of the war. Many people were coming back from the concentration camps, many had been victims of bombings, and Victor Frankl was a really essential spirit who helped a great many people at that time. At the same time he arrived in Vienna from Belsen, immediately resettling in the clinic where he had worked before, there was a couple who had returned from two different concentration camps. They had both survived. They met in Vienna, and they were incredulous; they could not believe it: "You are still. . . ." That was wonderful! They were together for about six months, and then the wife died of an illness that she had contracted in the concentration camp. The husband lost heart completely. He would just sit at home all the time, stopped talking to the people who tried to console him and who were telling him, "Think if she had died earlier! . . ." He did not react. Finally, someone managed to convince him to seek help from Victor Frankl. The man went to Frankl, and they talked for a long time, maybe two hours, maybe three. At the end of this conversation, Victor Frankl said to this man, "Let's assume God granted me the power to create a woman exactly like your wife: she would remember all of your conversations, she would remember the jokes, she would remember every detail; you could not distinguish this woman I would create for you from the wife you lost. Would you like me to do it?"

The man kept silent for a while, then said, "No, thank you!" They shook hands; the man left and started a new life. When I heard this story, I immediately asked Frankl, "Doctor, what happened? I don't understand." He answered, "You see, Heinz, we see ourselves through the eyes of the other. When she died, he became blind. But when he saw that he was blind, he could see!"

NOTE

This chapter was presented as the first Gregory Bateson Lecture of the Philadelphia Society for Adolescent Psychiatry, October 1985.

REFERENCES

Bateson, G. 1972. *Steps to an Ecology of Mind*. New York: Ballantine.
Langer, S. 1962. *Philosophy in a New Key*. New York: Mentor.
Wittgenstein, L. 1961. *Tractatus Logico-Philosophicus*. New York: Routledge & Kegan Paul/Humanities.
Wordern, F. G. 1959. EEG studies and conditional reflexes in man. In M. Brazier, ed. *The Central Nervous System and Behavior.* New York: Josiah Macy, Jr., Foundation.

7   THE RELATIONAL MATRIX: THE CONTRIBUTIONS OF INFANT RESEARCH TO A PSYCHODYNAMIC DEVELOPMENTAL PSYCHOLOGY

JOSEPH D. LICHTENBERG

The Relational Matrix in Normal Development

The conception of a relational matrix permits us to take the large view. From ecology, we learn that the survival of the species and the individual depends on finding a niche in a matrix of animate and inanimate supports. We can see that, from an evolutionary standpoint (Slavin and Kriegman 1992), individuals are constantly influenced by inheritances that silently lead to an unfolding and emerging of biological and psychological factors that assist or challenge the quality of their lives. The relational matrix also permits us to take the more focused view of the life cycle (Erikson 1959) of an individual within a family and a particular cultural group. Along with most psychoanalysts, my studies center on this more focused view. I have, however, attempted a very broad integrated approach based on infant research and have remained aware of the ecological and evolutionary perspective.

Freud is responsible for asking the right question: Why do people do what they do and develop the psychological illnesses that they have? Unfortunately, he made two bad bets in answering his question. He drew on nineteenth-century evolutionary biology for a concept of instincts that ethology has subsequently revised greatly, largely into a study of differential information processing and communicating within species. And he drew on a concept of energy discharge from Helmholtzian physics (Jones 1953) that has proved to be a metaphoric dead end. In consequence, the dedication of traditional psychoanalysis to a theory of drives, whether Eros and Thanatos or sexual and aggressive-destructive, forced other observers into independent psychologies. The most famous of these are learning theories such as Pavlovian conditioning (Pavlov 1927) and Piagetian schema building (Piaget 1954) and relational theories such as Fairbairn's (1952) object seeking and Bowlby's (1958) attachment concept.

I have taken the stand that psychoanalytic psychology (Freudian, Piagetian, object relational) is a theory not of structure but of structured motivation (Lichtenberg 1988), and I have tried to spell out how that structured motivation might best be conceived. I have used as my critical source of data observations over units of time in infancy and in the clinical situation that allow for recognition of motivational transitions (Lichtenberg 1989). For example, we observe two-month-old Janet sleeping and her mother taking a moment to relax with a book. The baby stirs; the mother alerts and returns to her book. Janet stirs again, awakens, crying mildly. The mother puts down her book and readies herself to feed the baby. She picks up the baby, who stops crying and, as soon as contact is made with the nipple, starts sucking vigorously. Then Janet pauses and, with nipple still held, rolls her eyes up as mother looking down meets her eyes and gives her a verbal greeting. At a moment indistinguishable in time, the mother jiggles the nipple, and Janet resumes sucking. The baby pushes out the nipple and frets. The mother swings her up to her shoulder, and the baby instantly quiets, her eyes scanning. After burping and ending the feeding, mother and baby make eye contact, the mother talking to the baby, the baby widening her eyes, reaching forward with her arms, legs, and head, making grasping movements with her hands. The mother notices that Janet's attention suddenly shifts, her eyes rolling up, her face reddening, and her abdomen tensing as she has a bowel movement. In changing her diaper, the baby fusses with the restraint, and the mother moves as quickly as possible. The mother then puts her in her play area, starting a mobile music box that the baby fixes her eyes on, her body alert, moving forward. Before long, the baby begins to tire, fret, and, finally, cry. The mother rocks her, soothes her, and puts her in her crib to go to sleep, patting her for several minutes as she drops off.

How can we regard this commonplace sequence from the standpoint of motivation? We can easily recognize that Janet has a shifting series of physiological needs for sleep, nutrients, gas release, elimination, tactile and proprioceptive stimulation, breathing, and general body care. She also has a set of innate and quickly learned response patterns that facilitate her mother's efforts to meet those needs—sucking, bowel and bladder releases, muscle movements, sleep and awakening thresholds. When a physiological need for, say, nutrient or gas release is ascendant, bodily sensations and affects of discomfort are triggered. As the need is met, the sensations and affects alter to relief and, in the case of hunger and thirst, to satiety. The basis for the psychic regulation that facilitates lifelong adaptive responses to physiological need arises from encoding patterns of repetitive successful lived experiences in the form of generalized episodic memory and procedural memory. With this statement, we return to the relational matrix since the same encoded episodic and procedural memories of Janet's *mother* facilitate, on the one hand, her regulation of her own physiological requirements and, on the other, her part—and it is no small part—in the regulation of Janet's eating, sleeping, elimination, etc.

Remembering the lived experience that I described, we note that, at a point when Janet had satisfied her initial intense hunger, she stopped sucking and looked up to be met by her mother's downward glance. After the feeding ended, mother and Janet had a conversation while facing each other. This kind of eye and vocal contact accompanied the diapering and the putting off to sleep. Mother and baby and father and baby learn each other's rhythms—looking, reaching, touching, vocalizing. And a message is shared—I like you, my eyes sparkle and widen when I look at you—the approval and affirming that we call "mirroring." Later (at nine or ten months), Janet will check her mother's and father's faces for an indication of their agreement or disagreement with her agenda. Matched emotions will convey a sense of intersubjective sameness, of an alter ego or twinship experience. Janet will also look at her mother with admiration, even awe, as she does such wonderful things as finding Janet's lost favorite toy. To these attachment experiences that begin in early life Janet will add others that also give vitality and variety to her life. Examples are relatedness with a mentor, a sponsor, a rival, a best friend, a lover. Still within childhood and continuing throughout life, Janet will derive a sustaining feeling of intimacy not only from *attachment* to her mother, father, siblings, pets, and baby-sitters but also from her *affiliation* with groups—first her family, then her classmates, religion, country, etc.

Two special moments in our domestic event require our consideration. In one, mother is reading a book while Janet sleeps. In the other, Janet, fed, changed, played with, and talked to, is scanning her mobile and listening to the music. Each is involved in exploring, one a book, the other a mobile; each is asserting a preference for a type of perceptual-cognitive subject matter. Each is in a state of disengagement from the needs of the other, but the shadow of the other hangs over in mother's half-cocked ear to Janet's awakening and in Janet's sense of mother's presence in the general vicinity as she explores. Stern's (1988) studies demonstrate that the mother's attuned gestures or vocalizing as a baby plays add vitality to the child's affect levels of interest and joy.

Not all the moments described involved positive affects of relief, satiety, intimacy, interest, and efficacy. Janet cried when hungry, fussed when needing to burp, frowned when held on the diaper table, and fretted before going off to sleep. If a loud noise had occurred suddenly, she would have startled. If left crying and unattended long enough, she could drift into a low-arousal apathetic state. What we recognize is that a relational matrix contains many moments or longer periods in which either or both partners are aversive to each other or to the situation in which they find themselves. Janet's mother did not show aversiveness to feeding or changing or playing with Janet in this sample experience, but at other times she inevitably will. Aversive motives are thus a part of the innate need and response patterns of both. The manifestations fall into the two broad groups of antagonism and/or withdrawal. The understanding that we draw from the observation of Janet is that her mother took the baby's indications of aversiveness as signals to which she responded. Thus, we note that Janet was not forced into organizing any of her emerging needs as a trigger for prolonged anger, fear, apathy, shame, or distress, as she might without her mother's responsiveness. To complete the relational matrix, we can add that the mother's sense of the efficacy of her caregiving was communicated to her by Janet's responsiveness and the baby's growing competence. This sense of her efficacy enables her to weather the deprivations in other areas of her life and the frustration of baby care without consolidating aversive reactions. Note that I say "consolidating" because aversive moments of anger, annoyance, and irritation, of loneliness and sadness, of anxiousness and uncertainty, of distaste and dissmell, and of shame, embarrassment, and guilt are inevitable.

Janet sucks for nourishment and for the pleasurable sensation that sucking triggers. She likes being rocked, being held close to her mother's warm body, the feel of soft clothes on her skin, the touching of her perineum as she is wiped, the sounds of her mother's cooing, and her sleeptime record. Just as she is bathed in a world of communication and attachment contacts, she is bathed in a world of potential sensual enjoyment. Some sensations come to her from her mother directly as in hugging (or being tossed about by her father). Some come from her own activity as in finger sucking and self-rocking. Some stir her up, as when tickled; some calm her down, as when patted off to sleep. Much is shared with her mother—maybe a bit more because she is a girl, more skin and mouth sensitive than a boy. Sexual excitement as such is not likely until late in the first year for Janet. For her mother, arousal sometimes occurs in their shared sensual moments— in breast feeding, in contact with the baby's soft skin, and in a stir of fantasy life. When accepted, this can add vitality to the relational matrix; when it is not, it can trigger guilt and avoidance.

From an examination of events such as this in the life of infants and from clinical exchanges, especially the analysis of process notes, I have concluded that five motivational systems can be readily identified. Each motivational system develops in response to a specific need; each stabilizes innate and learned patterns of responsive functioning; each may be dominant at any moment, the others being either collaterally active or dormant. The needs that trigger the functioning of each system are lifelong; the forms that needs and functioning take vary at each period. As is evident in the episode of Janet and her mother, the five motivational systems develop in response to the need for the psychic regulation of physiological requirements (nutrients, elimination, temperature control, tactile and proprioceptive activity, equilibrium, sleep, breathing, and health care), the need for attachment to individuals and later affiliation with groups, the need for exploration and assertion of preferences, the need to react aversively to ascendant states of unmet needs, breaches of expectancies, pain, loss, and distress by responses of antagonism and/or withdrawal, and the need for sensual enjoyment and later sexual excitement. As the five motivational systems organize and stabilize, a more overarching regulatory organization forms—the self. The self as I define it develops as an independent center for the initiation, organization, and integration of experience and motivation.

I am ready now to offer my first conclusion: the relational matrix must include more than any single theoretical focus taken within psychoanalysis or other psychologies. Thus, studies of the effect of physiological change and body-brain maturation, of attachment experiences of mirroring, alter ego sharing, and idealizing, of group dynamics, of conditioning and Piagetian learning, of manifestations grouped under the aggressive drive and the sexual drive, all must find a place that gives significance to their hierarchical importance and to the constant changes in hierarchical dominance.

My second conclusion is that a relational matrix requires three perspectives to appreciate any unit of observation: an intrapsychic, an intersubjective, and an assessment of state (Lichtenberg, Lachmann, and Fosshage 1992). The intrapsychic worlds of Janet at two months and of her mother are alike in their each having the same five motivational systems. Their intrapsychic worlds are markedly different in that Janet has only the beginning of an emergent self and that mother has a mature self. Janet is building her intrapsychic world through the recording of procedural and episodic memories of lived experiences, while her mother has a highly plastic representational world encoded in primary- and secondary-process modes. When viewed from the intersubjective dimension, Janet experiences her mother and interesting inanimate objects (along with sensations from her body) as powerful triggers for perceptions, actions, and affects. Her mother experiences her interactions with Janet co-continuously with an inner world of representations, many in the form of unconscious fantasies and beliefs that include a Janet in the making from probably when the mother was a little girl of three or four. The actual interactions trigger the mother's responses, confirming her sense of now having her very own little girl. An assessment of state reveals a smooth transition from sleep to crying to alertness to drowsiness and sleep on Janet's part and from quiet exploratory inwardness to attentive caregiving receptiveness to active attachment responsiveness on the mother's part. The mature self of Janet's mother assures her an integration across state changes with the flexibility for open responsiveness and well-functioning motivational systems. With the caregiving that Janet receives and her biophysiological intactness, Janet's developing self assures her flexible state changes. Picture the difference if Janet were a premature baby whose state was set by the need to hold stimulation to a bare minimum to be able to process it at all or if her state were set by the aversiveness of colic or a milk intolerance or tactile hypersensitivity. Picture the difference if Janet's mother were in a state of depression, or dissociated in a schizoid or multiple personality state, or in a toxic drug condition.

A further implication of the observation of Janet and her mother is that we can no longer hold to the view that normal development implies the overcoming of infantile psychosexual states of orality and anality or of autism and symbiosis or of schizoid and depressive positions or of primary envy and destructiveness. Janet and her mother and other caregivers have plenty of challenges to overcome for Janet to mature, but not the ones that psychoanalytic theory has read back into childhood from adult pathology. The tagging of borderline or narcissistic pathology to stages of infancy must be rethought. Traumatic disturbances could occur to Janet at any age and produce any variety of unpredictable outcomes.

Implications for a Theory of Technique

I hold that the relational matrix defines the optimal listening stance of a therapist as being able to sense the inner world, the inner state of mind of the patient. I call this disciplined attempt to position oneself in this way the "empathic mode of perception" (Lichtenberg 1981). This type of empathic listening, as Schwaber (1981) calls it, requires therapists to use the sensitivity gained from an awareness of motivations from their own five systems to entwine emotionally with the motivations of the patient as Janet's mother did with Janet. Thus, in an hour when a patient reports that she has just awakened from a nap and feels drowsy, that she did not have time to get the snack she planned, we know by "trial identification" that she is telling us her feelings about small disturbances in physiological regulation. If she then goes on to complain that the therapist is unresponsive and that she feels discouraged, the therapist can wonder if she wanted him to recognize with her, her feelings of wanting someone to help her get more order in her life—more of a feeling of someone being with her, helping to care for her physical needs.

If the therapist can convey in words her understanding of the patient's latent and then explicit wish for her response, the patient may feel that he has been able to get through to her and also that he has been understood, his desire acknowledged. This will encourage him to reveal himself in greater depth, as Janet was encouraged to interact freely with her mother. But what if the patient experiences the therapist as indifferent to his concerns, as stubbornly silent until he tells her about sexuality or about his problems with intimacy or his hatreds? Not that he does not want to talk about those concerns, but not now—not when the motivational system that is dominant has to do with the psychic regulation of physiological requirements.

The other side of this intersubjective exchange may or may not be as the patient reads it. The therapist may not be insisting on another agenda before she will speak. She may not be out of touch with his emotional-physical state; in fact, she could be too much in it, a bit slowed down herself. When he complains about her unresponsiveness and his discouragement, she may be ready to inquire into his feelings about her with interest and without defensiveness. But a therapist who is locked into a theory that to speak is to gratify, or that only conflicts are to be addressed and he was not expressing a conflict, or that a patient speaking of drowsiness and hunger is being resistant, will be in a mind-set that will not permit in this instance effective empathic listening.

The effect of an absence of effective empathic listening will be a disruption in what has been called the "holding environment" (Winnicott 1956), the "therapeutic alliance" (Zetzel 1958), "the working alliance" (Greenson 1967), or "self-selfobject relatedness" (Kohut 1971, 1977). Such disruptions may be minor—a diminution in interest, in investment in the inquiry at hand. Generally noting the change in tone may be enough to rectify the situation. The disruption may be more marked, often by a return to some familiar aversive litany such as, This treatment isn't helping, or, I know you think I'm stupid, but. . . . When this occurs, the change needs to be noted, and then, for the restoration to occur, a recognition of the therapist's contribution to the disruption as perceived by the patient may be necessary.

Occasionally with any patient, certainly with any adolescent, but most commonly with patients with borderline and narcissistic personality disorders, disruptions may be more severe and lasting. The patient may undergo a change in state, for example, experience narcissistic rage or withdraw into hurt depression, or dissociate into an apathetic affectlessness, or become extremely guarded and avoidant. This state may persist for several hours or considerably longer. When this occurs, the therapist will have to be patient, at times to what may seem the snapping point, and try to glean what he or she can as to the triggering source, often with little or no direct help from the patient. As the therapist's persistence in "being with" the patient, in trying to see the experience from the patient's point of view, however ineptly, rebuilds the matrix of their empathic relationship, the prior sharing of exploratory-assertive motivation is restored.

These reflections on disruption-restoration sequences bring us to a reconsideration of transference. If we say that the disruption was triggered by what the patient experiences as an empathic failure—a need of a motivational system either not met or not understood—we can ask whether the failure was "real." Traditionally, we would have answered that, while sometimes a real failure might occur as a countertransference intrusion, for the most part the perceived failure is a distortion of current reality based on a transference superimposition of a past relationship that was itself based on a distortion. Both past distortion and present distortion were attributed to unmastered drives.

Infant research raises serious objections. First, rather than distorting their experience, infants are remarkably equipped to respond to and record their actual lived experience (Stern 1985). Not until eighteen months and after can we consider the possibility of fantasy and imaginative renderings of experience. Second, what passes for distortion, that is, fantastic renderings of relationships and events, is often the result of the limitations of problem-solving efforts using the cognitive possibilities and information processing available at the time. This explanation holds not only for children but also for explanations by adults that, to others, are the prejudices of ignorance. Third, in childhood, and for the adolescent or adult patient, current actualities are perceived in terms of expectations. What we find is that patients who carry strong expectations into treatment can find or relatively easily evoke convincing evidence to confirm the actualizing of their assumptions. By investigating the evidence that the patient perceives—not denying it or calling it a distortion but putting themselves into the patient's experiential world—therapists can unravel the unconscious expectations that organize their patients' way of perceiving and interacting.

I have suggested that great therapeutic leverage can be gained through the construction of model scenes (Lichtenberg 1981, 1989; Lichtenberg, Lachmann, and Fosshage 1992). A model scene is a conception that therapist *and* patient form that epitomizes (provides a model for) significant communications from the patient about his life. Often, these communications appear in bits of transference experience, especially in role enactments into which the therapist is drawn. An adolescent analysand reacted to any silence on my part or refusal to respond directly to an appeal for immediate help as gross, unforgivable neglect on my part. On one occasion, his hearing me rattle paper precipitated a rage response that took weeks to subside. From dream images and the slow recovering of memories, we pieced together—he and I acting in concert, amending and adding—the model scene of his coming to the room where his mother worked behind a locked door. By insistent rapping, he could get her grudging attention. She would open the door, leaving the night latch on, answer him perfunctorily, and then, unseen, return to her work as he continued to speak, her diverted attention signaled to him by her rattling her papers. As you can imagine, the formation of this model scene helped explain much previously puzzling information, helped integrate bits of previous understanding, and initiated further exploration, especially of other disturbances of his attachment motivation.

For treatment to work, in fact, for positive change to be possible at any time during the entire life cycle, the therapeutic process must be resonant with a basic design for growth. I believe that infant studies point to two such basic designs for growth, which I designate as self-righting and the reorganization of symbolic representations. "Self-righting" refers to a biological principle of resilience. If an obstacle stops normal growth, the removal of the obstacle during the period when growth remains possible will result in the restoration—the self-righting of the cellular formation. In psychological terms, lifting of a mother's depression can restore the vitality to her baby's attachment and exploratory motivations. In my description of disruptions during treatment, I illustrated self-righting when the therapist noted the emotional shift, interpreted the intersubjective interchange, and, after providing a holding environment during the prolonged state change, investigated the experience.

The symbolic reorganization of representations refers to a more complex process. Here, the uniquely human (post-eighteen-month) capacity to play in action and in imagination with representations of self and others permits us to create internal actualities both in accordance and at variance with external actualities. All our lives, we seek solutions to the problems at hand, but the tools available shift with time, yielding different solutions. The dual coding of primary and secondary process provides the unique plasticity to have dynamically competing renderings of the same lived experience. This process occurs most remarkably with model scene construction. Simultaneously, two people are pulling together in a logical sequence, within a shifting but orderly frame, visual-auditory-affective experiences across time, place, and person (condensation and displacement).

Implications for Adolescence

When adolescence was conceptualized within the theory of sexual and aggressive drives, the assumption of stages parallel to the oral, anal, and oedipal stages of prelatency was widely accepted (Blos 1962). My clinical experience fails to confirm that comparable psychosexual stages advance in an orderly fashion during adolescence or that adolescence is inevitably characterized by "Sturm und Drang" conflicts. I find that changes in each motivational system occur asynchronously and unpredictably. Physiological growth may precede expanded attachments to individuals, or expanded affiliations with groups may precede expanded exploratory-assertive motives. And the strength of each motive varies greatly from individual to individual. One boy may be bowled over by sexual urgency, another hardly bothered. One girl may be deeply aversive to her pubertal changes, another proud, another relatively indifferent. Thus, as much as or more than at any other point in the life cycle, empathic entry into the state of mind of adolescents is required to apprehend their individuality.

One example of the complexity of individual maturation and development is the timing and effect of the cognitive shift from concrete to formal operations, that is, the ability to confirm or dispose of hypotheses using symbols rather than requiring concrete objects or events. When this emergent cognitive change occurs early, say, at ten or eleven, the boy or girl appears precocious; when it occurs late, at fourteen or fifteen, he or she appears slow. During the period of cognitive changeover, the adolescent experiences dialectic tension between a familiar way of learning and an untried approach, leading at times to school anxiety. Once complete, the adolescent can create a more personal system of values, ideals, and ethics. The effect spreads from the exploratory-assertive to the attachment-affiliative system. To quote Wolf, "The adolescent can no longer hide from himself the inevitable discrepancies between who he has imagined his parents to be and who the parents really are" (1982, p. 179). Parents must accept the loss of the prior, more consistent idealization with relatively good grace, especially their offspring's glee at finding their feet of clay. The result is generally a tilt from attachment to parents to affiliation with peer groups and older adolescents. Turning from parents to peer groups is mistakenly considered a phenomenon beginning in adolescence. Children from at least age three on learn and test many of their values, such as taking turns, property rights, altruism, and handling confrontation, from peer group activities (Damon 1977), just as early attachment is nowhere as mother centered as our theories would imply (Cath, Gurwitt, and Ross 1982). My point here is simply that the timing of a development in one system varies and, with it, the ripple effect on the cohesion of the self and motivations in other systems.

Having made my plea for the individuality of each adolescent's motivational development and dominance, I shall state some general trends that I have found. Adolescents are very heavily pressured by the here and now. Thus, agenda bashing often occurs when therapists with their belief in the overriding significance of explanations from the past struggle against their young patients' preferences. Here and now usually means what do I do, how should I feel, be my mentor, my sponsor, my restrainer. Thus, the common attachment motivations for mirroring, alter ego sharing, and idealization show a subtle shift toward the desire for a practical model and guide—one outside the pull toward childlike overdependence and rivalry, one who can stand up to a lot of pummeling of desires and demands without undue or unacknowledged resort to hypocrisy, manipulation, and defensive dissembling. But, because of the rapid shifting pressures of motivational dominance, adolescents may passionately want the therapist to be a dispassionate evaluator of an exploratory plan or a romantic goal one minute and a passionately attuned sharer of their internal arousal the next. As a consequence, therapists have difficulty maintaining an empathic mode of perception. I believe that the more flexible mapping of the terrain of the adolescent experience made possible by the five motivational systems improves the therapist's potential for empathic sensing. With many adolescents in exploratory therapy, the process centers on self-righting. Extensive reorganization of symbolic representations from interpretation and model scenes occurs less reliably than in adult analysis. I do not mean this to be heard as a statement of pessimism about the treatment of adolescents. Self-righting at any time is no small gain. The restoration of self-cohesion and vitality during adolescence promotes not only resilience at the moment but also the momentum of emergent developmental thrusts. The reorganization of symbolic representations does not have to rest so heavily on the therapist's shoulders; growth of the individual self will move forward according to its design, to paraphrase Kohut (1971), when obstacles are recognized and set aside by the empathic ambience of the relational matrix of the therapy. Self-righting facilitates the forward movements in the psychic regulation of physiological requirements, of attachment and affiliation, of exploration and assertion of preferences, of successful adaptive mobilization of antagonism, power, and discretion, and of the search for sensual enjoyment and sexual excitement.

Conclusions

1. The relational matrix calls for a broader account of motivation than any currently offered within competing psychoanalytic theories. A theory of five motivational situations and self attempts to provide this broader account by integrating other proposals.

2. A relational matrix requires three perspectives to appreciate any unit of observation: an intrapsychic, an intersubjective, and an assessment of state.

3. We can no longer hold to the view that normal development implies overcoming early stages or the view that psychopathological formations can be linked to specific stages of infancy.

4. The inevitable disruptions of a patient's optimal motivation during treatment that result from the patient's experiencing a failure in empathic listening provide unique opportunities for investigating the precise nature of the relational matrix of the particular patient with the particular therapist.

5. Exploring disruption-restoration sequences facilitates self-righting, the most consistent occurrence during the treatment of adolescents, while constructing model scenes facilitates the reorganization of symbolic representations.

6. Changes in each motivational system during adolescence occur more asynchronously and unpredictably than stated in most stage theories, requiring particular attention to empathic entry into the state of mind of each adolescent.

7. Along with a plea for an appreciation of the individuality of each adolescent, one generalization worth remembering during treatment is the strong sense of here-and-now pressure that coincides with rapid shifts in motivational dominance.

REFERENCES

Blos, P. 1962. *On Adolescence: A Psychoanalytic Interpretation*. New York: Free Press.

Bowlby, J. 1958. The nature of a child's tie to his mother. *International Journal of Psycho-Analysis* 39:350–373.

Cath, S. H.; Gurwitt, A.; and Ross, J. M., eds. 1982. *Father and Child*. Boston: Little, Brown.

Damon, W. 1977. *The Social World of the Child*. San Francisco: Jossey-Bass.

Erikson, E. 1959. *Identity and the Life Cycle*. New York: Norton, 1980.

Fairbairn, W. R. P. 1952. *An Object-Relations Theory of the Personality*. New York: Basic.

Greenson, R. 1967. *The Technique and Practice of Psychoanalysis*. Madison, Conn.: International Universities Press.

Jones, E. 1953. *The Life and Work of Sigmund Freud,* vol. 1. New York: Basic.

Kohut, H. 1971. *The Analysis of the Self*. New York: International Universities Press.

Kohut, H. 1977. *The Restoration of the Self*. New York: International Universities Press.

Lichtenberg, J. 1981. The empathic mode of perception and alternative vantage points for psychoanalytic work. *Psychoanalytic Inquiry* 1:329–356.

Lichtenberg, J. 1988. A theory of motivational-functional systems as psychic structures. *Journal of the American Psychoanalytic Association* 36(suppl.): 55–70.

Lichtenberg, J. 1989. *Psychoanalysis and Motivation.* Hillsdale, N.J.: Analytic.

Lichtenberg, J.; Lachmann, F.; and Fosshage, J. 1992. *Self and Motivational Systems: Toward a Theory of Technique.* Hillsdale, N.J.: Analytic.

Pavlov, I. P. 1927. *Conditioned Reflexes.* Translated by G. V. Anrep. London: Oxford University Press.

Piaget, J. 1954. *The Construction of Reality in the Child.* Translated by M. Cook. New York: Basic.

Schwaber, E. 1981. Empathy: a mode of analytic listening. *Psychoanalytic Inquiry* 1:357–392.

Slavin, M., and Kriegman, D. 1992. Psychoanalysis as a Darwinian depth psychology. In J. Barron, M. Eagle, and D. Wolitsky, eds. *Interface of Psychoanalysis and Psychology.* Washington, D.C.: American Psychological Association.

Stern, D. 1985. *The Interpersonal World of the Infant.* New York: Basic.

Stern, D. 1988. Affect in the context of the infant's lived experience: some considerations. *International Journal of Psycho-Analysis* 69:233–238.

Winnicott, D. 1956. Primary maternal preoccupation. In *Collected Papers.* London: Tavistock, 1958.

Wolf, E. 1982. Adolescence: psychology of the self and selfobject. *Adolescent Psychology* 10:171–181.

Zetzel, E. 1958. The therapeutic alliance in the analysis of hysteria. In *The Capacity for Emotional Growth.* New York: International Universities Press, 1970.

8   SUBJECTIVITY IN PARENT-INFANT RELATIONSHIPS: CONTRIBUTIONS FROM ATTACHMENT RESEARCH

CHARLES H. ZEANAH

An individual's subjective experience of others in intimate relationships has long been a focus of psychodynamic clinical work. Twenty-five years ago, Escalona (1967) challenged developmental researchers by declaring that the most vital question about development was neither about the infant's characteristics, nor about the environment's characteristics, nor even about their ongoing interactions, but was instead about the infant's subjective experience of the world. Recent developments in research on attachment between infants and parents have provided the beginnings of empirical exploration of this area. Results from these investigations bear on a number of important clinical concerns, including transference, the compulsion to repeat, and the importance of early relationship experiences.

According to Bowlby's (1969) attachment theory, relationship repetition occurs because internal experience and behavior in relationships are structured by representational or internal working models. These are dynamic internal representations that are hypothesized to structure and organize perception and the interpretation of experience (particularly social experience or experience in interaction with others). They generate a set of organized and consistent expectations about the environment and organize behavior with respect to the environment. Specifically, these models are believed to organize an individual's feelings and behaviors in attachment relationships (Bretherton 1985; Main, Kaplan, and Cassidy 1985). As such, they are not merely passive filters of experience but also contribute to an individual's active re-creation of relationship patterns (patterns of thinking, feeling, and behaving). Recent attachment research has attempted to operationalize the construct of internal representations in order to explain how infants experience and reenact relationship patterns.

Research on attachment in infants and adults has been concerned not merely with interactional behaviors but also with the subjective experience of the individual engaging in the behaviors. If results from attachment research do reflect individual differences in internal representations of relationships, then we ought to be able to detect associated differences in subjective experiences related to different patterns of attachment. The purpose of this chapter is to describe three different lines of preliminary research relevant to the question of subjectivity in parent-infant attachment relationships and, briefly, to consider their clinical implications. First, I consider investigations that have examined concordance in types of internal representations of attachment in parents and infants and the implications of this research for the intergenerational transmission of relationship patterns. Second, I consider how parents with qualitative differences in their internal representations of attachment perceive and interpret infant distress. Third, I describe differences in parents' perceptions and interpretations of their own infants depending on the infant's pattern of attachment. Finally, I offer some theoretical and clinical speculations about the implications of this research and describe what I believe it attempts to demonstrate about parent-infant relationship patterns and the self-reorganizations that underlie them.

Intergenerational Transmission of Relationships

Bowlby (1969) originally suggested that infants constructed representational models toward the latter half of the first year of life on the basis of real (as opposed to fantasied) experiences with the attachment figure. Infants who receive adequately sensitive and emotionally available caregiving, according to Bowlby, develop models of others as dependable and available and models of themselves as worthy of such care. Conversely, infants whose experiences are less than adequate in any number of ways develop angry and anxious feelings about others and feelings of insecurity about themselves.

Inspired by Bowlby's theory and its careful attention to observable behavior, Ainsworth and her colleagues developed the most widely used assessment of attachment relationships in infancy, the Strange Situation procedure (Ainsworth, Blehar, Waters, and Wall 1978). This laboratory procedure involves a series of increasingly stressful episodes for eleven- to twenty-month-old infants. On the basis of the infant's reunion behavior with a particular caregiver following a brief separation, it is possible to classify the infant's attachment to that caregiver into one of three major patterns.

According to attachment theory, infants should use their attachment figures as a secure base to explore the novel environment provided by the Strange Situation. Following the caregiver's return, an infant should seek to reestablish interaction with the caregiver and to seek comfort if distressed. When infants behave in this manner, they are classified as having *secure* attachment to that caregiver. In contrast, some infants seem surprisingly undistressed by their caregiver's leaving and actively avoid them on return, ignoring the caregiver's bid for interaction and focusing instead on the physical environment. The relationship between these infants and their caregivers is termed *avoidant*. In another pattern, infants protest separation from their caregivers vigorously but are unable to settle during reunions. Instead, they behave ambivalently, alternately demanding contact and then resisting it. Relationships characterized by this pattern are termed *resistant*. Most of attachment research in infancy has involved these three patterns.

Attachment theorists and researchers have asserted that certain patterns of caregiver-infant interaction during the first year of life precede each of these attachment classifications. Studies have demonstrated that secure behavior in the Strange Situation reflects secure behavior in the home (Vaughn and Waters 1990) and that sensitive and emotionally available caregiving predicts secure attachment in the Strange Situation (Ainsworth et al. 1978; Sroufe 1988). There is some evidence that the avoidant pattern is preceded by caregiver rejection of the infant's bids for comfort and closeness and by an emphasis on the infant's self-sufficiency (Main and Stadtman 1981). The avoidant behavior during Strange Situation reunions is hypothesized to represent an organized defense against the pain of anticipated rejection by the caregiver (Main and Weston 1981). Ainsworth et al. (1978) suggested that the resistant pattern was preceded by inconsistent caregiving behavior. The heightened distress during the Strange Situation reunions is interpreted as the infant's attempt to convey distress in terms that are unmistakable to a caregiver who is not consistently dependable. The cost to the infant, according to this line of reasoning, is that the arousal becomes so intense that it takes on a life of its own. As a result, attempts by the caregiver to settle the infant are unsuccessful.

Patterns of reunion behavior in the Strange Situation are believed to reflect differences in infants' internal representations of attachment relationships to particular caregivers. It is important to emphasize that it is internal representations and not infants that are classified in the attachment paradigm. Because patterns of behavior in the Strange Situation may be different with different adults, infant attachment classifications are said to be relationship specific rather than within-the-infant traits. Nevertheless, it is plausible, and there is some evidence to suggest, that temperamental characteristics such as emotional reactivity contribute to attachment classifications and, therefore, to internal representations.

Mary Main and her colleagues (Main et al. 1985; Main and Goldwyn, in press) reasoned that differences in attachment relationships ought to be reflected in individual differences in the internal representations of these relationships in adults as well as in infants. In order to explore this question empirically, George, Kaplan, and Main (1984) designed the Adult Attachment Interview (AAI) to develop a system of classifying adults' narrative descriptions of attachment relationships and experiences.

Main et al. (1985) also argued that, although internal representations of attachment might derive from nearly infinite varieties of specific events, their salient differences could be specified in terms of several critical formal features of subjects' narrative descriptions of their attachment relationships and experiences. Main and Goldwyn (1988, in press) described three major narrative patterns that emerged from studying verbatim transcripts of the interviews. Adults classified as *autonomous* valued caregiving relationships, described them in a coherent and open manner, and demonstrated a tolerance for imperfection without idealizing either themselves or their caregivers. Adults classified as *dismissing* devalued the importance of early experiences and relationships or dismissed the effects of attachment-relevant experiences either by being unable to recall them entirely or by remembering them without reexperiencing or recalling the emotions associated with them. The group classified as *preoccupied* described attachment relationships and experiences in a way that betrayed a seeming dependence on and excessive concern with their families of origin. Although remembering a large number of vignettes about their childhood, they exhibited either a passive incoherence or unmodulated anger that prevented them from providing a clear or objective overview of their experiences.

The Adult Attachment Interview was originally designed to provide a comparable measure for adults to the Strange Situation for infants. Nevertheless, it is interesting that, during these quite different procedures, a structured interview and a laboratory separation-reunion paradigm, individuals of concordant classifications behave similarly. For example, avoidant infants seem to ignore their distress during separations in the Strange Situation and suppress their need for comfort during reunions. To the casual observer, they appear unperturbed and unaffected by the stress of separation from their caregivers, although physiological measures suggest that they are quite highly aroused (Sroufe and Waters 1977). Similarly, adults classified as dismissing on the basis of their Adult Attachment Interview responses tend to idealize or normalize their experiences, but they have difficulty providing specific memories, or their memories fail to support their global descriptors. Adverse aspects of experiences are either acknowledged or said to have had no lasting effects. Implicit in both infant and adult behavior is a claim to independence, strength, and an emotional detachment from their own distress. Much like infants who appear avoidant during the Strange Situation, adults who provide dismissing descriptions experience high levels of physiological arousal during the Adult Attachment Interview (Dozier 1991). Cassidy and Kobak (1988) have argued that these parallels reflect common defensive processes in infants and adults, in which negative affects are masked or distorted by the individual in order to preserve the attachment relationship.

Studies that have examined the concordance between adult and infant attachment (defined as the pairing of autonomous with secure, dismissing with avoidant, and preoccupied with resistant) have produced impressive preliminary results. In the first study conducted on this question, Main and Goldwyn (in press) reported that 75 percent of mother-infant pairs (kappa = 0.61) and 60 percent of father-infant pairs (kappa = 0.41) were concordant, even though the Adult Attachment Interviews were administered five years after the Strange Situations (concordance is defined as autonomous mothers with secure infants, dismissing mothers with avoidant infants, and preoccupied mothers with resistant infants). In a second investigation of infant-mother attachment, Eichberg (1987) reported a 74 percent concordance (kappa = 0.47) between mother and infant attachment classifications. In her middle-class sample, Adult Attachment Interviews were administered six to twelve months after the Strange Situation procedures.

In another investigation in which the Strange Situations and the Adult Attachment Interviews were administered contemporaneously, Zeanah and his colleagues found a 75 percent concordance (kappa = 0.62) between the attachment classifications of mothers and their twelve-month-old infants (Zeanah, Benoit, Barton, Regan, Hirshberg, and Lipsitt, in press).

These studies raise the question of the direction of effects since parents' representations of attachment were measured either concurrently or after their infants' Strange Situation procedures. The psychodynamic hypothesis is that mothers who have accepted and integrated their own childhood experiences and who value relationships (and therefore would be classified as autonomous) are in the best position to provide sensitive care to their infants and to promote a feeling of security in them. On the other hand, it is possible that infants with more favorable temperamental characteristics may elicit sensitive caregiving in their mothers and that, as a result of these caregiving experiences with their infants, mothers may change their perspectives on their own childhood experiences. Three recent investigations administered Adult Attachment Interviews to pregnant women and assessed infants' attachment classifications in the Strange Situation one year later. These investigations produced remarkably similar findings of significant concordance ranging from 66 to 74 percent (kappas = 0.38–0.54) between mother attachment in pregnancy and infant attachment one year later (Benoit, Vidovic, and Roman 1991; Fonagy, Steele, and Steele, in press; Ward, Botyanski, Plunkett, and Carlson 1990). These results suggest either that the direction of effects in the first year of life is largely mother to infant or that some third factor explains attachment in both mothers and infants.

Main et al. (1985) and others (Bretherton 1985, 1987; Zeanah and Zeanah 1989) have interpreted findings of concordance between adult and infant attachment classifications as suggesting similarities in the qualitative features of internal working models or internal representations of attachment in both infants and adults. Although the evidence to date is compatible with that formulation, more work on the discriminant validity of attachment measures remains in order to demonstrate that the measures are really specific to attachment. The next formidable challenge for researchers is to delineate the mechanisms by which these representational processes are transmitted.

Mothers' Perceptions of Infant Distress and Attachment

Another important area of investigation is how parents perceive and interpret infant emotions. The way in which an individual responds to strong emotions is an important criterion in the adult attachment typology and is thought to be a basic component of an individual's internal representation of attachment relationships. If it is true, as has been suggested (Cassidy and Kobak 1988; Main 1982), that mothers of avoidant infants subtly reject bids for comfort of distress, then they might perceive and interpret their own infant's distress and perhaps that of other infants differently than mothers who do not respond with subtle rejection. Similarly, the putative inconsistent responsiveness of the mothers of resistant infants might indicate systematic biases about their interpretations of distress.

In order to begin to explore this area, our group assessed middle-class mothers' interpretations of infant distress (Zeanah, Benoit, Hirshberg, Barton, and Regan 1991). The mothers in this investigation observed a four-minute videotape and then completed various ratings about the infant's emotions and personality.

The tape is of a one-year-old infant in parts of episodes 4 and 5 of the Strange Situation procedure (first separation and reunion episodes). The child is quite distressed during the separation from his mother. He is not comforted by the stranger's attempts to soothe him. On his mother's return, he immediately seeks proximity to her. She picks him up, and he settles somewhat but continues to cry softly. She then puts him down, to which he responds by crying more vigorously. Again she picks him up, and again his crying diminishes somewhat as she walks him over by the toys. At this point, she puts him down once more and goes to a chair, where she sits down and begins looking at a magazine. The boy cries more intensely than ever and begins to walk around the room past his seated mother. He pounds on the one-way mirror several times with his fist as he continues to protest. He then walks over to his mother and swats at her magazine with his hand as he continues to cry. She continues to look at the magazine.

After watching this videotape, the subjects were asked to complete a twenty-item questionnaire about the child they watched, the Description of the Child's Behavior Questionnaire (DCBQ; Zeanah et al., in press). The first nine items on the scale are subjects' ratings of the degree to which the following emotions are apparent in the infant: angry, sad, afraid, disgusted, distressed, ashamed, shy, and happy. In the remaining eleven items, subjects are asked to rate the degree to which they imagine the boy's personality is clingy, loving, stubborn, flexible, mean, soothable, whiny, independent, spoiled, difficult, and secure. The instrument was designed to assess individual differences in mothers' interpretations of infants' separation and reunion distress.

Mothers of secure, avoidant, and resistant infants in this sample perceived the distressed infant in the videotape differently. All the positive and negative attributions were grouped together, and ANOVAs were conducted to assess differences in the three groups of mothers. Essentially, we found that mothers of avoidant infants perceived the infant most negatively and that mothers of resistant infants perceived the infant most positively. Mothers of secure infants rated the videotaped infant's emotions and personality traits in between these extremes.

The general pattern of results of DCBQ scores by mothers' adult attachment classification is similar. Mothers classified as dismissing on the AAI perceived the infant in the videotape to have more negative emotions and personality traits, mothers classified preoccupied perceived the infant to have more positive emotions and traits, and mothers classified autonomous perceived the infant's emotions and personality traits to be in between the other two groups.

Interestingly, of the thirteen cases in the Zeanah et al. (in press) investigation that were discordant for adult and infant attachment classifications, eight were composed of mothers classified as preoccupied with infants classified as secure. The eight preoccupied mothers with secure infants (discordant group) were significantly different from the seven preoccupied mothers with resistant infants (concordant group) in terms of their perceptions of distress on the DCBQ. Specifically, preoccupied mothers with secure infants perceived the infant in the videotape less positively than did preoccupied mothers with resistant infants. In other words, preoccupied mothers with secure infants interpreted infant distress more like autonomous mothers with secure infants than like preoccupied mothers with resistant infants.

Mothers' Representations of Their Own Infants

The next question is whether different internal representations of attachment are associated with different patterns of interpreting and experiencing one's own infant. In order to explore this question, a number of teams of investigators have independently developed and reported on instruments designed to characterize parents' representations of their own infants.

Inspired by Main's development of the AAI, our group was interested in attempting to classify parents' representations of a particular child. The Working Model of the Child Interview (Zeanah, Benoit, and Barton 1986) is a structured interview designed to inquire about the caregiver's experiences and perceptions of a young child. Parents respond to probes about their impressions of their infants' personalities and behaviors in a variety of situations as well as about their own emotional responses to the infants. Specific examples are frequently requested to augment and elaborate general impressions.

Interviews are tape-recorded, and verbatim transcripts are coded with a number of rating scales, some of which address the specific content of the interview and others of which assess qualitative features of the caregiver's descriptions of the child and of the relationship with the child. The qualitative scales include richness of perceptions, openness to change, intensity of involvement, and coherence. They are content free, in the sense that they concern not the specific characteristics that the caregiver perceives and describes about the infant but rather how the characteristics are perceived and described. Content scales include infant difficulty, caregiving sensitivity, acceptance, and fear for safety. The overall affective tones of the descriptions and perceptions are also rated.

An overall classification of the caregiver's representation of the child is determined by these ratings as well as by other distinctive features. Three major classifications were identified in the initial investigation: *balanced, disengaged,* and *distorted.*

Representations classified as balanced are characterized by narratives or interview responses that are coherently constructed, open to change, and richly detailed and convey a sense of the caregiver as engrossed in his or her relationship with the infant. The caregiver values the relationship with the infant and considers it to have effects on the infant's behavior and development. Balanced descriptions convey a sense of the infant as an individual (distinct from children in general) who is noticed and valued. If there are difficulties with the infant, these are acknowledged and placed into context. In general, a pervasive sense of respect and an empathic appreciation of the infant's experience characterize the interview. Descriptions and perceptions of the caregiving role convey feelings of "good-enough" competence in the relationship with the infant. The caregiver seems convincingly drawn to comfort the infant when he or she is distressed and describes how it feels to see the infant upset rather than merely describing what to do. Caregiving behavior is placed into a meaningful context. Negative affects in the caregiver toward the child are acknowledged but are modulated so that the infant is "protected."

The disengaged classification is identified by the caregiver's prominent disengagement from the relationship with the infant. This may take the form of emotional aloofness or a more pervasive distancing from or even aversion to the infant. This is particularly evident in the lack of caregiver engrossment with the infant and the relationship with the infant. Details about the infant are not particularly rich, or, if they are, they may seem unconvincing or forced, and there may seem to be little flexibility to accommodate changes in the representation over time. Descriptions and perceptions of the infant convey an unmistakable sense of coolness or distance from the infant. The caregiver seems not to know the infant as an individual so that descriptions may be minimal or may have a pat quality about them. Descriptions of the caregiving role also convey a limited involvement in the relationship with the infant.

Distorted representations are characterized by a struggle to be close to the infant, but one of several types of distortions makes the attempt unsatisfying. There is none of the coolness or distance as in the disengaged representations; instead, the caregiver is more involved and may have a lot to say, but it is difficult for the caregiver to convey a clear sense of the baby. The distortion involved is not with regard to "objective" reality but instead refers to an internal inconsistency and lack of coherence. The caregiver may have difficulty describing the infant and the relationship with the infant. The caregiver may seem preoccupied by or distracted by other concerns, confused and anxiously overwhelmed by the infant, self-involved and insensitive to the infant as an individual, or to look for comforting and caregiving from the infant in a role-reversed relationship pattern. Difficulties with the infant may be prominent, but they are not placed into context by the caregiver and may intrude into the interview in various ways. The caregiver may seem confused or disappointed by the infant or by the relationship with the infant. The infant's needs are not well recognized or understood, although the caregiver may seem to have a definite agenda for the infant.

In a study with forty-three middle-class families (Zeanah, Benoit, Hirshberg, et al. 1991), we classified mothers' descriptions and perceptions of their infants using the Working Model of the Child Interview. We compared mothers' representations of their infants to infant attachment classifications, predicting that mothers whose representations were balanced would be more likely to have infants classified as secure, that mothers whose representations were classified as disengaged would be more likely to have infants classified as avoidant, and that mothers whose representations were classified as distorted would be more likely to have infants classified as resistant. We found a 70 percent agreement (kappa = 0.51) between mothers' representations of their one-year-old infants and the infants' attachment classifications measured concurrently from Strange Situations (concordance is defined as above). These findings indicate that different types of internal representations of attachment in mothers are associated with different patterns of perceiving and interpreting one's own infant.

Clinical Implications

If the psychodynamic assertion that early relationship patterns are reenacted in subsequent relationships is true, then it is plausible that these patterns are mediated by similar representational processes in parents and infants. Specifically, as predicted by attachment theory, results from these studies indicate that autonomous mothers are more likely to have securely attached infants, that dismissing mothers are more likely to have infants classified as avoidant, and that preoccupied mothers may be more likely to have infants classified as resistant. These results suggest that there are important similarities in the representational processes by which mothers and their infants subjectively experience attachment relationships.

The preliminary evidence that we reviewed suggests that current methods of classifying internal representations do relate to differences in subjective experiences. The clinical implications of this line of research are that attachment patterns in infants and adults reveal an overall organizing theme of the parent-infant relationship, associated with a way of experiencing and enacting the theme (Zeanah and Zeanah 1989). Thus, it is possible to offer some tentative speculations about overall organizing themes of attachment relationship patterns. Autonomous/secure relationships are organized by emotional availability and responsiveness, dismissing/avoidant relationships by rejection and detachment from distress, and preoccupied/resistant relationships by a dissatisfying closeness.

The autonomous/secure pattern, characterized by emotional availability and responsiveness, is the "good-enough" pattern. Reasonably direct expression of needs for attention and comfort in the child are appreciated and responded to with adequate sensitivity by the caregiver. Positive and negative aspects of experiences in the relationship are accepted and integrated so that the individual has ready access to memories and feelings of seeking and obtaining comfort and security. As Bowlby (1969) emphasized, self-representations include a sense of the child as deserving of emotionally available and responsive care and as belonging to essentially gratifying, caregiving relationships.

In the dismissing/avoidant pattern, bids by the child for comfort or nurturance are turned away or rejected, especially at times when the child is distressed. This rejection ranges from a subtle disengagement from the child to a frank aversion to her. She learns to suppress her need for comfort by turning her attention away from her distress and from her caregiver. Instead, she maintains an outward appearance of self-reliance and strength, in order not to elicit rejection from the caregiver by a direct display of neediness. The self-organization underlying this pattern likely includes a powerful, self-reliant, dominant (perhaps victimizing) self-representation fused with a needy, weak, submissive (perhaps victimized) self-representation (see Harmon, Wagonfield, and Emde 1982; and Troy and Sroufe 1987). The more extreme the rejection the individual has experienced, the more extreme the split between these two extremes is likely to be. Because it is less painful, the former self-representation will be more conscious. For it to be maintained, however, the individual will be especially averse to stimuli (e.g., neediness) that threaten to elicit its more painful, less conscious counterpart. Thus, the adult in this pattern rejects his needy child as he shuns his own neediness. The child who experiences the rejection defensively constructs a similarly split self-representation, and the cycle continues.

In the preoccupied/resistant pattern, there is none of the coolness or detachment as in the dismissing/avoidant pattern. Instead, these relationships are characterized by an intense but dissatisfying involvement. The caregiver yearns for a relationship with the child that will be reparative and will satisfy myriad unmet needs from previous relationships. Unfortunately, the pressure of the caregiver's needs clouds appreciation of and consistent responsiveness to the child's needs. As a result, the child's bids for comfort or nurturance are responded to inconsistently by the caregiver, leading to angry and/or anxious reactions in the child. The caregiver experiences these reactions as critical rebukes and implicitly or explicitly pleads for the child to be reasonable. He struggles in an unsuccessful attempt to please the adult who cannot be pleased because of the intensely idealized nature of her longings. Self-representations in this pattern are suffused with doubt and frustration about being unable to please or to be satisfied by the other. This frustration and self-criticism breeds an intense yearning for an idealized relationship against which the actual relationship is compared and found wanting, adding even further to the disappointment.

Conclusions

Two caveats are necessary about these speculations. First, it should be emphasized that the latter two patterns are pathological only in their extremes. Many individuals in the dismissing/avoidant and preoccupied/resistant patterns will have generally successful adaptations, although significantly fewer than those in the autonomous/secure pattern. Second, especially after infancy, many other relationships beyond the dyad influence an individual's self-representations. Our focus on subjective experience in dyadic relationship patterns is only part of a complex and evolving process.

In the future, if investigators are able to confirm these formulations, then we may be able to understand more clearly how relationship patterns are transmitted between parents and children. Already it seems apparent, however, that the representational world and an individual's subjective experience of others' intimate relationships are of interest to researchers as well as to clinicians and theoreticians. This convergence of interests augurs well for the future of our collective efforts.

NOTE

Charles H. Zeanah was supported in part by a Research Scientist Development Award from the National Institute of Mental Health (MH 00691). Portions of this chapter have appeared in "Subjective Experience in Attachment Relationships: The Perspective from Research," in *Attaccamento e psicoanalisi,* ed. M. Ammaniti and D. N. Stern (Rome: Laterza, 1992).

REFERENCES

Ainsworth, M. D. S.; Blehar, M. C.; Waters, W.; and Wall, S. 1978. *Patterns of Attachment.* Hillsdale, N.J.: Erlbaum.

Benoit, D.; Vidovic, D.; and Roman, J. 1991. Transmission of attachment across three generations. Paper presented at the meeting of the Society for Research in Child Development, Seattle.

Bowlby, J. 1969. *Attachment and Loss: Attachment.* New York: Basic, 1982.

Bretherton, I. 1985. Attachment theory: retrospect and prospect. In I. Bretherton and E. Waters, eds. *Growing Points of Attachment Theory and Research.* Monographs of the Society for Research in Child Development, vol. 50, serial no. 209. Chicago: University of Chicago Press.

Bretherton, I. 1987. New perspectives on attachment relations: security, communication, and internal working models. In J. Osofsky, ed. *Handbook of Infant Development.* New York: Wiley-Interscience.

Cassidy, J., and Kobak, R. 1988. Avoidance and its relation to other defensive processes. In J. Belsky and T. Nezworski, eds. *Clinical Implications of Attachment.* Hillsdale, N.J.: Erlbaum.

Dozier, M. 1991. Psychophysiology in adult attachment interviews: converging evidence for deactivating strategies. Paper presented at the meeting of the Society for Research in Child Development, Seattle.

Eichberg, C. 1987. Security of attachment in infancy: contributions of mothers' representation of her own experience and child-care attitudes. Paper presented at the meeting of the Society for Research in Child Development, Baltimore.

Escalona, S. 1967. Patterns of infantile experience and the developmental process. *Psychoanalytic Study of the Child* 22:197–244.

Fonagy, P.; Steele, H.; and Steele, M. In press. Maternal representations of attachment during pregnancy predict the organization of infant-mother attachment at one year. *Child Development*.

George, C.; Kaplan, N.; and Main, M. 1984. Adult Attachment Interview. University of California, Berkeley. Typescript.

Harmon, R. J.; Wagonfield, S.; and Emde, R. N. 1982. Anaclitic depression: a follow-up from infancy to puberty. *Psychoanalytic Study of the Child* 37:67–94.

Main, M. 1982. Avoidance in the service of attachment: a working paper. In K. Immelman, G. W. Bariow, I. Petrinovich, and M. Main, eds. *Behavioral Development: The Bielfield Interdisciplinary Project*. Cambridge: Cambridge University Press.

Main, M., and Goldwyn, R. 1988. Adult attachment classification system: version 3. University of California at Berkeley. Typescript.

Main, M., and Goldwyn, R. In press. Interview-based adult attachment classifications: related to infant-mother and infant-father attachment. *Developmental Psychology*.

Main, M.; Kaplan, N.; and Cassidy, J. 1985. Security in infancy, childhood, and adulthood: a move to the level of representation. In I. Bretherton and E. Waters, eds. *Growing Points of Attachment Theory and Research*. Monographs of the Society for Research in Child Development, vol. 50, serial no. 209. Chicago: University of Chicago Press.

Main, M., and Stadtman, J. 1991. Infant responses to rejection of physical contact by the mother. *Journal of the American Academy of Child Psychiatry* 52:292–307.

Main, M., and Weston, D. R. 1981. The quality of the toddler's relationship to mother and father: related to conflict behavior and the readiness to establish new relationships. *Child Development* 52:932–940.

Sroufe, L. A. 1988. The role of infant-caregiver attachment in development. In J. Belsky and T. Nezworski, eds. *Clinical Implications of Attachment*. Hillsdale, N.J.: Erlbaum.

Sroufe, L. A., and Waters, E. 1977. Heart-rate as a convergent measure in clinical and developmental research. *Merrill-Palmer Quarterly* 23:3–28.

Troy, M., and Sroufe, L. A. 1987. Victimization among preschoolers: role of attachment relationship history. *Journal of the American Academy of Child and Adolescent Psychiatry* 26:166–172.

Vaughn, B., and Waters, E. 1990. Attachment behavior at home and in the laboratory: Q-sort observations and Strange Situation classifications of one-year-olds. *Child Development* 61:1965–1973.

Ward, M. J.; Botyanski, M. C.; Plunkett, S. W.; and Carlson, E. A. 1990. The concurrent and predictive validity of the AAI for adolescent mothers. Paper presented at the meeting of the Society for Research in Child Development, Seattle.

Zeanah, C. H.; Benoit, D.; and Barton, M. L. 1986. *Working model of the child interview*. Brown University. Typescript.

Zeanah, C. H.; Benoit, D.; Barton, M. L.; Regan, C.; Hirshberg, L.; and Lipsitt, L. In press. Representations of attachment in mothers and their one-year-old infants. *Journal of the American Academy of Child and Adolescent Psychiatry*.

Zeanah, C. H.; Benoit, D.; Hirshberg, L.; Barton, M. L.; and Regan, C. 1991. A typology of parents' representations of their infants: results using a structured interview. Brown University. Typescript.

Zeanah, C. H., and Zeanah, P. D. 1989. Intergenerational transmission of maltreatment: insights from attachment theory and research. *Psychiatry* 52:171–196.

9   ATTACHMENT AND THE PROBLEM
     OF COHERENCE: IMPLICATIONS FOR
     TREATING DISTURBED ADOLESCENTS

R. ROGERS KOBAK

I cannot help wondering how it is that the authorities can produce such smooth and precise histories in cases of hysteria. As a matter of fact the patients are incapable of giving such reports about themselves. They can, indeed, give the physician plenty of coherent information about this or that period of their lives; but it is sure to be followed by another period as to which their communications run dry, leaving gaps unfilled, and riddles unanswered; and then again will come yet another period which will remain totally obscure and unilluminated by even a single piece of serviceable information. The connections—even the ostensible ones —are for the most part *incoherent,* and the sequence of different events is uncertain. . . . That this state of affairs should exist in regard to the memories relating to the history of the illness is a *necessary correlate* of the symptoms and one which is theoretically requisite. [Freud 1905, pp. 16–18]

Freud suggests that incoherence in the hysteric's description of her illness forms a "necessary correlate" of her symptoms. Yet his comments indicate that most case histories tend to ignore the incoherence of patients' discourse. The comfort that medical authorities may draw from "smooth and precise" case histories may ultimately cost them understanding the client. Recent developments in attachment research have rediscovered the problem of incoherence in subjects' discourse.

Like much of attachment theory, this new work returns to an old problem with a fresh perspective. Central to an attachment perspective is the notion of defining a healthy, normative developmental pathway, which begins in infancy and moves through subsequent phases of development. From this perspective, an understanding of incoherent discourse must begin by specifying criteria for coherent discourse.

Analysis of conversation has provided researchers with a window on the development of child and adolescent attachment relationships. The importance of conversation becomes apparent during the transition from infancy to the formation of cooperative goal-corrected partnerships. In the next section, the importance of conversation to the maintenance of cooperative goal-corrected partnerships will be emphasized. If conversation mediates the child's access to attachment figures, discourse analysis should provide vital clues to understanding attachment security. Main's research linking infant attachment security to the development of coherent conversation highlights the contribution of discourse analysis. In the third section, the transition to adolescence is considered. During this period, the ability to maintain coherent conversation with parents develops into the ability to maintain coherent discourse *about* the self. Finally, treatment implications of discourse analysis will be considered. By focusing on criteria for conversation coherence, mechanisms for repairing incoherence become apparent. Thus, treatment of disturbed adolescents can be viewed as a movement toward reestablishing conversational coherence in the parent-teen relationship.

Infant Security and the Emergence of Cooperative Partnerships

The attachment literature provides strong support for the notion that sensitive and responsive parenting leads to a worthy and efficacious sense of self (Bretherton 1985; Sroufe 1989). In addition to a confident sense of self, the child also develops self-regulating strategies for maintaining access to attachment figures. Thus, the secure child uses emotion to organize behavior, signal caregivers, and monitor outcomes. Paradoxically, these same secure children show more self-reliance. For instance, they work more persistently in problem-solving situations, enlisting parental support only when personal resources have been exhausted (Matas, Arend, and Sroufe 1978). This capacity for flexible self-regulation has been documented with longitudinal predictions from infant security to observers' ratings of ego resiliency in the preschool and elementary school classroom (Sroufe 1983).

Although the infant's attachment sets the child on a favorable developmental pathway, the movement into early childhood requires that the parent and child form a cooperative partnership (Bowlby 1969; Marvin 1977). For such a partnership to form, the parent must continue to be sensitive and responsive to the child's growing cognitive abilities and accommodate accordingly (Greenberg and Speltz 1988). Early successes in gaining access to attachment figures lay the groundwork for successful developmental change. Thus, the secure infant learns to be an active partner in the relationship and provides the parent with continual information about the importance of the attachment relationship while he or she goes about the business at hand of asserting his or her need for increased autonomy. Sometime during the fourth year, the child's ability to understand and accommodate the parent's goals and plans allows the parent-child relationship to become a *cooperative partnership* (Bowlby 1969; Marvin 1977).

When the parent fails to read and respond to the infant's attachment signals successfully, deviations from the normative secure pattern are set in motion. The nature of the deviation depends on the particular ways that a parent fails to respond to the child's signals. One kind of parent may find the child's bids for proximity and bodily contact disruptive and reject or rebuff the child. In this situation, the child faces the dilemma of maintaining a relationship while avoiding conflict with the parent. Such a child may develop a self-regulatory strategy involving deactivating the attachment system, minimizing expression of needs for contact, and diverting attention away from situations that normally elicit attachment behavior. This type of strategy helps the child minimize anxiety about the relationship and reduce potential conflict with the parent. Alternatively, a child may experience inconsistent responses from a parent. In this situation, the child may develop a strategy involving close monitoring of the parent and exaggeration of attachment emotion and action tendencies in order to increase the likelihood of parental response. The conflictual underpinnings of this strategy may be manifested in anger that often accompanies contact with the parent.

Although both types of insecure strategies serve the child's short-term concerns with maintaining access to unresponsive parents, they have long-term maladaptive consequences. Children with insecure strategies may lack the self-confidence and self-efficacy needed to persist at new or challenging situations. As a result, both types of children may be more dependent on adult figures such as teachers (Sroufe, Fox, and Pancake 1983). By minimizing the expression of attachment needs, the child adopting a deactivating strategy may be less successful in using emotion to engage others in positive interactions. On the other hand, a child with hyperactivating strategies may tend toward withdrawn self-preoccupation. Although insecure strategies serve to maintain the attachment relationship, they also are likely to reduce the quality of cooperation with the parent.

Bowlby suggests that early attachment experiences play a critical role in shaping personality processes. Ainsworth's infant classifications have provided researchers with a way of understanding the contribution of attachment to personality. Further, the strategies that children develop in parent-infant relationships have been found to have long-term consequences for how the child adapts to peer and school situations (Bretherton 1985; Sroufe 1983). However, less is known about how early infant strategies for maintaining relationships with parents influence subsequent security in the parent-child relationship. In the next section, I consider how developmental change influences the way children maintain security with their attachment figures.

From Cooperation to Coherent Discourse

An important change occurs as the child shifts from proximity seeking to conversation as the means of regulating access to the attachment figure. As a result, the quality of conversation becomes a critical marker of the security of goal-corrected partnerships. Main, Kaplan, and Cassidy (1985) first drew attention to the importance of conversation in studying six-year-old children and their parents. Working with the transcripts of parent-child conversations during a three-minute reunion episode, a psycholinguistics student, Amy Strage, rated "discourse fluency." Ratings were assigned for balance of participation between partners, the flexibility with which partners maintained conversational focus, and the ease of access each participant had to relevant information. The fluency of this three-minute conversation was strongly linked to the child's security in the Strange Situation five years earlier. These findings provide remarkable empirical support for the link between infant attachment security and the development of coherent conversational discourse.

Several implications follow from the association between attachment security and parent-child discourse. First, if the set goal of the child's attachment system is access to the attachment figures (Ainsworth 1990), establishing fluent discourse during reunion would serve the function of an attachment behavior. Thus, cooperative conversation serves to reassure the child of his or her access to the attachment figure. Second, the conversational analysis conducted by Strage reflects the move toward a goal-corrected partnership in that the fluency of the discourse was dependent on both the child's and the parents' cooperative participation. Third, the association between infant security and discourse fluency supports a developmental pathway model of attachment. In this model, infant security facilitates the later transition to a cooperative goal-corrected partnership. The open communication and direct signaling that characterize the infant's secure strategies should support the child's transition to competent discourse partner. Finally, it is apparent that discourse fluency provides a means of assessing the quality of attachment. By six years of age, coherent discourse and attachment security are inextricably linked.

To date, discourse analysis has been used most extensively to assess adult attachment. However, instead of analyzing discourse with an attachment figure, Main and Goldwyn (1989) have examined adults' discourse about their own attachment history in the Adult Attachment Interview (AAI). The AAI interviewer asks subjects to recall memories from childhood and organize them into a coherent narrative. During the interview, individual differences in subjects' ability to deploy attention become apparent. For instance, subjects may access specific memories from childhood, involving separations, rejections, and threats of abandonment, with varying degrees of fluidity. Subjects also vary in their ability to generalize and gain perspective on their experiences. The challenging nature of the AAI tests subjects' ability to respond cooperatively to interview questions.

In order to assess coherence in adult's discourse, Main and Goldwyn drew from Grice's (1989) work in linguistic philosophy. According to Grice, the overarching principle for evaluating coherence involves the extent that participants recognize "a common purpose or set of purposes, or at least a mutually accepted direction" (p. 26). In the AAI, the interviewer establishes the purpose for the subject's discourse.

However, subjects may cooperate with this protocol to varying degrees. According to Grice, coherency can be evaluated with four maxims: Quantity, Quality, Relation, and Manner. Each maxim provides a norm that subjects may observe or violate. For instance, the maxim of Quantity states, "Make your contribution as informative as is required (for the purposes of the exchange)" (p. 26). It can be violated by providing either too much or too little information. Both kinds of violations may occur in the interview. For instance, when asked to provide a specific memory to support a description of a loving mother, subjects may either fail to remember or launch into an extended set of memories that distract attention from the initial question.

The maxim of Quality states, "Try to make your contribution one that is true" (p. 27). This may be violated either by saying what one believes to be false or by making statements for which the participant lacks evidence. Failure to support generalizations can occur through use of stereotypes, superficial generalizations or vague responses, or blatant contradictions of previous statements. The third maxim of relation states, "Be relevant." Observance of this maxim is continually tested by the progression in interview topics. With each new question, the subject must accommodate to the topic change in order to remain relevant. Finally, the maxim of Manner states, "Be perspicuous" (p. 27). To observe this maxim, subjects must be clear, orderly, and unambiguous in their choice of terms. Idiosyncratic or personalized meanings create problems in maintaining a cooperative discourse.

If everyone fully observed Grice's maxims, we would live in a world in which each person would be fully comprehensible to every other. Since we do not, it is useful to consider cases in which violations of specific maxims do not jeopardize coherency. "Licensed" and "unlicensed" violations of maxims are possible (Mura 1983). A violation is licensed when the speaker directly acknowledges difficulty observing a maxim in order to maintain the cooperative principle. For instance, if a subject lacks information to support a description of parents, this violation of the Quantity maximum can be licensed with an apology indicating difficulty and a continued effort to cooperate. "Unlicensed violations" occur when maxims are not acknowledged or "flouted." For instance, a subject who repeatedly fails to remember supporting memories may, at a certain point, imply that he or she has no intention of cooperating with the interviewer.

Main and Goldwyn (1988) use coherence criteria to infer subjects' discourse strategies in the AAI. If subjects observe Grice's maxims and license violations, they are rated as "secure" or "free to evaluate" attachment relationships. In contrast, if subjects show incoherence marked by lack of memory for childhood, idealization of parents, and defensive devaluation of attachment, they are presumed to be employing a "dismissing" discourse strategy. Alternatively, if subjects show incoherence marked by excessive detail, lack of integration of memory, and sudden vacillation in viewpoint, they are using a "preoccupied" discourse strategy. Parents' security or discourse coherence in the AAI predicts infants' attachment security in the Strange Situation. Thus, parents employing dismissing strategies tend to have infants who are avoidant, while those employing preoccupied strategies have infants classified as anxious/resistant (Green-Eichberg 1987; Main and Goldwyn, 1988). In extending the study of AAI discourse strategies to late adolescents, we found that teens with secure discourse strategies were rated by their peers as more ego resilient, less hostile, and less anxious (Kobak and Sceery 1988).

AAI Discourse Strategies and Cooperation in Parent-Teen Relationships

An important aspect of our recent work has been in developing an observational paradigm for assessing coherency in parent-teen discourse. For this purpose, we had mothers and teens participate in a ten-minute problem-solving discussion of a major area of disagreement. In developing this paradigm, we hoped to learn about mothers' and teens' ability to maintain cooperative discourse by observing them in a situation requiring reconciliation of conflicting goals. To remain coherent in this task, teens and mothers must be honest about their goals and yet discuss their disagreement in a manner that allows cooperation and topic progression.

To establish the topic, we asked mothers and teens to identify their major area of disagreement. Grades, communication, and siblings were the most commonly identified problem topics. We then separately interviewed the mother and the teen, audiotaped their statements of the problem, brought them back together, and replayed their tapes. After hearing each person's statement, mothers and teens were instructed to discuss the problem for ten minutes and try to reach a mutually satisfying solution.

Successful interactions tended to observe the maxims for coherent discourse. For instance, in order for the dyad to cooperate and sustain the focus of the interaction, both teen and mother had to provide adequate but not excessive information (Quantity maxim) about their position in a manner that was honest and forthright (Quality maxim). We considered observance of these maxims in terms of rating the teens' and mothers' effectiveness in communicating their point of view. Optimal performance was characterized by dyads that maintained balanced assertiveness in which neither mother nor teen dominated the interaction. A second scale assessed avoidance of problem solving (Relevance maxim) in terms of whether participants made contributions that maintained and developed the problem focus. Finally, a dysfunctional anger scale (Manner maxim) rated critical, hostile comments that disrupted the orderly flow of conversation.

In addition to evaluating mother-teen coherence during problem solving, we also interviewed teens with the AAI. These interviews were evaluated for coherency of discourse using a Q-sort rating. We expected that the coherence of mother-teen discourse should facilitate the teen's ability to employ a secure discourse strategy in the AAI. Our results supported this hypothesis (Kobak, Cole, Fleming, Ferenz-Gillies, and Gamble 1993). More specifically, lack of dysfunctional anger (manner violations), lack of avoidance of problem solving (relevance violations), and balanced mother-teen dialogue (observance of the Quantity maxim) predicted teens' security in the AAI.

Interpretation of directions of effects in our findings is difficult. On the one hand, a secure discourse strategy in the AAI may emerge from a parent-child relationship characterized by cooperative discourse. On the other hand, the teen's discourse strategy may contribute to his or her ability to maintain coherent discourse with a mother. The cross-sectional nature of our findings makes it impossible to resolve this ambiguity. However, we suspect that, by adolescence, the child's way of conversing with parents and about parents has become organized and self-regulating. The consistency we find between AAI discourse strategies and mother-teen conversation thus reflects a common way of organizing discourse in two different assessment contexts.

Treatment Implications: Threats
to Coherence and Cooperation in Therapy

If adolescent attachment security is viewed as the ability of adolescents to maintain coherent discourse with and about parents, breakdowns in discourse and cooperation may be viewed as "necessary correlates" (Freud 1905) of adolescent psychopathology. Yet insecure attachment and incoherent conversation are not sufficient to produce psychiatric casualties (Sroufe 1988). Teens' vulnerabilities become most apparent during times of stress or transition. The normative stresses involved in parent-teen relationships can be greatly exacerbated by socioeconomic and family factors. At few times during the course of development is the maintenance of conversation and negotiation so important for successful developmental change.

Despite the challenges of adolescence, most studies indicate that parents and teens manage to negotiate this period successfully. However, incoherent conversation with parents may put teens at risk for disturbances. For instance, teens' experience of movement toward autonomy might become problematic if they were unable to talk about those changes with their parents. Thus, moves toward autonomy would come at the expense of the family or by violating family norms.

Insecure discourse strategies not only limit teens' ability to maintain coherent discourse with parents but may make access to internal thoughts and feelings problematic. For instance, a child who dismisses attachment may be less able to communicate effectively with a parent and consequently display frustration and anger that seem situationally inappropriate. Parents' comments that their child seems unhappy often seem quite accurate to the outside observer, but feelings of unhappiness remain outside the teen's awareness. The inability to communicate with others makes feelings unavailable for reflection or self-understanding. Alternatively, a teen who is preoccupied with attachment may be prone to emotional lability, confusion, anger, and self-preoccupation. Both dismissing and preoccupied deviations from the secure norm jeopardize the cooperative underpinnings of a successful parent-child relationship.

When misunderstanding and misperception become pervasive, teens, or, in some cases, their parents, develop symptomatic behavior. For instance, a young male adolescent growing up in a family characterized by marital conflict and parental substance abuse learns to take care of himself and dismiss attachment feelings. By adopting this strategy, he managed a relatively symptom-free childhood. However, with increased stress from his parents' separation and his mother's financial difficulties, a distant relationship erupted into overt conflict. One day, his mother asked him to stop listening to his Walkman and clean his room. When he failed to comply, she took the Walkman, and he responded by calling her a "bitch." The conflict escalated as his mother dragged him to the bathroom and tried to wash his mouth out with soap. He became hysterical. The mother, doubting her ability to manage the situation, called his grandmother, who took him for two days. This breakdown in cooperation and extreme violations of conversational coherence led the mother to seek therapy for her son.

This case illustrates how symptomatic behavior and the decision to seek treatment often occur when parents have lost faith in their ability to manage relationships in which discourse violations have become pervasive. Therapeutically, the problem of reestablishing cooperative discourse can be approached through either individual work or family sessions. In this case, the son was seen for twelve months by an individual therapist. During this time, his ability to sustain coherent discourse about his problems was severely restricted. Through expressive play, he communicated uncertainty as to whether his mother loved him and talked extensively about his desire to return to his father's house, where he was less closely supervised.

Progression in treatment occurred when the therapist could reframe coherency violations into communications. Initially, when a maxim was violated, the therapist tended to experience confusion or uncertainty. Although subtle variations in cooperation occurred throughout sessions, probably the most obvious instances of coherency violations occurred at moments during sessions in which the therapist felt attacked. During one session, the client asked to stretch a slinky between himself and the therapist and then released it so that it snapped in her face. The therapist first called attention to the violation and then linked it to her understanding of the client's history of rejection. Although he did not immediately respond to these remarks, the client's attacking behaviors gradually ceased. During the course of treatment, coherent conversation slowly replaced the client's inchoate depression and frustration.

Although the therapist could actively work to license incoherence through her empathy, parents' discourse strategies may restrict their ability to reestablish cooperative conversation. In this case, the son's incoherent expressions of anger and rejection tended to increase his mother's rejecting or insensitive responses. Both mother and child lived with a constant threat of rejection by the other. Their fears increased as treatment moved from individual to family therapy. Family therapy began with a focus on increasing contact between mother and son. Initially, the mother reported satisfaction with her contact with her son and his apparent openness with her.

The fourth session brought a new threat to the relationship. On their way to the family session, the son asked the mother to mail a request to the court asking to move back with his father. The mother was hurt by this request and started to respond angrily. She presented her story to the therapist, indicating that she was fed up with her son. The son, attuned to his mother's anger, intensified his request to live with his father. With support in the family session, the mother accessed feelings of hurt and vulnerability that accompanied her son's rejecting. Licensing her anger was accompanied by crying. This repair in the mother-child discourse was followed by the son acknowledging the importance of the relationship. Inchoate feelings of anger and rejection were turned into cooperative conversation.

Conclusions

Attachment theory allows us to return to Freud's problem of incoherence in a new way. It suggests that problems of coherency cannot be separated from problems in relationships. To treat problems of incoherence, it is useful for the therapist to understand the relationship context that predates the formation of symptoms. By providing a window on the development of attachment relationships, recent research offers therapists a framework that may guide their understanding of clients' development. Such a perspective facilitates the therapist's ability to reframe coherence violations and reestablish cooperative communication. Attachment research also suggests new goals for treatment. Not only is the practical aim of treatment to remove symptoms and replace them by conscious thoughts (Freud 1905) or, in our terms, coherent discourse with a therapist. The therapist must also monitor the family context and attempt to reestablish cooperation in the client's attachment relationships. In this sense, successful individual and family treatment should be two sides of the same coin.

REFERENCES

Ainsworth, M. D. S. 1990. Epilogue: some considerations regarding theory and assessment relevant to attachments beyond infancy. In D. Cicchetti, M. Greenberg, and M. Cummings, eds. *Attachment in the Preschool Years*. Chicago: University of Chicago Press.

Bowlby, J. 1969. *Attachment and Loss*. Vol. 1, *Attachment*. New York: Basic.

Bretherton, I. 1985. Attachment theory: retrospect and prospect. In I. Bretherton and E. Waters, eds. *Growing Points of Attachment Theory and Research*. Monographs of the Society for Research in Child Development, vol. 50, serial no. 209. Chicago: University of Chicago Press.

Freud, S. 1905. Fragment of an analysis of a case of hysteria. *Standard Edition* 7:7–122. London: Hogarth, 1953.

Greenberg, M. T., and Speltz, M. L. 1988. Attachment and the ontogeny of conduct problems. In J. Belsky and T. Neworski, eds. *Clinical Implications of Attachment*. Hillsdale, N.J.: Erlbaum.

Green-Eichberg, C. 1987. *Quality of Infant-Parent Attachment: Related to Mother's Representation of Her Own Relationship History*. Baltimore.

Grice, P. 1989. *Studies in the Way of Words*. Cambridge, Mass.: Harvard University Press.

Kobak, R.; Cole, H.; Fleming, W.; Ferenz-Gillies, R.; and Gamble, W. 1993. Attachment and emotion regulation during mother-teen problem-solving: a control theory analysis. *Child Development* 64:231–245.

Kobak, R., and Sceery, A. 1988. Attachment in late adolescence: working models, affect regulation, and representations of self and others. *Child Development* 59:135–146.

Main, M., and Goldwyn, R. 1988. Adult attachment classification system. University of California, Berkeley, Department of Psychology. Typescript.

Main, M., and Goldwyn, R. 1989. Adult attachment rating and classification system. Department of Psychology, University of California, Berkeley. Typescript.

Main, M.; Kaplan, N.; and Cassidy, J. 1985. Security in infancy, childhood and adulthood: a move to the level of representation. In I. Bretherton and E. Waters, eds. *Growing Points of Attachment*

Theory and Research. Monographs of the Society for Research in Child Development, vol. 50, serial no. 209. Chicago: University of Chicago Press.

Marvin, R. S. 1977. An ethological-cognitive model for the attenuation of mother-child attachment behavior. In T. M. Alloway, L. Krames, and P. Pliner, eds. *Advances in the Study of Communication and Affect.* Vol. 3, *The Development of Social Attachments.* New York: Plenum.

Matas, L.; Arend, R.; and Sroufe, L. 1978. Continuity of adaptation in the second year: the relationship between quality of attachment and later competent functioning. *Child Development* 49:547–556.

Mura, S. S. 1983. Licensing violations: legitimate violations of Grice's conversational principle. In R. Craig and K. Tracy, eds. *Conversational Coherence.* Beverly Hills, Calif.: Sage.

Sroufe, L. A. 1983. Infant-caregiver attachment and patterns of adaptation in preschool: the roots of maladaptation and competence. In M. Perlmutter, ed. *Minnesota Symposium in Child Psychology,* vol. 16. Hillsdale, N.J.: Erlbaum.

Sroufe, L. A. 1989. Relationships, self and individual adaptation. In A. J. Sameroff and R. N. Emde, eds. *Relationship Disturbances in Early Childhood: A Developmental Approach.* New York: Basic.

Sroufe, L. A.; Fox, N.; and Pancake, V. 1983. Attachment and dependency in developmental perspective. *Child Development* 54:1615–1627.

10 ATTACHMENT, PERSONALITY, AND PSYCHOPATHOLOGY: RELATIONSHIP AS A REGULATORY CONTEXT IN ADOLESCENCE

DIANA S. ROSENSTEIN AND HARVEY A. HOROWITZ

The concept of attachment as it is manifest in adolescents is relatively unexplored. It is easy to understand the importance of attachment relationships for the well-being of infants and small children. However, if adolescence is conceptualized as a time of increased separation from parents, the need for direct parental promotion of security is less apparent. The attachment model provides a lens through which we can view the continuing influence of parents as attachment figures via internalized, abstract organizations of the relationship between attachment figures and the self. These internal working models of attachment are one of the basic regulators of affect and behavior in relationships throughout the life span and are essential to the development of personality and psychopathology.

This chapter will examine the relationship between attachment organization, personality development, and psychopathology. The study of the role of attachment in adolescent psychopathology presented here is part of a larger study of psychiatrically hospitalized adolescents at the Institute of Pennsylvania Hospital in Philadelphia. The Adolescent Research Group has also been examining the cognitive development and family structure of these adolescents. This group has come to think of relationship as providing the regulatory context in which behavior, affect, and cognition find organization in the developing individual (Horowitz, Overton, Rosenstein, and Steidl 1992; Overton, Steidl, Rosenstein, and Horowitz 1992; Rosenstein, Horowitz, Steidl, and Overton 1992; Steidl, Horowitz, Overton, and Rosenstein 1992). Attachment is one means of conceptualizing and describing a basic intrapsychic organization that Bowly (1973) has deemed a "tolerably accurate reflection" of actual relationship experiences.

Development and Self-Regulation

The developmental perspective taken is a constructivist one. Development proceeds from a state of globality to ever increasing states of differentiation and hierarchical integration. Change arises as new competencies direct new patterns of adaptive organization. The idea of adaptation implies a context in which adaptation takes place. Human relationships form that context, initially emerging from an infant-caregiver system that is embedded in a larger familial and societal context. The constructivist element in this perspective holds that meaning and knowing are co-constructed within a relationship through affective communication and shared experience. The individual is understood as emerging within the regulated context of the infant-caregiver relationship, evolving into a differentiated, constant, and coherent self, yet remaining embedded, connected, and interdependent within a relational system throughout the life span. The outcome of early experiences that provide effective dyadic regulation is self-regulation, that is, a coherent and adaptive pattern of affective, behavioral, and cognitive regulation. The outcome of ineffective dyadic regulation is a self-regulatory strategy that is incoherent and leads to patterns of organization that are adaptive only in the context from which they originated.

The individual and her personality, which includes the contribution of biological and genetic factors, such as temperament and maturation, are stable forms of organization of affect, behavior, and cognition across contexts. This is to say, not that the particulars of behavior remain the same across the life span, but that the organization of adaptation to the environment is stable (Sroufe 1979). This point is crucial to the understanding of patterns of attachment relationships across the life span. It is not the particular attachment behaviors, such as the clinging or crying for attention that is seen in infants and toddlers, that remain the same but the expectations that the individual holds about the subjective quality of the interaction and its capacity to provide satisfaction, positive affective tone, and reliability that drive ever changing sets of behaviors.

The links between early experience, early adaptations, and later disorder require a complex developmental view of the person-experience-environment interaction such as those proposed by epigenetic theorists, including Erikson (1963), Piaget and Inhelder (1969), Sander (1962), Sroufe (1979), and Werner (1957). These developmentalists propose a lawful sequence of salient developmental, adaptive issues that are integrative and include the affective, cognitive, and social domains. Furthermore, the outcome of the negotiation of issues at one period is seen as laying the groundwork for subsequent issues in subsequent periods as well as being of continuing and central relevance throughout the life cycle. Sander (1975) proposes an epigenetic sequence of adaptive issues negotiated over the first three years in the interactions between infant and caregiver. This epigenetic sequence describes the movement from dyadic organization and regulation within the infant-caregiver system toward self-regulation and inner organization—an ontogeny of self as a differentiation of basic self-regulatory mechanisms from a relational matrix. This movement is viewed as the central adaptational task of early development and reflects a commitment to a relational model shared by developmental and psychoanalytic theorists. The phases in the development of self-regulation are as follows:

Phase 1: Biological regulation. In the first three months of life, the infant's state, communicated to an available, responsive, and intervening caregiver, leads to the etablishment of the regulation of such biological functions as feeding, sleeping and waking, and elimination. The dyadic regulatory system establishes "phase synchrony," a rhythmicity to the periods of relative activity and quiescence. Infant state and caregiver intervention become coordinated, a reciprocal or bidirectional coordination of actions.

Phase 2: Modulation of affect. From four to nine months, the caregiver-infant dyad moves toward greater reciprocity within a more genuine relationship, through the coordination of complex infant-initiated affective and behavioral exchanges, affect attunement, and the "bifurcation" brought on with intentionality. The infant's subjective experiences of reciprocity and coordination, attunement, and bifurcation within the dyadic relational matrix are internalized, leading to the earliest differentiation of self and other. This structuralization of the affective self and the available or unavailable caregiver contributes to the capacity for affective sharing, self-soothing, and self-modulation, all essential to the self-regulation of affects.

Phase 3: Control of behavior. This phase, from nine to eighteen months, is marked by three changes in the relational system having to do with exploration/attachment, locomotion/containment, and language/prohibition, all of which contribute to the emergence of self-control. The central organizing and regulating function of the attachment relationship emerges during these months, resulting in the use of the caregiver as a "secure base" to resolve uncertainty or diminish fear when exploring the environment. With the development of locomotion, conscious intentionality, and early means-ends thought, the infant asserts herself and widens the determination of her own behavior, frequently in opposition to the caregiver's expectations. By providing protective containment and consistent limit setting while continuing to be emotionally available to the ambivalent toddler, the caretaker facilitates the development of autonomy and impulse control. The appearance of language adds a powerful new mode of mediation of impulse control and compliance balanced with initiative and autonomy.

Phase 4: Self-monitoring. From eighteen to thirty-six months, the emergence of the symbolic capacity, language, recall memory, and representational thinking contributes to the toddler's recognition of self. Self-awareness and shared awareness are differentiated. This differentiation is facilitated by caregiving that provides an experience of empathic constancy, clarity, and continuity, yielding a coherence of self and the self-regulatory core.

The manifest psychiatric symptomatology in adolescents is understood as an expression of an underlying vulnerability in the regulatory and adaptive activities of the self. More specifically, our model proposes that the clinical presentation in adolescence is the symptomatic outcome of patterns of relational dysregulation transformed to maladaptive patterns of self-regulation in the first three years. The symptomatology, the triad of affective instability, impulsivity, and nonreflectivity, is developmentally linked to vulnerabilities emerging from the phase-specific tasks of acquiring self-modulation, self-control, and self-monitoring. Affective instability refers to the failure of internalization of an available and attuned caregiver who modulates distress. The experience is one of states of agitation, rage, shame, hurt, and

153

loneliness. This compromise is expressed as an intolerance of distress and dysphoria and an inability to dampen the affective state or to contain and terminate the dysphoric event. In addition, there is little expectation of empathic responsiveness from others, from within-familial relationships where the communication of painful affects is integral to connectedness, trust, and the sense of well-being.

The symptoms that reflect dysregulation of behavior, behavioral impulsivity, are linked to the development of self-control in the dyadic context. Following this trajectory, ineffective dyadic regulation of exploratory activity, intentionality, and aggression compromise the differentiation of an active, intentional self and the internalization of a protecting, containing caregiver. The structural limitations in the capacity for self-control, challenged by the developmental tasks of adolescence, are expressed in the impulsivity, hyperaggressiveness, noncompliance, and self-destructive risk taking of adolescents predisposed to a maladaptive outcome.

The symptoms that reflect dysregulation in cognitive nonreflectivity are linked to the development of self-monitoring in the relational context. Following this trajectory, ineffective dyadic coordination and regulation of awareness, affect, and internal representations compromised the differentiation of affectively positive, complex, and coherent self- and other schemas. This lack of differentiation of a fundamentally good and lovable self and a good and loving other renders self-esteem unstable. The compromised developmental trajectory has two forms, an ambiguous/indistinct and a rigid/remote articulation. Ambiguity within the toddler-caregiver relationship, the inability clearly to articulate the complexity of affects, of shared and personal awareness, and of the fundamental continuity of mutually empathic relationship, disrupts the development of constant and complex categories of self and other and leads to instability in the maintenance of psychological boundaries, diffusion, and enmeshment. Rigidity, concreteness, and emotional distance in the relational system, the inflexibility and global articulation of fundamentally negative affective experiences of relationship, disrupt the development of coherent, complex, and essentially positive categories of self and other and lead to forms of relatedness that are egocentric and exploitative.

Constructs central to attachment theory, such as the secure base, sensitivity in caretaking, and promotion of autonomy, are embedded in this model of the development of self-regulation. The remainder of this chapter will focus exclusively on the ineffective adaptation in pathological adolescents that occurs with disruptions in their attachment relationships. The attachment model provides a lens through which we can view the continuing influence of internalized, abstract, organizational features of attachment relationships and of the self. These features, or internal working models, as they have come to be known in the attachment literature, are the basic regulators of affect and behavior in relationships throughout the life span and have far-reaching implications for the structure of personality.

The term "attachment" is often used loosely to describe any close, emotionally involved relationship. As first used by the British psychoanalyst John Bowlby (1958), the term was intended to refer to a specific form of affective relationship. That relationship is an enduring and deep emotional bond between one human and another. The attachment figure provides protection, soothing, comfort, and help, leading to physical security in the very young, but also to the experience of emotional security and well-being. This is not a model for describing any interpersonal relationship, nor is it the description of relationships only in infancy. As development proceeds, attachment behaviors are reorganized to include newly acquired skills that express the underlying, stable, attachment organization. The remainder of this chapter will describe the mechanisms by which the attachment organization retains its stability and the behavioral manifestations of that attachment organization in adolescence. The central organization of attachment remains the same throughout the life span, barring severe trauma or deliberate attempts to change the organization, for example, through psychotherapy or deliberative involvement in relationships that are experienced as healthier or more satisfying.

Attachment in Infancy

In infancy, the burden of assessing the need for and providing security rests with the caretaker. Sensitive, consistent care leads to expectations that security needs will be met and hence to a secure attachment. Ainsworth, Bell, and Stayton (1974) have shown that the quality of mother-infant attachment can be predicted from aspects of their interaction as early as the sixth week of life. The quality of infant attachment formed is based on the history of the mother's and the infant's interaction together. The standard assessment of attachment in infancy is the Ainsworth-Wittig Strange Situation procedure (Ainsworth and Wittig 1969). In a series of short episodes, an infant and her mother are brought together in a laboratory, joined by a friendly stranger, and then separated from one another. The infant is left with the stranger, then left alone, and finally reunited with her mother. Observation of both separation and reunion behaviors determines attachment classification. Three main infant attachment classifications exist, one secure and two insecure (ambivalent and avoidant) types. A fourth category, insecure-disorganized, has more recently been developed by Main and Solomon (1990). Secure infants are the largest group, comprising 65–75 percent of most middle-class American samples. In the Strange Situation, secure infants may show initial wariness of the novel situation, checking back with the mother (the "secure base" phenomenon) before beginning to play. The infant acknowledges maternal absence on separation, either through protest or through diminishment in the quality of play, but does greet the mother with pleasure on reunion. If distressed, the infants are calmed by the mother's return or ministrations, such as holding or reassurance. These infants have a working model of the mother as sensitively responsive to their needs. The term "sensitively responsive" refers to the caretaker's capacity accurately to understand and respond to the needs of the child. The infant's working model is not to be thought of as a conscious, reflective representation, as it may become in adolescence or adulthood with the advent of formal operational thought. Rather, the model is embedded in the behavior of the infant. Securely attached infants expect that their mothers will see their distress and also will see and respond to their signals about how to end their distress.

The second classification, the insecure-ambivalent attachment, is characterized by cyclical efforts to gain security from the attachment figure and avoidance of the attachment figure. These infants are distressed about the novel environment and cling to their mothers. On separation, they are excessively distressed and uncontrolled. On reunion, these infants alternate bids for physical contact with their mothers with angry rebuffs of her. They fail to be soothed by their mother's attention and, therefore, cannot use her as a secure base. They appear to be in unending conflict with the attachment figure. This is the rarest organization in infancy (less than 10 percent of a middle-class American sample) and is often associated with severely disordered relationships and sometimes with neurological compromise in the infant. These are infants who have experienced inconsistent sensitivity from their mothers (Ainsworth, Blehar, Waters, and Wall 1978), leading them to become uncertain of the mother's availability. The infant's inconsistent adaptation reflects the mothers' inconsistent caretaking. In order to elicit and maintain the mother's attention, the infant intensifies attachment behaviors (e.g., crying, clinging) and vigilance regarding the mother's whereabouts. However, because of the infant's anger over maternal unavailability, the infant cannot be soothed by the mother.

By contrast with their ambivalent counterparts, insecure-avoidant infants rarely show overt distress over separation in the Strange Situation. On reunion, they are indifferent to their mother's return and literally avoid interaction with her, usually turning their attention to toys, exploration of the room, or the company of the stranger. Like the other attachment organizations, infant avoidance reflects the relational history of the mother-infant dyad. These infants have relational histories that include emotional and physical rejection, particularly in times of distress (Ainsworth et al. 1978). The avoidant infant has created an adaptational strategy to deal with rejection and to regulate its affective response to this rejection. The rejection of attachment behavior leads to anger and anxiety within the infant. Avoidance serves to cut off interaction that might arouse attachment behavior, thereby avoiding the arousal of negative affect as well. Main (1981) further views the function of avoidance as maintaining the attachment relationship. Avoidance is a compromise between alienating the attachment figure with angry demands for attention and maintaining an intolerably angry, rejected position in the absence of a comforting attachment figure. Avoidance serves to cut off the affective arousal before it is experienced as distress. This allows the infant to regulate its affect, thereby maintaining its organization during times of distress, and to maintain some comforting physical proximity to the attachment figure. The presence of such a complex strategy in an infant as young as twelve months speaks to the early, organized, effective, and adaptive nature of internal working models.

The fourth category, disorganized, was derived by a careful review of the Strange Situation behavior of infants previously thought to be unclassifiable (Main and Solomon 1990). These infants do not possess a coherent and functional strategy for regulating their distress on separation and, therefore, engage in behaviors that seem inexplicable or contradictory in intent or function, behaviors such as "approaching with the head averted, stilling or freezing of movement with a dazed expression, walking backwards toward the mother, calm contented play suddenly succeeded by distressed, angry behavior" (Main and Solomon 1990, p. 122). In middle-class samples, infant disorganization is associated with mothers' unresolved mourning for their own attachment figures (Ainsworth and Eichberg, in press), which leads to frightened and frightening behavior by the mother with her own infant. The infant is placed in the intolerable position of having the source of her distress and her haven from that distress embodied in the same person—the attachment figure (Main and Hesse 1990). In high-risk samples (individuals with abusive, neglectful, or psychopathological attachment figures), infant disorganization is also related to the mother's lack of resolution of trauma, typically a history of abuse or neglect in childhood.

Attachment in Preschoolers and School-aged Children

If one expects that the infant's behavior in the Strange Situation is based on an internal working model, which is in turn based on a relational history, it would stand to reason that the internal working model would remain stable so long as the context from which it emerged remained stable. Empirical evidence supports this idea. Attachment classification with the mother (or primary caretaker) is quite stable through at least the first six years of life (Main, Kaplan, and Cassidy 1985). Internal working models are solidified in the preschool years and are difficult to change without conscious, effortful reflection on one's behavior and experience. In what Sroufe (1989) calls a "sophisticated sensitive period hypothesis" (p. 85), Bowlby (1973) claims that internal working models are difficult to change because "early prototypes of inner organization are not readily accessible to conscious awareness and continue to operate out of awareness" and because of a tendency to form new relationships that are congruent with earlier models and hence tend to reinforce the validity of those models. The latter point embodies the concept of recursion in development.

Observations of toddlers and young school-age children show the enduring and widespread effects of attachment organization on many aspects of their functioning, although primarily on emotional or social functioning. Toddlers with secure attachment histories as infants are more positive in their affect, more enthusiastic, confident, and persistent in problem solving, and better able to use adults effectively when distressed or needing assistance (Arend 1984; Erikson and Farber 1983; Matas, Arend, and Sroufe 1978; Sroufe, Fox, and Pancake 1983; Sroufe and Rosenberg 1980). They seem more confident and flexible in managing impulses, feelings, and desires (Egeland 1983). Socially, they are more engaged and empathic with other children and more cooperative and compliant with their mothers (Londerville and Main 1981) and other adults (Main 1973). As preschoolers, these children are more socially competent with peers (Waters, Wippman, and Sroufe 1979), have more positive affect and are less aggressive and disruptive (Silver 1991), depend less on preschool teachers (Sroufe et al. 1983), and are more ego resilient at age five (Arend, Gove, and Sroufe 1979). At age ten to eleven, secure children again were more socially competent, had more and deeper friendships, and were less dependent on adults (Sroufe, Egeland, and Kreutzer 1990).

Children with insecure attachment histories lack the positive attributes of their secure counterparts. At age two, their affect is more negative, frustration tolerance is low, and social competence poor. Adults are avoided angrily or clung to. Peer relationships are marked by negative affect, lack of empathy, and shallowness. Frustration and lack of persistence characterize efforts at problem solving. Behavior disorders are more common in this group (Speltz, Greenberg, and DeKlyen 1991), as is childhood depression (Armsden, McCauley, Greenberg, Burke, and Mitchell 1990). Follow-up of these children into adolescence is still in process in longitudinal studies at the University of Minnesota, directed by Alan Sroufe, and at the University of California, Berkeley, led by Mary Main.

Attachment in Adolescence

Cross-sectional studies of adolescent attachment have consistently linked the quality of adolescent relationships to their overall emotional adjustment (Rice 1990). Parental attachment security made an increased contribution to adolescent adjustment over and above the effect produced by peer attachment security, highlighting the causal role of parental attachment relationships in producing adequate relationships of all kinds into adolescence. Links between attachment insecu-

159

rity and psychopathology in adolescence have also been demonstrated. Insecure attachment is associated with symptomatic affects (depression and anxiety; Papini, Roggman, and Anderson 1991), problem drinking (Hughes, Francis, and Power 1989), and treatment noncompliance (Dozier 1990). Dismissing (avoidant) attachment in adolescence is associated with drug abuse (Allen and Hauser 1991) and eating disorders (Cole 1991), while preoccupied (ambivalent) attachment has been associated with depression (Cole 1991).

In the Adolescent Attachment Project at the Institute of Pennsylvania Hospital, sequelae of insecure attachment in adolescence, particularly the symptomatic presentation corresponding to each form of insecure attachment, are being described. The scant literature on adult and adolescent attachment provides some direction. However, a semistructured interview that captures the attachment classification of an adolescent or adult, developed by Main and her colleagues (George, Kaplan, and Main 1985), has greatly aided the understanding of the developmental outcome of insecure attachment. The Adult Attachment Interview does not purport to capture the quality of the literal attachment relationship when the adult in question was an infant; rather, it looks exclusively at components of the adult's current representation of attachment. The adult's current state of mental organization, rather than her history, is being assessed. This interview has been successfully used with several other groups of adolescents, but this is its first use with any adolescent psychopathological population. The interview asks questions regarding the basic structure of the family, about quality of caretaking, about affective tone, about security operations, and about experiences of loss. It is designed so that the subject is asked to support through memories or anecdotes the generalizations put forth earlier in the interview about the quality of her relationships with each of her parents. Classification parallels the infant classification scheme, although it is obviously based in the observation, not of behavior, but of the use of language in the interview and in the content of the interview. The adult or adolescent's coherence and consistency of description of attachment-related experiences form the core of the classification scheme.

The classification scheme derived from this interview embodies the four principles of development central to a self-regulatory system: (1) It has structure and process in that both the content of the individual's narrative regarding her childhood and the process by which that narrative is put into language are considered. (2) It is relational and contextual. The focus of the interview is on a description of the quality of relationships with parents. (3) It is constructivist. The meaning made by the individual of her childhood experiences is the information of interest. (4) It is cybernetic and recursive. The process by which the narrative of childhood is constructed reflects an abstraction and reintegration of processes inherent in the relationship itself. The internalization of the organization of earlier relationships is demonstrated in language in the interview.

From the Adult Attachment Interview, three major classifications can be made of adult attachment, one secure and two insecure forms. A fourth category, unresolved regarding loss of an attachment figure, supersedes the other three.

AUTONOMOUS ATTACHMENT

The analogue to the secure infant is an autonomous adult/adolescent. Autonomous individuals value attachment relationships and regard attachment-related experiences as influential. They are relatively independent and objective regarding any particular experience or relationship. The interview is coherent and consistent. The generalized description of relationships with parents is supported by specific memories. The parents are differentiated from one another. Their discourse is fluent, relaxed. The individual seems at ease with the topic and, therefore, able to reflect objectively on experiences with parents. She is largely free of idealization or angry preoccupation with unsupportive or incompetent parents. The individual's narrative is believable to a listener or reader.

The histories of these individuals include parents who served as a secure base in an ongoing way or who have had considerable productive reflection on the reason for parental failings and are now resolved regarding their disappointments in the relationship. The autonomous organization requires considerable effort and insight and requires the acquisition of formal operational thought. Moreover, most of these individuals possess what Main (in press) has termed "metacognitive monitoring," or the capacity to monitor and report on the processes of their thinking and recall as they speak. They are able to put their current thought processes in the context of their habitual ways of thinking, comment on their biases, distortions, etc., and recognize that others have viewpoints differing from their own. This metacognitive monitoring is the hallmark of cognition in an autonomous adolescent or adult. Since the internal working model of the self is the complement of the internal working model of the attachment figure, these individuals have a balanced view of self and others, value interdependence, and have a clear sense of identity.

Not always are they free from psychopathology, however. Many experience troubled periods in their lives and unsatisfying relationships. This is because the attachment function is only one of many functions of a relationship. Recall Bowlby's original definition of an attachment relationship as the regulatory function for the maintenance of security and the basis for confident engagement with the environment. However, one would expect an overall psychological resilience and flexibility in adaptation that is absent in the insecure groups.

PREOCCUPIED ATTACHMENT

The parallel to the infant insecure-ambivalent category is called preoccupied in adulthood and adolescence. As the name implies, for these individuals the influence of parents and attachment-related experiences can be neither dismissed nor coherently stated and seems to preoccupy attention. They appear highly conflicted and in an ongoing cycle of fruitless reflection on relationships with parents and disavowal of interest in maintaining these relationships. Two distinct subtypes are found, an active and a passive. Actively preoccupied individuals are marked by extreme anger that dominates their discourse. They blame parents for their own difficulties yet exhibit placating attitudes toward their parents. They are pseudopsychological, talkative, and ineffective in using their insight. Instances of role reversal or spousification with one parent are universal. Identity diffusion is common. These individuals have a history of inconsistent sensitivity from parents and failure of parental support for their autonomy. They experience enmeshed relationships with parents, with role reversal and guilt inducing efforts to control their behavior.

Passively preoccupied individuals can never settle on a characterization of their relationship with their parents. They may oscillate between a positive and a negative evaluation of parents or are so vague as to be incomprehensible. A sense of inchoate negativity about their relationships lingers, however. With respect to the self, they too exhibit identity diffusion. A third subtype can be classified on the basis of a response to trauma that leaves the individual overwhelmed and unable to construct a coherent overview of her childhood. The individual is either flooded with unintegrated memories or distressed by the lack of memory with respect to childhood. While this subtype is rare in a normal population, it is quite common in a psychiatric population.

DISMISSING ATTACHMENT

The third adult/adolescent classification, dismissing, parallels an infant insecure-avoidant attachment. The individual either dismisses the importance of attachment or relationships or, if she does value relationships, dismisses the extent of their effect on her. There is an idealization of the parents or a portrayal of negative experiences with the parents as normal. Frequently, these individuals lack memory for childhood, or, if negative memories do occur, they regard themselves as unaffected by them. Often, they highly value achievement, self-reliance, personal strength, or cunning. These qualities are sometimes cited as rationalizations for the lack of an effect on self of negative experiences. In a study by Kobak and Sceery (1988) of older adolescents, these individuals are the least likely of any attachment groups to avow internal distress. However, others view them as hostile and provocative, acting out their all too obvious inner disharmony and affective disregulation. The histories of these individuals include rejection by one or both parents and a pervasive lack of love and supportiveness. Since this description is identical to the description of the relational histories of avoidant infants, the question is raised whether the mothers of avoidantly attached infants do themselves have dismissing attachment organizations. Main et al. (1985) found this to be the case. There is a high correlation between maternal and infant attachment classifications for all three attachment organizations.

UNRESOLVED ATTACHMENT

The unresolved category is reserved for individuals who either are unable to resolve mourning in a timely way for an attachment figure who died when the individual was young or have not resolved traumatic experiences, typically childhood abuse. In both cases, unresolved individuals, like preoccupied individuals, cannot move beyond the events in question to form an abstract understanding of their effect. They continue to experience disorganization and disorientation, as manifest in irrational thought processes surrounding the events (e.g., an unfounded belief that in some way they caused the death of the attachment figure or encouraged their own victimization), unfounded fear, unfounded guilt, and continuing disbelief that the traumatic events occurred. While this category is frequently viewed as a separate attachment organization, it can theoretically occur in individuals who had any other attachment organization prior to the trauma or loss. Therefore, the preexisting, traditional attachment classification should be discernible.

Defensive Adaptation, Attachment Organization, and Prediction to Psychopathology

Insecure attachment forms a major risk factor in the development of impoverished or conflicting relationships, negative mood states (anxiety, hostility, and depression), and psychopathology. What is unclear and inconsistently supported by the existing empirical evidence is the prediction of specific forms of social/emotional/symptomatic dysfunction from knowledge of early or concurrent attachment organization. What follows are hypotheses about the relation between insecure attachments and specific forms of psychopathology in adolescence. These hypotheses are generated from existing empirical evidence from infancy through adolescence and from commonalities in the descriptions of adolescent/adult attachment classificatory criteria and in descriptions in the clinical literature of individuals with a variety of major psychiatric and personality disorders. What are the reorganized expressions of the infant adaptive processes in adolescence?

AVOIDANT/DISMISSING ATTACHMENT

In infants, avoidant attachment is an adaptational response to maternal rejection, lack of maternal emotional expressiveness, and maternal dislike of close physical contact. Avoidance serves to regulate affective arousal (to diminish anger and anxiety) and to maintain an attachment relationship, albeit compromised. The dismissing adolescent defensively excludes from awareness any information that may evoke attachment behaviors and hence put her in the position of being rebuffed and angered. For this individual, negative affects are not associated with ameliorating responses on the part of parents, nor does the individual have sufficient self-regulatory capacity to acknowledge and tolerate negative affect. Negative affects can be neither displayed nor tolerated in order to achieve mastery over threatening or frustrating situations. Hence, denial, repression, falsification of affective expression, or displacement of aggression are used as the primary defenses of dismissing individuals. The lack of memory central to this organization serves to disengage the attachment system and reduce the experience of negative affect by screening from consciousness information that might elicit either attachment-seeking behavior or the anger over disappointment, When this defensive organization fails, the symptomatic constellation of affective liability, behavioral impulsivity, and cognitive nonreflectivity emerges. Likewise, idealization serves an avoidant function in these individuals by also allowing selective ignorance of negative information relevant to attachment. Idealization also plays a part in what Bowlby (1980) calls "multiple contradictory models of attachment," that is, simultaneously holding contradictory ideas regarding the parent or attachment without awareness of the contradiction.

It is precisely this constellation of repressive defenses that is common to adolescents with externalizing disorders, that is, conduct and oppositional disorders and substance abuse. The central defensive style that underlies these disorders is exclusion of negative affect from consciousness. The widely observed affective regulatory function of substance abuse can be viewed from an attachment-theoretic perspective as a means to cut off awareness of negative affects surrounding attachment and as an effort to maintain an idealized view of attachment figures. These types of defenses are also likely to be the precursors to narcissistic and antisocial personality organizations. This connection also stands to reason, given the high rates of those personality organizations in comorbid (substance-abusing and psychiatrically disturbed) adolescents. The antisocial character's lack of affection and empathy, disavowal of the importance of relationships, impulsiveness, and displaced aggression are all seen in dismissing individuals. Similarly, the idealization found in dismissing individuals may be a precursor of a narcissistic personality organization. If one thinks of the complementary models of the self that are generated from internal working models of attachment figures, then dismissing individuals should have idealized views of themselves and their capacities. In the extreme, this may take the form of the grandiosity and excessive self-centeredness of the narcissist.

AMBIVALENT/PREOCCUPIED ATTACHMENT

Like their avoidant counterparts, ambivalent infants' central problem is the lack of expectation of maternal sensitivity and responsiveness. The avoidant infant is *certain* that her mother is unavailable. The ambivalent infant grapples with the *uncertainty* of maternal unavailability, coupled with the mother's inability to encourage exploration of the environment and autonomy. The infant, therefore, intensifies attachment behaviors in order to elicit and maintain the mother's attention and appears to be dependent or clinging. In addition, the infant intensifies her vigilance regarding the mother's whereabouts and frame of mind so as to monitor and maintain potential access to her. Several negative psychological outcomes emerge. The first is role reversal. The burden of maintaining emotional contact now rests with the child rather than the mother. The second is the heightened fearfulness of the infant, induced by her uncertainty about her mother's availability. The third deficit for the infant is in the reduction of her ability to explore beyond the mother. If the child's energies are engaged in securing maternal comfort, she has little time or energy left to explore the environment. As the infant becomes a toddler, her mother becomes *overly* available, discouraging autonomy and continuing to reinforce the child's dependency and preoccupation with the caregiver. Therefore, an ambivalent infant's bids for comfort are partially met and coupled with a maternal strategy that prevents disengagment from the relationship. Through partial reinforcement of distress or the overemphasis on closeness, the mother binds the child to her but never provides the child with the nurturance she desires. Ultimately, the child may become passive or depressed, as she gives up efforts to obtain nurturance and become competent (Main and Cassidy 1988).

On the basis of these findings, adolescents with backgrounds of ambivalent attachment can be expected to display heightened dependence on parents and increased levels of overt emotional distress, especially anxiety and depression. They should be especially prone to depression for several reasons. The first is the heightened neediness of these individuals, who have no experience with sensitive responsiveness and are prone to requiring exaggerated displays of caring from others. They are frequently disappointed that others cannot meet their excessive demands and despair of ever feeling loved. The second reason has to do with role reversal. The mothers of these adolescents require that the child become the attachment figure, satisfying maternal rather than child needs. However, following Cole (1991), the child finds herself in the position of continuously attempting to satisfy the needs of a parent who cannot be satisfied. This leaves the adolescent feeling as if she has failed and makes her susceptible to depression. In addition, these adolescents have failed to learn the skills necessary to regulate their negative affect because their mothers did not know how to do this themselves and never taught them, because of the child's lack of exploratory competence that would have allowed her to learn these skills from other sources, and because of the mother's need to heighten the child's distress in order to maintain the child's interest in remaining close to her.

Adolescent depression is not the only psychopathological expression that can be predicted from a history of infant ambivalence. Increased displays of any form of emotional distress would be expected, putting these adolescents at risk for affective and anxiety disorders and histrionic and dependent personality traits. The personality trait and disorder that should be most closely associated with a preoccupied attachment is borderline. Both borderlines and preoccupieds are entangled in their thoughts about early relationships and cannot move above their current preoccupation to a more abstract level, which would allow resolution of painful affects. Borderlines are characterized by instability of self-image, particularly a deep disturbance in the consistency of identity, poor interpersonal relationships (including stormy relationships, in which fears of abandonment predominate and alternate with idealization and devaluation of highly valued individuals), extreme affective lability, and intense, inappropriate, and unmodulated anger. Many of these characteristics resemble descriptions of angry preoccupied individuals on the Adult Attachment Interview. Fears of abandonment can be viewed in this context as an extreme form of vigilance for the whereabouts of the attachment figure.

Research Procedures and Results

Testing these hypotheses about the links between attachment classification, personality, and psychopathology proceeded in two ways.
The first was in looking at the relation between Axis I and Axis II
diagnoses and attachment classification. The second was by exploring
the connection between personality dimensions and attachment classification. The wide range of DSM-III-R psychiatric diagnosis has been
collapsed into four broad categories: conduct disorders, including oppositional defiant disorder; affective disorders, including almost exclusively major depression and dysthymic disorder; and substance abuse.
Multiple, concurrent diagnoses were also identified. Of this sample of
sixty admissions to the various adolescent services at the institute, 55
percent have affective disorders alone, 13 percent conduct disorders
alone, and 20 percent a combination of affective and conduct disorders. Seven subjects could not be included in these diagnostic groups,
two individuals with anxiety disorders, one with multiple personality
disorder, one with substance abuse alone, one with attention deficit
disorder, and two with atypical psychosis. Of the sixty subjects, half
have a comorbid substance abuse diagnosis.

With respect to attachment classification, the data were analyzed
using the system of four categories, including unresolved regarding
loss, and using the system of three categories, where those who were
unresolved were classified by their secondary classification. Results
using the three-category system will be discussed at length, with only
brief comments on some of the more striking findings regarding those
who are unresolved. Unless stated otherwise, all numerical differences
meet statistical significance. Of the total group, 47 percent are dismissing, 50 percent preoccupied, and 3 percent autonomous. For comparison, in a normal sample of older adolescents, 53 percent were autonomous, 32 percent dismissing, and 15 percent preoccupied (Kobak and
Sceery 1988). In looking at the relation between Axis I diagnosis and
attachment classification, individuals with conduct disorders over-
whelmingly have dismissing attachments, as predicted. Those individuals with affective disorders are twice as likely to have a preoccupied
attachment. Individuals with comorbid conduct and affective disorders
are twice as likely to be dismissing.

Of the larger group of sixty, thirty carry a substance abuse diagnosis.
A higher percentage of substance abusers have dismissing organiza-

tions when compared to non–substance abusers (60 vs. 33 percent). In the substance-abusing group, those with comorbid affective disorders are split between preoccupied and dismissing attachments. Adding in conduct disorder to this group shifts the attachment organization toward the dismissing. The higher rates of dismissing attachments, even when affective disorders are comorbidly present, are due to the propensity to act out, especially aggressively, inherent in the choice of substance abuse. Expanding this logic, all acting-out pathologies should be associated with dismissing attachments. By its nature, acting out precludes the conscious recognition of underlying unconscious affects and conflicts, an aspect of what we have called "cognitive nonreflectivity." This cognitive feature is shared with a dismissing attachment organization. Cole (1991) recently presented data supporting this claim. In her sample of college women, those with eating disorders were more likely to have a dismissing organization. Those with concurrent eating disorder and depression or depression alone have higher rates of preoccupied attachments. In our sample, the link between affective disorders and preoccupied attachment becomes even clearer when the non-substance-abusing subjects are considered. Non–substance abusers are twice as likely to be preoccupied as dismissing.

Clear patterns of sex differences in diagnosis and attachment organization emerge in these data. While affective disorders are the most common diagnoses among both sexes, males are more likely than females to be conduct disordered with or without affective disorder. Conversely, females show very high rates of affective disorder alone, with consequent low rates of conduct disorder. When substance abuse is added as a diagnostic category, no significant sex differences in the distribution of diagnoses were found. However, twice as many males as females have substance abuse diagnoses and, concomitantly, show higher rates of conduct disorders as compared to females. Half of comorbid females have conduct disorders.

Sex differences in attachment classification were also found. Males were significantly more dismissing than preoccupied (66 vs. 34 percent) and more dismissing than females (75 vs. 25 percent). Females are more preoccupied than dismissing (68 vs. 25 percent) and more preoccupied than males (63 vs. 37 percent). The two autonomous subjects were females. These data reflect the same pattern of sex differences in adolescent attachment classifications reported by Kobak and Sceery (1988) and Dozier (1990). Although we believe these data to reflect in part a developmental sex difference, the diagnosis of conduct disorder has an effect on the sex differences. The relationship is particularly strong between conduct disorders (with or without comorbid affective and substance abuse disorders) and a dismissing attachment for males. Males with affective disorders alone are equally likely to be dismissing or preoccupied. However, all preoccupied males have affective disorders. For females, the rates of conduct disorder were so low ($N = 4$) that the stastistical relation between affective disorders and preoccupied attachment may have been obscured. Nevertheless, nearly all affectively disordered females were preoccupied.

The second strategy used in assessing the relation between attachment and psychopathology was to examine the effect of personality disorders on attachment organization. Forty percent (twenty-four individuals) of our subjects have an Axis II diagnosis and all in addition to an Axis I diagnosis of affective disorder. A range of Axis II pathology exists, including histrionic, obsessive-compulsive, schizotypal, narcissistic, and borderline. Both subjects with obsessive-compulsive personality disorder are females and have preoccupied organizations, as predicted. Both subjects with narcissistic personality disorders are males and have dismissing organizations, as predicted. Both subjects with histrionic personality disorder are female, with preoccupied attachments. The subject with a schizotypal personality disorder is male and preoccupied. Only the borderlines occur in large numbers— fourteen of the twenty-four individuals with Axis II pathology. The majority are female and somewhat more likely to have a preoccupied than a dismissing organization. All these subjects have an Axis I affective disorder diagnosis that is predictive of a preoccupied attachment organization by itself. There is some indication that those subjects who also are substance abusers (i.e., substance abusing, affectively disordered, and borderline) are more likely to be dismissing. The effect of substance abuse in determining dismissing attachment organizations appears to be strong.

Personality traits were measured with two instruments. The SCL-90 (Derogatis 1977) is a checklist of ninety somatic and psychiatric symptoms to be endorsed for presence and severity by the patient. Following Kobak and Sceery (1988), we predicted that the dismissing group would be less symptomatic on all measures, consistent with their defensive exclusion of feelings of internal distress. On the SCL-90, the dismissing individuals see themselves as less symptomatic on all nine symptom scales and three severity scales when compared to their pre-occupied counterparts, although differences are not statistically significant. Consonant with prediction, they see themselves as less somatic, hostile, depressed, anxious, obsessionally preoccupied, sensitive, paranoid, phobic, or psychotic. A second assessment of personality was conducted through the MCMI, developed by Millon (1983) specifically to assess personality dimensions corresponding to Axis II diagnosis. On the MCMI, the dismissing individuals differ significantly from preoccupied individuals by being more narcissistic, histrionic, antisocial, and drug abusing and less avoidant and dependent. All findings are consistent with prediction. The preoccupied group, by contrast, is significantly more avoidant, dependent, schizotypal, and dysthymic. A trend emerges for psychotic depression, psychotic thinking, anxiety, and borderline symptoms. With the exception of schizoid and schizotypal, all findings are consistent with prediction. Although the findings of dismissive's histrionic nature and preoccupied's avoidant may seem counter to prediction, they are not, given the way in which these constructs are defined within the MCMI. Histrionic individuals on the MCMI highly resemble narcissistic and antisocial individuals in their interpersonal seductiveness, sociable self-image, stimulus-seeking behavior, and ability to "dissociate" dissonant information. The latter quality is more descriptive of a dismissing pattern of indifference to contradiction and lack of coherence. In Millon's system, avoidance does not mean disinterest or indifference to interpersonal relationships. Quite the contrary, these individuals seek interpersonal contact but are highly anxious about criticism or rebuff. Therefore, they are more like the conflicted preoccupied individual. The anomalous connection between schizotypal traits and preoccupied attachments may result from the substantial group of psychotic individuals who have preoccupied attachments.

One further area of investigation is the high rate (20 percent) of unresolved loss that this group has endured and its effects on attachment organization. Secondary classifications of those who were primarily classified as unresolved were randomly distributed across the other classifications. This validates Main's notion that the traditional adult/adolescent attachment classifications are developmentally prior to the unresolved status and that the traditional classifications can be discerned even when lack of resolution is present. Clinically, those with affective disorders are at greater risk for lack of resolution of mourning, and those with the broadest range of pathology (simultaneous conduct, affective, and substance abuse disorders) are most highly associated with the unresolved status. In psychotherapy, these individuals may benefit most from an attempt to resolve the mourning process prior to attempts to clarify the underlying insecurity in relationship to attachment figures.

NOTE

This chapter was originally presented as a paper at the meeting of the American Society for Adolescent Psychiatry, May 10, 1991, New Orleans. The research reported here was supported by grants from the Sigmund A. Miller Memorial Foundation and the 76 Fund of Pennsylvania Hospital.

REFERENCES

Ainsworth, M. D. S.; Bell, S. M.; and Stayton, D. J. 1974. Infantmother attachment and social development: "socialisation" as a product of reciprocal responsiveness to signals. In M. P. N. Richards, ed. *The Integration of a Child into a Social World*. London: Cambridge University Press.

Ainsworth, M. D. S.; Blehar, M. C.; Waters, E.; and Wall, S. 1978. *Patterns of Attachment: A Psychological Study of the Strange Situation*. Hillsdale, NJ: Erlbaum.

Ainsworth, M. D. S., and Eichberg, C. G. In press. Effects on infantmother attachment of mother's unresolved loss of an attachment figure or other traumatic experience. In P. Marris, J. Stevenson-Hinde, and C. Parkes, eds. *Attachment across the Life Cycle*. New York: Routledge.

Ainsworth, M. D. S., and Wittig, B. A. 1969. Attachment and the exploratory behavior of one-year olds in a strange situation. In B. M. Foss, ed. *Determinants of Infant Behavior*. London: Methuen.

Allen, J. P., and Hauser, S. T. 1991. Prediction of young adult attachment representation, psychological distress, social competence and hard drug use from family interactions in adolescence. Paper presented at the meeting of the Society for Research in Child Development, Seattle.

Arend, R. 1984. Preschoolers' competence in a barrier situation: patterns of adaptation and their precursors in infancy. Ph.D. diss., University of Minnesota.

Arend, R.; Gove, F.; and Sroufe, L. A. 1979. Continuity of individual adaptation from infancy to kindergarten: a predictive study of ego-resiliency and curiosity in preschoolers. *Child Development* 50:950–959.

Armsden, G. C.; McCauley, E.; Greenberg, M. T.; Burke, P. M.; and Mitchell, J. R. 1990. Parent and peer attachment in early adolescent depression. *Journal of Abnormal Child Psychology* 18:683–697.

Bowlby, J. 1958. The nature of the child's tie to his mother. *International Journal of Psycho-Analysis* 39:350–373.

Bowlby, J. 1973. *Attachment and Loss.* Vol. 2, *Separation, Anxiety and Anger.* New York: Basic.

Bowlby, J. 1980. *Attachment and Loss.* Vol. 3, *Loss, Sadness and Depression.* New York: Basic.

Cole, H. 1991. Worrying about parents: the link between preoccupied attachment and depression. Paper presented at the meeting of the Society for Research in Child Development, Seattle.

Derogatis, L. R. 1977. *SCL-90 Administration, Scoring and Procedures Manual—I.* Baltimore: Johns Hopkins University Press.

Dozier, M. 1990. Attachment organization and treatment use for adults with serious psychopathological disorders. *Development and Psychopathology* 2:47–60.

Egeland, B. 1983. Comments on Kopp, Krakow, and Vaughn's chapter. In M. Perlmutter, ed. *Minnesota Symposium in Child Psychology,* vol. 16. Hillsdale, NJ: Erlbaum.

Erikson, E. H. 1963. *Childhood and Society.* 2d ed. New York: Norton.

Erikson, M. F., and Farber, E. A. 1983. Infancy to preschool: continuity of adaptation in high-risk children. Paper presented at the meeting of the Society for Research in Child Development, Detroit.

George, C.; Kaplan, N.; and Main, M. 1985. An adult attachment interview: interview protocol. University of California, Berkeley, Department of Psychology. Typescript.

Horowitz, H. A.; Overton, W. F.; Rosenstein, D.; and Steidl, J. H. 1992. Comorbid adolescent substance abuse: a maladaptive pattern of self-regulation. *Adolescent Psychiatry* 18:465–483.

Hughes, S. O.; Francis, D. J.; and Power, T. G. 1989. The impact of attachment on adolescent alcohol use. Paper presented at the meeting of the Society for Research in Child Development, Kansas City.

Kobak, R. R., and Sceery, A. 1988. Attachment in adolescence: working models, affect regulation and representation of self and others. *Child Development* 59:135–146.

Londerville, S., and Main, M. 1981. Security of attachment, compliance, and maternal training methods in the second year of life. *Developmental Psychology* 17:289–299.

Main, M. 1973. Exploration, play, and cognitive functioning as related to child-mother attachment. Ph.D. diss., Johns Hopkins University.

Main, M. 1981. Avoidance in the service of attachment: a working paper. In K. Immelmann, G. Barlow, L. Petrinovich, and M. Main, eds. *Behavioral Development: The Bielefeld Interdisciplinary Project.* New York: Cambridge University Press.

Main, M. In press. Metacognitive knowledge, metacognitive monitoring, and singular (coherent) vs. multiple (incoherent) models of attachment: findings and directions for future research. In P. Marris, J. Stevenson-Hilde, and C. Parkes, eds. *Attachment across the Life Cycle.* New York: Routledge.

Main, M., and Cassidy, J. 1988. Categories of response with the parent at age six: predicted from infant attachment classifications and stable over a one month period. *Developmental Psychology* 24:415–426.

Main, M., and Hesse, E. 1990. Lack of resolution of mourning in adulthood and its relationship to infant disorganization: some speculations regarding causal mechanisms. In M. Greenberg, D. Cicchetti, and M. Cummings, eds. *Attachment in the Preschool Years.* Chicago: University of Chicago Press.

Main, M.; Kaplan, N.; and Cassidy, J. 1985. Security in infancy, childhood, and adulthood: a move to the level of representation. In I. Bretherton and E. Waters, eds. *Growing Points of Attachment Theory and Research.* Monographs of the Society for Research in Child Development, vol. 50, serial no. 209. Chicago: University of Chicago Press.

Main, M., and Solomon, J. 1990. Procedures for identifying infants as disorganized/disoriented during the Ainsworth Strange Situation. In M. T. Greenberg, D. Cicchetti, and E. M. Cummings, eds. *Attachment in the Preschool Years.* Chicago: University of Chicago Press.

Matas, L.; Arend, R.; and Sroufe, L. A. 1978. Continuity of adaptation in the second year: the relationship between quality of attachment and later competent functioning. *Child Development* 49:547–555.

Millon, T. 1983. *The Millon Clinical Multiaxial Inventory Manual.* 3d ed. Minneapolis: National Computer Systems.

Overton, W. F.; Steidl, J. H.; Rosenstein, D.; and Horowitz, H. A. 1992. Formal operations as regulatory context in adolescence. *Adolescent Psychiatry* 18:502–513.

Papini, D. R.; Roggman, L. A.; and Anderson, J. 1991. Early-adolescent perceptions of attachment to mother and father: a test of the emotional-distancing and buffering hypotheses. *Journal of Early Adolescence* 11:258–275.

Piaget, J., and Inhelder, B. 1969. *The Psychology of the Child.* New York: Basic.

Rice, K. G. 1990. Attachment in adolescence: a narrative and meta-analytic review. *Journal of Youth and Adolescence* 19:511–538.

Rosenstein, D.; Horowitz, H. A.; Steidl, J. H.; and Overton, W. F. 1992. Attachment and internalization: relationship as a regulatory context. *Adolescent Psychiatry* 18:491–501.

Sander, L. W. 1962. Issues in early mother-child interaction. *Journal of the American Academy of Child Psychiatry* 1:141–166.

Sander, L. W. 1975. Infant and caretaking environment: investigation and conceptualization of adaptive behavior in a system of increasing complexity. In E. J. Anthony, ed. *Explorations in Child Psychiatry.* New York: Plenum.

Silver, D. H. 1991. Representation of attachment and social behavior in preschool. Paper presented at the meeting of the Society for Research in Child Development, Seattle.

Speltz, M. L.; Greenberg, M. T.; and Deklyen, M. 1991. Attachment in preschoolers with disruptive behavior: a comparison of clinic-referred and nonproblem children. Paper presented at the meeting of the Society for Research in Child Development, Seattle.

Sroufe, L. A. 1979. The coherence of individual development. *American Psychologist* 34:834–841.

Sroufe, L. A. 1989. Relationships, self, and individual adaptation. In A. J. Sameroff and R. N. Emde, eds. *Relationship Disturbances in Early Childhood.* New York: Basic.

Sroufe, L. A.; Egeland, B.; and Kreutzer, T. 1990. The fate of early experience following developmental change: longitudinal approaches to individual adaptation in childhood. *Child Development* 61:1363–1373.

Sroufe, L. A.; Fox, N.; and Pancake, V. 1983. Attachment and dependency in developmental perspectives. *Child Development* 54:1615–1627.

Sroufe, L. A., and Rosenberg, D. 1980. Coherence of individual adaptation in lower SES infants and toddlers. Paper presented at the International Conference on Infant Studies, Providence, RI.

Steidl, J. H.; Horowitz, H. A.; Overton, W. F.; and Rosenstein, D. 1992. Family interaction as regulatory context in adolescence. *Adolescent Psychiatry* 18:484–490.

Waters, E.; Wippman, J.; and Sroufe, L. A. 1979. Attachment, positive affect, and competence in the peer group: two studies in construct validation. *Child Development* 50:821–829.

Werner, H. 1957. The concept of development from a comparative and organismic point of view. In D. Harris, ed. *The Concept of Development*. Minneapolis: University of Minnesota Press.

11 THE INTERPRETIVE COMMUNITY
OF SELF

POLLY YOUNG-EISENDRATH

Until only recently, it seemed radical, perhaps even provocative, to critique the individual self of personal autonomy, to consider the self to be a social product constrained by a cultural era. Although such critiques appeared throughout the 1980s, they tended to be received as an "outsider" view. Now, barely into the 1990s, we seem to have come into a new zeitgeist in which the "insider" view is that the self is originally and continually the product of a relational matrix and thus is neither free nor even individual.

Today, I imagine that most of us could accept the following premises for subjectivity that might have seemed radical only a few years ago: (1) that selves are created and developed in relationships; (2) that the geography (boundaries and domain) of selves is shaped by cultural contexts; and (3) that selves carry the local meanings of the folk psychologies that sponsor them, both on the level of particulars, such as gender, class, and ethnic meanings, and on the level of general design, such as degree of individuality.

These are the premises that I bring to this chapter, in any case, and I will begin by fleshing them out. This will lead naturally to a discussion of Jane Loevinger's model of ego development that I introduce with regard to a study conducted by me and some graduate students in human development at Bryn Mawr College. In answer to the question, What is psychotherapy? adults at different ego development stages narrated the self-other event of therapy. Let me begin, first, by making a distinction between persons and selves, to show how narrative is especially important for a self.

Persons, Selves, and Narrative

Several philosophers have contributed significantly to the premises of self that I listed above. For me, the most prominent are Rom Harre (1984), John MacMurray (1957), P. F. Strawson (1959), and Charles Taylor (1989). From their work especially I have come to define "self" as the set of attitudes, beliefs, images, and actions that permit a person to sustain individual subjectivity. Whereas the category "person" can be universally identified by public criteria (such as body form and expected powers), the construct of "self" is the product of an interpretive community, more local or homegrown, so to speak. Certain features are universal, however, in the way in which persons account for selves.

Charles Taylor (1989) centralizes the role of morality in self-formation. He connects identity to the fact that "we cannot do without some orientation to the good, that we each essentially are . . . where we stand on this" (p. 33). He also stresses that "one is a self only among other selves. A self can never be described without reference to those who surround it" (p. 35). Like Winnicott's famous dictum, "There's no such thing as a baby," Taylor can be paraphrased as saying, "There's no such thing as a self"—only selves.

Rom Harré (1989) urges us to see the significance of self-making in the development of a person: "Animate beings are fully human if they are in possession of a theory—a theory about themselves. It is a theory in terms of which a being orders, partitions, and reflects on its own experience and becomes capable of self-intervention and control." Harré challenges psychological investigators "to look for conversational practices in which a theory of the appropriate kind could be acquired by an animate being who is . . . organized in a strong unitary fashion" (p. 404). A person then is fully human only when she can narrate or construct self as unitary over time, space, and causality.

The state of being a unitary subject is sustained both by the experience of *coherence,* in the sense of the integration of complex subjective states into unity, and by *continuity,* in the sense of narrating oneself over time and space. Harré (1989) cautions us not to universalize a masterful, bounded *individuality* as the character of coherence or continuity. Depending on the forms available within an interpretive community, a person may have a *collective* self like that of the Copper Eskimo—"When one weeps, they all weep; when one laughs, they all laugh" (Harré 1989, p. 399)—or a powerfully *independent* self like that of the Maori, who view the *mana* of an individual to be a sort of physical force (Harré 1989, p. 400).

The psychologist Jerome Bruner (1990) builds on the claims of Taylor and Harré in seeing narrative as the major vehicle for self-construction. "Narrative" refers to a story that links past, present, and future. After young children have grasped the basic idea of reference necessary for language, their principal linguistic interests center on stories of human action. The self as narrator is perhaps born with the practice of language.

The self as *agent,* as a personal cause or prime mover, seems to be another universal feature of selfhood, emphasized especially by the philosopher John MacMurray and the psychologist Jean Piaget and his followers, who recognize the centrality of action in the development of thought. Agency and continuity are linked in narrative, as Bruner shows, because a basic requirement of narrative is to account for action in outcome.

From the work of John Bowlby and the investigators of the attachment model, we can fill out the claim that the self is relational by pointing to *affective relational patterns* that are ubiquitous features of subjectivity, patterns arising from the interdependence of persons, organized by human emotion across the life span.

What is perhaps most compelling about selves is their organizing power, their ability to draw into related meaning much that would be dissociated without them; perhaps this is why, fundamentally and universally, persons need selves.

Ego Development and Self in Psychotherapy

Jane Loevinger (1979) claims that her model of ego development is a "master variable" that "encompasses the complexity of moral judgment, the nature of interpersonal relations, and the framework within which one perceives oneself and others as people" (p. 3). Ego development is the type of theory specified above by Harré (1989), one based on a study of "conversational practices" that progressively organize the subject in a "strong unitary fashion." From my clinical and research experience, I believe that Loevinger's nine stages or frames of reference of self-other *are* exhaustive of types of subjectivity among adolescents and adults in our society.

Each of her stages is a paradigm of meaning derived from peoples' actual narratives collected via a sentence completion test. Each new stage reorganizes all that has come before, and thus it is impossible to skip a stage. Typically, a person moves expectably through early stages until a dominant one is reached, usually in young adulthood. A majority of Americans seem to stop developing after about the age of 21, and thus Loevinger's model serves as a typology of differences among adults. Stages are perspectives or frames of reference that cannot be directly observed but rather must be inferred from respondents' narratives. Loevinger's sentence completion test has been used reliably from the age of twelve years on.

I will briefly introduce the nine stages of ego development that fall along a continuum of self from less to more complex, from less to more integrated, from less to more internalized, and from less to more differentiated. As I describe each stage, I will also give an illustration from the study that I mentioned earlier. With the help of my students, I surveyed 210 people using the sentence completion test for ego development and a simple questionnaire about psychotherapy. We were interested in the self-other narratives of psychotherapy that might fall along the continuum of ego development. My brief illustrations are actual responses to the question, "What is psychotherapy?"

What I want to show is that the patient's self puts limits on the narrative of therapy as much as the therapist's self does. A stage of ego development represents not only an individual but a whole fabric of cultural exchange in which a person validates meanings. If one goal of psychotherapy *is* self development, then we must pay attention to the interpretive set of a patient's self. For my purposes here, I chose examples from people not in psychotherapy. Although their responses are exemplary of their stages, their language is not burdened by the jargon of a particular therapeutic culture.

The first stage of ego development is called "impulsive." The person tends to dichotomize the world into "nice to me" and "mean to me" and has difficulty controlling impulses. Emotional expressions tend to be limited to wishes and fears. What is psychotherapy at this stage? A fifty-six-year-old man and a woman of unknown age both said that it is a "doctor," "a doctor who helps people"—obviously defining "psychotherapy" as a person, a doctor person. What appears to us as a "confusion" between a concrete person and an abstract process is not confusion at this stage of development. There is as yet no differentiation of the person of the therapist from the process of therapy.

The "self-protective" stage signals an ability to control impulses and stay out of trouble. Luck and other people are to blame for life's difficulties. Feelings are expressed as quasi-physical states (such as "pissed off"). Psychotherapy for a fifty-three-year-old self-protective man is "analiss" in which the therapist is said to "cheat." Preoccupations with the therapist's "advantages" are common projective accounts of the patient's opportunism at this stage.

The "conformist" stage is a major paradigm shift from the first two because it focuses on trust in belonging, especially to a group or family. Conformity to rules and norms is expected, simple, and absolute. Feelings are described in generalities often associated with groups, for example, "Teenagers are rowdy." Identity corresponds to group membership and is usually described in terms of demographics—age, race, religion. What is psychotherapy? A man said, "Someone to talk to"; another man said, "When you talk about your problems"; a woman answered, "A person who listens to your problems"; and another man said, "To tell the truth, I really have no idea." At this stage, therapy is seen as "talking about problems" and getting advice. Clearly, this kind of discourse occurs everywhere, not only in therapy, so this last respondent may be implying that he cannot say what distinguishes therapy from anything else.

The "self-aware" stage is named for its hallmark of self-consciousness and rudimentary self-criticism, but a person is still quite captured by conformity to the group and the desire to belong. Feelings are more clearly expressed, but differences in attitudes, interests, and abilities are recognized mostly in global terms. Multiple possibilities are envisioned for the self that is often "future oriented," looking for success in the future. Moral values are of the greeting-card type, and people are judged in terms of how nice, good, and polite they are. (This stage appears to be the one at which the majority of adults in our society live.) About psychotherapy, a self-aware woman said, "It's a study where people's thoughts, actions, etc. are studied to try to find a way to help the person understand herself, know what she really wants, why she acts in some ways, etc." Another woman said, "The art of helping people through a relationship that allows a person to look at what hurts (?) in his/her life and gives him/her choices (?) on making changes. The relationship is mainly one-to-one and by conversation." Many people at the self-aware stage describe a form of helping through relationships, a process, or a knowledge base. It seems to me that the self-aware stage is developmentally the first interpretive context in which psychotherapy per se can be engaged. At earlier stages, counseling, guidance, and advice giving are a better match with self-other narratives.

The "conscientious" stage of development includes a richly differentiated inner life that matches a psychoanalytic narrative. The notion of *self-development* arises spontaneously at this stage, and life experiences are savored and appreciated, with a full awareness of the struggle for self-control of impulses. The birth of true empathy comes with an appreciation of the complexity of others' lives. Intentions, motives, and consequences of action are differentiated, as is the distinction between appearance and reality. The self is an active agent who holds the origin of her own destiny. From a woman at this stage, we hear that psychotherapy "explores a person's orientation of his surroundings and reality." Another woman says that therapy is "the process of engaging in a relationship with someone else in which you both devote your energies and your knowledge of human behavior toward understanding why the person in therapy is experiencing problems and toward finding alternative ways for the person to cope with these problems." The conscientious stage is a discourse on decentering of the self from itself.

The "individualistic" stage combines paradoxically what had seemed incompatible and contradictory before. For example, a person might see the link of personal intimacy and impersonal objectivity to be the unique character of psychotherapy, while, at the conscientious stage, this combination could not be imagined. Psychologically complex explanations replace statements of "reasons" or "problems." The stage is named "individualistic" because of its focus on the "struggle for autonomy" within conflicting needs. A woman sees psychotherapy as "a relationship between an objective person who has the knowledge and skill to accurately time comments, to diminish differences, and handle conflict and a client who is trusting enough to allow the process to happen." Another woman says, "Psychotherapy is an interpersonal process whereby a person is helped to an increased awareness of his or her feelings, thoughts, and behavior. Through this process the therapist helps an individual begin to change in ways that are growth producing and that will eventuate in an increased ability to deal with all aspects of living in a more gratifying way.''

The individualistic stage and the two stages that follow it obviously represent the interpretive community in which depth psychotherapy is sustained. These stages exist among a small minority of adults and probably a very small minority of our patient population. The ''autonomous'' stage includes understanding inner conflict with a continuing desire to transcend it. Feelings are expressed in rich and diverse ways. The person displays spontaneity, genuineness, intensity, and authenticity across many situations. At this and the next stage of ''integrated'' self, a person has a high tolerance for ambiguity and sees life as multifaceted. The final stage includes an acceptance of suffering and conflict as part of human life and a lively humor in response to life's ironies. Here is an example of an answer from a man in one of the final two stages. He has never been in psychotherapy, but he says, ''Psychotherapy is a disciplined process of diagnosing, identifying, and liberating persons from unhealthy or abnormal ways of thinking about or responding to life, which block a person's development of continuing growth as a human being.''

These stages of ego development and illustrations of therapeutic narrative are intended to show how the selves of our patients are constrained by their interpretive communities and perhaps to encourage a certain modesty about the therapeutic endeavor of self development. Although the therapist certainly cannot take the patient into paradigms, narratives, or attitudes unknown in the therapist's self, neither can the therapist evoke or discover narratives wildly beyond the patient's interpretive community. As the philospher Charles Taylor says, ''One is a self only among other selves. A self can never be described without reference to those who surround it'' (1989, p. 35).

REFERENCES

Bruner, J. S. 1990. *Acts of Meaning*. Cambridge, Mass.: Harvard University Press.

Harré, R. 1984. *Personal Being: A Theory for Individual Psychology*. Cambridge, Mass.: Harvard University Press.

Harré, R. 1989. The "self" as a theoretical concept. In M. Krausz, ed. *Relativism: Interpretation and Confrontation.* Notre Dame, Ind.: Notre Dame University Press.

Loevinger, J. 1979. The idea of the ego. *Counseling Psychologist* 8(2): 3–5.

MacMurray, J. 1957–61. *The Form of the Personal,* vols. 1, 2. Atlantic Highlands, N.J.: Humanities, 1978.

Strawson, P. F. 1959. *Individuals: An Essay in Descriptive Metaphysics.* London: Methuen.

Taylor, C. 1989. *Sources of the Self: The Making of Modern Identity.* Cambridge, Mass.: Harvard University Press.

12 RELATEDNESS AND AUTONOMY IN ADOLESCENCE: LINKS WITH EGO DEVELOPMENT AND FAMILY INTERACTIONS

STUART T. HAUSER AND HILARY A. LEVINE

In recent years, theorists and researchers have addressed a bias ingrained in Western developmental theory. Simply stated, this bias emphasizes themes of autonomy and separation while neglecting those of intimacy and connectedness. From this perspective, psychological development is viewed in terms of progression from an attached, dependent state toward an autonomous, independent existence. The notion that an individual frees him or herself from attachments in search of pure independence overlooks the roles that relationships play in the formation of the self. Gilligan (1982) remarks on this omission, "There seems to be a line of development missing from current psychological accounts, a failure to describe the progression of relationships toward a maturity of interdependence. . . . The truth of separation is recognized . . . but the reality of continuing connection is lost" (p. 155). Some feminist psychologists argue that the "reality of continuing connection" is particularly true in female development, contending that women tend to define themselves in relation to others whereas men more typically assert themselves as independent and separate from others (Chodorow 1978; Gilligan 1982; Surrey 1983).

It may be the case that systematic empirical studies will support the argument that women and men differ in how they engage in and/or value connections with other people. Yet there will remain a second matter worthy of careful consideration: the fact that forming and sustaining close relationships is surely important—often problematic—for children and adults of both genders. Along these lines, recent studies highlight the roles of relationships for both genders across the life span (Bar-Yam Hassan and Bar-Yam 1987; Grotevant and Cooper 1985, 1986; Jordan 1984; Loevinger 1966; Maccoby 1990; Selman 1980; Stechler and Kaplan 1980; White, Speisman, and Costos 1983). These contributions portray a complex picture of social development, involving both autonomy and connectedness. Needs to establish oneself in the world as an independently functioning, distinct person are balanced by needs to be connected to others. The interplay between these two seemingly polar orientations constitutes a lifelong dialectical process in which a person becomes more differentiated and independent within an evolving network of increasingly complex familial and peer relationships. If all goes well, autonomy and connectedness mutually enhance one another in important and varied ways across the life span (Ainsworth, Blehar, Waters, and Wall 1978; Bar-Yam Hassan and Bar-Yam 1987; Blatt 1990; Bowlby 1977; Franz and White 1985; Stern 1985; Sullivan 1953).

Basic Concepts

We use the terms "relatedness" and "autonomy" to represent those processes that contribute to the forming of interdependent relationships and to establishing independence. One optimal, but by no means certain, outcome of these intersecting forces is the adolescent's and adult's experience of a stable and differentiated sense of self. Other researchers have also discussed these aspects of development along the lines of relatedness and autonomy (Allen and Hauser 1988; Murphey, Silber, Coelho, Hamburg, and Greenberg 1963), attachment and individuation (Franz and White 1985), communion and agency (Bakan 1966; Bar-Yam Hassan and Bar-Yam 1987), connectedness and individuality (Cooper, Grotevant, and Condon 1983), and attachment and autonomy (Hill and Holmbeck 1986). Relatedness and autonomy appear in different forms throughout the life cycle. For instance, an infant's attachment to his parents is surely different from his teenage romantic relationship with a new girlfriend. So too, a toddler's defiant "no" reveals an early expression of autonomy, while a young adult's intense search for a career that suits her personal tastes and skills, rejecting conventional recommendations of well-known lucrative professional paths, reflects a later form of autonomy. The analyses that we present in this chapter trace orientations toward relatedness and autonomy as they are verbally expressed by young adolescent boys and girls. Of much interest to us, in light of recent work concerned with connections between these dimensions, is how autonomy and relatedness are linked during adolescence and how the developmental status of the adolescent may influence this linkage. In addition to focusing on adolescent development, we also explore how relatedness and autonomy are expressed within the family, a setting representing some of an adolescent's most salient and ancient relationships. Although we first consider relatedness and autonomy separately, the reader should bear in mind that our greater interest is in the linkages between these dimensions and how these linkages are aligned with advancing psychosocial development.

RELATEDNESS

COMPONENTS

"Relatedness" refers to the growing potential of an individual to form and sustain meaningful emotional and physical connections with others. One has the capacity for relatedness at all stages of life, but the quality and depth of the connection grows with maturity. There are many forms of relatedness. There is that between parent and child, a boy and his dog, sister and brother, therapist and client, two childhood friends, and romantic lovers, to name just a few. While these relationships differ, they are all sustained by processes of relatedness that encompass overlapping affective, behavioral, cognitive, and moral components.

The affective component of relatedness is the experience of feeling connected to a particular person. The "behavioral dimension" refers to the actions that a person takes to maintain this connection: the sharing of experiences over time (Selman and Schultz 1990), the self-disclosures (Jourard 1971), and the various compromises and negotiations (Selman and Schultz 1990). The more time people spend together doing a variety of activities, including sharing personal matters as well as participation in activities, the more likely significant, mutual experiences, such as intimacy, will develop (Berscheid, Snyder, and Omoto

1989). Like the other dimensions, the cognitive one is multifaceted. First, it involves conscious and unconscious expectations, generated in part from repeated interactions. For example, individuals differ in the extent to which they perceive others as trustworthy and/or responsive. These expectations are derived from past experiences and may guide the person's affective and cognitive experience in the relationship. In other words, behaviors and feelings also shape these important cognitions. More specific cognitions involved in relatedness include self-appraisals and perspective taking.

The "moral component" of relatedness refers to the overlap between those personal principles that are held separately from any given relationship—and the individual's specific connection with another person. Relationships often force us to reconsider our preexisting values. A feminist, very involved in her line of work and committed to the belief that people should not surrender or sacrifice their personal goals for a relationship, may in the context of her own deep romantic relationship decide to quit her job and move to the city where her partner lives (and is currently attending medical school) in order to preserve and strengthen the relationship. Under optimal conditions, this decision would be a product of the extensive and careful evaluation of all possible options and consequences by both partners. This is an example of what we might call an interpersonal moral issue. Although people usually organize their values and attitudes around a consistent frame of reference, they can (and do) reevaluate even their most strongly held views in special circumstances within a relationship.

DEVELOPMENT

Stern (1985) describes a basic sense of connectedness and affiliation as given from the moment of birth. Early forms of relatedness occur between infant and primary caretaker. An infant's facial expressions, eye contact, and vocalizations engage others and elicit attention. Such observations as these have led to an appreciation of the role that babies play in maintaining and strengthening relational bonds. Within the first year of life, babies can detect and respond to (albeit in a rather primitive way) the affective states of others (Stern 1985).

At about six months, babies begin to show preferential attachments to the people in their lives who are most familiar to them, their primary caretakers. In a series of theoretical contributions, Bowlby (1969) conceptualizes patterns of relational behaviors organized around attachment. Attachment behaviors are those in which the infant successfully attains or maintains proximity to another familiar individual who is perceived as better able to cope with the world. These behaviors are most evident in emergencies since they serve the biological function of protection.

If the attachment figure is consistently responsive to the infant's needs and desires, the infant develops a strong sense of security and trust. The infant's expectations regarding the responsiveness and reliability of the caretaker are synthesized into a representational model of this relationship. The securely attached infant remains confident that people are in general trustworthy and reliable and that the child, himself, is worthy of love and nurturance. In contrast, if the attachment figure is unresponsive, unavailable, and/or unpredictable, the infant is said to be insecurely attached and usually expresses anxiety, depression, and anger (Bowlby 1969).

Viewing infant relationships from the attachment perspective, the infant is seen as developing an organized pattern of relating to others, a pattern that plays itself out over and over again and in differing ways influences all subsequent relationships (Armsden and Greenberg 1987; Chodorow 1978). Such patterns, established early, but changing with continued attachment experiences, have been described by Bretherton (1985) as "internal working models." Children and adolescents who maintain internal working models characterized by distrust and anger run a high risk of having difficulty in future relationships. Furthermore, such models of attachment may predispose these individuals to serious adjustment difficulties, including acting out and delinquency (Allen et al. 1990; Kobak and Sceery 1988).

Entering the preschool years, children's social networks expand as they engage in more interactive play with their peers. At this age, children usually show greater assertiveness in relationships (Veroff and Veroff 1980), often demonstrated by their use of imperatives and demands when playing with friends. Rarely can preschool children cooperatively work toward the completion of a common goal. They will ultimately pull in opposite directions, unable to compromise. From a subjective vantage point, relationships at this early stage of development are experienced as desirable only in so far as they serve the individual (Selman 1980). Gradually, this egocentric perspective is challenged as the child's unilateral strategies prove ineffective in social interactions and she becomes more aware of the ways in which getting along with others can better serve her needs.

Young children are generally not capable of recognizing and taking into consideration another person's perspective (Selman 1980). They are generally unable to appreciate that their actions have consequences that affect other people. During early school years, one-sided relationships are usually transformed into more give-and-take, cooperative friendships (Piaget 1952; Selman 1980). In these friendships, children gain a greater awareness of their own internal states and of those of others, subsequently becoming more sensitive to the evaluations that others are capable of making about them. Gradually, the child who was characteristically opportunistic and self-serving becomes interested in external approval and acceptance and thus develops more socially grounded behavior.

Sullivan (1953) describes the need for intimacy as not coming to the forefront until late childhood, during the preadolescent years. In his conception of intimacy, Sullivan refers to a more mature closeness than is possible in the preceding years. This intimacy first develops in "chumships," intense and exclusive same-sex friendships in which each party provides complete validation of the other's personal worth. For the first time, in these relationships, the child gains a sensitivity to another's perspective, and the friend becomes almost equally important as the person himself: "Validation of personal worth requires a type of relationship which I call collaboration, by which I mean clearly formulated adjustments of one's behavior to the expressed needs of the other person in the pursuit of increasingly identical—that is more and more nearly mutual—satisfactions, and in the maintenance of increasingly similar security operations" (Sullivan 1953, p. 246). It is in these relationships that children go beyond cooperation toward a mutual goal and begin to do things for the good of their friend because of a genuine interest in the other's well-being.

While young adolescents define themselves in relation to and through the eyes of others, more mature adolescents, having internalized some of the approval and acceptance that they were once dependent on others for, are now able to venture away from stereotyped, conformist groups in a way similar to how a secure toddler will initiate exploratory behavior in the presence of her attachment figure. Adolescents begin to value the ways in which they differ from friends and family members and, with this recognition, are better able to explore a range of interests, values, and religious and spiritual beliefs. In Erikson's (1963) terms, this is the period during which identity consolidation becomes the principal task at hand.

During the early years of high school, adolescents seek affiliations with people and groups that affirm their experiences of themselves as increasingly differentiated and individuated. Older adolescents selectively align themselves with institutional systems, clubs, and activities that support their newly enriched understandings of themselves (Kegan 1982). These new affiliations with groups and individuals begin to affirm adolescents' views of themselves as both distinctly individual and connected to others. Relationships at this age become more complex as adolescents deal more fully with plurality, ambiguity, conflict, and diversity (Bar-Yam Hassan and Bar-Yam 1987). As the ability for relatedness grows and the individual experiences increasing autonomy, differences among people no longer pose a threat to his identity. Variations among others are now cherished, not merely tolerated. Individuals begin to appreciate the other as an autonomous being with distinct motivations and ideas (White et al. 1983). The roles that each partner plays in the relationship become more flexible and subject to change. More mature adolescents tend to use a morality of care that is dependent on a particular context rather than a preestablished moral code (Gilligan 1982).

Mature relationships are engaged in and experienced by individuals who have achieved the necessary individual and interpersonal skills for managing the complexities inherent in close relationships. While there are undoubtedly many types of relationships, the most intimate ones are those in which both partners develop a deep understanding of the other's feelings, thoughts, and behaviors and act sensitively in accordance with this knowledge. Intimate relationships are characterized by mutual trust (Selman 1980; Youniss 1980), empathy (Jordan 1984; Jordan, Surrey, and Kaplan 1982; Selman 1980), a relatively free yet regulated expression of emotion (Douvan and Adelson 1966), the sharing of personal thoughts, beliefs, and values (Berndt 1982; Berscheid et al. 1989), the tolerance and negotiation of conflict and disagreement (Selman 1980), and reciprocal and respectful probing of the other.

AUTONOMY

COMPONENTS AND THEIR DEVELOPMENT

Since the development of autonomy is critical in the progression of relatedness toward intimacy, we have already touched on issues around autonomy in our discussion of the unfolding of relatedness. Nonetheless, before considering the integration of autonomy and relatedness, we must separately consider the emergence of autonomy. "Autonomy" refers to the person's growing capacity to take control over his own life, making responsible, independent decisions along the way. At optimal levels, autonomy is usually demonstrated by an absence of excessive dependency on others, an ability to take the initiative in various contexts, and a willingness to assume responsibility for one's actions (Greenberger and Sorensen 1974). The attainment of substantial autonomy is critical for the development of an individuated and consolidated identity since identity formation entails being able to recognize and separate what one chooses to be (and do) from what one is expected to be (and do) by family, peers, and social standards (Erikson 1963).

Autonomy encompasses several related yet conceptually distinct components: affective,[1] behavioral, cognitive, and attitudinal. Similar categories have been proposed by Douvan and Adelson (1966) and Sessa and Steinberg (in press). Affective autonomy involves a reduction in the degree of emotional dependence that one has on one's parents and peers. As one gains autonomy, the need for excessive approval, acceptance, and affirmation from outside sources lessens and is replaced by internal confirmation. As described by Douvan and Adelson, "emotional autonomy" refers to the extent to which individuals resolve early ambivalent attachments to their parents so that they no longer idealize them in the same unquestioning manner that they did in earlier years (Blos 1967; Douvan and Adelson 1966). Freedom from excessive emotional dependencies allows for a more realistic perception not only of parents but of peers, teachers, and public figures as well.

Behavioral autonomy is marked by the degree to which an individual can manage her own responsibilities and affairs while making responsible choices and decisions. In order for a child to achieve a healthy proportion of functional independence, parents must be willing to grant the child a sufficient amount of behavioral freedom within which to explore. But, as Douvan and Adelson (1966) remark, behavioral autonomy refers less to what a person is allowed to do, which is more a reflection of parents and society, and more to how the person handles such freedom.

Cognitive autonomy includes those cognitive developments underlying the potential for autonomy and the subjective appraisal of self-reliance and independence. Among the key aspects of cognitive developments contributing to this dimension of autonomy are recognizing oneself as an active agent responsible for one's own behavior, assuming an internal locus of control (Greenberger and Sorensen 1974), and gaining the intellectual capacity for what Piaget (1952) has called formal operations, allowing for more complex, independent problem solving. The understanding that people are distinct, with individual feelings, thoughts, and qualities, sets the stage for more advanced autonomous endeavors, such as the ability for multiple perspective taking (Selman 1980). Cognitive autonomy is reflected in a person's subjective sense of independence, especially with regard to parental control and decision making (Douvan and Adelson 1966). Self-trust, self-reliance, and confidence in one's ability to make responsible decisions (Steinberg and Silverberg 1986) all contribute to a person's ability to function autonomously. Combined cognitive and behavioral processes allow for what Connell (1990) explains as a "self-regulation process," involving continual self-appraisals of why one is behaving in a particular manner in a given situation.

Finally, attitudinal (or value) autonomy involves the questioning of parental and social values and morals. Since it is based on use of principled or independent reasoning in moral, political, and social problem solving, this dimension of autonomy is unlikely to come about before a substantial development of affective, behavioral, and cognitive autonomy (Kohlberg and Gilligan 1971). Douvan and Adelson (1966) describe value autonomy as "the capacity to manage a clarity of vision which permits one to transcend customary structurings of reality" (p. 131). This capacity follows the gaining of more realistic, less idealized perceptions of parents. A child comes to think independently, thus differentiating her beliefs from those of the family and her peers (Erikson 1963). Parental values are not simply rejected in their entirety. Rather, there is a sifting through of the conglomeration of principles that have been explicitly and implicitly taught during the preceding childhood years. Gradually, with advancing independence in this sphere, she selects more personally meaningful values. Consequently, there is the emergence of a personal pattern of beliefs and opinions that aid in the process of individuation (Erikson 1963).

RELATEDNESS AND AUTONOMY

At first blush, relatedness and autonomy appear to signify opposing poles of a developmental spectrum. Yet theoretical and clinical observations remind us that they are complexly intertwined across the life span. Generally speaking, the more differentiated and self-governing a person becomes, the greater the potential for the forming and sustaining of interdependent, intimate relationships. Conversely, we know from personal observations and clinical experience that the history of one's relationships contributes to his inclinations and abilities to differentiate and form an increasingly coherent identity. As individuals become more competent in recognizing, coping with, and appreciating interpersonal differences, they gain additional opportunities for further self-discovery and independence. This in turn enhances the development of intimate relationships. Our recognition of the complex dynamics that go on between the autonomous and the relational aspects of an individual's life suggests many complexities that remain to be explored. For instance, relatedness is constrained by the developmental stage of the individual—a person cannot empathize with another if he does not have the cognitive skills that enable perspective taking. And it is likely that connections between relatedness and autonomy are deeply influenced by the individual's overarching psychosocial development.

Besides such developmental influences, there are other questions about how the individual's relational context may reflect, and influence, the extent of his autonomy and relatedness. How might the family interfere with or enhance the adolescent's growth toward autonomy and relatedness? These developmental and contextual issues are at the core of our analyses, as we trace ego development and family interactions with respect to adolescent relatedness and autonomy.

EGO DEVELOPMENT

While other stage theories describe the growth of the individual from a psychosocial perspective, none lend themselves as readily to system-

194

atic empirical research as does Loevinger's conceptualization of ego development (Loevinger 1966). This perspective, and its linked assessment, offers one way of indexing the interplay between relatedness and autonomy as the individual advances or regresses along specific stages. As we observed at the start of this chapter, many measures of individual development place more value on the attainment of autonomy than on the formation of relational skills. In contrast, this view of ego development considers aspects of evolving self-definition as they relate to interpersonal growth. As defined by Loevinger, Wessler, and Redmore (1970), "ego development" refers to an abstract continuum of the various frames of reference that an individual uses to organize and integrate experience. In this light, the primary function of the ego is to master, integrate, and make sense of experience (Loevinger 1969).

Loevinger's measure of ego development was designed to capture the various frames of meaning that one uses to integrate increasingly complex self-perspectives in relation to the external environment. The measure consists of thirty-six stems organized around issues involving parental and peer relationships, education, rules, morality, self-control, and identity (Loevinger and Wessler 1970; Loevinger et al. 1970). These stems include the following: *"When a child will not join in group activities—," "When she thought of her mother, she—,"* and *"Sometimes he worried that—."* Designed as a projective technique, the stems are left intentionally ambiguous to allow subjects the freedom to project their own thoughts, ideas, and feelings (their meanings) onto the incomplete sentences.

Ego development is best understood by examining the various stages along with their respective characteristics (Loevinger 1966; Loevinger and Wessler 1970). Seven stages and three transitional levels represent the ego development continuum (table 1).

The first stage of ego development includes the presocial and symbiotic phases. In the presocial phase, the infant is described as relatively undifferentiated from her social and physical surroundings and attentive only to the gratification of her immediate needs. In the symbiotic phase, the infant usually develops a more differentiated attachment to her primary caretaker, but she does not yet differentiate herself from her mother. Since the sentence completion test requires verbal proficiency, this stage cannot be assessed using this measure.

The first stage that can be assessed using the sentence completion test is called the *impulsive* stage. People at this stage tend to view the

TABLE 1

Loevinger's Stages of Ego Development

Stage	Impulse Control, "Moral" Style	Interpersonal Style	Conscious Preoccupations	Cognitive Style
Preconformist:				
Presocial (I-1)	...	Autistic	Self vs. nonself	...
Symbiotic (I-1)	...	Symbiotic	Self vs. nonself	...
Impulsive (I-2)	Impulsive, fear	Receiving, dependent, exploitive	Bodily feelings, especially sexual and aggressive	Stereotypy, conceptual confusion
Self-protective (Δ)	Fear of being caught, externalizing blame, opportunistic	Wary, manipulative, exploitive	Self-protection, wishes, things, advantages, control	
Transition from self-protective to conformist (Δ/3)	Obedience and conformity to social norms are simple and absolute rules	Manipulative, obedient	Concrete aspects of traditional sex roles, physical causation as opposed to psychological causation	Conceptual simplicity, stereotypes
Conformist:				
Conformist (I-3)	Conformity to external rules, shame, guilt for breaking rules	Belonging, helping, superficial niceness	Appearance, social acceptability, banal feelings, behavior	Conceptual simplicity, stereotypes, clichés
Transition from conformist to conscientious;				

self-consciousness (I-3/4)	Dawning realization of standards, contingencies, self-criticism	Being helpful, deepened interest in interpersonal relations	Consciousness of the self as separate from the group, recognition of psychological causation	Awareness of individual differences in attitudes, interests and abilities; mentioned in global and broad terms
Postconformist: Conscientious (I-4) ...	Self-evaluated standards, self-criticism	Intensive, responsible, mutual, concern for communication	Differentiated feelings, motives for behavior, self-respect, achievements, traits, expression	Conceptual complexity, idea of patterning
Transition from conscientious to autonomous	Individuality, coping with inner conflict	Cherishing of interpersonal relations	Communicating, expressing ideas and feelings, process and change	Toleration for paradox and contradiction
Autonomous (I-5)	Add: Coping with conflicting inner needs[a]	Add: Respect for autonomy	Vividly conveyed feelings, integration of physiological and psychological causation of behavior, development, role conception, self-fulfillment, self in social context	Increased conceptual complexity; complex patterns, toleration for ambiguity, broad scope, objectivity
Integrated (I-6)	Add: Reconciling inner conflicts, renunciation of unattainable	Add: Cherishing of individuality	Add: Identity	....

SOURCE.—Loevinger and Wessler (1970).

NOTE.—"Add" means in addition to description applying to previous level.

world from an egocentric perspective. They have difficulty restraining their actions, monitoring their speech, and delaying gratification of nagging desires. The notion of rules and standards is generally not understood or used as a guiding principle. Thus, these people's behaviors often need to be monitored and controlled by external sources.

Overwhelmed by the effort required to manage basic tasks and responsibilities in their own lives, people at the impulsive stage tend to be incapable of thinking much beyond themselves to the effects that their actions have on others. Furthermore, they lack the cognitive capacity to consider perspectives outside their own. Other people are appreciated, not for their individual qualities, but for what they have to offer. People at the impulsive stage will often make imperative demands and expect to be taken care of without any delay. This may reflect an early attempt to assert their autonomy. Not surprisingly, "impulsive" individuals are very much dependent on others.

As people learn to anticipate short-term consequences, they gain better control over their impulsive expression. Once the relationship between action and reward and/or action and punishment is understood, "rules" come to be regarded as stable and invariant. This stage of ego development is called *self-protective*. The central motivation around self-management is to avoid punishment. Adherence to rules aids in keeping behavior in check, so relationships with parents and peers differ from relationships engaged in at the impulsive stage. A child at the self-protective stage would be likely to handle being angry at his parents in a way different from a child at the impulsive stage. Rather than lashing out at his parents or throwing things in anger, a self-protective child might decide instead to bike over to a friend's house so as to avoid punishment. However, this behavior would also be indicative of a lack of awareness or concern for how his parents might worry over his unexpected absence, not to mention a lack of foresight; he may be punished on his return. The presocial, symbiotic, impulsive, and self-protective stages together constitute the "preconformist level" of ego development.

At the *conformist* stage, the individual's orientation toward the outside world has progressed from a once solipsistic perspective to a new appreciation of how the self is connected to others. In addition to being more adept at caring for oneself, a person at the conformist stage can attend to the more surface needs of others. Getting along and behaving are primary goals. Conflicts and differences that might threaten the

198

status quo are downplayed or ignored. Consequently, friends at this stage cloak themselves in bonds of exaggerated similarity. These bonds serve to validate each person's growing sense of self. Rules are adhered to simply because they are rules, and shame is experienced when rules are broken. This partial internalization of rules and standards is critical in helping people manage their own behavior. At the conformist stage, there may be a dawning recognition of reciprocity, yet the predominant concern is with material objects, popularity, and appearance. Obvious group differences are recognized, but subtle individual differences go unappreciated. Although there is some recognition of internal states, they are generally expressed through clichés, stereotypes, or moralistic language.

More flexible thinking, introspection, and subjective awareness characterize the *self-aware* transition. Right and wrong are not understood as static. They are now seen as shifting with different contexts. Because of their increased capacity for self-reflection and self-criticism, people at the self-aware stage rely more on their own judgment and ideas than on those of the social majority. Repeatedly, studies have found that more people function at this stage than at any other (Haan, Stroud, and Holstein 1973; Harakel 1971; Holt 1980; Lambert 1972; Redmore and Waldman 1975). The conformist and the transitional self-aware stages represent the "conformist level" of ego development.

In the *conscientious* stage, morality is internalized, and internal rules and standards more powerfully guide behavior than external peer and authoritative sources. The existence of inner moral standards leads to the experience of guilt when the individual behaves or thinks in ways that conflict with personal principles. Conscientious individuals are greatly concerned with the carrying out of ideals, achievements, and responsibilities. Building on the preceding transitional stage, the conscientious person is even more capable of self-reflection and self-criticism. Relationships tend to be richer, more intense, and more meaningful than those at earlier stages.

At the transitional stage between the conscientious and the autonomous stages is the *individualistic* stage, marked by the high value placed on interpersonal relationships. The complexity of thought characteristic of this stage is reflected in an increased ability to make sense of paradoxical ideas and to tolerate ambiguity. This capacity has many consequences. For instance, when both partners in a close relationship are functioning at this stage, they may be more capable of painstakingly understanding and talking about deep conflict, as opposed to trying to resolve their knotty problems immediately and superficially. Relationships between people at the individualistic stage approach interdependence. Autonomy and relatedness are viewed as interrelated and mutually enhancing rather than as at odds and inhibiting.

The *autonomous* stage is distinguished by the individual's effort to struggle with and resolve inner conflicts, such as discrepancies between desires and moral principles. Relationships continue to be highly valued. There is an added appreciation for one's own and the other's need for autonomy. As a result, relationships engaged in by people at this stage tend to be mutually interdependent. Salient issues for people at this stage involve individuality, differentiation, and self-fulfillment.

The highest stage of ego development is called the *integrated* stage, marked by the resolution of conflicting demands and the renunciation of that which is unattainable (Loevinger 1966). Individual differences and uniqueness are highly valued and esteemed. Responses at this stage are remarkably original and often poetic. The autonomous stage has been described as more theoretical than empirical since it is relatively unusual to see people scoring at this stage (Loevinger and Wessler 1970). The conscientious through the integrated stages make up the postconformist level of ego development.[2]

Loevinger's conception of successive stages of ego development incorporates the notion that the integration of the capacities for relatedness and autonomy is a critical component of higher levels of ego development. This view, that greater integration of autonomy and relatedness is inherent in the progression of ego development, is an important basis of our developmental studies.

CONSTRAINING AND ENABLING
FAMILY INTERACTIONS

Family processes both enhance and interfere with an adolescent's ego development (Hauser, Houlihan, Powers, Jacobson, Noam, Weiss, Perry, Follansbee, and Book 1987; Hauser, Powers, Jacobson, Noam, Weiss, and Follansbee 1984; Hauser, Powers, and Noam 1991; Stierlin 1974). In other words, an adolescent's repeated experience of certain interactive experiences within the family can contribute favorably and unfavorably to her continued ego development. When interactions are accepting, empathic, and stimulating, they will sustain, and at times evoke, advancing ego development. On the other hand, a family milieu in which one or both parents dismiss or undermine the adolescent—and one another—discourages adolescent explorations and new experiments—in thought and action—that are paradigmatic of ego development. Interactions believed to promote and enable advances in adolescent ego development include focusing, problem solving, curiosity, and acceptance. In contrast, interactions that undermine social conditions favorable to an adolescent's ego development are ones that distract, devalue, and ignore the young family member. The full array of enabling and constraining interactions is represented in tables 2–4. We know from previous studies that these interactions are linked with adolescent ego development (Hauser et al. 1984; Hauser et al. 1991). We now address a more specific question: whether adolescents' orientations toward relatedness and autonomy are connected with these characteristics of their family milieu.

Methods of Study

SAMPLE AND PROCEDURE

To study systematically how the evolution and integration of relatedness and autonomy might be connected to individual ego development and family processes, we studied sixty subjects (equal numbers of males and females) randomly drawn from a larger sample of 146 participants in the first year of a longitudinal study of adolescents and their families (Hauser et al. 1991). Previous findings (Hauser 1976) indicated that an average high school class was not representative of the full range of adolescent development. Consequently, half our subjects (from both this pilot study and the larger longitudinal study) were drawn from successive admissions of nonpsychotic, nonorganically impaired patients to a private psychiatric hospital. The other half were volunteers from a ninth-grade class of a local public high school. The average age of the subjects was 14.5 years. Almost all the subjects were living in families of upper-middle- and middle-class socioeconomic status (Hollingshead 1957).

Each adolescent filled out the Washington University Sentence Completion Test for ego development (Loevinger and Wessler 1970). Levels of relatedness, autonomy, and ego development were sepa-

TABLE 2
OVERVIEW OF THE CONSTRAINING CODES

Constraining	Description	Example	
Cognitive:			
Distracting	The speaker disrupts the discussion by interrupting another speaker or abruptly changing the topic in a way that directs others away from the task	M:	It's OK to steal if it's to save a life. Life is/
		A:	I'm going to try using that as an excuse sometime. Let's see how far it gets *me*. (A laughs.)
Withholding	The speaker is cryptic and nonresponsive, refrains from offering an opinion, evades direct questions	F:	What do you think A?
		A:	I already told you what I said.
		F:	Could you explain it again?
		A:	No!
Judgmental	The speaker evaluates negatively another's ideas or opinions, reasons dogmatically, speaks in terms of right and wrong	A:	I think the kid is old enough to decide for himself.
		M:	No, that's wrong. He should respect his parents' wishes.
Affective:			
Indifference/unyielding conviction	The speaker ignores another's opinion or question, repeatedly affirming his or her own stance	M:	I definitely think he should be punished.
		A:	Do you want to hear what I think?
		M:	I don't care if the guy is reformed; he still committed a crime.
Excessive gratifying ..	The speaker offers undue acceptance, agreement, or praise of another's position, often with the intent of ending the discussion	A:	I cannot disagree with you.
		F:	OK, I'll give in to you; I'll give in to you.
Devaluing	The speaker rejects, criticizes, or belittles the opinions of another person or the person himself or herself. The speaker may also be devaluing of the task	M:	I don't think there is anything wrong with having an all black or all Jewish club.
		F:	You really believe that, huh? I'm embarrassed for you.

NOTE.—"A," "F," and "M" stand for, respectively, adolescent, father, and mother.

TABLE 3
OVERVIEW OF THE ENABLING CODES

Enabling	Description		Example
Cognitive:			
Explaining	The speaker presents an opinion or offers information that contributes to the understanding of his or her stance	A:	Well, the important part is that the father made a promise. The child fulfilled his part of the deal, and if the father wants his son to trust him, he should keep his promise, too.
Focusing	The speaker rephrases or adds information to others' explanations to get them to think further about their position	F:	On the basis of what I see here. I would have reported the escaped convict.
		M:	What if you knew for sure he was innocent in the first place?
Problem solving ..	The speaker furthers the discussion by orienting the group to the problem at hand, clarifying the terms of the task, explaining his or her thinking process, or moving the group toward resolution	F:	Let's not get off the subject by talking about the druggist; the question is should Heinz steal the drug to save his wife.
Curiosity	The speaker attempts to further understand another's position by asking questions and encouraging further elaboration by another	A:	I don't understand. How would that make a difference?
Affective:			
Acceptance	The speaker acknowledges another's ideas by overtly agreeing, repeating the other's statement, or encouraging the other to continue	M:	She's 16, old enough to choose her own friends.
		A:	Right, I totally agree with you.
Active understanding ..	The speaker demonstrates an accurate, "tuned-in" understanding of another's statement by paraphrasing the idea, simultaneously using identical words, or accurately finishing the other's thought	A:	Somehow to talk to an old man and cheat him and betray him, and . . .
		F:	. . . play on his sympathies . . .
		A:	Yeah, it seems so base.

NOTE.—See table 2.

203

TABLE 4

OVERVIEW OF THE DIRECTION OF DISCOURSE CHANGE CODES

	Description		Example
Discourse change:			
Regression ...	The speaker shifts from an enabling speech to a constraining speech or from a more complex, coherent remark to a simpler, less coherent one	A:	So why do you think he should be reported?
		F:	It doesn't matter how good a person he is now; what matters is he stole.
		A:	Give me a break, Dad.
Progression ...	The speaker shifts from a constraining speech to an enabling speech or from a less complex, complete statement to a more complex and coherent one	A:	I said the captain should man the boat.
		M:	But the captain has more experience blowing up bridges than the other people do.
		A:	Yeah, but if he goes out and gets wasted, then the chances are greater that they will all die. The captain is the only one who knows how to lead the retreat.
Foreclosure ...	The speaker's second speech is no more complex or elaborated than the first and is, in fact, often redundant. The same interaction code is applied to both statements. The speaker has neither progressed nor regressed from his or her first speech	A:	Call her in!
		F:	Do you think we are finished?
		A:	Call her in!
Topic change:			
Regression ...	The speaker shifts the topic to one that is tangential or unrelated to the topic addressed in the first speech, and the second speech is not as clear, coherent, or strong as the first	M:	Explain why you said that?
		F:	I said parents should be able to trust their child.
		M:	Wouldn't it be nice if "A" gave us respect all the time.
Progression ...	The speaker changes the topic from the first to the second speech, and the latter speech is more complex and articulate than the first	M:	Look, that red light is flashing!
		A:	It's been doing that the whole time.
		M:	Never mind, I'm sure it's OK. Why do you think the father has the right to break his promise?
Equivalent ...	The speaker shifts the topic from the first speech to the second, but the level of complexity and clarity remains the same	F:	You don't think it was wrong?
		A:	I don't know.
		F:	Sit over here so I can hear you.
		A:	I don't want to.

NOTE.—See table 2.

rately scored from these written protocols. All coders were blind to the subject's ego development and family scores as well as to whether subjects were psychiatric patients or high school students. Ego development was scored by three coders trained in Loevinger's coding system (interrater reliabilities, using intraclass correlations, ranged between .70 and .80).

MEASURING RELATEDNESS AND AUTONOMY

In order to assess relatedness and autonomy, we devised a new coding system, one based on the conceptual considerations reviewed in the previous section. Using a detailed manual operationalizing these dimensions, three trained coders achieved acceptable intraclass interrater reliabilities (.86 for relatedness and .73 for autonomy).

RELATEDNESS

Relatedness was scored on the basis of the frequency and quality with which a person incorporated other people into her responses to all the stems. Many of the sentence stems, such as *"My mother and I—,"* *"When I am with a woman—,"* and *"Being with other people"* refer directly to relationships with others. Other stems often evoke, but do not demand, responses involving friends, family members, and other critical people in a person's life. For instance, an adolescent might write *"At times she worried about—*what other people thought of her" or *"I feel sorry—*for my mother, who's going through a hard time right now." Finally, there are some stems that only rarely elicit the inclusion of other people. And such stems may at times be completed with an unusual twist, at times indicative of the importance that others play in adolescents' lives. For example, one adolescent wrote, *"Education is—*something I get more from my friends than from my classes right now."

Responses making no mention of others or expressing overtly hostile feelings toward other people were scored as zero. Especially noteworthy were those cases where people avoided writing about connections with others when relationship-oriented responses were prompted by the stem: for example, *"My mother and I—*I don't know." Completions referring to other people were scored from 1 to 3 on the basis of the nature of those references and the degree to which the mention of others was prompted by the stem. The more specifically a person wrote about others, the higher the response was scored for relatedness. Thus, *"My father—*was really nice to me when I felt lousy the other day" would receive a higher relatedness score than *"My father—*is a good person."

We assumed that, through their ego development responses, adolescents were revealing their capacity to form and sustain close meaningful relationships. Not surprisingly, there was much variation in the expression of these relationships. There were those adolescents who tended consistently to leave others out of their sentences, probably reflecting a pattern that exists for these adolescents in their daily lives. For this group, responses that did include others were vague or egocentric: for example, *"Being with other people—*is important" or *"If my mother—*were young and fresh, I'd be happier." Some of these subjects completed the stem by restating it more concretely rather than expanding on the meaning of the sentence stem or adding a more personal reaction: for example, *"When people are helpless—*they have no one to help them."

Adolescents whose responses represented higher levels of relatedness conveyed unmistakably positive feelings about being with other people and, in general, about relationships: *"Being with other people—*makes me feel good"; *"My husband and I—*will have many children." Subjects often wrote about similarities with others in generalized terms, such as *"My mother and I—*are exactly alike." An appreciation of one's similarity with another was understood to reflect some sense of connection but on its own did not warrant a high score of relatedness.

At the highest levels of relatedness, adolescents wrote about both their similarities and their differences with others, or sometimes a person referred to important differences that she could appreciate: *"I am—*the black sheep in my family, but usually that doesn't get in the way of our getting along anymore." These responses depicted self-reflection in the context of relationships: *"My mother and I—*each have a lot of things to work out before we can have the kind of relationship we would both like to have." Some responses showed a person's initiative in working out the rough spots of a relationship. Verbal communication was not always seen as the fundamental component of relationships. There was an interest in caring for others, a desire to be cared for, an attempt to understand how others think, feel, or behave.

Other features of these responses included an appreciation of the multi-faceted nature of people and a clearly articulated expression of love and concern for another person. Sometimes this interest in attending to others could be seen in a hypothetical situation: *"When a child will not join in group activities*—I try to figure out what might be wrong so I can help him have more fun."

AUTONOMY

Autonomy was scored on the basis of how adolescents referred to self-differentiation, identity, responsibility, choice, and independence in their responses. Like relatedness, some of the stems were more likely to elicit responses around these themes than others: for example, *"What gets me into trouble—," "When his wife asked him to help with the housework—,"* or *"I am—."* However, *all* the sentence stems could be completed in ways that could express autonomy (e.g., *"A good mother*—is like mine because, while she loves me, she lets me decide most things for myself").

Our subjects showed much variation in their expressions of autonomy. Some responded in ways suggesting little or no differentiation from others: *"If my mother*—were to die, I'd die too." Other adolescents relished ways they differed from others: *"I am*—unique in that I am fourteen and still like to fingerpaint in the bathtub." A few repeatedly avoided using the first-person-singular pronoun "I," raising the possibility that they did not see themselves as active agents: compare *"When people are helpless*—someone should help them" with *"When people are helpless*—I try to figure out a way to help them feel less helpless." The first response implies how the adolescent might pass the responsibility to "someone" else, whereas the second completion suggests that the adolescent takes the initiative in helping others, possibly reflecting the value that she places on respecting another person's right of self-direction. Subjects at the higher levels of autonomy expressed even more clearly the importance of self-direction: *"The thing I like about myself*—is that I am as independent as I can be at this point of my life"; *"A good mother*—should give her children room to grow and make some mistakes."

Cognitive autonomy was marked by the presence of independent, creative, and original thinking. Most of the time, adolescents would respond to the sentence stems as they were written, but several tailored the wording of the stems: for example, "*A woman should always*—I don't believe there is anything that all women should do." Any alteration of a stem was taken as some indication of autonomy, but this particular modification is rich in autonomy for additional reasons, such as "Judy's" disdain for a uniform prescription of behavior for a large group of diverse people. In completing the stem, she is rejecting a gender stereotype. Many adolescents (and adults) respond in conventional ways to the incomplete stems referring to conceptions of gender, thereby voicing prevalent social norms. Yet Judy is questioning such traditional norms, implicitly declaring that women have the right to make choices and not be limited by restrictive gender roles.

Adolescents also expressed independent thinking about relationships with friends and families. For instance, one wrote, "*Usually she felt that sex*—was something she was going to wait on even though her boyfriend wants to now." In responding this way, this young adolescent recognizes that the girl (perhaps herself) and her boyfriend differ on how comfortable they feel in engaging in sexual activity at this time and that each of them must decide individually about such important matters.

Another index of autonomy involved how the subjects described controlling their behavior, particularly how they coped with conflict and intense affect. Adolescents expressing lower levels of autonomy provided simpler, often impulsive responses: "*When I am criticized*—I criticize them back"; "*When I get mad*—I throw things and yell a lot." Those expressing higher levels of autonomy depicted a more extensive repertoire of ways for dealing with difficult experiences. They wrote about handling their anger or disappointments by talking about the experiences with their parents, going for a bike ride, retiring to their room to read or listen to music, and thinking before acting.

Subjects also differed in the degree to which they viewed themselves as responsible for their behavior. At the lower end of the spectrum, there were adolescents who blamed others for their problems and expressed little, if any, self-reflection or insight about their actions. Several wrote variations on the sentence, "*What gets me into trouble is*—my friends." Others were more aware of how they might have caused difficulties for themselves and noted things about themselves that they would like to change: "*What gets me into trouble is*—not working as hard as I should in school." Some adolescents recognized that their actions had an effect on others: "*My conscience bothers me if*—I don't realize that someone has told me something in confidence and I happen to tell someone what I didn't know was personal information." At the highest levels of autonomy, adolescents understood their behavior as having an effect on a broader scale, such as their community or communities outside their own: "*At times she worried about*— the subtle ways she contributes to the prejudice in this world even though she is dedicated to fighting against such injustice."

Also of interest to us were relations between a person's self-awareness and independence in establishing his unique sense of self. One stem in particular, *"I am—,"* illuminated differences in self-conceptions ranging from simple and general descriptions to those that were multifaceted and unique. For instance, compare "*I am*—human" or "*I am*—tired" with "*I am*—who I am (a lover of mocha chip ice cream, sensitive, caring, a lover of milk chocolate, Katherine, and fifteen years old)."

MEASURING CONSTRAINING AND ENABLING INTERACTIONS

Constraining and enabling family interactions were assessed from transcripts of family discussions, generated by a revealed differences procedure (Strodtbeck 1958) in which family members defended their disagreements on moral dilemmas and then attempted to arrive at a family consensus (Hauser et al. 1984; Hauser et al. 1991). Reliably trained coders, applying the Constraining and Enabling Coding System, provided family interaction scores for each family member, scoring all members' speeches during thirty- to forty-minute family discussions.

Space limitations do not allow a full definition of all twelve types of interactions. Brief definitions of each are provided in tables 2–4. The constraining and enabling categories of interaction are composed of cognitive and affective components. Interrupting or distracting family members away from the discussion ("distracting"), withholding opinions or responses to questions ("withholding"), and being judgmental of another family member's position ("judgmental") are all coded as "cognitive constraining." Examples of the "affective constraining" category include showing indifference to another family member's contribution, such as repeatedly stating one's own position without regard for the questions and opinions of other family members ("indiffer-

209

ence'') and gratifying others by giving in to their point of view prematurely and devaluing the opinions of others or the discussion task itself (''devaluing'').

Explaining one's own position (''explaining''), making comments or asking questions about another person's position to make him think further about his stance (''focusing''), orienting the group, clarifying the terms of the dilemma, or talking about one's thinking process in response to the dilemma (''problem solving''), and posing questions to others (''curiosity'') are interactions coded as ''cognitive enabling.'' The ''affective enabling'' speech patterns are those that confirm or support another family member's position (''acceptance'') or demonstrate a seemingly empathic understanding of another person's point of view (''active understanding'').

In addition to the constraining and enabling codes, we also considered how adolescents' contributions furthered or hindered the course of the discussion. Discourse and topic changes were assessed across successive pairs of speeches. If the adolescent continued or elaborated on an idea expressed in her first speech, thereby moving the discussion forward, the second speech in the pair was coded as a ''progression'' in discourse. If the adolescent became less coherent or less complex in her second speech than in her first, the adolescent's second speech was coded as a ''regression'' in discourse. If the adolescent neither progresses nor regresses from the first speech to the second, the discourse change was coded as a ''foreclosure.'' If the change occurring between two consecutive speeches involved a change in topic, the intraindividual sequence was scored as a topic change ''progression,'' ''regression,'' or ''equivalent.''

Results

RELATEDNESS, AUTONOMY, AND EGO DEVELOPMENT

Ego development, as expected, was closely associated with both relatedness and autonomy. A one-way multivariate analysis of variance of these variables by ego stage score revealed a significant effect for ego development level. Using Wilks's lambda statistic, the overall effect of ego score was found to be significant, $F(12, 104) = 6.91$,

$p < .01$. The higher a subject scored on ego development, the higher he scored on relatedness and autonomy. Similar results were found in follow-up univariate analyses of relatedness, $F(6, 53) = 8.74$, $p < .01$, and autonomy, $F(6, 53) = 11.97$, $p < .01$. Consistent with these findings, ego score (item sum score) was strongly correlated with both relatedness ($r = .65$) and autonomy ($r = .69$).

Both male and female adolescents expressed more relatedness than autonomy. A paired t-test revealed that responses indicative of relatedness were significantly greater than those of autonomy, $t = 3.9$, $p < .0002$. Further analyses of these scores indicated that differences were occurring only for adolescents at the preconformist and conformist levels.

Finally, we found that relatedness and autonomy were significantly correlated for the whole sample, $r = .60$, $p < .01$. This finding remained significant even when ego development was controlled for using partial correlations, $r = .39$, $p > .002$. No gender differences were found with respect to relatedness, autonomy, or ego development.

RELATEDNESS, AUTONOMY, AND FAMILY INTERACTIONS

Higher levels of adolescent relatedness were closely associated, $r = .30$, $p < .02$, with the extent of their cognitive enabling (e.g., explaining, focusing, problem solving, and curiosity). Similarly, there was a connection between adolescents' relatedness and their affective enabling. There was a significant correlation between relatedness and affective enabling, $r = .35$, $p < .009$, as well as with each of the more discrete affective enabling categories (e.g., with empathy, $r = .39$, $p < .02$). Adolescents expressing higher levels of relatedness were more likely to show progressive change between their own successive speeches, drawing on the contributions of one or both parents.

In contrast, few associations were found for adolescents' autonomy. While adolescents who expressed higher levels of autonomy also showed more progressive discourse change, $r = .31$, $p < .02$, the only other significant correlation was with affective constraining (e.g., devaluing, excessive gratifying, indifference, and unyielding conviction). Subjects expressing lower levels of autonomy were more likely to express higher levels of affective constraining, $r = -.35$, $p < .04$.

Discussion

As predicted, adolescents' expressions of interests and understandings of long-term mutual relationships were associated with their ego development. In addition, also consistent with our expectations, adolescents' views about their assuming responsibility and control over their lives substantially correlated with their level of ego development. More specifically, adolescents with advanced levels of ego development tended to be more oriented toward (1) maintaining satisfying, close relationships with others, (2) achieving a well-differentiated, consolidated sense of self, and (3) responsibly managing their own affairs.

Since our newly devised coding system measures the ways in which an adolescent writes about relatedness and autonomy, it would be erroneous to assume that what we have detected necessarily reflects interpersonal skills or level of interpersonal competence. The fact that adolescents do not spontaneously respond to the sentence completion test with thoughtful references to relationship and/or autonomy matters could reflect their style of verbal expression rather than how they actually relate to others.

A second caution for us to consider here is that these discovered links between ego development and relatedness/autonomy could actually represent part-whole connections between important components of ego development—relatedness and autonomy—and the overall stage of development. However, our second set of analyses, focusing on adolescents' interactions with their parents during family discussions, reveals that the adolescents' expressions of relatedness and autonomy in their sentence completions are differentially associated with how they interact in their families. These family discussions were stimulated by a revealed differences task in which moral dilemmas, about which family members had specific differences of opinion, were presented to the family. The family's task was to defend their differences and attempt to reach a family consensus. When the constraining and enabling codes were applied to transcriptions of these audiotaped discussions, we found that adolescents who had showed high levels of relatedness in their sentence completions also tended to express more acceptance and empathy in their family interactions. Adolescents at higher levels of relatedness appeared to have more mutual and reciprocal relationships with their parents so that, for example, they not only responded to their parents' questions but were also interested in their parents' insights and thus stimulated further discussion. They were more likely than their peers at lower levels of relatedness to become engaged in heated, yet civil, discussions with their parents. Adolescents who scored lower on the relatedness scale often played a passive, indifferent, and/or subtly disruptive role in the family discussions.

Adolescents expressing higher levels of autonomy showed fewer constraining interactions in the family discussions. They were less likely to behave in devaluing or seductive ways and less likely to withhold their opinions from one or both parents. Similar to those adolescents expressing more relatedness, more autonomous subjects showed a clear progression in their discourse, speaking in more complex ways as the family's discussion unfolded.

Our results are consistent with recent findings reported by Allen and Hauser (1991). Using rating scales for autonomy and relatedness family behaviors, ego development was found to be positively correlated with behaviors that served to differentiate a person from others and those that served to strengthen a relationship through positive engagement, interest, and involvement in the other's feelings and ideas. Ego development was negatively related to those behaviors that reflected poor differentiation, little tolerance for differences of opinion, minimal involvement in the discussion, and little interest in the views of others.

To consider further how ego development, relatedness, and autonomy may appear in actual behaviors, we turn to case studies, assembled from the sentence completions and clinical interviews.[3] The adolescents whom we describe sketched themselves and their relationships to others by responding to the sentence completion test. They then elaborated on these first sketches through more expansive semistructured, clinical interviews, which took place shortly after they completed their sentence completions. The interviews show us ways in which the relatedness and autonomy themes initially observed in the sentence completions are closely connected with ways in which these adolescents experience autonomy and relatedness in their daily lives. Through the interviews, we see how increasing independence and self-definition may color relationships with family members and peers and how these relationships may inhibit or stimulate advancing self-governance and discovery.

TOM

A prominent aspect of Tom's life is his inability to regulate and control expression of strong feelings. This characteristic is indexed in his impulsive stage of ego development and in his expression of low-level relatedness and autonomy. As is typical of adolescents at the impulsive stage of ego development, Tom is seemingly unaware of how his actions affect others. He routinely acts on his impulses, leading to difficulties in beginning or sustaining friendships. He has particular difficulty controlling his anger:

> *Tom.* If someone double-crosses me or someone makes me bullshit or something, I want to whack them, and that's the way I feel, and I'll never change on that part.
> *Interviewer.* And what do you do? You want to whack them, do you?
> *Tom.* Yeah, I took a, I broke a kid's nose once cause he made me mad. . . . I can't talk when I'm bullshit because all I do is end up hollering, and I holler and I get louder and louder and louder, so I can't talk.

In his interview, Tom describes having no close friends. There is no one in his immediate or extended family to whom he feels close except for an uncle who is "all right." When speaking to the interviewer about other people in his life, Tom's voice sounds angry. Yet he does not spontaneously speak about this feeling, or other ones, in the interview.

Even when completing sentence stems that usually prompt expressions of sympathy or concern for another person, Tom gives no indication of any sensitivity toward another person's experience: "*When a child will not join in group activities*—he is stupid"; "*When people are helpless*—they are helpless."

KATE

Kate is at the self-protective stage of ego development. Consistently, she expresses higher-level relatedness and autonomy orientations than Tom. Kate's relationships with her family and peers are filled with conflict. She describes loving and hating the significant people in her life but sees no connections between these feelings. In both her sentence completions and her clinical interview, Kate comments at length on the people in her life. Yet these portraits are shadowed by pervasive hostility: *"Being with other people—sucks!"*

Despite her clear statement of disdain for being with others, Kate spends little time alone. In fact, she considers her main problem to be getting "too involved with people." Kate was one of the few adolescents who incorporated her friends by name into her sentence completions, at times suggesting a preoccupation with them: *"My conscience bothers me if—I* think about Michael."

When Kate becomes angry at people, or when she recognizes that they are angry at her, she stops talking to them, a pattern alluded to in one of her sentence completions: *"When they avoided me—I* avoided them." In her interview, Kate more clearly illustrates her transient rejecting and rejections. Kate explains what happens when she gets into a fight with her two friends:

Kate. I don't talk to them for around two days. And they get mad. They'll say, "Kate, do you want some of this," and I don't answer, and they get mad and don't talk to me either.

Interviewer. What happens next? How do you and your friends make up?

Kate. I either go . . . um . . . "I'll tell the teacher," or I just go up to her and say, "Now start talking." Or she does something for me. She gives me something.

Kate and her friends avoid talking about their problems. After a day or two, they may be ready to make up, but they do so only when one side gives in. As Kate so succinctly portrays it, either she orders her friends to start talking to her, or her friends bribe her to start talking to them.

This interaction style is common among adolescents at the preconformist level of ego development. Relationships at this stage are characterized by dependent, manipulative, and exploitative behavior. Of uppermost importance is *receiving*. People are valued primarily in terms of what they have to offer materially. In Kate's case, her friends are "forgiven" when they give her something. Resolution of difficulties does not result from a shared understanding of the conflict.

215

Later in the interview, Kate tells the interviewer that her father yells at her a lot:

> *Interviewer.*   How does it make you feel when your father yells at you?
> *Kate.*   OK. I usually just fall asleep in the middle of the yelling. Or I just leave.

By falling asleep, Kate probably tunes out her father; she "just leaves." Kate rarely sees associations among her feelings, thoughts, and ideas. Neither spontaneously nor in response to the interviewer's probes does she wonder about why her father yells at her or her reasons for leaving the scene.

JACOB

Jacob is at the transitional stage ("self-aware") between the conformist and the conscientious stages of ego development. Like the majority of adolescents at the conformist level, Jacob's relatedness orientations were considerably higher than those for autonomy. He expresses very positive, seemingly unconflicted, positive feelings about his parents: "*When he thought of his mother, he*—wished that someday his wife would be like that." And Jacob values the importance of spending time with loved ones and getting along with people: "*A man feels good when*—he's with the one he loves"; "*My main problem is*—getting along with my sisters." Particularly noteworthy is Jacob's sensitivity as he thinks about how to respond to a child who will not join in group activities: "*When a child will not join in group activities*—ask him what he would like to do, and then coax him a little bit."

Jacob feels very close to his family. His parents are separated, but he spends a significant amount of time with both of them. His three older sisters often make him feel as though he has "four mothers." They are always telling him what to do, what to wear, when to clean his room, when to study: "My mother, she'll remind me to clean my room, or something like that, but my oldest sister will rush me. She'll say, 'Do your room. You have to do it before Ma comes back. I want you to do it now!' And I don't like that. I just want to do it when I am ready to do it. But she makes me." Jacob is very conscientious about doing what he is told—by his sisters, his parents, his friends, or his teachers.

Jacob's orientations toward autonomy are at a different level. He recognizes that people have differing perspectives: "*When they talked about sex*—I tried to understand their point of view." Yet he focuses on his similarities with others and disregards the differences: "*Being with other people*—is great when you can agree on things." In his interview, Jacob reports not wanting to stand out from his peers. He tries to keep a low profile. The interviewer questions how he handles not understanding some of the material in his chemistry class: "Sometimes, if I am too shy to bring it up cause I think that the whole class might know it, then I won't say nothing; I feel too embarrassed. But if I really think it's something that the whole class is confused about, then I might bring it up." Worried over his peers' opinions of him, Jacob carefully refrains from doing or saying anything that would set him apart from them.

Jacob's social life is of central importance for him, so much so that it obstructs his work. In talking about how he spends his time in study hall, he says, "Well, sometimes, I try to do my work if I can. But usually when I'm around a group of people, I just get distracted, and just talk with them for the rest of the period." Spending time with his friends is such an attractive option that Jacob tends to neglect his studies. He spends a lot of time on the telephone at night and does not complete his homework during the day.

VALERIE

At the transitional stage between the conscientious and the autonomous ego development stages, Valerie expresses strikingly high levels of relatedness and autonomy. In her sentence completions, she refers to much warmth when writing about being with others and describes feeling close to both parents: "*Being with other people*—makes my life more interesting and exciting!!!" "*My mother and I*—are very close, more like friends, considering how open we are."

At the same time, Valerie describes herself as having a separate identity, being a person with her own interests and aspirations. Valerie has a strong awareness of her developing greater independence from her parents and older brothers. Yet she does not seek out independence at the expense of her relationships with her family. Her relationships expand to encompass her growing individuation. For instance, having always looked up to her two older brothers, she is beginning to gain a fuller picture of them, as she becomes more conscious of their weaknesses as well as their strengths: "I think that now I am closer to Charlie [her older brother]. Since we are in the same high school, I see more of him, so I see all his, you know, shortcomings. I know what other people think of him. Both of my brothers to me have always been kind of up on pillows. . . . I have always imagined my brother with girls trailing after him for miles. I think that my brother is really popular with girls, but they are hardly following him around the halls, like I imagined them. So, by seeing my brother [at school], it kind of takes him down a little, down to earth where he belongs."

Clearly, one reason that Valerie's relationships are as rich as they are is because of her considerable self-awareness and reflectiveness. She applies these strengths in many interpersonal situations, such as when she is having problems with friends and siblings. Valerie describes taking time to assess situations from her own perspective as well as someone else's. She tries to think before she acts, to gather enough information so that she can respond using her best judgment rather than reacting impulsively. A recent argument with her brother Marc began over whose turn it was to do the dishes. The altercation escalated until each was feeling furious with the other. Valerie was then tempted to tell him critical comments that she had heard about him in school. But she decided to restrain herself. Throughout the heated disagreement, she recalls trying to stay calm, a strategy that she thinks has been learned from watching her other older brother: "He said that I should listen to him and he was right and I was wrong, and I was wrong, and I was wrong. And I should listen to him and not move and to stay right there. . . . So I said, 'I'll listen to you if you'll keep calm, you know, don't yell at me.' So he said, 'I am not yelling at you,' and he was yelling while he said that. So I said, 'I am not going to listen to you if you're going to yell.' So I got up and went upstairs."

As Kate did with her father, Valerie ultimately walks away from the disagreement. However, unlike Kate's, Valerie's decision to remove herself from the heat was premeditated, based on an active decision rather than impulse. Her attempt to transform the fight into a discussion and her choice to delay speaking with her brother until he had calmed down are illuminating. Even in the midst of intense emotions, she could step back from the heat and make a balanced decision about how she wanted to handle the situation.

Valerie takes pride in the way she differs from others: "*I am*—different from a lot of kids, but I enjoy that." Her comfort in standing apart from her friends can be seen in her deciding to join extracurricular activities in which none of her friends participate. Valerie provides many examples of how relationships give her confidence in making new friends and exploring new interests. Considering why she finds it easy to develop new friendships, she says, "I think basically I'm willing to take the chance that they are not going to like me." The security that Valerie receives from her close friends and family makes her more comfortable initiating conversations with people she's never met before, an act that feels too risky for many adolescents—and adults.

Valerie recognizes the value of both taking care of her own needs and attending to those of others. In her sentence completions, she refers to this recognition: "*A good mother*—should love her family, but not neglect herself." Unlike the many adolescents who are so consumed by the demands of looking after themselves that they have little to offer in the way of psychological support to others, Valerie thinks about and responds to the needs of others: "*When people are helpless*—I want to help them"; "*When a child will not join in group activities*—they should be asked personally, maybe they are shy."

In her interview, this precocious sensitivity is even more visible. Many adolescents experience one-sided relationships with their parents where they give little thought to the needs or concerns of these adults. In contrast, Valerie has a serious interest in her parents' careers and their psychological well-being: "I have a different view of my father [a public official] than everybody, almost everybody in the town. There are people who hate him. There are people who love him, but I think there aren't that many people who really know what he goes through, how many late hours he works, and how long he works each day, and how many meetings he goes to in a week; how many battles he tries to fight. Sometimes I ask my father, 'Why do you do this to yourself? Why do you love this kind of job?' And he says he doesn't know. But during a vacation, he goes nuts because he loves that kind of job.'' Valerie shows an understanding of the complexity of her father's predicament. She responds empathically, recognizing both how hard he works and how much he enjoys it.

Conclusions

Increasingly enriched introspection and growing recognition of how one differs from others characterize more advanced stages of ego development. Assumptions and stereotypes are no longer taken for granted. At these stages, adolescents are more apt to recognize the nuances in people and situations, more likely to tolerate ambiguity and conflict. Growing cognitive complexity and tolerance of many simultaneous feelings contribute to more profound levels of self-discovery and also pave the way for enhanced intimacy with others. The capacity to recognize and cope with one's own inner conflict is an essential ingredient of being able to withstand and grow from conflicts in a relationship. People can be appreciated in a more complete and realistic way because interpersonal differences are less feared and more valued. They are less likely to need the security of exaggerated similarity because they recognize that differences and conflict are often an integral part of growing intimacy.

When an adolescent has achieved a more integrated and solid identity, the intensity of high levels of intimacy can be enjoyed rather than experienced as threatening. Less fearful, barriers to relationships are less rigid and more permeable. This breaking down of the ''protective armor,'' together with a more developed capacity for perspective taking, enables empathic communication—based on a genuine understanding of another's subjective experience. Relationships at this stage are grounded in sharing ideas, values, and feelings as well as shared participation in activities of mutual interest.

Both Valerie and Jacob describe strong connections with their families and peers, but their relationships are of a different nature. While Valerie's relationships are obviously important to her, their maintenance is not contingent on her sacrificing her independent interests, values, or beliefs in order to belong. On the other hand, Jacob resembles the majority of adolescents in our project, especially those at the conformist stages, in that his development of autonomy lags behind his development of relatedness and his relationships are affected accordingly. It may be that, by around fourteen years of age, most adolescents have developed a stronger basis for making connections with others than for functioning autonomously. This result corroborates findings that adolescents in the eighth and ninth grades are particularly susceptible to peer pressure, considerably more so than in early or late adolescence (Steinberg and Silverberg 1986). Perhaps at this age the need to make and sustain intimate friendships is so strong that it inhibits adolescents from venturing away from conventional group norms to discover and expand their unique interests and values.

It is likely that adolescents' lower levels of autonomy inhibit them from achieving the intimacy characteristic of the later stages. In the ninth grade, most adolescents are still living at home, under the supervision of their parents, under familial rules and regulations. They still rely very much on their parents for emotional support and guidance. In the midst of puberty, they are still adjusting to the physical and psychological changes characteristic of this age. While most adolescents are capable of looking after themselves and making some independent, responsible choices, parents still have considerable influence over their children's decisions such as who they befriend, which activities they partake in, when to study, and when to be home. Like those of others (e.g., Murphey et al. 1963), our findings suggest that the capacity for mature autonomous functioning is somewhat restricted and limited at this age. It has been well documented that the process of becoming autonomous is facilitated by the behavioral changes that follow leaving home (Murphey et al. 1963).

Correlational analyses are not sufficient for completely examining connections between relatedness and autonomy. Further research must look specifically at the complex interactions between these dimensions. One possibility to consider is turning again to the sentence completion test to develop a way to assess differences in the integration of these developmental tendencies. A sentence completion such as "*When they avoided me*—I felt bad and asked them why," reflecting how this adolescent goes about handling conflict with others, is revealing of both the related and the autonomous aspects of the self and how they are inextricably interwoven. This response suggests that this adolescent would not only acknowledge his feelings of sadness resulting from being avoided by his friends but also take the initiative in asking them why, what he had done to evoke such a response. This type of willingness to confront and resolve conflicts is indicative of an integration of autonomy and relatedness.

The present study explores several initial questions about the interplay of relatedness and autonomy during mid-adolescence. Our results suggest that these capacities are differentially expressed at different levels of ego development and most evenly balanced at the highest stages. However, further research is needed to understand this dynamic across a wider range of development and across the life cycle. This is one of the underlying considerations of a follow-up study in which we reexamine our original sample of adolescents, now in their young adult years (Allen and Hauser 1991; Hauser and Allen 1991).

Another question that we are currently investigating is how these orientations to relatedness and autonomy might be transmitted across generations. We have already looked at correlates between parents' and their children's levels of ego development and interaction styles (Hauser et al. 1984; Hauser et al. 1991). Parents may encourage their children's involvement in family discussions, and in social behavior in general, by being supportive of and interested in their children's views and ideas. They may ask focusing or provocative questions that affirm their respect and appreciation of their children's independent growth. In contrast, some parents tend to discourage and stifle their children's social behavior by being indifferent toward or disrespectful of their feelings and ideas. No doubt, adolescents influence their parents' contributions as well as being influenced by them. In the future, we plan to address how parents' orientations to these important issues may promote or interfere with their children's interaction patterns, ego development, and parenting of new offspring.

NOTES

1. Although there is some debate about the different connotations of "affective" and "emotional," we use these terms interchangeably throughout the chapter.

2. Supplementary descriptions of the stages can be found in Young-Eisendrath (in this volume), in the coding manual (Loevinger and Wessler 1970), and in an earlier review of the construct and measure (Hauser 1976).

3. All names and other identifying features used in this and the following case studies have been altered to maintain confidentiality.

REFERENCES

Ainsworth, M. D. S.; Blehar, M. C.; Waters, E.; and Wall, S. 1978. *Patterns of Attachment*. Hillsdale, N.J.: Erlbaum.

Allen, J.; Aber, J. L.; and Leadbeater, B. J. 1990. Adolescent problem behaviors: the influence of attachment and autonomy. *Clinics of North America* 13:455–467.

Allen, J. P., and Hauser, S. T. 1988. The autonomy and relatedness coding system. Harvard Medical School. Typescript.

Allen, J. P., and Hauser, S. T. 1991. Prediction of young adult attachment representations, psychological distress, social competence and hard drug use from family interactions in adolescence. Paper presented at the meeting of the Society for Research in Child Development, Seattle.

Armsden, G. C., and Greenberg, M. T. 1987. The inventory of parent and peer attachment: individual differences and their relationship to psychological well-being in adolescence. *Journal of Youth and Adolescence* 16:427–454.

Bakan, D. 1966. *The Duality of Human Existence*. Boston: Beacon.

Bar-Yam Hassan, A., and Bar-Yam, M. 1987. Interpersonal development across the life span: communion and its interaction with agency in psychosocial development. In J. A. Meacham, ed. *Contributions to Human Development*, vol. 18. Buffalo: Karger.

Berndt, T. 1982. The features and effects of friendship in early adolescence. *Child Development* 53:1447–1460.

Berscheid, E.; Snyder, M.; and Omoto, A. M. 1989. Issues in studying close relationships: conceptualizing and measuring closeness. In C. Hendrick, ed. *Review of Personality and Social Psychology*, vol. 10. Newbury Park, Calif.: Sage.

Blatt, S. J. 1990. Interpersonal relatedness and self-definition: two personality configurations and their implications for psychopathology and psychotherapy. In J. Singer, ed. *Repression and Dissociation: Implications for Personality Theory, Psychopathology, and Health*. Chicago: University of Chicago Press.

Blos, P. 1967. The second individuation process of adolescence. *Psychoanalytic Study of the Child* 1:183–198.

Bowlby, J. 1969. *Attachment and Loss*. Vol. 1, *Attachment*. New York: Basic.

Bowlby, J. 1977. The making and breaking of affectional bonds: aetiology and psychopathology in the light of attachment theory. *British Journal of Psychiatry* 130:201–210.

Bretherton, I. 1985. Attachment theory: retrospect and prospect. In I. Bretherton and E. Waters, eds. *Growing Points of Attachment Theory and Research*. Monographs of the Society for Research in Child Development, vol. 50, serial no. 209. Chicago: University of Chicago Press.

Chodorow, N. 1978. *The Reproduction of Mothering: Psychoanalysis and the Sociology of Gender*. Berkeley and Los Angeles: University of California Press.

Connell, J. P. 1990. Context, self, and action: a motivational analysis of self-system processes across the life-span. In D. Cicchetti, ed. *The Self in Transition: Infancy to Childhood*. Chicago: University of Chicago Press.

Cooper, C. R.; Grotevant, H. D.: and Condon, S. M. 1983. Individuation and connectedness in the family as a context for adolescent identity formation and role taking skill. *New Directions for Child Development* 22:43–60.

Douvan, E., and Adelson, J. 1966. *The Adolescent Experience*. New York: Wiley.

Erikson, E. 1963. *Childhood and Society*. New York: Norton.

Franz, C. E., and White, K. M. 1985. Individuation and attachment in personality: extending Erikson's theory. *Journal of Personality* 53:224–256.

Gilligan, C. 1982. *In a Different Voice*. Cambridge, Mass.: Harvard University Press.

Greenberger, E., and Sorensen, A. 1974. Toward a concept of psychosocial maturity. *Journal of Youth and Adolescence* 3:329–359.

Grotevant, H. D., and Cooper, C. R. 1985. Patterns of interaction in family relationships and the development of identity exploration in adolescence. *Child Development* 56:415–428.

Grotevant, H. D., and Cooper, C. R. 1986. Individuation in family relationships: a perspective on individual differences in the development of identity and role-taking skill in adolescence. *Human Development* 29:82–100.

Haan, N.; Stroud, J.; and Holstein, J. 1973. Moral and ego stages in relation to ego processes: a study of "hippies." *Journal of Personality* 41:596–612.

Harakel, C. M. 1971. Ego maturity and interpersonal style: a multivariate study of Loevinger's theory. Ph.D. diss., Catholic University. (*Dissertation Abstracts International* 32:1190B.)

Hauser, S. T. 1976. Loevinger's model and measure of ego development. *Psychological Bulletin* 83:928–955.

Hauser, S. T., and Allen, J. P. 1991. Antecedents of young adult ego development: the contributions of adolescent and parent ego development. Paper presented at the meeting of the Society for Research in Child Development, Seattle.

Hauser, S. T.; Houlihan, J.; Powers, S. I.; Jacobson, A. M.; Noam, G.; Weiss, B.; Perry, B.; Follansbee, D.; and Book, B. J. 1987. Interaction sequences in families of psychiatrically hospitalized and non-patient adolescents. *Psychiatry* 50:308–319.

Hauser, S. T.; Powers, S.; Jacobson, A.; Noam, G.; Weiss, B.; and Follansbee, D. 1984. Familial contexts of adolescent ego development. *Child Development* 55:195–213.

Hauser, S. T.; Powers, S.; and Noam, G. 1991. *Adolescents and Their Families: Paths of Ego Development*. New York: Free Press.

Hill, J. P.; and Holmbeck, G. N. 1986. Attachment and autonomy during adolescence. *Annals of Child Development* 3:145–189.

Hollingshead, A. B. 1957. Two-factor index of social position. Yale University. Mimeo.

Holt, R. R. 1980. Loevinger's measure of ego development: reliability and national norms for male and female short forms. *Journal of Personality and Social Psychology* 39:909–920.

Jordan, J. V. 1984. Empathy and self boundaries. Working paper. Wellesley, Mass.: Stone Center.

Jordan, J.; Surrey, J.; and Kaplan, A. 1982. Women and empathy. Working paper. Wellesley, Mass.: Stone Center.

Jourard, S. M. 1971. *The Transparent Self*. Rev. ed. New York: Van Nostrand–Reinhold.

Kegan, R. 1982. *The Evolving Self*. Cambridge, Mass.: Harvard University Press.

Kobak, R. R., and Sceery, A. 1988. Attachment in late adolescence: working models, affect regulation, and representations of self and others. *Child Development* 59:135–146.

Kohlberg, L., and Gilligan, C. 1971. The adolescent as philosopher. *Daedalus* 100(Fall): 1051–1086.

Lambert, H. V. 1972. A comparison of Jane Loevinger's theory of ego development and Lawrence Kohlberg's theory of moral development. Ph.D. diss., University of Chicago.

Loevinger, J. 1966. The meaning and measurement of ego development. *American Psychologist* 21:195–206.

Loevinger, J. 1969. Theories of ego development. In L. Breger, ed. *Clinical-Cognitive Psychology: Models and Integrations.* Englewood Cliffs, N.J.: Prentice-Hall.

Loevinger, J., and Wessler, R. 1970. *Measuring Ego Development,* vol. 1. San Francisco: Jossey-Bass.

Loevinger, J.; Wessler, R.; and Redmore, C. 1970. *Measuring Ego Development,* vol. 2. San Francisco: Jossey-Bass.

Maccoby, E. E. 1990. Gender and relationships. *American Psychologist* 45:513–520.

Murphey, E. B.; Silber, E.; Coelho, G. V.; Hamburg, D. A.; and Greenberg, I. 1963. Development of autonomy and parent-child interaction in late adolescence. *American Journal of Orthopsychiatry* 33:643–652.

Piaget, J. 1952. *Origins of Intelligence in Children.* New York: International Universities Press.

Redmore, C., and Waldman, K. 1975. Reliability of a sentence completion measure of ego development. *Journal of Personality Assessment* 39:236–243.

Selman, R. 1980. *The Development of Interpersonal Understanding: Developmental and Clinical Analysis.* New York: Academic.

Selman, R., and Schultz, L. H. 1990. *Making a Friend in Youth: Developmental Theory and Pair Therapy.* Chicago: University of Chicago Press.

Sessa, F. M., and Steinberg, L. In press. Family structure and the development of autonomy during adolescence. *Journal of Early Adolescence.*

Stechler, G., and Kaplan, S. 1980. The development of the self: a psychoanalytic perspective. *Psychoanalytic Study of the Child* 35:85–106.

Steinberg, L., and Silverberg, S. B. 1986. The vicissitudes of autonomy in early adolescence. *Child Development* 57:841–851.

Stern, D. N. 1985. *The Interpersonal World of the Infant: A View from Psychoanalysis and Developmental Psychology.* New York: Basic.

Stierlin, H. 1974. *Separating Parents and Adolescents.* New York: Aronson.

Strodtbeck, F. L. 1958. Husband-wife interaction over revealed differences. *American Sociological Review* 16:468–473.

Sullivan, H. S. 1953. *The Interpersonal Theory of Psychiatry.* New York: Norton.

Surrey, J. 1983. The self in relation: a theory of women's development. Working paper. Wellesley, Mass.: Stone Center.

Veroff, J., and Veroff, J. B. 1980. *Social Incentives: A Life Span Developmental Approach.* New York: Academic.

White, K. M.; Speisman, J. C.; and Costos, D. 1983. Young adults and their parents: individuation to mutuality. In H. D. Grotevant and C. R. Cooper, eds. *New Directions for Child Development,* vol. 22, *Adolescent Development in the Family.* San Francisco: Jossey-Bass.

Youniss, J. 1980. *Parents and Peers in Social Development.* Chicago: University of Chicago Press.

13 THE RELATIONAL SELF: IMPLICATIONS FOR ADOLESCENT DEVELOPMENT

JUDITH V. JORDAN

Prevailing theories of "the self" focus on its bounded, separate, and agentic qualities. Clinical and developmental approaches have emphasized autonomy and individuation. The capacity to use abstract thought, a sense of self as origin of action and intention, increased exercise of self-control, and movement toward self-sufficiency characterize the mature Western self. This tends to be a decontextualized and reified picture of the self. Several theorists in the psychology of women have suggested that such a notion of self may not accurately represent women's self experience (Gilligan 1982; Jordan 1989; Jordan, Kaplan, Miller, Stiver, and Surrey 1991; Miller 1984; Surrey 1985); alternative descriptions have included "self-in-relation" (Jordan and Surrey 1986; Surrey 1985), "being in relation" (Miller 1984), and "relational self" (Jordan 1989).

The study of the self as a kind of molecular entity is based on the Newtonian model of physics in which discrete, separate entities are taken as the primary data; these are secondarily seen as interacting with each other in predictable ways. While physics has moved on to an understanding of matter as being centrally about movement, interconnections, and flow, psychology has continued to conceptualize the self as atomistic—separate and discrete.

Another influence on theory building about the self came from the sociopolitical assumptions of Western, democratic societies. Very generally speaking, these involve the celebration of individualism, personal freedom, self-sufficiency, and personal rights. In this model, we expect the fully mature individual to be able to take care of himself or herself (and possibly a family) and to be free of dependence on others.

Classic Freudian theory stressed the power of innate instinctual forces and the need to develop intrapsychic structure to manage these impulses; relationships were seen as secondary to the satisfaction of drives. In this theory, the primary source of motivation is the pleasure principle; satisfaction of need is seen as the central motivating influence as the organism attempts to achieve some relief from unpleasant stimulation (hunger, thirst, sexual appetite, etc.). Although not using the language of "the self," Freud's original *das Ich,* later translated as "ego," performs many of the functions that "the self" does in others' theories. This ego was importantly there to protect the organism from the onslaught of impulses from within and demands from without. He noted, "Protection against stimuli is an almost more important function for the living organism than reception of stimuli" (Freud 1920, p. 27).

The object relations theorists made some modifications of classical Freudian theory and placed relationships at the center of human development. They were, however, unable completely to free themselves of the core drive concepts in Freudian theory and continued, in their language, to view the other person as "object" of the subject's needs. The bias of a basically self-interested organism, driven by personal greed and innate aggression, is honored in this theory. Thus, Melanie Klein (1953) traces the development of a capacity for love to the infant's wish to make reparations to the mother for harm inflicted. Winnicott (1963) carries this notion forward in his work on the development of a capacity for concern.

Fairbairn (1952) and Guntrip (1973) succeeded in moving more in the direction of the primacy of relatedness. In particular, Fairbairn appreciated the ongoing dependence of human beings, and Guntrip emphasized the importance of mutuality in relationships. However, in this country, the dominant object relations theory appears to derive from the Kleinian position, which emphasizes the primacy of aggression and injury, rather than primary positive relatedness, in the establishment of concern or love.

Sullivan (1953), Horney (1926), and Thompson (1941) made major contributions to the building of an interpersonal theory of self. Sullivan noted, "A personality can never be isolated from the complex of interpersonal relations in which the person lives and has his being" (1953, p. 10). What was missing in this construction, however, was the notion of a self actively engaged in mutual interaction. Sullivan tended to see the self as somewhat inactive in this process, constructed of "reflected appraisals."

Erikson's (1963) ego identity may come close to what others refer to as "a self." While Erikson successfully moves away from the psychosexual model of development, stressing the importance of psychosocial factors, his delineation of ego identity importantly rests on the development of a sense of autonomy. Intimacy comes later. In fact, the main thrust of development, until late in life, seems to be toward mastery, industry, and separation.

Kohut's (1984) theory also has recognized the importance of relationships; his work, however, stresses the centrality of empathy and mirroring from others for the development of the individual's self-esteem. Late in his life, he seemingly reluctantly acknowledged the ongoing need for selfobjects throughout life. Needing selfobjects, however, is not the same as needing other people. Selfobjects are under the fantasied control of the individual, and they continue to be used by the person to perform some function for the self (self-esteem regulation); they are indeed objects of a need. Further, there is an implication that, in the best of all possible worlds, the selfobject function would be internalized and the self would be narcissistically sufficient unto itself.

Daniel Stern's work on mother-infant interaction has articulated the primary relatedness between infant and mother; he speaks of "being with the other" (Stern 1986). Early patterns of differentiation and relatedness, in which mother and infant participate in a mutually regulated relationship, are traced in his work. Trevarthan (1979) studied the "primary intersubjectivity" in human beings, which he considers as innate and unfolding. Earlier, George Klein had posited the existence of "we" identities, an "aspect of one's self construed as a necessary part of a unit transcending one's autonomous actions" (Klein 1976, p. 178).

A contextual-relational perspective of self also resonates with the work of the symbolic interactionists (Baldwin 1897; Cooley 1902; Mead 1925). And there are similarities to the existential approach, which emphasizes "being-with-others" (Tiryakian 1968). Some have also described development through the movement of dialectical schema (Basseches 1980). Basically, all these works are seeking a fuller representation of context in the understanding of the person; there is also a movement from a primary emphasis on structure to process. Thus, the notion of self-boundaries, often seen as providing protection, form, and demarcation between inside and outside in the more traditional conceptualizations of self, might better be understood from a relational point of view as being about communication, exchange, and receptivity. Piaget's (1952) model of adaptation, with accommodation and assimilation occurring in an ever-shifting process of equilibration, is helpful in conceptualizing the changing, ongoing, and interactive quality of relational development. One's interpersonal reality is changed in interaction just as the other's reality is altered; there is a fluidity of relational images. The negotiation of sameness and difference is crucial to relational development.

In the past decade, the impetus for rethinking our concepts of self has come very importantly from feminist psychologists. These scholars have been increasingly dissatisfied with the application of traditional models of self to women; in almost all cases when male standards of self development are applied to women, their differentness is viewed as deficiency. This has been most obvious and distressing in the area of relatedness or connection versus separation.

As Gilligan notes, "The disparity between women's experience and the representation of human development, noted throughout the psychological literature, has generally been seen to signify a problem in women's development. Instead, the failure of women to fit existing models of human growth may point to a problem in the representation, a limitation in the conception of the human condition, an omission of certain truths about life" (Gilligan 1982, pp. 1–2). Very specifically, Gilligan, Miller (1976), and others note the failure of previous theories of "human development" to appreciate the relational nature of women's sense of themselves. Miller explicitly questions whether the concept of self as we use it is applicable to women's experience.

This new body of theory, a relational model of development, is being created by a number of different researchers and clinicians (Belenky, Clinchy, Goldberger, and Mattuck 1986; Chodorow 1978; Gilligan 1982; Jordan 1984, 1985; Jordan et al. 1991; Jordan and Surrey 1986; Kaplan 1984; Miller 1976; Stiver 1984; Surrey 1985). It is an intersubjective perspective that focuses on the movement of mutual initiative and responsiveness; mutual empathy and empowerment are seen as core organizing dynamics in women's lives. The primary feature of

231

development is increasing empathic responsiveness in the context of interpersonal mutuality.

The development of mutual empathy, characterized by the flow of empathic attunement between people, alters the traditional model of boundedness and separateness. In full mutual empathic understanding, the sense of "separate self" is experientially altered. Empathy has been described as "sharing in and comprehending the momentary psychological state of another person" (Schafer 1959, p. 345). When two people join in empathic attunement, the distinctions between subject and object blur; knower and known come together in mutual empathy. Both become subjects and objects in the process of understanding. The resonant physiological mirroring that often accompanies empathy (sometimes called vicarious affective arousal) furthers this experience of "joining with" the other person, lessening one's subjective sense of separate self. Typically, women experience more vicarious affective arousal than men do in situations of empathic arousal (Hoffman 1977).

Studies of one- to two-day-old infants support the notion that there is a readiness for responsiveness to another's experience, possibly the early underpinnings for more elaborate empathic responsiveness later in life. Thus, at one to two days of age, infants demonstrate distress cries to other infants' wails of distress (Sagi and Hoffman 1976; Simner 1971).

While I have been suggesting that, in general, we may need to rethink our conceptualizations of self, it is also possible that we have two broadly different patterns of socializing individuals by gender that lead to very different experiences of self. I would like to speculate (and share clinical impressions to support these speculations) about some differences in male and female functioning around the notion of a more contained, separate self versus a relational, contextual self. Empathy is an important factor in the development of a relational sense of self; the capacity for empathy depends a great deal on one's openness to affective arousal, vulnerability to being moved by inner and outer experience, clear articulation of emotions, and lack of a need for a certain kind of control or power over others.

The way in which we conceive of self boundaries greatly influences our interactions with our world. And the way in which we conceptualize our place in the world broadly affects interpretive, meaning-making, value-generating activity. The nature of relatedness and of our understanding of self boundaries shapes our openness to new experience and the quality of revelations about inner experience that occur between people. If "self" is conceived of as separate, alone, "in control," personally achieving, and mastering nature, others may tend to be perceived as potential competitors, dangerous intruders, or objects to be used for the self's enhancement. A system that defines the self as separate and hierarchically measurable is usually marked in Western cultures by power-based dominance patterns. In such a system, one seeks to exercise self-control, minimize affective display (particularly those feelings suggesting loss of control), and maintain independence. Abstract logic is seen as superior to what has been called "connected knowing" (Belenky et al. 1986). While somewhat caricatured here, this represents much of the prescribed socialization for males in Western societies. I have suggested this be called the "objectifying/power/control mode" (Jordan 1987). Relationships in this system are in important ways about power, entitlement, hierarchy (being better than or higher than); one feels safe and clear in separation rather than in connection.

If, on the other hand, the individual is socialized toward connection and empathic responsiveness, as are girls, the experience of self may be quite different. While men feel most vital and "at home" in separation, women feel most themselves, most safe, most alive, in connection (Pollak and Gilligan 1982). Where connection shapes one's sense of self, self boundaries are more flexible and open, as the longing for connectedness is seen as a powerful need and an end in itself. In other words, relationships are not means to some end, as they are when power is the main dynamic. When they are mutual and growth enhancing, relationships are intrinsically satisfying and sought. The motivational principle operating here suggests that we move toward "expansion rather than satisfaction" (Jordan 1987). As Jean Baker Miller (1984) has suggested, good relationships lead to the desire for more relatedness.

Several explanations have been put forward regarding these gender differences in the experience of boundedness and self. Chodorow (1978) suggests there is a much longer preoedipal period for the girl; this allows the girl a prolonged time of closeness and primary identification with the mother, which is interrupted at an earlier age for the boy. In her modification of the object relations/analytic depiction of development, Chodorow further points to the abrupt shift in identification away from mother that the boy must make at an early age. Noticing differentness, defining himself as "different from mother," then, becomes very important as the young boy seeks to establish secure masculine identification. Chodorow further notes that the boy is treated more as "object" by the mother. These differences in intrapsychic development, in Chodorow's opinion, lead to more "permeable boundaries" in girls and a greater premium on separation and protection from others in boys.

Lynn (1962) hypothesized that the nature of identification is different for boys and girls by virtue of the roles that mothers and fathers play in the socialization of young children. Owing to father's absence, boys are left identifying with a distant father, an "abstract role" rather than a particular, interacting person in a rich context of relatedness. Girls, on the other hand, identify with the present, real, and contextual mother.

I would also like to suggest that boys are socialized toward a power/dominance experience of self while girls are socialized toward a love/empathy mode of self (Jordan 1987). The former stresses discontinuity between self and other and decreased empathic attunement; the latter enhances the movement of mutual effect and growth. These ways of organizing self-experience have far-reaching effects on many aspects of our lives.

These two diverging, gendered ways of experiencing our sense of ourselves often collide in adolescence. The differences become paramount particularly in the ways in which boys and girls handle intimacy and sexuality. On the one hand, boys move into establishing themselves clearly as men; as such, they are to be powerful, in control, instrumental, nonemotional, increasingly abstract, rational, and independent. On the other hand, they are to prove themselves as heterosexually competent. Their sexuality is usually portrayed as being peremptory, powerful, pushing for discharge. Sexuality often becomes a part of a general system of performance; it can be competitive and part of an effort to achieve the status of a grown-up, sexually mature man. Both sides of this pressure are captured in statements by two different men about their first experience of sexual intercourse: the first noted, "I just wanted to get it over with and hoped I wouldn't be too humiliated." The other, reflecting on the powerful importance of this event, noted, "After I had sex the first time, I said to myself, 'OK, now I can die.'"

Desire for sexual intercourse makes the boy aware of his need of the other person (the girl), which conflicts with his increasing need to present himself as manly and superindependent. His need for the other is then often repudiated. Frequently, as a result, the girl is treated like a sex object or denigrated in some fashion. The emphasis on power and the establishment of "manliness" takes the boy away from the centrality of the relationship and his own real vulnerability in these sexual explorations.

From the girl's point of view, the story unfolds differently. In recalling their adolescent sexuality, few women speak about the surge of genital strivings that is so often written about in describing adolescent sexuality. This may be another instance of "male development" being inaccurately described as "human development." Rather, most women speak about remembering the importance of relationships with boys when they were adolescents; they speak about the excitement and the initiative being taken by the boy. They recall being very aroused in early sexual explorations, but, more often in referring to their most intense pleasure in sexuality, they speak of intimacy, tenderness, and feeling loved. While orgasm is noted as a powerful experience, it seems to be less sought in a goal-oriented way in relationships by adolescent girls. For them, the meaning and joy of sexuality largely derives from the interpersonal joining and sharing.

The adolescent girl, then, often experiences herself as being the object of the boy's peremptory sexual urge rather than fully getting to know her own sexuality. There is a shared notion that the boy's pressure for sexual discharge must be alleviated, that there is some entitlement to sexual intercourse if the boy is aroused. And the socialization of the girl toward accommodation and caretaking, as well as her investment in the relationship, often leads to a sexuality organized more around the boy's needs than the girl's during adolescence. In these interactions, the boy becomes more agentic, centered on his own needs, developing a sense of sexual entitlement and more concerned with assuming his place in the male hierarchy. The girl, on the other hand, feels less in touch with her own body experience and more responsive to the needs of the other. The shared delight of mutual exploration and excitement can be lost in these early sexual exchanges.

Adolescent failures of mutuality may be largely determined by the disparate ways in which girls and boys organize their sense of self. These differences show up later in life in the profound difficulties that men and women have communicating with one another. Men become less self-disclosing (Jourard 1971), while women seek emotional ex-

235

pressiveness and define intimacy often in terms of close, open, verbal sharing. In groups, men seek clarity about power hierarchies and quickly establish patterns of dominance (O'Leary, Unger, and Wallston 1985), while women focus on creating connections that minimize patterns of dominance. Typically, women seek help when having trouble, while men attempt to solve the problem for themselves. When couples encounter difficulty, men often suggest more sexual engagement as a way through the problem, while women often insist that the relational difficulty must be solved before sexual intimacy can occur.

In summary, relational abilities and competencies exist from the time of birth and develop over the course of our lives. In most cultures, the ideal self is organized in complex and compelling ways along gender lines. In this culture, we value the image of a separate, autonomous, powerful, and objective male, while, in women, we encourage the capacity to connect with people, empathy, and nurturance. Different values, motivational patterns, ways of knowing (Belenky et al. 1986), moral systems (Gilligan 1982), organization of interpersonal experience (Jordan 1987), and spheres of influence have been delineated by gender.

From a relational perspective, human beings are seen as experiencing an essential need for connection and emotional joining. While the initial arena for studying this has been in reworking our understanding of the psychology of women, I am suggesting that a larger paradigm shift from the primacy of "separate self" to "relational being" must be considered in order to expand and deepen our understanding of all human experience.

NOTE

Portions of this chapter appeared in *The Self: Interdisciplinary Approaches,* ed. J. Strauss and G. Goethals (New York: Springer, 1991), and in J. V. Jordan, "The Relational Self: A New Perspective for Understanding Women's Development," *Contemporary Psychotherapy Review* 7 (1992): 56–72, and are reprinted here with permission.

REFERENCES

Baldwin, J. 1897. The self-conscious person. In C. Gordon and K. Gergen, eds. *The Self in Social Interaction.* New York: Wiley, 1968.

Basseches, M. 1980. Dialectical schemata: a framework for the empirical study of the development of dialectical thinking. *Human Development* 23:400–421.

Belenky, M.; Clinchy, B.; Goldberger, N.; and Mattuck, J. 1986. *Women's Way of Knowing: The Development of Self, Voice, and Mind.* New York: Basic.

Chodorow, N. 1978. *The Reproduction of Mothering: Psychoanalysis and the Sociology of Gender.* Berkeley and Los Angeles: University of California Press.

Cooley, C. H. 1902. The social self: on the meanings of "I." In C. Gordon and K. Gergen, eds. *The Self in Social Interaction.* New York: Wiley, 1968.

Erikson, E. 1963. *Childhood and Society.* New York: Norton.

Fairbairn, W. 1952. *Object Relationships and Dynamic Structure: An Object Relations Theory of Personality.* New York: Basic.

Freud, S. 1920. Beyond the pleasure principle. *Standard Edition* 18:3–64. London: Hogarth, 1955.

Gilligan, C. 1982. *In a Different Voice.* Cambridge, Mass.: Harvard University Press.

Guntrip, H. 1973. *Psychoanalytic Theory, Therapy and the Self.* New York: Basic.

Hoffman, M. 1977. Sex differences in empathy and related behaviors. *Psychological Bulletin* 84(4): 712–722.

Horney, K. 1926. The flight from womanhood. In H. Kelman, ed. *Feminine Psychology.* New York: Norton, 1967.

Jordan, J. 1984. Empathy and self boundaries. Working Paper no. 16. Wellesley, Mass.: Stone Center.

Jordan, J. 1985. The meaning of mutuality. Working Paper no. 23. Wellesley, Mass.: Stone Center.

Jordan, J. 1987. Clarity in connection: empathic knowing, desire and sexuality. Working Paper no. 29. Wellesley, Mass.: Stone Center.

Jordan, J. 1989. Relational development: therapeutic implications of empathy and shame. Working paper. Wellesley, Mass.: Stone Center.

Jordan, J.; Kaplan, A.; Miller, J. B.; Stiver, I.; and Surrey, J. 1991. *Women's Growth in Connection.* New York: Guilford.

Jordan, J., and Surrey, J. 1986. The self-in-relation: empathy and the mother-daughter relationship. In T. Bernay and D. Cantor, eds. *The Psychology of Today's Woman: New Psychoanalytic Visions.* New York: Analytic.

Jourard, S. 1971. *The Transparent Self.* New York: Van Nostrand.

Kaplan, A. 1984. The self-in-relation: implications for depression in women. Working Paper no. 14. Wellesley, Mass.: Stone Center.

Klein, G. 1976. *Psychoanalytic Theory: An Explanation of Essentials.* New York: International Universities Press.

Klein, M. 1953. *Love, Hate, and Reparation.* With Joan Riviere. London: Hogarth.

Kohut, H. 1984. *How Does Analysis Cure?* Chicago: University of Chicago Press.

Lynn, D. 1962. Sex role and parental identification. *Child Development* 33(3): 555–564.

Mead, G. H. 1925. The genesis of the self. In C. Gordon and K. Gergen, eds. *The Self in Social Interaction.* New York: Wiley, 1968.

Miller, J. B. 1976. *Toward a New Psychology of Women.* Boston: Beacon.

Miller, J. B. 1984. The development of women's sense of self. Working Paper no. 12. Wellesley, Mass.: Stone Center.

O'Leary, V.; Unger, R.; and Wallston, B. 1985. *Women, Gender and Social Psychology.* Hillsdale, N.J.: Erlbaum.

Piaget, J. 1952. *The Origins of Intelligence in Children.* New York: Norton.

Pollak, S., and Gilligan, C. 1982. Images of violence in thematic apperception test stories. *Journal of Personality and Social Psychology* 42(1): 159–167.

Sagi, A., and Hoffman, M. 1976. Empathic distress in newborns. *Developmental Psychology* 12:175–176.

Schafer, R. 1959. Generative empathy in the treatment situation. *Psychoanalytic Quarterly* 28:342–373.

Simner, M. 1971. Newborn's response to the cry of another infant. *Developmental Psychology* 5:135–150.

Stern, D. 1986. *The Interpersonal World of the Infant.* New York: Basic.

Stiver, I. 1984. The meanings of "dependency" in female-male relationships. Working Paper no. 11. Wellesley, Mass.: Stone Center.

Sullivan, H. S. 1953. *The Interpersonal Theory of Psychiatry.* New York: Norton.

Surrey, J. 1985. Self-in-relation: a theory of women's development. Working Paper no. 13. Wellesley, Mass.: Stone Center.

Thompson, C. 1941. Cultural processes in the psychology of women. *Psychiatry* 4:331–339.

Tiryakian, E. 1968. The existential self and the person. In C. Gordon and K. Gergen, eds. *The Self in Social Interactions*. New York: Wiley.

Trevarthan, C. 1979. Communication and cooperation in early infancy: a description of primary intersubjectivity. In J. M. Bullower, ed. *Before Speech: The Beginning of Interpersonal Communication*. New York: Cambridge University Press.

Winnicott, D. 1963. The development of the capacity for concern. *Bulletin of the Menninger Clinic* 27:167–176.

14 THE EPIGENESIS OF RELATIONAL SYSTEMS: A REVISED DEVELOPMENTAL PERSPECTIVE

LYMAN C. WYNNE

This chapter builds on the core hypothesis that relational processes within families and other enduring interpersonal systems follow one another in a certain developmental sequence. Do distortions of sequential patterning in the development of relational systems predictably lead to distress or to constrictions of growth? If so, what are the implications for assessment and intervention?

The present preliminary formulation builds on and revisits earlier hypotheses. My starting point for these ideas was the outline of a theory of relatedness. My colleagues and I postulated that a *dilemma* emerges in interpersonal systems because of the universal primary "striving for relatedness to other human beings" and the simultaneous striving "to develop a sense of personal identity" (Wynne, Ryckoff, Day, and Hirsch 1958, p. 206).

The Concept of Epigenesis

In 1965, we (Singer and Wynne 1965, p. 208) noted that our view of development was encompassed by the *epigenetic* principle:

The interchanges or transactions of each developmental phase build upon the outcome of earlier transactions. This means that constitutional and experiential influences recombine in each developmental phase to create new biological and behavioral potentialities which then help determine the next phase. If the transactions at any given developmental phase are distorted or omitted, all the subsequent developmental phases will be altered because they build upon a different substrate. We hypothesize that the family environment needs to provide certain kinds of influences in each maturational phase of the individual. What is appropriate and what may have psychopathological consequences thus varies over time and must always be considered in this developmental context.

For psychologists and psychiatrists, the most familiar reference to the "epigenetic principle" is by Erik Erikson (1956), who proposed a schema of stepwise, successive changes in ego formation out of a "ground plan" from which parts arise, "each part having its time of special ascendency" (p. 92). He identified eight stages in the individual life cycle, beginning with basic trust, proceeding in adolescence to the consolidation of identity, and going on to generativity and integrity in the final developmental stages. Erikson (1968, p. 93) argued that "the healthy child, given a reasonable amount of proper guidance, can be trusted to obey inner laws of development, laws which create a succession of potentialities for significant interaction with those persons who tend and respond to him and those institutions which are ready for him. While such interaction varies from culture to culture, it must remain within 'the proper rate and the proper sequence' which governs all epigenesis."

Here I am proposing that the principles and processes of epigenetic development in relational systems, beyond the person or personality as a system, be explicitly considered. I take it as axiomatic that relatedness and relational systems of more than one person constitute a system level different from that of individual psychology. I believe that it is possible and useful to distinguish those relational systems that Charles Cooley (1909) called "primary groups": "those characterized by intimate face-to-face association and cooperation" with a unity, not of "mere harmony," but always "a differentiated and usually a competitive unity, admitting of self-assertion and various appropriate passions; but these passions are socialized by sympathy and come, or tend to come, under the discipline of a common spirit" (p. 23). The principal example of a primary group is, of course, the family. In broad agreement with Cooley, I believe that the patterning and quality of relatedness are more crucial issues than the specific number

1. Attachment/ caregiving	Emotional overinvolvement	"Flat" detachment	Criticism/ hostility
2. Communicating	Amorphous communication deviance	Constrictive guarded communication	Fragmented communication deviance
3. Joint problem solving	Cyclic "solutions" and ruptures	Evasion of problem solving	Disruptive disagreement
4. Mutuality	Unstable pseudomutuality	Rigid, syntonic pseudomutuality	Pseudohostility
(5. Intimacy)	(Romanticized relatedness)	("Ho-hum" relatedness)	(Coercive/ submissive relatedness)

Fig. 1.—Major processes, and illustrative dysfunctions, in the epigenesis of enduring relational systems. The sequence may stop progressing at any stage. Intimacy is not essential for enduring relatedness, but, if and when it becomes *reliably* available, intimacy is a subjective corollary of mutuality.

of persons or the name given to the primary group (family, marriage, intimate friendship, etc.).

My primary purpose here is to introduce what I believe has been a neglected perspective, a developmental, epigenetic view of the *processes* of relational systems. Four processes appear to unfold epigenetically in relational systems: (1) *attachment/caregiving,* complementary affectional bonding; (2) *communicating,* sharing foci of attention and exchanging meanings and messages; (3) *joint problem solving* and renewable sharing of tasks, interests, and activities; and (4) *mutuality,* patterns of reengagement, renewing and deepening each of the preceding modes of relatedness in a shifting pattern linked to the internal states of the participants and the external context.

Relational Processes as Dimensionalized Systems

As figure 1 suggests, each of these four concepts can be regarded as the "positive" pole of a dimension or a domain. The corresponding "negative" pole, or side, for each is some form of relational distancing, divergence, differentiation, or relational failure. The positive side of each process, such as attachment/caregiving, implies (evokes?) the potentiality of a negative counterpart, such as separation. For example, the intensity of attachment/caregiving is strengthened by appropriately timed separation, whereas excessively prolonged and poorly timed separation can lead to detachment/rejection. In relational systems, experiences of detachment/rejection are as essential to the further development of relatedness as are the experiences of attachment/caregiving. The potentiality of impasse and disorder is implicit in the concept of a fluctuating range of functioning at each stage. But impasse may also be a precondition for creative new solutions. This point is reminiscent of what I once called "the anguish, and creative passions, of *not* escaping double binds" (Wynne 1976, p. 243; italics added).

The Family Life Cycle

In an extensive literature in both family sociology (Duvall 1962; Hill 1964) and family therapy (Carter and McGoldrick 1980; Grunebaum and Bryant 1966; Haley 1973; Solomon 1973), family development has been studied in terms of the concept of the family life cycle. The most pivotal criterion for making transitions between stages in the family life cycle has been the exit and entry of family members, that is, changes in the formal structure or composition of the family with births, deaths, marriage, divorce, and geographic moves. The partial departure of children from the family system, first into the school system, and later into extrafamilial adolescent life, and the family as a launching center for adolescents who are leaving home provide marker points in the normatively defined family life cycle. Much has been written about the problems for *individuals* who are not developmentally or experientially ready for those transitions. My concern here is with the problems for the relational system when the quality of relating is inappropriate or provides a poor fit between persons at the time of these structural changes. Therefore, conceptually, the family life cycle is not, except in an idealized norm, a truly epigenetic process in which each stage builds on the preceding stage in an expectable form. What is crucial for my present formulation is the point that many of these life-cycle changes in family role structure proceed regardless of the quality of relating of the participants at that time.

Attachment/Caregiving

Bowlby's 1958 paper "The Nature of the Child's Tie to His Mother" sparked a massive amount of research and speculation under the loose heading of "attachment theory." Some of these studies focused on unidirectional attachment behavior of the infant to the mother and did not refer to the mother-infant relational system. Other researchers (Klaus and Kennell 1976; Leiderman and Seashore 1975) have observed what they call "bonding" in the direction of mother to infant that takes place abruptly almost immediately after the birth of an infant, provided that conditions are optimal. The fully complementary "attachment" of infant to mother develops only gradually during the infant's first six months or so of life. There is also evidence (e.g., Peterson, Mehl, and Leiderman 1979) that fathers may become affectively "bonded" to their infants.

Unidirectional models of attachment and bonding are being replaced by more systemic and transactional concepts (Svejda, Pannabecker, and Emde 1982). Bowlby (1969, 1980) carefully noted that attachment behavior takes place in a feedback system in which the complementary function is caregiving. Some authors (e.g., Svejda et al. 1982) have broadened their use of the term "attachment" to refer to both the parental growth of love for the infant and the reciprocal tie from infant to parent. Hinde (1982) uses the term "attachment behavior system" much as family system theorists would refer to the feedback processes that "incorporate sensitivity to and expectations about the other participant—what Bowlby called a 'working model' of the other" (p. 54). Similarly, Sroufe, Fox, and Pancake (1983, p. 1616) note that the concept of a situationally "flexible *organization* of behavior" in the service of the "affective bond" between the prototypical infant and caregiver is now a central feature of attachment theory.

Present-day attachment theory also specifies that "attachment/caregiving" refers to the relatedness between infant and a hierarchy of specific caregivers, in contrast to dependency and other behaviors of the child toward people *in general* (Ainsworth 1982; Sroufe et al. 1983). Interestingly, this specification of certain persons, rather than others, is also a distinction, made from an entirely different research starting point, by Brown, Birley, and Wing (1972), Vaughn and Leff (1976), and other researchers working with the concept of "expressed emotion" (EE). Expressed emotion is operationally defined in terms of the attitudes expressed by a relative about a *specific* family member (patient) with whom there has been considerable face-to-face contact. The EE concept is nontransactional and unidirectional (from relative to patient), not measuring feedback and multiperson processes; but the two major components of EE, emotional overinvolvement and criticism, can readily be understood as special forms of attachment/caregiving that are likely to lead to dysfunctional communicating, problem solving, and intimacy.

As Ainsworth (1982) notes in an excellent review, there is not yet full consensus about the terminology and criteria used in attachment theory, and further research is needed. Nevertheless, much animal and human research on the basic concept of attachment/caregiving has gone far toward validating this construct as the starting point for what I am calling the epigenesis of relational systems (Ainsworth, Blehar, Walters, and Wall 1978; Sroufe 1979; Weiss 1982).

To be relevant to a generalized model of relatedness, the concept of attachment/caregiving should be applicable throughout life, not just to parent-infant transactions. Weiss (1982) has written a valuable review of the unfolding of attachment/caregiving systems into adolescence and adulthood. He particularly identifies three criteria for attachment: need for proximity to the attachment figure in situations of distress; heightened comfort and diminished anxiety in the company of the attachment figure; and marked increase in discomfort and anxiety on the discovery that accessibility to the attachment figure is threatened. Weiss considers whether these criteria characterize all "face-to-face" enduring relationships of the kind Cooley (1909) referred to as "primary." Weiss concludes that "attachment in adults is an expression of the same emotional system, though one modified in the course of its development, as is attachment in children" (1982, p. 175). He notes that these differences include, first, that "attachment in adults is not nearly so capable of overwhelming other behavioral systems as it is in infancy" (p. 173). Second, attachment after infancy draws increasingly on affiliative relationships with peers. Third, attachment is then more often directed toward a figure with whom a sexual relationship also exists. The concept of affiliative systems needs to be understood better in comparison with attachment/caretaking systems. Weiss has shown that friendship affiliations do not substitute for the loneliness that occurs after, for example, the ending of a marital attachment.

The most striking instance of attachment in later life, which actually may overwhelm other behavioral systems, is "falling in love," a relational change that is not unlike maternal bonding toward the newborn infant in its intensity and abrupt onset. (This phenomenon should not be confused with "intimacy," in the sense in which I shall use that term.) Another form of intense attachment/caregiving emerges more gradually in long-standing marriages, again not necessarily in combination with "love" or intimacy. In later life, role reversals between the caregiver and the recipient often occur if the relational system is organized in a situationally flexible manner. This point is relevant to Bowlby's (1975) definition of attachment behavior: "Any form of behavior that results in a person obtaining or retaining proximity to some other differentiated and preferred individual, usually conceived as stronger and/or wider" (p. 292). Ainsworth (1982) comments that, "in a good marriage, each partner on occasion plays the role of stronger and wiser figure for the other, so that each derives security and comfort from the other, as well as wishing to be with the other and protesting actual or threatened separation" (p. 26).

In addition, the pattern of parental caregiving appears to be influenced by the pattern in which caregiving was received from the parents. As I have suggested, "In early infancy a reciprocal relatedness between mother and infant on a nonverbal basis appears to influence the later development of communicative language" (Wynne 1968, p. 187). Singer and I (Singer and Wynne 1965, 1966; Singer, Wynne, and Toohey 1978) have taken the position that a necessary precondition for communicating is shared focusing of attention, leading to potentially shared meanings. We have also formulated the concept of communication deviance (CD) in which "a listener is unable to construct a consistent visual image or a consistent construct from the speaker's words" (Singer et al. 1978, p. 500). Communication deviance and affective style, the counterpart of EE studied with direct observation of family interaction, were poorly correlated with each other, but both of these family measures contribute significantly to the prediction of outcome of schizophrenia and schizophrenia-spectrum disorders at a fifteen-year followup. A broader conclusion that can be drawn is that attachment and communicating are indeed qualitatively different processes and are given priority at different times.

In figure 1, I have indicated that, through recursive, "circular" processes (spiral when viewed through time), the quality of communicating, for example, will modify subsequent attachment/caregiving. Certainly, this "feedback" occurs in enduring familial and marital relatedness. In addition, it can be noted that the sheer repetition of shared communicational (and problem-solving) patterns in the workplace, and in some cultures in arranged marriages, may actually generate attachment/caregiving. Weiss (1982) comments that the "institution of marriage" tends to foster attachment, whatever the initial relationship of the couple.

Joint Problem Solving

In accord with my epigenetic schema, the effects of dysfunctional communication patterns emerge most vividly at the next stage when joint problem solving becomes more primary. Although behavioral therapy has emphasized problem solving for some years, only more recently has the concept of *joint* problem solving as a task for healthy family relatedness been given much attention in family therapy. Individual problem-solving skills, industry, and task mastery are surely a major phase of psychological development. Erikson (1950) described "industry versus inferiority" as the fourth stage in ego epigenesis. Some of the learning of such skills takes place through individual trial and error. What I wish to underline here is that *joint* problem solving and *shared* engagement in sustained and renewed tasks involve relational processes that create a potentiality for new relational growth.

Clearly, negotiation through life-cycle transitions requires joint problem-solving skills. But, without a background of attachment/caregiving and communicational skills, joint problem solving is doomed to be muddled and dysfunctional. For example, if a family at the adolescent-launching stage is still deeply enmeshed and emotionally overinvolved or is still communicating in an amorphous, fragmented, or constricted manner (Singer and Wynne 1965), problem solving will be difficult indeed. Most of the structural changes of the family life cycle move on inexorably as the "fallout" of gradual aging or of "random" events such as illness, death, divorce, and remarriage that occur in "fits and starts." In contrast, both the epigenetic processes of family relatedness and those of individual psychological growth and identity formation optimally march at the pace of their own drummers. Therefore, at any given point in time, the quality of functioning in family relational processes frequently does not fit with the more arbitrary progression of the family life cycle. In current "schools" of family therapy, the emphasis on joint family problem solving (Epstein and Bishop 1981; Falloon, Boyd, McGill, Strang, and Moss 1981; Haley 1976) has constituted a major focus for effective change.

A feature of Falloon's (Falloon et al. 1981) approach to behavioral family therapy is directly relevant to my present epigenetic formulation. He emphasizes the teaching of communicational skills as a prior and necessary step when efforts to help families with problem solving have failed. His assumption is that successful use of communicational skills is a more basic task before effective problem solving can proceed. Also, in any family therapy approach, family members must be sufficiently emotionally attached to one another before they are willing to come together in order to learn communicational skills or anything else. With high levels of EE or CD, family problem-solving difficulties will be inevitable. However, assisting couples or families to work on simple problems together may promote their becoming more comfortable affectively and their communicating more successfully. More complex and sustained problem solving, I believe, presupposes prior success in earlier developmental stages.

Mutuality

The final stage in my epigenetic schema centrally involves the processes of long-term relational renewal and reengagement. "Mutuality," the term that I am using in a special way to characterize this stage, begins with the recognition of difficulties that cannot be resolved within the framework of prior forms of relatedness and involves renegotiation and sometimes transformation to new patterns of relating. The possible new patterns include "ending" this relational system, which may actually be a shift to relatedness at a greater distance, for example, in divorce.

At each stage in the epigenesis of relatedness, difficulties are inevitable. In figure 1, some of the possible adaptive "solutions" (forms of impasse) are outlined at each stage. The stage of mutuality builds most directly on joint problem solving because, in a sense, the problem to be solved is whether the relationship should or will continue and, if so, under what conditions. This implies a stocktaking about the current quality of relating and about the circumstances that are affecting it—illness, growth, and aging of each family member, transitions in the family life cycle, and involvement in other systems (at work, with extended family, and with other persons). Mutuality differs from the other forms of relating considered so far in that it requires that each person "observe," temporarily, the functioning of the system in which he or she has been participating, that is, take a metaposition partially outside the system.

Mutuality does not necessarily or automatically emerge after the sequence of attachment/caregiving, communicating, and joint problem solving has developed, but it does draw on accrued relational experience and skill from each of these stages in order to return selectively to whatever form of relatedness is appropriate to changing internal and external contexts. Mutuality is a superordinate concept that is specifically oriented to the issue of relational change over time in the face of conflict and divergence. As I and my colleagues (Wynne et al. 1958, p. 207) have formulated it, "With growth and situational changes, altered expectations inevitably come into any relation. Then at least transient nonfulfillment of expectations—that is, noncomplementarity—necessarily occurs. . . . Mutuality is experienced as having a larger context than a particular role. . . . Genuine mutuality, unlike pseudo-mutuality, not only tolerates divergence of self-interests, but thrives upon the recognition of such natural and inevitable divergence."

Enduring relatedness requires periodic stocktaking, with each person taking into account his or her own needs and preferences, those of each other, and the quality of what goes on between them. The results of such stocktaking may alter the previous relationship. It may move into "pathological" forms, what I have called pseudomutuality (Wynne et al. 1958) and pseudohostility (Wynne 1961), in which the preservation of a fixed pattern of relatedness takes priority at the expense of individual needs and despite changing circumstances. In other instances, change is not negotiated but simply asserted by one person, or a dyad, seemingly at the expense of the others. Finally, of course, without some degree of mutuality, the relation may break up quite abruptly (Weiss 1982), with little genuine exploration of options, including whether there is any point to a fresh start.

"Renegotiation" in mutuality may be quite explicit, for example, in the planning of a new life-style after retirement or organizing household chores when a wife takes on a full-time job when there are children at home. In other situations, the new pattern may be established without discussion or even awareness, for example, when an ailing parent or the workplace gradually becomes all absorbing at the expense of the marriage or the nuclear family.

The changes within the context of mutuality may involve not only expansion of relatedness but also narrowing of the range of involvement with others. For example, when young adults leave the nuclear family to establish a new household of their own, a warm and diversified parent-offspring mutuality does not evaporate but, rather, changes into a new pattern. This changed pattern will include attachment/caregiving that is now more episodic, with less need for face-to-face accessibility. In later years, the attachment/caregiving will need to be reorganized again, perhaps with role reversal when circumstances change with aging and illness. Given a clear but flexible framework of attachment/caregiving, there can be a resumption of communicating and joint problem solving in an altered mutuality that is not so intense as in earlier years but is still highly meaningful. Thus, the concept of mutuality does not imply that there is an optimal, necessary direction that relatedness must take. Instead, this concept, as I am using it, involves repeated changes of direction and a high degree of flexible variation over time.

Intimacy

The place of intimacy in a conceptualization of relational processes is extraordinarily difficult to delineate. Intimacy is often touted in today's popular (and family therapy) literature as the ideal type of highly valued relatedness. More sober reflection has led me to conclude, however, that, historically, across the full range of social class and cultural variations, intimacy has been more of a luxury than a developmental necessity in relational systems. For example, in the many cultures in which arranged marriages have been customary, attachment/caregiving slowly builds out of the realities of proximity, eventually leading to fine-tuned mutuality, but not necessarily with much intimacy.

Perhaps it is not surprising that reliable sharing of intimate experience between men and women is the exception, a current Western ideal that over the course of world history has been seldom sought and more rarely achieved. By contrast, in enduring marriages and some friendships, especially in times of cultural stability, there may quite regularly be considerable mutuality in the sense in which I have used the term.

In my current version of an epigenetic schema, I locate recurrent intimacy as an inconstant stage beyond mutuality (see fig. 1). Intimacy is sometimes sought as a quality valued in itself. Persons with this goal as an ideal are overrepresented in the offices of marital therapists. A common difficulty of "modern" couples is that they are so preoccupied with maintaining intimacy that they fail to give adequate priority to the necessities of day-to-day problem solving. There may be much global talk about intimate "caring," but little attention given to problem resolution or to the restructuring of attachment/caregiving and communication patterns.

When there is reciprocal respect between persons who have well-defined roles, a considerable degree of genuine mutuality can develop, even without much intimacy. However, when life circumstances change rapidly or drastically, intimate understanding of one another's needs and experiences can greatly facilitate the discovery of new ways of relating. Intimacy can infuse joint problem solving with new ingredients, and, at the same time, unfettered efforts at problem solving set the stage for deepened experiences of intimacy.

Concluding Note

A fundamental proposition underlying the approach described in this chapter is that one cannot properly conceptualize the reciprocity of relatedness by using only the perspective of individual persons, even when one recognizes that persons are social beings. I have noted that life-cycle changes in family structure usually proceed at a different pace than the unfolding of relational processes during development. The epigenetic model has implications for identifying points of family impasse and for giving priorities to preventive and therapeutic interventions that are likely to be effective. For example, this formulation points specifically to the desirability of strengthening joint problem-solving skills in therapy before mutuality and intimacy can be expected to stabilize. In other instances, the focus of intervention must move further back to the behavioral building of communicational skills and to elemental experiences of affectional bonding.

NOTE

This chapter was originally presented as a paper to the meeting of the American Society for Adolescent Psychiatry, New Orleans, May 11, 1991.

REFERENCES

Ainsworth, M. D. S. 1982. Attachment: retrospect and prospect. In C. M. Parkes and J. Stevenson-Hinde, eds. *The Place of Attachment in Human Behavior*. New York: Basic.

Ainsworth, M. D. S.; Blehar, M. C.; Walters, E.; and Wall, S. 1978. *Patterns of Attachment: A Psychological Study of the Strange Situation*. Hillsdale, N.J.: Erlbaum.

Bowlby, J. 1958. The nature of the child's tie to his mother. *International Journal of Psycho-Analysis* 39:1–23.

Bowlby, J. 1969. *Attachment and Loss*. Vol. 1, *Attachment*. New York: Basic.

Bowlby, J. 1975. Attachment theory, separation anxiety, and mourning. In D. A. Hamburg and H. K. M. Brodie, eds. *American Handbook of Psychiatry*, vol. 6, *New Psychiatric Frontiers*. New York: Basic.

Bowlby, J. 1980. *Attachment and Loss*. Vol. 3, *Loss: Sadness and Depression*. New York: Basic.

Brown, G. W.; Birley, J. L. T.; and Wing, J. K. 1972. Influence of family life on the course of schizophrenic disorders: a replication. *British Journal of Psychiatry* 121:241–258.

Carter, E. A., and McGoldrick, M., eds. 1980. *The Family Life Cycle: A Framework for Family Therapy*. New York: Gardner.

Cooley, C. H. 1909. *Social Organization*. New York: Scribner's.

Duvall, E. M. 1962. *Family Development*. Rev. ed. Chicago: Lippincott.

Epstein, N. B., and Bishop, D. S. 1981. Problem-centered systems therapy of the family. In A. S. Gurman and D. P. Kniskern, eds. *Handbook of Family Therapy*. New York: Brunner/Mazel.

Erikson, E. H. 1950. *Childhood and Society*. New York: Norton.

Erikson, E. H. 1956. The problem of ego identity. *Journal of the American Psychoanalytic Association* 4:56–121.

Erikson, E. H. 1968. *Identity: Youth and Crisis*. New York: Norton.

Falloon, I. R. H.; Boyd, J. L.; McGill, C. W.; Strang, J. S.; and Moss, H. B. 1981. Family management training in the community care of schizophrenia. In M. J. Goldstein, ed. *New Developments in Interventions with Families of Schizophrenics*. San Francisco: Jossey-Bass.

Grunebaum, H. U., and Bryant, C. M. 1966. Family diagnosis on an in-patient service. II. a theory for the family diagnostic. In I. M. Cohen, ed. *Family Structure, Dynamics, and Therapy*. Research Report no. 20. Washington, D.C.: American Psychiatric Association.

Haley, J. 1973. *Uncommon Therapy: The Psychiatric Techniques of Milton H. Erikson, M.D*. New York: Norton.

Haley, J. 1976. *Problem-solving Therapy*. San Francisco: Jossey-Bass.

Hill, R. 1964. Methodological issues in family development research. *Family Process* 3:186–206.

Hinde, R. A. 1982. Attachment: some conceptual and biological issues. In C. M. Parkes and J. Stevenson-Hinde, eds. *The Place of Attachment in Human Behavior*. New York: Basic.

Klaus, M. H., and Kennell, J. H. 1976. *Maternal-Infant Bonding*. St. Louis, Mo.: Mosby.

Leiderman, P. H., and Seashore, M. J. 1975. Mother-infant neonatal separation: some delayed consequences. In *Parent-Infant Interaction*. CIBA Foundation Symposium no. 33 (new series). Amsterdam: Elsevier.

Peterson, G. H.; Mehl, L. E.; and Leiderman, P. H. 1979. The role of some birth-related variables in father attachment. *American Journal of Orthopsychiatry* 49:330–338.

Singer, M. T., and Wynne, L. C. 1965. Thought disorder and family relations of schizophrenics. IV. results and implications. *Archives of General Psychiatry* 12:201–212.

Singer, M. T., and Wynne, L. C. 1966. Principles for scoring communication defects and deviances in parents of schizophrenics: Rorschach and TAT scoring manuals. *Psychiatry* 29:260–288.

Singer, M. T.; Wynne, L. C.; and Toohey, M. L. 1978. Communication disorders and the families of schizophrenics. In L. C. Wynne, R. Cromwell, and S. Matthysse, eds. *The Nature of Schizophrenia: New Approaches to Research and Treatment*. New York: Wiley.

Solomon, M. A. 1973. A developmental conceptual premise for family therapy. *Family Process* 12:179–196.

Sroufe, L. A. 1979. The coherence of individual development: early care, attachment and subsequent developmental issues. *American Psychologist* 34:834–841.

Sroufe, L. A.; Fox, N. E.; and Pancake, V. R. 1983. Attachment and dependency in developmental perspective. *Child Development* 54:1615–1627.

Svejda, M. J.; Pannabecker, B. J.; and Emde, R. N. 1982. Parent-to-infant attachment: a critique of the early "bonding" model. In R. N. Emde and R. J. Harmon, eds. *The Development of Attachment and Affiliative Systems*. New York: Plenum.

Vaughn, C. E., and Leff, J. P. 1976. The influence of family and social factors on the course of psychiatric illness: a comparison of schizophrenic and depressed neurotic patients. *British Journal of Psychiatry* 129:125–137.

Weiss, R. S. 1982. Attachment in adult life. In C. M. Parkes and J. Stevenson-Hinde, eds. *The Place of Attachment in Human Behavior*. New York: Basic.

Wynne, L. C. 1961. The study of intrafamilial alignments and splits in exploratory family therapy. In N. Ackerman, F. Beatman, and S. Sherman, eds. *Exploring the Base for Family Therapy*. New York: Family Therapy Association of America.

Wynne, L. C. 1968. Methodologic and conceptual issues in the study of schizophrenics and their families. *Journal of Psychiatric Research* 6(suppl. 1): 185–199.

Wynne, L. C. 1976. On the anguish and creative passions of not escaping double binds: a reformulation. In C. Sluzki and D. Ransom, eds. *Double Bind: The Foundation of the Communicational Approach to the Family*. New York: Grune & Stratton.

Wynne, L. C.; Ryckoff, I.; Day, J.; and Hirsch, S. 1958. Pseudo-mutuality in the family relations of schizophrenics. *Psychiatry* 21:205–220.

PART III

DEVELOPMENTAL ISSUES IN ADOLESCENT PSYCHIATRY

EDITORS' INTRODUCTION

Virtually all adolescent psychiatrists are developmentalists. They maintain a constant awareness of the teenager's developmental past, the tasks of the future, and the unfolding of maturational factors in the treatment process. While many psychotherapists do not seek the uncovering of genetic memories as a curative force, they do value their importance when they spontaneously emerge or are reenacted in the treatment relationship.

Richard P. Kluft and Rosalyn Schultz describe a series of adolescents with multiple personality disorder (MPD), a condition similar to some of Freud's early patients, who present disturbances of identity and memory. The authors conclude that the study of multiple personality disorder has barely begun and that adolescent psychiatrists have a unique opportunity to intervene before the condition has become chronic and fixed.

Eitan D. Schwarz, Janice M. Kowalski, and Steven Hanus explore the place of memories in human psychic function. They compare the maturity of lush personal and collective memories with traumatic memories that grow from violence and can be destructive of our humanity. Posttraumatic stress disorder (PTSD) is the psychiatric equivalent and is described as deriving from an unusual stressor and yielding three clusters of symptoms: reexperiencing; avoidance; and arousal. The authors coin the term "malignant memories" to highlight the central role of memory in PTSD development and emphasize that human response to trauma is a neurobiological as well as psychosocial phenomenon. Their review of the literature reveals linkage to Freud, Janet, and Penfield and, more recently, to Horowitz, Foa, and Perry that sufficient stress may actually induce structural changes. The authors conclude that developmental factors may play an important part in how an individual reacts to violence. Adolescents are particularly sensitive to biopsychosocial shifts that include hormonal changes, sexual stimulation, affects and behaviors, cognitive shifts, development of values, and other growths. As such, they are at high risk for exposure to violence.

Jonathan Cohen presents a broad overview of the factors that can directly and indirectly interfere with adolescents being able to use their most basic and complex cognitive/ego function: attention. Three types of disorders are described: verbal or nonverbal learning disabilities; a selective attention disorder; and an attentional skill deficiency. Cohen describes some of the developmental, diagnostic, educational, and clinical implications of the psychobiological spectrum of disorders; the most serious is that attentionally disordered adolescents are at risk for developing psychopathology and misdiagnosis may result in profound neglect.

Barbara Fajardo extends the study of adolescent development by considering young adulthood, the next developmental period in the life span. Unlike earlier stages, such as infancy, latency, and adolescence, there are no obvious biological or endogenously generated imperatives that confer uniqueness on the experience of young adulthood. Therefore, since adolescence should be considered a phase of life, not a career, the young adult is faced with alternatives of intimacy and work versus isolation. The correct resolution of this psychosocial task produces an adult connectedness to society. Fajardo uses metaphor to illustrate the observation that development is a process rather than a succession of stages.

15   MULTIPLE PERSONALITY DISORDER IN ADOLESCENCE

RICHARD P. KLUFT AND ROSALYN SCHULTZ

Multiple personality disorder (MPD) is a complex and chronic dissociative psychopathology. Contemporary scientific investigators conceptualize it to be a posttraumatic syndrome of childhood origin (Kluft 1985b, 1985c, 1987c, 1991b; Putnam 1985, 1989; Schultz, Braun, and Kluft 1989; Spiegel 1984, 1986b, 1991). Significant childhood mistreatment is reported in the histories given by 97–98 percent of the MPD patients in recent series (Putnam, Guroff, Silberman, Barban, and Post 1986; Schultz, Braun, and Kluft 1985, 1989) and appears to be a major factor in the etiology of most cases. Multiple personality disorder was long considered a rarity, but in 1987 Kluft (1987c) listed eleven individuals or groups reporting clinical contact or research with ten or more contemporary MPD patients and noted that many additional large series had been presented at conferences on multiple personality/dissociative states. Many experts with wide experience, such as Cornelia B. Wilbur and the late David Caul, are known to have seen over 100 such patients, but they have never presented or reported their large series systematically.

Among the larger series in the literature is one of the 355 MPD patients contributed by 355 individual therapists described Schultz et al. (1985, 1989); the 100 patients submitted by ninety-two therapists to the series of Putnam et al. (1986); the 236 MPD patients about whom Ross, Norton, and Wozney (1989) collected data from 203 therapists; the 210 patients interviewed by Kluft (1985b); and the fifty patients exhaustively evaluated by Coons, Bowman, and Milstein (1988).

These series also demonstrated that, on the average, MPD patients spend approximately seven years between their first mental health assessments for symptoms that prove referrable to MPD and their receiving an accurate diagnosis, being given in the meantime an average of 3.6 erroneous diagnoses (Putnam et al. 1986). Since MPD patients do not recover in therapies that fail to address their core psychopathology (Kluft 1984d, 1985b, 1986a), these simple statistics bespeak considerable excess morbidity, human suffering, and waste of resources.

The condition's alleged rarity, the incredulity that surrounds retrospective complaints of abuse (Goodwin 1985), and the frequently dramatic nature of MPD phenomena all are prone to inspire both countertransferential fascination and skepticism. Consequently, the mental health professions have been reluctant to take MPD seriously and have often demonstrated considerable hostility to this area of study (Dell 1988; Morris 1989).

Recent studies, however, have necessitated the revision of many long-standing preconceptions about MPD. Although females continue to outnumber males from four to one to nine to one in most series (Kluft 1984b), MPD has been found in patients of both genders from childhood to the later years of life (Kluft 1985a; Putnam et al. 1986; Schultz et al. 1985, 1989). Its presentation is quite variable both across patients and in the same patient over time (Kluft 1985b, 1991a). Most patients try to disguise rather than flaunt their condition, rendering the diagnostic process rather difficult (Coons 1980, 1984; Kluft 1985a, 1985b, 1987a, 1987b, 1987c, 1991a, 1991b; Loewenstein 1991; Putnam, Loewenstein, Silberman, and Post 1984; Solomon and Solomon 1982). Since MPD may be accompanied by symptoms that suggest alternative and/or concomitant diagnoses, it is useful to have a high index of suspicion for it, especially when a patient who appears to have another mental disorder fails to respond to the interventions that usually prove effective with that disorder (Kluft 1985a, 1987c, 1991a; Putnam et al. 1984).

The purpose of this chapter is to bring together observations and reports on MPD during adolescence and to offer some thoughts on the treatment of MPD in this group of patients.

Diagnostic Criteria and Clinical Characteristics

MPD involves a disturbance of both identity and memory (Nemiah 1985). The presence of recurrent episodes of amnesia (or other distortions of memory) and repetitive instances of separate identities assuming executive control of the mind distinguish it from other mental disorders (Putnam et al. 1984). Excepting forensic situations, in which malingering must always be considered and ruled out, if signs of the disorder are documented, MPD should be regarded as present, a superordinate diagnosis under which many manifestations may be encompassed (Putnam et al. 1984). The current diagnostic criteria (American Psychiatric Association 1987, p. 272) for MPD are (1) the existence within the persona of two or more distinct personalities or personality states (each with its own relatively enduring pattern of perceiving, relating to, and thinking about the environment and the self) and (2) at least two of these personalities or personality states recurrently taking full control of the person's behavior.

It is important to realize that, since the personalities may be covert for long periods or influence one another from behind the scenes, patients are encountered who fulfill these criteria at one point in time but not at another (Kluft 1985b, 1991a). Many patients with the structure of MPD fall short of DSM-III-R diagnostic criteria and should receive the diagnosis of dissociative disorder not otherwise specified.

Amnesia is a commonly associated feature that many (e.g., Coons 1984; Putnam 1989) consider essential to MPD. Often, however, it cannot be documented early in treatment, may take many confusing forms, and can be difficult to quantify. Also, there are many other dissociative dysfunctions of memory that do not involve actual forgetting (Kluft, Steinberg, and Spitzer 1988). This makes amnesia an equivocal diagnostic criterion, although it is proposed as criterion C for DSM-IV (Kluft 1991b). Only about two-thirds of MPD patients have clear-cut psychogenic amnesia at first assessment, but nearly all manifest amnesia as the treatment progresses (Putnam et al. 1986; Ross et al. 1989; Schultz, Kluft, and Braun 1986).

Contemporary MPD cases show a modal range of eight to thirteen personalities (Kluft 1984b). Two studies show that approximately half have ten personalities or less, while half have eleven or more (Kluft 1984b; Schultz et al. 1985, 1989). Several large series suggest that the average in contemporary cases is between thirteen and sixteen (Kluft 1984d; Putnam et al. 1986; Ross et al. 1989; Schultz et al. 1989). Cases with over 100 personalities have been reported and treated successfully (Kluft 1986a, 1988). The personalities may experience and represent themselves (in self-description and in overt behavior) as different in any dimension of self-concept or self-representation: gender, age, appearance, sexual orientation, values, and beliefs. They may have separate wardrobes, possessions, food and other preferences, pursuits, or interpersonal styles. Some manifestations are quite overt, some well hidden. Psychophysiological differences between alter personalities have been described and researched (reviewed recently by Coons [1988]). The personalities may show different handedness as well as different handwritings and artistic styles. Their voices, movement characteristics, speech patterns, memories, vocabularies, accents, and even languages of choice may vary.

The personalities' awareness of one another may range from total mutual amnesia (i.e., no personality is aware of the existence or activities of the others), to one-way amnesia, to partial shared awareness, to co-consciousness (Ellenberger 1970). Often, several patterns are found within the alters of a single patient. Many areas of knowledge may be held in common. Personalities' sense of separateness and narcissistic investment in remaining separate may vary widely. The personalities may have complex inner relationships among themselves, including friendships, agreed-on areas of cooperation, protection arrangements, and inner enmities and civil wars. Their degrees of definition and their distinctness from one another may range over a wide spectrum. Vaguely formed and quite similar personalities are encountered, especially in very complex cases (Kluft 1988, 1991a). It is crucial to appreciate that the personalities' senses of their autonomy may well be held with a degree of conviction that may be termed pseudodelusional (Kluft 1984b). They may act on the illusion that they can attack the body to punish, mutilate, or kill some other personality without injuring themselves.

The personalities have come into existence to serve defensive purposes. When an overwhelmed child cannot take flight from deleterious circumstances, she may turn inward, dissociating the damage, segregating certain aspects of experience from others in a relatively rule-bound way (Spiegel 1986a, 1991), and developing alternate personalities. Stereotypical conceptualizations of MPD lead to the expectation that the personalities will be polarized opposites of one another. In fact, they often enact alternative coping strategies (Kluft 1987c). No types are universally encountered (Kluft 1991b). Both Kluft (1984b) and Putnam et al. (1986) have listed types commonly seen: children; protectors and helpers; ones who retain particular memories; ones who maintain a continuous awareness; depressed and suicidal alters; guardians of secrets; alters who are critical, punitive, and/or violent to other alters (often thinly disguised identifications with their abusers); alters who express interpersonal aggression; expressors of sexuality; avengers against and apologists for abusers; ones who feel no pain (so-called anesthetic personalities); and alters who are based on lost love objects etc. More than half of MPD patients have alters of both sexes.

The etiology of MPD appears to be determined by several factors. In the interests of brevity, we will summarize a theory presented elsewhere (Kluft 1984d). It holds that the individual who develops MPD has the capacity to dissociate, whether this is primarily biological or induced by exposure to abuse, which has been shown to increase this capacity (Sanders, McRoberts, and Tollefson 1989). When such a person's nondissociative adaptive capacities are overwhelmed by traumatic events or circumstances, that capacity is mobilized for defensive purposes. Naturally available psychological substrates serve as the building blocks for personality formation. These include imaginary companions (Schultz et al. 1985), normative ego states, hidden observer structures, state- and mood-dependent phenomena, the vicissitudes of the libidinal phases, difficulties in the intrapsychic management of introjection/identification/internalization processes, miscarried mechanisms of defense, problems in the separation-individuation continuum (especially rapprochement issues), and mishaps in the achievement of cohesive self- and object representation. Dividedness becomes reinforced and fixed by a failure on the part of significant others to protect the child against being further overwhelmed and/or to provide positive and nurturing interactions that allow traumata to be "metabolized" and early or incipient dividedness to be abandoned. Materials that confirm aspects of this theory have been summarized elsewhere (Kluft 1986b).

Although there are no published controlled studies concerning the treatment of MPD, follow-up studies tracing patients from integration through reassessment two and five years after integration indicate that the prognosis for motivated patients in intense individual psychotherapy with therapists experienced in work with MPD is excellent indeed (Kluft 1984d, 1986a). Over 90 percent reassessed after two years show no behavioral evidence of MPD, and over 75 percent do not continue to use dissociative defenses. However, the unusual characteristics of the therapists in these series make it unlikely that generalizations can be drawn from these studies. Patients in treatment with less experienced therapists are less likely to achieve integration so readily or to hold it so well (Coons 1986; Schultz et al. 1986).

MPD during Adolescence

The literature of MPD in adolescence is fairly sparse. The celebrated May Reynolds and Felida were both in their teens when observed and studied (Ellenberger 1970). A number of articles indicate that adolescents were among the cohort reported but do not single them out in any way. Recently, Bowman (1990), reviewing the older literature, discovered a number of long-overlooked reports of adolescent cases and compared their features with those found in modern cohorts. Some modern single case studies (Bowman, Blix, and Coons 1985; Fagan and McMahon 1984; Gruenewald 1971; Weiss, Sutton, and Utecht 1985) and two series of adolescents with MPD have been reported, one summarizing findings with sixteen patients (Kluft 1985b) and another describing eleven (Dell and Eisenhower 1990).

During adolescence, a transition occurs between the childhood form of MPD, which is readily treatable and in which the alters usually are not very narcissistically invested in retaining their separateness, and the more familiar and entrenched adult form (Kluft 1985b). The personalities become more invested in their separateness and their senses of themselves apart from the defensive purposes they serve. They often become more detailed and specialized.

The developmental tasks of adolescence are often the occasion for further dividedness. For example, the development of additional alternate personalities, some of which may appear to be precocious and mature, may give the adolescent with MPD an illusion of increased separateness and independence that covers strong dependency needs (Schultz 1990). Alters may be created to manage age-appropriate sexual concerns and the conflicts they engender, to acquire more complex and autonomous social roles, and to develop new skills. As dividedness increasingly becomes an approach to mastery as well as a defense against overwhelming traumata, complexity increases. If there is a combination of developmental demands with ongoing traumatization, large numbers of new entities may be formed. To illustrate, a girl trying to handle her own emerging age-appropriate sexuality, ongoing incest, her use in prostitution and pornographic movies, an after-school job, maintaining honor grades, teaching Sunday school, and developing her considerable creative potential developed many rather specialized alters to address these demands. Most of them were complex and elaborated but had relatively limited time in sole control of the body.

Also, it is during adolescence that most of the more complex MPD patients develop their elaborate inner systems and societies of personalities (Kluft 1985b, 1988). Furthermore, the personalities of many adolescents with MPD now, for the first time, have increasing freedom and opportunities to develop separate lives of their own.

The diagnosis and successful treatment of MPD in adolescence is rarely reported. MPD adolescents rarely either disclose their condition or reveal the stressors that led to it. Even though one retrospective study of 142 adult MPD patients reported that 81 percent of the sample had experienced prolonged incestuous activity during childhood and adolescence (mean age of onset 3.7 years, mean age of cessation 15.5), the majority did not disclose the incest prior to adulthood (Schultz, Braun, and Kluft 1987). Thirty-four percent did disclose their incest before age eighteen; however, most were not believed by the person they first informed (mother, school personnel, mental health professionals), and a significant percentage were either punished or removed from their homes after the disclosure. In common with other abused adolescents, most MPD adolescents keep their mistreatment hidden because of anxiety, shame, and realistic fears regarding blame, punishment, abandonment, or family disruption (Schultz 1990). Unfortunately, this need for secrecy profoundly affects consolidation of personality development at the end of this transitional phase and contributes to developmental fixations (Schultz 1990).

Furthermore, those diagnoses and treatments that are reported often are not documented in a way that allows objective assessment as to whether the interventions were definitively effective. Gruenewald's (1971) patient ceased to show overt MPD phenomena but continued to use dissociative defenses while under study. She was unavailable for follow-up. Fagan and McMahon's (1984) patient, Ellen, did not do well and required hospitalization. The fate of the patient described by Bowman et al. (1985) was not documented. In the six older case studies summarized by Bowman (1990), two cases appeared to demonstrate the apparent remission of dissociative phenomena, two cases showed their persistence, and two integrated in the course of therapy. Kluft

(1984d, 1986a) recorded the successful treatment of MPD adolescents. Five of his sixteen adolescent patients integrated and did well, but eleven dropped out of treatment, were removed from therapy by their families, or, having been seen in consultation only, were treated by therapists who either elected not to accept the MPD diagnosis, attempted to bypass it in treatment, or adopted treatment strategies not known to be effective with MPD (Kluft 1985b). Dell and Eisenhower (1990) reported that three of their eleven MPD adolescents had integrated, three remained in therapy directed toward integration, and five had quit therapy. Most of those who dropped out did not fare well, requiring rehospitalization and further treatment. On follow-up, only one was in treatment that addressed the MPD.

Despite the small number of reported successes, our anecdotal experience suggests that MPD in adolescence is very treatable if the patient is motivated and if it is possible to protect the therapy situation and achieve continuity of care. However, our experience is that this may be difficult to achieve with this age group. The problems usually encountered appear more correlated with general issues of adolescence than with phenomena unique to MPD in this age group. There appear, however, to be some massive resistances associated with the unique features of certain adolescent patients' MPD psychopathology.

Discussion

The diagnosis of MPD is a complex subject (Coons 1980, 1984; Fagan and McMahon 1984; Kluft 1984b, 1985a, 1985b, 1987b, 1987c, 1991a, 1991b; Loewenstein 1991; Putnam 1989; Putnam et al. 1984; Ross 1989; Solomon and Solomon 1982). The presenting symptoms of adult patients with MPD have been summarized elsewhere (Kluft 1991a, 1991b). Unfortunately, adolescent presentations are difficult to characterize. Bowman's (1990) attempt to tabulate characteristic symptoms in older and more modern cases were compromised by the fact that, in each era, different symptoms were considered important and noted. Therefore, data from different eras are difficult to correlate. We will summarize some well-known vignettes.

At about nineteen years of age, Mary Reynolds was found in a field near her home, having lost consciousness. On recovery, she was blind and deaf for weeks. Months after her apparent recovery, she awoke from a deep sleep with a global amnesia. Initially unable to speak, she gradually acquired or recovered skills and knowledge. Weeks later, she awoke in her natural state, unaware of the passage of time. In her natural state, she was quiet, sober, thoughtful, and prone to depression. In the emergent second state, she was gay, cheerful, and fun loving. These states, which differed in many respects, alternated for the next decade and a half, after which she remained in the second (Ellenberger 1970).

Azam (1887) followed Felida from age fifteen to age fifty. From age thirty on, she had reported headaches, neuralgias, and a wide variety of symptoms. Usually taciturn and sullen, she would feel (almost daily) an acute pain in her temples, become lethargic for a few minutes, and then awaken gay, vivacious, and symptom free for several hours. There were numerous differences between the states, which continued to alternate, but in the first she was always amnestic for behaviors in the second (Ellenberger 1970).

Gruenewald's (1971) seventeen-year-old patient had been in treatment for five years prior to diagnosis. She was failing in school, was unable to adjust, and had multiple somatic complaints. Confusional and amnestic episodes were documented. She was considered borderline. Hospitalized for a suicide attempt, she was depressed, confused, and aware that she did "crazy things." She admitted to hearing voices arguing in her head. Seen by Gruenewald for psychological testing twice in one day, she did not recognize Gruenewald on the second occasion and protested having to take the other personality's tests. She acknowledged her responsibility for several unexplained periods of time and bits of behavior and described forcing the presenting personality to act self-destructively. There was a verified history of incest; her stepfather had molested her for several years.

Fagan and McMahon's (1984) thirteen-year-old patient, Ellen, was referred for lying and difficult behavior. She oscillated between sweet and unmanageable behavior. Her father was unknown, her mother had died when she was young, and her stepfather did not supervise her adequately. She denied sexual activities witnessed by other informants. In her fifth session, a second alter emerged and introduced herself to the therapist.

The fifteen-year-old girl described by Bowman et al. (1985) was an incest victim who had been removed from her family and placed, after foster care, in a preadoptive setting that also proved abusive. Her second preadoptive family brought her for evaluation. She had many regressive behaviors and strong evidence of amnesia. She also showed abrupt differences in affect and behavior. In her first interview, she revealed awareness of another part of herself that behaved differently; in the second, she dissociated spontaneously into a different personality.

Kluft (1985b) sunmmarized the presentations of sixteen adolescents, four males and twelve females. The four males were referred with an assortment of putative diagnoses (temporal lobe epilepsy, mania, schizophrenia, and Tourette's syndrome plus character disorder). All had problematic, aggressive propensities in at least one alter, including arson, destructiveness of property, armed robbery, and wanton assaultiveness. They handled their amnesias in ways that raised suspicion as to their veracity. They sometimes denied their inappropriate behaviors or rationalized them as drug related, only to admit them with bravado at other times. They often said that they would rather represent themselves as "bad" than admit that they had no true memory of their offenses and risk being considered liars or "crazy." Two were successfully treated and ceased their aggressive behaviors. One preferred to accept a legal penalty rather than acknowledge and disclose his disorder.

Kluft noted that adult MPD patients who had remained in intact albeit dysfunctional families during their teens had not been diagnosed in adolescence because their alters were suppressed or learned to pass for one another and/or the families forbade them to seek help. Eight of his twelve female adolescents with MPD did not live with their families. Many had run away from abusive situations, usually involving father-daughter incest. Several knew that they had been promiscuous, suffered a rape, or had become pregnant but had no actual memory of the incidents or behaviors. Three were heavy drug users and one floridly sociopathic. Somatoform complaints and suicidal gestures were common. In their initial interviews, all dissociated and switched quite obviously, but their personalities did not identify themselves openly. Most acknowledged numerous passive influence experiences and hallucinations (Kluft 1987a). They had learned that their disavowals of disremembered behaviors would not be believed. Out of despair, confusion, and expedience, their denials frequently crumbled into false admissions of being liars.

The remaining four females showed less overt turmoil. They were withdrawn. One immature girl showed the structure and characteristics of childhood MPD. Two showed typical adult presentations: a neurasthenic and depressed alter complained of headaches, of amnesias, and of being confronted with out-of-character behaviors. The last appeared to be deteriorating into a refractory schizophrenic process. She was screened for MPD because she had not responded to treatment appropriate for her apparent diagnosis. All four readily accepted treatment and recovered. The hopeless apparent schizophrenic rapidly became medication free, was discharged in short order, integrated rapidly, went on to graduate from college, and was well on five-year follow-up.

Dell and Eisenhower (1990) tabulated the symptoms elicited in their first three clinical contacts with eleven adolescent MPD patients and also studied behavior problems endorsed by observers on the Behavior Problem Checklist (BPC) of Fagan and McMahon (1984). The most common clinical findings were depression, hearing voices in the head, amnesia, and school problems, all found in 82 percent of the patients. Behavior problems were noted in 72 percent, nightmares in 64 percent, headaches in 55 percent, drug abuse in 36 percent, violence in 36 percent, self-mutilation in 27 percent, and both phobias and eating disorders in 18 percent. The most common phenomena noted by observers and indicated on the BPC were very changeable school work (100 percent); dazes, trances, and forgetfulness (91 percent); big changes in personality, lying, perplexing professionals (82 percent); a failure to respond to discipline (73 percent); suicidality, stealing or destructive behavior, many illnesses and/or injuries (64 percent); and odd changes in physical skills, behavior problems at school, being stoical in the face of punishment, using more than one name, and being aggressive or homicidal (55 percent).

Treatment of Adolescents with MPD

Multiple personality disorder adolescents may present with a residual or late-onset juvenile form of the condition, tumultuous or withdrawn presentations, or may already manifest a well-defined classic adult syndrome. The optimal treatment approach may vary quite widely from case to case, depending on such considerations as the safety of the patient, the danger the patient may pose to self and others, and the patient's accessibility to treatment. At times, the adolescent MPD patient's pain and conflicts may be expressed in behaviors that make the use of a hospital setting advisable.

It is not possible to offer effective treatment to an MPD adolescent who is subject to ongoing abuse or whose own behavior is placing herself or others in jeopardy. This may involve the removal of the adolescent from a pathological setting, arranging for the treatment of the family and/or its individual members, and the placing of structure and constraints on behaviors that, if unchecked, could prove detrimental (Bowman et al. 1985; Dell and Eisenhower 1990; Fagan and McMahon; Gruenewald 1971). Those MPD adolescents who are well motivated and highly self-controlled, have childhood MPD–like structures, are withdrawn, and who were not abused by members of the family with which they reside all constitute subgroups that are inclined to engage in productive therapy with little delay.

There are many instances, however, in which the early months of treatment are often dominated by efforts to arrive at a reliable format in which the therapy of an individual with severely alloplastic behavior and ambivalent motivation can proceed with safety. The adolescent's alters have the strength, skill, and knowledge at their disposal to carry out their separate plans of action. They may each, in their own ways, pursue efforts to become independent and solidify their separate identities. The problem can be understood as one of identity diffusion or as a chaotic clash of sets of simultaneously ongoing and inevitably competing efforts to achieve cohesiveness. The therapist must be cautious not to collude with the adolescent's illusion of having multiple separate persons within her. At one and the same time, the therapist acknowledges the subjective reality of the personalities' experience of separateness while indicating that the several personalities are aspects of the function and experience of a single human being.

Having established a viable format for and locus of the treatment, work with the adolescent with MPD follows an amalgamation of the sequences observed in work with MPD children (Kluft 1986b) and adults (Braun 1986; Kluft 1991b; Putnam 1989; Ross 1989). The MPD adolescent is often less inclined to value psychotherapy than are most adults and children with this condition. While some are in pain and quite eager to cooperate, most are trying to develop independence and distance themselves from parent figures. The majority were mistreated by the authority figures on whom they were dependent. They are loath to allow yet another authority figure into their lives and permit themselves to be influenced and changed by such a person. Hence, issues of mistrust and the testing of the therapist may be pursued with noteworthy dedication, tenacity, and even ferocity. Thus, provocative behaviors may be intense and extreme and be encountered anew with several of the separate personalities. The adolescent will not accept the therapist as an agent of his best interests without some rigors. The management of one's countertransference can also prove challenging since, as with all adolescents in treatment, regardless of diagnosis, countertransference issues may constitute the greatest potential obstacle (Giovaccinni 1974).

The treatment of MPD is usually an intense, individual psychodynamic psychotherapy facilitated, when indicated, by hypnosis. Although hypnosis is widely accepted in the treatment of MPD, its use may prove either undesirable or even unacceptable in work with MPD adolescents, who may perceive such interventions, no matter how well established their efficacy, as controlling, manipulative, and intrusive. Group therapies and family interventions may have some circumscribed roles but are not successful as primary modalities. No medications affect the core psychopathology, but they may ameliorate associated symptoms (Barkin, Braun, and Kluft 1986; Braun 1990; Kluft, 1984a; Loewenstein 1991; Loewenstein, Hornstein, and Farber 1988).

In the process of the therapy, the personalities are assisted to empathize with one another, identify with one another, and, thereby, separateness becomes redundant and unnecessary (Kluft 1984d, 1991b). As the therapist assists the adolescent to tolerate the affects that have been disavowed and denied in an attempt to repudiate reality from consciousness, the need for dissociation diminishes and ceases to serve a psychodynamic need or adaptational purpose. Therefore, dividedness can be ceded.

The course of therapy has been described as occurring in a number of stages, which can be described as a sequence, but commonly overlap (Braun 1986; Dell and Eisenhower 1990; Kluft 1984c, 1986b, 1991b; Putnam 1989; Ross 1989). As the therapy becomes established and protected, it becomes crucial to establish a preliminary sense of safety and a rudimentary therapeutic alliance. The patient must be helped to understand and accept the nature of his or her condition; only with this foundation of understanding can the patient begin to understand what the therapy is all about and the actual treatment of the MPD begin. It is important to establish communication with the several alters, and the treatment must evolve ways of achieving this. Here, if hypnosis can be used without otherwise impeding the treatment, it may have a valuable role. Once alters are accessible, many therapists attempt to get contracts with the several personalities to abstain from harming one another, the body they share, or external others (Braun 1986). However, the usefulness of this step with MPD adolescents has yet to be established. It is useful to elicit the history and concerns of each alter, either systematically or in the process of the treatment. Their origins, functions, problems, and inner relationships are assessed. The treatment addresses their individual and shared difficulties, working both with individual alters at some times and with the patient addressed as a "whole" at others. The therapist should treat the personalities with complete evenhandedness. In the process, the therapist comes to better understand the system of the personalities and can move to facilitate the alters' communication and cooperation. Many therapists find hypnosis invaluable in this regard. The therapist may serve as a mediator or negotiator among the personalities. Some personalities make active efforts to assist the therapy; others vigorously oppose it.

Gradually, as the alters share and cooperate increasingly, an integration (a spontaneous or facilitated blending of the personalities) becomes possible. Generally, the personalities integrate one at a time or in groups rather than all at once. A complete integration includes all personalities. The integrated patient must develop nondissociative patterns of adaptation and resolve residual issues. Considerable working through and ongoing support is essential, and long-term follow-up is advisable.

Certain developmental issues of adolescence, universal in their importance, raise particular issues with regard to the treatment of adolescent MPD. Completion of the phase-specific developmental tasks and challenges that lead the adolescent into adulthood usually have not been successfully negotiated by the MPD adolescent. These include the second individuation process, the achievement of ego continuity, the loosening of parental ties, the resolution of residual trauma, and the solidification of sexual identity (Blos 1962, 1967, 1968, 1977). In order to negotiate these issues, the MPD adolescent must be helped to regain memories of abuse and trauma that have been hidden by dissociative defenses, disengage pathological objects and their internalized representations, and work through intense feelings of rage, shame, and guilt. The MPD adolescent usually has had sufficient early trauma and betrayal to render the development of trust and the establishment of the therapeutic alliance problematic to patient and therapist alike.

Although the issue is hotly debated (and polarized views are held in this area), many are convinced that most MPD patients have severe preoedipal difficulties (Schultz 1990). In work with adult MPD patients, it is uncommon to find that the issues of separation and individuation have been negotiated successfully. In Erikson's (1959) terms, the individual with MPD has been unable to resolve the identity crises characteristic of adolescence and remains in a state of identity diffusion. Many MPD patients remain enmeshed with their childhood objects, unable to face either their inner or their outer reality. Since a primary developmental challenge of adolescence involves disengagement from pathological objects and their internal representations, and since it often appears that this has not been successfully negotiated, MPD patients may not have achieved satisfactory object constancy and firm self- and object representations. Consequently, a secure and cohesive sense of identity and autonomy may not have developed. The MPD adolescent may resist coming to grips with disengagement issues in treatment, appearing to utilize dissociation and alloplastic activities in an attempt to cope with problematic situations, persons, and confrontations within the therapy.

In the course of and following the integration of a dissociatively fragmented self, the MPD adolescent, with increased cognitive capacities, must achieve ego continuity. The adolescent must form an appreciation of his or her individual past, present, and future, that is, engage in "a kind of historical reality testing" (Blos 1977). Especially, the adolescent has to deal with misrepresentations of reality that others willfully inflicted, with the consequence that she believed to be real what she was told was real (Blos 1977). Ideally, a factual history can be discovered and shared in the course of the therapy, although it is often possible to do no more than achieve a coherent narrative that approximates the patient's subjective psychological truth. Blos is eloquent: "A reality distortion which is willfully imposed from the outside . . . has to be rectified by a rational or truth-loving environment of which the therapist is the representative and guardian" (1977, p. 14). The MPD adolescent must be helped to recover a traumatic past and assisted to overcome abusers' injunctions to forget or to misrepresent experiences, injunctions often reinforced by punitive alters and alters protective of the abusers.

Residual trauma is inevitable in life and is understood as a driving force toward mastery. However, the MPD adolescent has been so grossly traumatized as to make this concept meaningless until the adolescent has been treated to the point of recovering the past and working through the traumata. If the MPD patient is not understood to be carrying an intolerable burden and is not given extensive opportunities to work through overwhelming experiences, the residuum is more often a severe masochistic adjustment than an impetus to mastery.

The establishment of a sexual identity is an exceedingly difficult matter for the MPD adolescent. Most have suffered sexual traumatization, and their efforts at self-cure in this area beget behaviors that further retard their resolution of these issues. They tend to reenact abusive constellations or seek out individuals they perceive as somehow safe, the opposite of their abusers. Usually, extensive work on the issues outlined above and painstaking attention to masochistic patterns of interpersonal adaptation are necessary before MPD adolescents can distinguish appropriate sexuality from exploitation, pain, and concerns about being "good" or "bad."

It is appropriate to add a note of caution. Our experience is consistent with that of Dell and Eisenhower (1990; personal communications, 1989–1991): a considerable number of MPD adolescents rebuff and frustrate the most energetic, competent, and well-informed efforts to address their dissociative psychopathology. It is not uncommon for adolescents either to refuse to deal with their dissociative difficulties and the traumata that underly them or to become so overwhelmed by such therapeutic efforts that they must be curtailed. With this subgroup, it is important to establish a good ongoing relationship in which as much therapy as is tolerated can be achieved, in which the therapist can attempt to intervene to minimize damage to the patient's life trajectory and future options, and in which the adolescent can feel sufficiently accepted so that he will have the confidence that he can either move toward addressing the MPD when this proves tolerable or return, at some later date, for definitive treatment.

Conclusions

The study of adolescents with MPD has barely begun. This chapter has reviewed the available literature and synthesized the findings of those few clinicians who have developed some experience with this population. As knowledge about MPD becomes increasingly disseminated and more readily available, increasing numbers of these patients will be identified in all age groups. The psychotherapist who works with adolescents and encounters MPD teenagers has a unique albeit challenging opportunity to intervene before the condition has become as chronic and fixed as the adult form and save the patient from years of misdiagnosis, ineffective treatment, considerable pain, and significant morbidity.

One of the unresolved issues in the treatment of the adolescent with MPD and other adolescents who have suffered overwhelming life events is the interface of developmental and dynamic processes with the trauma response. To date, our efforts to comprehend this interface and provide a concise general formulation have been frustrated by the diversity of the patient material that we have had the opportunity to study. The same has proved to be the case with MPD adults. This group of patients is remarkably heterogeneous. To the extent that a general formulation has not yet emerged, each treatment of an adolescent with MPD requires of the therapist a willingness to embark on a demanding, challenging, and novel adventure.

REFERENCES

American Psychiatric Association. 1987. *Diagnostic and Statistical Manual of Mental Disorders*. 3d ed., rev. Washington, D.C.: American Psychiatric Press.

Azam, E. E. 1887. *Hypnotisme, double conscience et altération de la personnalité*. Paris: J. B. Baillière.

Barkin, R.; Braun, B. G.; and Kluft, R. P. 1986. The dilemma of drug therapy for multiple personality disorder. In B. G. Braun, ed. *Treatment of Multiple Personality Disorder*. Washington, D.C.: American Psychiatric Press.

Blos, P. 1962. *On Adolescence*. New York: Free Press.

Blos, P. 1967. The second individuation process of adolescence. *Psychoanalytic Study of the Child* 22:162–186.

Blos, P. 1968. Character formation in adolescence. *Psychoanalytic Study of the Child* 23:245–263.

Blos, P. 1977. When and how does adolescence end: structural criteria for adolescent closure. *Adolescent Psychiatry* 5:5–17.

Bowman, E. S. 1990. Adolescent MPD in the nineteenth and early twentieth centuries. *Dissociation* 3:179–187.

Bowman, E. S.; Blix, S.; and Coons, P. M. 1985. Multiple personality in adolescence: relationship to incestual experience. *Journal of the Academy of Child Psychiatry* 24:109–114.

Braun, B. G. 1986. Issues in the psychotherapy of multiple personality disorder. In B. G. Braun, ed. *Treatment of Multiple Personality Disorder.* Washington, D.C.: American Psychiatric Press.

Braun, B. G. 1990. Unusual medication regimens in the treatment of multiple personality disorder patients. I. noradrenergic agents. *Dissociation* 3:144–150.

Coons, P. M. 1980. Multiple personality: diagnostic considerations. *Journal of Clinical Psychiatry* 41:330–336.

Coons, P. M. 1984. The differential diagnosis of multiple personality. *Psychiatric Clinics of North America* 7:51–68.

Coons, P. M. 1986. Treatment progress in 20 patients with multiple personality disorder. *Journal of Nervous and Mental Disease* 174:715–721.

Coons, P. M. 1988. Psychophysiologic aspects of multiple personality disorder: a review. *Dissociation* 1(1): 47–53.

Coons, P. M.; Bowman, E. S.; and Milstein, V. 1988. Multiple personality disorder: clinical investigation of 50 cases. *Journal of Nervous and Mental Disease* 176:519–527.

Dell, P. F. 1988. Professional skepticism about multiple personality. *Journal of Nervous and Mental Disease* 176:528–531.

Dell, P. F., and Eisenhower, J. W. 1990. Adolescent multiple personality disorder: a preliminary study of eleven cases. *Journal of the American Academy of Child and Adolescent Psychiatry* 29:359–366.

Ellenberger, H. F. 1970. *The Discovery of the Unconscious.* New York: Basic.

Erikson, E. H. 1959. *Identity and the Life Cycle.* Psychological Issues Monograph, vol. 1, no. 1. New York: International Universities Press.

Fagan, J., and McMahon, P. P. 1984. Incipient multiple personality in children. *Journal of Nervous and Mental Disease* 172:26–36.

Giovaccinni, P. L. 1974. The difficult adolescent patient: countertransference problems. *Adolescent Psychiatry* 3:271–288.

Goodwin, J. 1985. Credibility problems in multiple personality disorder patients and abused children. In R. P. Kluft, ed. *Childhood Anteced-*

ents of Multiple Personality. Washington, D.C.: American Psychiatric Press.

Gruenewald, D. 1971. Hypnotic techniques without hypnosis in the treatment of dual personality. *Journal of Nervous and Mental Disease* 153:41–46.

Kluft, R. P. 1984a. Aspects of the treatment of multiple personality disorder. *Psychiatric Annals* 14:51–55.

Kluft, R. P. 1984b. An introduction to multiple personality disorder. *Psychiatric Annals* 14:19–24.

Kluft, R. P. 1984c. Multiple personality in childhood. *Psychiatric Clinics of North America* 7:121–134.

Kluft, R. P. 1984d. The treatment of multiple personality. *Psychiatric Clinics of North America* 7:9–29.

Kluft, R. P. 1985a. Making the diagnosis of multiple personality disorder (MPD). In F. F. Flach, ed. *Directions in Psychiatry,* vol. 5. New York: Hatherleigh.

Kluft, R. P. 1985b. The natural history of multiple personality disorder. In R. P. Kluft, ed. *Childhood Antecedents of Multiple Personality.* Washington, D.C.: American Psychiatric Press.

Kluft, R. P. 1985c. The treatment of multiple personality disorder (MPD). In F. F. Flach, ed. *Directions in Psychiatry,* vol. 5. New York: Hatherleigh.

Kluft, R. P. 1986a. Personality unification in multiple personality disorder: a follow-up study. In B. G. Braun, ed. *The Treatment of Multiple Personality Disorder.* Washington, D.C.: American Psychiatric Press.

Kluft, R. P. 1986b. Treating children who have multiple personality disorder. In B. G. Braun, ed. *The Treatment of Multiple Personality Disorder.* Washington, D.C.: American Psychiatric Press.

Kluft, R. P. 1987a. First-rank symptoms as a diagnostic clue to multiple personality disorder. *American Journal of Psychiatry* 144:293–298.

Kluft, R. P. 1987b. Making the diagnosis of multiple personality disorder. In F. F. Flach, ed. *Diagnostics and Psychopathology.* New York: Norton.

Kluft, R. P. 1987c. An update on multiple personality disorder. *Hospital and Community Psychiatry* 38:363–373.

Kluft, R. P. 1988. The phenomenology and treatment of extremely complex multiple personality disorder. *Dissociation* 1(4): 47–58.

Kluft, R. P. 1991a. Clinical presentations of multiple personality disorder. *Psychiatric Clinics of North America* 14:605–629.

Kluft, R. P. 1991b. Multiple personality disorder. In A. Tasman and S. M. Goldfinger, eds. *American Psychiatric Press Annual Review of Psychiatry,* vol. 10. Washington, D.C.: American Psychiatric Press.

Kluft, R. P.; Steinberg, M.; and Spitzer, R. L. 1988. DSM-III-R revisions in the dissociative disorders: an exploration of their derivation and rationale. *Dissociation* 1(1): 39–46.

Loewenstein, R. J. 1991. An office mental status examination for complex chronic dissociative symptoms and multiple personality disorder. *Psychiatric Clinics of North America* 14:567–604.

Loewenstein, R. J.; Hornstein, N.; and Farber, B. 1988. Open trial of clonazepam in the treatment of posttraumatic stress symptoms in multiple personality disorder. *Dissociation* 1(3): 3–12.

Morris, R. A. 1989. *Multiple Personality: An Exercise in Deception.* Hillsdale, N.J.: Erlbaum.

Nemiah, J. C. 1985. Dissociative disorders (hysterical neurosis, dissociative type). In H. I. Kaplan and B. J. Sadock, eds. *Comprehensive Textbook of Psychiatry/IV,* vol. 1. Baltimore: Williams & Wilkins.

Putnam, F. W. 1985. Dissociation as a response to extreme trauma. In R. P. Kluft, ed. *Childhood Antecedents of Multiple Personality.* Washington, D.C.: American Psychiatric Press.

Putnam, F. W. 1989. *The Diagnosis and Treatment of Multiple Personality Disorder.* New York: Guilford.

Putnam, F. W.; Guroff, J. J.; Silberman, E. K.; Barban, L.; and Post, R. M. 1986. The clinical phenomenology of multiple personality disorder: review of 100 recent cases. *Journal of Clinical Psychiatry* 47:285–293.

Putnam, F. W.; Loewenstein, R. J.; Silberman, E. K.; and Post, R. M. 1984. Multiple personality in a hospital setting. *Journal of Clinical Psychiatry* 45:172–175.

Ross, C. A. 1989: *Multiple Personality Disorder: Diagnosis, Clinical Features, and Treatment.* New York: Wiley.

Ross, C. A.; Norton, G. R.; and Wozney, K. 1989. Multiple personality disorder: an analysis of 236 cases. *Canadian Journal of Psychiatry* 34:413–418.

Sanders, B.; McRoberts, G.; and Tollefson, C. 1989. Childhood stress and dissociation in a college population. *Dissociation* 2:17–23.

Schultz, R. 1990. Secrets of adolescence: incest and developmental fixations. In R. P. Kluft, ed. *Incest-related Syndromes of Adult Psychopathology*. Washington, D.C.: American Psychiatric Press.

Schultz, R.; Braun, B. G.; and Kluft, R. P. 1985. Creativity and the imaginary companion: prevalence and phenomenology in MPD compared to major depression. Paper presented at the Second International Conference on Multiple Personality/Dissociative States, Chicago, October.

Schultz, R.; Braun, B. G.; and Kluft, R. P. 1987. The relationship between post-traumatic stress disorder and multiple personality disorder. Paper presented at the Fourth International Conference on Multiple Personality/Dissociative States, Chicago, September.

Schultz, R.; Braun, B. G.; and Kluft, R. P. 1989. Incidence of abuse in multiple personality disorder: phenomenology of selected variables in comparison to major depression. *Dissociation* 2:45–51.

Schultz, R.; Kluft, R. P.; and Braun, B. G. 1986. Interface between multiple personality disorder and borderline personality disorder. Paper presented at the Third International Conference on Multiple Personality/Dissociative States, September.

Solomon, R. S., and Solomon, V. 1982. Differential diagnosis of multiple personality. *Psychological Reports* 51:1187–1194.

Spiegel, D. 1984. Multiple personality as a post-traumatic stress disorder. *Psychiatric Clinics of North America* 7:101–110.

Spiegel, D. 1986a. Dissociating damage. *American Journal of Clinical Hypnosis* 29:123–131.

Spiegel, D. 1986b. Dissociation, double binds, and post-traumatic stress disorder. In B. G. Braun, ed. *Treatment of Multiple Personality Disorder*. Washington, D.C.: American Psychiatric Press.

Spiegel, D. 1991. Dissociation and trauma. In A. Tasman and S. M. Goldfinger, eds. *American Psychiatric Press Annual Review of Psychiatry,* vol. 10. Washington, D.C.: American Psychiatric Press.

Weiss, M.; Sutton, P. J.; and Utecht, A. J. 1985. Multiple personality in a 10-year-old girl. *Journal of the Academy of Child Psychiatry* 24:495–501.

16   MALIGNANT MEMORIES:
SIGNATURES OF VIOLENCE

EITAN D. SCHWARZ, JANICE M. KOWALSKI,
AND STEVEN HANUS

In the futuristic science-fiction film classic *Blade Runner* (1982), androids are commercially manufactured to substitute for humans on hazardous distant planets. Eventually, they become too human-like and rebel. But how did they become more human?

Memories.

On their own, these nonhumans accumulated and patterned memories that enabled them to become human, integrating identities, relationships, aesthetics, emotions, and free will. But they were too child-like—preadolescent at best—and lacked the refinement that comes with full development into civilized beings who can function reasonably in society.

Also, they became too autonomous, aggressive, and dangerous. So, the manufacturer "gifted" his latest models with rich pasts of actual human memories. But, when Rachel, a beautiful, state-of-the-art, latest edition android, a postadolescent woman in every way, discovered that her memories were not her own, she felt betrayed. Yet she was able to grieve this loss and form a loving, mature, romantic relationship with the human hero. Even though not her own, a remembered past made this android human in a fuller sense.

In the musical *Cats* (1981), the haunting tune "Memories" laments, "Has the moon lost her memory? She is smiling alone. . . . I remember the time I knew what happiness was—let the memories live again." Cats were humanized individually and as a community through the endowment of lush personal and collective memories. Proust (1956) in

Remembrances of Things Past reminds us how memory can surprise us so agreeably. Suddenly, a rich and pleasant tapestry of complex images, sensations, and affects begins to envelop us, prompted merely by a seemingly trivial tasting of a "petite madeleine" pastry.

But there is another side. Traumatic memories lie at the core of human experience on the opposite extreme from memories of joy, love, soothing, safety, nurturance, even yearning, that enrich our existence or even make it possible. Memories that grow from violence can be invasive and tenacious and destroy the core of our humanity. In Shatan (1974), a soldier described his experience during a fifteen-second terror-filled ambush as "your whole world feels as if it slides through a membrane." Years later, he still looks to a therapist to assist him "back through the membrane of reality." Shatan quotes Yuri Suhl's poem "Survivor": "*Memory* is the enemy now. . . ."

Wiesel (1969) embodies the struggle to hold on to our humanity and give meaning to personal and collective memories in spite of the unspeakable atrocities of the Holocaust. Wiesel is haunted by an image of the indifferent, passive onlooker who stands by and does nothing as his neighbors are systematically destroyed. Additionally, there has been growing interest in the popular media, especially American television and film, in the enigmatically enduring effects of violence. Recent films, including *Jacob's Ladder* (1990), *The Prince of Tides* (1991), and *The Fisher King* (1991), depict tormented individuals haunted by traumatic memories.

Posttraumatic Stress Disorder

Posttraumatic stress disorder (PTSD) is a syndrome that has gained much attention since the Vietnam War and has recently also been studied in children. PTSD is characterized in DSM-III-R (American Psychiatric Association 1987) as deriving from an unusual stressor and distinguished by three clusters of symptoms: reexperiencing, avoidance, and arousal.

To illustrate, data were gathered in the aftermath of a shooting at a local school where a child was murdered and several were wounded (Egginton 1991). Table 1 (Schwarz and Kowalski 1991) shows the range of PTSD symptoms and how they are organized in clusters and yield diagnoses in children, mean age eight, and adults, mean age forty-four, and displays the differences between children and adults.

TABLE 1

DSM-III-R PTSD Symptoms, Cluster, and Diagnosis Frequencies, Differences between Adults and Children, Diagnosis and Cluster

	Adults (%) (N = 66)	Children (%) (N = 64)
Was event an extreme stressor?	55	91[a]
Reexperiencing (at least one) . . .	81	92
Recurrent recollections/play . .	42[dc]	88[ac]
Recurrent distressing dreams	6	30
Sudden feeling event recurrent	6[b]	39[a]
Distress at reminders	78[bc]	25[d]
Avoidance (at least three).	20[d]	30[d]
Thoughts or feelings	29[dc]	23[dc]
Activities or situations	29[dc]	52[dc]
Inability to recall	11	
Lost interest/regressed	10	41[ac]
Detached from others	9[dc]	39[acd]
Restricted range of affect	17[dc]	48[adc]
Future foreshortening	5[dc]	
Arousal (at least two).	46[d]	55[d]
Insomnia.	22[c]	30[dc]
Irritability/anger		14
Difficulty concentrating.	17[d]	33[c]
Hypervigilance	73[c]	
Exaggerated startle response. .	31[c]	67[ac]
Physiological reactivity	28[cd]	23[cd]
PTSD diagnosis	19	27

Note.—χ^2 analysis Yate's Correction $p < .002$.
[a] Children > adults.
[b] Adults > children.
[c] Associated with cluster.
[d] Associated with diagnosis.

Malignant Memories

We coined the term "malignant memories" to highlight the central role of memory in PTSD development and to emphasize that human response to trauma is a neurobiological as well as a psychosocial phenomenon (fig. 1). A malignant memory is a relatively stable, pernicious, persistent, biologically rooted configuration that embeds itself after a trauma, linking cognitive, perceptual, and affective functions. A malignant memory invades experience and is associated with high levels of arousal and opposite tendencies to attentuation that include cognitive distortions, affective numbing, and behavioral and affective

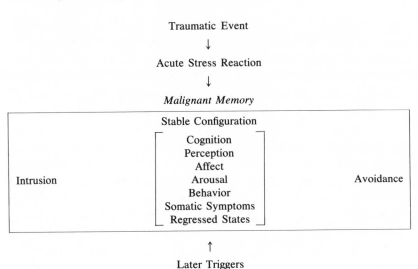

FIG. 1.—Schematic representation of the structural component of a malignant memory

avoidance (Schwarz and Kowalski 1991). Such memories are later activated with specific triggers.

The concept of malignant memory is not new, and a body of theory and experimental evidence has accumulated since the early days of modern psychiatry linking experience, memory, behavior, and brain structure and function. For example, recognizing the central role of memory almost a century ago, Breuer and Freud (1893, p. 7) wrote, "Hysterics suffer mainly from reminiscences," and suggested abreaction as a cure.

Freud speculated about the underlying neurophysiological organization of traumatic memories: "As a result of the experience of pain the mnemonic image of the hostile object has acquired an excellent facilitation to . . . key neurones" and may involve "endogenous stimuli consist[ing] of chemical products, of which there may be a considerable number" (Freud 1895a, p. 321). Note his prediction of the discovery of facilitatory processes and neurotransmitters.

Freud went still further to distinguish posttraumatic memories from ordinary "mnemic images": "Particularly large and repeated binding from the ego is required before this facilitation to unpleasure can be counterbalanced" and before an "untamed mnemic image" that interrupts thought and is associated with "sensory qualities" and "manifestations of affect and defence" is finally modified and "come[s] to resemble other mnemic images" (Freud 1895b, p. 380). He offered a model for neuronal organization underlying memories that involved progressive rearrangements or "registrations of memory traces." Speculating about how memories ordinarily diminish in intensity, he noted that, the more often a painful memory recurs, "the more inhibited does its release finally become"; otherwise, it would be "behaving as if it were some current event" (Freud 1896, p. 236). Confirming Freud's speculation that the passage of time does not necessarily help these distinctive types of memories, we recently found that PTSD-symptomatic adults reporting their experiences the day of the shooting tended to exaggerate at eighteen months what they reported at six months after the shooting (Schwarz, Kowalski, and McNally, in press).

Janet (reviewed in van der Kolk and van der Hart 1989, p. 1532) posited a certain type of memory as unique to trauma. Events accompanied by "a vehement emotion . . . produce their disintegrating effects in proportion to their intensity, duration, and repetition. . . . Memory traces linger as subconscious fixed ideas that cannot be 'liquidated' as long as they have not been translated into a personal narrative and instead continue to intrude as terrifying perceptions, obsessional preoccupations, and somatic reexperiences, such as anxiety reactions."

Later, Freud (1920, p. 30) conceptualized trauma as "a breach . . . in the protective shield" resulting in flooding of the mental apparatus with stimuli that require binding, but he did not pursue his interest in specific processes of memory. Yet the concept of repetition compulsion was always central in psychoanalytic thinking. Horowitz and Becker (1972) supported its manifestations in traumatic experiences by showing that stimulus-repetitive intrusive thoughts followed stress of watching a film even in individuals without a psychiatric diagnosis. On the whole, however, psychoanalytic theory and practice evolved away from studying the neurophysiological basis of memory toward exploration of their content, especially memories of early experiences and their associational links, vicissitudes, and influences on later experience and behavior. The heart of psychoanalytic treatment has been the development and analysis of a transference neurosis, a rich reliving in the transference of unconscious patterned memories or fantasies

(Freud 1926), and the distinction between memory and fantasy has become unclear (see, e.g., de Saussure 1982).

From a behavioral/cognitive viewpoint, Foa, Steketee, and Rothbaum (1989) distinguished traumatic from other memories, using Lang's (1977) concept of "fear structures" that exist in memory. Such fear structures include information about the feared stimulus or situation, responses (including physiological), and interpretation of its meaning, especially danger, and form a program for escape or avoidance. Accordingly, PTSD fear structures differ from phobias in the persistence of intensity of responses, size and accessibility of the structure, high arousal, and low threshold for activation.

More recently, there has been renewed interest in the biological basis for stress (see the review in Chrousus and Gold 1992). A stressful experience can have profound effects on the organism mediated by the hypothalamic-pituitary-adrenal axis and the locus ceruleus/norepinephrine sympathetic system. These systems are activated with stress to restore adaptation and homeostasis but can malfunction when stress is overwhelming or chronic. Stress affects arousal, behavior, cognition, and physiological functioning of most body systems and can affect reproductive, growth, thyroid, and immune functions.

Stressful experiences are recorded in the brain via neuronal mechanisms. Evidence for the basis of memory in brain structure and function was offered by Penfield and Jasper (1954), who called the temporal cortex "memory records" after evoking memories from patients stimulated there. Horowitz, Adams, and Burton (1968) suggested a more complex and dynamic model that does not posit static localized memory engrams.

Mesulam (1990) summarized a modern model for the neurological foundations of memory, mapping the phenomena at the level of multifocal neural systems that give rise to brain-behavior relationships that are both localized and distributed. The widely distributed but tightly connected limbic network is critical in making new experiences storable and old experiences retrievable. Enabling association between multimodal sensory information and affective states related to fear and reward, the amygdala elicits the recall of emotionally charged memories. Furthermore, Mesulam notes that activation states of the entire cerebral cortex, modulating the tone and coloring of experience, can be shifted by five projection systems, each arising from a relatively small group of subcortical neurons using a single neurotransmitter. Li and Spiegel (1992) offered a neural network model for dissociative disorders including PTSD.

Recent studies are providing empirical evidence that PTSD may be not only a psychological or a mind phenomenon but also a brain phenomenon (reviewed in Bremner, Southwick, and Charney 1991; Friedman 1991), involving catecholamine, benzodiazepine, and endogenous opioid systems. Recent reports (Brodsky, Doerman, Palmer, Slade, and Munasifi 1990; Ornitz and Pynoos 1989) link PTSD to neurophysiological disturbances, intimating the distinctiveness of traumatic memories. Additionally, studies (Pitman, Orr, Forgue, de Jong, and Claiborn 1987; Pitman, Orr, Forgue, Altman, de Jong, and Herz 1990; van der Kolk, Greenberg, Orr, and Pitman 1989) are showing that sounds and sights of battle combat–related stimuli evoke peripheral signs of physiological arousal, as well as analgesia, in combat veterans with PTSD but not in those without PTSD. Moreover, Bremner et al. (1991) discussed how the preference of PTSD patients for benzodiazepines might result from long-term alterations in benzodiazepine systems induced by trauma. Emotional numbing and analgesia may derive from release of endogenous opioids (Pitman, van der Kolk, Orr, and Greenberg 1990).

Sufficient stress may actually induce structural changes—changes in the "hard wiring"—of the brain. Studying children, Perry (in press) hypothesized that abnormal patterns of catecholamine activity associated with and induced by traumatic events may result in altered development in which a dysregulated brain stem results in permanently abnormal brain stem functioning. In abused and neglected children, he found altered cardiovascular regulation, affective lability, behavioral impulsivity, increased anxiety, increased startle response, and sleep abnormalities. Perry hypothesized that young children victimized by trauma are at risk for developing permanent vulnerabilities rooted in permanent changes in neuronal differentiation and organization. Perry's preliminary findings show that symptoms respond to clonidine, which attentuates noradrenergic-mediated arousal.

Malignant Memories and Adolescence

Following the school shooting, when comparing adults' to children's reactions, we found that developmental factors may play an important part in how an individual reacts to violence. For example, adults needed more specific cues to trigger reexperiencing memories, while older children and adolescents were more angry in response to the shooting (Schwarz and Kowalski 1991), and younger children's reactions were more interactive with parental symptoms (Schwarz and Kowalski 1992a).

It is reasonable to ask how traumatic events affect individuals at differing stages of development. Adolescence is an important period in the developmental process. It is characterized by complex biopsychosocial shifts that include hormonal changes, stimulating sexual features, affects, and behaviors; cognitive shifts, enabling more abstract and moral thinking regarding the meaning of self in the world and in time; increases in affective coloring and intensity; shifts in personality organization and crystallization of identity; and shifts in relations with family and peers.

Adolescents are at high risk for exposure to violence. We know that adolescents are participants in, or witnesses of, family and street violence at least as much as younger children or adults. After all, many combatants in wars and victims of rape are adolescents. In the United States, twenty-nine adolescents, compared with nineteen children, out of a thousand are abused ("Teens Abused More Than Children" 1992).

In the poignantly tragic song "Next" (from *Jacques Brel Is Alive and Well and Living in Paris*), a veteran remembers his traumatic battlefield initiation into sex as an adolescent: "I was still just a kid when my innocence was lost in a mobile army whorehouse, gift of the army free of cost. . . . next, next. . . . I would always recall the brothel truck, the flying flags. . . . Me, I really would have liked a little bit of tenderness, maybe a word, a smile. . . . It is the voice of nations, it is the thick voice of blood. . . . And since then, each woman I have taken to bed seems to laugh in my arms, to whisper through my head . . . next, next. . . . Oh, the naked and the dead should hold each other's hands as they watch me scream at night in a dream no-one understands . . . next . . . next. . . ."

Yet a search of the Medline data base, cross-referencing rape or trauma with adolescence, showed relatively few studies of how trauma affects adolescents as a group or the adolescent process. Reports are anecdotal, retrospective, and uncontrolled and lump adolescents together with children or do not discuss in detail how adolescents respond differently from younger children, from adults, or from each other.

Many authors have noted that exposure to extreme stress in adolescence or childhood produced symptoms later. Klein (1971) described social adjustment and families of Holocaust survivors currently living in a kibbutz. Kahana (1981) discussed the effect on an adolescent boy of his father's traumatic experiences in the Holocaust. Jackson (1982) described arrested moral development in adolescent combatants. Glover (1984) highlighted the development of profound mistrust in adolescent Vietnam veterans. Gidycz and Koss (1989) reported that sexually victimized adolescent girls later scored higher on the Trait Anxiety Inventory and the Beck Depression Scale. Beck and van der Kolk (1987) reported incest as a risk factor for intractable psychosis in chronically hospitalized adult women. Burgess, Hartman, and McCormack (1987) showed that sexual abuse was associated with higher risk for later drug use and sociopathy. Edwards and Donaldson (1989) and Lindberg and Distad (1985) showed that adult victims of childhood and adolescent incest showed PTSD symptoms. Stoddard, Norman, Murphy, and Beardslee (1989) noted that children and adolescent burn victims suffered posttraumatic enuresis and phobic and overanxious disorders. Kinzie, Sack, Angell, Manson, and Rath (1986) and Kinzie, Sack, Angell, Clarke, and Rath (1989) followed a group of Cambodian adolescents exposed as children to the Pol Pot atrocities and found continuing PTSD and depressive symptoms in a substantial number. Herman, Perry, and van der Kolk (1989) suggested a link between early abuse and later development of borderline personality disorder. Terr (1987) explored how early trauma influenced the creative product of writers and artists.

In contrast, Leon, Butcher, Kleinman, Goldberg, and Almagor (1981) questioned the intergenerational transmission of psychopathology in Holocaust survivors. Elder and Clipp (1989) reported that adolescents exposed to heavy combat in World War II and the Korean War displayed more resiliency as adults, and Saigh (1985) reported that traumatized adolescents did not differ from nontraumatized Lebanese adolescents.

Several authors reported on the treatment of traumatized adolescents: Stocking (1989) described the psychotherapy of an adolescent girl who witnessed parental murder-suicide. Van der Kolk (1985) noted the vulnerability of adolescent combatants to battle loss of a buddy— they suffered narcissistic injury and threat to group cohesion that motivated revenge but responded to group therapy aimed at restoring group

TABLE 2
TRAUMA DURING CHILDHOOD REACTIVATED IN ADOLESCENCE

Traumatic event
Sexual abuse/physical abuse/neglect/multiple foster placements and moves

Malignant memory
Cognition: repression, cognitive constriction, inattention
Affect: shame, dysphoria, guilt, lability
Arousal: anxiety/panic, flashbacks, intrusive imagery, insomnia
Behavior: avoidance, overcompensation, dependency, pseudomaturity, superficial
  cheerfulness
Somatic: headaches, fatigue
Regressed states: splitting, indiscriminate attachments, idealizing or caretaking
  transference

Triggers/cues
Molestation at age thirteen
Puberty, particularly development of secondary sexual characteristics
Heterosexual contacts

identity. Saigh (1988) used flooding therapy to treat adolescents with PTSD. Deblinger et al. (1990) noted improvement with treatment in sexually abused children and adolescents.

Case A:
Childhood Trauma Reactivated in Adolescence

Miss A (see table 2) was hospitalized at age thirteen because she left a suicide note describing vague sexual advances by a male household member and intense feelings of fear and shame that prevented her from telling her adoptive mother, therapist, or teachers. Reportedly a single incident, this event precipitated a serious depression. During hospitalization, Miss A exhibited behavioral disorganization, dissociation, sleep disturbance, hypervigilance, and diffuse fear reactions suggesting more serious prolonged abuse. She began to verbalize strong wishes to reunite with her father, now absent many years, and guiltily blamed herself and feared rejection by her adoptive mother.

The little developmental history that was available included early neglect, physical abuse, and multiple moves. She was removed from her parents at age six after sexual abuse by a stepsibling. She began psychotherapy at the age of eight as part of planning for a permanent adoptive home with few reported behavioral or psychological difficulties, except for a chronic mild sleep disturbance and oversolicitous behaviors toward younger siblings. She presented as a compliant and eager-to-please child who exhibited great difficulty when speaking about herself. She persisted in denying memories of her earlier home life and past abuse but appeared guilty and ashamed whenever the subject was brought up.

Although treatment at the age of eight was successful in helping Miss A adapt to her new home and maintain good grades, winning several awards of recognition, she remained on the fringes of her peer group, typically serving as a peacemaker and caretaker. She preferred the company of adults, from whom she sought praise and attention, and of younger children, whom she mothered.

As early adolescence approached, Miss A exhibited little interest in dressing or acting like her peers and preserved a younger appearance. However, by thirteen, physical changes attracted comments from boys, to which she responded angrily. Refusing to acknowledge her development, she demanded not to be called a "teenager."

In this case, Miss A's malignant memories of early neglect and abuse were triggered by her own emerging sexuality and the potential for abuse again. Except for a mild sleep disorder, her defensive avoidance, repression, denial, and reaction formation allowed for relative equilibrium through latency. Triggered by an overstimulating experience at the onset of her adolescent sexuality, malignant memories flooded her with intense affect and arousal, strongly coloring her interpretation of current experience.

Case B: Trauma in Adolescence

At fourteen, Miss B (see table 3) suddenly began to have severe headaches and up to ten daily "blackout spells" of twenty-five to thirty seconds, characterized by unresponsiveness and staring. Typically, she experienced a prodrome of dizziness, tingling, and weakness in the upper extremities and a gradual and rapid dimming of vision, "like I was looking through a screen," progressing to a brief loss of consciousness. A thorough neurological investigation, including direct observations and EEGs during these episodes, revealed no abnormalities.

History revealed development as normal, and she was pleasant, easy, compliant, and a well-behaved "mother's helper." Current symptoms began after a short visit to a relative's home in Texas.

TABLE 3
Trauma in Adolescence

Traumatic event
Rape/physical assault, terror

Malignant memory
Cognition: cognitive constriction, amnesia, inattention, confusion, flashbacks
Perception: derealization, depersonalization, hallucinations
Affect: dysphoria, lability, irritability, shame, guilt
Arousal: pseudoseizures, anxiety, flashbacks, intrusive imagery, tachycardia with
 amitriptyline, response to benzodiazepines
Behavior: suicidality, school avoidance
Somatic: headaches, visual changes, blackouts
Regressed states: dissociation, hallucinatory states, idealizing transference

Triggers/cues
Heterosexual contact
Confinement in close quarters
Proximity to site of trauma

Although she initially denied violence, Miss B soon remembered fragments of molestation by a nineteen-year-old stepcousin in Texas during the visit. Terrified of his retribution, she was frightened of angering her family and worried that no one would believe her. When recalling the events, she became dysphoric, irritable, tearful, and confused. Intense anxiety was accompanied by dissociative symptoms of depersonalization and derealization and a feeling of having "lost time" with long periods of time passing without her conscious awareness.

She experienced flashbacks of repetitive, intrusive visual images of the cousin laughing at her and often developed headaches afterward. She felt guilty and worthless, and difficulty in concentrating interfered with her schoolwork. She was angry at her mother for allowing her to visit a potentially dangerous setting yet feared setting off a depression in mother.

An attempt to treat her headaches with amitriptyline was unsuccessful because of tachycardia, which persisted after discontinuation. After intensive individual and group psychotherapy in the hospital, and with one milligram of alprazolam per day, symptoms remitted, and Miss B returned to home and school. Unfortunately, she soon relapsed, this time also having auditory hallucinations of her cousin's laughter and intense suicidal ideation, after she was taken to Texas against medical advice. Again hospitalized, she recalled other aspects of the trauma, which included being raped several times.

After six months of additional outpatient psycho- and pharmacotherapy, she felt ready to visit benevolent grandparents in Texas. On returning, she felt triumphant that she was no longer being "punished" by the memories of the abuse. Miss B is still wary of being alone with teenage boys and fears that she will not be able to date successfully.

Miss B illustrates many issues related to PTSD and malignant memories in adolescents. It is important to have a high level of suspicion, no matter what the presenting problem, whether somatic, cognitive, affective, or behavioral. Goodwin, Simm, and Bergman (1979) and Gross (1979) described hysterical seizures following incest. Malignant memories of the rape were organized and expressed initially through such symptoms, regressed states, avoidance, and perceptual distortions. There were physiological as well as psychosocial components to this presentation. Use of alprazolam was successful, while amitriptyline probably exacerbated an autonomic system dysregulated by trauma.

Without an intensive holding environment providing nurturance and safety, dampening of arousal with alprazolam, and opportunity for cognitive reappraisal, Miss B could have become developmentally arrested and left with persistent malignant memories.

Case C:
Trauma in Childhood Not Clinically Detected in Adolescence but Surfacing in Adulthood

At thirty-six, Mr. C (see table 4) was a bright, articulate, talented, and successful executive and devoted father. Suddenly, on the breakup of his third marriage, he became tormented by intense nightmares and sought treatment. Initially, he was totally amnesic for the first ten years of his life. Reporting an adolescence marked by family conflict, Mr. C reported social, athletic, and academic success and seemed to suffer little. However, he did not experiment sexually and eventually married a high school sweetheart.

Associations to nightmares began triggering piecemeal recall of two traumatic constellations. The first, during toddlerhood and early childhood, consisted of severe eczema for which he was tied down supine

TABLE 4
TRAUMA IN CHILDHOOD NOT DETECTED IN ADOLESCENCE

Traumatic events
Eczema, tied down supine—toddlerhood, early childhood
Beatings (victim, witness)—middle/late childhood

Malignant memories
Cognition: amnesia, concrete "black and white" thinking, confusion, distractability
Perception: skin sensations
Affect: rage, anxiety, depression, numbness, guilt
Arousal: insomnia, nightmares, agitation, response to medication
Behavior: suicidality, agitation, avoidance
Somatic: skin burning/cold, hives, alopecia
Regressed states: object hunger, splitting, idealizing transference

Triggers/cues
Divorce
Toddlerhood of son
Empathic disruptions
Contact with family of origin

in the crib for long periods in order to prevent scratching. The second set of memories was of vicious "cold-blooded" beatings by a sadistic father that made him feel as "garbage," coupled with neglectful intrusions and emotional neglect by an obsessive, perfectionistic, and possibly episodically depressed mother.

Mr. C quickly became flooded with intense rage, becoming increasingly agitated, disorganized, and suicidal. He developed dermatological symptoms of alopecia and "burning skin," or would feel numb and have "cold skin" with specific memories. He required intensive psychotherapy and medication, including neuroleptics, anxiolytics, and lithium carbonate and a brief hospitalization for suicidality.

We discovered that his success in business and his choices of spouses were expressions of a grandiose self that survives, plays "perfect son," and mediates family conflict—the "superman" corporate man. Eventually, Mr. C reintegrated around an idealizing transference and holding environment of intensive therapy and used his considerable intellect to cognitively reappraise the violence of his childhood. To avoid reexperiencing malignant memories, Mr C broke off all contact with his entire family. His grandiosity, drivenness, and exaggerated expectations of himself and others lessened. He terminated the first treatment episode calmer and hopeful in a new marriage and a renewed sense of self.

However, as in rapprochement, Mr. C would "touch base" for an office visit or two several times a year for four years when triggers such as empathic failures by his wife or intrusive calls from his father reactivated brief relapses from which he quickly recovered.

Mr. C had a relapse when his new son entered toddlerhood. He felt the intense dilemma of being trapped in a business and marriage that were denying his intense needs for narcissistic mirroring. He reexperienced pain, rage, and "hot skin" alternating with emptiness, numbing, and "cold skin." Thinking again became concrete and "black and white." He felt as "garbage" again. Often, the only solution appeared to be suicide. Obtaining considerable relief in interacting with his son, with whom he felt intense joy and loving, Mr. C could not maintain these states when separated from him. Intensive psychotherapy to provide an empathic center for rapprochement and restoration of self-soothing representations, together with lithium carbonate, fluoxetine, and alprazolam to attenuate his affective intensity and lability, again stabilized him. With a stronger therapeutic alliance, rooted in a more stable holding environment and transference, enabling identification with the male therapist, Mr. C continues to attempt to integrate split off parts of the self. Small slights by his wife, or even just her presence, still trigger injury, rage, numbness, somatic symptoms, and avoidance, which he recognized as irrational but which precluded intimacy with her. These symptoms remitted temporarily with the addition of clonidine.

In summary, during adolescence, we can hypothesize that, although heterosexual intimacy eluded him, Mr. C adaptively refined the grandiose "perfect son," identifying with and sublimating his father's aggression and perfectionistic demandingness of an obsessional unempathic mother. He utiiized considerable cognitive and social abilities to form a rigid psychic structure while splitting off the injured, enraged aspects of his self. This developmental period, albeit partially arrested, may have enabled his adaptation. Only specific triggers in adulthood reactivated the malignant memories.

Conclusions

We have observed case vignettes of trauma during childhood reactivated in adolescence, trauma during adolescence, and malignant memories from childhood activated only in adulthood. These illustrate that presentation of sudden decompensation in an adolescent or adult should lead us to suspect that malignant memories have been triggered. Overwhelming shame, guilt, depression, disorganization, and suicidal behavior often accompany such presentations.

Intervention must sometimes be quite massive and include establishment of a safe holding environment in a long-term therapeutic relationship, medication to subdue arousal or rage, and careful attempts to reappraise the traumatic experiences, integrating avoided and walled-off memories. The patient must be given control over the pace at which efforts to uncover are made. Because psychic trauma might induce structural brain changes, especially in younger children, it may ultimately not be possible to achieve a cure.

Trauma before and/or during adolescence can affect the developmental process, and intervention with adolescents can be especially rewarding because so much of the personal narrative is reworked, reformed, and integrated with the group narrative during this period. Yet adolescents present difficult challenges because of their, as yet, immature cognitive capacities. Additionally, striving for autonomy and individuation, adolescents resist therapeutic alliances, and many utilize holding environments poorly. Sometimes we may best serve an adolescent's adaptation by strengthening defenses and assisting efforts at avoidance, rather than exposing memories.

Treatment of the adolescent often demands interpreting his or her experience to family members and enlisting their cooperation, if not offering them treatment as well. Yet it is in the family that so much trauma may have occurred. Additionally, malignant memories of parents deriving from their own traumatic adolescence may be triggered during the adolescence of their offspring, leading to complicated family problems and difficulties in accessing the parent or adolescent. Avoidance symptomatology may result in reluctance in both the adolescent and the family to utilize mental health services (Schwarz and Kowalski, 1992b).

It is hoped that the concept of "malignant memories" will serve to organize thinking about the complex multidimensional human response to violence and lead to interventions preventing their formation, as well as detoxifying them, restructuring their configurations, or uncoupling relationships among reexperiencing, arousal, and avoidance. For example, animal studies show that there may be a critical period before which a fear memory is transferred from temporary storage in the hippocampus to permanent storage (Kim and Fanselow 1992). Therefore, in the immediate aftermath of trauma, would aggressive provision of intensely reassuring, nurturing, and safe experiences undermine their formation? Would dampening neurophysiological arousal with pharmacotherapeutic agents during or in the immediate aftermath of a trauma lessen the likelihood of formation of such memories?

Memory is formed by and also informs experience. Its importance cannot be overstated. Once an event is over, psychological effects derive only from memories of the event. Memories form the tapestry of our personal narratives that make us human and are woven into the collective narrative that forms our group identities. It is in our memories that our developmental achievements are stored.

As mental health professionals, we are beginning to recognize how violence—be it in the home, media, street, genocide, or war—leaves sometimes indelible signatures on the human psyche, on brain function and possibly structure as well as mind and soul. We have important roles to play in the deterrence of violence, in the prevention of malignant memories, in subduing their pernicious effects on our patients' lives, and in studying the biopsychosocial mechanisms that link exposure to stress with enduring changes in brain structure and function, experience, behavior, and development.

NOTE

This chapter was originally presented in part at the third international congress of the International Society for Adolescent Psychiatry, Chicago, July 15, 1992.

REFERENCES

American Psychiatric Association. 1987. *Diagnostic and Statistical Manual of Mental Disorders*. 3d ed., rev. Washington, D.C.: American Psychiatric Association.

Beck, J., and van der Kolk, B. 1987. Reports of childhood incest and current behavior of chronically hospitalized psychotic women. *American Journal of Psychiatry* 144:1474–1476.

Bremner, J.; Southwick, S.; and Charney, D. 1991. Animal models for the neurobiology of trauma. *PTSD Research Quarterly* 2(4): 1–3.

Brodsky, L.; Doerman, A.; Palmer, L.; Slade, G.; and Munasifi, F. 1990. Post traumatic stress disorder: an eclectic approach. *International Journal of Psychosomatics* 37:895–898.

Burgess, A.; Hartman, C.; and McCormack, A. 1987. Abused to abuser: antecedents of socially deviant behaviors. *American Journal of Psychiatry* 144:1431–1436.

Chrousus, G., and Gold, P. 1992. The concepts of stress and stress system disorders. *Journal of the American Medical Association* 267:1244–1252.

Deblinger, E.; McLeer, S. V.; and Henry, D. 1990. Cognitive behavioral treatment for sexually abused children suffering post-traumatic stress: preliminary findings. *Journal of the American Academy of Child and Adolescent Psychiatry* 29(5): 747–752.

de Saussure, J. 1987. Dreams and dreaming in relation to trauma in childhood. *International Journal of Psycho-Analysis* 63:167–175.

Edwards, P., and Donaldson, M. 1899. Assessment of symptoms in adult survivors of incest: a factor analytic study of the responses to the childhood incest questionnaire. *Child Abuse and Neglect* 13:101–110.

Egginton, J. 1991. *Day of Fury*. New York: William Morrow.

Elder, G., and Clipp, E. 1989. Combat experience and emotional health: impairment and resilience in later life. *Journal of Personality* 57:311–341.

Foa, E.; Steketee, G.; and Rothbaum, B. 1989. Behavioral/cognitive conceptualizations of post-traumatic stress disorder. *Behavior Therapy* 20:155–176.

Freud, S. 1895a. Project for a scientific psychology. I. *Standard Edition* 1:321. London: Hogarth, 1966.

Freud, S. 1895b. Project for a scientific psychology. III. *Standard Edition* 1:381–382. London: Hogarth, 1966.

Freud, S. 1896. Stratification of memory traces. *Standard Edition* 1:233–236. London: Hogarth, 1966.

Freud, S. 1920. Beyond the pleasure principle. *Standard Edition* 20:29–31. London: Hogarth, 1955.

Freud, S. 1926. Inhibitions, symptoms, and anxiety. *Standard Edition* 20:77–175. London: Hogarth, 1959.

Freud, S., and Breuer, J. 1893. On the psychical mechanism of hysterical phenomena: preliminary communication. *Standard Edition* 2:3–21. London: Hogarth, 1966.

Friedman, M. 1991. Biological approaches to the diagnosis and treatment of post-traumatic stress disorder. *Journal of Traumatic Stress* 4:67–91.

Gidycz, C., and Koss, M. 1989. The impact of adolescent sexual victimization: standardized measures of anxiety, depression, and behavioral deviancy. *Violence and Victims* 4:139–149.

Glover, H. 1984. Themes of mistrust and the posttraumatic stress disorder in Vietnam veterans. *American Journal of Psychotherapy* 38:445–452.

Goodwin, J.; Simm, M.; and Bergman, R. 1979. Hysterical seizures: a sequel to incest. *American Journal of Orthopsychiatry* 49:697–703.

Gross, M. 1979. Incestuous rape: a cause for hysterical seizures in four adolescent girls. *American Journal of Orthopsychiatry* 49:704–708.

Herman, J.; Perry, J.; and van der Kolk, B. 1989. Childhood trauma in borderline personality disorder. *American Journal of Psychiatry* 146:490–495.

Horowitz, M.; Adams, J.; and Burton, B. 1968. Visual imagery on brain stimulation. *Archives of General Psychiatry* 19:469–486.

Horowitz, M., and Becker, S. 1972. Cognitive response to stress: experimental studies of a "compulsion to repeat trauma." In R. Holt and E. Peterfreund, eds. *Psychoanalysis and Contemporary Science*. New York: Macmillan.

Jackson, H. 1982. Moral nihilism: developmental arrest as a sequela to combat stress. *Adolescent Psychiatry* 10:228–242.

Kahana, R. 1981. The aging survivor of the Holocaust: discussion; reconciliation between the generations; a last chance. *Journal of Geriatric Psychiatry* 14:225–239.

Kim, J., and Fanselow, M. 1992. Modality specific retrograde amnesia of fear. *Science* 256:675–677.

Kinzie, J.; Sack, W.; Angell, R.; Clarke, G.; and Rath, B. 1989. A three-year follow-up of Cambodian young people traumatized as children. *Journal of the American Academy of Child and Adolescent Psychiatry* 28:501–504.

Kinzie, J.; Sack, W.; Angell, R.; Manson, S.; and Rath, B. 1986. The psychiatric effects of massive trauma on Cambodian children. I. the children. *Journal of the American Academy of Child and Adolescent Psychiatry* 25:370–376.

Klein, H. 1971. Families of Holocaust survivors in the kibbutz: psychological studies. *International Psychiatry Clinics* 8:67–92.

Lang, P. 1977. Imagery in therapy: an information processing analysis of fear. *Behavior Therapy* 8:862–886.

Leon, G.; Butcher, J.; Kleinman, M.; Goldberg, A.; and Almagor, M. 1981. Survivors of the Holocaust and their children: current status and adjustment. *Journal of Personality and Social Psychology* 41:503–516.

Li, D., and Spiegel, D. 1992. A neural network model of dissociative disorders. *Psychiatric Annals* 22:144–147.

Lindberg, F., and Distad, L. 1985. Post-traumatic stress disorders in women who experienced childhood incest. *Child Abuse and Neglect* 9:329–334.

Mesulam, M. 1990. Large scale neurocognitive networks and distributed processing for attention, language, and memory. *Annals of Neurology* 28:597–613.

Ornitz, E., and Pynoos, R. 1989. Startle modulation in children with posttraumatic stress disorder. *American Journal of Psychiatry* 146:866–870.

Penfield, W., and Jasper, H. 1954. *Epilepsy and the functional anatomy of the human brain.* Boston: Little, Brown.

Perry, B. In press. Neurobiological sequelae of childhood trauma. In M. Murberg, ed. *Catecholamine Function in Post Traumatic Stress Disorder: Emerging Concepts.* Washington, D.C.: American Psychiatric Press.

Pitman, R.; Orr, S.; Forgue, D.; Altman, B.; de Jong, J.; and Herz, L. 1990. Psychophysiologic responses to combat imagery of Vietnam veterans with posttraumatic stress disorder versus other anxiety disorders. *Journal of Abnormal Psychology* 99:49–54.

Pitman, R.; Orr, S.; Forgue, D.; de Jong, J.; and Claiborn, J. 1987. Psychophysiologic assessment of posttraumatic stress disorder imagery in Vietnam combat veterans. *Archives of General Psychiatry* 44:970–975.

Pitman, R.; van der Kolk, B.; Orr, S.; and Greenberg, M. 1990. Naloxone-reversible analgesic response to combat-related stimuli in posttraumatic stress disorder. *Archives of General Psychiatry* 47:541–544.

Proust, M. 1956. *Swann's Way.* New York: Modern Library/Random House.

Saigh, P. 1985. An experimental analysis of chronic posttraumatic stress among adolescents. *Journal of Genetic Psychology* 146:125–131.

Saigh, P. 1988. The use of an in vitro flooding package in the treatment of traumatized adolescents. *Journal of Developmental and Behavioral Pediatrics* 10:17–21.

Schwarz, E., and Kowalski, J. 1991. Malignant memories: posttraumatic stress disorder in children and adults following a school shooting. *Journal of the American Academy of Child and Adolescent Psychiatry* 30:937–944.

Schwarz, E., and Kowalski, J. 1992a. Malignant memories: associated posttraumatic reactions to a school shooting in children and parents. Typescript.

Schwarz, E., and Kowalski, J. 1992b. Malignant memories: reluctance to utilize mental health services after a disaster. *Journal of Nervous Mental Disease* 180:767–772.

Schwarz, E.; Kowalski, J.; and McNally, R. In press. Malignant memories: posttraumatic memory disturbances in adults after a school shooting. *Journal of Traumatic Stress*.

Shatan, C. 1974. Through the membrane of reality: "impacted grief" and perceptual dissonance in Vietnam combat veterans. *Psychiatric Opinion* 11:6–15.

Stocking, M. 1989. Catastrophe and the capacity to withstand it: an adolescent responds to personal tragedy. *Adolescent Psychiatry* 16:412–434.

Stoddard, F.; Norman, D.; Murphy, J.; and Beardslee, W. 1989. Psychiatric outcome of burned children and adolescents. *Journal of the American Academy of Child and Adolescent Psychiatry* 28:589–595.

Teens abused more than children, researchers find. 1992. *American Medical News* (May 11), p. 14.

Terr, L. 1987. Childhood trauma and the creative product. *Psychoanalytic Study of the Child* 42:545–572.

van der Kolk, B. 1985. Adolescent vulnerability to posttraumatic stress disorder. *Psychiatry* 48:365–370.

van der Kolk, B.; Greenberg, M.; Orr, S.; and Pitman, R. 1989. Endogenous opioids, stress induced analgesia, and posttraumatic stress disorder. *Psychopharmacology Bulletin* 25:417–421.

van der Kolk, B., and van der Hart, O. 1989. Pierre Janet and the breakdown of adaptation in psychological trauma. *American Journal of Psychiatry* 146:1530–1540.

Wiesel, E. 1969. *The Town beyond the Wall*. New York: Avon.

17 ATTENTIONAL DISORDERS IN ADOLESCENCE: INTEGRATING PSYCHOANALYTIC AND NEUROPSYCHOLOGICAL DIAGNOSTIC AND DEVELOPMENTAL CONSIDERATIONS

JONATHAN COHEN

Paying attention is like breathing: we do it automatically and throughout our waking life. But paying attention is not simply a constitutionally based, unlearned activity: we also learn to pay attention for a variety of cognitive and psychodynamic reasons. In any case, when we have difficulty paying attention, it always affects learning and development. There are psychogenic, cognitive, and biological factors that can complicate and disrupt an adolescent's ability to pay attention. Understanding what is complicating or interfering with an adolescent's ability to pay attention makes a difference: it critically informs and to some extent dictates how we can be helpful. And, when we misunderstand the nature of an attentional problem, we can do damage. For example, if we mistakenly believe that a disorder is biologically based (e.g., an attention deficit/hyperactive disorder or an affective illness) and/or psychologically/emotionally based (e.g., anxiety) when it is in fact largely a cognitively based attentional problem (e.g., a receptive language problem) with secondary emotional concerns, we may inadvertently mistreat the adolescent.

In this chapter, I will focus on the psychobiological spectrum of attentional disorders that we often see in adolescents who are having difficulty learning and developing. I describe the range of not uncommon psychological, cognitive, and biological factors that result in attentional disorders in adolescence, make a clinical statement about the differential diagnosis of attentional problems in childhood and adolescence and the experience of these disorders, and elucidate clinical and developmental implications.

Attention and Attentional Disorders

Attentional problems in adolescence are common sources of underachievement and school-related problems. Although epidemiological data are lacking, clinical reports from psychiatrists, clinical psychologists, and neuropsychologists suggest that more than half of all adolescents present with attentional problems (Cohen 1992b). But what does it mean to pay attention? And what are the various factors that complicate adolescents' ability to attend? Think about your attentional experience now. As you read these words, what are you doing right now? The brain has a limited ability to process information. Our nervous system relies on a complex process to narrow the scope and focus of information to be processed and assimilated. Attention is really a term used to focus on a group of hypothetical mental mechanisms that collectively serve this function for the organism.

Attention is not a single mental process. In fact, it is one of the most difficult processes to describe in cognitive psychology because so many neurocognitive processes interact with and result in the process of paying attention. There have been many attempts to differentiate various distinct aspects of the attentional process that have ranged from relatively simple distinctions (e.g., involuntary vs. voluntary attention) to much more complex and long lists of attentional dimensions with related, cascading lists of factors that affect and are affected by these dimensions of attention (e.g., Goldstein and Goldstein 1990; Levine 1987; Shaywitz and Shaywitz 1988, 1992). These authors have been systematically researching the relations between various aspects of attention and the process of learning. This has the potential to tell us more about the specific aspects of attention, any of which individually could result in an attentional disorder. But I do not believe that we yet have an empirical basis on which to decide what is the most useful model to use. On the other hand, most students of attention would agree that there are two or three basic interrelated aspects of attention: (1) *Sustained attention* refers to the ability to persist or begin to and then sustain attention until the task is completed. For example, the adolescent who is unable to remain on a task for a sufficient amount of time to complete the task satisfactorily would have a problem with sustained attention. (2) *Focused attention* refers to the ability to focus the mind on one thing and screen out other input. In other words, this refers to the capacity not to be distracted. Some researchers have thought of this attentional process as involving two distinct processes—focusing and screening—and some have thought of them as integrally linked. (3) *Selective attention* refers to the cognitive capacity to pick out what is important in the range of stimuli. In other words, after you have decided to begin to focus on the page or the speaker and you have narrowed your attentional focus to this page or speaker, selective attention allows us to be able to discern what is important to remember.

Biological and/or psychological disorders can play a major role in the first two components of attention: being able to sustain attention and then to focus and screen. Although all mental processes are ultimately biologically based, the third component of attention—selective attention—is often conceptualized as a cognitive capacity. I am now going to describe in more detail the range of attentional disorders that adolescents evince.

Attentional Disorders: Subtypes

It is useful to conceptualize three overlapping types of attentional disorders: psychological, cognitive, and biological. Sometimes adolescents show only one of the difficulties that I will now describe, but often we see several of these problems simultaneously. Table 1 summarizes the subtypes of attentional disorders.

PSYCHOGENICALLY BASED ATTENTIONAL DISORDERS

There are no adequate epidemiological studies yet that shed light on the prevalence of the various childhood and adolescent attentional disorders described here. However, it is my impression that the purely psychodynamically based or "emotional" concerns and conflicts that are often described are the most common source of attentional disorders. In fact, I believe that the vast majority of attentional disorders that adolescents evince today are due to psychodynamic factors alone.

TABLE 1
ATTENTIONAL DISORDERS: SUBTYPES

Psychological/emotionally based attentional disorders
A. Primary psychological disorder (initially unrelated to learning or attention)
B. Reactive psychological disorder
C. Lack of interest

Cognitively based attentional disorders
A. Verbal and nonverbal learning disabilities
    1. A cognitive weakness itself can complicate and/or look like a problem
       in attention
    2. The psychological/emotional effects of a learning disability organize personality
       development and can result in attentional and related problems
B. A selective attention weakness
C. Attentional "skills" deficiency

Biologically based attentional disorders
A. Fatigue and arousal disorders
B. Temperament and temperamental factors
C. Various medical conditions
D. ADHD
E. Affective disorders

At a recent interdisciplinary seminar,[1] on average 80 percent of these youngsters presented with attentional symptoms as an important aspect of the presenting problem. And, on average, 80 percent or more of these youngsters were evincing attentional difficulties for psychogenic reasons alone (Cohen 1992a). Although this perspective about prevalence is shared by other experienced clinicians (e.g., Silver 1990), epidemiological studies need to be undertaken to confirm or disconfirm this impression.

There is a wide array of ongoing and/or reactive experiences that can result in psychic distress, conflict, preoccupations, anxiety, or depressive concerns (e.g., an underlying neurotic or more severe psychological conflict; a reaction to family disorders or difficulty in school or with friends). It is well known that psychological distress, anxiety, and depression can and do interfere with our basic ability to attend (as well as a number of other cognitive capacities, like memory, expressive language, and perception). There are three basic types of psychologically based attentional problems: a primary psychogenic disorder that is initially unrelated to problems in learning or attention; a reactive psychological disorder that is initially in response to problems in learning or attention; and a lack of interest.

PRIMARY PSYCHOGENIC DISORDERS

There are many psychological and social difficulties that are initially unrelated to problems of learning or attention. For example, a death in the family will naturally result in certain kinds of expectable psychosocial dysfunction. And it is well known that anxiety and depression can and do interfere with a host of basic cognitive abilities including speech, memory, and/or attention. In fact, we all know that everyday anxieties or depressive concerns can and do interfere with these basic cognitive abilities. And normal adolescent developmental struggles can interfere with our ability to pay attention. For example, if we are worried that we will not get somewhere on time, or if we are concerned about how we will do on a test, attentional abilities are often adversely affected.

For characterological reasons, we may not want to know certain things. For example, some youngsters who have experienced the loss of a parent will develop a characteristic aversion to consciously experiencing and expressing anger, having imagined (in a normal, early childhood/egocentric manner) that their angry feelings killed the parent. This fantasy and the developing characteristic ways of coping with these memories, ideas, and fearful expectations (e.g., "I could kill again if I get angry") can powerfully contribute to youngsters being both generally anxious (which would tend to undermine attentional efforts) and more specifically distractable when issues around aggression and death emerge in and out of the classroom.

A REACTIVE PSYCHOLOGICAL DISORDER

Some youngsters do not begin to develop significant anxieties or depressive concerns until cognitive weaknesses, unrelated to attention, begin to interfere with learning. This in turn leads to anxious expectations and negative representations of themselves.

In the early childhood years, it is particularly important to distinguish between psychological disorders that are directly (reactively) related to a learning problem and those that are initially quite independent of a learning problem. This distinction has implications for how we, the family and eventually the child, will come to understand their experience. However, it is also important to know that, as the child moves into the middle and late latency-age years, this distinction begins to break down. What may initially have been a reaction to educational frustration and failure begins to become an internalized, ongoing aspect of how they remember themselves and others as well as what they anxiously expect and depressively remember. In other words, as I have described in detail elsewhere, these initially reactive experiences become an integral aspect of their developing character (see Cohen 1984).

Primary or reactive psychogenic disorders can and do affect all three basic aspects of the attentional process: focusing and sustaining our attention as well as interfering with our ability to identify (or select) the main points in a chapter or a lecture. Typically, psychogenic disorders most significantly interfere with attention (and any number of other cognitive processes) when the youngster is upset or conflicted and/or the primary psychological problem is being activated in some way. For example, if a youngster is consciously or unconsciously remembering a parent who has died, this memory and the associated emotions and defensive operations that are evoked may complicate any of these three basic aspects of attention. However, as I have noted above and will detail more below, when a psychological disorder continues to be a force in a youngster's life for a period of time (e.g., longer than six months), it potentially enters the nooks and crannies of the mind: it begins to become a part of the child's character (Cohen 1984). This can contribute to the youngster's developing characteristic styles that complicate attention (or any number of other cognitive abilities). For example, a youngster who becomes a "jokester" as a way of attempting to cope with an emotional difficulty may in time show these characteristics in a more ongoing or characterological manner for a variety of reasons.

A LACK OF INTEREST

Not all psychologically based attentional problems are indicative of psychopathology. Many children and adolescents do not pay attention because they are simply not interested in the material or experience before them. Although boredom is often a psychological defense (e.g., the youngster who is afraid that she cannot accomplish the task will feign boredom to protect herself from anticipated failure), there are many adolescents who are not being stimulated intellectually and/or are not interested in the material being presented.

This pattern has most often presented itself in situations where the adolescent is quite gifted and not being challenged at school. Characteristically, the adolescent is labeled "a problem" by educators and the mental health professional at the school because she is not fitting in. And it is certainly true that sometimes, when adolescents are told that they have a problem and/or are being treated as if there is a problem, they do develop actual emotional concerns, often rapidly. Tension and conflicts between parents, teachers, and the adolescent ensue. Adolescents can come to feel that it is their fault that they are not being stimulated intellectually. A lack of interest characteristically affects the ability to focus and sustain attention, but not a selective attentional capacity.

COGNITIVELY BASED ATTENTIONAL DISORDERS

The term "learning disability" is used in various ways. I find it useful to think of learning disabilities as specific neuropsychologically based cognitive weaknesses. As such, a biologically or neuropsychologically based attentional disability (e.g., attention deficit/hyperactive disorder [ADHD]) can be conceptualized as one type of learning disability. There are two other major classifications of learning disabilities: verbal (or language-based) and nonverbal disabilities (Shepherd 1991). The term "learning disorder," or "attentional disorder," refers to a difficulty where the origin of the problem is unknown.

There are two ways in which verbal and nonverbal learning disabilities can complicate attention: (1) a verbal and nonverbal learning disability—a cognitive weakness—can complicate paying attention in a particular mode and, hence, look like a problem in attention; and (2) the psychological/emotional effects of a learning disability organize personality development and can result in attentional and related problems.

A cognitive weakness can complicate attentional processes in a particular mode and, hence, look like a problem in attention. For example, an auditory processing weakness or receptive language disability (both verbal learning disabilities) may make it difficult for the adolescent to understand verbalizations. This can appear to be the result of the adolescent not paying attention. Or a visual processing disability (a nonverbal disability) that results in the reversal and rotation of visual percepts may complicate and frustrate the adolescent's ability to concentrate on the blackboard or the page. The abilities to focus and sustain attention are most often affected here.

Obviously, these and other kinds of cognitive disabilities will make specific types of listening, memorizing, and/or attending more frustrating. This is quite common, and, too often, professionals incorrectly believe that a teenager who evinces verbal and/or nonverbal learning disabilities has a more pervasive and biologically based attention deficit disorder (e.g., ADHD). There are many reasons why biologically based attention deficit disorders are overdiagnosed. One reason has to do with the fact that, although verbal and nonverbal learning disabilities initially complicate attention only in the domain being affected, the experience of being learning disabled sometimes leads to more generalized anxiety. Generalized anxiety, even at a low level, can lead to relatively ongoing states of inattention, impulsivity, and/or overactivity. It is to this process that I will turn in a moment. It is important to add that the manner in which the youngster copes with the specific cognitive weakness (e.g., avoidance or denial) can also become generalized and an ongoing, characteristic defensive style (Cohen 1984). Virtually all of us evince some areas of relative weakness. And it seems that the way that children cope with significant weaknesses (e.g., weaknesses that come to have significant meaning) is one of the critical forces that determine the development of particular defensive styles. And it is well known that our defensive styles have major implications for how and to what we attend (e.g., Shapiro 1965).

As noted, the adolescent's psychological reactions to the frustration and failure that verbal and nonverbal learning disabilities engender is the other way that these cognitive weaknesses may inadvertently and indirectly cause attentional problems. The experience of being learning disabled tends to result in anxiety, decreased motivation, and poor self-esteem that can profoundly undermine one's ability to attend and learn (Rourke and Fuerst 1991; Silver 1974). But this is not the only process that can lead to anxiety, depression, and attentional difficulties.

Mild to moderately severe cognitive weaknesses tend to be intermittent and, hence, unpredictable experiences, and this seems to have subtle but profound effects on personality development and the characteristic emergence of low-level anxiety that so often characterizes learning-disabled youngsters. When a difficulty (e.g., a word-finding disability) is intermittent, it engenders a sense of unpredictability and helplessness that quite naturally leads to anxiety and helplessness (when is it going to happen again?). In addition, the repeated experiences of helplessness (not being able to predict the difficulty and do much about it) are sometimes emotionally wounding.

In my clinical research study of fifteen learning-disabled adolescents, I have also found that the intermittent nature of these mild to moderately severe learning disabilities often leads to the depressing fantasy that there is something wrong with one's brain and that one has lost something that one once had (Cohen 1984). Thus, in a multitude of ways, learning-disabled adolescents are vulnerable to becoming anxious and depressed.

As the adolescent grows older, it is typically these often unconscious psychological dynamics (which in turn result in behavioral problems) that are as debilitating, if not more so, than the cognitive weakness itself. There is always a cyclical and ongoing interaction between current educational and psychic experience and remembered abilities, frustrations, failures, and how we have selectively understood these experiences.

SELECTIVE ATTENTION

The ability to determine which details are important in a page or in a lecture is a cognitive capacity in and of itself (Levine 1987). If this selective attentional ability (or what Levine refers to as "saliency determination") is an area of weakness in an adolescent, it complicates attentional functioning. This is a cognitive capacity that we can teach an adolescent to utilize more effectively.

Typically, both these kinds of cognitively based attentional difficulties will appear only when the weak cognitive function is being called on or utilized. Hence, the situation-specific appearance of the attentional difficulty is diagnostically important. On the other hand, it is important to remember that, when this kind of cognitive weakness is not identified relatively early in the adolescent's life, and when there are not other sources of pleasure and success, these youngsters characteristically develop anxious expectations, concerns, and, sometimes, character pathology that can result in more chronic, psychologically based attentional problems as well as other psychosocial difficulties.

The process of paying attention involves a series of steps that most youngsters learn without ever being instructed. To become alert, aware of the task, to listen and/or look in a sustained and focused manner, to think about the experience and then become reaware of the task, is a process or series of attentional skills (as well as many other cognitive skills). There are some youngsters who have not learned to make sure that they proceed through all these steps in a relatively orderly manner but whose basic attentional capacities are intact.

There are four (potentially overlapping) groups of youngsters whom I have seen who present this kind of problem: (1) adolescents who come from very chaotic homes in which there are always psychological factors (e.g., the parents not appropriately structuring and empathically listening) that also complicate attention; (2) adolescents who evince an ADHD that has complicated focused and sustained attentional functioning for years; (3) adolescents who present with an array of frontal lobe–related or "executive functioning"–related difficulties (e.g., planning and self-monitoring capacities); or (4) quite brain-damaged youngsters.

Children who grow up in chaotic, unstructured, unempathic homes tend to develop an array of psychopathologies. Because of understandable concerns, conflicts, and maladaptive defensive inclinations, these children sometimes do not learn basic cognitive skills that range from being able to read to being able to organize one's thoughts in an essay. Being able to plan, anticipate, and sustain one's attention in a flexible manner is also a skill that we need to learn. And youngsters from these home environments sometimes need assistance learning to do just this.

There are other youngsters who have difficulty with attentional skills because of frontal lobe–related weaknesses. Frontal lobe dysfunction undermines our capacity to plan, monitor, and flexibly shift (Stuss and Benton 1984). As I will describe, there seems to be a subgroup of youngsters evincing ADHD who present with frontal lobe pathology. There are also some youngsters who present with these attentional skills difficulties and who perform very poorly on traditional measures of frontal lobe functioning (e.g., the Wisconsin Card Sort test or the Stroop) who do not evince ADHD. And there are also adolescents whom I have seen who present with significant brain damage (due to a car accident or mental retardation) that may affect frontal lobe functioning as well as brain function in other areas.

Cognitive behavior modification, self-motivating strategies, comprehension-fostering strategies, and modeling can all be helpful here. These are important strategies to know about because they are the same ones that can often help teachers and parents help adolescents with severe attentional disorders, be they of biological or psychological origin.

BIOLOGICALLY BASED ATTENTIONAL PROBLEMS

Biological factors clearly affect our capacity to attend. In fact, attention is a process that is so interrelated with so many neuropsychological functions (e.g., verbal and nonverbal perception, remembering, integration, processing, and expression) that biologically based disruption in any number of these systems can adversely affect attentional abilities. Research in neurology informs us that there do seem to be critical centers of attentional processes (e.g., the frontal lobes and the reticular activating system). Severe damage to these areas does seem to affect various aspects of our attentional abilities dramatically and adversely.

There is recent research that is beginning to attempt to differentially assess dysfunction in different parts of the brain. However, there is no simple neurological center of attention because attention is more than one process and it is so interrelated with many other cognitive/neuropsychological functions. I now describe five sets of biologically based attentional disorders that clinicians tend to see most often: (a) temperament and the question of the fit; (b) fatigue and arousal disorders; (c) various medical conditions; (d) ADHD; and (e) affective disorders. In adolescence, all attentional disorders that are biological have an important psychogenic component. All biological disorders come to have particular psychological and also social (which, then again, has psychological) meanings for the youngster. And the narrative that youngsters come to tell themselves, consciously and unconsciously, is as important, if not much more so, than the original biological disorder. For organizational and differential diagnostic purposes, I have categorized attentional disorders into three groups: psychological, cognitive, and biological. But these groups are actually overlapping processes viewed from different perspectives.

Temperamental factors are biologically based phenomena and not necessarily biologically based problems. But temperamental factors influence childrens' and, then to a lesser extent, adolescents' ability to pay attention in particular situations. The idea of "temperamental types" has been used since the time of Hippocrates. Although definitions of "temperament" have changed over time, this dimension of the person has always referred to patterns of action and mood that are presumed to have a constitutional basis. These biologically based inclinations and moods do not necessarily represent a weakness or dysfunction but are rather part of the package that we are all born with. To a very great extent, how the person understands (or misunderstands) this package and how it fits with the environment determine the ways in which the temperament becomes a strength and/or a weakness.

Temperamental dimensions matter clinically because they often affect the child's caretakers: they are experienced as easy to abrasive or desirable to undesirable in relation to the caretakers' own values, expectations, and temperament. A "goodness of fit" results when the expectations and demands of the caretaker fit, or are in accord, with the child's capacities, motivations, and style of behavior. On the other hand, "poorness of fit" involves discrepancies and a lack of accord between the environment and the child. When this occurs, development and learning are always adversely affected. For example, some children need to be very gently stroked to be soothed. When this child is held by an adult who is either unattuned to this temperamentally based need or unable to stroke in a gentle manner, we have an unhappy, overstimulated, overwhelmed baby who will tend to withdraw. Or a child who is very active will "fit" or "not fit" into a classroom in part on the basis of the teacher's capacity to tolerate and support this behavior (Carey and McDevitt 1989).

Some children are born with what has been called a difficult temperament, and difficult or extreme temperamental types may also importantly contribute to attentional difficulties. The idea of difficult temperament was introduced by Thomas, Chess, and Birch (1968). They found that certain behaviors in the first years of life (arhythmic, low in approach and adaptability, negative in mood but low in activity and intensity, or excessively persistent, distractible, or active) were significantly predictive of latter psychiatric problems. Recently, Turecki and Tonner (1985) have taken basic temperamental dimensions and usefully shown how extreme temperamental dispositions make for a difficult child. Initially, being a difficult child is importantly different than being a problem child. And parent guidance can help create a better fit and minimize the potentially complicating aspects of having extreme or difficult temperamental features.

Kagan's (1988, 1989) recent research on the temperamental dimension of extreme sensitivity also has a bearing on attentional abilities and disabilities. Kagan and his coworkers have studied twins and found that there are some children who are temperamentally very "shy" or, at the opposite end of the spectrum, very outgoing. More specifically, he has found that roughly 15 percent of children are born with a physiological tendency, a hypersensitivity, that causes them to avoid novelty. He suggests that this cortically based initial reaction to unfamiliarity is linked with more exaggerated physiological reactions to stress (e.g., higher heart rates, greater pupil dilation, greater muscle tension, and higher secretion of norepinephrine). Kagan and other researchers have suggested that these shy kids will then tend to avoid and withdraw from numerous novel experiences, including social ones. They will fail to explore and play with new social situations/problems.

Researchers have followed these children only to the age of three or four. In attentional terms, these young children may not be able to attend to certain kinds of novel and/or high-intensity experiences. It is not entirely clear how this temperamentally based shyness will show itself in adolescence. But it is likely that it may be a force in the child's and the adolescent's attentional style.

I believe that some difficult temperamental types overlap with other groups in this section on biologically based attentional disorders. In fact, some of the extreme temperamental types are the same syndrome as some of the neuropsychological dysfunctions described, but from different points of view. For example, the child whose temperament can be characterized as high activity, highly distractible, high intensity, and low persistence may also be described as evincing a biologically based attention deficit (ADHD). What importantly differentiates these perspectives is that temperament is always viewed as being a part of an interaction—a fit or relative lack of fit between the child and his environment—whereas ADHD is viewed as being due to the child's biological dysfunction. Both points of view may be true. But one's point of view may have profound consequences for how we think about intervention: psychopharmacology and/or working with the parent and perhaps the child psychotherapeutically. Clinicians who work with adolescents are in a unique role to be able to educate parents, teachers, and the adolescents themselves about the usefulness of an interactive (goodness-of-fit) model, regardless of what the overall treatment plan is.

How a difficulty is labeled has potentially profound consequences for the youngster's conscious and unconscious representations of self. It is certainly unproductive ever to minimize a problem. However, it does have very different consequences to label a problem in the context of the strengths and weaknesses that the adolescent evinces (and how she interacts with the environment) as opposed to a biological disorder. These labels are obviously not mutually exclusive.

FATIGUE AND AROUSAL

To pay attention effectively, we need to be alert. There are a number of factors that contribute to children and adolescents being underaroused and/or fatigued. For children and some adolescents, fatigue is a surprising source of difficulty sustaining attention and, in fact, learning in general. And there are a great number of youngsters who simply do not get enough sleep. For children, this is often seen in quite disordered families but also not infrequently because working professional parents do not want their children to go to bed until after they have come home from work. When parents do not come home until 8 o'clock, keep their children up until 10 or 11 o'clock, and then need to wake them at 7 to go to school, it is often simply not enough sleep for the children. Fatigue can affect all three basic aspects of attentional functioning. And I have been surprised by the number of instances in which loving, very well-meaning parents have inadvertently contributed to their child not getting enough sleep and fatigue has then been the cause of attentional problems. There are a variety of other emotional/behavioral factors that contribute to adolescents creating the situation of not getting enough sleep: normal adolescent experimentation and rebellion; drug use; poor study habits; and, of course, psychosocial concerns and disorders.

Sleep-arousal imbalances can also result in the youngster being tired, underaroused, and inattentive during waking hours. Usually, the term "sleep-arousal imbalances" refers to a presumably biologically based disorder that results in difficulties falling asleep or being restless during sleep and/or erratic, disrupted, or frenetic sleep (Luisada 1969). Anxious and/or depressive emotional concerns can also result in similar patterns of sleep difficulties. Hence, it is important to assess emotional functioning and the way the youngsters tend to manage their emotional life as well as simple scheduling issues (i.e., whether the child is getting to bed early enough). My clinical impression is that the vast majority of sleep problems in adolescents are caused by not letting them get enough sleep for nonbiologically based reasons and/or emotional concerns. However, there are certainly a number of relatively rare biological disorders and disturbances of sleep-wake states in childhood that need to be considered as a part of the psychobiological spectrum of factors that can result in fatigue and/or other problems of arousal (see Keener and Anders [1986] for a review in this area).

MEDICAL CONDITIONS

There are a range of medical problems that can disrupt attentional processes and/or appear to be attentional problems (see Goldstein and Goldstein [1990] for a recent review). Undiagnosed ear or vision problems, developing diabetes, eye-tracking problems, seizure disorders (e.g., petit mal epilepsy can be mistaken for an attentional disorder because children with frequent absences may be mistaken for attention deficit disorder kids), sensory difficulties, myopia or hearing loss, hyperthyroidism, pinworms, sleep apnea, iron deficiency anemia, and allergies are just a few of the many medical problems that can interfere with attention and alertness. On the other hand, there are conditions that are correlated with biological attentional disorders and are not remedial (e.g., prenatal factors, previous ear infection, brain injury or encephalitis, previous lead poisoning, and, most commonly, heredity). In addition, certain medications may create excessive fatigue and thereby interfere with attention. Antihistamines, theophylline-containing compounds (often used to treat bronchial asthma), and barbiturates may all blunt sustained selective attention. I am not going to detail the list of medical problems that can lead to attentional disorders, but it is obviously important that the clinician understand whether biological or medical disorders are operative before making a diagnosis.

Inattention, impulsivity, and hyperactivity may represent the most common reason why youngsters are referred to mental health practitioners in the United States. These behavioral difficulties are also the most common reason why children are labeled "behavior problems" in the classroom. There is growing evidence to support the idea that there are chronic and pervasive attentional disorders that are biologically based (e.g., Zametkin et al. 1990). ADHD is the most recent label for children and adolescents who evince a relatively chronic and pervasive pattern of difficulties with attention, impulsivity, and/or overactivity.

It is unclear how many children diagnosed with ADHD will continue to be plagued into adolescence and adulthood, but the numbers are high. Various professionals believe that 50–80 percent diagnosed in early and middle childhood will show the disorder in adolescence and that 25–70 percent of these adolescents may continue to manifest the disorder into adulthood (Barkley 1990; Silver 1990).

The key diagnostic dimension of ADHD is the relative chronicity and pervasiveness of inattentive, impulsive, and overactive behavior. However, children and adolescents diagnosed with ADHD are a heterogeneous group who show significant variations in the severity and pervasiveness of their symptoms. There are many recent and excellent reviews on the diagnostic and treatment considerations of ADHD (e.g., Barkley 1990; Greenhill and Osman 1991; Silver 1992). Hence, I will only briefly describe some of the general issues surrounding this much diagnosed disorder. I will then focus on some new and important research that has the potential to shed further light on the heterogeneous nature of ADHD.

General issues. The relatively chronic and pervasive nature of this disorder is diagnostically critical but complicated. It is diagnostically critical because these attentional, impulse control, and hyperactive problems tend to be relatively chronic and pervasive in a way that is not so with purely psychologically based, cognitively based, and even many other biologically based attentional problems. For example, psychologically and/or learning-disability related attentional problems tend to evince themselves in a nonchronic and nonpervasive manner: they are expressed when the emotional wound or cognitive weakness is being affected, whereas adolescents with ADHD evince these difficulties at home, school, and with friends since infancy and across the whole range of activities (e.g., emotionally laden and neutral moments). However, this is not always so: moderately severe and severe psychopathology sometimes does result in relatively chronic and pervasive cognitive impairment (e.g., Bettelheim and Zelan 1982). I believe that this has complicated and continues to complicate defining the disorder, research, and communication between clinicians who have very different perspectives (e.g., psychoanalytic and psychopharmacological).

What further complicates this diagnostic evaluation is the fact that motivation (e.g., how much the youngster wants to do a given task) and structure (e.g., the extent to which a situation is defined and monitored) profoundly affect symptom presentation in children and adolescents who really do seem to evince ADHD. Children and adolescents with biologically based attentional problems typically perform much better on a one-to-one basis than they do in a group situation. Group settings are more stimulating, and these youngsters may not have the physiological mechanisms to manage this. Also, one-to-one settings tend to be emotionally safer, more secure, and more structured than group situations. Thus, an individualized clinical situation may not elicit the typical group behavior. To help determine the youngster's pattern of functioning, it is always essential to have parents and teachers report behavioral patterns over time.

There are two other, overlapping factors that make the diagnosis of ADHD complicated: determining normalcy and differential diagnosis. We all have difficulty paying attention sometimes. And this raises the basic question of what is normal and how we define the problem. In extreme clinical cases (e.g., severe ADHD), this is typically not a problem. However, in more marginal situations (mild ADHD), knowing what to call normal can be difficult. Recent research suggests that ADHD kids have most difficulty on tasks that are repetitive and boring (Barkley 1990). But what does this mean? All children have some (if not a lot) of difficulty on repetitive and boring tasks, unless they have been successfully beaten into "the school mold." Emotional concerns and being distracted for any number of reasons (psychologically, socially, or biologically) will increase difficulty on repetitive and boring tasks. What is further complicating is that ADHD in adolescence never exists in isolation. Virtually all adolescents who evince attentional problems have other problems as well. In assessing attentional problems, we must watch for disorders that overlap and may be confused with attentional problems. In fact, having an attentional problem predisposes one to having educational and psychological problems. Therefore, the clinical challenge is not to isolate a single trait but to ensure that we account for the multiple sources and complications often associated with these traits.

Currently, the only way to make this differential diagnosis is for the clinician to talk directly with the adolescent and with the parents, teachers, and other professionals who have been working with the adolescent (Silver 1992). Meeting with the adolescent and his or her whole family is also invaluable. This direct clinical contact and comprehensive understanding of all facets of the adolescent's life provides the basis for understanding the youngster's cognitive strengths and weaknesses as well as how psychological and family dynamics help and/or hinder cognitive functioning. This kind of integrative evaluation allows the clinician to develop an impression over time and across situations that leads to knowing whether the attentional problems are relatively chronic and pervasive in nature and the extent to which psychogenic factors are causative.

The current DSM-III-R (American Psychiatric Association 1987) diagnostic guidelines do not require this kind of integrative understanding and, hence, are inadequate. However, they are important to be familiar with as they represent the research findings and, to some extent, clinical understanding. I am not going to review the recent and present DSM-III (American Psychiatric Association 1980) and DSM-III-R diagnostic guidelines as the reader is probably familiar with these. I will briefly note what is being planned for DSM-IV as this reflects recent research findings and overlaps with the subtyping research that I shall present shortly.

In DSM-IV, there are plans to differentiate the symptoms of ADHD into two categories: developmentally inappropriate degrees of inattention and impulsivity/overactivity (Greenhill 1992). This distinction represents a return to the DSM-III distinction of an attention deficit disorder with hyperactivity and an attention deficit disorder without hyperactivity, which was removed in DSM-III-R. Many professionals believe that ADHD has been overdiagnosed. As a result, there are plans to make DSM-IV diagnosis of an attention deficit disorder contingent on symptoms leading to impairment or marked distress. And it has been suggested that the following criteria be added to the DSM-IV manual: that the ADHD symptoms "must be present to a strong degree in a structured setting demanding task completion, such as school or work" (Greenhill 1992, p. XIV-5).

Heterogeneity and the subtyping of ADHD. Another fact that may make diagnostic efforts in this domain difficult is that ADHD does not seem to be a single disorder; it is heterogeneous. The most interesting and potentially the most useful research now under way in this area is the attempt to distinguish different types of the disorder. There are five areas of research that illustrate current work attempting to clarify the various subtypes of ADHD: (1) ADHD versus ADHD without hyperactivity; (2) inattention/cognitively impaired versus impulsive/aggressive; (3) the low-risk, high-yield group versus the low-risk, low-yield group versus the high-risk, low-yield group; (4) underfocusing versus overfocusing; and (5) a subgroup of youngsters diagnosed with ADHD who in fact evince an underlying biological depressive disorder.

Recent research supports the idea that one valid nosological distinction for attention deficit disorders is an attention deficit with hyperactivity (ADHD), on the one hand, and an attention deficit without hyperactivity, on the other (Barkley 1990; Shaywitz and Shaywitz 1988, 1992). This distinction is akin to the past DSM-III criteria and, apparently, in accord with the upcoming DSM-IV criteria (Greenhill 1992). There is mounting evidence that ADHD and ADHD without overactivity may in fact be two distinct disorders. For example, the Shaywitzes have found spinal fluid differences between these two groups of children, and this is one of a number of biologically based differences that support this notion.

While the attention deficit disorder without hyperactivity group of youngsters do not seem to manifest the intrusive, externalizing behaviors of the ADHD kids, they do perform poorly in school and are at serious risk for long-term academic and social problems. These children and adolescents seem to have more trouble with focused attention and cognitive processing speed rather than sustained attention and impulse control problems. They do not evince a pattern of behavioral self-control problems: they are not so impulsive, intrusive, and unable to delay gratification to a degree that is abnormal for their mental age. This is the less well-studied group of youngsters. The attention deficit disorder without hyperactivity youngsters overlap much more with the so-called conduct-disorder children and adolescents.

The attention deficit disorder with and without hyperactivity distinction overlaps with research that has used the Continuous Performance Test (CPT) to reveal a dual diagnostic discrimination between the following two groups of children and adolescents who present with attentional problems: inattentive/cognitively impaired versus impulsive/aggressive. There has been much effort made to develop objective measures of attention. The CPT is one instrument that is increasingly being used to assess inattention, impulsivity, and dyscontrol. A letter is visually presented for 200 milliseconds, with a 1.5-second interstimulus interval. And the child is told to respond when she sees an "A" followed by an "X." Various aspects of children's abilities here have been and are being studied (e.g., Matier, Halperin, Sharma, Newcorn, and Sathaye 1992). We do not yet know how diagnostically useful or even how valid this measure is. But many researchers agree that CPT omission errors reflect an attentional disorder. It is unclear whether errors of commission are an indication of impulsivity.

In a series of studies utilizing CPT measures, researchers have found support for the idea that there may be two subgroups of ADHD youngsters: a group that can be characterized primarily by attention and cognitive problems and another group that can be characterized more by aggression or conduct problems, without significant attentional or cognitive dysfunction (August and Garfinkel 1989; Halperin, Newcorn, and Sharma 1991). In a series of past and ongoing studies, Halperin and his coworkers are investigating the finding that there does seem to be these two distinct groups of children who meet "teacher report" profiles of evincing ADHD (Halperin, personal communication, 1992). They are looking at presenting symptoms, antecedent predictors, neurobiological disturbances, treatment response, and long-term outcome from a variety of perspectives (e.g., biological, behavioral, neuropsychological, pharmacological).

At present, it is unclear whether the subgroup that can be characterized as having conduct problems (as opposed to the other group that evinces inattention and learning problems) is simply psychogenically troubled. Sometimes, psychopathology expresses itself as a conduct problem, and these children can meet DSM-III-R criteria for ADHD. Nonetheless, the attempt to utilize psychophysiologically based measures of attention in conjunction with comprehensive evaluations will potentially be quite fruitful.

Another interesting and quite important line of subtyping is being conducted by Urion (personal communication, 1991) at Children's Hospital in Boston. He is conducting a retrospective study with 176 nine- to eleven-year-old boys. In an earlier study, Urion (1989) used youngsters' responses to ritalin in conjunction with neurological findings (patternings of soft and hard signs) to identify three subgroups of youngsters who have met the diagnostic criteria for ADHD: (1) youngsters who respond positively to ritalin and whose reticular activating system may be affected (the low-risk, high-yield group); (2) a group of youngsters (one in five) who respond positively to ritalin and who evince mild frontal lobe findings (the low-risk, low-yield group); and (3) youngsters who quickly experience complicating side effects to ritalin and evince an abnormal neurological exam with parietal lobe dysfunction (the high-risk, low-yield group).

Urion is now attempting to replicate and extend these retrospective study findings with three additional studies: a prospective study ($N = 150$) again focusing on ritalin response, a "SPEC" brain scan study ($N = 40$), and a comparative study using another stimulant medication (disiprimine) that in some important ways seems to work on neural transmitters that are related to the frontal lobes and not the reticular activating system. Preliminary results from the disiprimine study seem to replicate the three subgroups described above (Urion, personal communication, 1991).

It has been suggested that distinguishing between youngsters who overfocus and those who underfocus may represent another subtype classification of ADHD (Kinsbourne 1991). Kinsbourne suggests that both subgroups are inattentive to ongoing instruction. But the more typical impulsive and sensation-seeking temperament that is typical in many ADHD youngsters is inattentive owing to rapid attentional shifting. On the other hand, it is suggested that overfocusers become stuck or too overly focused on an earlier stimulus. A series of studies using Kinsbourne's "Focus of Attention Rating Scale" and the DSM-III diagnostic criteria revealed that, in contrast to the "more usual underfocusers," the overfocusers tended to show the following patterns: they will finish things that they start but may still be doing them tomorrow; they tend to evince preservative trends and hence do not "often act before thinking"; they act impulsively only when trapped in situations in which they cannot avoid becoming overstimulated; overfocusers do not have "difficulties waiting their turn in games of group situations" and, in fact, tend to hang around the fringes and wait longer than necessary; they do not show characteristic ADHD impulsive and hyperactive behavior (e.g., difficulty staying seated, fidgeting when seated, running, and climbing excessively); and they do not really have difficulty sustaining attention because they sustain it to excess.

In addition to these difficulties, Kinsbourne has identified a number of additional characteristics of this group of "attentionally disordered" youngsters: they tend to be shy and to withdraw socially and are un-skilled interpersonally (especially with strangers); they prefer same-ness and are upset by changes in routine; they tend to work slowly and may be compulsive; they resist being hurried or told to do more than one thing at a time; they evince organizational difficulties, espe-cially at the beginning of tasks; they are bothered by loud noises; they evince a narrow scope of interest; they are worried and anxious; they have difficulty reading nonverbal cues (e.g., faces); they have difficulty remembering more than one thing at a time; they are quite vulnerable to explosive outbursts; and they tend to engage in repetitive move-ments.

This subgroup of youngsters does not appear simply to evince an attentional disorder. As can be seen, these youngsters show a num-ber of social/communicative and right-hemisphere-related difficulties. Kinsbourne postulates that the attentional disorder of overfocusing may be an attempt to correct for an underlying, unstable arousal sys-tem. This may be true. But attention is only one of these youngsters' difficulties. In fact, these overfocusing youngsters may very well evince a high-level autistic disorder (Allen 1988; Cohen 1992a; Wing 1988).

Some investigators suggest that there is a subgroup of children diag-nosed with ADHD who in fact evince an underlying biological de-pressive disorder (see Brumback and Weinberg [1990] for a recent review). And it is suggested that the pharmacological treatment of the disorder with antidepressant medication results in the removal of the attentional symptoms as well as the depression and associated right-hemisphere-related learning disabilities. What is very clear is that there can be and often is a complicated relation between attentional disor-ders and depressive disorders. Attentional disorders can and often do result in (understandable) reactive depression. And biological de-pressive illness (unipolar or bipolar disorders) can result in attentional problems. It is to these issues that I now turn.

AFFECTIVE DISORDERS

Attentional disorders and affective disorders can be confusing to diagnose differentially (e.g., Brumback and Weinberg 1990; Jenson, Burke, and Garfinkel 1988; Weinberg, Rutman, and Sullivan 1973; Werry, Reeves, and Elkind 1987). They share symptomatology, and they may both coexist within a given child. A number of clinicians have anecdotally reported the observation that childhood ADHD sometimes seems to convert into a major depression in late adolescence or young adulthood (e.g., Popper, personal communication, 1990). This has not been supported in the few research studies that have examined this (e.g., Barkley 1990). However, some other investigators are beginning to believe that ADHD may be a form of an "affective spectrum disorder." In other words, there is evidence that there may be a common underlying physiological basis to major depression and ADHD as well as the following six disorders; bulimia; panic disorder; obsessive compulsive disorder; migraine; irritable bowel syndrome; and cataplexy (Hudson and Pope 1990). I now briefly review how the two syndromes overlap symptomatically.

We cannot always tell whether an adolescent has ADHD and/or an affective disorder. All the features of ADHD can be seen in mood disorders at times, so ADHD is a diagnosis that we reach after ruling out a mood disorder. Popper (1989) was one of the first to describe his comparative and contrasting clinical impressions of these two groups. In conjunction with Popper's (1989) impressions, I have reviewed my own clinical experience, the Fisher Landau Interdisciplinary Seminar on Attentional Disorders report (Cohen 1992b), and others clinical experience (e.g., Kestenbaum 1992), and I now summarize major trends in the (1) similarities, (2) slight differences, and (3) significant differences between ADHD and affectively disordered adolescents (e.g., youngsters with a bipolar illness or a major depression).

1. They can be similar in that both can show problems with attention, impulsivity, hyperactivity, and labile emotional and behavioral control. Both can show low energy level (although ADHD adolescents can also show normal or increased energy level) and motor restlessness during sleep (bipolar adolescents are physically restless at night when high, although they may have little physical motion during sleep when low). They may have self-image problems and problems with school

learning. Stimulant and antidepressant medication is often helpful. And family history often includes mood disorders.

2. They are somewhat different in the following ways: The mood of the affectively disordered adolescent tends to be sad and that of the ADHD child labile and intermittently dysphoric. Both groups of adolescents can act destructively, but the mood-disordered youngster tends to do so in anger while the ADHD youngster does so not only when angry but when careless as well. The appetite of the ADHD adolescent tends to be normal or increased, whereas the mood-disordered adolescent's appetite tends to be poor or increased (although, in bipolar, we see marked fluctuations).

3. They are significantly different in the following ways: The sleep difficulties of the mood-disordered adolescent tend to be insomnia or too much sleep (with severe nightmares sometimes), and with the ADHD youngster we can see sleep-arousal imbalances with difficulty falling asleep sometimes. The interest of a mood-disordered youngster is lessened (there is a loss of interest or pleasure in usual activities), and, with the ADHD adolescent, the interest often seems inconsistent. Suicidal intent or thought is common with the mood-disordered adolescent and much more rare for the ADHD youngster. Finally, psychotic symptoms and primary-process thinking sometimes occur in the mood-disordered adolescent and are extremely rare in the ADHD adolescent.

Another major diagnostic marker that usually makes this differential diagnosis clear is frequency of symptoms: with ADHD, we see relatively chronic and pervasive symptomatology; with a mood disorder, we tend to see a pattern that is not simply chronic and pervasive but cyclic and/or recurrent and/or more severe over time. When ADHD is a factor, we sometimes see a positive family history for this disorder. The parent (more often the father) often does not realize that he, too, evinced (and may still evince) ADHD until the diagnosis of his child or adolescent is under way.

The consequences of ADHD (lack of control, frustration, and, often, academic and social difficulties) do diminish opportunities for pleasure and hence often result in a psychogenic (dysthymic) depressive disorder. The fact that this is often not recognized and addressed is one of the reasons why so many of these children go on to develop moderately severe to severe character pathology and maladaptive behavioral patterns.

However, in considering the diagnosis of dysthymia, the clinician must be aware that one of the key diagnostic issues may be determining whether irritable mood stems from symptoms of helplessness and depression or is simply a characteristic of the ADHD child's overarousal and impulsivity. But ADHD youngsters with significant overarousal and hyperactivity problems and long histories of environmental failure appear at greater risk of developing symptoms of dysthymia. In fact, DSM-III-R notes that ADHD is a predisposing factor for dysthymia.

Attentional Disorders and Developmental Implications

How do attentional disorders affect the conscious and unconscious narratives that adolescents have come to tell themselves, about themselves, others, and the world? There is no simple relation between any of the psychological, psychobiological, and, initially, purely biologically based attentional disorders, on the one hand, and personality development, on the other. But it is clear that, whatever our weaknesses and our strengths are, they have a molding influence on what we think and feel about ourselves and others as well as on our past and future. As such, an ongoing attentional disorder will be one aspect or force in personality development. There are several trends and questions worth noting, however, regarding attentional disorders and psychosocial development as they have important clinical implications: the psychodynamically heterogeneous nature of this group; the risk factor—regardless of etiology—of attentional disorders; the psychological power of the frequency and severity of the attentional disorder; the question of how realistically aware the adolescent is, or is not, about her attentional problem; and the relation between a neuropsychological deficit and conflict.

Psychodynamically, adolescents with attentional disorders are a heterogeneous group. In other words, having a given type of attentional disorder—whether a symptom of a particular set of conflicts and anxieties, an auditory discrimination diability, or ADHD—does not simply result in a particular set of conflicts, self-representations, concerns, or the utilization of particular defenses. It does not even necessarily result in what would be the understandable conscious concern that one has difficulty paying attention. For example, the adolescent who denies that he has any problem paying attention (with or without the aid of illicit drugs, which are so often used to self-medicate) may not experience any conscious concerns in this area.

Personality, like the weather, is an unpredictable phenomenon that is influenced by a countless number of variables that interact in ways that we can begin to describe but never fully understand. However, an attentional disorder—like a strong "cold front"—is always a force in the development of personality. Our ability to pay attention is one of the most fundamental aspects of ego functioning or an integral part of the foundation of mental functioning. As such, it will always affect and interact with the myriad other factors and processes that determine psychological and social functioning. As I have noted above, there is never a purely biologically based attentional disorder in adolescence.

Adolescents who evince an ongoing attentional disorder that has a clear biological etiology (e.g., an eye-tracking disorder due to occular-motor imbalance or unmanaged diabetes or a bipolar illness) always attribute meanings to the disorder. Hence, it becomes interrelated with all the other narratives that the adolescents consciously and unconsciously tell themselves about who they are, what they can and cannot do, what their body has and does and does not have and cannot do, to name but a few of the narrative tales that adolescents importantly tell themselves.

Clinically, what is always most critical is to begin to understand the following questions: What is the nature of the attentional disorder? What effect has it had in school, in affecting the adolescent's experience of self, others, and the process of learning? How has this particular weakness been understood consciously and unconsciously by the adolescent? How has it interacted with the youngster's strengths, weaknesses, wishes, fears, and other affects, dreams, and coping/defensive styles? Although few simple predictions can be made about the effect of attentional disorders on psychological functioning, I believe that it can be said that they certainly contribute to the child and the adolescent being "at risk" for developing psychopathology.

Attentional disorders do not necessarily result in psychopathology, but they do seem to be a factor that makes youngsters "at risk." This has been clearly established for a number of disorders that I have described above. For example, there is clinical and research evidence suggesting that the following factors place children and adolescents at risk for developing adolescent psychopathology: learning disabilities (e.g., Cohen 1984; Rourke and Fuerst 1991); extreme temperament (e.g., Thomas, Chess, Birch, Hertzig, and Korn 1963); ADHD (e.g., Barkley 1990); and affective illness (Akiskal, Hirschfeld, and Yerevanian 1983; Kestenbaum 1992; Winokur, Clayton, and Reich 1969). It is not surprising that youngsters who have difficulty controlling one of the most basic aspects of mental functioning would be "at risk" for consciously and unconsciously telling themselves that "there is something wrong with me." This experience and related disparaging narratives about oneself and one's body naturally will, to a greater or lesser extent, become interrelated with all the other stories that the adolescent is telling himself. The adolescent's narrative about his attentional experience will always be colored by two specific dimensions of the particular attentional problem: frequency and severity.

Clinical experience suggests that, the more intermittent, and hence unpredictable, the attentional problem is in childhood and adolescence, the more complicating it will be psychologically. The frequency (i.e., ranging from constant to intermittent) of a disorder is a psychologically potent dimension. Early infant research underscores that one of the most basic motivational systems has to do with our built-in predisposition toward self-regulation, mastery, and a need to organize experience or "make sense" of the world (e.g., Emde 1989; Stern 1985). Unpredictability complicates and interferes with youngsters' ability to organize experience. Psychologically, a disorder that is constant (e.g., blindness or a complete inability to pay attention due to a severe trauma) tends to be easier to understand, adjust to, and cope with emotionally than a disorder that is intermittent. I have detailed elsewhere how mild to moderately severe verbal learning disabilities (e.g., a word-finding disability or a reading disability) are intermittent in nature: they do not occur in a consistent, predictable manner. The intermittent and, hence, unpredictable nature of the disorder is one of the central factors that contributes to a sense of subtle but significant helpless and cumulative trauma in childhood and adolescence (Cohen 1984).

Some of the attentional disorders that I have described above are more intermittent than others. For example, an adolescent who evinces a mild version of ADHD will experience attentional functioning as being more intermittently affected as compared to a youngster with a severe ADHD. Or an adolescent who does not pay attention in a particular class because he is genuinely not interested or because he is profoundly conflicted about his feelings toward a particular teacher or topic will tend to have difficulty paying attention more constantly in that situation. However problematic this attentional symptom may

327

be academically, it will tend to be less complicating psychologically because the youngster will be able to understand it relatively easily: "I'm bored," or, "Yeah, I'm uptight, of course I have trouble paying attention." Even when it is not understandable, it is more predictable. On the other hand, an intermittent attentional symptom (e.g., an adolescent who is beginning to become hypomanic for the first time or when there is an auditory discrimination disorder that is problematic only when there is a lot of noise, like an air conditioner or a lot of voices in the background) means that the adolescent will have much more difficulty "making sense" of the experience. The frequency of the disorder always interacts with the severity of the disorder.

Clinical experience suggests that, the more severe the attentional problem is in childhood and adolescence, the more complicating it will be psychologically. A very mild attentional disorder, whatever the cause, will tend to be less problematic than a severe disorder. Generally, there is no agreed on way to assess severity (or frequency) of these disorders. In DSM-III-R, there was a beginning attempt to rate ADHD as "mild," "moderate," or "severe." I suspect that future clinical research will fruitfully develop more systematic ways of assessing these two basic dimensions: frequency and severity. However, it will always be the clinician's task to understand, with the adolescent, the meanings that have come to be associated with the particular nature of the actual, imagined, and remembered attentional disorder.

The extent to which the adolescent is able to assess his weaknesses (and strengths) realistically is always a central psychological/developmental process. This primary adolescent task has particular importance for youngsters with attentional disorders. This is equally so for youngsters with other types of verbal and nonverbal learning disorders and disabilities. Who are we? What are our interests, strengths, and weaknesses? It is usually painful for adolescents to begin to come to terms with their inadequacies and weaknesses. And it is characteristically most painful and often quite shameful when these weaknesses have profoundly affected their experience in school and relationships, which are two of the spheres that attentional disorders so often complicate. Adolescents often have developed very unrealistic ideas or narratives about their attentional disorders: "I am a dumb person and I can't learn anything in school"; "I am a lazy person who is lacking in some fundamental, ineffable way"; "I am a problem to other people"; "There is something very wrong with me. . . . No one understands me, there is something 'bad' in me.'' These are typical beginnings of narratives of attentionally disordered adolescents. Consciously or unconsciously, each youngster "fills in" specifics (e.g., what is the nature of the "bad") and elaborates these opening sentences into the tapestry of their own, idiosyncratic story of the many aspects of themselves. The more unclear the adolescent is about the specific nature of her attentional disorder, the more vulnerable and "at risk" she is to develop complicating, unrealistic, and often problematic narratives, conflicts, and a sense of shame.

Mental health professionals have a unique opportunity to help adolescents, their parents, and the youngsters' teachers understand what is the specific nature of the attentional problem. A clear and realistic understanding allows adolescents to perceive themselves in a more coherent and integrated manner. It also enhances the chance that youngsters will be able to experience their weakness, not only as the weakness that it is, but potentially as a strength or linked to strengths. As adolescents and adults gradually come to realize, there are often critical links between our weaknesses and our strengths. For example, many adolescents who evince ADHD are quite gifted in athletic activities that require extremely rapid kinesthetic action (e.g., zooming down a slalom course or racing around the soccer field). In this kind of context, their inclination to shift their attention rapidly, to be "filled with energy" and move around a lot, is not a liability; it is an asset. It is not uncommon that kids who have any number of disabilities— including attentional disorders—become particularly sensitive to others who have handicaps: empathic capacities are enhanced. Athletic abilities and the enhanced interpersonal sensitivities are examples of strengths that can emerge from a weakness or be the "flip side" of a weakness. But, for adolescents to understand, appreciate, and integrate these strengths and weaknesses into a coherent sense of self, they (and their families) often need the help of professionals in a number of ways. It is to these considerations that I now briefly turn: further clinical considerations and implications of having an attentional disorder.

Before turning to more specific clinical considerations, I want to add a note on neuropsychological deficit and conflct. Attentional disorders that have a neuropsychological basis (e.g., affective illness, ADHD) raise interesting questions regarding deficit and conflict. These types of attentional disorders do constitute a deficit in an aspect of the autonomous functioning of the ego. The attentional problem is not simply due to a conflict. However, it is simplistic to say that the psychological effects of this neuropsychological deficit are or can ever be unrelated to conflict. The adolescent's experience of what he can and cannot do (attentionally and otherwise) becomes integrally intertwined with the story lines that he tells himself consciously and unconsciously about self (or selves), others, wishes, self-deceptions, and more. To acknowledge the nature of the actual weakness and then to be able to go on to collaboratively understand how this experience has become "folded into" the myriad of other wishes, defenses, affects, and self- and object representations is clinically most useful.

Further Clinical Considerations

There are several clinical considerations that I want briefly to describe now that emerge from the psychobiological spectrum of attentional disorders that I have described. Some of my comments will pertain just to the adolescent's self-experience and some to the adolescent, his family, and his experience in school.

Attentional disorders can affect functioning in all spheres of the adolescent's life: intrapsychically, interpersonally, at home, and learning in and outside school. The process of diagnosis must be a comprehensive and integrative effort. As follows from the psychobiological spectrum of attentional disorders described here, it is essential that the clinician have a comprehensive understanding of the adolescent's psychodynamic, cognitive, neuropsychological, psychiatric, medical, family, social, and school functioning. Sometimes, this understanding can and will emerge from an initial extended consultation phase in which the clinician meets with the adolescent and his family and talks with teachers and/or tutors and past clinicians/diagnosticians. To the extent that we need to understand how chronic and pervasive an attentional disorder is, it is usually essential that teachers as well as parents be interviewed. Sometimes, an extended clinical consultation does not provide information that we need to make a diagnosis. For example, we may know that the adolescent is extremely anxious and evincing pathological narcissistic disturbances. And we may sense (from our own direct experience and teacher reports) that sometimes the adolescent does not seem to "register" what is being said to him. But we may not be able to confirm or disconfirm the presence of a receptive language problem or an auditory discrimination problem or another form of a memory and/or attentional disorder. In such cases, a comprehensive and integrated neuropsychological/educational/psychodynamic evaluation may critically clarify the nature of specific cognitive (e.g., language) strengths and weaknesses (see Cohen [1983] and Rothstein, Benjamin, Crosby, and Eisenstadt [1988] for details).

Comprehensive diagnostic evaluations should ideally be conducted by a neuropsychologically and educationally trained diagnostician who is psychoanalytically informed and can administer projective tests. This provides the invaluable opportunity for the tester to see how the adolescent's strengths and weaknesses interact with wishes, defenses, affects, central concerns, and self- and object representations. An educational or a neuropsychological evaluation without this clinical/psychoanalytic integration may provide very valuable information about the adolescent. But it will not clarify what are always critical clinical questions: how the actual weaknesses and strengths interact with psychodynamic processes.

A comprehensive understanding of the adolescent's attentional disorders in conjunction with an understanding of her other weaknesses, strengths, and psychodynamic, social, family, and school functioning provides the basis for an informed and potentially effective plan of intervention and treatment. A comprehensive diagnostic understanding of a learning problem—be it an attentional problem or a verbal or nonverbal problem—can be a powerful therapeutic and educational intervention in and of itself. Often, the adolescent, the family, and the school are confused about the adolescent's difficulties. The mental health professional who directly or indirectly conducts a comprehensive evaluation can then begin to accomplish three important goals: to develop an informed treatment plan; to educate the adolescent, her family, and the school (where appropriate); and, where appropriate, to develop a team to assist the adolescent in an ongoing manner.

The treatment of attentional disorders in adolescence is sometimes relatively simple and straightforward: individual psychotherapy alone may be the recommended treatment, for example, when a youngster is conflicted about succeeding in school and is defending against conscious and unconscious fears by "not paying attention." On the other hand, attentional disorders are sometimes quite complex. An attentional disorder that stems from ADHD or a bipolar illness affects many aspects of the adolescent's life and the family's emotional and social life as well. In any case, the treatment or treatments (whether individual psychotherapy, psychoanalysis, family therapy, pharmacological, educational, and/or social) always need to be based on a comprehensive understanding of the problem, the person, and the context.

One of the first therapeutic interventions that we characteristically make is to initiate or continue the process of educating the adolescent about the nature of the problem. This is particularly important with many attentionally disordered adolescents who have very unrealistic and convoluted ideas about their strengths and weaknesses. To help them and often their families and schools understand what is a weakness (or deficit) and what difficulties are due to other factors (e.g., anxiety and maladaptive defenses), we need to set in motion a process of education about the specific nature of the adolescents' experience, strengths, and weaknesses.

Ultimately, no one cares more about the youngster than the parents. When the learning-disabled youngster is a child, I think that it is virtually always critical that the parents become educated about their child's weaknesses, strengths, and psychoeducational functioning. This allows them to become effective advocates for their child and provides necessary opportunities for an ongoing dialogue with the child and the school about these issues. This allows the parents to help the child develop more experiential coherence and mastery and to become the most effective advocate for himself. But all this is much more complex in adolescence. The adolescent is in the process of separating from the parents, so that educating the parents can be a complicated and sometimes conflictual process for reasons that have nothing to do with the attentional disorder. As is generally the case, there is no simple answer or guideline here. An understanding of the specific nature of the adolescent's attentional (and other) disorder(s), developmental experience, and how this affects family functioning will often suggest pathways to discuss with the adolescent and, perhaps, the family and, sometimes, the school. When the attentional problem is not due to psychogenic factors alone, it is often clinically helpful for the adolescent to know that there is a team of people who understand and will help with the problem.

Adolescents who evince attentional problems that have a cognitive and/or a biological basis (as well as an inevitable psychogenic component) typically do have a team of adults who are directly and/or indirectly involved with the problem: teachers, parents, and sometimes tutors and/or mental health professionals. Too often members of this team do not talk to each other. The adults may even have quite different conceptualizations of the nature of the problem, goals, and an evolving sense as to what is changing and what is remaining the same. Sometimes, all the members of the team should not talk to each other. For example, to the extent to which a psychoanalytic psychotherapy is an integral aspect of the treatment plan, the analyst or psychoanalytically oriented psychotherapist should not talk to others as it sometimes can so easily undermine the alliance and the ability to use the emerging transference and countertransference. But this is not always the case. In any case, I would suggest that, even when one member of what is in fact an interdisciplinary team of a sort chooses not to communicate with the other team members, it is sometimes quite useful to conceptualize the adults working together with the adolescent as a team. And there should be periodic meetings of all members of the team that can and want to come, including the adolescent.

There are a number of quite simple but educationally and clinically powerful factors that contribute to the team being a useful idea and forum. If the attentional disability (or verbal or nonverbal learning disability) is affecting various sectors of the adolescent's life (e.g., school, social, home, self-experience), it can only be helpful to think about these spheres in an integrated manner. Goals, progress and/or lack of progress, problems, and helpful and unhelpful solutions can be profitably and integratively discussed. Even if the psychoanalyst/ psychotherapist does not attend these meetings, this information can be communicated to the therapist (e.g., by the adolescent) and used as invaluable "grist for the mill." But the idea of the "team" needs to rest on the adolescent's willingness to allow it to develop. Ideally, the adolescent becomes in time the leader of this team. Interestingly, most adolescents who have been given the opportunity to join such a work group welcome the chance. On the other hand, it has been more common that one or more of the adults have initially been quite anxious about such a gathering.

This process of developing a meeting of the adults involved with the adolescent is extremely educative in and of itself. To have the adults talking together in an appreciative, collaborative manner with the adolescent is often an extremely useful diagnostic process (e.g., where do we see the problem now?) and a powerful supportive intervention that can lead to useful questions, ideas, and plans. In addition, this gathering of the team ideally—and usually in reality—contributes to a sense of genuine caring and support, which is, after all, one of the basic therapeutic factors that facilitate change (e.g., Wallerstein 1986). Furthermore, it is quite empowering for the adolescent when the goal is to gradually make the youngsters themselves the leader/coordinator of the team. This experience can importantly contribute to a sense of mastery, control, and experiential coherence, which is the basis for narcissistic well-being.

It is well known that one of the most common and potentially complicating effects of any learning disability is unrealistic, negative representation of self (i.e., poor self-esteem). Since some of Freud's earliest writings (Breuer and Freud 1893), there has been the idea that an event or experience becomes pathological because it cannot be integrated into the person's psychological organization. Learning disabilities— whether attentional, verbal, or nonverbal in nature—tend to complicate and interfere with the child's and adolescent's ability to integrate a realistic sense and appraisal of strengths and weaknesses. There are a number of reasons why this tends to be so. Weaknesses that characteristically result in frustration, failure, confusion, and shame tend to be consciously and unconsciously remembered (and anticipated) with greater and undue psychic weight. In fact, the psychic confusion (e.g., "It must be that I am lazy, 'cause I can pay attention if I really try . . . but I'm not lazy!") and cumulative trauma that learning disabilities engender lead to the youngster wanting either to avoid the activity or to experience it as a critical challenge to be overcome. In either case, the experience (in this case, "paying attention") tends to be psychically loaded in a way that makes psychic integration and realistic appraisal of the actual weaknesses difficult. And all these learning disabilities—attentional, verbal, and nonverbal—tend to undermine a sense of mastery and experiential coherence as well as increasing the experience of helplessness and passivity. Clinically, one of our central tasks with these adolescents is to help them shift these trends, experience a greater sense of mastery and experiential coherence, and reduce their passivity and helplessness. But how do we do this? Obviously, there is no simple answer to this question.

Ideally, we need to help the adolescent actually experience success, pleasure, and mastery in external areas that come to have meaning for her as well as developing insight and a sense of emotional/psychic mastery. On the one hand, any experiences that actually result in more moments of success, pleasure, and mastery help. In fact, without these actual external experiences, understanding alone is often not enough: the backload of negative experience is a force that undermines the utilization of insight. Psychoanalysts have sometimes been too uninvolved with thinking about what actual experiences (e.g., shifts in the academic schedule, or ways of making the adolescent's strengths shine more brightly, or volunteer apprenticeship or job situations) can enhance and further facilitate mastery. But it is often painfully apparent that further experiences of mastery alone may not undo an unconscious inclination neurotically to recreate the experience of being unable and/or "dumb" and/or confused and/or a failure to confirm the unconscious and sometimes conscious sense of being helpless, victimized, and/or misunderstood.

Psychic understanding and a gradual, growing sense of psychological and relational mastery that can sometimes emerge only within the psychotherapeutic process often need to go hand in hand with other kinds of successes. It is here that the analyst's understanding of the original strengths and weaknesses (the "deficit") in conjunction with a sense of how these deficits have become interrelated with the narratives, conflicts, concerns, dreams, defenses, and representation of self and others is so critically helpful. But rigidity is a factor that often interferes with and inhibits this process of understanding, on the one hand, and emotional and behavioral experimentation and change, on the other hand. It may be that, for several reasons, attentionally (as well as verbally and nonverbally learning) disabled youngsters characteristically show significant mental rigidity, which is often a stumbling block to change. The ability to think and act in a nonrigid or flexible manner may be the single most important factor that determines success and pleasure in late adolescence and adulthood.

Flexibility is a multidetermined process that develops over time and operates in a number of domains (e.g., verbal, visual, mathematical, kinesthetic, musical, intrapsychic, and interpersonal). Being flexible in one domain does not necessarily imply great flexibility in other domains. I believe that it is useful to think about cognitive flexibility in the following ways: Cognitive flexibility is the ability to entertain several different formulations, solutions or interpretations in a simultaneous or dialectical manner to accomplish the task. Rigidity is an antonym of flexibility.

Rigidity is always a force that complicates growth. In fact, all neurotic, character-disordered, and borderline-level psychopathology can be viewed as patterns of rigid mental processes. There may be three overlapping factors that contribute to learning-disabled adolescents showing significant and, often, pathological mental rigidity: educational, psychodynamic, and biological.

To some extent, flexible or rigid problem-solving styles are learned. The extent to which a youngster grows up in a family and educational culture where flexibility and/or rigid behavior is valued will have a profound effect. Some parents and school systems value "disciplined, obedient behavior" over all else. Naturally, this will be a molding force on how the youngster attends and thinks about as well as attempts to solve problems. A growing awareness that being a flexible problem solver is one—if not the most—predictive factor in adult satisfaction (e.g., Heath 1991) has resulted in a great deal of recent research (e.g., Hamburg 1992) and educational programs in this area (e.g., cooperative education). It is probable that significantly attentionally disordered adolescents—whatever the etiology—are often hampered or even unable to utilize educational programs that do attempt to enhance flexible problem-solving capacities. Although to some extent flexibility is a learned ability, psychodynamic factors are probably the major force that limits this ability in many attentionally disordered adolescents.

Psychodynamically, many of these adolescents utilized defensive strategies in a relatively rigid manner. In other words, they tended to rely on a limited number of defensive operations, which they used with little regard for the actual situation. They also showed an exaggerated and tense deliberateness of behavior, which reflects a special kind of self-consciousness. This rigidity was not a manifestation of any one character structure: it was an important aspect of functioning regardless of character type. Many of the attentionally disabled adolescents felt (understandably) an unstable sense of mastery. And they often evinced a need continuously to reinforce a sense of mastery and self-control. Rigidity may be an important solution to this set of experiences.

Being attentionally disabled can lead to doubts of one's ability to be in control and to find ways to avoid the repeated experience of helplessness. Acting in a rigid manner may help the adolescent feel more in control. In addition, it is possible that, as the adolescent anxiously struggles and then gradually learns what helps compensate for the disorder and to defend against the experience of helplessness and distress, she then clings to and rigidly maintains these coping strategies.

Rigidity in learning-disabled adolescents may also be colored by biological processes. It is well known that severe brain damage characteristically results in rigidity: it limits some aspects of cognitive flexibility by eliminating some of the parallel processes among which normal individuals can choose in approaching a situation or a problem. In fact, extreme rigidity is sometimes used to confirm the diagnosis of brain damage. The extent to which an attentional disorder—like an attention deficit disorder—is due to brain dysfunction may mean that mental rigidity is another manifestation of this. But at present we do not know how to tease apart what is biological and what is psychological when disorders are on the more "mild" end of the spectrum. Our psychological/emotional reactions become so interrelated with our biologically based strengths and weaknesses that it is characteristically quite difficult to distinguish the two.

Conclusions

Adolescents who are seen in mental health clinics and in the consulting room often present with difficulties paying attention in conjunction with any number of other problems. Typically, clinicians believe that attentional symptomatology is due to psychogenic factors (e.g., anxiety or dysthymic conditions) or an ADHD. And this is often the case. But many factors can directly and indirectly interfere with adolescents being able to utilize this most basic and complex cognitive/ ego function: attention.

There is a psychobiological spectrum of factors that can complicate adolescents' ability to pay attention: to sustain and focus attention as well as selectively to determine what is most important to attend to. A clinical schema has been presented that describes the range of psychogenic, cognitive, and biological factors or disorders that can complicate and disrupt adolescents' ability to pay attention. Psychologically, three experiences were described that can and do most often lead to attentional disorders: a primary psychogenic disorder that is initially unrelated to problems in learning or attention; a reactive psychological disorder that is initially in response to problems in learning or attention; and a lack of interest. Three types of cognitively based attentional disorders were described: verbal or nonverbal learning disabilities; a selective attention disorder; and an attentional skill deficiency. And five sets of biological factors were described that can directly or indirectly complicate adolescents' ability to pay attention: temperamental factors; fatigue and arousal disorders; various medical conditions; ADHD; and affective disorders.

Some adolescents do evince biologically based conditions that complicate their ability to pay attention. However, there is never a purely biologically based attentional disorder: the experience of the disorder has inevitably come to be understood (and misunderstood) unconsciously and consciously in ways that are clinically critical to understand. In addition, many adolescents evince more than one factor that is complicating their ability to pay attention. The differential diagnosis of these various factors can and must inform clinicians working with children and adolescents who present with attentional disorders. It is typically true that treatment planning needs to follow diagnosis. And it is particularly the case here: when a misdiagnosis is made, the patient can be harmed inadvertently.

I have also begun to describe some of the developmental, diagnostic, educational, and clinical implications for the psychobiological spectrum of attentional disorders that I have presented here. Although attentionally disordered adolescents are a heterogeneous group (in general and within each of the subgroups), problems that do complicate this most basic of cognitive or ego functions put youngsters "at risk" for developing psychopathology. A number of factors were discussed that contribute to this: the psychological power of the relative frequency and severity of a given attentional disorder; the adolescent's tendency to have an unrealistic perception of his strengths and weaknesses; the tendency of attentional disabilities (like verbal and nonverbal disabilities) to undermine a sense of mastery and experiential coherence and increase the experience of helplessness and passivity. Finally, a number of diagnostic and treatment suggestions were made.

NOTE

1. A "Fisher Landau Interdisciplinary Seminar at Dalton" was organized to study this issue. Ten clinicians (psychoanalysts, clinical psychologists, psychiatrists, neuropsychologists, and school psychologists) had seen a total of roughly 700 children and adolescents in the last year (in consultation, through supervisees, or in treatment).

REFERENCES

Akistal, H. S.; Hirschfield, M. A.; and Yerevanian, B. I. 1983. The relationship to affective disorders: a critical review. *Archives of General Psychiatry* 40:801–810.

Allen, A. A. 1988. Autistic spectrum disorders: clinical presentation in preschool children. *Journal of Child Neurology* 3:48–56.

American Psychiatric Association. 1980. *Diagnostic and Statistical Manual of Mental Disorders.* 3d ed. Washington, D.C.: American Psychiatric Association.

American Psychiatric Association. 1987. *Diagnostic and Statistical Manual of Mental Disorders.* 3d ed., rev. Washington, D.C.: American Psychiatric Association.

August, G. J., and Garfinkel, B. D. 1989. Behavioral and cognitive subtypes of ADHD. *Journal of the American Academy of Child and Adolescent Psychiatry* 28:739–748.

Barkley, R. A. 1990. *Attention Deficit Hyperactivity Disorder.* New York: Guilford.

Bettelheim, B., and Zelan, K. 1982. *On Learning to Read: The Child's Fascination with Meaning.* New York: Knopf.

Breuer, J., and Freud, S. 1893. Studies on hysteria. *Standard Edition* 2:1–18. London: Hogarth, 1955.

Brumback, R. A., and Weinberg, W. W. 1990. Pediatric behavioral neurology: an update on the neurological aspects of depression, hyperactivity and learning disabilities. *Neurologic Clinics* 8(3): 677–703.

Carey, W. B., and McDevitt, S. C., eds. 1989. *Clinical and Educational Applications of Temperament Research.* Berwyn, Pa.: Swets North America.

Cohen, J. 1983. Learning disabilities and the college student: identification and diagnosis. *Adolescent Psychiatry* 11:177–198.

Cohen, J. 1984. Learning disabilities and adolescence: developmental considerations. *Adolescent Psychiatry* 12:177–196.

Cohen, J. 1992a. The psychobiological spectrum of social disorders in adolescents. Paper presented at the third annual congress of the International Society for Adolescent Psychiatry, Chicago, July 12.

Cohen, J. 1992b. A report on the second Fisher Landau Interdisciplinary Seminar at Dalton: attentional disorders in childhood and adolescence. New York. Typescript.

Emde, R. 1989. The infant's relationship experience: developmental and affective aspects. In A. Sameroff and R. Emde, eds. *Relationship Disturbances in Early Childhood*. New York: Basic.

Goldstein, S., and Goldstein, M. 1990. *Managing Attention Disorders in Children*. New York: Wiley.

Greenhill, L. 1992. Disruptive behavior and attention deficit disorders: review in the era of DSM-III and IV. In J. O'Brien, ed. *Seventeenth Annual Review in Child and Adolescent Psychiatry*. New York: American Academy of Child and Adolescent Psychiatry.

Greenhill, L. L., and Osman, B. B., eds. 1991. *Ritalin: Theory and Patient Management*. New York: Mary Ann Liebert.

Halperin, J. M.; Newcorn, J. H.; and Sharma, V. 1991. Diagnostic comorbidity: ADHD, disorders of conduct, and cognitive problems. In L. L. Greenhill and B. B. Osman, eds. *Ritalin: Theory and Patient Management*. New York: Mary Ann Liebert.

Hamburg, D. A. 1992. *Today's Children: Creating a Future for a Generation in Crisis*. New York: Times Books, Random House.

Heath, D. H. 1991. *Fulfilling Lives*. San Francisco: Jossey-Bass.

Hudson, J. I., and Pope, H. G. 1990. Affective spectrum disorder: does antidepressant response identify a family of disorders with a common pathophysiology? *American Journal of Psychiatry* 147(5): 552–564.

Jenson, J. B.; Burke, N.; and Garfinkel, B. D. 1988. Depression and symptoms of attention deficit disorder with hyperactivity. *Journal of the American Academy of Child and Adolescent Psychiatry* 27:742–747.

Kagan, J. 1988. Biological bases of childhood shyness. *Science* 240:167–171.

Kagan, J. 1989. *Unstable Ideas: Temperament, Cognition, and Self*. Cambridge, Mass.: Harvard University Press.

Keener, M. A., and Anders, T. F. 1986. New frontiers of sleep-disorders medicine in infants, children, and adolescents. In R. Michaels and J. O. Cavenar, eds. *Psychiatry: Child Psychiatry*. New York: Basic.

Kestenbaum, C. 1992. The treatment of bipolar disorder in adolescence: a dual-track treatment approach. *International Annals of Adolescent Psychiatry* 2:119–125.

Kinsbourne, M. 1991. Overfocusing: an apparent subtype of attention deficit–hyperactive disorder. In N. Amir, I. Rapin, and D. Branski, eds. *Pediatric Neurology: Behavior and Cognition of the Child with Brain Damage*. Basel: Karger.

Levine, M. D. 1987. *Developmental Variation and Learning Disorders*. Cambridge, Mass.: Educators Publishing Service.

Luisada, P. V. 1969. REM deprivation and hyperactivity in children. *Chicago Medical School Quarterly* 28:97.

Matier, K.; Halperin, J. M.; Sharma, V.; Newcorn, J. H.; and Sathaye, N. 1992. Methylphenidate response in aggressive and nonaggressive ADHD children: distinctions on laboratory measures of symptoms. *Journal of the American Academy of Child and Adolescent Psychiatry* 31:219–225.

Popper, C. 1989. Diagnosing bipolar vs. ADHD. *Newsletter of the Academy of Child and Adolescent Psychiatry* (Summer), pp. 5–6.

Rothstein, A.; Benjamin, L.; Crosby, M.; and Eisenstadt, K. 1988. *Learning Disorders: An Integration of Neuropsychological and Psychoanalytic Considerations*. Madison, Conn.: International Universities Press.

Rourke, B. P., and Fuerst, D. R. 1991. *Learning Disabilities and Psychosocial Functioning: A Neuropsychological Perspective*. New York: Guilford.

Shapiro, D. 1965. *Neurotic Styles*. New York: Basic.

Shaywitz, S. E., and Shaywitz, B. E. 1988. Attention deficit disorder: current perspectives. In J. F. Kavanagh and T. J. Truss, Jr., eds. *Learning Disabilities: Proceedings of the National Conference*. Parkton, Md.: York.

Shaywitz, S. E., and Shaywitz, B. E., eds. 1992. *Attention Deficit Disorder Comes of Age: Toward the Twenty-First Century*. Austin, Tex.: PRO-ED.

Shepherd, M. J. 1991. Consider the hypothesis of primary social disabilities associates with mathematics and motor disabilities. Paper presented at the Teachers College Conference "Learning Disabilities: Social, Emotional, and Attentional Difficulties," Columbia University, November 1.

Silver, L. B. 1974. Emotional and social problems of children with developmental disabilities. In R. E. Weber, ed. *Handbook on Learning Disabilities*. Englewood Cliffs, N.J.: Prentice-Hall.

Silver, L. 1990. An evolving biological of ADHD: implications in clinical practice. Paper presented at the meeting of the New York Orton Dyslexia Society, New York, March 23.

Silver, L. B. 1992. *Attention-Deficit Hyperactivity Disorder: A Clinical Guide to Diagnosis and Treatment.* Washington, D.C.: American Psychiatric Press.

Stern, D. 1985. *The Interpersonal World of the Infant.* New York: Basic.

Stuss, D. T., and Benton, D. F. 1984. Neuropsychological studies of the frontal lobes. *Psychological Bulletin* 95:3–28.

Thomas, A.; Chess, S.; and Birch, H. G. 1968. *Temperament and Behavior Disorders in Children.* New York: New York University Press.

Thomas, A.; Chess, S.; Birch, H. G.; Hertzig, M. E.; and Korn, S. 1963. *Behavioral Individuality in Early Childhood.* New York: New York University Press.

Turecki, S., and Tonner, L. 1985. *The Difficult Child.* New York: Bantam.

Urion, D. K. 1989. Response to desipramine in attention deficit hyperactive disorder is predicted by neurological subtype. *Annual of Neurology* 26:481.

Wallerstein, R. 1986. *Forty-two Lives in Treatment: A Study of Psychoanalysis and Psychotherapy.* New York: Guilford.

Weinberg, W. A.; Rutman, J.; and Sullivan, L. 1973. Depression in children referred to an educational diagnostic center. *Journal of Pediatrics* 83:1065–1073.

Werry, J. S.; Reeves, J. C.; and Elkind, G. S. 1987. Attention deficit, conduct, oppositional, and anxiety disorders in children. I. a review of research on differentiating characteristics. *Journal of the American Academy of Child and Adolescent Psychiatry* 26:133–143.

Wing, L. 1988. The continuum of autistic characteristics. In E. Schopler and G. Mesibov, eds. *Diagnosis and Assessment of Autism.* New York: Plenum.

Winokur, G.; Clayton, P.; and Reich, I. 1969. *Manic-Depressive Illness.* St. Louis: Mosby.

Zametkin, A. J.; Nordahl, T. E.; Gross, M.; King, C. A.; Semple, W. E.; Rumsey, J.; Hamburger, S.; and Cohen, R. M. 1990. Cerebral glucose metabolism in adults with hyperactivity of childhood onset. *New England Journal of Medicine* 323(20): 1361–1366.

18   PSYCHOANALYTIC DEVELOPMENTAL PERSPECTIVES ON THE TREATMENT OF A YOUNG ADULT

BARBARA FAJARDO

According to a familiar developmental perspective, young adulthood is a stage, a unique period in the life span, beginning approximately at twenty-two and ending about twenty-eight years of age. In the tradition of Erikson (1950), there are eight stages of life, each defined by biological and/or social imperatives that are operative during a particular time period in the life span. Biological imperatives are physiological (e.g., cognitive, maturational, and hormonal) forces, and social imperatives are the expectations imposed by the culture. By the time a person reaches the threshold of young adulthood, he or she will have completed cognitive and physical maturation, and nature's hormonal rushes will be settling down. Unlike earlier stages, such as infancy, latency, and adolescence, there are no obvious universal biological or endogenously generated imperatives that confer uniqueness on the experience of young adulthood. While endogenous problems can surface during this period, evolving from earlier conflicts and developmental failures, these are unique in the life of each individual and cannot be generalized to all lives.

Regarding social imperatives, the young adult is expected to find a marriage partner or significant other and to be directed in search of a specific vocation within a chosen field of life work. The young adult will be pressed with some urgency to "fit in," to take a place as a member of a "couple," and to function as a productive participant in the workplace. Erikson (1950) tells us that the young adult is faced with alternatives of intimacy and work versus isolation. Successfully negotiating this task produces an adult connectedness to society.

The defining criterion of young adulthood, then, is the adaptational task of mastering this social imperative. Havighurst (1952) has defined a developmental task as one that arises during a certain period in the life span. Successful completion of a developmental task leads to happiness and later satisfaction, whereas failure leads to unhappiness, social disapproval, and difficulty with later tasks.

Often, young adults seek treatment because of failures in their capacity to master the tasks posed by social imperatives of finding a love partner and a life work. This describes the precipitant and the manifest content of their struggles but says nothing about the particular experience, the intrapsychic origins of distress, or the dynamics of their intrapsychic life. Such an emphasis on the exogenous or social pressures as critical in young adulthood has led some writers (e.g., Adatto 1980) to recommend making technical adaptations in treatment to respond to these issues. Others (e.g., Brockman 1984) instead recommend focusing on the intrapsychic and for the therapist to follow the standard technique for adults.

In this chapter, I will take a different perspective, that development is a process rather than a succession of stages. My thesis is that, as clinicians, our strategies for learning and listening are inevitably tied to how we think of development and its relevance for treatment. Using the metaphor of a flowing river for developmental process, in the coursing of the waters during life experience, the terrain adjacent to the banks may influence the currents in the water by limiting or permitting access to the water. But this influence is like the precipitant of psychological problems, important but not as influential as rocks, branches, or sunken debris in the water itself. As precipitants, the contents of the surrounding terrain or social imperatives of young adulthood are important, but attending to them may not be helpful and can even be distracting for treatment.

The Eriksonian tradition is useful for marking young adulthood as a unique period regarding social contextual imperatives. However, being universal in the culture does not make them particular to the individual's psychological experience and functioning, which has to be the focus of treatment.

So what is a "developmental perspective" for a psychoanalytic psychotherapist or psychoanalyst who is working with the process of her own and her patients' unique emotional lives? Returning to the river metaphor, if you were to stand on the banks of the river as it meanders gently or churns with a spring thaw, you would see many movement patterns. Eddies and currents are apparently related to a branch, a rock, or perhaps something invisible below the surface; perhaps you would speculate that the bend twenty yards upstream or an old sunken rowboat on the riverbed caused the movement patterns. You would feel confidence in your explanations if you had studied movement patterns and currents in other rivers. On the basis of this past empirical observation, you could assume connections between the visible rock and a swirl of current just below it so that, when you see a rock in this particular river, you look with certainty for the swirl in the ambiguity of movement patterns nearby. This perspective is like the first observational posture that can be taken by a developmentalist therapist. He might expect, for instance, that manifest concerns about control and dominance will rest on underlying conflicts that universally relate to the anal period of development.

As another possibility, the developmentalist could look to the sky to see the movement patterns of clouds above, noticing perhaps how the lower layer moves rapidly in one direction while the clouds higher and deeper in the sky appear to stand still, unperturbed. Maybe the movement pattern in the heavens is a useful metaphor for the forces in the dark river that cannot be seen. If you can see and understand the evolution and fate of currents above, you may then know something important about the currents below in the water. A similarly organized psychoanalytic developmental view, for instance, would consider studying mother-child interaction when parents go out for a social evening leaving baby behind, as a method of learning about patients' experiences of vacation or other interruptions in the therapy.

Taking yet a third developmental posture, you might instead wade into the waters to feel what is there below the surface, to get a closer look, while taking care not to go too far, lose your footing, and be swept away. However, the mass of your body will create another series of currents so that, as you reach in to discover, you will influence and alter the forces you had intended to observe. Does this invalidate your observations? Maybe that does not pose a problem if you shift your study to the interaction between the currents and your body as you move through the water. Perhaps the understanding of this interaction leads to all that is important to know about currents.

Development from this view is the process of the interaction between you and the water. For the psychoanalytic therapist, development in this perspective is studied in situ during the process of the therapy itself, in a hermeneutic fashion where the exploration, construction, or discovery of here-and-now experience is the developmental process itself.

Emotional life is like this river, and knowing about another person's or one's own experience is like learning about the river's currents and movement patterns. Whether for knowing the river or for knowing emotional experiencing, a developmental perspective is essential because currents in each are in motion, an ongoing process in a field of multiple forces with a past, present, and future. The concept "development" often implies a connection between the flux and forces of the present and those of the past. The past is one more or less important source of influence on the currents. What happens in the river where we stand is affected by the events and obstacles around the bend upstream, beyond our immediate perception. Also important is the snowfall three months ago in the mountains a thousand miles away where the river originates. But, from our vantage point, how can this be known? How important is it anyway to what sense we make of the currents before our eyes?

As this applies to knowing and then therapizing another's life, another's emotional experience, there are different ways of observing and of making a developmental perspective useful. I will now describe a twenty-three-year-old patient and a session in her analysis, which is like the river we can see from our position on the banks. After introducing her to you, I will go on to a session fourteen months after treatment began, relating it as process. Following this, we will hear from three imaginary consultants about how each listens to this material, how they understand the currents and patterns in the session, and how each uses a developmental perspective.

Case Example

Lisa is beautiful and vivacious. She sat on my couch confidently as she flashed her sparkling and infectious smile. She had everything: looks, family wealth, friends, and opportunity. College had been one long party. Her complaints now were that she hated her job in her father's business and did not know what kind of career she wanted.

She was also having trouble with men because the ones who had a social background that matched hers were unexciting and all the others were so awed by her, knowing that they could not equal her, that they did not pursue her. I felt spellbound, as many others apparently have felt.

Her sessions were a torrent of affect and associations, rich but disorganized and even chaotic. It was very difficult for me to understand details. Although the words she was using made sense, I could not grasp a thread of meaningful continuity in her sentences, almost as if she were speaking a language I did not know well. It felt like looking at an impressionist painting from too close; I could see the dots of paint but not know what the picture was about.

Lisa is the oldest of three children raised in a reconstituted, nuclear family; neither sibling is doing well now. She is her mother's child from an earlier marriage, and she always felt "different," not quite belonging to the family. The separation and divorce took place when she was three or four. Nothing was ever spoken to her about these early years, and no photographs remained to document them. There were many secrets about this period, apparently because of her parents' anger and shame about their marital situation. When the divorce occurred, her mother abruptly moved with her out of her father's household into a new one with the man who became her stepfather. The story of these events was not narrated to her until she was in college, and many important details were not disclosed until her insistent questioning during treatment.

Over the first several sessions, I learned about her mother's emptiness and social ambition, about her father frequently disappointing her in their weekly visits during her childhood, and about her stepfather's power and business success. She admires him most of all and especially wants his understanding and approval. He was the one who encouraged her to excel in sports, which is important to both of them. She believes that she is like a son to him. As a child she longed for closeness, especially with mother, but rarely permitted herself to be held. She yelled a lot and caused trouble in the family. She felt no one paid attention to what she knew was going on and what she wanted for herself. Instead, she was given all the material goods and advantages that money could buy.

There were two particularly vivid stories about herself, told with intense feeling. One was about a book she made in kindergarten, which

she brought to show me. The title was "I Want to Be an Artist," and
it was an illustrated statement about what she liked about art. Tearfully, she spoke of her family's disapproval of artistic ambition because
it was not important enough work, and now she herself agrees. Desperately seeking a positive response, she is easily seduced and compliant
until she is overcome with rage that the others want her to be just like
them rather than authenically herself. The other vivid story was that
at age thirteen she was in an accident, narrowly escaping death and
injury, while the girl sitting next to her in the place she had been
assigned was killed. Although her well-being is often disregarded by
those responsible for her, through her own wit and energy she has
always been the survivor. She thought she felt a bit guilty about always
being the winner.

Psychoanalytic Session, Fourteen Months Later

Lisa is ten minutes late. Today she was more organized than usual
and engaged in dialogue about a dream:

> *Patient:* Lots has happened. Had lunch with Mom Friday, she
> said she'd keep paying for analysis even though Dad refuses; I
> mentioned she'd once again be keeping secrets, but didn't get into
> it more. She went on about stupid things she's doing like her club,
> and I felt unfulfilled. I had a dream Friday night, wrote it down.
> Today I went to the vocational counselor and felt so frustrated.
> And this morning I went running, but I'm so competitive I couldn't
> run with anyone. Anyway, I *like* to run alone, I give up when I'm
> not alone and then I go slow. I told the counselor I was frustrated,
> I was all over the place. I showed her what I have been doing,
> and she said it was obvious I was visual and into images and TV.
> *Everyone* gives me advice. But here's the dream:
>
> I was in flatlands with my family and friends. A plane dropped
> bombs, and everyone ran. I found a path to get away. I looked
> back and saw two little boys and ran back to get them; I hid with
> them and chose *not* to follow my family. We ran to a castle that
> swirled inside, the structure was swirling. I'd been there before.
> A woman who looked like you greeted me, I knew it was safe.
> She and I communicated in French. She smiled, I knew my French
> was not perfect but was OK to use with her. I was inside and safe

when I realized I had forgotten my passport. A guy told me not to worry, he was going to call people to tell them my situation. But I couldn't figure out how to pay for it. Then I saw a little boy, and we were looking at lots of red planes outside, threatening. I grabbed him and ran out, back to where we had been at first where there were enemies. My passport was there, but I couldn't get it. I got away, ran past a kitchen, and saw my friend Joan.

The patient went on to comment on her dream:

Patient: Once again I am lost, how am I going to survive as my family goes on. I save the two little boys.
Analyst: Boys?
P: A choice I made, to protect them or myself. Two eight- and ten-year-old boys I knew on vacation, they looked up to me, cute and innocent, full of life. I've had this dream before about bombing and red planes.
A: Dangerous.
P: Yes. That's how I'm feeling. I opened up to a man on a job interview; he responded, but we got off track onto *his* thing. There is not a job for me there.
A: You put a lot of energy into it, and nothing came of it.
P: Yes. A few names he gave me, but I'm feeling frustrated.
A: Maybe you're losing track of what direction you want?
P: Yes, I feel so disheartened, my video interest isn't realistic.
A: Red planes in the dream?
P: In the sky, visible and all over. And I run to the castle, it's safe with you. But I have to leave again. The planes came back again.
A: Safe for only a while.
P: Mom will pay for treatment for a few months or a little more.
A: Is *that* the danger, the red planes? You have to flee from the castle.
P: Yes, I feel I have to face the *world*—my anxiety, the dangers. Saturday night I felt betrayed by John; he was with another girl who he was set up with. I open myself up, and then the sword is thrown at me.
A: You leave the castle?
P: Yes, there is danger, and I can't retrieve my identity, which

is my purse with my passport. Then we open the door; it is red inside at the kitchen. Two men are peeking out, and I saw my friend Joan. I had opened the wrong door again, there was no way out, and I was trapped. The vocational counselor suggested I research schools for video and TV.

A: You're very frightened; maybe you feel beyond my help.

P: Money and power is a way of life, and the whole thing is *sick.*

Consultant 1

This consultant relies on his theory and experience with similar situations and other patients, posing a priori connections between the present and the past and between manifest and latent meanings. He is like the river watcher who stands objectively on the dry banks, sees a rock, and then expects a swirl of current a certain distance downstream (see Blos 1971, 1983; Blos 1991; Esman 1985; Kernberg 1991).

The consultant comments that it is very important to note from the history what has failed to be accomplished in earlier development since that failed area is likely to surface again under the strains of the young adult's developmental task to separate from family and to establish his or her own autonomous place in the world. Lisa is clearly struggling with finding her own identity, especially regarding her career, expressed as the lost passport in the dream. It is my experience that, if in early years, particularly during latency, the protective parental object relations are not given up and gradually replaced by growth-enhancing identifications, this becomes a significant problem in late adolescence and young adulthood when autonomous functioning is expected. Lisa was overindulged rather than encouraged to develop interests, talents, and skills. Her anger about the divorce was suffered rather than acknowledged. Her infantile relationship with her parents, with whom she was enraged and disappointed, was never replaced by a comfortable sense of herself as separate and enriched by their influences. Now, as a young adult, she remains angry, needy, and helpless with her parental objects. The deeply felt conflicts with them were denied, in spite of the angry acting out throughout her childhood. She could not manage the ambivalence toward them and form useful identifications.

Only through conflict and resolution can maturity occur. The painful depressive and angry affects were not tolerated in latency and early childhood. Therefore, she is unable to find positive identifications and to acquire the capacity to sustain painful affect in young adulthood when it is needed vis-à-vis the frustrations of encountering new responsibilities and expectations. Her treatment must allow her to reexperience these conflicts, to revisit them, and finally to resolve them, as she missed doing in her latency years. The dream of finding safety with you in the castle and then being driven out by the red bombers portrays a reexperiencing with you of the safety with mother that she expects will again be disrupted by anger (related to being unable to pay for treatment) before she could learn (identification) how to express something of herself, the French language, with fluency.

The consultant goes on to suggest the importance of a certain kind of listening, which he says is interactive and empathic, and describes how he believes he comes to these conclusions about the patient. His explanation actually tells us less about his interactions and empathy with the patient and more about his use of developmental theory for observation.

This kind of listening provides the therapist with information that is unintentionally conveyed by the patient and goes beyond what is literally communicated. The trained faculty of hearing what is communicated by the patient without his conscious awareness lifts the act of listening onto a special plane quite remote from the receptivity of a natural good listener. This kind of listening proceeds in a state of suspended judgment to which we refer as free-floating attention. Content and sequence of the patient's communications are constantly viewed against the backdrop of psychoanalytic theory. While listening, the clinician elaborates hypothetical formulations in his mind, letting the clinical evidence that follows render the verdict whether the tentative construct was accurate. The therapist should be pleased with whatever the verdict might be because it brings the truth closer within his reach. The therapist simultaneously listens to his own inner prompting, which never fails to be elicited by the help-seeking individual as a patient and as a person. This prompting receives its buoyancy from the therapist's personal associative sensitivities, thus evoking in him a state of empathy (Blos 1983).

Consultant 2

The second consultant, still standing on the dry banks of the river, is more willing to step into the currents of the patient's experiencing, however cautiously. When she is up to her knees, or even up to her waist, she believes that what they are enacting and observing is a metaphor for early childhood experience (eventually the patient agrees). Or is it the other way around, that the earlier experience is a metaphor for the present interaction (see Basch 1980; Giovacchini 1973; Kohut 1977; Novick 1983; Stern 1985)?

The consultant comments that the feeling of confusion with Lisa at the outset, in the diagnostic sessions, is an important indicator of her own inner confusion, particularly related to affects. This is in contrast to the session reported now, over a year into the treatment, where there is an orderly sense of working together to understand her dream. And, in the dream, Lisa portrays herself as finding refuge with the therapist and speaking a common language, where her imperfect French is acceptable and she is understood. Essential in treatment is the patient's and therapist's mutual creation of a common language, in Winnicott's sense a transitional space for the "as if" experience.

Lisa's difficulty initially to organize and communicate ideas and especially affect indicates the earlier developmental failure to make herself understood and to feel understood. Whether the patient is a child, where this common language is communication with play, or an adolescent, where often it is communication through mutual enactments, or an adult, where more often it is through verbal free association, only after the common language is established can other early developmental failures be recapitulated. It is likely that her confusion and affective disorganization and her inability verbally to describe her present-day experiences originated with her experience around age three of her parents' divorce, the abrupt relocation in a new household with a new father, and the subsequent lack of opportunities for her feelings about the disruption and loss to be recognized and verbally articulated.

What comes alive in treatment are the developmental failures of early childhood and the developmental lacunae that inevitably ensue in functions that build on that faulty foundation. The therapist's knowledge of child development is crucial in her listening to the patient, giving her the ability to recognize and formulate those developmental failures and then to respond in the needed way so that they can be corrected or filled in. The therapist looks at childhood developmental experiences and sequences in order to focus on patterns and currents in the present-day process of therapist-patient interaction. The therapist can then know how to become a new corrective object for the patient.

In Lisa's dream, her passport is her passage into the adult world and refers to her childhood inability to take an initiative that was officially recognized. The passport is lost when the safe conversation in a unique common language with the therapist is disrupted by the bombers or her uncontrolled affects. We can expect that, by the end of treatment, she will have completed many conversations with you and therefore can comfortably direct her steps out on her own into the world.

Consultant 3

This third consultant is like the river watcher who believes that the only way to observe is to get all the way into the water, feel the currents, and notice what the movement patterns are like in response to her presence. She believes that any theory about empirical a priori connections between past and present, or the softer connections suggested by metaphor, is simply a distraction from observations being directed by the subjective experience of the present here and now with this patient. For this consultant, the developmental perspective is that treatment is itself development, and the therapeutic action of treatment is the same as the fuel for all development, at any age. That fuel is the recognition through the discovery or through the construction of the patient's present unique experience within a process between therapist and patient (see Gill 1982; Sander 1983; Schafer 1983; Schwaber 1983; Stolorow 1992). The consultant and her like-minded colleagues identify themselves with the hermeneutic trends within psychoanalysis. Discovery or reconstruction of the patient's past is unimportant and perhaps not even possible. Memories are viewed not as repositories or structures from the past but as constructions or inventions in the present. The here and now of the interaction in treatment is focal.

The consultant emphasizes the importance of the therapist's efforts to elucidate with Lisa her experience in the transference that was a part of the evocation of the dream. The patient's recounting the dream and the subsequent gathering of her associations to its details are only the beginning. What could have happened in the immediately preceding sessions between therapist and patient that contributed to her experience that safety and communication in the castle with the therapist is disrupted? The therapist must go back to her notes and find some reason. Better yet, on the spot, she would engage the patient in this research by inquiring into her here-and-now experience of the disruption of safety with the therapist that is communicated through the dream.

Discussion

Going back to my process notes of this treatment, I find that, in the several preceding sessions, the patient has been telling me of her reluctance to see the vocational counselor, how she had canceled several appointments with her and had not looked up a newspaper article I had mentioned. The counselor had been my referral several months ago in response to her railings about having no ideas and no guidance about job-market possibilities. Directed then by my therapeutic intent to address the realities of her passage into young adulthood, I had chosen to respond to the manifest content rather than to inquire into her experience about asking me for this help. It begins to seem more probable that the dream is about her experience of anger at me for making suggestions to do things my way rather than continuing to listen to the language she chose to speak. Sympathetically, the consultant acknowledges how easily one can fall into listening to a patient's experience independently of one's own participation in it. The systematic search for one's own place in the context of another's psychic experience is a task most difficult to sustain (see Schwaber 1983). However, it must be accomplished, albeit falteringly, for the resumption of development in treatment to occur.

Conclusions

The first developmental perspective on young adulthood described here is that proposed originally by Erikson, specifying a developmental task of intimacy versus isolation, defined by social imperatives. Three other perspectives, more germane to the therapeutic process itself, have each been represented by imaginary consultants commenting on a case of a young adult.

Although, at points, each of these three perspectives may seem to blend with another, I have tried to illustrate how they each direct our listening and our technique quite differently and also how they conceive of therapeutic action differently. In our excursion into ways of listening to patients, we began with a metaphor of river watching, describing different investigational perspectives in terms of the position of the observer, the varying breadth of field for observation, and the focus or phenomena for observation.

Being a purist about any one perspective could lead to the condemnation of all the others as wrong. Does that mean that only one way is "right"? Certainly there are those who will always believe that. However, the richness of all these perspectives challenges us to accept the legitimacy of many voices, in the best spirit of postmodernism (Flax 1990): to acknowledge that we may never be authorities about our patients' experience and that a great deal can be learned from thinking about them from all these developmental perspectives.

REFERENCES

Adatto, C. P. 1980. Late adolescence to early adulthood: psychoanalytic contributions toward understanding personality development. In S. Greenspan and G. Pollack, eds. *The Course of Life,* vol. 2, *Latency, Adolescence, and Youth.* Washington, D.C.: National Institute of Mental Health.

Basch, M. 1980. *Doing Psychotherapy.* New York: Basic.

Blos, P. 1971. The generation gap: fact or fiction. *Adolescent Psychiatry* 1:5–13.

Blos, P. 1983. The contribution of psychoanalysis to the psychotherapy of adolescents. *Psychoanalytic Study of the Child* 38:577–600.

Blos, P., Jr. 1991. Sadomasochism and the defense against recall of painful affect. *Journal of the American Psychoanalytic Association* 39:417–430.

Brockman, D. 1984. *Late Adolescence: Psychoanalytic Studies.* New York: International Universities Press.

Erikson, E. 1950. *Childhood and Society.* New York: Norton.

Esman, A. 1985. A developmental approach to the psychotherapy of adolescents. *Adolescent Psychiatry* 12:119–133.

Flax, J. 1990. *Thinking Fragments: Psychoanalysis, Feminism and Post-Modernism in the Contemporary West.* Berkeley and Los Angeles: University of California Press.

Gill, M. 1982. *Analysis of Transference,* vol. 1, *Theory and Techniques. Psychological Issues* Monograph no. 59. New York: International Universities Press.

Giovacchini, P. 1973. Character development and the adolescent process. *Adolescent Psychiatry* 2:402–414.

Havighurst, R. 1952. *Developmental Tasks and Education*. New York: McKay.

Kernberg, O. 1991. Sadomasochism, sexual excitement and perversion. *Journal of the American Psychoanalytic Association* 39:333–362.

Kohut, H. 1977. *The Restoration of the Self*. New York: International Universities Press.

Novick, K. K. 1983. Modes of communication in the analysis of a latency girl. *Psychoanalytic Study of the Child* 38:481–500.

Sander, L. 1983. Polarity, paradox and the organizing process in development. In J. D. Call, E. Galenson, and R. Tyson, eds. *Frontiers of Infant Psychiatry*. New York: Basic.

Schafer, R. 1983. *The Analytic Attitude*. New York: Basic.

Schwaber, E. 1983. A particular perspective on analytic listening. *Psychoanalytic Study of the Child* 38:519–546.

Stern, D. 1985. *The Interpersonal World of the Infant*. New York: Basic.

Stolorow, R. 1992. *Contexts of Being*. Hillsdale, N.J.: Analytic.

PART IV

PSYCHOPATHOLOGY IN ADOLESCENT EMOTIONAL DISORDERS

EDITORS' INTRODUCTION

This part concentrates on the nature and presentation of psychopathology in difficult-to-treat children and adolescents. The selection of topics focusing on severe pathology provides a review of current research findings in diagnostic issues, assessment, and treatment.

Derek Miller views adolescent suicide from a biopsychosocial perspective. He writes that adolescence is a period during which self-destructive behavior is likely to occur since it is at the service of developing a sense of autonomy. In order for the process to succeed, mastery of helplessness, grandiosity, and body sense is obligatory. With a dysfunctional family to contend with, however, the alienation cannot be adequately resolved, and the young person is rendered vulnerable to unstable affective storms. Miller describes the etiology of suicidal behavior, the environmental response to suicide attempts, types of suicidal behavior (intentional, marginally intentional, and accidental), and the evaluation of suicidal potential in clinical practice. Further discussion of social determinants considers biological and psychological factors. Miller outlines a series of diagnostic clues to determine suicidal ideation: the revelation on inquiry of suicidal ambivalence; the revelation of a history of previous treatment for suicidal intentions; the presence of unresolved problems with separation and bereavement; and evidence of sending a message via friends and relatives. An outline of treatment clarifies the approach to suicidal disorder.

Robert M. Gluckman discusses physiological, physical, and psychological stress in adolescents. He postulates that, during this period of development, young people are subjected to as much distress during health as illness. Major psychobiological tasks must be completed during the adolescent phase of life. These include puberty, a major reorganization of the self, a second separation-individuation, and a whole reworking of identity formation. Gluckman discusses the effects of these stressors, which may create turmoil and psychological malfunctioning, and provides a number of case examples to illustrate the efforts to master, by means of somatic symptoms, the state of psychobiological maturation.

Approaching the demography of severe adolescent psychopathology, Adrian D. Copeland studies symptom clusters of childhood maladjustment. He found a predictive criterion in the data that did not predict specific diagnoses but revealed sensitive indicators that a close association between certain specific clusters of childhood behavior and psychopathology.

Linda Greenberg and Aaron H. Esman explore the role of interdisciplinary consultation in dealing with acute adolescent psychopathology. They catalog the countertransference responses of the hospital staff and present psychoanalytic understanding of the adolescents' transference behavior. A discussion by Hervé Benhamou confirms the value of transference analysis.

Robert M. Galatzer-Levy explicates the role of narcissistic rage in adolescent violence, using the approach of self psychology. He explains that self psychology is helpful in explaining adolescent violence, particularly meaningless violence, and adolescent violence is best understood as an attempt to restore cohesive and vital self-experience.

19   ADOLESCENT SUICIDE: ETIOLOGY AND TREATMENT

DEREK MILLER

The biopsychosocial etiology of suicidal behavior means that, in a diagnostic assessment, multiple determinants need to be understood before adequate therapy can be undertaken. Certain psychiatric disorders (depression, schizophrenia, bipolar disorders, and panic disorders) are linked to a high frequency of attempted suicide. The same is true for behavioral syndromes such as drug and alcohol abuse. Adolescence, however, is a period during which self-destructive behaviors are likely to occur; from 1970 to 1980, reported juvenile suicide rates rose 66 percent with 6,000 adolescent suicides a year (Pardes 1985).

An understanding of adolescent development clarifies the reason for this vulnerability. The psychological responses to the physiological changes of puberty are not the same as the psychosocial processes of adolescence that depend on puberty to have validity (Miller 1978b). Without puberty, adolescence is hollow. Pubertal change, however, does not necessarily imply that the child can achieve psychological adolescence.

Adolescence manifests itself as a biopsychosocial process necessary to develop a sense of autonomy, a sense of a separate and independent self. The psychosocial reactions to puberty involve a struggle to deal with a number of psychological issues. In particular, these include the mastery of a biologically induced sense of helplessness, along with a profound split-off sense of one's own omnipotence and a preoccupation with the bodily self. During puberty, thinking, which may have begun to be more formal (Piaget and Inhelder 1969), may regress to less sophisticated cognitive modes: the capacity for empathy may be impaired, the ability to experience ambivalence may be temporarily lost, and the sense of the future and the past can be highly attenuated.

In twentieth-century Western society, a sense of self, one's status as a person, no longer depends on the individual occupying the same role as the parents. Furthermore, a masculine sense of self-worth depends on being loved and valued as much by the mother as by the father, and a female sense of self-value as a person requires paternal as well as maternal love. It is not then surprising that suicidal adolescents are commonly alienated from their families in early childhood by parental attitudes—which may be quite subtle—of resentment, hostility, and rejection (Sabbath 1969). Statistically, young suicides show more frequent parental abuse and rejection than a control group (Shafii, Corrigan, Whittinghill, and Derrick 1985).

Further, recent changes in society make adolescence, the end of preadulthood, as a significant developmental period almost impossibly complex. Especially in the United States, there has been a massive disintegration of the nuclear and extended family. Parenting divorce is almost as common as marital divorce, which, in any case, almost invariably puts an end to shared parenting. There is often little reality against which to resolve oedipal conflicts; boys often have no stable male identification figure, and girls do not experience being loved by males for themselves, not for their sexuality. There has been a breakdown of the extended family, and consistent social ties have disintegrated owing to vertical and horizontal social mobility. The easy availability of regressive drugs of abuse and alcohol has made it difficult for many young people to become meaningfully emotionally involved with others. The attenuation of attachment, especially in the nuclear family, produces a particular vulnerability in young people to processes of splitting in the individual's representation of the self at times of stress. When, in adolescence, vulnerable young people are frustrated, they may consciously or unconsciously recall images of parental figures who were rejecting, controlling, or demanding. They may then attempt to avoid psychic pain by reckless behavior with automobiles, alcohol, or drugs, with violence directed toward others, or with suicidal behavior. The failure to learn to tolerate frustration is thus etiologically significant in the treatment of destructive behaviors.

Adolescence has been divided into three separate, if overlapping, stages (Miller 1974). Early adolescence, lasting approximately three years, which encompasses puberty, is associated with a high degree of internal turbulence. Middle adolescence, a stage of identity consolidation lasting two to three years, is the period in which conformity to adult norms appears (Offer 1973). Late adolescence, which exists only in those who are engaged in further training, is a period of coping, a period in which a new sense of self is tested, experimented with, and enlarged.

Except for those young people who avoid significant drug and alcohol abuse, who have an intact family, who have significant extrafamilial relationships that are valued, and who have a broad educational experience that includes cognitive, creative, and imaginative stimulation, adolescence in these terms may now hardly exist. Many young people have difficulty in developing an autonomous sense of self. Instead, they become in a psychological sense other-directed adults who, when isolated, may experience a paralyzing sense of aloneness (Hendin 1991). Such young people may then experience "a state of vacant cold isolation accompanied by varying degrees of terror" (Maltsberger and Biue 1989). A feeling of self-worth comes to depend almost entirely on the approval of others (Reisman 1954). Unless tension is constantly reduced, often by peer group involvement or a sense of concordance with an amorphous "they," autonomy is hardly present, and escape from an intolerable affective state becomes vital. The experience of rage, hopelessness, emptiness, and despair may be drowned by alcohol and drugs, masturbatory behavior, which may superficially involve others, and self-destructive suicidal activity.

The Etiology of Suicidal Behavior

The large number of young people who depend for a sense of worth on being valued by others are particularly vulnerable to psychological stress. Their internal world often appears devoid of conscious fantasy, and they depend for psychological stimulation on external forces, often music and drugs of abuse. When individuals are vulnerable to stress in a society that implicitly (and sometimes explicitly) devalues living, suicide becomes a common technique of attempted conflict resolution. Suicide in the United States is now the second most common cause of death in the eighteen- to twenty-four-year-old age group and the third most common cause of death in the fifteen- to-nineteen-year-old age group, greater than leukemia and appendicitis (Weissman 1974), but ranking behind homicide and accidental death (Hendin 1985). In the ten- to fourteen-year-old age group, suicide causes as many deaths as appendicitis and diabetes. Many adolescent suicides are thought wrongly by authorities to be accidental deaths, and reliable statistics are thus unavailable (Petzel and Cline 1978). This is because young people generally do not leave a farewell note. In addition, the problem, like many adolescent difficulties, tends to be either overexaggerated or denied by the culture. It is probable that there are five times as many suicides as are actually reported and ten times as many attempted suicides as there are completed acts. However, the incidence of suicide varies from country to country. This variation is not necessarily related to religion; Roman Catholic Austria has almost the highest suicide rate in Europe, Roman Catholic Ireland the lowest.

The recognition of the implication of suicidal behavior by any one individual requires an accurate concept of the meaning of death. However, suicidal behavior is possible even though the individual may have no awareness of this. The sense that "life is impossible without change" (Hendin 1991), the experience of desperation and intolerable anxiety in those who are already depressed (Fawcett, Shelfner, Fogg, Clark, Young, Hedeker, and Gibbens 1990), can lead to suicidal behavior. The concept of irrevocable loss depends partly on whether a significant loss of loved figures has been experienced as well as on the type of thinking of which a youngster is capable. The fantasy of reunion with lost figures (Zilborg 1938) is more likely in adolescents whose time sense is, in any case, not yet fully developed. Furthermore, the developmental omnipotence of adolescents is more likely to overcome the dread of death, and the adolescent fantasy of immortality and grandiosity makes young people particularly vulnerable to an act that in its symbiotic fusion with a powerful lost object has similar implications (Pollock 1975). Thus, suicidal behavior is possible without an understanding of the finality of death.

The blurring and attenuation of the adolescent developmental period mean that many adolescents inappropriately maintain an early adolescent attitude through chronological early adulthood, a profound conviction about the ease of the act and the probability of survival. These individuals may then play Russian roulette with their own sense of omnipotence and hopelessness by repeated attempts (Peterson, Awad, and Kendler 1973). They seek a superman type of mastery to deal with their own helplessness.

Since the span of today's adolescence has become elongated, chronological young adults may be as much prisoners of the present as would be expected from an early adolescent in a more traditional developmental mode. The sense of omnipotence in the young is further reinforced as significant bodily aging does not occur in adolescence. There is often very little real awareness on the part of the individual of physical fragility, an issue that is also relevant in homicidal behavior and drug abuse.

The perpetuation of a sense of omnipotence and a failure to develop a capacity for ambivalence, both of which are still present in many chronologically late adolescents, may mean that individuals who ought to be able to mourn an irrevocable loss are not able to do so. The concept of death is then further denied.

Omnipotence, as helplessness, has nowadays many social reinforcements. Most urban adolescents are no longer tested against natural forces. Contact sports, which enhance an awareness of physical vulnerability, are the preserve of the few. Finally, a false sense of personal power is given to adolescents who are allowed to drive automobiles when many have not yet developed a final sense of their own body image and still have poor reality testing about their own relative impotence.

The decline in the quality and availability of developmentally significant relationships for children and adolescents helps the understanding of the increasing emotional disturbance among young people and the general increase in self-destructive behavior; it does not explain why some attempt suicide and others do not. There are a number of clinically assessable factors that help the understanding of this.

Biological etiology is of obvious, if not necessarily specific, significance in self-destructive behavior. It has been divided most usefully (Siever and Davis 1991). Cognitive/perceptual organization is of significance in the schizophrenic syndromes and is related to disorganization and psychotic-like symptoms, thought disorder, and social isolation. Individuals suffering from these types of disorders show eye movement dysfunction and high levels of homovanillic acid, which is an index of dopamine metabolism (Siever, Coccaro, Zewishlany, and Silverman 1987).

Impulsivity and violent behavior, which may have a direct relation to suicidal activity, are associated psychologically with externalization and dissociation. Biologically, they occur with a diminution of seroti-

365

negic functions and reduced concentrations of 5 hydroxyendole acetic acid, a serotonin metabolite. These have been reported in patients who have attempted suicide (Brown, Ebert, Boyer, Jameson, Klein, Bunney, and Goodwin 1982). Affective lability with marked affective shifts, which is commonly present in suicidal adolescents, may be related to an excessive cholinergic response and hyperresponsiveness of the noradrenergic system. On the other hand, hyporesponsive catecholamine function is associated with classic affective disorders.

Finally, in the anxiety disorders, states of anxiety-inhibition are clearly related to biological factors, and these may be etiologically significant in suicidal behavior.

Depressed adolescents with a specific type of nonverbal learning disability (Rourke, Young, and Leaners 1989) that modifies an individual's ability to develop effective adaptation to his or her physical limitations have a syndrome that is related to a high risk of suicide (Bigler 1989). These children show psychomotor clumsiness, problems in tactile sensitivity, and visual/spatial organizational deficits. They are unable to reflect on the nature of their problems (anosognosia), and they have marked difficulty in appreciating the implications of both subtle and obvious nonverbal communications. They are thus ostracized by their peers.

There may be an increase in the incidence of depression among young people (Klerman 1986). Biologically based mood disorders are certainly diagnosed with increasing frequency and should always be considered. One variable, significantly associated with suicide, is the diagnosis of unipolar depression in a patient with a family history of a bipolar disorder (Goldstein and Black 1991). However, the failure to provide adequate psychosocial nurture in infancy, childhood, and adolescence leads to an increase in deprivation depression (Miller 1986), which apparently produces exactly the same intrapsychic pain as may be produced by neuroendocrine disorder, although the variation in affect is different in the latter.

The Prediction of Suicidal Behavior

The prediction of suicidal behavior depends primarily on clinical assessment. The change in the mourning rituals of society makes it harder for adolescents to deal with the deaths of those who are loved, but there is some question as to whether this has statistical validity

(Barraclough 1987). However, the recent death of a loved person is significant in those who make suicidal attempts.

When a loved individual dies, adolescents may deny the significance of the death and feel that the person they have lost is still alive inside themselves. It is as though they keep internal ghosts. These ghosts may be made into a type of transitional object (Winnicott 1953). A loved internal figure is talked to as in the past a child might have talked with a teddy bear. When life becomes difficult, the concept is to join these internal images of the loved one. So inquiries should be made about recent loss, and young people should be asked whether they think of dead friends, parents, siblings, and grandparents, along with the frequency of this occurrence. A particular problem of sibling death is that the preoccupation of parents with a dying child and then with their own mourning means that they are likely to withdraw emotional investment in their living children. The dead child is looked on as a wonderful person, and survivors, particularly of the same sex, often feel that the only way to be loved is to die.

Of particular significance is whether the adolescent, when under stress, thinks of the dead loved one. When adolescents deal with loss by internalizing this image, this can also create realistic emotional deprivation. Involvement with an intrapsychic ghost can lead to emotional withdrawal from real people; the adolescent becomes more isolated, deprived, and empty. The experience of stress is then even more likely to create a wish to join the lost one, particularly as the feelings about such an individual are inevitably mixed. The rage felt at abandonment makes self-destructive behavior in the survivors more likely.

There are a number of affective and cognitive ethical factors that make young people vulnerable to suicidal behavior and assist in diagnosis. A crucial attitude that has implications for the length of treatment is that the adolescent thinks that an individual is entitled to do whatever one wishes with one's own life. This can easily slip into an attitude of "retaliatory abandonment" (Hendin 1963). It also allows young people to maintain the illusion that they have complete control over their own destiny, particularly in those who suffer from a recurrent depression associated with mood disorder. Vulnerability to suicide is then intense as the individual has no built-in protection.

Suicide is not uncommonly a vengeful act directed toward parents. Such adolescents are filled with hatred for their parents and are well aware that they will, by a suicidal act, project onto their parents the same feelings of helplessness, guilt, abandonment, and despair that they themselves experience. This type of suicidal behavior is not uncommon in those who have been psychologically as well as physically abused.

Suicidal adolescents often have an astonishing amount of intolerance directed toward the self. Such individuals have an image of perfection that they are unable to attain, a failure based on their perception that they could never attain the level of achievement they perceive in idealized others, especially parents. Their ego ideal cannot be lived with; this is an attitude common in the subtle self-destructive behavior of patients with eating disorders. Suicide in these adolescents is often associated with the idea that they are too worthless to stay alive. It is clinically important to inquire about the dreams of such adolescents in that irrevocable destruction is a common implicit theme in their content. Of equal importance is the implicit familial permission to behave in a suicidal way. Suicide is disproportionately frequent among the first- or second-degree relatives of suicidal adolescents (Schaffer, Garland, Gould, Fischer, and Traunta 1988).

The issue of intolerable guilt is related to the failure to develop a sense of trust, and, if the capacity to be ambivalent cannot be developed, without constant external support adolescents are likely to remain dependent on an archaic superego. Thus, they constantly need to seek freedom from external sources for the ensuing guilt (Fenichel, 1945; Freud 1917; Menninger 1931). If mother is either loved or hated, inevitable before ambivalence becomes possible, one solution to unbearable hatred is to fuse with the attacking object (Zilborg 1936). As suicide is also one defense against unresolved oedipal conflicts (Glover 1955), vulnerability is further increased. Finally, adolescents with no sure sense of themselves are extraordinarily vulnerable to separation (Miller, Visotsky, and Carlton 1992), and suicide is a significant defense against this.

The Environmental Response to Suicide Attempts

If an adolescent conmmits suicide, the response aroused in parents and all those who have been involved with the youngster is generally that of anxiety and guilt. If the suicide is not successful, the environmental response may be similar to that often seen in the relatives and professionals involved with a dying patient; an initial experience of anxiety and guilt is often followed by denial, rage, depression, and fear before there is an ultimate acceptance of the situation. Parental denial and rage may be inevitable, and, if they are not assisted with these psychological responses, such parents may find themselves the unwitting agents of a successful future attempt by their child. For example, it is not unusual for an adolescent to attempt suicide more than once, using medication that is repetitiously left in a medicine cabinet or a carelessly left automobile allowing suffocation by exhaust fumes. Often, when adolescents in treatment begin to say, in a premature fashion, that they are now recovered, these parental responses make it likely that they will be tempted to believe their youngster and collude in the premature termination of necessary treatment. Society is also collusive with this because the financially induced excessively short stay in the hospital implies that immediate symptomatic relief has solved the problem of suicidal intent.

Types of Suicidal Behavior

Suicidal behavior can be classified in a variety of ways. However, apart from its possible consequences, the severity of problem behavior in adolescents is not necessarily indicative of its etiology or the prognosis of the underlying psychiatric illness. All problem behavior fulfills an economic function in the psyche. A suicidal crisis (Klerman 1987) can be an attempt to relieve the intrapsychic tension often associated with the dramatic prominence of the patients' unique psychodynamic constellation of affect, cognition, and internal conflict with all its meanings (Grey 1972; Zilborg 1937). The crisis behavior can also be a stimulant for a further crisis. However, the thought of suicide may protect an individual from its actual performance.

For example, a sixteen-year-old girl had a two-year history of uncontrollable intrusive thoughts. These were either sexual or self-destructive and included visual hallucinations of throwing herself out the window. Throughout this two-year history, she felt that she would not actually kill herself. Outpatient psychotherapy having failed, she was referred to an adolescent treatment center. She was placed in their special care unit and diagnosed as suffering from a schizophrenic reaction. She was given haldoperidol (two milligrams) twice daily. The intrusive thoughts disappeared, but for the following weeks she was acutely suicidal.

On the other hand, the thought may be the precursor of the act. A sixteen-year-old boy was admitted to an adolescent treatment center with a history of repeated self-mutilation in which he had attempted to knife himself. Under stress, he became acutely delusional and heard a voice telling him to kill himself. This was a precursor of the suicidal behavior. He also used threats of killing himself as a way in which he could get his parents to grant his quite unreasonable wishes (e.g., a desire to be married). Adequate medication with phenothiazines ended the hallucinatory episodes. The resolution of the characterological problem in which he was threatening suicide, so as not to be suicidal, was more difficult.

If hallucinatory or delusional invitations to attempt suicide are removed psychopharmacologically with no effort made to resolve the conflict around the suicidal wishes, an attempt is more likely.

Intentional Suicidal Behavior

A common pervasive feeling prior to suicide is that of extreme helplessness and a frantic need to act. It appears to the patient that the only effective way of changing the situation is self-destruction. Sometimes the helplessness is related to an overpowering feeling of rage. Intentional suicidal behavior is associated with efforts at self-destruction that appear deliberate to others, although that may not be the adolescent's intent. Often, the behavior is preceded by more or less subtle warnings that may not be conscious. If they are ignored, such efforts at communication may well reinforce the likelihood of the act occurring. Thus, all suicidal threats should be taken seriously, and skilled intervention should be sought. In this respect, the transient expression of the feeling "I wish I were dead" is not the same as "I am going to kill myself."

The warning of intent is sometimes done by subtle throw-away lines. One reaction to such a death in the involved survivors, particularly those in helping professions, is to wonder whether the situation could have been averted. Nowhere is this more evident than in a hospital when a patient commits suicide, although suicidal threats are often implicitly not taken with sufficient seriousness by hospital staff, particularly if they are repeated. For example, a seventeen-year-old boy attempted suicide in a hospital by throwing himself out of a fourth-floor window. He was a patient on an adolescent ward and made repeated suicidal threats and gestures. Whenever he stopped these, there was a tendency on the part of the staff to assume that they were "only" attention-getting remarks. During a period in which he denied his suicidal risk, some three to four hours after he had threatened to kill himself, he was taken to a less secure area of the hospital for a therapeutic group. It is hypothesized that the staff did not want to face the fluctuation of affect that is present in some suicidal adolescents, and their denial was not dissimilar to that seen in staff who care for seriously ill and severely psychologically disturbed patients.

One type of intentional suicide is associated with a cognitive, conscious decision to kill the self. This is a type of predatory violence (Grey 1972) directed against the self. There may be no evidence that such violence is necessarily directed against a bad introject (Zilborg 1937). The suicidal decision may be secret in an individual who has shown no previous evidence of the intent.

A similar story, when there is no evidence of previous intent, occurs when an apparently well-adjusted adolescent who never gives trouble to anyone inexplicably commits suicide. Such young people often do not have an overt history of psychiatric illness. Two types of individuals are involved. Some, retrospectively, have been withdrawn, isolated people who have not made a significant emotional investment outside themselves; they are individuals with acquaintances but not true friends. Since conformity is often highly valued in the educational system and nuclear family, particularly in some parts of Europe and in the United States, these youngsters are not perceived as having problems. Diagnostically, when seen after a failed attempt, these may be highly schizoid individuals whose suicidal attempt is a despairing rejection of their profound feelings of emptiness, or, alternatively, they may be overtly schizophrenic. Some have suffered from depression for years, on the basis of either emotional deprivation or neuroendocrine vulnerability or both. Often, the act is preceded by the additional presence of acute anxiety or guilt about previous behavior.

Others have not been withdrawn and seem to have been healthy offspring of healthy families. The explanation for their death seems to be as follows. Some individuals under stress are genetically vulnerable to depression (Miller 1978a). They avoid psychic pain by seeking and conforming to consistent environmental expectations. If the nuclear family has been consistent in its explicit and implicit messages, such young people may appear quite healthy. The unavoidable stress is the ultimate psychosocial demand for autonomy and separation that appears toward the end of high school. At this point, acute depression occurs, and suicide may supervene.

Apart from psychological immaturity, some young people who abuse drugs and alcohol have potential genetic neuroendocrine vulnerability. Impulsive suicide may occur when they are intoxicated. The stress that leads to such suicides may be psychological, biological, or both. These young people are ill prepared to meet the normative persecutory experience that is a concomitant of helplessness or the recognition that one cannot be loved as one would wish (Masterson 1970). The intoxicated suicidal adolescent may, from a dynamic viewpoint, be destroying a bad introject as alcohol or drugs may weaken superego controls. On the other hand, alcohol or drugs may significantly affect brain biochemistry in a genetically vulnerable individual.

The development of the sense of self requires the capacity to introject and then incorporate the perceived image of emotionally significant individuals and the interaction between them (Miller 1974). The development of a bad introject is often associated with the physical and sexual abuse of the child or adolescent or an early exposure to violence (Hendin and Hass 1991). To deal with these stresses, children and adolescents identify with such behavior either overtly or covertly (Miller and Looney 1976). Such young people may become intentionally suicidal, homicidal, or both. When homicidal, such adolescents may project the bad internalized object onto others; when suicidal, although they make such a projection, they internalize the bad object. In its destruction, they destroy themselves.

Intentional suicide also takes place in association with acute emotional deprivation, the experience of loss or separation, which is felt as abandonment. The depriving figures are then felt as deserving of punishment, and this may be associated with the wish to kill oneself to gain revenge on others, usually parents. Self-destruction is the ultimate punishment inflicted on others. However, when some adolescents kill themselves in a narcissistic rage, the issue of revenge is irrelevant; at an emotional level, others do not exist. The rage is often associated with the acute feeling that one cannot receive that to which one is entitled.

A type of intentional adolescent suicide is associated with public self-immolation. Altruism and self-sacrifice are common in adolescents. These may represent an ascetic psychological defense against

372

infantile greed and dependence. Vulnerable to social contagion, some young people may destroy themselves under chronic or acute group pressure. Chronic contagious group pressure for self-destruction is transmitted by the media. Reports of monks burning themselves to death in Saigon produced imitators in Prague and thence imitations in the West. The suicide is designed to save the world or to convey to the world an awareness of its deficiencies.

Some adolescents who have no real sense of an autonomous self gain other-directed support by joining cults. If, under acute stress, a charismatic leader convinces a group that self-destruction is better than being destroyed from outside, group suicide or homicide becomes the preferred solution. This type of suicide has a long and revered history, particularly among minority groups who are or see themselves as being persecuted: for example, the Israelites of Masada, the Jews of York in the thirteenth century, and the followers of the Reverend Jones in Guyana. In the latter case, the group's perception of the hostility was seen by the outside world as unjustified; this could not be said of the first two episodes.

The etiology of mass suicide is not dissimilar to that of the mass homicide that may occur in atrocities (Gault 1971): (1) the enemy is everywhere; (2) the responsibility for the act is shared; (3) the pressure to act out self-destructively is expected, and this pressure is reinforced by a charismatic leader who shares the conflicts of the group; (4) the leader reinforces in the group the concept that life is irrelevant; dehumanization of the self is easily reinforced as the group feels dehumanized by others. The etiology of intentional suicidal behavior thus includes neuroendocrine vulnerability, schizophrenia, and unipolar and bipolar illness; serious character disturbance, especially in those who suffer from borderline syndrome or from pathological primary narcissism. The suicidal act requires an identification with a societal attitude that devalues the significance of human life. This may exist along with an altruistic or revenge leitmotif, often existing in parallel with each other.

Marginally Intentional Suicide

This is usually chronic and is typically seen in those individuals who severely neglect the self, those suffering from anorexia nervosa, or those who are accident prone. Adolescents who are repeatedly involved in car accidents, motorcyclists who do not use protective clothing, driving when intoxicated on alcohol, marijuana, or other drugs are all examples of marginally intentional suicidal behavior. This type of activity, which is especially related to the regressive reinforcement of omnipotence, requires societal collusion. Drug and alcohol abusers are particularly vulnerable to marginally intentional suicidal behavior. This group includes the middle-class youth who drives when intoxicated and the ghetto youngster, normally street wise, who exposes himself on the turf of hostile gangs. The chronic heroin abuser, who knows that the cut of the drug varies yet continues to use it, is also marginally suicidal.

On clinical examination, these individuals are omnipotent and narcissistic, but they often consciously suffer from a pervasive sense of low self-esteem (Boyer and Giovacchini 1967). Sometimes these individuals make suicidal attempts with the concept that they will be found and saved. A lethal dose of sedatives is taken just before parents are due to return home; sometimes telephone help services are used. Adolescents may refuse to give their names or location, threaten self-destruction, and wait to see whether they are rejected by the telephone being put down.

Accidental Suicide

Some schizophrenic adolescents have no conscious intention to commit suicide but do so because of a wish to reconciliate or fuse with another part of the self. This has been seen in twin studies (Maenchen 1968) of schizophrenic adolescents who perceive themselves as having living introjects. Such deaths can also be a symbolic self-castration with a desire to engage in a fantasied (Resnik 1972) experience. For example, adolescents who tie themselves up in order to masturbate may accidentally hang themselves.

Accidental suicide may occur in those social systems that reinforce adolescents in self-destructive behavior. For example, bodily mutilation in psychiatric hospitals is almost always an institutional symptom. Self-mutilation is often highly eroticized and aims to reduce intrapsychic tension. It is also apparently designed to project helplessness and rage into the environment and at the same time have the environment return negative attention. Typical behavior includes the making of suicidal threats; cutting wrists, arms, abdomen, or thighs; or putting hands through glass. Although this behavior is rarely suicidal, it may lead to accidental suicide. In vulnerable individuals, who gain environmental permission for this type of symptomatic behavior, intentional suicide may follow. In a statistically significant way, suicidal gestures may be followed by suicide (Patel 1974).

Not all accidents are suicidal. They may be related to the inability of some young adolescents, especially males, to be aware of their own physical limitations. Many brought up in cities, adequately protected by their parents, have little or no actual awareness of their own physical limitations. Accidental deaths due to poor judgment occur in adolescents who are skating, swimming, or sailing. Such young people are like small boys climbing inappropriately large trees. On the other hand, when mountain climbers are killed when they climb alone, these are marginal suicides, not accidental deaths. The abuse of toxic drugs, particularly LSD and hallucinogens, often produces an acting out of an omnipotent wish. The relation between dreams that one can fly from high buildings and infantile fantasies is clear. Omnipotence is reinforced by regressive drug abuse. Under the influence of hallucinogens, omnipotent fantasies may become acted-out delusions.

The Evaluation of Suicidal Potential in Clinical Practice

The initial interview with adolescents helps indicate the likelihood of self-destructive behavior. Even if the adolescent has made a positively felt relationship with an interviewer, ideas of suicide are unlikely to be volunteered unless the youngster is acutely distressed. Even then, the subject may appear only if the inquiry is made about thoughts or previous attempts at killing oneself. If the question is not asked, the information is rarely volunteered. In evaluating the likelihood of suicide, a careful study of the potential social, biological, and psychological determinants of such behavior is necessary. In initial interviews, treatability is assessed primarily on the issues of the adolescent's ability to make a relationship with a therapist such that problem behavior can be contained.

With behavior that is dangerous to the self or others, there is no room for symptomatic maneuverability. The behavior must be stopped. At issue is whether the adolescent is able to commit himself or herself to the therapist or others such that efforts at self-hurt will not be made without giving the therapist a chance to intervene. A therapist or staff member in a hospital cannot function with the persistent anxiety that a boy or girl in treatment is likely to attempt suicide. If such an assurance cannot be obtained, inpatient treatment is certainly indicated, although this may be necessary anyway for other reasons. Adolescents are almost always honest about suicidal intent. If they are unable to agree not to kill themselves without first contacting the therapist and offering a chance for appropriate intervention, they will make this clear. Those who make suicidal attempts and immediately thereafter deny a suicidal wish may be experiencing a relief of acute stress; they may also be consciously dishonest.

Social Determinants of Suicidal Behavior

Young people who are vulnerable to suicide often have a long history of social and psychological problems that may include antisocial behavior. Drug abuse, including drug dealing, is common. A history of a failure to make satisfactory interpersonal relationships along with a description of a pervasive experience of a feeling of emptiness and boredom may be obtained. These experiences are often associated with the presence of major mood disorders. The youngster may come from a subgroup of society in which life is especially devalued. Particularly vulnerable are minority groups; victims of society's prejudices unconsciously identify with society's social and verbal devaluation. Many incorporate into their self-belief the notion that they are in some way inferior.

A history of parental suicide makes the adolescent particularly vulnerable (Maxmen and Tucker 1973). The explicit and implicit message of this act is that such behavior is acceptable. Mourning in children and adolescents for lost parents is almost always incomplete, and this is especially true when a parent has committed suicide. The child who loses a parent of the same sex may have to attempt to replace that parent with the one who survives. After parental suicide, if the remaining parent remarries (another loss), the child may then become a greater suicidal risk as a living individual has made what may be felt as a final abandonment. Apart from suicide, other types of parental hostility are common in the etiology of adolescent suicide. Parents may be significantly overly involved with their youngster, and they may be highly intrusive. They may depersonalize their child by being overpermissive or overrestrictive. Prior to an attempt, a history of significantly perceived parental rejection is not unusual.

Biological Factors

Unipolar and bipolar illnesses and schizophrenia are still commonly misdiagnosed in children and adolescents because of their atypical presentation (Miller 1986). Either passive compliance or focal anger directed toward objects or individuals who come to represent an externalization of the image of an unloving parent is commonly found. Depression should be suspected when a behavior disorder is initially monosymptomatic and occurs at apparently inexplicable intervals, if there is a history of mental illness in the family, if there is an eating or sleeping disorder, and if the world is felt as particularly persecutory early in the day. Pregnancy, menstruation, and physical illness are all of some significance in the etiology of suicidal behavior. Adolescents who suffer from epilepsy, particularly with a temporal lobe focus, may be particularly vulnerable.

Psychological Factors

Patients who are serious suicide risks generally have a plan. There is no evidence that direct questioning about this puts it into operation. It is important to check whether patients have the means to kill themselves. If they are known to have the means and the means are not withdrawn, this puts the therapist in a position of colluding with the intent, a common situation for the family.

The personality organization of adolescents who attempt suicide is crucial in understanding the meaning of the act. The latter may be related to the need to be free of unbearable guilt. It may be a homicidal act directed against the self. The suicidal act may represent both a rebirth and a fusion with an ambivalently felt internal representation of a dead loved one or a living parent whose hated infantile image is introjected into the personality.

In summary, the diagnostic clues to potential suicide are as follows. (1) On inquiry, the patient will reveal that the idea of suicide has occurred and is ego syntonic, but reasons for not doing this may be unsatisfactory: I'm afraid I will fail; I don't want to damage myself. Depression is present due either to neuroendocrine dysfunction or to deprivation. The act is associated with guilt, anger, and thoughts of revenge; depression may be felt as an emptiness. (2) There may be a history of previous treatment and its failure; sometimes the failure of treatment may be in physical illness; thus, adolescents who are fearful of a recurrence of a serious illness such as carcinoma may attempt suicide. For example, a fifteen-year-old boy thought that he had a secondary malignancy of a bone carcinoma in his arm, and he attempted to shoot himself. (3) There may be unresolved problems with separation and bereavement: death tends to cause guilt in surviving children; those who feel acutely guilty may attempt to kill themselves. This is also related to the fantasy wish of joining loved ones. (4) Relatives or friends, especially peers, may be told by the patient that he or she is thinking of suicide while the patient will not indicate this to the physician; if this is not reported, the inaction of the relatives or the psychiatrist is taken as permission. Finally, there may be a history of repeated accidents, especially in automobiles.

The basic personality structure prior to the attack is significant; faced with overwhelming despair, many patients who previously had a highly organized compulsive personality may attempt suicide. Immature personalities who make repeated attempts ultimately may be successful; these attempts should not be dismissed as attention-getting behavior.

Treatment

Initially, an assessment must be made of the need of the patient for protection. To some extent, this need is assessed in terms of a review of the social, psychological, and biological systems that impinge on the patient. If the suicidal crisis is a reaction to an overwhelming stress, it is clear that the patient needs emergency protection. This is a particularly relevant issue if divorce or death is the stress precipitant. When either occurs, apart from the effect on the adolescent, the social system in which the patient lives is less supportive than it otherwise might be.

Sometimes the suicidal crisis is a representation of an internal decompensation; the equivalent of the fourth-order reaction of Menninger (1931). The decompensation may not be the result of a reality stress; the issue is the patient's perception. Whether the patient has to be hospitalized will depend on the strength of the relationship that is made with the interviewer, whether the therapist knows that he or she can offer continuity of care, and whether other people in the patient's world are willing to aid the patient if necessary.

Some adolescents are so emotionally bankrupt—chronic drug abusers or alcoholics—that they have no significant object in their lives. This may be an issue particularly when the adolescent has been involved in drug dealing because drug dealers alienate others; the dealer is an exploiter. The adolescent's family and friends are alienated. His or her survival then seems to be quite irrelevant to others. These individuals may become highly suicidal, and, since larger social system protection is missing, they require hospitalization.

If the patient has to be hospitalized, the issue of appropriate precautions against suicide is relevant. Ultimately, it is not possible to protect a patient who is determined, whatever the situation, to kill himself or herself. However, if suicidal precautions respect the dignity of the patients, overt self-destructive efforts within a hospital setting are less likely. Some hospitals, in their attempt to prevent suicide, strip the patient of every appurtenance of self-worth. If every object of value is removed from the patient, this implicitly devalues the individual as a person. The likelihood of suicide then becomes even greater. In other words, some suicidal precautions implicitly seem to imply that there is an expectation that the patient will attempt self-destruction; this reinforces the likelihood of the act. Hospital design is highly relevant: whether it is easy for the patient to hurt himself or herself, whether adequate protection from drugs and weapons is possible with adequate numbers of staff. An essential attitude on the part of a program that looks after potential suicidal individuals is an expectation that people will survive, that life is worth living. Suicidal precautions on programs that provide adequate specific and nonspecific care need not be as stringent as on units that are emotionally depriving.

If the patient is suffering from unipolar or bipolar illness, appropriate medication is called for. However, most antidepressant drugs do not have an immediate effect, and there is always the possibility that, when they do begin to take effect, the patient will become suicidal. This is because the anergic depressed patient may become more energetic under the influence of medication before its antidepressant effect takes place. Sometimes adolescents with a bipolar disorder may appear to be suffering from a major depression. If they are given a serotonin inhibitor, they may respond to the medication by becoming manic. Grandiose depressed delusions—"the devil is telling me to kill myself"—often indicate a bipolar type of disorder. The inappropriate use of phenothiazines to tranquilize such individuals may make them suicidal as a grandiose delusion may cover profound depression.

There is no indication for the use of electroshock therapy in adolescents. When adolescent depression is attenuated with medication, there are a number of psychological problems. Alcohol and drug abuse may be particularly psychotoxic if the adolescent is taking antidepressants; if lithium carbonate is being used, its effect is attenuated with alcohol. If the effect of medication and therapy is to assist the postpubertal teenager become adolescent, the individual may stop taking medication inappropriately as part of the struggle for autonomy.

In psychotherapy, there are a number of significant issues. In depression, as in phobias and eating disorders, symptoms may become a learned response, and depression becomes a typical stress reaction even though the biological substrate may have been removed. When adolescents call their therapists as part of the agreement to give their therapist the chance to help them not behave suicidally, immediate success is a two-edged sword. The adolescent may feel that allowing the intervention may carry the implicit promise that the psychic pain will not occur again; they project their own omnipotence onto the therapist. If the suicidal wish occurs again, they may then ragefully make an attempt, directing it toward the therapist who has failed them.

Often parents collude with or provoke suicidal behavior in their offspring. Family intervention thus becomes crucial. Apart from necessary family or parental therapy, insofar as family relationships are concerned, the parents should be warned, as with adults, that the period of recovery from depression is when the patient is most vulnerable. The family should be told that safety cannot be guaranteed in the course of treatment because absolute protection makes treatment impossible because of its regressive connotations. This is an essential part of the informed consent procedure. In suicidal adolescents, every parameter of good therapy is necessary; treatment procedures aimed only at dealing with acute crises, which encapsulate brief interventions, lead at best to chronic illness, at worst to the ultimate death of the adolescent.

REFERENCES

Barraclough, D. 1987. *Suicide: Clinical and Epidemiological Studies.* New York: Grune & Stratton.

Bigler, E. D. 1989. On the neuropsychology of suicide. *Journal of Learning Disabilities* 22(3): 180–185.

Boyer, L. B., and Giovacchini, P. L. 1967. *Psychoanalytic Treatment of Schizophrenic and Characterological Disorders.* New York: Aronson.

Brown, G. L.; Ebert, M. H.; Boyer, P. F.; Jameson, D. C.; Klein, W. J.; Bunney, W. E.; and Goodwin, F. K. 1982. Aggression, suicide and serotonin: relationship to CSF metabolites. *American Journal of Psychiatry* 139:761–766.

Fawcett, J.; Shelfner, W. A.; Fogg, L.; Clark, D. C.; Young, M. A.; Hedeker, D.; and Gibbens, R. 1990. Time related predictors of suicide in major affective disorder. *American Journal of Psychiatry* 147:1189–1196.

Fenichel, O. 1945. *The Psycho-Analytic Theory of Neurosis.* New York: Norton.

Freud, S. 1917. Mourning and melancholia. *Standard Edition* 14:237–258. London: Hogarth, 1959.

Gault, W. B. 1971. Some remarks on slaughter. *American Journal of Psychiatry* 128(4): 82–86.

Glover, E. 1955. *The Technique of Psychoanalysis.* New York: International Universities Press.

Goldstein, R. B., and Black, D. W. 1991. The prediction of suicide: sensitivity, specificity, and predictive value of a multivariant model applied to suicide among 1906 patients with affective disorders. *Archives of General Psychiatry* 48:418–422.

Grey, J. S. 1972. The structure of emotions and the limbic system in physiology and emotional and psycho-somatic illness. *CIBA Symposium* 8:92–93.

Hendin, H. 1963. The psychodynamics of suicide. *Journal of Nervous and Mental Disease* 136:236–244.

Hendin, H. 1985. Suicide among the young: psychodynamics and demography. In M. L. Peck, N. L. Faberow, and R. E. Litman, eds. *Youth Suicide, 19–38.* New York: Springer.

Hendin, H. 1991. Psychodynamics of suicide, with particular reference to the young. *American Journal of Psychiatry* 148(9): 1150–1158.

Hendin, H., and Hass, H. P. 1991. Suicide and guilt as manifestations of post-traumatic stress disorder in Vietnamese combat veterans. *American Journal of Psychiatry* 148:586–591.

Klerman, G. L. 1986. *Suicide and Depression among Adolescents and Young Adults.* Washington, D.C.: American Psychiatric Press.

Klerman, G. L. 1987. Clinical epidemiology of suicide. *Journal of Clinical Psychiatry* 68:33–38.

Maenchen, A. 1968. Objects cathexis in a borderline twin. *Psychoanalytic Study of the Child* 23:438–456.

Maltsberger, J., and Biue, D. 1989. The psychological vulnerability to suicide. In David Jacobs and H. David Brown, eds. *Suicide: Understanding and Responding*. Madison, Conn.: International Universities Press.

Masterson, J. 1970. Depression in adolescent character disorders. *Proceedings of the American Psychological Association* 59:242–257.

Maxmen, J. S., and Tucker, G. J. 1973. No exit: the persistently suicidal patient. *Comprehensive Psychiatry* 14:71–79.

Menninger, K. A. 1931. Psycho-analytic aspects of suicide. *Archives of Neurology and Psychiatry* 25:1369.

Miller, D. 1974. *Adolescence: Its Psychology, Psychopathology, and Psychotherapy*. Northfield, N.J.: Aronson.

Miller, D. 1978a. Affective disorders in adolescence: mood disorders and the differential diagnosis of violent behavior. In F. J. Ayd, ed. *Depression: The World's Major Public Health Problem*. Baltimore: Ayd.

Miller, D. 1978b. Early adolescence: its psychology, psychopathology, and implications for therapy. *Adolescent Psychiatry* 6:434–447.

Miller, D. 1986. *Attack on the Self*. Northfield, N.J.: Aronson.

Miller, D., and Looney, J. 1976. Determinants of homicide in adolescents. *Adolescent Psychiatry* 4:231–254.

Miller, D.; Visotsky, H.; and Carlton, B. 1992. Treatment of emotional disturbances in adolescents: practical and theoretical considerations. *Adolescent Psychiatry* 18:26–43.

Offer, D. 1973. *The Psychological World of the Teenager: A Study of Normal Adolescent Boys*. New York: Basic.

Pardes, H. 1985. *Youth Studies*. New York: Springer.

Patel, N. S. 1974. A study of suicide. *Medicine, Science and the Law* 14:129–136.

Peterson, A. M.; Awad, G. A.; and Kendler, A. C. 1973. Epidemiological differences between white and nonwhite suicide attempts. *American Journal of Psychiatry* 130:1071–1076.

Petzel, S. V., and Cline, D. W. 1978. Adolescent suicide: epidemiological and biological aspects. *Adolescent Psychiatry* 6:239–266.

Piaget, J., and Inhelder, B. 1969. *The Psychology of the Child*. New York: Basic.

Pollock, G. H. 1975. On mourning: immortality and utopia. *Journal of the American Psychoanalytic Association* 23:334–362.

Reisman, D. 1954. *The Lonely Crowd*. Garden City, N.Y.: Doubleday Anchor.

Resnik, H. L. P. 1972. Eroticized repetitive hanging: a form of self-destructive behavior. *American Journal of Psychotherapy* 26:4–21.

Rourke, B. P.; Young, G. C.; and Leaners, A. A. 1989. A childhood learning disability that predisposes these affiliated to adolescent and adult depression to suicide risk. *Journal of Learning Disabilities* 20(3): 169–174.

Sabbath, J. C. 1969. The suicidal adolescent: the expendable child. *Journal of the American Academy of Child Psychiatry* 8:272–289.

Schaffer, D.; Garland, A.; Gould, M.; Fischer, P.; and Traunta, P. 1988. Preventing teen age suicide: a critical review. *Journal of the American Academy of Child and Adolescent Psychiatry* 27:675–687.

Shafii, M.; Corrigan, S.; Whittinghill, J. R..; and Derrick, A. 1985. Psychological autopsy of completed suicide in children and adolescents. *American Journal of Psychiatry* 142:1061–1064.

Siever, L. J.; Coccaro, E. F.; Zewishlany, Z.; and Silverman, J. 1987. Psychobiology of personality disorders: pharmacological implications. *Psychopharmacological Bulletin* 11:576–589.

Siever, L. J., and Davis, K. L. 1991. A psychological perspective on the personality disorders. *American Journal of Psychiatry* 148(12): 1647–1658.

Weissman, M. D. 1974. The epidemiology of suicide attempts, 1960–1971, *Archives of General Psychiatry* 30:737–746.

Winnicott, D. W. 1953. Transitional objects and transitional phenomena: a study of the first not-me possession. *International Journal of Psycho-Analysis* 34:89–97.

Zilborg, G. 1936. Differential diagnostic types of suicide. *Archives of Neurology and Psychiatry* 35:270–291.

Zilborg, G. 1937. Considerations of suicide with particular reference to the young. *American Journal of Orthopsychiatry* 7:15–31.

Zilborg, G. 1938. The sense of immortality. *Psychoanalytic Quarterly* 7:171–199.

20 PHYSICAL SYMPTOMS AS A MASK FOR EMOTIONAL DISORDER IN ADOLESCENTS

ROBERT M. GLUCKMAN

As we are all so well aware, the adolescent developmental stage subjects the individual boy or girl to many stressful demands and conditions, in health as it does in illness. There may well be no other period of life when one is subjected to this degree of physiological, physical, and psychological distress.

Adolescence is a phase of life during which major psychobiological tasks need to be accomplished to master the dynamic process of maturational change from childhood to adulthood. The work of puberty plays no small role in this process as a motivator and integrator of this whole phenomenon. From a developmental, psychological perspective, a major reorganization of the internal percepts of one's self (mother, father, siblings) has to take place. A reexperiencing of separation and individuation occurs, with all the conflicts this engenders for the adolescent, both within the self and with the outer world (Blos 1974).

There is thus a whole reworking of identity formation, so as to become a very particular person, in a specific sense. The adolescent now has to make decisions and adaptations that were never required before. We must keep in mind, in the face of all this, that the adolescent is still immature and vulnerable and feels more a victim than a participant.

All this may result in inner turmoil on the part of this young person just coming out of childhood. The question raised, however, is what within the individual at this time of life is causing this turmoil. Several issues come to mind: physiological changes (neuroendocrinological and neurochemical) introduce and produce the phenomenon we call pubescence; there is the psychological counterpart to the physiological phenomena; there is a reworking of tasks mastered earlier (a major undertaking and not rapidly accomplished); and there is a modification of the personality to enable the individual to become his or her own self, which too often means becoming alienated from his or her past security, objects, persons, and values.

The inner stress with which the adolescent is struggling places great demands on the self-regulating mechanisms. When this adapting, coping, sublimating, integrating function is not up to the task demands, regression or disintegration may result in the self-organizing and self-regulating structures of the personality.

It is at this point that symptoms of identifiable psychological malfunctioning may occur. This is also when symptoms of a physical or physiological nature may attempt to camouflage (or disguise) the underlying personality breakdown or may occur as the most evident manifestation of it. Blos (1974) noted that all adolescent disturbances reflect the existence of developmental impasse at an early stage of adolescence. When physical symptoms do occur, they may do so as various kinds of physical disorders, often making the underlying psychological disturbance difficult to detect.

There are a number of different general diagnostic categories of physical symptoms that we have to keep in mind as possible manifestations of underlying emotional or personality disorders in adolescence. Perhaps the most frequent are those symptoms secondary to anxiety and depression. As Wolman (1988, p. 213) points out, "The psychosomatic reactions to fear and anxiety are much the same; both involve the autonomic nervous system, specifically its sympathetic part, resulting in disturbances of the gastrointestinal system, adrenal gland secretions, respiration, heart rate, as well as various symptoms secondary to arousal of the peripheral nervous system." Hysterical conversion phenomena with physical symptomatology occur as a result of internal emotional conflict with resolution through mechanisms of repression, displacement, and overcompensation.

Wolman comments that often conversion symptoms enable one to avoid a noxious activity or to get support from the environment that might otherwise not be forthcoming. Physical and physiological disorders due to regressive disintegration of the individual's ego or self-integral functioning are another source of stress. These symptom complexes are referred to by Alexander (1950) as true psychosomatic illnesses and involve initial organ tissue destruction. Examples are duodenal ulcer, essential hypertension, ulcerative colitis, and even thyroiditis, rheumatoid arthritis, and diabetes mellitus. Hypochondriasis (using Wolman's definition) is an unrealistic interpretation of various physical signs or bodily sensations as being abnormal, leading to preoccupation with the fear or belief of having a serious illness. Another category would be in the case of an emotional illness; while not having physical and physiological symptoms initially, as the illness progresses physical symptoms may become dominant.

Psychosomatic medicine may have had its earliest beginning in the philosophical thoughts of Descartes (1927), who drew a clear distinction between the mind as a "thinking entity" and the body as a "nonthinking entity." However, modern-day thinking and advocacy regarding mind-body unity in illness dates to Dunbar (1974), who, in her pioneering book on psychosomatic medicine, stressed that psyche and soma are "two aspects of a fundamental unity."

In the first edition of its journal *Psychosomatic Medicine,* the American Psychosomatic Society emphasized a monistic approach to the mind-body dichotomy. Engel (1967) pointed out that psychophysiological symptoms may occur when conversion symptoms have failed to dissipate anxiety. Thus, continuing anxiety states may activate biological systems and result in physiological changes. Adolescence, as a specific developmental phase, may readily serve as a vulnerability factor.

Many others have written on this subject as it pertains to children and adolescents as well as to adults. For instance, Bettelheim and Sylvester (1949) stated, "In children, the origin, persistence, and dissolution of somatic symptoms result from the integrative tasks to be mastered at that moment" (p. 358). They further added, "A child may frequently be forced to attempt mastery by means of somatic symptoms because of the particular nature of the interpersonal constellation in which he finds himself. The choice of symptoms, however, will depend on the state of psychobiological maturation he has reached" (p. 359).

Laufer (1977, p. 249) wrote, "Adolescent pathology is a breakdown in the process of integrating one's physically mature body as part of the representation of oneself. It is a breakdown that occurs at puberty and has a cumulative effect throughout adolescence." He adds, "The range of pathology in adolescence is vast, and each has its own explanation and meaning for the individual."

Mattson and Agle (1979) have written that psychophysiological disorders include those illnesses where emotional factors significantly contribute to the onset or course of the illness. The physiological changes involved are those that normally accompany certain emotional states, but in these disorders the changes are more intense and sustained.

The following clinical examples are illustrative.

Clinical Example 1

Mary, a seventeen-year-old girl in a special education program at a nearby suburban high school, was first admitted with a diagnosis of seizure disorder. From the very beginning, her seizures were recognized as unusual. They occurred at irregular times, and the patient would just fall to the ground, as her legs would suddenly give way. She would become semiconscious, have a glassy, distant stare, and appear to be out of contact. She was put on carbamazepine, improved, and was discharged ten days later, with a diagnosis of idiopathic seizure disorder and cerebral palsy.

Mary was readmitted two months later with the same diagnosis. The admitting resident noted there was no tongue biting, no incontinence, and immediate lucidity on recovering from a seizure. In the hospital, these seizures were now observed as periodic, wild thrashing episodes that could be stopped with aromatic ammonia; her speech would become slightly slurred, her pulse was rapid, and her skin was highly flushed. The patient was always apologetic afterward and expressed anger at her mother, who said she did not believe the seizures were real. An electroencephalogram taken immediately after recovery from a seizure was not contributory. A psychiatric consultation was requested when the neurologist introduced the possibility of there being emotional causes involved.

In my consultation note, I remarked that the falling spells and dissociation phenomena would seem to have as a purpose escaping from reality, owing to a lack of inner resources for coping with stress. I felt that marked ego regression produced the dissociative reaction. During this period, the patient remained in bed or was in a wheelchair, as staff feared she would hurt herself. I thought it very important to encourage her to be dressed and walking, even though a special nurse had to be provided. I was now seeing the patient regularly in psychotherapy. The anticonvulsion medication was reduced to a level below the effective clinical dosage, yet improvement continued. The therapy began to deal with the various ways in which both conscious and unconscious conflicts could cause physical symptoms. In three weeks, Mary was symptom free and had not had a seizure for five days. She began to complain of being infantilized by her private nurse, but she was much more cheerful.

Her therapeutic sessions focused on her conflicted feelings related to her twin sister, who had always been socially adequate, brighter, and sophisticated. Also, feelings about her mother, brother, father, and grandmother began to emerge. By one month, the ataxia had completely abated, the anticonvulsant was discontinued, and she had not had seizures for ten days. Mary was discharged with primary diagnosis of cerebral palsy (spastic diplegia).

Mary continued in outpatient treatment, but three months later she was readmitted, having overdosed on phenobarbital. She had become depressed and anxious one day when home alone. She was transferred to the psychiatric unit for intensive care. Mary's history revealed that her parents were divorced when she was about three years old. Her mother remarried when she was six, and she was subsequently adopted by her stepfather. The family moved to California, where Mary developed asthma. They returned to the Midwest, and her asthma subsided. She had always felt inferior to her twin sister, a condition reinforced by the sister and mother. The mother openly preferred the sister, and Mary always felt afraid of her mother, who would whip her as punishment. Mary's chronic complaint was of being picked on by peers and family and of having no friends. She particularly felt deserted when her sister began a close relationship with a boy.

On this admission, the patient showed regressive symptoms of confusion, slurred speech, lethargy, and unsteadiness of gait. The overdose was seen as a way of getting back into the protective, warm care of the hospital. She was also quite anxious about increasing difficulties between her parents and the possibility of divorce. Her course in the hospital was an uphill struggle. The whole therapeutic program was geared toward helping her develop stronger ego resources, better adaptive functioning, and more self-sufficiency. This was viewed, however, as a long-term therapeutic course, and she was transferred to a psychiatric hospital for adolescents with a diagnosis of borderline personality disorder with dissociative regressive manifestations. The question of the coexistence of true organic brain syndrome was not completely settled at the time of her transfer. She remained a patient in the adolescent hospital for almost two years and was discharged to home, functionally much improved, with a discharge diagnosis of organic brain syndrome; hysterical neurosis, dissociative type; and immature personality.

Clinical Example 2

Amelia, age sixteen, was admitted to the neurological service with a diagnosis of convulsive disorder. Previously she had been well until January of that year, at which time she developed fever, headache, earache, and a cough. She was hospitalized on the medical service with a diagnosis of mycoplasma pneumonia. Within two weeks, the symptoms of pneumonia abated, and she was discharged. Shortly thereafter, she began having involuntarly jerking of her hands, arms, and head.

When admitted in March, her neurological exam was normal, except for repetitive, frequent myoclonic arm jerking, which was reported as highly atypical. An electroencephalogram was moderately abnormal, with spiking and three- to five-second waves, but not in rhythm with the myoclonus. A second EEG was reported as normal. She was treated with clonopin to control the spasms. Some weakness of the flexor and extensor muscles of her upper and lower extremities was noted, and the myoclonic movements were absent during sleep. She was discharged a week later with a diagnosis of encephalomyelitis with myoclonus.

Amelia was readmitted to the hospital in April with a diagnosis of myoclonus because four milligrams of clonopin daily did not control the seizures. A larger dosage was to be given in the hospital. A CT scan, lumbar puncture, and EEG were performed, and all were reported as normal. At this time, the patient also complained of frontal headaches. It was noted by nursing that the myoclonic movements were reduced in intensity when Amelia did not know she was being observed and that she remained alert and talkative during seizure-like movements. She was started on haloperidol when the neurologist noted that he suspected a hysterical basis or component in addition to the neurological condition present. A psychiatric consultation was also requested.

The psychiatric consultation revealed a history of the family moving from the Middle East a year and a half before, under stressful conditions. The entire family had a very difficult adjustment period for the first year, but especially the patient, who was entering high school. She suffered depressive and withdrawal symptoms, escape into fantasy, and excessive eating. She also had fears of death, especially of her parents and younger sister, which resulted in fears of being alone and not being able to care for herself. There were also guilt feelings over increasing adolescent desires to be like her peers, in America, because such desires meant that she was "bad." Also revealed was a hidden, hostile aggressive, and sexual fantasy life.

I began to see Amelia for psychotherapy, and she was continued on haloperidol. She described a great deal of sadness, feelings of isolation, marked fears, excessive eating with weight gain, conflicted feelings over adolescent image change, and lowered self-esteem. She could not experience consciously repressed anger, for anger to her meant being "bad." With hospital therapy, her myoclonus became greatly reduced, and she was discharged with a diagnosis of myoclonic seizure disorder, etiology unknown. Haloperidol was continued in ambulatory care, as was psychotherapy.

Amelia was readmitted on May 1, this time directly under my care on the psychiatric unit. She now had severe myoclonic spasms of the head, arms, and legs. In the hospital, the psychotherapy provided opportunity for catharsis and insight. She was encouraged and helped to bring out her areas of greatest inner conflict. With much support, through the hospital care and therapeutic relationships, she did become consciously aware of her angry feelings and memories (but cautiously). She was also involved in the adolescent milieu program.

The course in the hospital was to encourage involvement of positive relationships with staff—the redirection of tensions from outside influences—and reduction gradually of the medication. While the psychotherapeutic process was effective, ambivalence about giving up the myoclonus was also noted. As guilt feelings became more consciously worked with, homesickness became prominent. Her self-image improved as she worked on and through her conflicts around obesity and overeating. She was able to become angry at staff members and at me, in relation to not gratifying all her wishes, and that anger became associated with the anger at her parents for coming to America. This led to dependence conflicts and anger at her parents for overprotecting her. She became able to experience adolescent sexual feelings and fantasies without guilt. Her own child-adolescent conflicts came out and were dealt with. The haloperidol was discontinued one week before discharge, at which time she was completely myoclonus free, a much more relaxed and happy person.

Clinical Example 3

June, age sixteen, was first admitted to the pediatric inpatient service in November, with a diagnosis of anorexia nervosa, and was discharged two weeks later as improved. Her history revealed that she had begun dieting nine months prior to admission, when she weighed 126 pounds. At the time of her hospital admission, she weighed 76 pounds, standing five feet, six inches tall. Although menstruation had begun at age thirteen, she had not menstruated for several months. No other physical symptoms were present at the time.

Early in her hospital stay, I saw June in consultation. The psychiatric evaluation revealed that she had a very depreciated and distorted self-image. She had been dieting because of feeling fat and ugly. She also complained of being unpopular. The dieting itself had become a compulsion, and she was unable to stop. She had a great fear that, if she began eating normally, she would lose control of her weight. She could no longer see herself as others saw her. June had been working in a doughnut shop and also told of enjoying baking. Yet she would not eat anything she baked. During this period of hospitalization, she seemed motivated to improve, and weighed eighty pounds on discharge.

Two to three weeks later, June's parents called, as she had lost weight again and they were concerned. Since her weight had dropped to close to seventy pounds, I decided to hospitalize her on the psychiatric unit. The patient was physically weak, tired, and depressed. Her pulse rate, respiratory rate, and blood pressure were all below normal. June was put on a 2,500-calorie diet, with supervised meals. Psychotherapy was begun on an intensive basis, focusing on developing insights as to the cause of her behavior, family problems, and how she was using dieting to manipulate and control her environment.

June discovered that, early in her life, she was fearful of not receiving enough love and attention from her parents, particularly her mother. This was also revealed in her behavior in the hospital, when her lowered frustration tolerance, caused by delay and denials of gratification, came out in hurt and angry feelings. Hunger for food became associated with hunger for love and attention, with strong defenses, such as denial, being manifested. Much of the therapeutic work centered on her reasons for becoming anorexic—how this related to her conflicts regarding self-image, self-identity, and early childhood dependency. While in the hospital this time, June gained eighteen pounds; she appeared to be fairly well stabilized and ready to continue therapy as an outpatient. Discharge was exactly one month after admission, to resume a full daily life living at home. She continued to maintain the weight gain—stabilizing at between ninety-five and one hundred pounds. However, she continued exercising excessively, got a job in a restaurant, and occasionally ate in binges. As an outpatient, she became increasingly resistant to exploring her deeper conflicts. She was in therapy as an outpatient for about five months. Even though I thought she was not ready to end therapy, she did so, with her parents' support. There were still some important adolescent conflicts that needed to be worked through. However, I did hear from her again, when she reported that she felt that she was getting along pretty well.

Discussion

In the foregoing clinical material, I have attempted to clarify and make explicit how the process and work of adolescence as a phase of development involves physical, physiological, and psychological changes that are taking place simultaneously, both separately and interrelatedly. While the majority of adolescents are able to experience this transitional process from childhood to adulthood without much turmoil, many are not mature and may manifest expressions of psychological upheaval.

Many of the emotional, mental, and adjustment disturbances of the adolescent are expressed primarily or solely through a form of psychological disorder. However, others who basically have a disturbance of mental or emotional functioning are either primarily or secondarily expressing this through the biological systems and structures of the body. While physical symptomatology may be the selected means for expressing psychic disturbance, it may also be used (unconsciously) to hide from oneself as well as from others that a mental or emotional disturbance actually exists.

REFERENCES

Alexander, F. 1950. *Psychosomatic Medicine.* New York: Norton.

Bettelheim, B., and Sylvester, A. 1949. Physical symptoms in disturbed children. *Psychoanalytic Study of the Child* 3/4:353–368.

Blos, P. 1974. The genealogy of the ego ideal. *Psychoanalytic Study of the Child* 29:43–86.

Descartes, R. 1927. *Descartes Selections.* New York: Scribner's.

Dunbar, F. 1974. *Mind and Body: Psychosomatic Medicine.* New York: Random House.

Engel, G. L. 1967. A reconsideration of the role of conversion in somatic disease. *Comprehensive Psychiatry* 9:316–326.

Laufer, M. 1977. A view of adolescent pathology. *Adolescent Psychiatry* 5:249–250.

Mattson, A., and Agle, D. P. 1979. Psychophysiological aspects of adolescence: hemic disorders. *Adolescent Psychiatry* 7:269–280.

Wolman, B. 1988. *Psychosomatic Disorders.* New York: Plenum.

21 CHILDHOOD SYMPTOMS OF MALADJUSTMENT: A PROGNOSTIC INDICATOR OF ADOLESCENT PSYCHOPATHOLOGY

ADRIAN D. COPELAND

Aberrant behavior in children is difficult to understand in terms of clinical significance, difficult to classify (Rutter and Shaffer 1980), and difficult to predict in terms of outcome (Lundy 1990). What appears atypical or abnormal may reflect a subcultural norm rather than true psychopathology (Achenbach and Edelbrock 1981). Some behaviors seen in mentally ill children are seen in normal children as well (Rutter and Schaffer 1980).

With regard to classification, DSM-III-R (APA 1987), the current diagnostic standard, is based on categories that are qualitatively different, and while it constitutes a significant improvement over prior systems, it still has many oversights, ambiguities, and unresolved issues (Simmons 1987). Focusing on these shortcomings, Edelbrock and Achenbach (1980), Achenbach, Connors, Quay, and Howell (1989), Swett, Surrey, and Cohen (1990), and others have instead developed a number of quantitatively differentiable categories of psychopathology, empirically derived, based on commonly occurring, frequently associated symptom clusters of childhood and adolescent maladjustment. Unfortunately, however, these typologies and pathological profiles often do not relate either to one another or to DSM-III-R, nor do they predict the fate of these symptoms. While such prognostication is far from a science, Kestenbaum (1988) did, however, relate attentional problems of childhood to later psychopathology.

Currier (1990) saw an association between pavor nocurnus and affective disorders, and Simmons (1987) noted that attention deficit hyperactivity disorders and conduct disorders were often associated with subsequent diagnoses of antisocial personality disorder. He added, however, that some associated, more subtle variables could be specific indicators.

My psychiatric evaluation of over 300 male adolescent residents of the St. Francis Homes for Boys revealed a close association between certain specific symptoms of behavioral maladjustment reported in their childhood and current major psychopathology of adolescence. These were (1) nail biting; (2) finger or thumb sucking past age three; (3) enuresis past age five; (4) nightmares causing awakening; (5) fire setting; and (6) running away. Encopresis, cruelty to animals, and sleepwalking were also reported, but less frequently. The clinical significance in any one of these symptoms is unclear, however. For instance, Shaffer (1988) did not consider enuresis to be a sign of mental illness, while Gerard (1939) and Kolb and Balla (1976) did, and enuresis is listed as an elimination disorder in DSM-III-R. Gabel (1981) generally regarded maladjustment symptoms only as transitory stress reactions, but Heller, Ehrlich, and Lester (1984) found fire setting to be closely associated with strong antisocial trends. In a review of the literature, Moffat (1989) cited several authors who found clusters of behavioral symptoms more common in enuretic than in nonenuretic children.

The focus of this study is to determine whether the presence of clusters of three or more of the often-reported childhood symptoms of maladjustment constitutes an adequate criterion for predicting major adolescent psychopathology. The cluster was chosen rather than the single symptom inasmuch as the clinical significance of any one symptom is controversial. Each subject was evaluated in terms of the presence or absence of a positive cluster history, a history of prior psychiatric treatment, and a current diagnosis of major psychopathology.

Method

Two groups of subjects were studied sequentially. Group 1 consisted of 131 residents of the St. Francis Homes for Boys. They were all male and ranged in age from twelve to seventeen, of whom 85 percent were black, 1 percent Hispanic, and 14 percent white. Group 2 consisted of seventy-four Catholic school students from inner-city Philadelphia. There was an equal number of males and females, and the subjects' ages ranged from nine to sixteen. Twenty percent of the group were black, 30 percent Hispanic, and 50 percent white; 16 percent were age thirteen years or older.

Definition of "Major Psychopathology"

The St. Francis adolescents were adjudicated dependents of the court, having major life disruptions, with histories of drug-using parents, broken homes, and abandonment. They presented a variety of disturbed behaviors best characterized as stress reactions or adjustment disorders. The majority, however, presented symptoms of more deep-seated, severe psychopathology. Their DSM-III-R diagnoses included conduct disorders, overanxious disorders, major depression with suicidality, various substance-abuse disorders, atypical psychotic disorders, pedophilia, and oppositional disorders. Thus, "major psychopathology" is defined in this study to refer to all adolescents with diagnoses other than adjustment disorders.

Sequences of the Study

The 131 St. Francis adolescents were studied first. I personally evaluated each boy psychiatrically on his entering the institution, thereby providing a high degree of diagnostic reliability. In the majority of cases, these initial diagnoses were independently corroborated by prior evaluations from other institutions or by subsequently performed intramural psychological tests, thus affording a high degree of validity.

The subjects were then divided into two groups, according to whether or not they reported histories of clusters of three or more of the specific symptoms of childhood maladjustment described. Each of these subgroups was then compared in terms of histories of prior psychiatric treatment.

The second group of seventy-four Catholic school students was randomly chosen. They were well adjusted, presenting neither academic nor behavior problems. They were interviewed by experienced school counselors who had been oriented in terms of the significance and

TABLE 1

Group	Prevalence of Symptom Clusters (%)
1 ($N = 131$)	66
2 ($N = 74$)	0

mode of administration of the brief questionnaire. The brevity and simplicity of the questionnaire reduced problems of reliability. However, validity of the students' responses cannot be adequately determined, and there was possible underreporting of symptoms of childhood maladjustment by this group.

Results

As would be predicted, the more disturbed population of St. Francis adolescents had a much higher prevalence of childhood maladjustment symptom clusters than the Catholic school, well-adjusted students (see table 1). Despite the fact that the two groups were not well matched, and despite possible underreporting of symptoms by the latter group, the difference is still so distinct as strongly to suggest that the specific maladjustment symptom clusters technique employed was a sensitive criterion for differentiating the two groups. This was further substantiated by the dramatic differences in the subjects' incidence of mental health treatment (see table 2).

When the two well-matched St. Francis subgroups 1A and 1B were compared, the presence of these specific childhood maladjustment symptom clusters differentiated those subjects with major adolescent psychopathology from those with less severe adjustment disorders to a very statistically significant degree ($p < .01$; see table 3). This differentiation was further substantiated by differences in their prevalence of prior mental health treatment ($p < .05$; see table 4).

TABLE 2

Group	Prevalence of Prior Mental Health Treatment (%)
1 ($N = 131$)	57
2 ($N = 74$)	1.3

TABLE 3

Group	Prevalence of Major Psychopathology (%)
1A, St. Francis "clusterers" (N = 88)	61
1B, St. Francis "nonclusterers" (N = 43)	34

Note.—$z = 3.25; p < .01$.

One may conclude from these data that these symptom clusters of childhood maladjustment were forerunners of later major psychopathology and, thus, constitute a predictive criterion. They did not, however, predict specific diagnoses but were instead broad, sensitive indicators.

Conclusions

This study is significant from several standpoints. (1) It helps clarify the clinicopathological significance of certain childhood symptoms of maladjustment by linking them to prognosis and, to a lesser extent, diagnosis. Symptoms such as nail biting and enuresis, the most prevalent ones noted in the St. Francis group, have never been well understood, leaving clinicians uncertain about the need for therapeutic intervention. This uncertainty, articulated by Rutter, Lundy, and others, was compounded by a paucity of relevant long-term studies. By treating this group of commonly occurring maladjustment symptoms as clusters rather than individually, the prognostic significance became

TABLE 4

Group	Prevalence of Prior Mental Health Treatment (%)
1A, St. Francis "clusterers" (N = 88)	66
1B, St. Francis "nonclusterers" (N = 43)	48

Note.—$z = 2.25; p < .05$.

clear in this retrospective study and could provide a basis for therapeutic intervention. (2) The study provides a bridge between the quantitative "pathological profiles" classification system and the qualitative categorical system of DSM-III-R. While both nosological approaches are valid and still developing, their ultimate reconciliation is necessary if the field of psychiatry is to advance and mature. This study, in conjunction with the work of Currier, Heller, Kestenbaum, Simmons, and others, helps bridge this gap. (3) The study provides the rationale for further investigation of childhood maladjustment symptoms. While it provided a sensitive prognosticator of later psychopathology, it was nonspecific. Further research could possibly identify specific childhood symptom clusters that predict specific DSM-III-R diagnoses in adolescence and adulthood.

REFERENCES

Achenbach, T.; Connors, C.; Quay, H.; and Howell, C. 1989. Replication of empirically derived syndromes as a basis for taxonomy of child/adolescent psychopathology. *Journal of Abnormal Child Psychology* 17(3): 299–323.

Achenbach, T., and Edelbrock, C. S. 1981. Behavioral problems and competencies reported by parents of normal and disturbed children aged four to sixteen. *Monographs of the Society for Research in Child Development,* vol. 46, no. 1, serial no. 188.

American Psychiatric Association (APA). 1987. *Diagnostic and Statistical Manual of Mental Disorders.* 3d ed., rev. Washington, D.C.: American Psychiatric Association.

Currier, B. 1990. Adult night terrors and associated psychopathology. Paper presented to the meeting of the American Psychiatric Association, New York, May.

Edelbrock, C., and Achenbach, T. 1980. A typology of child behavior profile patterns: distribution and correlates for disturbed children aged six to sixteen. *Journal of Abnormal Child Psychology* 8(4): 441–470.

Gabel, S. 1981. *Behavioral Problems in Childhood.* New York: Grune & Stratton.

Gerard, M. 1939. Enuresis: a study of etiology. *American Journal of Orthopsychiatry* 9:48–58.

Heller, M.; Ehrlich, S.; and Lester, D. 1984. Childhood cruelty to animals, firesetting and enuresis as correlates of competence to attend trial. *Journal of General Psychology* 110:151–153.

Kestenbaum, C. 1988. The clinical assessment of children and adolescents. In C. Kestenbaum and D. Williams, eds. *Handbook of Clinical Assessment of Children and Adolescents,* vol. 2. New York: New York University Press.

Kolb, D., and Balla, D. 1976. *Delinquency and Psychopathology.* New York: Grune & Stratton.

Lundy, M. 1990. Childhood psychiatric status and criminality. Paper presented to the meeting of the American Psychiatric Association, New York, May.

Moffat, M. 1989. Nocturnal enuresis: psychologic implications of treatment and nontreatments. *Journal of Pediatrics* 114(suppl.): 697–704.

Rutter, M., and Shaffer, D. 1980. DSM III: a step forward or back in terms of classification of child psychiatric disorders. *Journal of the American Academy of Child and Adolescent Psychiatry* 19:391–394.

Shaffer, D. 1988. The clinical management of bedwetting in children. In C. Kestenbaum and D. Williams, eds. *Handbook of Clinical Assessment of Children and Adolescents,* vol. 2. New York: New York University Press.

Simmons, J. 1987. *Psychiatric Examination of Children.* 4th ed. Philadelphia: Lea & Febiger.

Swett, C.; Surrey, J.; and Cohen, C. 1990. Sexual and physical abuse histories and psychiatric symptoms among male psychiatric outpatients. *American Journal of Psychiatry* 147:632–636.

22 THE ROLE OF INTERDISCIPLINARY CONSULTATION: COUNTERTRANSFERENCE DURING THE ACUTE PSYCHIATRIC HOSPITALIZATION OF THE ADOLESCENT

LINDA GREENBERG AND AARON H. ESMAN

In a previous work (Greenberg, Haiman, and Esman 1987), my colleagues and I discussed the emergence of countertransference during an acute hospitalization as an inevitable and crucial aspect of work with adolescents. This presentation represents an elaboration and refinement of our understanding of countertransference phenomena that emerge when working with adolescents in such a setting. We will describe a consultative methodology that we have evolved to aid staff in identifying and resolving interdisciplinary countertransference within a brief setting. Attention will be paid to the role of identificatory and separation-individuation processes as well as a new way of looking at the "adoption process" (Palmer, Harper, and Rivinus 1983). A literature review on countertransference with adolescents in an acute setting will follow, and, in conclusion, a description of a seventeen-year-old patient will flesh out theory and demonstrate the importance of the interdisciplinary staff's awareness and capacity to monitor countertransferential reactions.

An acute psychiatric hospitalization offers a unique opportunity to the adolescent to develop and experience powerful transferential reactions toward staff. Such reactions can evoke interdisciplinary staff countertransference. We and others (Rinsley 1968; Steinberg 1986) believe that hospitalization, which involves the physical separation of the adolescent from his or her family, represents a profound developmental impasse within the child, who struggles with dynamic conflicts over separation and consolidation of identity. In our former paper, we noted the maladaptive aspects of the "adoption process," a phenomenon in which interdisciplinary staff assume aspects of the parental environment and, in the extreme, may play out pathologically projected roles. Such behavior reinforces the adolescent's proclivity toward splitting as well as the family's feelings of alienation from the hospital and, ultimately, from the child. We view the emergence of the adoption process with its concomitant rescue fantasies as unavoidable in the context of an adolescent's hospitalization.

Furthermore, through our present lens, we view the adoption process as a countertransferential process—crucial to treatment. When made conscious, this process can and must inform the staff about the adolescent's intrapsychic conflicts. A compelling and potentially curative aspect of the adoption process is the adolescent's adoption of the hospital staff experienced within a "parental transference" (Rinsley 1965, p. 407). The capacity of the adolescent to reach out for adoption not only sets the stage for development of the transference but, at the same time, allows for the establishment of a therapeutic alliance. It is this alliance that allows the adolescent to begin to work through within the transference his or her identificatory conflict regarding the good versus the bad introject. In many adolescents, this conflict symbolizes "an intrapsychic representation of the [conflict] between the parents" (Greenson 1954, p. 203). During the regression that ensues prior to the hospitalization, erotic and aggressive instincts are defused, and separation may mean "death, dissolution, starvation, loss of external controls for self-destruction, or liquidation . . . of identity." It is during the mutual "adoption process" (the dialectic between transference and countertransference) that mourning may take place through an "exchange of introjects" (Rinsley 1965, p. 418).

A phase of "infantile depression" (Rinsley 1968) emerges approximately two to four weeks after admission, immediately following the initial "honeymoon phase" in which there exists a mutual idealization of adolescent and staff (Greenberg, Haiman, and Esman 1987). It is against a backdrop of early object loss and its concomitant fear of dissolution that deep-seated fears of abandonment can be addressed within the transferential aspects of the hospital experience.

Literature Review

Generations of psychotherapists have learned about the special intensity of countertransferential reactions evoked by adolescents and have stuggled to find ways of addressing these reactions in therapeutically helpful ways. Ironically, discussions in the literature about countertransference regarding adolescents have been rare and, until our 1987 paper, nonexistent for acute inpatient settings.

In our paper, we emphasized the "totalistic," as opposed to the "classical" (Kernberg 1976), definition of countertransference that incorporates the entire emotional response of the therapist to the patient in the treatment situation. Totalistic countertransference includes conscious and unconscious reactions of the treatment staff to the patient's reality as well as to the patient's transference. This definition allows for both positive and negative countertransference to emerge (Halperin, Lauro, Miscione, Rebhan, Schnabolk, and Shachter 1981).

Although most of the literature on countertransference in residential treatment deals with long-term facilities, the problems are, if anything, more intense and demanding in short-term acute settings. As we have noted elsewhere, the very nature of such a setting makes it difficult to pause and reflect on the messages that characterologically disordered patients communicate through their acting out (Greenberg, Haiman, and Esman 1987). Such patients demand immediate action, but those demands also necessitate a thoughtful consideration of the staff's conscious and unconscious reactions. Treatment of these patients challenges staff to learn to feel comfortable with intense dependency, primitive rage, erotic feelings, and provocative behavior.

Furthermore, when patients constantly come and go, staff members tend to protect themselves against growing too close to adolescent patients. Thus, a disengaged or overinvolved attitude may defend against feelings of separation and loss. On short-term, acute units, staff members rarely have the opportunity to be part of the resolution of the adolescent's conflict, which can leave them feeling unfulfilled and frustrated. When anger, helplessness, frustration, and guilt color reactions to patients, countertransference is naturally intensified.

A major contribution to staff countertransference is the proclivity of adolescents (particularly those with personality disorders) to employ splitting as a major mode of defense. Unwary staff members can readily take on, by way of the dyadic process of projective identification, the role that the patient imposes on them as "good"/nurturing or "bad"/rejecting parent surrogates. Such countertransference splits may lead to serious inconsistencies in treatment practice, to internecine conflicts among staff members, and to potentiallly dangerous acting out on the part of both patient and treatment personnel. It is by now a well-established principle that such disruptive events on a treatment unit can often be traced to unexpressed and unresolved countertransference reactions (Stanton and Schwartz 1954).

Interdisciplinary Consultation

Since brief hospitalization demands rapid assessment and intervention, the tendency to act impulsively is rampant, particularly among staff who treat disturbed adolescent inpatients. Rinsley (1968) sees a polarity between what he calls the "patch and dismiss" unreflective approach in acute settings and an intensive "interpretive" approach, in which one may have several months or years to allow interdisciplinary transference and countertransference to unfold.

Our approach takes into account the necessity of rapid decision making and a dynamic understanding of the object relations of adolescent patients as they emerge in the transference-countertransference. Within this brief model, clarification and interpretation are utilized.

We subscribe to Erlich's (1976) paradigm of an integrative theory that weaves together perspectives of individual treatment, family treatment, educational rehabilitative approaches, and nursing care interventions. Our philosophy is particularly informed by a belief that family work is essential with adolescent inpatients in an acute setting. Since it is necessary to formulate rapid interpretive interventions, it is helpful to view the actual parental figures on whom the internal self-representations are based, thus providing a "shortcut" to understanding. Moreover, when parents are involved, there is less opportunity for them to become alienated and scapegoated, which, in turn, can lead to either avoidance or too much emphasis placed on the adolescent's internalized conflict.

Our consultative philosophy is based on our belief that interdisciplinary staff functions as a therapeutic or dysfunctional family, depending on their capacity to be aware of and monitor countertransferential reactions. These reactions are dealt with in individual supervision, regularly scheduled adolescent interdisciplinary group meetings, and joint family therapy supervisory sessions.

404

In individual supervision, each professional is urged to become curious about issues as they reflect intense, personalized, or unusual reactions that may impinge on objectivity and therapeutic intervention. Since we are an academic center that trains young professionals, particular attention is paid to identification of the young trainees with adolescents who are close to their age.

Adolescent group meetings are led by the chief adolescent psychiatrist and attended by the social work family supervisor, head nurse, and specialized adolescent activities therapy supervisor. In these meetings, open expression of affect is encouraged, and empathic support is given. There is a commitment to move beyond affect to conceptualize staff disagreements and splitting as reflective of the psychopathology of the patient/family. Development of treatment strategies takes place to minimize mutual acting out within the countertransference. Didactic teaching about limit setting, adolescent psychopathology, and countertransference encourages mastery and diminution of staff reactivity.

Joint family therapy supervision allows the psychiatric resident and social worker an opportunity to explore the powerful influence of family dynamics as it reverberates within their countertransferential reactions. Encouragement is given to open discussion of differing views that may serve as a mirror of the family's psychopathology. The joint nature of the supervision strives for a synthesis of individual and systemic points of view, which is crucial, given the intense feelings evoked by distressed, frightened families of adolescent inpatients.

Impromptu meetings are scheduled by any of the supervisors to explore what may be viewed as countertransferential crises. These meetings are attended by all supervisors and trainees and aim for a resolution of countertransferential impasses and a development of revised treatment strategies, if indicated.

In all these forums, we strive for a "holding environment" of sorts, where professional staff can feel safe to struggle, disagree, explore feelings and conflicts, and, ultimately, come to a resolution of countertransferential roadblocks.

The following case will illustrate the dynamic effect of countertransference in working with adolescents in an acute setting and ways in which the interdisciplinary consultative team intervenes.

Jennifer, a waif-like, ethereal looking, seventeen-year-old girl of unusual charm and intelligence, lived with her mother and father, who were both ministers in the same church. Jennifer's two older brothers attended colleges in different cities. Jennifer dated the onset of her problems to the previous year, when her two closest friends began dating boys and she felt alone, rejected, detached, and suicidal. At the time, she developed angry outbursts at her mother, whom she screamed at, but she refused to talk about her feelings afterward. She felt that she was "taking up space" and should "move on by dying." During the three weeks prior to admission, Jennifer made three minor suicide attempts: one after a fight with her mother; a second after her twenty-nine-year-old boyfriend sought to change the nature of their relationship to a "friendship"; and a third after she missed a service at her parents' church. Only after the last of these did her mother seek psychiatric attention. At admission, Jennifer reported mild insomnia, bored mood, fatigue, and poor concentration. On admission, she saw herself as getting along better with her father, who was more intellectual than her "anxious" mother, with whom she felt she could not talk.

In spite of her symptoms, Jennifer continued to receive all As at a prestigious private school. The September prior to admission, marking the first school year at home without her brothers, she described as lonely, as the family spent little time together. Although she had friends, her role was the confidante. She felt uncomfortable sharing her own worries with girlfriends. She had always been the easy, "good" girl in her family. The patient's social life revolved around her family's church, but she had recently considered conversion to Judaism because of a sense of belonging that she perceived Jews to have.

Jennifer's mother revealed symptoms of depression for the preceding year. She had experienced recent deaths of her two closest female friends and her own mother's deteriorating course of Alzheimer's disease. She had felt closest to her own mother, in whom she confided her innermost thoughts. Just prior to the admission of her daughter, she had accepted a job in another church, where she would be chief minister and which was further away from the family home.

The patient's father was quiet, pensive, removed, and closed and appeared seductive with his daughter, who allied with her father against her mother. The father described having gone through a "midlife" crisis seven years prior to Jennifer's admission. He had stopped work for four months, found himself contemplating the meaning of life, and had intermittent thoughts of suicide.

The parents as a couple appeared concerned about Jennifer but constricted, controlled, and difficult to engage. There appeared to be rivalry about who was the better parent in the midst of an overt agreement about parenting issues.

Course of Treatment

Jennifer signed herself into the hospital. She wrote, "I believe I should go in because I do not think the problem can be dealt with from my own home and I need a different environment to figure things out."

Jennifer was hospitalized for four months on an acute psychiatric inpatient unit that provides treatment to patients of varying ages and diagnoses. She was treated with individual psychotherapy by a psychiatric resident and attended the hospital school and group activities as part of a separate adolescent program. The psychiatric resident and social worker treated the family in weekly sessions.

On admission, Jennifer seemed like an "empty shell" with a remoteness similar to that of her parents. She was relieved to be in the hospital and felt that she would become suicidal if she returned home. Early on, her parents revealed that they had kept Jennifer's suicide attempts hidden from her brothers, at the same time questioning the necessity of hospitalization. Jennifer reported feeling "shamed" and spoke of "something missing—new or old, comfortable or secure."

During the course of hospitalization, significant secrets unfolded that had dramatic reverberations within Jennifer, her parents, and the interdisciplinary team. The revelation of these secrets precipitated countertransferential crises that, when understood and monitored, led to deeper understanding and progression of treatment.

The first secret was that Jennifer's boyfriend was a hospital staff member. The psychiatrist and social worker initially kept this fact a secret from unit staff and the family supervisor; in supervisory sessions, they appeared lifeless and uninvolved (as the patient and family did). Although Jennifer feared that her boyfriend's career might be in jeopardy, the liaison was revealed to the parents, and a recommendation was made to transfer the patient to another hospital. The parents felt we were "trying to sweep our problems under the carpet." Some staff believed that Jennifer ought to be transferred because of confidentiality and the risk of objectivity being compromised. Given the patient's age, there was vociferous outrage as well about the inappropriateness of this liaison. Once a decision was made to keep the patient in our hospital, Jennifer developed vegetative signs of depression and became visibly sad. She expressed alternating rage and profound concern about her mother's incessant crying. It had by now become clear that Jennifer's mother had parentified her.

The second secret was revealed by Jennifer's mother. A year prior to hospitalization, she told Jennifer that her birth had been an "accident," reassuring her that she had been a "special gift," nonetheless.

The family therapists felt "burdened" by the mother's sadness, tears, guilt, rage, and ambivalence about keeping Jennifer in the hospital. They also experienced anger about the mother's expectation that Jennifer nurture her and the fact of Jennifer's accidental conception. In individual and joint supervision, after affect was explored, the therapists were encouraged to view their feelings of burden and anger as part of an identificatory process with the patient.

The third secret was revealed indirectly by the father's seductive behavior toward Jennifer in a family session. The family therapists found themselves "looking away." They raised the issue in individual and family supervision, where they discussed their outrage and discomfort about the incestuous tone of the father-daughter interaction. The therapists confronted the issue with the father, who revealed that his wife had battled with him about inappropriately touching the patient in the past.

Jennifer's father revealed a fourth secret. Seven years prior to the hospitalization, he had had a "platonic" affair with a woman in the parents' church. Jennifer's mother spoke about her sorrow about this liaison, which had not been terminated, as promised. It was at this point that Jennifer's mother revealed that her move to another church was motivated by her humiliation about her husband's relationship and also an attempt to protect his reputation. After the secret was shared with the family, Jennifer began more openly to express longing for comfort, predictability, and nurturing. Interdisciplinary staff encouraged her to ventilate her yearning and anger while confronting her perceived lack of concern and aloofness of the staff as Jennifer's projections based on fear of closeness and disappointment. Whereas initially Jennifer had been remote and compliant but disdainful toward the nurses, a turning point occurred during her psychiatrist's vacation. A team decision was made that the patient be urged to talk to nursing staff before and after passes since it was at these times that she tended to have tantrums and suicidal impulses. After returning from her mother's farewell party at church, Jennifer spoke of her sadness about her mother's moving on, leaving the family behind. Nurses noted Jennifer was more affectually authentic and no longer abrupt with them.

Further pivotal countertransferential points revolved around the therapist's vacation, outpatient treatment, and termination. During the therapist's vacation, a plan was formulated to mobilize Jennifer's return to her prestigious private school. Staff was split around this decision. Jennifer's therapist felt that it was important to get the patient back to her former functional level. The activities therapist felt that the patient's poor concentration and depression militated against her return. Jennifer left school the day prior to the therapist's return because of difficulty concentrating. In the first session after vacation, she spoke of her loneliness but felt that she could "rediscover her feelings" now that her therapist had returned. The therapist explored her unrealistic expectation of having needed to see Jennifer as a "prize" who could function intellectually while she was away.

After the therapist returned from another vacation, Jennifer's mother reported an "explosive fight" with her daughter. Jennifer agreed that most of her anger at her mother was due to her anger about her therapist's vacation. Jennifer said, "I know I really need you now. It's hard to admit that. I don't want anything to jeopardize our relationship. I guess I'm afraid you'll leave me. I need to be your good girl too." In the last phase of hospitalization, Jennifer was verbal about her anger at her therapist. At the same time, she exhibited playfulness, was more related to other adolescents, and engaged in more normative adolescent behavior.

Heated debates about follow-up outpatient psychotherapy dominated family sessions. When the mother revealed her preference for a seventy-eight-year-old female psychiatrist as a therapist for Jennifer after discharge, Jennifer's therapist was outraged and suggested that she treat Jennifer. The patient had hoped for this offer but had feared being a burden on her therapist. A stalemate existed until the therapist explored her anger at the mother, whom she viewed as demanding and narcissistic. In a family session, the mother admitted to feeling mistrusted, disdained, treated as the real patient, left out of decisions about school and treatment, and, most important, envious of the therapist's and Jennifer's relationship. The therapist reassured the mother about the ongoing importance of her continuing relationship with Jennifer and also promised continued communication with the parents

about Jennifer's progress in outpatient treatment. The parents ultimately agreed to allow their daughter to continue with the therapist in
outpatient psychotherapy.

During the final phase of hospitalization, the interdisciplinary staff
had difficulty setting a discharge date. Supervisory and group meetings
revealed that the staff's reluctance to set a date was based on feelings
of loss, deep pleasure in the work with this rewarding patient, and
hesitation about acknowledging the impending end of the intense inpatient stay.

On the day of discharge, Jennifer left a parting note that read:

Dear Next Inhabitant:
    This is now your room, as it was mine for four months. I hope
you will not be here as long as I have; however, it is not a bad
place as long as there are people here who you get along with
pretty well. It can even be fun sometimes, believe it or not. A few
tips: 1) Don't be afraid of the people here. We aren't a bunch of
psychopathic axe-murderers; 2) The toilet in the bathroom does
not work . . . Don't worry; that's not urine in the bowl. It's just
aged water. The bathtub is barely functional as well. I've written
a note to get it fixed, but who knows when they will come and
what they will do. Everything was okay before except that one
had to pump the toilet many times for it to flush; the workmen
came and somehow reduced everything to its present state; 3) A
sense of humor is a necessity here. Don't take everybody and
everything too seriously.
    This room will be your "blank sheet" to make your personal
statement on. You can make your room a temporary home, and
learn what is essential to you as well. Good luck, and may your
life be free soon.

Discussion

It was Freud's (1905) abortive effort to treat an adolescent girl, Dora,
that brought him face to face with the phenomenon of countertransference. Ironically, there are some striking similarities between Dora and
Jennifer. Both girls were approximately the same age, treated for three
to four months, and ostensibly more attached to and identified with
their fathers. For both, themes of blackmail, revenge, threats of sui-

cide, and annihilation predominated. More important, for both, the seductive and more conscious tie to the father disguised an unconscious preoedipal yearning for the maternal object. In the case of Jennifer, the capacity of the interdisciplinary staff to recognize and deal with countertransferential phenomena allowed for an unfolding of Jennifer's core, internalized conflict within the interdisciplinary transference.

Jennifer's object relations transpired at a preoedipal level in which oral and anal conflicts predominated. The regression that ensued to an "angry anacliticism" can be viewed as a struggle over "basic identity" and an attempt to achieve "mastery and control" (Rinsley 1968).

We see Jennifer's conflicts around separateness, mastery, and control of impulses compounded by her "family's regressive use of each other" (Rinsley 1968). Her adolescent developmental tasks of separation-individuation could not proceed until her "identity crisis" (or resolution of split-off self-representations of the parental objects) could be addressed. Her identity seemed an amalgam of the disparate aspects of her parents. She had, thus, developed a "false self" (her charming, "good-girl" facade) in which she was confidante and "special gift" to both parents. Her quest for identity and individuation and her profound yearning for belonging may be found within the viscissitudes of the transference-countertransference paradigm.

The hospital staff passionately adopted this articulate, insightful girl, who mutually adopted the staff. Positive transference and countertransference predominated in the beginning phase of hospitalization, characterized by intense rescue fantasies (Esman 1988). The staff viewed the family as crucial to Jennifer's recovery and involved them in treatment. A negative aspect of the adoption process began as the family therapists overidentified with Jennifer, tending to view the family as withholding and resistant. They saw the mother as more pathologically disturbed than the father, echoing Jennifer's tendency to utilize splitting as a defense.

A dramatic countertransferential crisis was addressed when the "forbidden secret" of Jennifer's clandestine relationship with a hospital staff member was shared with the family therapists. Their identification with the patient replicated the secretive mode of the family by withholding the "secret" from the supervisor. The horror, disbelief, and titillation that developed among the interdisciplinary staff centered around professional ethics, incestuous relationships, and the retaliatory act of seeking hospitalization at her boyfriend's hospital. Reactions to erotic and aggressive acting out were explored in the staff's individual supervision. Interdisciplinary staff meetings moved the group beyond intense countertransferential reactions to a formulation of focused goals. The adolescent team consultant and social work and activities therapy supervisors concurred that we could engage Jennifer in further treatment. Couple sessions were conducted with the patient and boyfriend to set limits on acting out. The ability of the staff to transcend their reactivity made it possible for Jennifer to remain in the hospital and discover her "true self."

The next period ushered in rich clinical material about Jennifer's longing for belonging, along with a burgeoning of the positive transference to the therapist, who became the good introject. The split-off bad introject was projected onto nurses, who were perceived as unavailable. Nurses discussed their negative countertransference, thereby controlling their tendency to act out the "bad introject" by withdrawing.

Countertransference was again evoked by the father's seductiveness with Jennifer. A flurry of emotionally laden discussions ensued, with treatment delayed. Once the issue was taken up in supervision and in the group conference, the father was confronted, and the therapeutic field was again clear to deal with Jennifer's preoedipal yearning for the maternal object.

Other secrets that unfolded allowed the staff more fully to appreciate Jennifer's valiant attempt to understand and to resolve painful affect and conflicts about identity. Positive countertransference toward Jennifer, along with rescue fantasies, increased at the revelation of her father's clandestine "affair," her symbolic meaning as a "special gift" to both parents, and her having been an unwanted child. These secrets, however, aroused negative countertransference toward the parents, who were viewed as having used Jennifer as a narcissistic extension for their own unmet needs. Ironically, the last two of these secrets were mirrored in the staff's premature decision to send Jennifer back to school during her therapist's vacation.

Unrecognized countertransference contaminated the decision. This reflected the staff's adoption of Jennifer while ignoring her intense separation anxiety, reenacting the trauma of abandonment within her family. After the vacation, staff reassessed the school decision, noting the seductive pull toward viewing Jennifer as their "brilliant, special child."

Negative countertransference toward the mother climaxed around the choice of an outpatient therapist. Competition over control may be seen as a reenactment of the struggle between the parents and, on a deeper level, as the mother's feeling abandoned by the therapist in the transference, replicating the loss of her own mother as confidante—thus her preference for an elderly female therapist for Jennifer. An empathic alliance with the mother increased after exploration of countertransference in individual and family supervision.

Countertransference again colored the setting of a termination date, as Jennifer had become a "special prize" patient who offered unusual narcissistic gratification to the inpatient staff. Group meetings focused on the former issue as well as mourning and separation. As Jennifer's parting note indicates, the mutual "adoption process," as part of the transference-countertransference dialectic, had been resolved. Jennifer was, thus, able to separate from her adopted "temporary home."

Conclusions

The experience of working within an interdisciplinary countertransferential model makes for a mutually exciting learning experience for both supervisor and supervisee. Within a short-term setting, it represents a commitment to maintaining a reflective, analytic stance while, at the same time, working quickly to formulate behavioral intervention. This approach challenges us to look within both ourselves and our adolescent patients in the midst of fiscal constraints, pressure to discharge rapidly, and a tendency to search for easy answers to perplexing, complicated problems.

NOTE

This chapter was presented in Paris on November 17, 1990, at a conference entitled "Journée Nationale 'Perspectives Psychiatriques' le Passage à l'Age Adult: Pathologies et Strategies Therapeutiques."

REFERENCES

Erlich, H. S. 1976. Growth opportunities in the hospital: intensive inpatient treatment of adolescents. In A. H. Esman, ed. *The Psychi-*

atric Treatment of Adolescents. New York: International Universities Press, 1983.

Esman, A. H. 1988. Rescue fantasies. *Psychoanalytic Quarterly* 56:263–270.

Freud, S. 1905. Fragment of an analysis of a case of hysteria. *Standard Edition* 7:7–124. London: Hogarth, 1953.

Greenberg, L.; Haiman, S.; and Esman, A. H. 1987. Countertransference during the acute psychiatric hospitalization of the adolescent. *Adolescent Psychiatry* 14:316–331.

Greenson, R. 1954. The struggle against identification. *Journal of the American Psychoanalytic Association* 2:200–217.

Halperin, D.; Lauro, G.; Miscione, F.; Rebhan, J.; Schnabolk, J.; and Shachter, B. 1981. Countertransference issues in a transitional residential treatment program for troubled adolescents. *Adolescent Psychiatry* 9:559–577.

Kernberg, O. 1976. *Borderline Conditions and Pathological Narcissism*. New York: Aronson.

Palmer, A. J.; Harper, G.; and Rivinus, T. M. 1983. The "adoption process" in the inpatient treatment of children and adolescents. *Journal of the American Academy of Child Psychiatry* 22:286–295.

Rinsley, D. B. 1965. Intensive hospital treatment of adolescents: an object-relations view. *Psychiatric Quarterly* 39:405–429.

Rinsley, D. B. 1968. The theory and practice of intensive residential treatment of adolescents. In A. H. Esman, ed. *The Psychiatric Treatment of Adolescents*. New York: International Universities Press, 1983.

Stanton, A. H., and Schwartz, M. S. 1954. *The Mental Hospital*. New York: Basic.

Steinberg, D. 1986. *The Adolescent Unit: Work and Teamwork in Adolescent Psychiatry*. New York: Wiley.

23   DISCUSSION OF

GREENBERG AND ESMAN'S CHAPTER

HERVÉ BENHAMOU

The works of Esman and Greenberg, from New York Hospital–Cornell Medical Center, on institutional and psychotherapeutic treatment of adolescents are often referred to in the United States and deserve to be much better known in Europe.

The richness of their account, as much on the clinical as on the institutional level, shows the quality of their experience. It is a great stimulation to our own reflection on the similarities and differences between the techniques used here in France and across the Atlantic.

My own experience in France in an evening intensive-care unit for preadolescents suffering from severe behavioral disorders naturally leads me to such a process of comparison. In this unit, thirteen is the upper age limit; it was deliberately chosen because of its quasi-ritual value, precisely connected with "reaching adulthood," the theme of this national symposium. This reaching begins as early as preadolescence when the revision of identity and sexuality takes place at the time of psychical puberty, which can at times precede and anticipate biomorphological puberty in the setting of an overstimulating environment. A first comment could actually be made about the issue of therapeutic support for some youths reaching puberty and for their families. In the reported case, if one calculates, one notices that, at the age of ten, Jennifer was confronted with two difficult situations at the same time. On the one hand, her father, a minister (and a seducer), became possessed by the demon of the mid-life crisis and was unfaithful to his wife. His daughter's oncoming puberty may have increased his sexual arousal, which he then displaced onto a faithful follower of his church. Jennifer and her mother consequently felt abandoned.

On the other hand, almost at the same time, the mother was shaken by the onset of her mother's Alzheimer's disease and used Jennifer as her confidante. Jennifer, therefore, approached puberty under difficult circumstances that complicated the disentanglement of the reactivated Oedipus complex all the more since oedipal anxieties were linked with preoedipal ones, as Greenberg and Esman have clearly outlined.

Our American colleagues have not reported any precise anamnestic elements about the progress of Jennifer's puberty. In other cases, there are some more or less discrete psychical peripuberty symptoms that call for our attention. The staff must be vigilant on both clinical as well as countertransferential levels so that they can positively support a young person confronted with the accession to sexuality under problematic circumstances. Quite often, as in Jennifer's case, puberty goes on almost unnoticed within the family, with delayed effects after the event, as, for example, in the case of a later disappointment in love.

The disappointment Jennifer suffered with a man older than she was is a nodal point of the report. The breakup was followed by a suicide attempt. A second attempt took place after Jennifer missed a church service where she could have had an uncomfortable encounter with her rival, the woman still loved by her father. Coincidentally, Jennifer managed to sign herself into the very hospital where her ex-boyfriend worked. The fact that this man belonged to the hospital staff was initially kept as an institutional secret, and that leads me to a second remark. Remember that this is a secret shared, on the one hand, by Jennifer, by the resident psychiatrist (who is at once her individual therapist and a joint family cotherapist), and by the social worker trainee (who is also the family cotherapist) and, on the other hand, by the rest of the team, including the supervisors.

One begins to wonder if the secret was not partly maintained because of the very setting of supervision and teaching. Indeed, in such a setting, relatively organized into a hierarchy, supervisors are particularly subject to superego projections from both patients and staff members—for example, the social worker and the psychiatrist trainees.

For example, if one considers the psychiatric resident, one of the administrative psychiatrists was the supervisor during Jennifer's hospitalization; this psychiatrist, who contributes to institutional analysis, holds responsibilities within the institution and is also a teacher who might have an influence on the resident's educational experience. During group meetings, this plurality of functions might well interfere with the resident's free expression of both pleasure and aggression, not only toward patients but also toward other members of the staff and above all toward the supervisors, to the extent that they are the focus of forbidding superego projections, as in Jennifer's case.

A psychoanalyst dealing exclusively with the institution could be most useful in overcoming the difficulties of analyzing institutional countertransference created by the intermingling of hierarchy and reality. This psychoanalyst, who would not hold any responsibility within the hierarchy and who would not directly meet the patients and their families, would have less difficulty in spotting projective and repetitive phenomena induced by the patients. Nevertheless, the treatment setting pursued by our American colleagues was effective if we consider Jennifer's development throughout her hospitalization, which came to an end with a letter she wrote as a gesture to the next patient who would occupy the room, as well as to the staff. Fortunately, Jennifer was not transferred, as her mother had been when she moved to another church. Even her ex-boyfriend's belonging to the hospital staff was cleverly dealt with, and the high risk of confusion between fantasy and reality was finally averted rather quickly.

We know that the rapid discharge of patients in the United States is due in part to financial contraints from insurance companies and that it complicates the working through of investment and separation within the institution. We also know that adolescents favor acting over sexualized thought. All this combines to hamper our thinking—hence the necessity to carry on, especially with foreign colleagues, our consideration of the most efficient methods of analyzing institutional countertransference, in order to outline the most appropriate therapeutic strategies.

NOTE

This discussion was presented in Paris on November 17, 1990, at a conference entitled "Journée Nationale 'Perspectives Psychiatriques' le Passage à l'Age Adulte: Pathologies et Strategies Therapeutiques." It was translated for publication here by Claude Sevestre.

ROBERT M. GALATZER-LEVY

Adolescent violence has become an overwhelming problem in this country. Approximately 15 percent of persons arrested for violent crimes are under eighteen years of age, virtually all of them adolescents (Federal Bureau of Investigation 1978–1987, quoted in Benedek and Cornell 1989). FBI data also indicate that, during the last decade, approximately 8 percent of homicide arrests are violent adolescents. The objects of adolescent violence are most likely to be other adolescents, but the victims of adolescent violence are not limited to those directly physically harmed. Very considerable psychological trauma is associated with witnessing violence, a common occurrence in violent communities (Eth 1989). Homicide is a significant contributor to excess mortality in black ghetto populations (McCord and Freeman 1990), where the problem of adolescent violence is of overwhelming social significance.

Psychiatric and sociological investigations have demonstrated a wide range of determinants of adolescent violence (Cornell 1989; Katz 1988; Marohn 1990). Despite careful investigations of adolescent populations, little of the depth psychology of violent adolescents has been clarified. This partly reflects the heterogeneous nature of the population, the multiply determined nature of any complex action, and the difficulty in studying violent adolescents from a psychological standpoint. However, in my clinical experience, and in the experience of many workers who have approached adolescent violence from a variety of viewpoints, certain issues do seem to recur, especially those issues that have to do with the relation of violence to the adolescent's experience of the self.

This chapter reviews psychoanalytic contributions to the study of adolescent violence, difficulties in the psychoanalytic study of violent adolescents, and the relation of self psychological concepts to adolescent violence. It is proposed that much adolescent violence is best understood as an attempt to restore cohesive and vital self-experience.

Problems in Studying Violence from a Psychoanalytic Viewpoint

Violence is hard to study because of our own attitudes toward it. Although violence pervades all historical eras, there is an equally pervasive view, at least in Western European societies, that violence is abnormal. Although war, murder, and assault are concrete realities in most people's lives, acts of violence are almost always regarded as anomalous, aberrant intrusions into normal living. The study of the psychology of violence is further complicated because it is often evaluated differently depending on how successfully it is rationalized. Especially when conducted on a large scale, violent acts are almost always rationalized as means to achieve otherwise unreachable ends. Mass killings and destruction of populations are explained as efforts to "civilize" the victims, to protect them from evil ideologies, or to ensure their economic well-being (Fein 1979; Staub 1989). We must understand the nearly universal need to rationalize and deny violence as a first step in comprehending adolescent violence.

Adolescent gangs, like nations, almost always explain violence on a rational basis. No one avows a wish to fight, but avoiding a fight can risk turf, honor, or assault from unscrupulous rivals (Keiser 1969; Rosenberg and Silverstein 1969; Suttles 1967; Yablonsky 1966). Maintaining honor or ideology is the best rationale for violence. The code of the old West, which dominated the lives of adolescents and young men in the southwestern United States in the latter half of the nineteenth century, is, "I'd rather die than run." A significant portion of Americans in the middle of this century believed, "Better dead than Red." In the exceedingly violent fourteenth-century Chinese classic *Outlaws of the Marsh,* many passages recount the care with which opponents arrange for dignity to be affronted to justify violence. In many episodes of this book, mortal enemies are invited to share dinner so that their poor table manners may justify their decapitation (Shi Nai'an and Luo Guanzhong 1988). Ethnic or ideological differences are also good reasons for violence. In the United States today, the thinness of this rationalization becomes evident. Significant numbers of youngsters have been killed because the color of their clothing was incorrect in that it either suggested that they claimed membership in gangs to which they did not belong or indicated membership in gangs to which their assailants were opposed. Thus, youngsters' statements, like those of adults, about the reason for their violence are poor guides to understanding their actions. They may, however, give hints about underlying motives.

Psychoanalysts tend to share the common idea that violence is a means to an end. Let us briefly consider psychoanalytic thinking about violence. For most of his career, Freud believed that violence and aggression were the logical consequences of competitive biological forces. He derived his ideas from Darwin. Darwin (1859) believed that nature is "bloody of tooth and claw" because beating sexual competitors in the struggle for mates leads to reproductive fitness. Until the end of the First World War, Freud adopted a position consistent with the social Darwinism of his age—man is forced to fight on the rational basis of sexual opportunity and reproductive fitness. He thus viewed competitive aggression as part of our biological endowment (Sulloway 1979). This instrumental aggression, however, did not reflect a primary urge toward destruction.

Following the First World War and the death of his beloved daughter Sophie, Freud reformulated his conceptions about violence and aggression. He took a far gloomier position, holding that there is a primary destructive impulse in man (Freud 1920). His ideas were politely ignored by most of the psychoanalytic community, perhaps because they were so therapeutically unpromising.

Ferenczi (1938) wrote poetically of the impulse toward death, but Melanie Klein (1927, 1935, 1945, 1975) was the first not only to concur with Freud in the idea of a primary death instinct but also to detail the psychological mechanisms operative in hate, destruction, and envy. She showed how a variety of psychological phenomena could be explained on the basis of destructive motives, but, more important, she demonstrated several means, such as projection, splitting, and projective identification, by which the individual might deal with these problematic impulses. Each of these mechanisms shares the feature that bad impulses are expelled from the experience of the self and good objects. It is not I who hates him but he who hates me. I do not love and hate the same person at once, but rather there are two psychologically distinct people, one of whom I love because he is good, the other I hate because he is evil. Studies of hatred and destruction by Klein and her followers, continuing into the present, are a rich source for understanding how it is that humans can commit so many "inhuman" acts (Segal 1988). If I regard another person as basically unhuman or as a pure culture of evil and corruption, I feel little compunction about destroying him. I may even regard it as a moral responsibility to overcome the squeamish sentimentality that stands in the way of my violence. If I, like many of the doctors who worked in Nazi concentration camps, separate the unpleasant, dirty work that I must do to earn a living from my true, kindly, family-oriented self, I can perform the most heinous acts while continuing to see myself as a man of virtue (Lifton 1986a, 1986b).

Outside the Kleinian group, psychoanalysts continue to regard aggression as basically instrumental. Aggression is seen as a means toward other aims. People act to obtain pleasure and sometimes must overcome obstacles that stand in their way. A primary aggressive energy was postulated that is to be used in the ultimate service of pleasure. To be civilized, the child must tame this energy and bring it under the control of the ego (Hartman 1939, 1950; Hartman, Kris, and Loewenstein 1946; Hartman and Loewenstein 1962). The problem of "unacceptably" violent people is the inadequate ego structures that fail to contain aggression and ensure its effective instrumental expression. Empirical research using this point of view illustrated how environmental failures can lead to lack of control over aggressive impulses. Parents can stimulte aggressive impulses that are too strong to be managed by immature egos by unduly frustrating children and making premature demands for independent functioning or by providing inadequate models of the control of aggression (Parens 1973, 1979, 1987).

Consider the child who is beaten. At the same moment as intense aggression is mobilized in her, she is shown a model in which aggressive impulses are violently enacted. She is terrified to direct her own aggression against the person who hurts her. It is little wonder that overt aggression will find expression elsewhere.

Other psychoanalytic theorists have emphasized the normal role of aggression in separation-individuation. In this point of view, to be a separate person requires pushing others away and angry leaving (Parens 1987).

Thus, psychoanalytic theorists have approached the problem of violence from several viewpoints. But none of these approaches, I believe, adequately addresses the central question of what violence is all about. It was a step forward to posit a primary aggressive drive because this concept moved away from the denial of violence. But this postulation simply disguised our ignorance by moving it into the area of biological or psychological givens of the individual. The very useful understanding of the mechanism by which people disguised the intensity of their aggression from themselves helped explain how aggressive impulses could be so little affected by morality but still left the sources of the aggression unclear. Similarly, describing the violent person in terms of inadequate ego resources says little about the meaning and motive for aggression within the person.

The problem of developing an adequate psychoanalytic theory of violence is further exacerbated because violent individuals tend not to be engaged in psychoanalysis. The psychoanalyst's most formidable research tool, in-depth exploration of a patient's psychology in the psychoanalytic situation, is rarely available to understand violence. Many of the psychoanalytic explorations of violence in young people were so dominated by the need to control, manage, and treat patients that it is hard to differentiate true psychological insights into the youngster's psychology from charismatically asserted principles that aided in the management of these very difficult situations (Friedlander 1960; Redl and Wineman 1952). But clarifying the psychological needs that are partly met by providing adequate structure for the action-prone adolescent is a far more subtle matter (Marohn, Dalle-Molle, McCarter, and Linn 1980). Violent youths can often be controlled by rigorous military discipline, but this hardly implies that these youngsters' problems resulted from not being raised in a boot camp or that their solution lies in such institutions. Likewise, the effectiveness of programs designed to promote children's ego development does not imply that the children's problem lay in faulty development of psychological structures.

The researches of general psychologists have supported many commonsense notions about aggression like the intimate association of frustration with aggression (Dollard et al. 1939). But the depth-psychological understanding of aggression and violence remains elusive.

422

ROBERT M. GALATZER-LEVY

The Self and Self Pathology

Starting in the late 1950s, Heinz Kohut (Kohut 1957) began a revolution in psychoanalytic thought. Like many analysts of the time, he was frustrated with psychoanalytic theory that explained human experience through its reduction to physiological tension (Cohler and Galatzer-Levy 1991; Galatzer-Levy and Cohler 1990). Many psychological phenomena could be explained in terms of ego psychology. This perspective assumed biological drives that sought discharge and an ego that mediates between drives, morality, and external reality. However, many of the explanations seemed strained and forced. They often gave the impression of intellectual sleight of hand. Careful study of ego psychology revealed that often its apparent explanation evaporated into tautologies or the renaming of clinical phenomena. A large group of analysts in the early 1970s rejected psychoanalytic metapsychology while retaining the clinical theories of psychoanalysis (Klein 1976).

Clinical problems were more important than these theoretical issues in leading many analysts away from classical theories. A substantial group of patients was unresponsive to interpretive work rooted in ego psychology. Kohut, along with many other psychoanalysts, most notably Winnicott, Fairburn, and Mahler, noted that many of these patients suffered from experiences of a self that was incoherent, fragmented, or lacking in vitality. The patients sometimes spoke directly of not knowing who they were or what they desired. At other times, they seemed to suffer from empty depressions, feelings of lifelessness, ennui, and meaninglessness. These feelings might be expressed directly or in symbolic form as hypochondriasis (Galatzer-Levy 1982; Kohut 1971; Kohut and Wolf 1978). Other patients seemed to have difficulties because they formed relations with other people designed to compensate for the distressing feelings about their selves. They formed addictive relationships or unrealistic idealizations because, without these relationships, they felt incomplete, fragmented, or lifeless. A final group of patients attempted to reestablish a vigorous cohesive self through actions of various kinds. These patients were said to suffer from narcissistic behavior disorders. A variety of enactments, including many sexual perversions and many forms of substance abuse, could be understood in this context as attempts to regulate self-states.

Kohut (1984), along with researchers like George Klein (1976), realized that Freud's psychological theories, so-called metapsychology, are not the core of psychoanalysis. Freud's metapsychology was one, among many, attempts to apply the ideas of nineteenth-century physics to psychology. It was never a satisfactory theory, but, by the mid-twentieth century, its inadequacies became glaring. What was and is uniquely valuable is Freud's psychoanalytic method and the understanding of meanings and motives that comes from it.

The psychoanalytic setup allows the analyst the unique opportunity to immerse himself, in depth, in the subjective world of another over extended periods of time. Using an exploration of the patient's experience of the analyst and the analyst's trained empathy, a rich picture of how the patient constructs meaning and the nature of his wishes and needs emerges in the psychoanalytic setting. This method proved enormously fruitful in understanding and treating neurosis. Neurotic patients regularly formed intense transferences to the analyst that reproduced early pathogenic experiences with the parents. As these transferences were worked through, the unconscious pathogenic ideas were reworked, and the patient liberated from his neurosis. These patients' major concerns centered on their conscious and unconscious love and hatred of other people.

As early as 1911, Freud recognized that an important group of patients was dominated by concerns about their self-experience (Freud 1911). Their psychological energies seemed to be directed toward themselves. Freud believed that they could not be treated using psychoanalysis since they lacked the basic interest in others that was required to form significant transferences—the main tool of psychoanalytic work, the analysis of the transference, was therefore unavailable in their treatment.

Kohut's most important contribution was the discovery that Freud was mistaken in this regard. Kohut recognized that these patients, who were referred to as suffering from narcissistic personality disorders or disorders of the self, could be analyzed. In the analytic situation, they engaged with the analyst intensely. These engagements were not based on an experience of the analyst as the object of love or hate. The analyst was not primarily experienced as a person with an independent initiative of his own. Instead, the patient's experiences of the analyst were rooted in the analyst's function as necessary for the intactness of the patient's self. The patient might feel good and alive because he felt responded to or invigorated because he was in relation to someone whom he conceived as powerful and wise. Kohut described three major groups of transferences of this type. In idealizing transferences, the patient feels alive and good because he is in relation to a powerful, admired figure. In mirror transferences, the experience of being appreciated and responded to leads to a sense of a coherent self. In twinship transferences, the patient's self is supported through the sense of being with someone who is like himself.

Transferences like these had been noticed by many psychoanalysts before Kohut. However, earlier analysts interpreted the transferences as derivatives of the well-understood competitive and loving transferences observed in neurosis. They were generally understood as means to disguise more basic drives toward the analyst. Idealization, for example, was seen as a defense against the wish to denigrate the analyst (Fenichel 1945). The conscious wish for the analyst's enthusiastic response was interpreted as a disguise for exhibitionistic longings. Kohut believed that premature interpretations of these transferences, in terms of such defensive purposes, were not only mistaken but interrupted and confused the development of the transferences. If instead of making these interpretations the analyst adopted a truly neutral attitude, allowing transferences to emerge and interpreting primarily the way the patient avoided knowing of the existence of the transference, a large group of patients formed intense transferences to the analyst in which the analyst was used to support an endangered self. He called these transferences "selfobject transferences."

The systematic exploration of these transference situations allowed new and more profound insights into what came to be called "disorders of the self." A wide range of ideas emerged from these investigations. The most important of these ideas is the notion of "selfobject function." The experience of self-continuity, coherence, and liveliness depends on experiences with other people, who in this context serve to support the self-experience or may be aspects of it.

Selfobject functioning is particularly obvious in infancy and early childhood, when selfobject failures result in immediate and manifest distress. Several investigators besides Kohut (e.g., Bowlby 1973, 1982, 1988; and Winnicott 1958, 1960, 1964, 1965) described aspects of early selfobject function. However, selfobject functioning ordinarily continues across the course of life (Cohler and Galatzer-Levy 1990; Galatzer-Levy and Cohler, in press). More mature forms of selfobject function are more difficult to describe because the need for selfobjects is less obvious as the individual grows older. Selfobject functioning becomes integrated with different uses of other people, so that "pure cultures" of selfobject function occur less frequently. The individual develops a larger repertoire of selfobjects so that interference in one selfobject relationship has a less profound effect. And the person responds less immediately to selfobject function failure. For the relatively healthy individual, when selfobjects function well, they are virtually invisible. They are like the oxygen we breathe—a matter of little or no interest when it is available but urgently distressing in its absence.

In the analysis of disorders of the self when the selfobject function of the analyst is interrupted for whatever reason, the symptoms of an endangered self become apparent, either in loss of vigor or coherence of the self or in emergency efforts to maintain the self such as a return to urgent searches for external confirmation, perverse sexual activity, or addictive behaviors.

Narcissistic Rage

One of the most important of the responses to the loss of selfobject function is narcissistic rage (Kohut 1972). Unlike instrumental aggression, narcissistic rage does not aim at the achievement of a concrete goal. Sometimes thinly rationalized as attempts to achieve some desirable end, narcissistic rage appears to be almost a pure culture of destructiveness. It combines a sense of profound urgency, a feeling that something is desperately wrong, and a wish to harm, damage, or destroy. In mild cases, it involves a sense of smashing or damaging. It is essentially without object; striking out at anything handy will do.

The experience of mild versions of narcissistic rage is common. Think of stubbing your toe. Most people feel momentarily furious at such an accident. There is an irrational desire to kick or break the offending piece of furniture and a sense that something must be done to rectify the wrong. Similarly, if an appliance such as a computer, an automobile, or a can opener fails to operate, people often feel overwhelming frustrated fury, assaulting or attempting to smash the offending object. The thing should simply work. The flow of life has been unfairly interrupted. The experience arises from an interruption of a sense of an effective and cohesive self. In fact, the fault lies in our coordination when we stub a toe. Goldstein (1947) was the first to describe narcissistic rage as part of the "catastrophic reaction" to brain injury when the individual discovers that she can no longer function properly.

A sense of self-righteousness and entitlement often accompanies these states of rage. The offending object is either experienced as part of the self or was supposed to function as an extension of the self, to simply do its job without coming to awareness, in much the same way that our bodies do as they are supposed to do. Interruptions in experiences that are supposed to "just happen" when we intend them commonly lead to intense rage and dismay.

Narcissistic rage can be acute or chronic. A sense of fury and needing to make up for past wrongs can be a way of life. Chronic narcissistic rage can range in its expression from a crusade against evils that becomes the main theme of life to a chronic sense of bitterness.

The rage may be directed internally or externally. The goal of self-injury is not to hurt the self but rather to damage the world. Fantasies of damaging the world and others through self-injury or self-harm are commonly associated with narcissistic rage. The idea, seen so commonly in adolescents, that "I'll show them!" points to several important aspects of narcissistic rage. First, it implies that the theme of revenge and the sense of righteousness are more important to self-cohesiveness than what we usually think of as the self's well-being. Second, it points to the source of difficulty in the self. Selfobject failures have led to disruptions in the self-experience, and it is the selfobject that must be punished. For these reasons, when self-destructive behavior is motivated by narcissistic rage, appeals to rational self-interest fail. In this state of mind, revenge is the route to an intact self. Until the wish for vengeance is adequately addressed, the self-damaging behavior cannot cease.

Kohut's observations about narcissistic rage have remained relatively unexplored even within self psychology. This is largely because self psychologists regard narcissistic rage as something analogous to a fever. A fever usually indicates the presence of an infection, and the doctor's job is primarily to treat the infection. Narcissistic rage indicates that something has gone gravely amiss in the central selfobject transference, and following Kohut's (1972) recommendation, the difficulty in selfobject function, rather than the rage itself, is usually investigated by self psychological psychoanalysts. As a result, self psychologists have tended not to explore the nature of this rage in depth.

This is a pity because narcissistic rage can be a fairly subtle matter. As I discussed earlier, states of rage are usually rationalized so that the recognition that one is dealing with narcissistic rage is often difficult. These rationalizations often take the form of moral righteousness or the upholding of standards. Much analytic work may be necessary before patient and analyst come to understand that apparently high ideals disguise chronic states of destructive rage. These moralistic states, whether manifest in the faculties of psychoanalytic institutes or among the members of violent street gangs, are invariably experienced as necessary to the well-being of the community, high minded, and independent of individual needs (Kernberg 1976, 1980a, 1980b, 1986). In fact, when chronic narcissistic rage is expressed as moralism, it is usually experienced consciously as selfless. The combination of narcissistic rage with identification with group ideals is such a powerful support of self-experience that most people hold on to it tenaciously.

More detailed explorations of narcissistic rage have come from sociologists and criminologists. These researchers have not associated their work with psychoanalytic investigations, but the phenomena they study seem to me to be clearly the same as those to which self psychologists refer as narcissistic rage.

Sociologists and criminologists have been consistently impressed with the extent to which violent acts are not instrumental. They do not lead to consciously desired goals. In fact, the purpose of violence, when explored in depth, seems, in many instances, to be the reestablishment of a sense of effectiveness and dignity.

Jack Katz, a sociologist, has employed observational methods that Kohut (1957) regarded as the core of psychoanalytic investigation, empathic emersion in the psychological world of the subject. In his remarkable book *The Seductions of Crime,* Katz (1988) discusses the most common form of murder, that of a spouse. The killing of spouses, with horrifying regularity, is precipitated by materially minor failures on the part of a spouse. In a case that came to my attention, a man beat his wife to death because she smoked the last cigarette in a pack. His experience as he killed her was one of righteous indignation. She had not respected him and had made him feel like less than a man by not saving the last cigarette for him. He knew that he was killing her as he beat her, but at the same time he thought that he would "teach her a lesson" by killing her. This sort of "righteous slaughter" for the purpose of reestablishing self-worth and dignity through violence is a far more common cause of homicide than violence committed in the course of committing crimes like armed robbery.

Even when violence occurs in the course of the commission of other crimes, the experience of the perpetrator is often that the victim failed to play the assigned role or did not treat the criminal with the respect that he felt was his due. The armed robber may kill precisely because his victim is not felt to fear the weapon adequately. The sense of reestablishing a vigorous, active, respected, and admired powerful self through violence is probably the leading psychological motive for violent acts. In these instances, it is the failure of selfobject transferences that precipitates violence. The gun that should have brought a mirroring response of terror and respect has failed to do so, and now it is used in the expression of narcissistic rage.

The traumatic interruption of idealization also produces narcissistic rage, often with a paranoid caste. Much adolescent fury at parents comes from the youngster's disappointment in the parent, and common denigrations of parents are statements of contrasts between the longed-for ideal parent and the disappointing perceived actuality. The "old fools," "money-grubbing pigs," and "complete wimps" are all fallen idols. The violence in most such deidealization is limited to verbal assault. However, therapists who treat borderline and psychotic adolescents should be aware that intense idealizations can be transformed into equally intense narcissistic rage when the idealized therapist fails in his role. For example, a brilliant paranoid youngster held his psychiatrist at gunpoint for several hours with every intention of killing him after discovering that some of the psychiatrist's intellectual pretensions were a sham.

The Joy of Violence

The sense of action and activity associated with actual or contemplated violence is described by many individuals as an incomparable thrill. We have only to listen to that master of violence, Genghis Khan, to sense how alive and whole violence can make an individual feel. The young man, Temuchin, later to be known as Genghis Khan, was discussing the greatest joy in life: "The greatest joy that a man can know is to conquer his enemies and drive them before him, to ride their horses and deprive them of their possessions, to make their beloved weep, and to embrace their wives and daughters" (Morton 1980, p. 115). Like satisfying sex, satisfying violence focuses the person's whole being in one direction, creating a sense of unified good function that supports the experience of the self. In trying to understand violent youngsters, the sheer joy of violence should never be underestimated.

Emilio Estavez's characterization of Billy the Kid in the movie *Young Guns* appears to have been true to the historical nineteen-year-old outlaw in many respects. In particular, killing seems to have left the young outlaw in a state close to delight. A sixteen-year-old-boy who I treated described feeling "high as could be, completely tough, totally cool," as he strode toward a high school gymnasium planning to assault another youngster who had offended him. Substitute gratification may lessen the loss. Athletics, with its thinly disguised violence, has often been successfully substituted for overt violence among delinquent youths because it provides much of the same experience of good bodily function. To some extent, the social approbations, its more regular availability, and the pleasure in the higher levels of skill required for athletics help make up some of the intensity of overt violence.

However, the adolescent who gives up violence experiences a real loss. Kohut (1971) observed that people who give up perverse sexuality, even as a result of successful psychoanalytic work, often complain that their more ordinary sexual experiences are not as intense as the perverse, narcissistically driven ones. He understood this as resulting from the confluence of narcissistic and libidinal gratifications that are commonly part of perverse sex. So too, violence carries with it an intense narcissistic gratification of excellent bodily function and power that is hard to achieve in any other way. The loss of these pleasures must be appreciated and the adolescent allowed to mourn them. Such mourning should not be suppressed for fear that the youngster will be drawn back into unacceptable conduct. It is a necessary component of making the repudiation of violence into a stable, internal psychological position.

Violence and Helplessness

Violence in adolescence is almost always the reverse side of a sense of helplessness. Sometimes it is a simple matter of being taken seriously. A sixteen-year-old whom I had seen diagnostically and to whom I had recommended analysis was unable to convince his parents of the need for such intensive treatment until he drove the family car into the side of the parents' house.

Violent youngsters often accurately perceive on some level that unresponsive selfobjects may be coerced into better functioning by the adolescent's actions. In working with violent teenagers, it is of the greatest importance that their perceptions in these matters not be realistic in regard to the therapist. If the youngster knows that violence and threats of violence are effective means of altering the therapist's emotional attitude toward him, he has little motive to abandon this effective tool in his relationship to the therapist.

In terms of doing psychoanalytic work with violent youngsters, this means that the analyst needs to be acutely and accurately aware of the conditions necessary to maintain an analytic stance. These conditions vary among analysts: some are extremely uncomfortable unless they can ensure that violence inside and outside of sessions can be completely and physically controlled if necessary; others of us are at ease with considerably less control. In any case, in order to work effectively from a psychoanalytic position with violent adolescents, the therapist must arrange for a degree of personal comfort that permits an analytic stance. Incidentally, I have worked with violent adolescents who understand the need for my comfort quite well and have been able to forgo violence as part of our working alliance because of their wish for psychoanalytic assistance.

It is, however, a mistake to think that violence is simply a powerful interpersonal manipulation by which the adolescent adopts a new tool for interpersonal interaction. For the adolescent who feels helpless, ineffective, or lifeless, violence is an instant route to a sense of power. The intensity of empowerment associated with violence is beautifully illustrated in the work of Algerian psychoanalyst and revolutionary Franz Fannon. In *The Wretched of the Earth,* Fannon (1968) first demonstrates the overwhelming psychological damage associated with colonialism. From the side of the colonized people, the experience is one of loss of a valued self. The only route to a sense of vigor and power is through identification with the oppressor. But this inevitably produces incredible tension since it entails self-hatred. Fannon sees violence as therapeutic in this context. He believed that violence is an effective tool for materially removing colonial power. But this was not his central concern. He believed that the inner life of the violent revolutionary is transformed through his actions. With regard to the immediate experience of violence, we can agree with him. He has captured the central feature of chronic narcissistic rage.

This is close to the experience of many violent youngsters. Their internal world is dominated by an everlasting sense of degradation,

431

triviality, and meaninglessness. It is against this experience that violence brings, at least temporarily, relief. Of course, this is also the problem with violence. I have not seen individuals whose sense of self is smoothly stabilized by way of violence, although this may be a limitation of my clinical experience.

The Selfobject Environment in the Origin and Treatment of Adolescent Violence

Approaches to the problem of violence that fail to address the self-experience of the adolescent must inevitably fail because, in the context of an enfeebled self, the need to reestablish a satisfying state of cohesion and vigor are matters of psychological life and death.

The environment that should have increased their sense of self-worth by providing enthusiastic responses and providing idealizable models for their development has commonly not only failed to give violent adolescents these provisions but actively attacked their sense of self-worth. The sudden, premature discovery that an idealized selfobject cannot be admired is a common source of enraged pain for adolescents. The psychologically or physically abusive parent is often the object of rage because the adolescent is traumatically confronted with the impossibility of admiring the parent at the same moment that his experience of being treated as a human being, the ordinary mirroring function of the environment, is precipitously shattered.

A thirty-year-old man in analysis scrupulously avoided any criticism of the analyst, although his associations suggested that he noticed and disapproved of a variety of the analyst's foibles. The patient deeply longed to admire the analyst and anticipated a catastrophe if he confronted any of the analyst's failings. His dreams suggested that the catastrophe lay not in the consequences of competition but in a destruction of the world if the idealization were interrupted. In fact, the patient had pleasant, ego-syntonic fantasies about athletic and intellectual competition with the analyst. In these fantasies, the analyst was not always the victor, but he *was* the perfect sportsman.

A dream clarified the situation. In the dream, the patient and the analyst were playing chess. The analyst seemed distracted and made an error that cost him his queen. He seemed increasingly confused, yelled at the patient, and started hurling chess pieces at him, making it impossible to continue the game. The dream continued with scenes of the patient wandering alone through the ruins of a burnt-out city. When the analyst asked for the patient's associations, the patient burst into tears and spoke for the first time of a fight between himself and his father. Father was a heavy drinker who beat his wife and children when drunk. When the patient was sixteen, he came home one evening to find father, once again, slapping mother. This time the adolescent intervened, stepping between them. The father tried to push the boy out of the way, but the youngster would not budge. Finally, father started grappling with him. The son pushed the father to the floor, and father struggled to get up, threatening all the time to kill the boy. The patient remembered being overwhelmed with grief and rage at this point, longing for a father he could admire and having instead an abusive "fool" who could not even beat a sixteen-year-old boy in a fight.

The willingness of violent youths to risk personal destruction to enact their rage becomes comprehensible once we understand that being violent is being psychologically alive. When the core of a person's true being is at stake, the destruction of his body matters very little. In certain contexts, this phenomenon is regarded as noble. When soldiers are willing to give up their lives for their country or more often, from a psychological point of view, for their comrades, the experience is often not one of risking life but rather one of sustaining group existence.

A major lesson of self psychology is that the boundaries of the self are not at the skin. While self-preservation is a universal human motive, the self that is preserved varies with the context. Often, youngsters' apparently irrational acts become comprehensible when it is understood that they are very actively attempting to preserve a self that they understand differently from the therapist's perception of their self. People generally, and adolescents in particular, commonly equate their selves with the group. Americans' strong emphasis on the ideal of individuality tends to obscure the greater psychological reality of the group self that is explicitly avowed in many cultures (Doi 1985). The destruction of the group is equated with loss of self. At the same time, personal death may even be regarded as strengthening the group. Youngsters whose self is enfeebled can often find that the powerful combination of group membership and violence provides an intense and sustaining self-experience that can be achieved in no other way.

This perspective is exceedingly useful in understanding terrorist youths. Often massively traumatized in childhood and, as a result, chronically in danger of fragmentation of the self, these young people commonly have their first vigorous experience of self in a context that combines committed group membership with violence. It is this heady combination that makes the many forms of nationalism that seem so irrational to the external observer such a powerful motivation for violence throughout history.

Many adolescents are much concerned with their personal integrity. They often question the depth of their own commitment and seriousness, just as their elders do. Violence provides a sense of serious commitment, a proof that "I really mean it," that the youngster can accomplish in no other way. Really meaning it, being someone to be taken seriously, and similar feelings are both interpersonal and intrapsychic states. Especially for people whose selves are otherwise enfeebled, it is a psychological life-and-death matter to be taken seriously. Often such individuals grew up in a selfobject world that did not take them seriously, and violence or the threat of violence is the only means available to them to coerce respect from an unresponsive internal and external environment.

The self as established through an amalgam of violence, group membership, and personal integrity is a major theme of the classic kung fu movie. Bruce Lee's *Enter the Dragon* is the best known of this genre to Western audiences. The movie is set during the Japanese occupation of China. This historical setting is in itself of little personal meaning to the protagonists. However, the Japanese incursion into the kung fu school and its community is deeply personally offensive. The young people, whose major identity is by way of membership in this quite meaningless organization, struggle mightily and perform acts of brave violence in its support. Their actions are to no avail. The Japanese karate group, supported by the Japanese officials, take over the school completely. However, this does not foreclose the possibility of reestablishing the group self. In a final triumphal moment of utter personal integrity, commitment to the group, and glorious physical action, the Bruce Lee character performs a magnificent flying side kick toward a battery of Japanese machine guns, presumably being killed in midair. In this single gesture, he achieves a state of heroic selfhood through committed personal annihilation.

Such behavior and belief is not limited to the movie screen. Late adolescent Japanese recruits at the end of the Second World War engaged in kamikaze missions fully aware of the inevitable physical outcome (Haito 1989). They did, however, firmly believe in their group selves, in the sense of the country and historical immortality as well as their personal joining of a group of "Thunder Gods." The Japanese military leadership was clearly reluctant to use the youngsters in this fashion, and their doing so reflected a failure to value them in the context of a disintegrating group self-experience. The disintegration of centrally important psychological groups that support the self-experience is a common context in which a fairly healthy self is imperiled. Since we believe that the individual's self is supported throughout life by a selfobject milieu (Galatzer-Levy and Cohler, in press), times of social disintegration imperil even the healthy self.

Society's Values

It is uncertain to what extent societal disintegration and violence are interrelated. Certainly, when institutional structures break down, violent acts become of greater importance. Similarly, acts of violence commonly disrupt the social order. Society also acts on the individual in another way. It commonly interdigitates with other mechanisms of self-support, such as group membership.

There is a group of individuals whose core experience of self is not nearly so much in danger but whose normative self-development during adolescence has been profoundly shaped by violent environments. In late adolescence, when a definitive identity ordinarily emerges, young people whose only opportunities for meaningful identities are related to violence may adopt it as a central aspect of their personalities. I suspect that this is true of many ghetto youths. During the time when the only powerful black figures portrayed in movies and television were "Superfly" characters, it is hardly surprising that many black youngsters who were isolated from the broader culture commonly adopted cynical violence as a committed position.

I have seen a similar phenomenon among Vietnam veterans. Often inducted into the military in late adolescence, these individuals, at a critical moment in life, found only two, not mutually exclusive identities available to them. They could settle rapidly into cynical indifference, attempting to survive and avoid psychic pain, or they could come to value violence in its own right. The effect of cultural experience on the enactment of violence is a difficult matter about which to generalize, and many trivial statements are possible. Yet, unless he is a moral

435

genius, the young person in search of a way to be in the world is limited by the models presented to him.

The results of violence and the opportunities to act violently profoundly depend on the historical moment. We do not know whether the psychology of youngsters armed with chains is much different from those armed with semiautomatic weapons. The consequences of the difference are enormous. The psychology of the elders who arrange for the slaughter of the young deserves our investigation. As with the problem of nuclear weapons, the psychoanalyst can rationalize his inattention and say that it is beyond his scope and expertise (Levine and Simmons 1988). This is morally wrong. In addition, it reflects a psychological resistance that is of the greatest importance in understanding deadly violence. Hannah Segal (1988) has proposed that the very intensity of the nuclear threat is such as to provoke primitive defense operations like splitting, projection, and denial in the parties involved. It is characteristic of these primitive defenses that they build on themsleves since they interfere with the feedback of material reality to the individual (Kernberg 1976). I believe that something quite similar happens in communities as lethal violence becomes commonplace. The need to purify the self-experience of the capacity to destroy and murder leads regularly to the projection of these qualities onto an enemy who is seen, increasingly, as inhuman, hateful, deserving of destruction, and, in particular, beyond empathic understanding. The pain of recognizing the brutal indifference of the older generation in failing to provide safeguards against violence and the enormous difficulty of addressing this indifference leads to inattention to the environment's failure as a selfobject of adolescents. Muslin (1982) demonstrated how the cynical indifference of the parental generation led each of its principle representatives to fail Romeo and Juliet as selfobjects and so led inevitably to their destruction. As a community, our failure to remove the principle immediate cause of intentional death, handguns, from violent adolescents reflects a similar group failing (Sloan et al. 1988).

Conclusions

In sum, the urgency of maintenance of the self lies at the heart of the dynamics of violence. Violence commonly takes its origin in the narcissistic rage that results from the self being endangered. The chief form of danger to the self is failure of selfobject functions, and the rage is often directed against failed selfobjects or symbolic representatives of failed selfobjects. When rage is enacted, it commonly leads to further impairment in the self-experience and consequent defensive operations that support further violence. These understandings are the beginnings of therapeutic work with many violent young people.

REFERENCES

Benedek, E., and Cornell, D. 1989. *Juvenile Homicide*. Washington, D.C.: American Psychiatric Press.

Bowlby, J. 1973. *Attachment and Loss*. Vol. 2, *Separation, Anxiety, and Anger*. New York: Basic.

Bowlby, J. 1982. Attachment and loss: retrospect and prospect. *American Journal of Orthopsychiatry* 52:664–678.

Bowlby, J. 1988. Developmental psychiatry comes of age. *American Journal of Psychiatry* 145:1–10.

Cohler, B., and Galatzer-Levy, R. 1990. Self, coherence and meaning in the second half of life. In R. Nemiroff and C. Colarruso, eds. *New Dimensions in Adult Development*. New York: Basic.

Cohler, B., and Galatzer-Levy, R. 1992. Psychoanalysis, psychology, and the self. In J. Barron, M. Eagle, and D. Wolitsky, eds. *Interface of Psychoanalysis and Psychology*. Washington, D.C.: American Psychological Association.

Cornell, D. 1989. Causes of juvenile homicide: a review of the literature. In D. Cornell and E. Benedek, eds. *Juvenile Homicide*. Washington, D.C.: American Psychiatric Press.

Darwin, C. 1859. *On the Origin of Species by Means of Natural Selection*. London.

Doi, T. 1985. *The Anatomy of the Self*. New York: Kodansha.

Dollard, J.; Doob, L.; Miller, N.; Mowrer, O.; Sears, R.; Ford, C.; Hovland, C.; and Sollenberger, R. 1939. *Frustration and Aggression*. New Haven, Conn.: Yale University Press.

Eth, S. 1989. The adolescent witness to homicide. In D. Cornell and E. Benedek, eds. *Juvenile Homicide*. Washington, D.C.: American Psychiatric Press.

Fannon, F. 1968. *The Wretched of the Earth*. New York: Grove.

Fein, H. 1979. *Accounting for Genocide*. New York: Free Press.

Fenichel, O. 1945. *The Psychoanalytic Theory of Neurosis*. New York: Norton.

Ferenczi, S. 1938. *Thalassa: A Theory of Genitality*. New York: Norton.

Freud, S. 1911. Psycho-analytic notes on an autobiographical account of a case of paranoia (dementia paranoides). *Standard Edition* 12:3–82. London: Hogarth, 1958.

Freud, S. 1920. Beyond the pleasure principle. *Standard Edition* 18:3–64. London: Hogarth, 1955.

Friedlander, K. 1960. *The Psycho-analytic Approach to Juvenile Delinquency: Theory, Case Studies, Treatment*. New York: International Universities Press.

Galatzer-Levy, R. 1982. The opening phase of the treatment of hypochondriasis. *Psychoanalytic Psychotherapy* 9:389–413.

Galatzer-Levy, R., and Cohler, B. 1990. The developmental psychology of the self: a new worldview in psychoanalysis. *Annual of Psychoanalysis* 18:1–43.

Galatzer-Levy, R., and Cohler, B. In press. *The Essential Other*. New York: Basic.

Goldstein, K. 1947. *Human Nature in the Light of Psychopathology*. Cambridge, Mass.: Harvard University Press.

Haito, T. 1989. *Thunder Gods*. Translated by M. Ichiwan. New York: Kodansha.

Hartman, H. 1939. *Ego Psychology and the Problem of Adaptation*. New York: International Universities Press.

Hartman, H. 1950. Comments on the psychoanalytic theory of the ego. In *Essays on Ego Psychology*. New York: International Universities Press.

Hartman, H.; Kris, E.; and Lowenstein, R. 1946. Comments on the formation of psychic structure. In H. Hartman, E. Kris, and R. Loewenstein, eds. *Papers on Psychoanalytic Psychology*, Psychological Issues 14. New York: International Universities Press.

Hartman, H., and Loewenstein, R. 1962. Notes on the superego. In H. Hartman, E. Kris, and R. Loewenstein, eds. *Papers on Psychoanalytic Psychology*, Psychological Issues 14. New York: International Universities Press.

Katz, J. 1988. *The Seductions of Crime: Moral and Sensual Attractions in Doing Evil*. New York: Basic.

Keiser, R. 1969. *The Vice Lords: Warriors of the Street*. New York: Holt, Rinehart & Winston.

Kernberg, O. F. 1976. *Object-Relation Theory and Clinical Psychoanalysis*. New York: Aronson.

Kernberg, O. F. 1980a. Adolescent sexuality in the light of group processes. *Psychoanalytic Quarterly* 49:27–47.

Kernberg, O. F. 1980b. *Internal World and External Reality*. New York: Aronson.

Kernberg, O. F. 1986. Identification and its vicissitudes as observed in psychosis. *International Journal of Psycho-Analysis* 67:147–159.

Klein, G. 1976. *Psychoanalytic Theory: An Exploration of Essentials*. New York: International Universities Press.

Klein, M. 1927. Criminal tendencies in normal children. In *Love, Guilt and Reparation and Other Works, 1921–1945*. New York: Delacorte, 1975.

Klein, M. 1935. A contribution to the psychogenesis of manic-depressive states. In *Love, Guilt and Reparation and Other Works*. New York: Delacorte, 1975.

Klein, M. 1945. New York: The Oedipus complex in the light of early anxieties. In *Love, Guilt and Reparation and Other Works, 1921–1945*. New York: Delacorte, 1975.

Klein, M. 1975. *Love, Guilt and Reparation and Other Works, 1921–1945*. New York: Delacorte.

Kohut, H. 1957. Introspection, empathy, and psychoanalysis: an examination of the relationship between mode of observation and theory. In P. Ornstein, ed. *The Search for the Self*. New York: International Universities Press.

Kohut, H. 1971. *The Analysis of the Self*. New York: International Universities Press.

Kohut, H. 1972. Thoughts on narcissism and narcissistic rage. *Psychoanalytic Study of the Child* 27:360–400.

Kohut, H. 1984. *How Psychoanalysis Cures*. Chicago: University of Chicago Press.

Kohut, H., and Wolf, E. 1978. The disorders of the self and their treatment: an outline. *International Journal of Psycho-Analysis* 59:413–425.

Levine, H., and Simmons, B. 1988. Introduction. In H. Levine, D. Jacobs, and L. Rubin, eds. *Psychoanalysis and the Nuclear Threat: Clinical and Theoretical Studies*. Hillsdale, N.J.: Analytic.

Lifton, R. J. 1986a. *The Nazi Doctors*. New York: Basic.

Lifton, R. J. 1986b. Reflections on genocide. *Psychohistory Review* 14:39–54.

McCord, C., and Freeman, H. P. 1990. Special article: excess mortality in Harlem. *New England Journal of Medicine* 322:173–177.

Marohn, R. 1990. Violence and unrestrained behavior in adolescents. *Adolescent Psychiatry* 17:419–432.

Marohn, R.; Dalle-Molle, D.; McCarter, E.; and Linn, D. 1980. *Juvenile Delinquents: Psychodynamic Assessment and Hospital Treatment.* New York: Brunner/Mazel.

Morton, W. 1980. *China: Its History and Culture.* New York: McGraw-Hill.

Muslin, H. L. 1982. Romeo and Juliet: the tragic self in adolescence. *Adolescent Psychiatry* 10:106–117.

Parens, H. 1973. Aggression: a reconsideration. *Journal of the American Psychoanalytic Association* 21:34–60.

Parens, H. 1979. Developmental considerations of ambivalence: part 2 of an exploration of the relations of instinctual drives and the symbiosis-separation-individuation process. *Psychoanalytic Study of the Child* 34:385–420.

Parens, H. 1987. Cruelty begins at home. *Child Abuse and Neglect* 11:331–338.

Redl, F., and Wineman, W. 1952. *Controls from Within: Techniques for Treatment of the Aggressive Child.* New York: Free Press.

Rosenberg, B., and Silverstein, H. 1969. *The Varieties of Delinquent Experience.* Waltham, Mass.: Xerox College Publishing.

Segal, H. 1988. Silence is the real crime. In H. Levine, D. Jacobs, and L. Rubin, eds. *Psychoanalysis and the Nuclear Threat: Clinical and Theoretical Studies.* Hillsdale, N.J.: Analytic.

Shi Nai'an and Lou Guanzahong. 1988. *Outlaws of the March.* Translated by S. Shapiro. Beijing: Foreign Language Press.

Sloan, J. H.; Kellermann, A. L.; Reay, D. T.; Ferris, J. A.; Koepsell, T.; Rivara, F. P.; Rice, C. G.; Laurel, G.; and LoGerfo, J. 1988. Special article: handgun regulations, crime, assaults, and homicide: a tale of two cities. *New England Journal of Medicine* 319:1256–1262.

Staub, E. 1989. *The Roots of Evil: The Origins of Genocide and Other Group Violence.* New York: Cambridge University Press.

Sulloway, S. 1979. *Freud, Biologist of the Mind: Beyond the Psychoanalytic Legend.* New York: Basic.

Suttles, G. 1967. *The Social Orders of the Slums: Ethnicity and Territory in the Inner City.* Chicago: University of Chicago Press.

Winnicott, D. 1958. *Collected Papers*. New York: Tavistock.

Winnicott, D. 1960. The theory of the parent-infant relationship. *International Journal of Psycho-Analysis* 41:585–595.

Winnicott, D. 1964. *The Child, the Family, and the Outside World*. Baltimore: Penguin.

Winnicott, D. 1965. *The Maturational Process and the Facilitating Environment*. New York: International Universities Press.

Yablonsky, L. 1966. *The Violent Gang*. Baltimore: Penguin.

PART V

PSYCHOTHERAPY OF ADOLESCENT EMOTIONAL DISORDERS

EDITORS' INTRODUCTION

Psychoanalysts have tended to be cautious about analyzing adolescents, and many therapists have introduced supportive techniques encouraging repression. One pioneer in adolescent therapy was Max Gitelson, whose perspective was that the therapeutic task not only be directed to psychic analysis but should result in a synthesis of the adolescent's character. Whatever approach is required to engage the adolescent may be used, but only as a means to the end: eventual dyadic engagement. The three chapters in this part focus on in-depth engagement of the severely disturbed adolescent.

Jacquelyn Seevak Sanders documents her long experience with children at the Sonia Shankman Orthogenic School of the University of Chicago and presents many ideas dealing with developmental issues, parenting, and education of children and adolescents. Arthur Salz examines a different population of adolescents but one also suffering from the stress of social, economic, and educational problems that are all too normal in Western societies. These are children who require nurturing and benefit from a long-term relationship. The final therapeutic example is a self-learning experience that Michael D. Miller writes about, which occurred during his training. He believes that the adolescent patient learned that "loving could feel good and that human relationships could provide sustenance for life as well."

25 SEVERELY EMOTIONALLY DISTURBED CHILDREN: FORESEEING, AVOIDING, AND AMELIORATING THEIR PAIN

JACQUELYN SEEVAK SANDERS

This chapter is about very difficult children: children who are difficult to live with, difficult to treat, and difficult to understand. They are the children with whom I have spent much of my life as a counselor and then director of the Sonia Shankman Orthogenic School of the University of Chicago. They are very frustrating because they are not schizophrenic or psychotic (although in my earlier professional days, from the 1950s even into the 1970s, they often were so diagnosed), have no intellectual or identifiable organic deficiency, and seem to be able to relate, yet they do not respond in the usual way to the usual treatment. They, unlike the ordinary neurotic child, are unable to return to normal life after being helped with the resolution of conflicts. These children are now called by a variety of names—such as "borderline," "narcissistic," "behavior disordered." These diagnoses mean different things to different people. These children have in common that they cannot manage their lives or relationships, nor can they accomplish what they want to in life. According to Freud, the measure of mental health is the ability to love and to work. The measure of child mental health is the ability to have friends, get along with family, and do the work of the growing child, which in our society is school. At the Orthogenic School, we deal with those children who are not able to do any of these three. These are the children with whom this chapter is concerned.

Although it would make things simpler if we could give a name—or a clear diagnosis—to these children so that we could identify exactly the problem that we are exploring, I actually prefer this less certain way. I prefer to talk about people without using diagnoses. Useful as they may be for theoretical purposes, I have found that, whenever a therapist uses a diagnosis in talking about a patient, it invariably means a distancing from the patient. When one of our staff describes a child as being in a "psychotic state," the meaning is, "I don't understand, and it frightens me." In our work, we need to be as close as possible to our patients, not as distant as possible from them. If I think of these children as "borderline," they are different from me; if I think of them as "difficult," they are like me.

I have been asked to address what are, of course, the most important issues—prevention and early intervention. On the basis of what we know, ideally, the guardian of every embryo should make certain that both parents are physically healthy and that there is no known history of mental disturbance on either side. Then, the parents should have a satisfying marriage, be firm and consistent but loving, and be sure to allow no disruptive influences at any of the critical stages of development. On the basis of my experience, there would be fewer severely disturbed youngsters, but there would still be some. That is, there seems to be some constitutional fragility in many of these children. In many, the course of their life, particularly their early life, has been disrupted. Disruptions have often come at critical times in their development; but, for some of our children, none of this has been true, and, in reflecting back, there is no way to have foreseen the future difficult course of these youngsters' lives.

In this chapter, I will be using what we have learned from years of work with these children to suggest some useful ways of avoiding the intensity of disturbance by seeing early signs, providing early support, and designing early treatment. I will be presenting some examples of our children and our work with them to explain these ideas. However, any serious consideration of early detection has to make use of the valuable longitudinal studies that have been done over the past decades and continue (Rutter 1988; Wadsworth 1991). When we use only the methods of retrospective analysis, rich as that may be, we do not know what would have happened to these children if they had been simply left alone—whether, for example, they would have "outgrown" their problem. Further, we often do not have descriptions of the children made at early ages, rather only what parents remember from those early ages. The large studies of entire cohorts can give us interesting

447

information not provided in retrospective studies. In discussing continuities in psychiatric disorders from childhood to adulthood in the children of psychiatric patients, Michael Rutter and his colleagues state, "Simple models linking adult disorders to single traumatic early experiences or to the press of current events or to biological dispositions do not provide an adequate explanation for most psychiatric problems. An approach is required that considers interactions between behaviors, dispositions, and environments" (Quinton, Rutter, and Gulliver 1990, p. 259). Thus, broad studies confirm what narrower experience suggests: we cannot look for a simple sign of future emotional distress.

In "Epidemiology of Child Psychiatric Disorder," Rutter and Sandberg (1986, pp. 564–565) summarized what have been found to be some of the early signs: "Thus, psychiatric disorders were more frequent in children with general or specific cognitive disabilities (such as language delay or reading difficulties), in those whose parents had a mental disorder, and in those from discordant, quarrelsome homes." They further delineated some of the criteria derived from the epidemiological data that pointed to the likelihood that the problem would be a significant one:

First, the pattern of symptomatology was relevant. Some features, such as poor peer relationships and hyperactivity/inattention, are not only strongly associated with other indicators of psychopathology, but also relate to a worse prognosis. Other features, such as nail-biting and thumb-sucking, proved to be of little psychiatric import. Secondly, in general, disorders that are pervasive over situations tend to be more persistent over time. Many childhood problems are largely situation-specific; these may be quite severe and incapacitating at the time, but on the whole, they reflect maladaptive patterns of interpersonal interaction and they respond to changes in such patterns. It is evident that knowledge regarding the situational-specificities in children's problems may have important implications for therapeutic interventions. Nevertheless, it should be noted that child psychiatric disorders associated with severe environmental stressors (such as parental mental disorder or family discord) frequently do generalize across situations and often persist over time. Thirdly, disorders associated with a wide range of emotional or behavioral difficulties tend to have a worse

448

outcome than those associated with a single "symptom" or a narrow range of problems. Indeed, isolated transient emotional or conduct problems are very common in normal children; on their own, such problems usually have little clinical significance. Fourthly, on the whole, problems that are out of keeping with normal developmental trends usually have a worse outcome than those that constitute exaggerations of age-appropriate phenomena. Thus, delinquent activities tend to peak in adolescence; delinquency that begins in early or middle childhood is more likely to be associated with recidivism. Conversely, separation anxiety is normal in preschoolers, and exaggerations of this in the form of elective mutism or school refusal about the time of school entry tend to have a good prognosis. Similar problems arising later in childhood are more likely to be persistent and to be associated with generalized psychosocial malfunction. It seems that it is not early or late onset per se that matters most, but rather, the developmental inappropriateness of the problems.

The longitudinal study is useful not only in identifying those early signs that are likely to predict greater problems but also in tracing those factors in the life histories that protect against the development of severe emotional problems. In "Adult Outcomes of Institution-reared Children," Rutter, Quinton and Hill (1990) present the finding that, although the overall outcome of institution-raised girls was worse than that of a control group, there was still heterogeneity. That is, some of the institution-raised children had good outcomes. The investigators, therefore, analyzed the findings to ascertain what the "protective factors" might be. They found that "planning" was significant—it was a factor that came from the individual's conviction that she could influence her life. This was often associated with education. Furthermore, it often led to the selection of a mate who was supportive.

These findings, as you will see, lend support to some of the conclusions that I have drawn from my experience, both as to what are early indications of severe emotional problems and as to ways to treat them.

Before I report on my retrospective analysis, I would like to tell you a little about the school where I have done my work. The Sonia Shankman Orthogenic School of the University of Chicago is a residential treatment institution for thirty children and adolescents where we practice psychoanalytically oriented milieu therapy. This "consists of

449

a physical environment, a human environment, a theory and a therapy. The physical environment is a school that we try to make as warm, beautiful, safe, and manageable as possible. The human environment is the staff. The theory that informs our action in, and arrangement of, these environments is that of psychoanalytic ego psychology, modernized with some more recent psychoanalytic concepts. The therapy is the gradual and consistent education of the ego. This involves the modification of, on the one hand, the external environment and, on the other, the internal environment, to suit the capacity of the weak or malformed ego. It involves at the same time the provision of ego support to help the student develop various ego functions'' (Sanders 1989, pp. 6–7).

The physical environment is designed to provide safety, comfort, enticement into life, and messages that convey our respect for these youngsters who have been failures all their lives. Like Maria Montessori, we feed them on china dishes, not plastic, both to let them know that they are worthy and to help them learn to manage their lives carefully. At the same time, our environment is very ordered and clear. Space is designed so that staff can always easily supervise the children, and nothing dangerous is permitted in their areas.

The staff who are with them most—counselors and teachers—are familiar with the life histories of their youngsters, their frailties, and their misperceptions and are involved with understanding how best to deal with them. The life of the institution is designed so that all its children will have abundant access to nurturance, reduced stress, and appropriate challenge. They live in groups of five or six, with an adult always present, and are expected to learn how to live well with others. Although many modes of expression are available to them and encouraged, destructive expression is not permitted. We make use of psychoanalytic understanding to understand better what they need and what their actions tell us and, only on rare occasions, to interpret to them. With this understanding, we are better able to construct an environment that they can learn to master, and, thereby, become strong. We also offer them opportunities to form positive identifications, at times by avoiding actions that would encourage negative transferences. The positive identifications around more neutral events contribute to their strength. Children are able to stay at our school for several years so that we are able to provide for all aspects of their environment in these growing years. We also, therefore, know our youngsters very well.

As I review the stories of some of our children, I will be describing something more of the Orthogenic School. I have by now dealt with about 250 children who spent an average of seven years at the school. The generalizations that I will make about their early histories is from a specific review of the thirty youngsters who have left in the past ten years and from my own impressions about the early histories of all the children that I have known at the Orthogenic School.

I would first divide the "early signs" into two categories: those shown by the children and those shown by the families. Signs shown by children at very early ages (i.e., the first two years of life) can again be divided in two: those of extreme overactivity and those of extreme underactivity. Of course, I refer only to behavior that cannot be traced to a physical cause. It is my unscientific opinion that many of these children outgrow these early signs—I, personally, know of some. Their course out of their aberrant behavior is sometimes facilitated by an extremely "attuned" (as Stern [1985] would put it) caregiver and sometimes by their own maturity. As an example of attunement, an experienced mother has described having had two different reactions to an infant's reluctance to nurse. Her firstborn's passivity in nursing made her feel rejected, and, therefore, she became more stiff and awkward, thus exacerbating the problem. With a later born, she realized that it was simply a matter of temperament and, therefore, was able to tune her actions appropriately and coax and stimulate the sucking response, thereby alleviating the problem. Again, one parent can see an overly active infant as alert and creative and, therefore, be pleased and only gently curtail the activity, while another can see the same child as difficult and demanding and, therefore, try unsympathetically to curtail the child. However, there are children who are excessively active or excessively passive and difficult for even the most empathic caregiver to attune to.

In reviewing what psychiatrists and other psychotherapists have said to and about the parents of some of our over- or underactive children, I have come to the conclusion that we in our profession have frequently done more harm than good by imputing the negative reaction to the neurosis of the parent rather than to the difficult stimulation of the child. With these infants who exhibit such problematic early behaviors, the value of early identification is to provide for the needs of both child and parent. Children need, on the one hand, frequent gentle stimulation and, on the other, frequent, gentle calming. It is equally important to provide for the parents' needs. Parents need help in dealing with the difficult behavior of their children, not because of their neurotic reaction to it, but because of their quite natural reaction to it. For example, a former student of the Orthogenic School found her second child to be unresponsive to comforting, hyperactive, and demanding. Because the mother had a number of emotional stresses concurrent with the birth of her daughter, and because her nature tended toward easy emotional expression, it was easy to interpret her daughter's problems as related to the mother. When the mother was distraught and frustrated with her own inability to cuddle and calm her daughter, it was tempting to attribute it to other stress. However, the baby was truly an "arching," tense infant, who slept little, had little self-soothing ability or ability to be soothed. The little girl gradually has become better, with the mother developing modes of coping—and especially being reassured that the girl's difficulty came with her nature, not from her mother.

I know of no way of predicting which of those children with these extremes of behavior will be able to right themselves without intervention and which will not. I cannot think, however, of any damage that could be done by the intervention that I (and many early childhood advocates) suggest. That is, the parents or caregivers should be helped to find ways of coping with the difficult infant and be reassured about their competence rather than criticized. In my experience, it has been rare that the parents of these children have sought psychiatric or psychotherapeutic help. If early intervention is to be provided for these children, then pediatricians have to be better educated and informed as to what kind of help is needed and what sources of help are available. When a parent has been concerned about a less than active baby, the pediatrician will most likely say that the baby will grow out of it. When a parent has been concerned about a more than active baby, the pediatrician will either say the same thing or prescribe a sedative. The problem of educating parents of the very young to be parents is intensified in the United States by the disruption of the extended family. For example, if a young mother does not know how to swaddle an infant to give it security and calm, there is less often a grandmother or an aunt to show her how. A good measure of prevention would be to provide this help.

Many parents, especially first-time parents, have not known that their baby was overly active or overly passive because they have not had any other children with whom to compare. The first sign, then, is when the child goes to nursery school or kindergarten. With the greater incidence of day care in the United States, there is more opportunity for alerting the caregivers to this kind of problem.

Early environmental signs of trouble have been in the family. Some of our youngsters have had very clearly abusive early years, and some have had nonabusive but clearly disrupted family situations. I will give examples of each of these together with the kind of treatment that was effective with them. I will also give examples of youngsters who had none of these very early signs, from neither themselves nor their families. The youngsters whom I will be discussing have by now left the Orthogenic School, so we have a good idea about the outcome of our treatment efforts.

We have had three children who had, as far as we can tell, very abusive and neglected early years and were then adopted by middle- or upper-middle-class, well-educated families who were very stable and devoted to them. I use these as examples because removing them from the problem situation and providing a stable, nonabusive environment was clearly not enough. Therefore, their treatment can suggest what more specific elements proved to be critical for their rehabilitation.

These youngsters were not able to relate to their adoptive families and were so disruptive that, after several years, the parents sought residential placement for them. As an example, Paul had been taken from his mother in infancy because of her abuse and neglect. He spent two years with a foster family with regard to whom there was also suspicion of abuse. Although the foster father had wanted to adopt Paul, because of an unforeseen illness of this father plans changed, and Paul was abruptly left with his new adoptive family on his third birthday. The new family was told little about his previous history. After a short honeymoon period, he became completely unmanageable. At first, the parents thought that they simply did not know how to deal with a boy (they had an older girl, their biological child). When they realized that they had a child with problems, they struggled to try to get help. The mother describes never being able to be at peace with Paul around, never knowing what disruptive thing he would do next. Although trying very hard, the mother could not empathize with the depth of despair that could lead to such actions or fathom how all her ministrations and gifts could not feel enough for him. She could only view his destructive behavior as manipulative. The parents finally brought him to a psychiatric hospital for children, where long-term residential placement was recommended because he was considered to be unable to form attachments. He was obviously very bright, could be personable, and often presented himself as an attractive, normal-acting youngster. However, he seemed to be totally lacking in conscience and did destructive things for reasons that others could not understand.

On his admission to the Orthogenic School, we began to detect relatively soon that he did form attachments but was terrified of showing those attachments and, therefore, put on a very hard exterior. I saw this myself on the day that he came to the school. He calmly said goodbye to his parents in a way that convinced his mother that he was not at all bothered by leaving her; he then walked upstairs, lay on his bed, buried his head in his pillow, and cried.

Nine years later, he left the Orthogenic School after successfully attending a local high school, playing on the sports teams, getting good grades, and making friends. He has been accepted at the college of his choice, where he will go in the fall. At his graduation party, he cried in front of all the school as he told the assembled staff and students that, although he was eager to leave the confines of a residential school, he was terribly sad at leaving the people in it.

It took many years before he was able to acknowledge the importance of his relationships. For the first several years of his stay, we were able to do the following. (1) We gave him the consistent nurturance and care that he had not had in his early life, but in a way that did not force him to be dependent on his caregivers or to show gratitude. This "care" is part of the institutional mores of the Orthogenic School, a care to which all are entitled no matter how they act. This not only gives a kind of emotional sustenance but affirms the worthiness of youngsters who are beset by feelings of unworthiness. Since it is "institutional," it does not necessitate a dependence that, because of early trauma in dependency, is so threatening to children who have suffered early abuse. (2) Paul's acting out of his anger was permitted, but only within safe limits. Even when it had to be curtailed, he was not rejected because of the acting out. So he had the opportunity to abreact some of his anger, but not in a way that could be destructive and, thereby, accrue ill toward him. (3) He was provided with many ways of expressing his feelings without having to confront them. This can provide for a working through that does not arouse the intensity of anxiety associated with a more direct confrontation with feelings. Much of what we do can be conceived of as play therapy on a grand scale. That is, we provide our youngsters with the means of acting out significant issues in a safe environment. (4) Finally, Paul was taught how to master the tasks of his particular stage of development successfully. He began to learn in school and became a good sportsman. These provisions are all part of the regular life of the Orthogenic School.

Paul was also offered individual sessions, but he vociferously rejected them for many years. He developed the strongest relationship with his teacher. As he slowly became a good student, he would confide in his teacher. For example, when he would engage in mischief in the dormitory, to all around he would show a bravado, but to his teacher he would confess that he knew it was wrong and that he was ashamed of himself. He could show his neediness only symbolically, through, for example, his interest in the nurturing of wild animals in a science class.

After many years, he began to accept individual sessions and make use of them. He never did so, however, in a reconstructive sense. It is my belief that the abuse and neglect of the early years were so traumatic that, until he had developed significant strength, he could not risk the possibility of coming close to the experience by putting himself in a position of proximal dependence—particularly with a woman. The teacher, who was sympathetic, was so clearly committed to developing his mastery of the world that he felt safe to acknowledge attachment. It was only after Paul had substantial security in that mastery and the toughness of his defenses that he could risk the close encounter of a session room. The kind of analytic work that he then did was of the analysis of current relationships rather than the reconstruction of past ones.

Two other children with similar beginnings were similarly unable to take full advantage of the very stable families into which they were adopted. One little girl, from a very chaotic and abusive situation in a European country, was adopted by a well-to-do American couple living in another European country. This couple was totally unable to comprehend why the little girl continued to be delinquent and destructive despite their giving her all kinds of considerations and comforts. They were further unable to have any empathy with the possibility of her continued attachment to the abusive environment. This is a very

frequent problem confronted by people who deal with abused youngsters. That is, we expect that the abused youngster will be happy to
leave the abuse and be grateful for a comfortable existence. However,
these youngsters often maintain strong attachments to their abusers.

On placement of this girl at the Orthogenic School, the difficulty in
providing an empathic environment continued. She was strong and
healthy enough to feel that she could get her needs met without risking
dependency and trust—however, her identifications remained such
that her mode of doing this was frequently destructive and asocial.
The staff would find it very difficult to understand why, after all the
kindness and material comforts she received, she had to be sneaky,
steal, destroy, etc. After several years of our continued institutional
nurturing, accepting her acting out without rejection or dire consequences, we were able to see a beginning of a kind of trust. It became
manifest after her behavior had become so dangerous that she was
threatened by us with expulsion. She was then able to acknowledge
her attachment, her behavior markedly improved, and she was able to
stay at the school. She was by then able to risk some dependency in
interaction on a symbolic level with an individual therapist. Unfortunately, her parents decided to transfer her to another program before
this development was secure. She had only the bare beginnings of a
new kind of identification and any ability to have an analytic interactional view. She, too, was not at all able to confront the pain of her
earliest years. She has kept in touch with us—informing us of what
she was doing—and brought her baby to see us about a year ago. How
she is able to treat this child is likely to be the final demonstration of
the success or failure of our intervention.

The third youngster who suffered abuse and neglect for the first
two years of life and then was adopted by an intact and apparently
well-functioning family was different from the first described in that
his first years with his adoptive family were harmonious and pleasurable. The parents lived in a country setting and were very laissez-faire
in their approach to him. Very little conformity was required of him.
He became unable to manage when the family moved to another community and a larger school, where more was expected of him. He then
became disruptive and unmanageable.

The course of his treatment at the Orthogenic School was, however,
similar to that of the first two youngsters described. He was provided
with both nurturance and gentle but firm limitation. It was most impor-

tant to him in accepting these limitations that he felt that he was understood, that we could empathize with the distress that led to his sometimes destructive acting up. There would be times when he would rampage, sometimes verbally and sometimes physically, vigorously enough so that he would have to be restrained. When, however, a staff member would be able to listen empathically and respond to his perspective as to why he was upset or angry, he would immediately calm down and become compliant. One of the most important relationships that he developed was with a female classmate who was a little older than he was. Although he had a number of very positive attachments, he, too, would never approach the emotion of those early years. He developed a reflective approach to himself and to his affairs and would discuss this with the staff. This, again, was in the nature of interactive rather than reconstructive analysis.

In our experience with these youngsters who had abusive early years, the very early intervention of removal from the abusive situation was not adequate to ameliorate it. The parents who then provided for them might have been better able to do so if they would have been helped to be empathic with the depth and violence of their children's reaction to their early history. Further, our experience was that such youngsters could not make use of reconstructive therapy—the early trauma was too intense for their still fragile egos to reexperience. It is possible that, with further success in life, they might become strong enough to go back and sort through those experiences, if they find that their intimate lives are being interfered with. It is also possible that the nurturance and discharge, coupled with new identifications, have reduced the effects enough to enable them to live successfully.

A second kind of early familial sign is that of a disrupted or dysfunctional family life—although not physically neglectful or abusive. Two of our girls, both now successfully in college, came to us from such families at relatively young ages. K was described as being disruptive, sometimes self-destructive, and unable to stay at a task. She showed some signs of thought disorder and was inappropriate in her approach to strangers. Her parents were divorced, but both were very loving of and concerned about her. At the placement prior to her coming to the Orthogenic School, the professional conviction was that, if her mother would provide a more stable existence, K would be all right. The mother, however, was not able to provide a stable environment until K had been at the school for several years, when she married a highly

457

respected physician (this was her fourth marriage). Before this, her life-style had always been unconventional and chaotic.

P's mother was similarly unconventional, providing an inconsistent and chaotic environment. She was highly emotional and very warm toward her daughter. P spent much of her time with her grandparents, who offered stability. The grandfather, however, although loving toward P, was abusive of his wife. The mothers of both K and P were very committed to finding a good place for their daughters, recognizing their own inability to provide what the child needed. P also displayed, more flagrantly, some signs of a thought disorder. The precipitant to her placement was the allegation that she had set a rug on fire and then claimed that "Sitting Bull" had ordered her to do it. Years later, her brother confessed to having lit the fire.

These girls both seemed to need a very long period of consistent and structured care. They were both able to form attachments easily and engage in the psychotherapeutic process. However, it took many years of this kind of treatment before they were able to develop the inner strength necessary to maintain a mastery of the world. K was very susceptible to any kind of delinquent acting out; P could easily be carried away by her own fantasies of grandeur. Although the work of analytic understanding was important to both these girls, it seemed that the protection and structure was of greater importance, to allow them time to grow. Academic success was also an important strength that they both had time to acquire. This, perhaps, contributed to their development of the ability to plan, as described by Rutter et al. (1990), and, thereby, feel able to be in control of their lives: not at the mercy of, in the case of K, outer pressures or, in the case of P, inner pressures. From a very young age, P had exhibited very great potential, while K appeared more limited. The limitation, it became apparent, was the result of psychological issues rather than true limitation. They were both able to work hard and, therefore, were able to continue their growth in the relatively sheltered environment of a college campus following graduation from the Orthogenic School.

The question of what to do ideally with such youngsters is a continuing societal problem. Their environment cannot be called neglectful or abusive, so there is no reason to take them out of it, but it does not provide the kind of minimal consistency necessary for growth. I am convinced that there are many more children like P and K who suffer from even less stability and simply have to do the best they can.

There is another kind of disrupted familial situation with which we have had experience that calls for a somewhat different treatment emphasis. That is that of divorce—the disruption to the familial structure that seems to precipitate a kind of breakdown. In our experience, the retrospective accounts of the early lives of such children indicate some earlier fragility that was not remarkable but was intensified with the loss of the familial security. Again, this interaction is supported by the studies of Rutter and his colleagues (e.g., Rutter and Sandberg 1986).

C was such a youngster who came to us at fourteen, showing some signs of psychosis. She reported that she had auditory hallucinations, and her behavior was extremely oppositional. Her extreme oppositionality can be seen as a very healthy striving. Since she had been able to develop a psychic structure, it was extremely important for her to hang onto it. For her, the imposition of any external structure was a threat to her own very fragile structure and, therefore, to her very existence. This made the problem of keeping her safe and containing her aggressive impulses a very serious one since she would fight any externally imposed limits. She was, however, able to relate, to form strong attachments, and to benefit from a kind of reconstructive analysis. We could, therefore, discover with her that the traumas of her earlier years were two. The first centered around the death of her beloved grandmother, of whom she had been a favorite and who had been a major caregiver. This grandmother had given her the impression that she could not die until C told her that it was OK, and that seemed to happen. She died shortly after a visit with C when C told her that it was OK for her to let go of life. C was, therefore, beset by the idea that it was her word that had precipitated her grandmother's death. The second trauma—the direct precipitant of her hallucinatory activity—was a humiliation by a somewhat deranged teacher, who had made C kneel in front of her class.

C was very articulate about what was important in our treatment of her. She said that we were able to convey to her that we did not reject her because of her destructive outbursts. This was conveyed by, for example, the staff staying with her through a tantrum when she broke a dish and continuing to be concerned about her reasons for doing so while picking up the pieces and imposing a moderate fine. She herself was terrified by her destructive tendencies; however, when they were simply curtailed, she viewed it as a rejection of her very being and, therefore, was impelled to engage in them even more vehemently.

459

When we were able to clearly recognize the justification for her anger and convey to her that we did, we could then be experienced by her as joining forces with her to master her impulses. It was then possible, for example, when she felt destructive, to permit her to go for a walk by herself and to work by herself in the library, until she felt that her impulses had subsided and that she could manage in the company of others.

C also presented that intermingling of biological and psychological issues. She very clearly had hallucinatory experiences. She also had insomnia. For several months, one of her counselors would stay with her during her times of insomnia. Eventually, it became apparent that, although to some extent clearly psychologically related, the hallucinatory experiences tended to occur after a time of significant sleep deprivation. There was no clearly documented evidence that this was so, but it seemed that she had a biological propensity for sleeplessness that was exacerbated by psychological issues; the sleeplessness, again combined with psychological issues, then produced a hallucinatory experience. C was always clearly able to know the difference between her hallucinations and reality.

She left us after three years to go to an environment that was less structured than ours—that gave her greater freedom—and put her at greater risk. There she was still able to get help in self-reflection and mastery at her own pace. She successfully went on to college and interaction with parents and sibling.

Those youngsters who have developed a certain degree of psychic strength and then lose a significant amount of support—by such things as divorce or a move to a larger and stranger environment—also need to know that their destructiveness will be contained. But, for them, unless they are convinced that those who are containing it are doing so in their best interests, the containment will lead only to more intense protest. This is so because the containment is perceived as a threat to their own psychic integrity and, therefore, a threat to their very being. Long ago, a teenager put it succinctly: "I will do what you or Dr. B tell me, even if I don't agree, because I know that you have my best interest at heart; but I will not do what R tells me because I don't believe that of him."

Although these youngsters, whose severe difficulties were precipitated by divorce or other disruption, may have had earlier problems that a very sensitive person might have identified, it is equally possible that, without the disruption, those problems could have been worked out without any intervention. This suggests that an easily identifiable time for intervention is at the time of these major disruptions. Studies (e.g., Wallerstein and Kelly 1980) have supported the notion that intervention at the time of a divorce can ameliorate potential problems. When parents are divorcing, they are not able to have the emotional energy to provide the support that their children need and that they are ordinarily able to provide. Thus, at the time of great loss, the children have even less of their usual support. In addition, neither of the divorcing parents is likely to be empathic with either the feelings of loss that the child experiences or the feelings of anger that inevitably must be present.

Another time of potential loss and trauma is the transition to a dramatically larger setting. In the United States, this is frequently in the transition from grade school to high school. In grade school, classes are small and usually with one teacher so that the child knows all the children in the class and the teacher has a good sense of all the students. In high school, every hour presents a different class with different teachers and different classmates. Some youngsters are able and ready to master this, but some are not and could make good use of support.

Then there are those youngsters for whom there seem to have been no early signs, either in the youngster or in the family. We have had a number of children whose very early histories describe the infant as progressing quite normally and the families as stable with no more than the usual amount of disruptiveness. One speculates that, for these youngsters, there is likely to be an unidentifiable and, therefore, undetectable and untreatable innate fragility and that the combination of that fragility with unfortunate timing of external events has led to the youngster's inability to develop a secure structure and having a view of the world as hostile and threatening. We have had a number of girls with such backgrounds, who have had their disturbance manifest after the onset of puberty. Their disturbance was manifest usually in self-destructive behavior and very stubborn withdrawal from investing their energy in the tasks of the world. Their successful treatment has been a combination of structure and understanding—one never being able to be emphasized at the cost of the other.

Some have been anorexic. If we would be only "understanding" of their need for control, their oral incorporative fantasies, and their

461

difficulty in accepting their femininity, they would become more involved in not eating and waste away to the point of danger. On the other hand, should we be only insistent on eating, they would become more stubbornly resistant and waste away even faster. Our consistently successful treatment of anorexia has been an absolute insistence that the person eat, an insistence that is accomplished very personally and consistently. For example, a counselor would stay with Kate until she ate—she simply would not leave her. Sometimes we would ply the youngster with offers of any kind—even the most exotic—of foods. Sometimes we would force feed a youngster by hand. Insistence that is less personal or consistent can end only in real force feeding or intravenous feeding. A very personal insistence usually in the end evokes a grudging cooperation. Similarly, Kate would sometimes hurt herself by scratching herself with a pen. The staff then began to hold her hand at all times. This provided her with both the contact that she desired and the supportive containment that she needed.

Some of these youngsters were actually already reexperiencing some of their early experiences and could, then, articulate their early view of life and the events that were, to them, traumatic. They sometimes would reenact these early events in their current lives. For example, Kate perceived her mother as uncaring and would accuse her counselor of being so, despite much effort and hours spent in her care. The understanding derived from a psychoanalytic perspective was then helpful to the staff in understanding what was being reenacted toward them. This understanding could, for example, permit them not to feel rejected by Kate's accusations. Therefore, they could react in ways that were not retaliative to some very hostile actions on the part of the youngster. This experience, in itself, is therapeutic.

Another way of working through some of the issues from the past was in symbolic action. Kate, for example, acquired a number of stuffed animals that she used to represent different aspects of her personality: "Mr. Bear" was security and protection; "Merlin" was a rabbit of gentleness; a lion hand puppet called "Bite" represented aggressiveness; a leopard called "Stink" represented budding sexual feelings; a large lion represented the clash of ambivalent feelings; and a monkey represented integration. Although a teenager at the time, she was able to use these animals to work through some of her pressures and conflicts.

These young women would usually be able to make good use of a traditional psychotherapeutic approach once they had acquired some balance in their lives. Kate, having successfully graduated from college, is now a teacher.

The young men seem to have more difficulty in dependency and, therefore, will be less open about their use of an analytic, particularly a reconstructive analytic, approach. A was one such young man whose problems seemed to become evident when he entered school and, despite some efforts by a school counselor and psychiatrist at helping him, worsened. Finally, at age thirteen, he was considered to be untreatable outside a residential facility because of his lack of superego formation. He was oppositional in school, engaged in delinquent acts, and, according to his family and therapist, had no consideration for anyone but himself. In the successful treatment of this young man, it was important that he was surrounded by the same conditions that were necessary for the other youngsters whom I have described: that is, clear structure and understanding. However, it was critical that he was not forced to accept any of it. He had to proceed on his own terms because he could not risk exposing his own fragility. Our speculation is that this terror of revealing his shortcomings was a result of his parents' overidealized view of him as exceptionally brilliant. When he entered school and found that he could not immediately master everything, he perceived this as a threat to the core of his parents' love of him. If he did not live up to their grandiose view, he would lose their love. The result was the puzzle of a very bright youngster who was panicked by the possibility of failure and, therefore, refused to attempt any task.

He presented himself to me as a very independent person who wanted to live on his own terms, who was deeply concerned about those people about whom he cared, and had an individualistic but very strong sense of morality. Others saw him as extraordinarily manipulative and narcissistic. It was many years before he would make any attempt to cooperate with an individual therapist—although he would take in what was talked about. The combination of sympathy and demand finally gave him enough security to enable him to study what he had to in order to complete high school and then go on to a college that permitted him the freedom to be a highly moral anarchist. It is, of course, speculative, but possible, that the girls' ability to accept a dependent attachment enabled them to avail themselves of a reconstructive therapeutic effort whereas such a position was a threat to the young man's identity.

Conclusions

What do these reflections indicate for early detection, prevention, and treatment? I think that what has most importantly run through our experience with these more than neurotic, less than psychotic children is that they need a combination of structure and understanding, that the one without the other is simply not enough. It seems a simple and obvious prescription, but, unfortunately, our therapies and approaches are usually dichotomized: "Freudian" is caricaturized as meaning that an understanding of causes and conflicts is enough to cure, and behaviorism is caricaturized as meaning that there is nothing but externals to influence an individual. The question of how the necessary intermeshing of approaches can be accomplished outside an institutional setting is one that I have had an opportunity to explore in my supervision of psychology residents at the University of Chicago Clinics.

This clinic services youngsters from some highly dysfunctional families, youngsters who have multiple problems, organic and psychological. The children are brought to the clinic for a variety of reasons, sometimes mandated by the Department of Children and Family Services, sometimes through the concern of the parents. The services are paid for either by insurance or by the state. Often, the attendance at weekly sessions is very erratic. When this is the case, it seems that the whole family system needs help, not just the child who is brought for treatment. It is usual that the kind of help these families need is general educational support—like how to feed a family and how to have a well-organized household. They need help in their own environment more than at a clinic. With those children who do come regularly to their sessions, I have seen some of the principles used at the Orthogenic School function very effectively. The fact of their regularity seems to reflect that the support system is supportive enough to maintain them and help them utilize the strength gained from the sessions. Interns tend to see the practice of a "psychoanalytic" or "psychotherapeutic" approach as providing a safe, defined setting for the youngsters to express whatever is important to them to express. They will present the purpose of the session that way, presenting themselves as understanding and accepting. For the kind of youngster about whom we are now concerned, this presentation is very scary since it invites the surfacing of overwhelming anxiety. Talking about one's worries makes one worry more, and youngsters like ours are not then able to confine these worries to a session room. Any youngster, therefore, with a shred of integration will be very resistant to this invitation lest it destroy that still fragile integration. On the other hand, since there is a strong press for those important issues to be expressed, when a really safe environment is provided with the safeguards that ensure that the concurrent anxiety will not be overwhelming and there is hope of some mastery, the youngster will reveal those most important issues. These safeguards to our children are demonstrated more often and effectively in action than in words.

A compelling example of this occurred when I was supervising a young woman who was treating a little girl, of limited cognitive capacity, who had suffered sexual abuse. Despite much encouragement, the little girl never talked with her therapist about this abuse. However, she talked openly at some length about it t a psychometrician. This psychologist had tested her one afternoon, after which her grandmother failed to pick up the child. The psychologist then waited with her until a family member did appear. During this time, the psychologist tried to occupy and reassure the girl by playing games, reading to her, etc. It was during this period that the little girl told the psychologist about her abuse. By staying with her, being kind, and teaching her, the psychologist had demonstrated her concern but also indicated that she was going to stay within the context of reality and the present.

The psychometrician subsequently became the girl's individual therapist. In this position, she was somewhat conflicted about establishing certain parameters. However, she was able successfully to continue to help the little girl develop by first laying down very clear limits. The girl was very curious about the therapist, but the curiosity was intermingled with aggression, so the therapist had to establish the limits of her exploration very definitively: she could look in some of the drawers, but some were to stay locked; she could feel her face, but, when she hit the therapist, the session was terminated. The therapist further used her knowledge of the trauma that the girl had suffered to understand intense anxiety about other incidents that occurred during the course of her sessions. For example, when the little girl cut herself on a soap container after toileting, the therapist used the opportunity to be sympathetic with her anxiety about injury and to teach her some of the things that she needed to know about protecting herself. The therapist's concentration on empathically developing the little girl's controls, teaching her means of establishing safe limits for herself, and teaching her simple modes of better expression (both through simple speech and drawing) led to warm and constructive interchange in the sessions. Although it is not possible to say how lasting the effects were, we had evidence that there was a carryover at least in her classroom, where the therapist had contact with school personnel who reported a marked improvement in the child's behavior.

There is then the question of an even earlier detection and intervention, before the child has become so distressed that all interaction is negative and stressful. I believe that it is almost impossible to say which children will "grow out" of their difficulties and which will need help. I know of very many instances when a child has shown ominous signs and in a year has regained balance. Even with a very sensitive therapist, psychotherapeutic sessions can have the negative effect of conveying to the child that there is something wrong. There are well-known developmental and situational periods that often evoke behavior that seems very problematic: the compulsive cleanliness of three- or four-year-olds, for example, or the misbehavior of a child when the more authoritative parent is absent for a while.

There is a means, however, of prevention that does not require expert assessment or risk the possibility of conveying to the child that something is wrong—that is, that those responsible for the social milieu of the child be educated to understand their developmental needs. Very frequently, the demands of a school reveal the weakness of the child's psyche. If, however, the school would be sensitive to the potential weaknesses, there could be built-in means of imposing the new demands in more ego-syntonic ways so that, rather than a blow to the child's course of development, the experience can be an enhancement to it. By no means do I want to imply that this means to place fewer demands on children; the demands should be more appropriate. The knowledge we have of children and what we know of the meaning that learning has for them, derived from our psychoanalytic understanding, can be invaluable in planning classroom arrangements and selecting learning experiences that will enhance mental health. We have found, for example, that unmanageable children can be enchanted by learning about unmanageable animals. The primitive processes of the animals speak directly to the needs and preoccupations of these children. Such a curriculum can both attract them and contribute to their emotional as well as cognitive mastery. This is a very small example of how emotional understanding can be incorporated into the education of our children.

Parents, of course, need to be both educated and supported. I think this education needs to be not in detecting disturbance but in the avenues for healthy growth. They need to be educated in some of those things that we later see when they become intensely problematic: that anger is a natural phenomenon—both the anger of parent and the anger of child; that fascination with dirt is a natural phenomenon, as is the fascination with genitals and sex; that children are not shrunken adults but slowly growing beings who only gradually can see and understand the world (they will, of course, misinterpret it so that it is up to the adult to explain reality gently); that adults will be able to do that better if they try first to see the world from the child's point of view; and that these slowly growing beings need both understanding of their primitive thoughts, feelings, and desires and teaching of how to master them.

I believe that, if all parents were so educated and all teachers so astute, we would have fewer of these children who are more disturbed than those neurotic children who respond to our interpretive psychotherapeutic ministrations and less disturbed than those psychotic children who seem of a different dimension. I believe, however, that there would still be some who will require that we help them build there psychic structure as well as understand and tame those forces that assault it.

REFERENCES

Quinton, D.; Rutter, M.; and Gulliver, L. 1990 Continuities in psychiatric disorders from childhood to adulthood in the children of psychiatric patients. In L. Robbins and M. Rutter, eds. *Straight and Devious Pathways from Childhood to Adulthood*. Cambridge: Cambridge University Press.

Rutter, M. 1988 *Studies of Psychosocial Risk: The Power of Longitudinal Data*. Cambridge: Cambridge University Press.

Rutter, M.; Quinton, D.; and Hill, J. 1990. Adult outcomes of institution-reared children: males and females compared. In L. Robbins and M. Rutter, eds. *Straight and Devious Pathways from Childhood to Adulthood*. Cambridge: Cambridge University Press.

Rutter, M., and Sandberg, S. 1986. Epidemiology of child psychiatric disorder: methodological issues and some substantive findings. In S. Chess and A. Thomas, eds. *Annual Progress in Child Psychiatry and Child Development*. New York: Brunner/Mazel.

Sanders, J. S. 1989. *A Greenhouse for the Mind*. Chicago: University of Chicago Press.

Stern, D. 1985. *The Psychological World of the Infant*. New York: Basic.

Wadsworth, M. E. J. 1991. *The Imprint of Time: Childhood, History, and Adult Life*. Oxford: Clarendon.

Wallerstein, J. S., and Kelly, J. B. 1980. *Surviving the Breakup: How Children and Parents Cope with Divorce*. New York: Basic.

26 KIBBUTZ SASA: NURTURING CHILDREN AT RISK

ARTHUR SALZ

The dream of the early Zionists was the creation of a Jewish state or homeland that would be normal, that would be, in important characteristics, like all the other nations of the world. The new Jewish entity was to have its own government, its own flag, its own army, its own educational and cultural institutions like any other country. Chaim Weizman, the first president of Israel, quipped in prestate days that he would know they had indeed created a nation when the first Jewish policeman arrested the first Jewish criminal on the streets of Tel Aviv. Indeed, since its inception in 1948, the State of Israel has developed into a vibrant, thriving society encompassing all aspects of modern life (Ben-Gurion 1972; Elon 1971; Laqueur 1972).

But along with the blessings of normalization has also come a wide range of social, economic, and educational problems that, unfortunately, are all too "normal" in Western societies. Thus, in Israel, one finds a segment of the population, usually second- or third-generation immigrants from Middle Eastern countries, that is economically depressed and disproportionately underrepresented in the upper echelons of government, the army, higher education, or industry. The children in this group are less successful in school, and the adults, discouraged and frustrated at their lack of progress within society, feel inadequate, with some turning to drugs and crime. In Hebrew, these people are called *toanay tipuach,* those in need of nurturing, and this chapter examines a program on an Israeli kibbutz that has successfully salvaged the lives of scores of these children at risk. Although kibbutz society differs in many fundamental respects from our American way of life, several important principles emerge from this study that could well provide guidance in our own work with children in need of nurturing.

The Setting

It is my second day at Kibbutz Sasa, and the youngsters are getting used to seeing me around. During the morning break between classes, the seventh graders invite me into a game of basketball. It is their passion, and they guess correctly that, as an American, I share their love of the game. We play for a while, I dazzle them with a couple of 1950s hook shots and "back-door" moves, and my impression is that these are a bunch of very normal, "together" kids. I know that these are not the youngsters who grew up on the kibbutz but rather a group of twelve-year-olds who come from troubled backgrounds and have been selected by Youth Aliyah and the kibbutz to be integrated into the kibbutz program for the six years of junior and senior high school. But, when they hit a few jump shots or rebound, they seem like any other group of teenagers I know.

Only later in the day, when I sit and talk with Inbal, the group's educator, do I get some insight into what is seething below the surface behavior of each child. One youngster comes from a family of nine that has disintegrated following the tragic accidental death of one of the children. The mother has suffered a nervous breakdown, the father shows little interest in the children, and there is a history of stress in the family. Another child, on returning from a home visit, confessed to Inbal that she can no longer "stand the violence at home and wants to remain at Sasa" on all weekends. One of the boys is badly abused by his virile father, who favors his younger brother and has no patience for this youngster's shy, retiring manner. There is practically no communication between father and son. In another situation, in sharing with the group her role in the preparation on Fridays for the Sabbath, a girl unwittingly discloses the fact that she was a virtual "slave" in her own household. While the other youngsters tell of their mothers' delight in cooking various special dishes and the family's cooperative role on Fridays, this girl described caring for her younger siblings, cleaning the house, doing the shopping, cooking all the meals, and cleaning up afterward. She has done this every day, had absolutely no idea how unusual her role was, and even had difficulty understanding the different situations her peers described.

Another youngster had been abandoned by his mother six years ago when she abruptly left the country and has been brought up by his father ever since. However, the mother returns once a year to persist in a court fight over his custody, which adds to the turmoil the child is feeling. He is extremely shy and quiet, wets his bed at night, rarely speaks, and often will go entire days without eating. Two other youngsters come from settings where violence is common and worry incessantly about conditions at home. One girl is so concerned for her mother's safety that she must speak to her at least twice a day. And from other groups there are reports of children who have had scalding water poured on them because they soiled their pants and those who have bounced around from one institutional boarding school to another most of their lives. Inbal's assessment is that, of her group of thirteen youngsters, only two come from reasonably stable home environments.

The question, of course, is what would prompt a small number of Israeli settlers, faced with their own serious economic problems, to create this children's community, called Anne Frank Haven, for such troubled youngsters? Why would a community like Sasa, located atop a magnificent *tel* on the northern border of Israel, isolated from social and educational problems found in other parts of the country, voluntarily integrate into its kibbutz children with such serious problems and whose backgrounds were so different from those of its own youngsters? The answer is threefold, with two of the responses being of the most practical nature. First, the early years at Sasa, beginning in 1949, were fraught with tremendous hardship and struggle, so much so that, nine years later, 73 percent of the founders had left the kibbutz (Snarey 1982, p. 91). There was a desperate need for new members, and inviting socially and economically disadvantaged youngsters whose families had recently immigrated to Israel from Arab-speaking countries was a way to attract potential new members. Successfully attracting these high school students was one of the factors that saved the kibbutz.

The second practical reason had to do with the desire of parents to keep their youngsters on the kibbutz during their high school years. As a very small kibbutz, Sasa could not justify having its own high school. Instead, its students were to go to the regional high school at another kibbutz, a long, difficult drive away. This meant that their children would have had to board at that kibbutz, returing to Sasa only for the short weekend. The people at Sasa were most unhappy with this arrangement, and, by enticing a sufficient number of city youths to study at their kibbutz, they were able to have the requisite number of children to warrant creating a high school on their isolated site (Snarey 1982).

To understand the third reason, one must have a sense of the ideological roots of this entire movement. Zionism in general, and the kibbutz movement in particular, had a powerful idealistic impulse driving it from the very beginning. That thousands of young men and women traded relatively comfortable lives in Europe and North America in the first half of this century for back-breaking physical work in the hot sun, for primitive living conditions, for bouts of malaria and other serious disease, for attacks from marauding Arabs, and for the uncertainty that their efforts would ever amount to anything bespeaks a desire to participate in the creation of a nation whose purpose transcends material well-being. For many, and especially those affiliated with the left-wing socialist movement of Hashomer Hatzair, which developed over seventy-five kibbutzim of which Sasa was one, the goal was the creation of a just society (B'Ari 1964; Blasi 1986; Laqueur 1972; Lurie 1952; Snarey 1982; Spiro 1956).

Kibbutzim, writes Snarey (1982, p. 1), "are intentionally created collective communities in Israel characterized by communal child-rearing, collective economic production, and direct participatory democracy. Kibbutzim can be understood as working class communities, since most members are engaged in and have a strong sense of the inherent dignity of blue-collar work. Kibbutzim can also be understood as intellectual communities because they grew out of a philosophical commitment to socialism, Zionism, and democracy, and because ideology continues to be valued when it is applied to practical social-moral issues." Kibbutzim were to be classless communities guided by the Marxist maxim, From each according to his ability, to each according to his needs. "Rewards were to be separated from performance, and the goal was to create a more just social order and, thereby, a new kind of person" (Snarey 1982, p. 2).

Although the dream of the early kibbutzniks of creating an entire country of collective communities in Israel did not materialize, with only 3 percent of the population currently living on kibbutzim, the more than 250 kibbutzim that do exist have to a considerable extent accomplished the goal of creating a democratic, egalitarian society. However, in the mid-1960s it was apparent to the members of Sasa that to have created an island of fairness and equity did not allow them to ignore the problems that beset others in the larger society, and out of this grew a commitment to integrate a group of city youngsters into the life of their kibbutz each year. Today, many years after that decision, when I ask Uri, the current principal of the Anne Frank school, what he is proudest of, he unhesitatingly talks of the integration program, the success he has with these children from the streets, and the contribution the kibbutz is making to the state and the Zionist movement. The idealism does not seem to have waned.

The Program

Each year, twenty or so boys and girls, twelve years of age, come to Sasa after having been identified by Youth Aliyah as in need of nurturing. An organization founded in 1933 to help bring children out of Nazi Germany and eventually all war-torn Europe, Youth Aliyah had evolved within Israel as the organization caring for needy children. At the time the Sasa program was beginning, Youth Aliyah was responsible for 10,000 youngsters in Israel in several types of programs and institutions, including kibbutzim. The youngsters are selected from a larger group of applicants after a very careful intake procedure involving not only academic testing but also an interview with the child, one with a parent, and a third with both child and parent. Uri, the principal, indicates that the magnitude of the family problem does not worry the kibbutz educators; they will take troubled kids from the most difficult backgrounds. What the child must have, however, is reasonable potential to succeed in his or her high school work because in one year the youngster will be integrated into the regular program. Sasa is careful not to create the type of integration experience where kibbutz youngsters consistently succeed academically and city kids fail, thus perpetuating the stereotype.

But, apparently, success in school, while important, is more of a means to enable the rest of the program to attain its objectives. When I ask Uri about his personal goals for the youngsters, he talks first about their remaining in Israel, retaining the Zionist love of country, remaining on the kibbutz, and becoming good, useful citizens in their society, including providing the best service one is capable of in the army. Only after stating these goals does he talk about passing the *bagrut,* the formal matriculation exam that determines entrance into the university, and then only as a way of structuring a youngster's education and giving him some direction. This ordering of priorities is indicative not only of the values of a newly emerging country but also of the great emphasis kibbutz education places on the collective welfare of the group and the individual's responsibility to contribute to this common good.

Toward the end of the summer, the city kids arrrive at Sasa to begin the program that will eventually immerse them fully in the life of the kibbutz, but for the first year they are kept rather starkly isolated. They live in a separate house with two or three children sharing a room and eat all their meals there rather than in the kibbutz dining room. They study in a classroom on the ground floor of this house rather than in the large, beautiful high school, and in all aspects their lives are tightly circumscribed. Even their physical movement is severely limited to the garden surrounding their home, and one eighth grader recalled how his friend was punished the previous year for retrieving a ball on an adjacent basketball court, which was out of bounds for them.

This "magnificent isolation" of the seventh graders has two very specific purposes. Academically, it is to give them an entire year of intensive, extremely supportive assistance in preparing themselves for entrance into the high school on a level that promises success. Emotionally and socially, it is to give the youngsters time to work through the rather difficult adjustment to kibbutz life and, of great importance, to help the group of newcomers build identity and solidarity. In one short year, they will be asked to integrate with youngsters who have lived together literally from the day they were born. The *kvutzah,* the small age-graded peer group, develops a powerful identity over those twelve years, and the educators at Sasa are convinced that integration will work only if the new group is reasonably cohesive. But this isolation may sound worse than it is. Many older kids look back on the seventh grade as the "best year of their lives," and, in their culminating theatrical presentation, one class of seniors played the entire scene behind bars to express their sense of being bound up in that first year. Yet it was played tongue in cheek, and one senses a bit of pride in their ability to follow those tough rules, as compared to their lives prior to coming to Sasa.

The youngsters are supervised by two people who will have tremendous influence on their lives, the *metapelet* (house mother) and the *mechanechet* (educator). These adults are with the youngsters from daybreak until lights out at 10:30 P.M. The house mother provides the physical and emotional sustenance these youngsters require as well as the careful supervision over the children's health, general behavior, and care of themselves and their home. The educator may teach the children one or more subjects, but her role is vastly broader than that. In an era when educational jargon glibly talks about caring for the whole child, academically, emotionally, socially, and physically, Kibbutz Sasa really expects this from the educator. She is in constant contact with parents, she will serve as liaison between a child and a teacher, she may conduct group process sessions, she will counsel individual children, she will help her youngsters organize special group programs or presentations, and she will arrange for some of her kids to go off the kibbutz for special instruction. All this is done in addition to her teaching responsibilities and will keep her busy from 7:00 in the morning until late at night, six days a week. And those are the good days, when major problems have not developed.

What are the seventh grade youngsters doing all day? They are up at 6:00 A.M., have washed up and cleaned their rooms, and are surprisingly wide awake for their first class, Hebrew grammar, at 6:30. Following this, the kids have breakfast, and those assigned assist the house mother in setting out the food, the utensils, and the cleanup. After breakfast, the kids clean the house but manage to squeeze in a short basketball game before their 8:15 class in English. There are also classes that morning in Hebrew literature and mathematics, and most of the children participate enthusiastically. Later that morning, the youngsters go with Inbal to a special learning center that is set up to allow the children to pursue individual projects of their own choice. One child is engaged in a study of animals using filmstrips, another is working on an art history project, a third child is developing a book of proverbs, and another child is doing a study of protected animals and flowers. The children work extremely well individually, and I am impressed with their sense of discipline, both in this setting and earlier that morning when they voluntarily stopped a game of basketball in which they were totally absorbed when one boy realized that the break was over and it was time for the next class. And this was only November—the kids had been at Sasa for a little more than two months.

Classes were finished for the day at 12:30 P.M., as is typical in Israel.

Other days in the six-day school week the children study history and Bible, computers, physical education, art, and, their great love, drama. But the children are not free after lunch. For those assigned to serious cleaning chores of the house, the mops, pails, and squeegees are out, and the kids claim that they really like this job. Actually, the work around their home is the initial step in the development of a very deeply held kibbutz ethic of the value and dignity of physical work, and this will be expanded in the coming years. This home is now theirs: eventually the entire kibbutz will belong to them. In helping with the preparation of meals, cleaning the house, and caring for their own rooms, they are acquiring a personal and collective pride in their involvement in the kibbutz.

Following this there is the daily shower for all, and, contrary to expectations, there is little resistance. They then return to their class-room in order to do their homework under the watchful and assisting presence of a teacher. The youngsters are then free until 5:00, at which time they have the first of what will be an increasing number of con-tacts with the kibbutz: they meet their seventh-grade counterparts from the kibbutz—the *B'nai kibbutz* (lit., the sons of the kibbutz)—for sports and recreation supervised by older kids. The kibbutzniks come by and pick up the city kids and from all reports are usually quite gracious in allowing the newcomers to choose the activities. Basketball and soccer are favorites, but so are table tennis and chess. In early fall, they may go together to pick apples, which is Sasa's main crop. In November, the youngsters were still in the stage of feeling each other out, a process that will be heightened sharply the following year when the groups come together to live as a unit. But, at this stage, things are quite tentative, and one senses from the remarks of the city kids their feeling of inadequacy. They are convinced that the kib-butzniks are better athletes than they are and also believe that the kibbutzniks do not like them. When pressed why they have this feeling, they talk about how often they bother the kibbutzniks, cause trouble, and do not listen to the counselors. If the integration process is to work properly, these feelings will have to change and be replaced by a new ego strength, but there is time; it is only November of the first year of the program.

Another vitally important contact that the city youngsters have with the kibbutz is their adoption, each individually, by a kibbutz family. On kibbutzim throughout Israel, the late afternoon hours are devoted to family, and it is a very beautiful time on any kibbutz. During the hours before supper, the city kids go to the home of their surrogate parents, interact with the children in the family, who may be of any age, have a little treat of candy or cake, and participate in the life of a real family. The youngster will keep his adopted family through the six years at Sasa and often return to visit them during his army service. As youngsters in the senior class commented, sometimes the chemistry is perfect and the relationship wonderful, and sometimes it is less so. But in the first years the surrogate family plays an important role in the lives of the newcomers.

After supper, the children are generally free—one hears music being played on the recorder in several rooms, and one sees many youngsters on the telephone. The children are allowed, indeed encouraged, to call home as often as they wish. Two kids are playing chess; one or two are reading. The program, in Inbal's words, is giving the youngsters some time and space to themselves. The mood is very mellow. Sometimes the children are free through the evening. More often, however, a program is organized, perhaps a group counseling session or a recreational activity. On Friday evening, the beginning of the Sabbath, a special program is planned. It is a busy, rich day, and the entire week is filled with valuable experiences. Saturday is free, and parents are encouraged to visit their children on that day. Unfortunately, for a host of reasons, few do. Every third week, the children go home for an extended weekend (Israel has only a one-day weekend), leaving Thursday afternoon or Friday morning and returning on Sunday. These visits home are very important, and both the recently arrived seventh graders as well as the hardened eighteen-year-olds talk with great feeling about missing their families. At the same time, after they have been home for a day or so, many of them also say that they are anxious to return to Sasa, that they miss their friends there, the eating and playing together, the camaraderie, the good times. Contact with the home is essential, and Inbal keeps in touch with the parents through the newsletter she sends out regularly as well as by individual letters and telephone calls when necessary.

The first year at Sasa is a difficult adjustment for the city kids. As they look back on it, they are aware that, even though they and their parents requested involvement in the program, they really had no idea what kibbutz life was all about. Most of the kids talked about the tough rules, and, no doubt, for the majority who came from loosely organized backgrounds, the tight schedules, the structure, and the sheer novelty of living together with a group of fifteen to twenty other children had to contribute to problems of adjustment. The one rule that seemed to be most disturbing was the prohibition against informal fraternization with their kibbutznik peers, yet, in retrospect, the older kids feel that their isolation contributed significantly to the creation of a strong, unified group that was essential the following year when integration took place. The youngsters do not admit to having had any academic problems when arriving at Sasa, but the educator Rachel recalls that many children had significant learning gaps. Despite these academic problems, the youngsters stressed how helpful and supportive the teachers were during this transition period.

Although the goal of the program is integration, we have seen that most of the experiences the city youngsters have had keep them isolated from the rest of the kibbutz. This is intentional. However, one experience, toward the end of the year, is especially designed to begin the integration process. A program that began on Kibbutz Kfar Blum, and has been adopted by many other kibbutzim, is the group Bar Mitzvah project. Bar Mitzvah, in the Jewish tradition, is the coming of age of the thirteen-year-old boy, at which time the child symbolically takes on the responsibilities of adulthood, the obligation of doing *mitzvot* (good deeds). (Increasingly, girls are celebrating the Bat Mitzvah, the corresponding ceremony for them.) In searching for a model that would place this rite of passage in a modern context, many kibbutzim have created a program in which the group of thirteen-year-olds perform thirteen good deeds, such as a project on a special aspect of Jewish history, a study trip to Jerusalem, an activity enhancing the environment, or the development of a sustained relationship with children from a local Arab village. At Sasa, the theme involves moving out from within a series of concentric circles, beginning with "me and myself" and going on to a concern for the larger world, and involves the city youngsters and kibbutzniks working jointly on such activities as an archaeological project involving a second-century synagogue on Sasa's *tel,* a study about Jews throughout the world at the Diaspora Museum in Tel Aviv, and similar projects. The group Bar Mitzvah culminates in a major theatrical production, written and produced by the youngsters, which is presented to the entire kibbutz in its impressive auditorium, and it is this all-consuming event that really begins the process of binding the two very disparate groups of children together. Its impact must be very great. Almost five years later, the seniors can recall vividly each of the thirteen activities in detail and discuss their Bar Mitzvah with enormous animation and enthusiasm.

The Eighth-Grade Experience

The isolation of the seventh-grade city kids from the kibbutzniks has built up a tension, and they are both frightened and fascinated with the prospect of living together. In fact, each group I spoke with talked about that illicit midnight visit made by the kibbutzniks to the dorms of their city peers in what has become something of a tradition late in the seventh grade. The kibbutzniks are delighted with the opportunity of living with a large group of new kids and view it with great excitement. Yet, at the same time, a very definite set of social patterns and status has been established over twelve years. This was about to be disrupted as the "new" kids would begin to vie for position and role within the enlarged group. The city kids, for their part, generally held the kibbutzniks in very high regard, and the thought of living together was anxiety provoking. Yet, at the same time, it meant increased status as they moved toward integration into the kibbutz.

The excitement of meeting new youngsters is, in part, sexual. Kibbutz boys and girls in the same age group have grown up sharing sleeping quarters and shower facilities. "Despite the 'Freedom' with respect to viewing the body of the opposite sex," Rabin and Beit-Hallahmi (1982, pp. 33–34) write, "kibbutz taboos and prohibitions with regard to sex play and sexual contacts are strict and unrelenting. These taboos apply primarily to members of the peer group, with whom the contact is continuous for many years. The taboos are not unlike the brother-sister taboos in the conventional family. It is probably due to this fact that there are no marriages between members of the same group in the kibbutz" (see also Bettelheim 1969; Spiro 1958). However, in the eyes of the kibbutz youngsters, the city kids fall into a different category; they are not viewed as siblings, and intimate relationships between kibbutz and city youngsters do sometimes develop. Rachel, the educator of the twelfth-grade group, introduced me to one of the couples, a boy from Tiberias with considerable musical talent and a lovely kibbutz-raised girl. She and several other educators at Sasa have told me that, in the case of serious, mature relationships, the youngsters will be given an opportunity for privacy and that additional counseling is given the couple concerning contraception.

Indeed, most of the youngsters indicated that there were many difficulties and problems during the eighth year, some no doubt exacerbated by this new sexual dimension. They talked about the realignment of friendships, the development of cliques, the struggle for power, and the uncertainty of one's position within the group. The kibbutzniks did not like the rough language and behavior of the city kids. They were miffed that the new kids did not respect some of the mores of the kibbutz, for example, that the space around one's bed was sacrosanct. They were also convinced that the teachers leaned over backward to favor the city youngsters. Typically, the city kids were sure that everyone favored the kibbutzniks, that they always got what they wanted, and that they were pampered, as one senior said, like flowers grown in a hothouse.

But gradually, for most groups, a strong, cohesive bond develops. The youngsters live three or four in a room, a mix of city and kibbutz kids. They are together in classes, in activities throughout the entire day and evening, at meals and at work, and this very intense and protracted contact provides the potential for close friendships. Nurit, the educator of the eight grade this year, tells me that the whole secret is to get the kids doing things together rather than talking. She chides the kibbutzniks for loving to talk about "their problem" and much prefers getting the youngsters involved in art projects or sports rather than holding endless group discussions. Nurit's convinced that integration works more smoothly for the boys, who are more apt to play ball together, who tend to be less sensitive, and, in the case of the city kids, who do better in school than the girls. However, she does hold group discussions with her youngsters regularly, and one of the perennial topics is the acceptance of those who may be less competent than you. On the other hand, Rachel, the educator of the twelfth grade, does a great deal of group process with her youngsters. Her current group was not very cohesive, she says, when she became their educator in the ninth grade. In her regularly scheduled group meetings, Rachel used a large variety of projective devices, including the writing of letters, stories, and poems and role playing, to give the children an opportunity to vent their feelings about various problems and concerns. She recalls that the youngsters were tremendously responsive and that out of this sharing of feelings developed an openness that enabled the group to be as unified as it was now in the twelfth grade.

The eighth-grade program begins to expand the youngsters' horizons in many ways. The children now attend the very attractive high school, and, in addition to the full range of academic subjects (mathematics, biology, chemistry, physics, Hebrew literature and language, world and Jewish history, Bible, geography, and English), they begin their technical studies. Three shops, in electronics, metal work, and home economics, are available, and the youngsters spend half a year in each shop as a general orientation to the field. Some youngsters will pursue these studies at a higher level in the future. In each shop I visited, the youngsters seemed highly motivated, the teaching was enthusiastic, the work was done with rigor, and the cakes baked by the home economics class were delicious. Roni, the teacher of electronics as well as math and physics, admitted that the city kids often grasp the work more slowly, but, with the extra help that he provides, most have no trouble catching up.

At the same time as the eighth graders start attending the high school, they begin their role as workers on the kibbutz, putting in an hour and a half daily, four days a week, in one of the various branches of the kibbutz economy. The boys often choose or are assigned to the cowsheds, the chicken coops, the orchards, or the packing house. While the girls may choose these same jobs, more often than not they work as assistants to the *metapelet* (nurse/educator) in the children's houses. The work period is taken seriously by the youngsters and increases in time and responsibility as they become older. The adults at Sasa view the youngsters' work as a real contribution to the economic life of the community, over and above the very powerful educational message concerning the value and dignity of manual labor. Both in the way the youngsters swaggered off to work after lunch and in the way they spoke about it in evening meetings, I sensed that they took considerable pride and pleasure in their ability to give something back to the kibbutz. Work provides the youngsters with their most valid connection to the larger kibbutz community and links them strongly to specific adults. This tie is so great that young people on leave from their army service, and free to relax for a day or two, invariably spend those days in the branch in which they worked in school. What an important lesson for all those involved with adolescent education.

On returning from work, the youngsters have some free time, then shower, do their homework, and, perhaps later in the afternoon, visit their real or surrogate families on the kibbutz. The period before and immediately after supper is filled with many special activities that are optional—basketball practice, tennis, volleyball, folk dancing, art, literature programs, and music—in what is an enriching aspect of their education. Later in the evening, each group comes together, for a movie one night, a program on kibbutz ideology on another, and, of course, the Friday evening Welcoming of the Sabbath with a cultural event. Two other nights are devoted to education in democratic living and require some explanation. The first evening enables youngsters to serve on a committee whose function it is to contribute to the life of the group. Committees deal with maintenance of the house and classrooms, the group's smooth functioning, the preparation of a monthly publication, and the development of Friday evening programs. Once a week, the committees meet under the guidance of the house mother, the educator, or another member of the kibbutz. For example, the group responsible for the upkeep of the grounds around their house meets with a kibbutznik skilled in landscaping. Here we have another area where the youngsters are learning to be responsible for the general welfare of the entire group.

The other evening devoted to democratic living is the group meeting and is of the utmost importance. Here, in *sichot* (conversation), is a "formalized opportunity for a *kvutza* (group) and its staff to discuss an issue or a problem which immediately confronts a group" (Reimer 1977, p. 221). There is only one radio in the eighth-grade home, and some of the youngsters complain that it is on too loud. What is the solution? Should each child get his or her own transistor radio? The educator sees that as an answer. The youngsters disagree. The issue is unresolved and must be dealt with at the next meeting. The seventh-grade boys have been fooling around in the shower, caused in part by their concern that girls are trying to look at them. Remedies are discussed, and the educator talks of the larger issues of trust and responsibility. The youngsters agree to follow the rules that only four can be in the shower at one time. The tenth graders are worried about the matriculation *bagrut* (exam) that they will take in their senior year and are asking that more testing be introduced into the school program. They show concern for the weak students, yet they are seeking more pressure in the school. The staff members listen attentively and tell the youngsters that they will consider their feelings and eventually make a decision (Reimer 1977, pp. 209–21).

Most issues are resolved through talking and reaching a generally accepted solution. It is rare that a vote is taken; rather, consensus is sought since the goal is group cohesiveness. All the participants are encouraged to present their feelings and thoughts, the approach is democratic, and the decision is binding on the group. This procedure for problem solving is analogous to that of the kibbutz and in this way serves as a very powerful and practical education in real democratic process.

Beyond the Eighth Grade

With most groups, the eighth-grade experience has achieved its goals. It has brought children from two very different sets of backgrounds together in a living experience, and it has made strides toward creating a cohesive group. The youngsters have studied together in school, worked together in the cow barns or the infants' homes, played as a group, eaten all their meals together in the kibbutz dining hall, and worked to solve their problems together. The succeeding four years build on this progress with the goal of eventually achieving full integration. Academically, the youngsters continue with the Ministry of Education curriculum, including mathematics, biology, chemistry, physics, Hebrew literature and language, world and Jewish history, Bible, geography, and English. While in grades 7–9 all children follow a prescribed curriculum, from the tenth grade on the youngsters concentrate on a broad area such as humanistic, scientific, or technological studies. In the eleventh grade, preparations begin for a major research project to be conducted in the senior year, and most students take one or two matriculation exams. In the twelfth grade, the academic focus is on the senior project and the matriculation exams. Outside school, the youngsters are very committed to the branch of work that they have chosen and are now contribuing the equivalent of one day a week of serious work. In addition, their "extracurricular" activities, including the basketball team, folk dancing, arts and crafts, and other choices, are central to their lives as new levels of skill are attained. But most significant for the twelfth graders is their impending induction into the army. The three-year (or more, depending on choice of branch or selection for officers' training) stint for boys and the two-year service for girls looms as the single most important event in their future, and it is the rare eighteen-year-old who talks very much about plans beyond the army.

The twelfth graders, in looking back on the entire experience in the

Anne Frank Haven, talk about the initial difficulties of living with children very different from themselves, the vying for status and leadership roles within the group, being excited but anxious about meeting new youngsters, and the tremendous effort made by adults and children to forge a unified class. But now, as I chatted with the group in the middle of their senior year, "it felt so good," said Shirali, "sitting with people here like brothers and sisters, real friends." At this stage, youngsters and adults no longer differentiate between children of the kibbutz and "city kids." They are now all very much part of the kibbutz.

This haven, however, does have its problems, some of which prove intractable. Kibbutz education, throughout the country, is conducted on a very high level. Over and above the fiscal allotment from the Ministry of Education, kibbutzim supplement their education budgets in money and person power and thus are able to maintain excellent adult-child ratios at every level from the infants' homes through high school. In a country where class size usually is close to forty, kibbutzim keep classes at about twenty youngsters. The kibbutzim that I am familiar with have modern facilities, some utilizing an "open plan," beautiful, well-stocked libraries, and excellent sports facilities. Young adults wishing to study to become teachers are selected with great care by their fellow kibbutzniks, many of whom are or will be parents of school-age children, and this accounts, in part, for the high quality of instruction on the kibbutz. Overall, a tremendous commitment is made to excellence in education, and the schools are the pride of each kibbutz. Sasa is no exception.

Into this setting walk twenty or so "city kids," seventh graders whose own educational background in many cases has been poor. Although the youngsters are reluctant to admit it, Rachel indicates that they do come with many learning deficits. The entire first year, in which they are isolated from the rest of the kibbutz, is devoted to eliminating these gaps. The teaching that I observed was skillful and very supportive, and the groups were small.

Several of the projects were individualized so that children had choices and could pursue a project of particular interest to them. A structured afternoon homework session was part of the schedule, and during that time the children could seek assistance if required. Tutoring or enrichment continues to be available in all grades. Despite this great effort, some of the youngsters, for a host of reasons, find the academic work too difficult and are asked to leave the program. In Rachel's twelfth-grade group, which is considered a very successful, integrated cohort, four of the twenty youngsters from the city dropped out over the years.

Behavioral problems revolving around social relationships and infraction of rules are a continuous issue to be dealt with in the program. For the city youngster, the adjustment to kibbutz life can be very difficult: group living, challenging academic work, separation from family, and a set of behavioral requirements that are often very different from what had been experienced earlier in life: in short, a completely different environment. Expectations are high, but the adults are supportive and helpful, and at times this is taken for weakness. The tough city kid is vying for status, but he or she is up against the kibbutznik, who somehow is the better athlete, is more relaxed in the setting, knows his or her way around the kibbutz, and is someone everyone naturally looks up to. Added to this are the regular visits home, every third weekend, often with a renewal of the tension and problems in the house or on the street, and then a return to Kibbutz Sasa, which is so very different. It has to be a confusing, stressful situation for many of the city kids, seriously affecting their interpersonal relationships.

An inordinate amount of time is spent by the house mother and group educator in working with youngsters on these matters, usually with success. In addition, the school psychologist and other kibbutzniks with a special relationship with a youngster, like an adult with whom the youngster works in an occupational branch, will be involved in dealing with the problem. Again, every effort is made over a long period of time to deal with the issue, but in the end some children are removed from the program for improper behavior. While no one in Rachel's group had been removed for nonacademic reasons, in the current tenth-grade class, which was much less cohesive than Rachel's owing to several turnovers in house mothers and educators, six children had been removed for serious long-term misbehavior.

The Results

On the basis of the indices of success established by the kibbutz, the results of the program are impressive. On average, 70–80 percent of the city children complete the six-year program and pass their matriculation exams. While no controlled experiments have been carried out, comparable youngsters who remain in their home setting have considerably lower rates of success in high school in Israel. Second, because there is almost universal conscription at age eighteen, and because of the importance of the Israeli army in defense of the country, successful participation in army service is another criteria for evaluating youngsters. Problematic youths, not unlike many who arrive at Sasa at age twelve, are often deemed unacceptable for army service when they are of age or, if inducted, are often dishonorably discharged before completing their three years. This is a serious, permanent stigma on the individual. Youngsters who complete the program at Sasa are successful in the Israeli army.

A third criterion of the kibbutz is to help each troubled youngster become a *mensch,* that is, a good human being. There is considerable evidence that, in fact, these youngsters who arrive with a very low level of moral judgment make remarkable gains in their moral development and are comparable to their *B'nai Kibbutz* peers by completion of high school (Reimer 1977; Snarey 1982).

The final criterion of the kibbutz is the number of city children who eventually become members of Kibbutz Sasa. This choice is made after their army service, which is at least three years beyond completion of the program. True, many of the youngsters spend their army leave time back on the kibbutz, but there is a considerable lapse of time between the experience of the tight-knit school group and their return to the kibbutz. In addition, as with most Israelis, following army service a year or more is spent traveling outside the country or living in one of the big cities of Israel. This means that, in some cases, five or six years may have elapsed between graduation and the decision whether to return to the kibbutz. Throughout Israel, about 50 percent of the children of kibbutzim return to live there as adults; at Sasa, 70 percent of the city youngsters have returned to become members.

Conclusions

The program at Kibbutz Sasa achieves these results for two fundamental reasons. First, at Sasa the youngster is totally integrated into every aspect of kibbutz life. Following the preparatory seventh grade, the city and kibbutz-reared children live and study together twenty-four hours a day. Indeed, their youth community serves as a miniature replica of the larger Sasa society. Further, the children are adopted by kibbutz families and, in addition, are in continuous interaction with other adults in their daily work in the orchard, the cowshed, or the children's home. Surrounded by this all-embracing experience, the city youngsters imbibe the common values of the kibbutz community, including participatory democracy, collective economic endeavor, and the goal of creating a just society. Kibbutzim that have similar programs but do not integrate the city children as fully do not have the same degree of positive impact.

The other reason for the significant change in the city youngsters is the extraordinary care and nurturing they receive from their educator and their house mother. These two professionals support each youngster academically and emotionally through these difficult years, and their deep concern for each individual child is almost palpable. To the greatest extent possible, a child's experience at Sasa is custom tailored: a youngster interested in dentistry is given his work assignment in the dental clinic; the boy with musical talent is sent twice a month to study at the Conservatory in Tel Aviv, three hours away; a girl is allowed to spend time in Zfat, the nearby city, in order to study business subjects, a course not given at Sasa. Paradoxically, in this collective community, great stress is placed on the well-being of each individual. A seventh grader who had been at Sasa only a few months told me how helpful her teacher was in enabling her to understand some complicated schoolwork. Then, reflecting back on her previous experience, she said, "It's better here at Sasa." It sure is.

REFERENCES

B'Ari, S. 1964. Fifty years of a kibbutz movement: Hashomar Hatzair. *New Outlook* 7(1): 44–50.

Ben-Gurion, D. 1972. *Israel: A Personal History.* New York: Herzl.

Bettelheim, B. 1969. *The Children of the Dream.* New York: Macmillan.

Blasi, J. 1986. *The Communal Experience of the Kibbutz.* New Brunswick, N.J.: Transaction.

Elon, A. 1971. *The Israelis: Founders and Sons.* New York: Holt, Rinehart & Winston.

Laqueur, W. 1972. *A History of Zionism.* New York: Holt, Rinehart & Winston.

Lurie, Z. 1952. Twenty-five years of struggle and growth: anniversary of Kibbutz Artzi. *Israel Horizons* 1(1): 1–14.

Rabin, A. I., and Beit-Hallahmi, B. 1982. *Twenty Years Later: Kibbutz Children Grown Up.* New York: Springer.

Reimer, J. B. 1977. A study in the moral development of kibbutz adolescents. Ph.D. diss., Harvard University.

Snarey, J. R. 1982. The social and moral development of kibbutz founders and sabras: a cross-sectional and longitudinal cross-cultural study. Ph.D. diss., Harvard University.

Spiro, M. E. 1956. *Kibbutz: Venture in Utopia.* Cambridge, Mass.: Harvard University Press.

Spiro, M. E. 1958. *Children of the Kibbutz.* Cambridge, Mass.: Harvard University Press.

27 THERAPEUTIC EFFECTS OF A NEAR-DEATH EXPERIENCE IN ANOREXIA NERVOSA

MICHAEL D. MILLER

Anorexia nervosa is a common psychiatric disorder associated with considerable morbidity and increased mortality. The illness typically affects young women between the ages of twelve and twenty-five with a prevalence of one in 250 (APA 1987). Reviewing data from twelve major outcome studies of anorexia nervosa, Schwartz and Thompson (1981) found the average mortality rate to be 6 percent after 5.3 years of follow-up. Mortality increased over time, reaching nearly 20 percent in those patients followed up after fifteen years. Although suicide occurs in 1 percent or more of anorexics, the complications of self-starvation, malnutrition, excessive exercise, and antacid, diuretic, and laxative abuse account for most deaths attributed to the disorder (Schwartz and Thompson 1981; Halmi, Broadland, and Rigas 1975).

Typically, the symptoms of the medical complications of anorexia nervosa are denied by patients, who maintain meticulously groomed appearances and cheerful countenances. Despite presenting a facade of normalcy and well-being, many anorexics suffer medical complications with significant rates of morbidity and mortality.

Less common, and more easily prevented, are complications arising iatrogenically during refeeding. This chapter reports a case of an adolescent patient with anorexia nervosa who developed profound hypophosphatemia with severe neurological sequelae during the course of oral realimentation. This case illustrates the potential dangers of aggressive nutritional management in the severely malnourished and physiologically fragile anorexics as well as how this patient's near-death experience influenced the course of psychotherapy and catalyzed her recovery.

Clinical Case Example

A seventeen-year-old adolescent female became preoccupied with her food intake as well as her body shape and weight during the summer of 1988. She began restricting her caloric intake and exercising compulsively. Prior to this point in her life, she stated that she had enjoyed food greatly and was unconcerned about her body weight or shape. Over the course of the summer and ensuing fall, her weight dropped from a baseline of 105 pounds to sixty-five pounds.

In October, she experienced an episode of loss of consciousness and was resuscitated in a local emergency room, where her blood glucose level was noted to be twenty-two milligrams/deciliter. Apparently, her body's glycogen stores had been depleted, and she could no longer generate sufficient glucose catabolically to sustain life. After being stabilized, she was transferred to a tertiary care hospital with a psychiatric unit that specializes in the treatment of eating disorders. Over the course of a three-month admission, she was treated medically with parenteral hyperalimentation and later psychiatrically with a cognitive-behavioral approach on an eating-disorders unit.

She was discharged in late December, weighing seventy-eight pounds, without meaningful psychiatric follow-up. She quickly reverted to her preadmission anorexic behavior and lost the weight that she had begrudgingly gained while hospitalized. In January 1989, she experienced another episode of loss of consciousness and was again treated in her local emergency room, where her blood glucose level was noted to be seventeen milligrams/deciliter. Her weight was fifty-five pounds at this time.

After spending two weeks in the intensive-care unit of her community hospital receiving parenteral hyperalimentation, she was transferred back to the hospital where she had been initially treated for her eating disorder. She was maintained on hyperalimentation for another month. During this period, she suffered a number of serious medical complications, including aspiration pneumonia, candida sepsis, and rhabdomyolysis. She remained significantly anemic, was thrombocytopenic, and was, at times, found to be hypoglycemic, hypocalcemic, and hypomagnesemic. Most alarming, however, was the fact that, in spite of parenteral hyperalimentation, she failed to gain significant weight.

Her treating physician described her as extremely resistant, highly manipulative, and often quite deceptive. Her efforts to undermine treatment were legion. When being treated with hyperalimentation in the intensive-care unit, she required continuous nursing supervision because of persistent self-destructive behavior such as opening her hyperalimentation port to air or diverting the hyperalimentation solution from her central-line catheter to the trash can beside her bed. On a number of occasions, she was discovered to be attempting to deceive her physicians as to her oral intake by hiding food in her hospital gown. She would try to appear to be gaining weight by "water loading" and by placing coins in her underwear for extra weight. Because of her failure to respond to treatment at this institution, she was transferred to our hospital when she was deemed medically stable. Her weight was fifty-six pounds at the time of her admission to our eating-disorders unit in March 1989.

Initially, she appeared as a frightened, cachectic, heavily made-up, but attractive white, adolescent female with facial lanugo. She was dressed in a baggy pink sweat suit. She was cooperative, although tired. She maintained good eye contact. There were no adventitious motor movements, and she ambulated slowly but without difficulty. Her speech was soft and normal in rate, tone, and prosody. She described her mood as "tired." Her affect was sad, but at times she appeared animated and bright. Her thoughts were logical and goal directed. There was no evidence of hallucinations, delusions, or distortions of body image. She stated clearly that she believed herself to be too thin. Suicidal ideation or intent was denied, as was binging, purging, and laxative or diuretic abuse. She had little insight into her condition. She was alert and oriented to person, place, and time and appeared to be of low average intelligence.

On admission to the unit, she was oppositional and defiant and failed to cooperate with the parameters of treatment, which included expectations of food intake. When told by the unit administrator that she would have to accept feedings via a nasogastric tube, she flatly refused and demanded to leave. The administrator advised me to have her involuntarily committed and attempt to transfer her to another hospital with more readily available medical backup. This proved to be impossible. In the end, I prevailed on her to stay and accept tube feedings temporarily by offering to help her in any way I could to make her hospitalization worthwhile.

The eating-disorders unit staff's anxiety about her low weight was dramatically reinforced by her death-camp appearance. Now that access to her gut was secured, an aggressive refeeding schedule was initiated to ensure rapid weight gain as a margin of protection against medical demise. She was started on four cans of full-strength high-calorie liquid nutrition on tube-feeding day 1 and was rapidly advanced to six cans daily on tube-feeding day 3 via a Dobhoff nasogastric tube. This supplied her with 2,160 kilocalories/day, which was far in excess of her metabolic demands at the time, her body having long before adapted to a starvation equilibrium.

Seven days after beginning to receive nasogastric feedings, she began to complain of "feeling dizzy" and reported difficulty in ambulation. Roughly twenty-four hours later she began to complain of muscle weakness in all extremities as well as parasthesias periorally, lingually, and distally in all extremities. Initially, these complaints were mild. Her vital signs were stable, and her EKG was normal. Despite the concerns of the nursing staff, we elected to observe her on the unit overnight. Laboratory studies including a CBC with differential, electrolytes, and a biochemistry profile were sent to the laboratory to be done that evening.

The next morning found her to be markedly worse. She was now significantly quadraparetic and dysarthric. She had difficulty swallowing and complained of marked parasthesias in all extremities and in her face. At this point, she was transferred to the emergency department of our hospital, which is located at another site.

Initial laboratory studies were normal, except for the serum phosphate, which was 0.4 milligrams per deciliter (the normal range is 2.5–4.5). Shortly after admission to the neurological intensive-care unit, she developed significant respiratory compromise and was electively intubated prior to respiratory collapse.

The following day, an EMG with nerve conduction velocities was performed. The study revealed a marked decrease in motor amplitudes with a normal DL, a normal CV, and normal sensory amplitudes. The results were diagnostic of an acquired demyelinating polyneuropathy or Guillain-Barre syndrome.

By the third hospital day, her serum phosphate had been restored to normal, but clinically she remained quadraparetic and unable to ventilate without mechanical support. She gradually recovered motor strength and was successfully extubated on hospital day 11, when her vital capacity had increased to 900 cubic centimeters. Because of a persistent absence of a gag reflex, she received feedings via a nasogastric tube. By hospital day 14, she demonstrated the ability to eat and was permitted to do so cautiously. On hospital day 19, her strength had recovered to $4+/5$ throughout. Her gait was wide based, and she had bilateral foot drops, but she was considered to be medically stable and was transferred back to our psychiatric facility for ongoing care. Her discharge diagnosis was Guillain-Barre syndrome secondary to hypophosphatemia.

During the course of her admission to the medical division of our hospital, I visited her four or five times each week. Spending this time together under such dire circumstances helped us forge a warm and meaningful therapeutic relationship. When she returned to the eating-disorders unit, she was highly motivated and engaged in treatment. Her struggle with food intake continued, however, as did her manipulative and deceptive games with the nursing staff, although both to a far lesser degree than before her neurological collapse. For the first time since beginning treatment, she exhibited a willingness to work with, and not against, her treatment team. She fought hard to overcome the anorexic thinking and behaviors perfected during the course of her illness.

The fear of neurological decompensation motivated her recovery. As she put it, "I don't want to ever lose control like that again." She continued to improve in the milieu and gain weight slowly. We established a good working alliance, and I enjoyed basking in the glow of a positive transference. In therapy, I tried to help her articulate feelings the intensity of which terrified her and that would not have been tolerated at home. Her murderous rage toward her emotionally abusive, alcoholic father as well as the anger and sadness she felt because of her perceived unimportance to her mother predominated in the therapy. She maintained a hostile dependence on her mother, and she was caught in a struggle to separate and individuate. The patient, "K," barely had any sense of self defined outside the context of her largely inadequately nurturing family. One of the central tasks of psychotherapy was, I believe, to help her begin to develop a sense of herself through the experience of her relationship with me.

Nine weeks after her return from the medical hospital, her weight was seventy-eight pounds. Unfortunately, at this time I went abroad to begin an elective. Her care was entrusted to a resident colleague of mine, who was to cover her during my ten-week absence. K decided, virtually a priori, that she did not like her substitute doctor and was unable to work collaboratively with him. Three weeks later, her weight unchanged, she left the hospital and returned home.

On my return, seven weeks after her departure from the hospital, I contacted her, and she came in to see me as an outpatient. To my surprise, she had continued to gain weight and had not resumed her anorexic behaviors. Her weight was ninety-five pounds at this time. Although she did not keep regular appointments, her weight continued to increase, and, on her last visit in February 1990, she appeared stable at 105 pounds. She stated that she was no longer preoccupied with her weight or body shape. Her relationships with family members and friends remained chaotic as characerological and situational problems persisted. Nevertheless, she was employed and enjoyed an active social life.

In May 1992, I called K and initially spoke with her mother, who informed me that K was doing well. She had moved into an apartment with a girlfriend, was working, and had a remarkably supportive boyfriend. With the exception of some bulemic symptoms in the past, she detected no evidence of K's eating disorder and reported that K's weight had stabilized at 110–115 pounds. My conversation with K was equally uplifting as she enthusiastically regaled me with her recent accomplishments.

Discussion of the Clinical Case Example

This case dramatically illustrates the potentially catastrophic effects of aggressive refeeding efforts in the physiologically fragile anorexic. Moreover, it highlights the constructive therapeutic consequences of a near-death experience in a highly resistant patient.

The patient reported in this chapter is the first case report of an anorexic in whom hypophosphatemia-induced Guillain-Barre syndrome was precipitated by enteral realimentation. The only other similar case previously reported was by Sheridan and Collins (1983). They reported a case of hypophosphatemia in a laxative-abusing anorexic patient who, during the course of tube feedings, took an overdose of antacid. Her phosphate dropped from the low normal range (2.7 milligrams/deciliter) on admission to 0.4 milligrams/deciliter after the overdose. She suffered an abdominal ileus, necessitating parenteral nutrition and intensive-care-unit monitoring but no neurological insult. Fortunately, this patient recovered on phosphate repletion as well.

One of the more compelling aspects of the case presented is the degree to which this patient's medical illness provided a fortuitous opportunity for me to connect with her psychotherapeutically. When I initially accepted her into treatment, I was counseled not to be optimistic that she would survive her anorexia. Her drive for self-starvation appeared resistant to human intervention. I was advised by my psychotherapy preceptors to be aware of any understandable, but misguided, rescue fantasies I might harbor in deciding to work with her.

I certainly believed, or at least wanted to believe, that I could make a meaningful difference in the course of this girl's life. My hope was that the relationship that we might establish could provide a context for her to experience herself and her life in new ways that might be life sustaining. K's decision to stay in the hospital and accept a feeding tube after she became intrigued by my offer of a supportive therapeutic relationship only strengthened my conviction that she was in fact engageable and treatable. Her hunger for meaningful, empathic human contact was intense. Unfortunately, her determination to prevail in control battles with her mother at home and with her physicians during her first course of treatment had made more constructive engagements with caretakers virtually impossible. Like many primitive patients, her powerful needs to frustrate and defeat served to alienate potential self-objects in her life.

I believe that my warm, sincere interest in her during her first few days in the psychiatric hospital were crucial in establishing the beginning footholds of a therapeutic alliance. I found her compelling and was touched, as well as horrified, by her emaciated physical presence. As a therapist and as a human being, I wanted to help her find a more life-affirming path than the path of self-denial and self-destruction that she was committed to.

When, after just a few days, she decompensated medically and had to be admitted to the neurological intensive-care unit, I was initially relieved. I would no longer have to be responsible for the burden of her care or have to suffer the pain of her possible demise. With the encouragement of one unusually adventurous preceptor, however, I elected to embrace the challenge of the situation and meet with her while she was in the medical hospital as often as I reasonably could. In addition, sharing responsibility for her acute care with others freed me to focus directly on enhancing our relationship.

My goal was to try to use the catastrophe of her medical collapse to forge a meaningful connection with her. I saw her almost every day. My involvement was made more powerful by the fact that her mother visited her only twice and her father not at all during this hospitalization. I held her hand when she could not move it and tried to articulate what I imagined she might be feeling as she lay paralyzed on a respirator. I tried to imagine myself in her place and spoke to her of the terror I saw in her eyes. I told her how frightening it must be not to be able to move, to speak, or to breathe. I tried to help her feel less alone when she was paralyzed, intubated, and completely helpless. I shared her fear of death and the impotent rage that accompanied her loss of control. When she began to recover function, I shared many of the small victories that constituted her eventual recovery.

Control was perhaps K's most paramount concern in life and one that she exercised tenaciously with her anorexia. Paralyzed and helpless, her most feared anxiety had become a reality. She could no longer maintain the illusion that she was in control of her life, that everything would be fine, and that she could live with her eating disorder. She had hit rock bottom and found herself completely out of control. This experience, however, enabled her to realize that she really would die if she did not fight her anorexia. All my caring would not help; her determination to starve was beyond the limits of my abilities to save her unless she were willing to fight to live. This occurred in her only as a consequence of having faced the limits of her mortality.

When K returned to the psychiatric hospital, she became an important and well-liked member of the therapeutic community. She engaged constructively in her treatment, both in the milieu and in individual sessions with me. K's denial of the severity of her illness was broken by her experience of total decompensation. Her pathological determination to lose weight had been transformed into a determination to get well.

For the first time in her life, she began to learn that she could experience feelings safely and share them with other people without catastrophic consequences. In our individual sessions, we spent a great deal of time discussing the enormous rage she felt toward many people in her life, especially her emotionally abusive, alcoholic father. She admitted to me on more than one occasion that, if she were to speak of all the people that she wanted to murder, she feared that she would never be released from the hospital. I helped her articulate those murderous feelings and learn the difference between thoughts and deeds.

K and I often had our sessions outdoors as the unit protocol dictated that she not be permitted to exercise because of her low weight. As a staff psychiatrist, however, I was administratively exempt from the rules of the unit. For K, a vigorously athletic adolescent, our walks were an important parameter of her treatment. My unique ability literally to open doors and take her outside made visits with me even more special.

When, as inevitably expected, she would get into control battles with nurses on the unit and would complain about how nasty or unfair someone had been to her, my responses, more often than not, would be on the order of, "Well, nurse so-and-so can be a bitch, you know." My overriding concern was to preserve the therapeutic alliance by tolerating splits between myself and various members of the nursing or administrative staff. This was a means of diverting negative projections away from me onto other figures, whom we could "hate" together. Later, when passions had cooled a bit, I would challenge some of these hostile projections and attempt to have her gain perspective on a given situation from her developing observing ego.

I was very much aware that such a therapeutic approach was not only untraditional but potentially counterproductive as well. I knew that my more classically minded colleagues could accuse me of colluding with my patient's pathology in not confronting her splitting more aggressively. My feeling, however, was that only by attempting to stay close to her within her highly narcissistic system of perceptions and projections could I ever hope to gain enough of a foothold into her emotional life to be able to challenge these and help expand her observing ego without precipitating a negative therapeutic reaction and the destruction of our relationship.

In taking this type of therapeutic stance, I was guided by ideas that Havens (1986) has so eloquently articulated in his *Making Contact*. Havens advocates the use of what he terms "counterprojective" statements such as my comment about the nursing staff to assist in "reducing the projections on the therapist to a manageable level" (p. 138). The patient's interpersonal world—instead of the therapist, as is encouraged by classical technique—becomes the screen on which internal object relations are projected.

By experiencing her powerful rage and frequent outrages with me by her side, K could borrow my ego strength and learn new ways of managing her passions more constructively. The more I could identify with and help her express her feelings, the more I felt she could identify with my more mature ways of coping with them.

Over time, my hope was that K would identify with me and internalize our relationship. Eventually, I hoped to become an important player in her intrapsychic object world. In a sense, I was providing myself and our relationship as food for her psyche to help modify the malignant internal objects with which she was at war and that clearly had references in her real-world experience with her parents.

K came to see me as a "good" parental figure with both maternal and paternal dimensions. I avoided control battles, something her mother could not resist. I also tried to understand and appreciate her in ways her mother was unable to. Unlike her father, I was consistent and reliable in my sincere affection toward her. I grew to have warm, tender feelings for her, which she was undoubtedly aware of.

I also will admit to being narcissistically gratified in having her as my patient. She was clearly the most dramatically ill patient anyone had seen in the hospital for quite some time. On my walks with her, I often felt like I was taking some rare species (a kind of praying mantis, perhaps) out for a walk. I enjoyed the reputation of being the resident bold enough to take on such a challenging patient.

My exhibitionism was gratified by the knowledge that we were noticed wherever we went because of K's profoundly disturbing thinness. My own gratification in treating her posed an interesting problem for me in terms of my analysis of the countertransference. Was I merely "getting off" on having the most dramatically appearing patient in the hospital, or were my feelings reflective of something within her that I was experiencing via a form of projective identification?

Besides whatever narcissistic gain I earned in being her therapist, was I being made aware, more important, of K's powerful desires to be noticed? Her appearance was truly shocking. She was an outrage against nature and nurturance. I had the feeling that her cachexia was her primitive but effective way of screaming, "Look at me, notice that I exist and I need too." Her anorexia was more than just punitive self-denial or an attempt to bind her murderous rage. It also served as a vehicle to express her longings for love and was an affirmation of her powerful needs for emotional nurturance. These primitive object needs remained unmet at home and would have to be met in some attenuated fashion by me and the hospital staff for treatment to be successful.

Weekly family meetings with her mother helped me understand some of the family dynamics involved in the genesis of her psychopathology. K was the second of four children born to a woman who was clearly overwhelmed by the demands of child rearing. She was only twenty-one herself when K was born. Father was alcoholic and unemployed at the time of her illness and had been so for much of the marriage, relegating even more of the household responsibilities to mother. K was described by mother and mother's sister, who attended the first meeting, as having been formerly "the family angel." She had been mother's helper until mid-adolescence and had maintained a posture of strict compliance with mother's will. Mother reported that K regularly awoke before the rest of the family on the weekends and cleaned the entire house before anyone else had got out of bed. This changed the year before she manifested any symptoms of her eating disorder, when mother reports that she underwent a "personality change" and became hostile, argumentative, and defiant. The family angel had become the family devil, seemingly without cause. Developmentally, we can understand this as the familiar dawning of the adolescent's struggle to separate from mother and individuate. Her anorexia seemed to be the compromise formation with which she continued this struggle.

Family sessions, more important, allowed a space for the two women to rediscover tender feelings for each other and begin to communicate about things other than K's weight or caloric intake. Father would not participate in treatment at all and did not visit her at any time during her hospitalization. During our last family meeting, K, her mother, and I all ate lunch together, and K and I shared an ice cream sandwich for dessert.

A day before my departure for Europe and shortly before our goodbye lunch, K and I met outside for a last session and exchanged gifts. I had wanted to give her a gift that would serve as a transitional object to help remember me and our time together. I decided on a small stuffed teddy bear wearing a jersey on which was printed, "I love my Daddy." I framed the gift as "symbolic" and told her that, because she and I both knew that her Daddy was not very nice, I had come to think of myself as a sort of substitute father for her. I asked her to hold the bear for me until I returned.

After I gave it to her, she was initially speechless. Fearing the worst, I stated, "You don't like it," to which she softly responded, "Oh, no. I love it." She went on to explain, "I just can't believe it because I wrote you a letter last night and I was going to tell you that I think you've become so important to me because I never had a nice father, but I was too afraid to say it." With that, she gave me a card in which she lovingly expressed how much I had come to mean to her over the course of the preceding few months.

K's presumed anger and disappointment about my departure was never fully addressed despite my attempts to help her do so. The interpretation made repeatedly by my covering colleague and by the nursing staff that she was displacing her anger from me, who had left, to my colleague, who had taken over, was consistently rejected. This may have demonstrated her need to protect me, the good object, from her destructive hostility.

Conclusions

The presentation is only a brief outline of a complex case. My intention is to highlight how K grew from a frightened, angry adolescent determined to starve into an adolescent with some hope for the future and some capacity to express herself in less self-destructive ways. Before her metabolic and neurological decompensation, she did not have an appreciation of how serious her condition was. Her two syncopal episodes did not reverse the course of her self-starvation. Rather, it was only her complete loss of control when paralyzed that afforded her a pause to ponder her fate and decide to become a patient engaged in treatment.

K was able to convert her self-destructive anger into a constructive effort to fight her anorexic thinking and behaviors. Paralysis, or loss of control, was a realization of her most feared anxiety, which her anorexia was an attempt to pathologically control. For a girl who felt internally so out of control, the only aspects of her existence that she felt she could control were her food intake, her body shape, and her weight. These she controlled with a determination that was formidable and almost killed her a few times over.

It is difficult to speculate what the effect of her paralysis would have been on the course of her illness in the absence of a meaningful psychotherapeutic relationship such as the one she established with me. Perhaps she would have done well merely out of fear of losing control again, but I doubt it. I think an anorexic solution at a somewhat higher weight would have been more likely. K's experience in psychotherapy helped her have hope that it is possible to negotiate life's challenges more easily and that human relationships offer more than disappointments or control battles. I think that K learned that loving could feel good and that human relationships could provide sustenance for life as well.

REFERENCES

American Psychiatric Association (APA). 1987. *Diagnostic and Statistical Manual of Mental Disorders*. 3d ed, rev. Washington, D.C.: American Psychiatric Association.

Halmi, K.; Broadland, G.; and Rigas, C. 1975. A follow up study of 79 patients with anorexia nervosa: an evaluation of prognostic features and diagnostic criteria. In R. Wirt, G. Winokur, and M. Roff, eds. *Life History Research in Psychopathology*. Minneapolis: University of Minnesota Press.

Havens, L. 1986. *Making Contact*. Cambridge, Mass.: Harvard University Press.

Schwartz, D., and Thompson, M. 1981. Do anorectics get well? current research and future needs. *American Journal of Psychiatry* 183(3): 319–323.

Sheridan, P., and Collins, M. 1983. Potentially life-threatening hypophosphatemia in anorexia nervosa. *Journal of Adolescent Health Care* 4:44–46.

PART VI

PERSPECTIVES ON MANAGED CARE

EDITORS' INTRODUCTION

During the past decade, the practice of medicine has been buffeted by enormous social and economic pressures affecting the access, costs, financing, and utilization of health care services. Spurred by the sky-rocketing costs of health care, business, industry, and the public have increasingly demanded not only cost containment measures but a continuum of care ranging from full hospitalization to partial hospitalization, brief hospitalization, and outpatient psychotherapy. Physicians have had to incorporate into their lexicon the strange new alphabet soup of HMOs (health maintenance organizations), PPOs (preferred provider organizations), IPAs (individual practice associations), and DRGs (diagnostic related groups). The practice of psychiatry in general and adolescent psychiatry in particular has not been immune to these changes. This special section is devoted to new developments in the delivery of adolescent psychiatric services and includes chapters on managed health care, the financing of adolescent psychiatric care, and, finally, partial hospitalization.

Harold Graff, writing from extensive clinical experience, views current clinical perspectives on managed care. He focuses on the history, current issues, and the dynamics of managed care, presenting an overview of managed care approaches. He describes some of the types and motivations of managed care companies, including freestanding facilities, capitated companies, and, finally, indemnity insurance companies. He provides rare insight to the practitioner into the business decisions affecting clinical care. Finally, he provides both case illustrations of the operations of different managed care companies and clinical case examples. Graff concludes that, rather than attempting to turn the clock back, physicians must be advocates for good managed care in the current economic climate, which focuses primarily on cost controls. He stresses that involvement of practitioners directly with managed care companies is more likely to allow for trust, accessibility, and the likelihood of providing appropriate treatment services for adolescent psychiatric patients.

Steven S. Sharfstein, from his vantage point as the chief executive officer of a well-established psychiatric hospital, describes the current financing of child and adolescent mental health care. He stresses the great paradox that exists in today's medical marketplace, including the twin problems of unmet need and lack of access combined with uncontrolled costs. He describes recent statistics indicating that over 20 percent of all children and adolescents were in need of mental health services, yet less than 25 percent of these children were actually receiving psychiatric treatment. Sharfstein highlights recent stories in the media focusing on the high cost of hospitalization, including issues of the potential for abuse of hospitalization. He believes that artificial financial barriers in our current system limit the treatment options available to seriously emotionally disturbed children. These have been, primarily, hospitalizations, residential treatment, and outpatient treatment. He believes that our current system, if unchanged, will continue to foster an unhealthy prescription of continuing high costs with low accessibility. He believes that the entire health care system needs to be drastically improved and modified to expand resources, contain costs, and provide for a continuum of care that would include short-term hospitalization, residential treatment in group homes and specialized foster care, day treatment, evening treatment, in-home crisis stabilization, and, finally, outpatient care. Sharfstein concludes that greater collaboration between the public and the private sectors is needed to expand the range of treatment services for more children and adolescents and that refinancing of the system is necessary so that the needs of a majority of children with severe emotional problems will be met, allowing good accessibility and cost containment.

Susan Daily and Consuelo Reddick describe their experiences in adolescent day treatment at the University of Alabama Medical Center. They define the concept of partial hospitalization, describing some types of partial hospitalization, treatment program models, and current therapies available, and focus on the adolescent day treatment process. They describe extensively their own experiences with a day treatment program, focusing in detail on 100 patients admitted to their program over a nine-year period. They indicate that adolescents presenting in the program have generally fallen into five major diagnostic groups: (1) disruptive behavior disorders, including conduct disorders, attention deficit, hyperactivity, and oppositional disorders; (2) pervasive development disorders; (3) adolescent psychoses; (4) adolescents with medical and psychiatric disorders; and (5) miscellaneous groups, including adjustment disorders. They note that psychotic disorders have approximately the same length of stay as the disruptive behavior disorders, approximately ten months. They conclude that day treatment, which reduces the regression associated with institutionalization and keeps the adolescent with her family, allows for greater cost effectiveness (reducing the cost of treatment up to 80 percent) and emphasize that partial hospitalization in day-care treatments are likely to grow in importance in the network of adolescent health care systems during the coming decade. They emphasize that further research into efficacy, funding, and outcome is still needed.

Martin H. Stein presents a rationale for widespread use of day treatment. He believes that a majority of patients can now be successfully treated in these programs. He focuses on the dynamics of day treatment with special attention to control and safety issues. Stein compares and contrasts approaches to patient control in both day treatment and hospital programs. He attributes much of the success of day treatment to emphasizing to the patient that the latter is always in control and must assume responsibility for her own safety with appropriate staff and patient concern. He perceives key elements of day treatment as empathic responsiveness of staff and patients, positive expectations that the patient can survive daily, development of a mutually supportive network of sustaining relationships, active involvement of the family, extensive use of group therapy, and artful use of psychopharmacology. Stein presents a series of clinical vignettes focusing on creative solutions to clinical impasses avoiding power struggles by the staff's "therapeutic use of the self." Stein concludes that day treatment is successful for many patients by trading overt control of patients by staff for sustaining relationships through a network of staff and patient relationships.

HAROLD GRAFF

Increasingly, clinical decisions in the psychiatric treatment of adolescents, hospitalized and outpatient, are being influenced by managed health care. Managed care is a system of management employing utilization review to control the cost, duration, medical necessity, and treatment for both adult and adolescent inpatients and outpatients. It is the purpose of this chapter to present clinical perspectives based on personal experiences with managed care during the past decade. I will focus on the history and an overview of managed care, current issues, and types of programs and will present case illustrations as well as clinical examples.

The History of Managed Care

As recently as 1980, the practice of medicine and psychiatry was essentially a "cottage industry." During the past three decades, spurred by both increased awareness and increased needs for adolescent mental health care, the public has increasingly demanded that insurers provide coverage for both inpatient and outpatient psychiatric treatment. Rising alcohol and drug abuse and juvenile delinquency have all contributed to this trend. These trends contributed, not only to the growth of general hospital psychiatry, but also to the rise in for-profit chain hospitals. Spiraling costs have contributed to a strong backlash by business and the insurance industry, determined to bring costs under control.

When I started practicing psychiatry, many patients did not have health insurance covering psychiatric care. Some families chose not to use insurance, wishing to maintain confidentiality. Most of the adolescents referred to me were able to afford private care since a number were from affluent families. It was possible to expect the development of a true therapeutic alliance that could be supported for at least several years of twice-weekly or more psychotherapy.

Psychoanalytically oriented psychotherapy practices were small, and waiting lists abounded. The increase and broadening of insurance coverage for psychiatric treatment presented a mixed blessing. Many psychoanalysts were notably ambivalent about these developments. Concerns were expressed that the use of health insurance for analysis introduced a third party into a therapeutic alliance that affected both transference and countertransference. Anxiety was expressed concerning the effect of third-party payment on the analysand's valuation of treatment; in other words, would there be less gain with less pain? Additional concerns focused on confidentiality. We had been taught to believe that all communications between patients and therapists were privileged. This principle often extended to proscribing note taking, with the exception of the presentation of ongoing cases to supervisors. Notes were often not written on hospital charts but kept in locked files in private offices with no requests for review. Gradually, insurance companies began to request weekly summaries. When resistance occurred, these companies finally mandated a "no documentation, no pay" stipulation. Currently, charging without documentation is considered by insurers to be fraud subject to investigation and prosecution.

Today, all hospitals, whether long established or new community hospitals, are equal targets for managed care. The call for cost containment reflects what some economists see as abuses that the hospitals have allowed with a rationale for lengthy hospitalization, concealing a profit motive. Insurers have not been convinced that the case for cost effectiveness has been made, especially when rates of $800–$1,000 daily for several months are charged.

Recently, there has been a trend by many insurers toward finding less costly hospitals that focus on crisis resolution and a continuum of services ranging from inpatient hospitalization to partial hospitalization to outpatient therapy programs. All these interventions are supported by careful monitoring so that appropriate dispositions can be made.

Current Issues in Managed Care

My experience with managed care was one that was thrust on me by the economic dynamics of my practice area, dominated by a few major corporations with many employees. As medical costs escalated, these companies sought ways to control their expenses by embracing managed care. Many practitioners felt that it was a matter of "join or die."

Both the insurers and the managed care industry have perceived treatment of mental illness as presenting special problems distinct from the rest of medicine owing to the difficulties of making clear, uniform diagnoses and providing procedures leading to quick resolutions. This lack of certainty is anathema to actuaries working for insurers if they cannot thoroughly predict risk. The response is to deny or drastically limit funding. A second problem is the lack of constituency for mental health among the vast majority of the potentially insured. Most people believe that it cannot happen to them. One poignant example was provided by a mother whose daughter was hospitalized briefly after running away. When the managed care reviewer allowed a total of only four days hospitalization, the mother acknowledged that she never dreamed that she would be confronted with the necessity for larger benefits.

If given a choice among options, such as cardiac, dental, pediatric, or mental health care, it is not hard to guess the option likely to be eliminated. As a corollary, members likely to select mental health care are those who already utilize services or have in the past. This choice raises the frightening specter of adverse selection to the insurer. Briefly, adverse selection means that members most likely to choose the benefit are those most likely to use it. This is counterproductive to the implied contract between insurer and insured. The insured bets that he will benefit directly from the service, and the insurer bets that the insured will not. If the member frequently wins and the insurer loses, the latter risks bankruptcy. Thus, insurers want to avoid insuring members most likely to utilize services. The insurance company can protect itself by resorting to claiming a preexisting condition that bars the member from using benefits. Insurers also believe that, the more benefits there are available, the more likely they are to be used. This process contributes to adverse selection and leaves insurers to justify decreasing benefits and limiting the number of practitioners authorized to offer services. Insurers believe that, the more providers on their panels, the more services likely to be provided. Thus, a trend is developing to limit the number of providers certified to provide services through credentialing processes or deliberately setting fees so low as to be a disincentive. This varies from region to region. The president of a large managed care firm was surprised that few psychiatrists wanted to provide services for his clients, noting that, in some areas with an excess of psychiatrists, he had no difficulty finding providers who would accept a fee of forty dollars for a full therapy session.

An Overview of Managed Care Companies

In order to understand the dynamics of managed care programs, it is desirable to have an overview of the various types of companies and their modus operandi. It is essential for the clinician to recognize at the outset that these programs are profit-making businesses.

Profits may be affected either directly or indirectly. The direct method is to organize a program in which a specific sum is allocated for mental health utilization. The indirect method is to manage care with specific goals in mind, such as saving 10 percent. The approach chosen may well not only determine how care is delivered but also help providers view managers and their programs.

A number of types of managers have entered the field of managed care. These include entrepreneurs with no medical experience, hospitals, groups of physicians, and major insurance companies. Some companies assume direct responsibility for the management of care, while others exist only to certify and set limits, leaving the responsibility of delivery of services to others. The combination of these different types of programs generates anxiety and confusion for the therapist. Often, both patient and therapist are not aware of restrictions until therapy has been initiated. The advent of managed care has forced mental health professionals to spend additional time, organization, and management, often unreimbursed, in a manner previously unknown and not deemed necessary to actual patient care.

Experiences with managed care firms have demonstrated to me that health care providers, insurers, and businessmen speak different languages. To negotiate with managers, it is necessary to hire a manager to be most effective. This approach changes the role of physicians, who become providers of services, and companies, who become purchasers of services. This subtle change of function permits an atmosphere in which negotiations can take place. Managed care companies are open to negotiations regarding fees, better provision of services, or referrals. Once this process is recognized, the potential for alleviating or diminishing conflict between the two groups can be greatly enhanced.

Types of Managed Care Programs

Some types of managed care programs attempt to control costs by providing their own clinical facilities with hired "in-house" therapists. Participating outside clinicians are not allowed to provide services until the patient is initially interviewed and approved personally by the managed care clinicians at their own facilities. In one program, most patients were not referred and were treated by "in-house" therapists. As psychiatrists dropped off the list of available therapists, the program was left with one hired psychiatrist who provided medication management and brief hospitalization services to both adults and adolescents. Many purchasers of health insurance view this type of program as too restrictive.

A second type of managed care provider works via the capitation method. Briefly, this means that the insurance company has carved out the delivery of mental health benefits to a for-profit company whose goal is to ensure provision of services separately from the primary insurers. Let us assume that a primary insurer has 10,000 lives insured and wishes to carve out all mental health insurance benefits. The company may offer the contract out for bids. For example, mental health management company A bids $1,200,000 while mental health management company B bids $1,000,000. More often, the calculation is based on dollars per insured life per month. This results in company A bidding $10.00 a month per life and company B $8.33 a month. In the normal course of events, company B wins. Now company B has $1 million in its pocket to provide all services, including hospital costs, costs of therapists, and ancillary expenses. If company B spends $999,999.99, it has made $0.01 profit. If it spends $1,000,000.01, it has lost $0.01. One must not forget that this $1 million also includes salaries for secretaries, managers, physicians, and corporate officers. Thus, there are fewer dollars for actual provision of care.

These types of companies have several ways of making sure that they do not spend too much. First, care is designated as crisis care, especially for hospitalization, with limited outpatient services, stressing symptom reduction or removal. Second, the fee provided for psychiatric care is substantially lower than the current full fee charged in the psychiatric community. Third, the company will recruit a group of psychiatrist providers who are willing to accept fees approximately 60 percent lower than the fees charged by full-fee psychiatrists. Currently, one such company has seemed to be less concerned about length of stay than creating a negative incentive for lengthy hospitalizations. By establishing a "case rate" system, the psychiatrists have agreed to provide the full hospitalization at $700 total. Other companies will approve hospitalization only on a day-to-day basis, demanding communication between psychiatrist and a manager to certify that single day. A third company demands that a full daily written report be sent to the manager even if there is certification for five days. Thus, most adolescents in these programs are hospitalized for brief crisis intervention. Once the crisis subsides, the adolescents are discharged to a limited number of outpatient sessions.

Another type of managed health care program is represented by large, nationally known companies that are self-insured. In these circumstances, a managed care company provides certification, and the insurance company provides financial management. In my experience, these care managers tend to be more generous, allowing up to thirty days of hospitalization and up to twenty outpatient visits annually.

Traditional or "indemnity" insurance companies, as exemplified by Blue Cross and Blue Shield, continue to be major players in the health care insurance market. In recent years, however, market forces have been driving purchasers of health insurance away from "indemnity" insurance to managed care companies with HMOs (health maintenance organizations) and PPOs (preferred provider organizations) as their base. Increasingly, some indemnity insurance companies are developing their own PPOs.

The market for indemnity insurance is shrinking rapidly. Since employers are the purchasers of insurance, it is clear that they will look for the least expensive product frequently. Insurance companies are very aware of the plight of business. Insurance company actuaries have reviewed their statistics to determine the cost of benefits, and the marketing department has the task of selling the product to the insured in a very competitive market. In the current economic climate, an insurance company must maintain market share or cease to exist. To do so, it must offer lower prices than the competition, with resultant lowering of benefits and limited availability of services. Mental health services are but a minor part of the mix and, having a small constituency, are easily trimmed. Nevertheless, certain of the managed care companies are well aware that they must offer services or (1) cease to exist or (2) be labeled as too restrictive and thus avoided.

An Example of a Managed Care Company

Company B had already had some experience in managed care through its subsidiary, a health maintenance organization. The HMO employed several "in-house" therapists plus an independent network of psychiatrists who were authorized to provide services. There was also a separate provider organization that had psychiatrists, psychologists, and social workers as providers on a referral basis. In general, the HMO and PPO lists were congruent. There were also two psychiatrists who were consultants to the director, an experienced clinical social worker. Recognizing the need to develop a formal managed care system, company B organized a program built on an existing model. The director was given the authority to organize and direct a program that encompassed all company B's insurance except for policyholders who chose not to participate. The program consisted of a group of managers who authorized care after an initial outpatient visit or hospital admission on the next business day. The two advisers became the psychiatric approval officers. Their role was to plan, advise, and assist providers in ensuring timely care within the guidelines of the policies. Their potential liability was recognized and covered. The provider list was created from mental professionals already authorized by the HMO and PPO. Any exclusions from the list were based on egregious performance by the provider after several warnings. Additionally, an advisory and appeals panel was formed by the company. This panel was composed of two providers from each of the appropriate professional societies. The panel also met to develop guidelines for the managed care program.

Supervisors of programs saw their task as ensuring the continuity of care appropriate to each case, which was monitored twice weekly. This task was accomplished by identifying a continuum of hospitals, day programs, intensive home programs, and therapists who would handle each problem appropriately.

Case Example

Let us review an ideal case to see how the program works. Lisa, a mid-teenager, had attempted suicide and was hospitalized on an emergency basis after being treated in the local hospital emergency room on a Sunday evening. On Monday, she was examined by her psychiatrist to determine the severity of her problems. The psychiatrist then contacted the managed care intake worker to describe the adolescent's crisis, her diagnosis, and a treatment plan. Three days later, her case was discussed by the program director and the two consulting psychiatrists. The adolescent psychiatrist consultant contacted the treating psychiatrist to discuss Lisa's situation. Lisa's suicide attempt was stimulated by a breakup with her boyfriend. If she were not a danger to herself, she would have to be discharged after a total of five days of hospitalization. If the psychiatrists were concerned about ensuring that Lisa was no longer in acute danger of self-harm, a weekend pass would be authorized. If the patient handled her pass appropriately, she would then be discharged the next day, to be followed up in outpatient therapy.

Often, cases are much more complicated. Adolescents may be hospitalized on the same day after a suicide attempt. They present with depression, substance abuse problems, and suicide attempt while coming from a highly dysfunctional home. They may be sent to a substance abuse program after being deemed no longer suicidal. Alternately, the patient may be provided with an intensive in-home therapeutic program after discharge. However, if the home situation is too unstable to allow for safe discharge, consideration of residential treatment for follow-up care would be an option.

In some cases, hospitalization can be shortened because the psychiatrist can refer to one of several day hospital programs while continuing to treat the patient. Occasionally, it is possible to begin intensive treatment at a day hospital, thus avoiding the cost of full hospitalization. Each of these choices must be selected with full awareness of the needs of the individual patient and the stability of the family.

Utilizing this format with its success in containing costs, it has been even possible to flex benefits, thus providing less costly care for a longer period of time than the original policy permitted. This development presents a major benefit of good managed care since it falls within the parameters of appropriate services to the patient.

Good managers must be advocates for health care in a climate that concerns itself primarily with cost control. By attempting to lower costs, physicians are in a better position to influence health insurance company policy. The development of trust in a working relationship with managed care companies often allows for more services to be provided when deemed necessary.

Conclusions

The treatment of many adolescents is a long and difficult task. Physician involvement with managed care companies frequently mitigates most flagrant restrictions of managed care while still allowing for appropriate care. We may anticipate continuous changes in managed care programs within the decade.

29 FINANCING CHILD AND ADOLESCENT MENTAL HEALTH CARE

STEVEN S. SHARFSTEIN

There is a great paradox in today's medical marketplace. What class of disorders simultaneously combines unmet need and lack of access with uncontrolled costs and allegations of unconscionable profiteering? The answer is treatment for children and adolescents with mental and substance abuse disorders. This chapter will review the dimensions of this scandalous issue, initially focusing on the extent of the problem, reviewing recent studies on the costs of care, and then proposing an approach that may lead us out of this wasteland.

Unmet Need and Lack of Access

Twenty years ago, I was the director of a community mental health service in a small comprehensive health center in a neighborhood in Boston. I was working with an idealistic pediatrician who had received a grant from the state government to conduct a comprehensive physical and psychological screening of the children in three elementary schools that were located in our neighborhood. There were approximately 900 children in all, and this required an extensive mobilization of families and teachers in order to conduct this particular survey. From the beginning, I had misgivings about the project since such case findings might lead to high expectations from the local community for care and treatment beyond the resources of the small health program that was conducting the study. After the study was completed several months later, the results were astonishing. It was determined from the survey that 600 of the 900 children suffered from "emotional problems." This pediatrician colleague tried to reassure me by focusing on 50 of the 600 who were in need of immediate diagnosis and treatment for severe emotional disturbance. At that point in time, I was able to take one additional referral. It was this gap between expectation, need, and reality that struck me as a fundamental issue for clinicians, policymakers, and concerned citizens.

Studies in more recent years of the epidemiology of mental disorders and substance abuse among children and adolescents have borne out that clinical experience in Boston two decades earlier. Knitzer (1982) estimated that 3 million children were severely mentally ill and in need of care. This represented approximately 5 percent of all children, and "serious mental illness" is defined as having a duration of over one year and known to two or more agencies. The U.S. Office of Technology Assessment (1986) estimated that 12 percent of the nation's children, or nearly 8 million children under the age of eighteen, were in need of mental health services. The Institute of Medicine (1989) estimated that 22 percent of 14 million children and adolescents were in need of mental health services. They further estimated that 2 million were in need of urgent and immediate care, but only 0.25–0.5 million were actually in treatment. These overwhelming needs of children and adolescents have exposed a deficiency in our health care system of epic proportions.

Uncontrollable Costs, Unwanted Hospitalization

Many recent stories in the media have highlighted the high costs of questionable hospitalization of adolescents. Today, we are witnessing a strong backlash from the payers, especially private payers, to the extensive and extended hospitalization of adolescents, in part spurred by the growth of for-profit hospital beds in the last five years. Nineteen percent of all discharges from psychiatric hospitals in 1986 were of children and adolescents. This increased to 22 percent in 1988 and then 25 percent in 1989. During this time, the number of psychiatric beds in private hospitals increased by 40 percent, an increase due entirely to the growth of the for-profit chains. Much of this increase was for adolescent care. Between 1984 and 1988, there was an increase of 160 hospitals (private psychiatric hospitals), an average 13 percent growth in hospitalization, and an 11 percent growth in admissions (Frank, Salkever, and Sharfstein 1991).

In order to get a more specific fix on what is happening in relation to cost increases and the reactions of the payers, the American Psychiatric Association and the Johns Hopkins University collaborated in a study utilizing Medstat data on 1.3 million enrollees and dependents from 1986 to 1989. This data set (Medstat) consists of employees and dependents of several major corporations distributed across the country and from a variety of industries. All the health plans reflected in the data set are self-insured. The data are not entirely representative of the U.S. population, but they do provide information on costs and use for a large and well-insured segment of the population.

Substance abuse and psychiatric treatment were covered by the health insurance plans during the study period. Benefits did not change significantly between 1986 and 1988. At the beginning of 1989, however, benefits did change significantly for a portion of the population. That year, insurance benefit changes were imposed on mental health and substance abuse care. Over half the enrollee populations had their benefits curtailed during that time period.

During 1986 and 1988, the charges for psychiatric and substance abuse treatment rose at rates substantially above the rate for all health care—20.1 percent and 32.4 percent, respectively, compared with an overall rate increase of 13.0 percent. Regarding information on inpatient use from 1986 to 1988, what was noteworthy was that inpatient care for both psychiatric and substance abuse problems increased more rapidly than did charges for all inpatient care. Most of this increase in payments, 72 percent for psychiatric care between 1986 and 1988, was due to an increase in utilization by children and adolescents. Charges and payments for inpatient treatment for substance abuse grew at high rates for both adults and juveniles during this time. Days for inpatient psychiatric care for children and adolescents grew from three to five per hundred enrollees, and the growth in inpatient care to children and adolescents accounted for all growth in the use and costs of psychiatric care.

In 1989, however, the picture changed. Inpatient use by children and adolescents now being subject to a thirty-day annual limit on reimbursable stays led to a 16 percent decrease in use by this population and an overall decrease in use of psychiatric care.

It is important to note that, in the Medstat data, increases in mental health charges contributed only 2.5 percentage points of the 13 percent increase in health charges between 1986 and 1988. The changes between 1988 and 1989 illustrate that, when there are limits imposed on mental health care, these cuts and increases of mental health spending do little to reduce growth in overall charges, which continued to rise at a rate of close to 12 percent.

So, here we are—underutilized and overpriced with the prospect of further cuts in private coverage creating an ever growing crisis in access for children and adolescents.

The Current System for Children and Adolescents: A Prescription for High Costs and Low Access

The current system of care largely consists of three options: hospitalization, residential treatment, and outpatient treatment. This is so because of the payment system that reimburses on the basis of hospital stays, to some extent residential care, and to a lesser extent outpatient treatment. These artificial financial barriers convert into the only available settings for treatment or care. Seriously emotionally disturbed children are then either hospitalized, treated in costly extended inpatient or residential care, or inadequately handled through spotty outpatient services and the general health, educational, and social service capacities of our community. Sometimes they are totally abandoned and neglected in the social welfare and juvenile justice systems. What is essential here is the translation and the reprogramming of resources devoted to the expensive few for resources devoted to many of those in need in a much more diversified treatment setting.

The Desired Treatment System to Expand Resources, Contain Costs, and Provide Care

An improved system for children and adolescents would include not only acute short-term hospitalization but also residential treatment in group homes and specialized foster care. Day treatment, which has been shown to be a cost-effective alternative to inpatient and residential care, should be provided on both a full- and a half-day basis, independent as well as a part of a therapeutic school, or in relation to a therapeutic vocational placement. Evening treatment is also an option for children who are in regular school. Outpatient care should be expanded, and a new innovative approach of in-home crisis stabilization is necessary to try to avoid expensive hospital stays. We need the full funding of the range of treatment, a collaboration of the public and private sectors to expand services for more children and adolescents, and a refinancing of the system in a way consonant with the needs of a majority of children with severe emotional problems.

Discussion

In the 1990s, we are emerging from several decades of rapid growth of hospitalization for adolescents. This growth has been financially driven on the basis of the economic opportunity afforded by private health insurance and the large epidemiology of adolescent behavioral problems. This economic opportunity from time to time deteriorated into economic opportunism with the scandals in Texas and elsewhere regarding recruiting adolescent patients for hospital beds.

We are also experiencing intense managed-care cutbacks, which are also financially driven. Here the imperative is cost containment. Stays in the hospital are being shortened and hospitalization averted. This has led to a reevaluation of the need for alternatives to hospital care and for methods to pay for those alternatives.

Several issues remain. The epidemiology issue is critical. What are the boundaries of mental disorder in adolescents, and what do these kids really need? Which kids require the highest-intensity specialty psychiatric care? Can this care be organized in an effective and efficient manner outside the twenty-four-hour inpatient hospital? Will the private and public payers finance these alternative settings for care?

Priorities must be set and choices made. In order to do so in addition to a more refined specific epidemiology, we desperately need standards and practice guidelines. Today, the criteria established by managed care companies for medical necessity and appropriateness substitute for what should be a professionally driven system of treatment protocols. These protocols should enable the rational funding of a continuum of care, the proper role of involving families early on in treatment, and the correct integration of education and therapeutic services.

We continue to struggle with issues of unmet need and neglect for children. We should do better.

REFERENCES

Frank, R. G.; Salkever, D. S.; and Sharfstein, S. S. 1991. A new look at rising mental health insurance costs. *Health Affairs* 10(Summer): 116–123.

Institute of Medicine. 1989. *Research on Children and Adolescents with Mental, Behavioral, and Developmental Disorders*. Washington, D.C.: Institute of Medicine.

Knitzer, J. 1982. *Unclaimed Children*. Washington, D.C.: Children's Defense Fund.

U.S. Office of Technology Assessment. 1986. *Children's Mental Health: Problems and Services*. Durham, N.C.: Duke University Press.

30   ADOLESCENT DAY TREATMENT:
AN ALTERNATIVE FOR THE FUTURE

SUSAN DAILY AND CONSUELO REDDICK

Day hospitalization is a relatively new concept in the treatment of psychiatric disorders, with few programs existing prior to the 1970s. In the 1960s, a number of changes led to conditions conducive to the growth of day hospitalization. These changes included the development of milieu and group therapy, advances in psychotropic medications, generalization of patient treatment to nonphysician professionals, sociological studies illustrating the negative effects of institutionalization, and the passage of the Mental Retardation Facilities and Community Mental Health Center Construction Act of 1963 that mandated the inclusion of partial hospitalization in the community and mental health model (Casarino, Wilner, and Maxey 1982). There has since been an explosion in the number and variety of partial hospitalization programs.

As the number and types of programs expanded, the need arose to establish standards for a definition of partial hospitalization. This need led to the formation of the American Association for Partial Hospitalization. This organization's most recent definition of partial hospitalization is hospital-level treatment, less than twenty-four-hour daily care, specifically targeted for the diagnosis and treatment of psychiatric disorders in which there is a reasonable expectation for improvement or to prevent relapse or hospitalization ("Medicine and Behavior Definition . . ." 1990).

Although day hospitalization originally was utilized for treatment of chronic adult patients, it is now being used to treat a variety of patient populations, including acute psychotic patients, substance abuse patients, geriatric patients, and child and adolescent patients. Adolescent patients may especially benefit from day hospitalization. Adolescence is generally a period of turbulence and confusion. Adolescent day treatment programs are geared to provide intensive treatment while allowing the adolescent to continue to function as much as possible at home, in the neighborhood, and in the outside peer group (Baenen, Stephens, and Glewick 1986).

With regard to adolescents, the most frequently utilized form of hospitalization is the psychoeducational day-school program. The psychoeducational model views inner emotional conflicts as the source of behavior disorders and focuses on the resolution of such conflicts through positive identification with a teacher-therapist. This type of program provides treatment for adolescents with severe emotional and behavior problems who are unable to function in regular school systems. Two other models are the behavioral and the ecological. The behavioral model views these disorders as learned behavior patterns and restructures the educational environment to teach and reinforce more appropriate behavior. The ecological model conceptualizes behavior problems as an incongruity between a child's behavior and environmental expectations (Baenen et al. 1986).

Most programs established since 1970 utilize integrated service models that incorporate a multidisciplinary treatment team, parent counseling, and group therapy. This combination was pioneered by psychoeducationally oriented programs. These programs also use the high degree of structure and attention to academics promoted by the behaviorally oriented programs. The treatment components generally include but are not limited to group psychotherapy; individual counseling or individual psychotherapy; pharmacotherapy; occupational therapy; recreational therapy; goal-oriented social groups; creative expressive therapies such as art, dance, poetry, or music; community meetings; development of daily living skills; organization of motor skills; family evaluation and counseling; home visits; prevocational evaluation; and aftercare (Baenen et al. 1986; Casarino et al. 1982).

The purpose of this chapter is to discuss a retrospective review of data from an urban university day-treatment program that serves an eclectic patient population. We will first describe our program and then present the data that we have reviewed. We will also present cases that illustrate the patient population and then discuss whether day treatment placement has had any mitigating effect on the expected course of the adolescent client's illness.

Program Description

The Adolescent Day Treatment Program was developed in the late 1960s to provide an academic program within a structured, treatment-oriented milieu for adolescents with emotional problems. The program has been developed through joint efforts of the UAB Comprehensive Community Mental Health Center and local boards of education. The goal of the program is to provide a form of partial hospitalization services to adolescents whose special mental health needs cannot be met within the public schools. The program often serves as an intermediary between inpatient treatment and outpatient treatment and is designed to maximize the patient's success in learning appropriate ways to solve personal problems, in developing interpersonal skills, and in mastering academic material.

Referral sources are varied, with the majority of referrals from local schools. Patients are also referred by psychiatrists, psychologists, social workers, community mental health centers, residential treatment facilities, or family members. The patient and the family are then seen by a multidisciplinary evaluation team. The patient's school records and previous testing are reviewed, and further psychological or psychometric testing is conducted when indicated. The patient and the family are given a tour of the facilities.

On completion of the screening process, the application is accepted or rejected. If accepted, the final admission plans are decided, which include expectations of the program and staff, expectations of parental involvement, fee and payment of services, and date of admission. Generally, patients are admitted for a four-week initial evaluation period as a specific treatment plan is developed and implemented. Most admissions are for at least one school semester (fig. 1).

The psychoeducational program is implemented by counselors and educational specialists who are trained to work with emotionally conflicted adolescents. The program is under the direct supervision of an adolescent psychiatrist. Team psychologists, social workers, master's-level nurse clinicians, and occupational therapists are involved in the

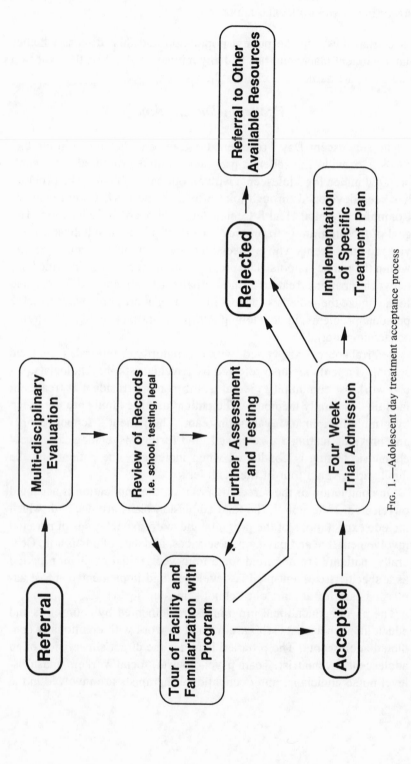

FIG. 1.—Adolescent day treatment acceptance process

patient's treatment program. Because the program operates in a medical school setting, trainees in the disciplines listed are also involved in patient care.

The Adolescent Day Treatment Center (DTC) Program runs from September through May of each calendar year. The program operates on the local school schedule with classes from 8:00 A.M. to 3:00 P.M., Monday through Friday. Spring break and holidays parallel the local school schedule. A separate eight-week summer program is often offered by the clinic, but the data from that program are not included in this study.

The academic program is set up on an individualized educational program basis that is geared to the specific level of academic functioning of an individual student. Classes are set up with the idea that natural consequences are the result of certain behaviors. Patients are on a levels system and earn privileges on the basis of their compliance with the rules of the program, their identification of individual problem areas, and their demonstration that they are effectively trying new ways to deal with problem areas.

In addition to the individualized academic instruction and the levels system, patients are seen for individual therapy and attend group therapy sessions once each week, occupational therapy twice weekly, affective classes once each week, health classes taught by a master's-level psychiatric nurse clinician twice each week, and adventure classes. Goal review classes and therapeutic community meetings afford the patients an opportunity to review their weekly progress with the staff and with peers. Individual and group activities are structured in order to provide essential practice for developing appropriate behavior patterns and interpersonal skills. The goal of the approach is for a teenager to internalize adaptive patterns of behavior that will carry over to other situations. The ability of the adolescent to generalize these acceptable behavior patterns to her home or school environment is continually assessed.

Treatment progress is monitored and assessed in a weekly staff meeting. Any concerns of the staff, changes in the level of functioning of the patient, changes in the adolescent's social circumstances, and/or changes in medications are discussed. Updates on progress or difficulties are sent to referral sources. Ongoing communication with the adolescent's family is an important part of the treatment program. Parents or those individuals providing the parental role are encouraged to meet regularly with the staff and to work toward maintaining consistency between the structure at home and the structure at school.

The cost of the day treatment program is billed to the referring school system or to the family. Few third-party payers in our state are funding day treatment services. Because we serve as part of a comprehensive community mental health center, the charges for catchment area patients are determined on a sliding-scale basis. Funding, however, has been an ongoing problem since the inception of the program.

The decision to discharge a patient is made by the multidisciplinary team. The discharge is considered to be not a terminal point in the patient's treatment but rather a step in the process of rehabilitation. The possible recommendations at discharge include referral to a more restrictive environment, referral to vocational rehabilitation services, or return to a public school setting with ongoing outpatient follow-up. Of course, some patients leave the system and do not comply with follow-up recommendations.

The patients who have presented to our program have generally fallen into five major diagnostic groups: (1) disruptive behavior disorders including conduct disorders, attention deficit hyperactivity disorders, and oppositional disorders; (2) pervasive developmental disorders; (3) adolescent onset psychotic disorders including schizophrenia, bipolar affective disorder, and atypical psychosis; (4) adolescents with medical and psychiatric disorders, that is, malnutrition, diabetes mellitus, sensory deficits, and pregnancy; and (5) other disorders including adjustment disorders, anxiety disorder, etc. Although our review data do not lend themselves to rigorous statistical analysis, a number of our observations merit further discussion.

Data Analysis

We have reviewed the available records of the adolescents admitted to the day treatment program from 1980 to 1989. A total of 100 patients were admitted to the program. For the purpose of this review, thirty-two patients who participated in the program for less than two months were omitted. These patients were participants in the eight-week summer programs, six-week trial evaluations that were either withdrawn or referred to another program, or brief crisis admissions.

Of the sixty-eight remaining charts, fourteen had incomplete data for the purpose of this review, leaving a total of fifty-four charts that were reviewed. The data obtained included date of admission, age at admission, referral source, diagnosis, IQ scores (primarily WISC-R or WAIS-R), length of stay, and sex. In addition, through chart review and contact with therapist or other caregivers, the Global Assessment of Functioning (GAF) was applied and scores given to each of the fifty-four identified clients.

Analysis of the data reviewed a sample composed of thirty-seven males (69 percent) and seventeen females (31 percent) ranging in age from twelve to nineteen, with a mean age at admission of fifteen. Thirteen and fourteen were the model ages of admission. The primary source of referral was the educational system where previous interventions had usually been attempted. Other referral sources included family court, private psychiatrists and psychologists, residential treatment facilities, and the Department of Human Resources. For the purpose of this review, diagnoses were divided into the five categories indicated, that is, psychotic disorders, pervasive developmental disorders, disruptive behavior disorders, combined medical/psychiatric disorders, and others. A graph of these categories by frequency reveals the most commonly admitted diagnostic category to be psychotic disorders and the second most common to be disruptive behavior disorders (fig. 2).

Length of stay was estimated in months (one month is defined as four weeks for the purpose of this review), with the range being two and one-quarter months to thirty months. The mean length of stay was ten months and the most frequent stay nine months. When the length of stay is considered by diagnostic category, the pervasive disorders remained the longest, with an average stay of eighteen and a half months. Psychotic disorders had approximately the same length of stay as the disruptive behaviors disorders that averaged ten months. The medical/psychiatric clients remained seven and a half months, and the "other" clients averaged nine and one-quarter months (figs. 3, 4).

Global Assessment of Functioning estimates for each category reveal the lowest level among the pervasive disorders, followed by the psychotic disorders, the medical/psychiatric combination group, the disruptive behavior disorders, and the "others" category. The mean full-scale IQ was eight-two.

The following cases illustrate the referring problems and course of treatment of four typical referrals to our program.

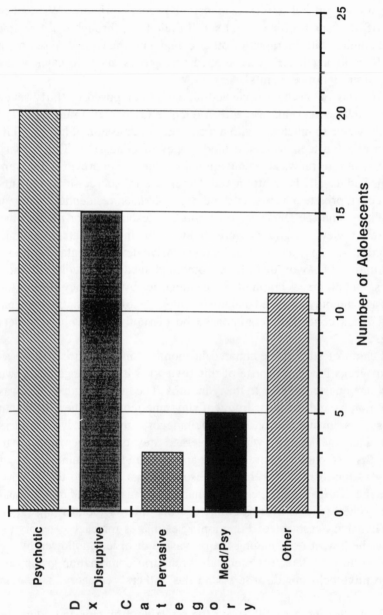

FIG. 2.—Diagnostic category vs. number of adolescents

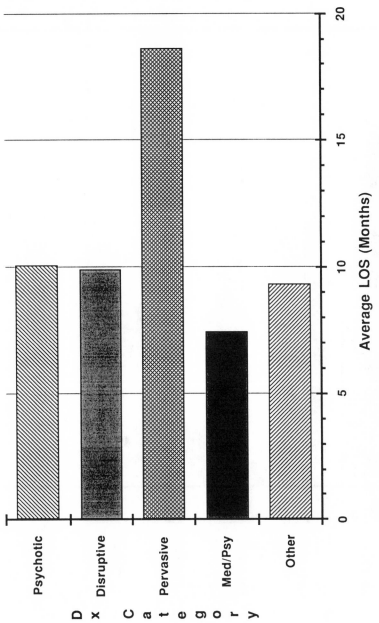

Fig. 3.—Diagnostic category vs. average length of stay (LOS)

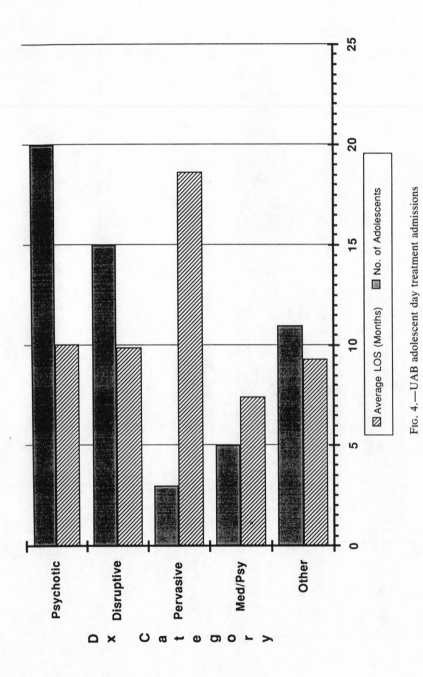

Fig. 4.—UAB adolescent day treatment admissions

Clinical Case Example A

Patient A, a sixteen-year-old Asian-American male, was referred to the day treatment program by his psychiatrist after he had been expelled from a public school setting. He had experienced problems in school since the fifth grade that included fighting, poor peer relationships, poor academic performance, and truancy. The problems began after his fifty-year-old father died with a myocardial infarction.

Patient A was initially admitted to an inpatient unit at age fifteen because of a suicide attempt. He was depressed, angry, and experiencing extreme conflict within the mother-son relationship. He had issues of unresolved grief related to the death of his father, and he met the criteria for a major depressive episode. He was treated with individual and family therapy and nortriptyline. On discharge, he was placed in a short-term treatment-oriented group home, where he remained for six months. The patient then returned home to his mother and to public school. After several aggressive incidents with peers at school, he was transferred to a self-contained class for the emotionally conflicted within the public school setting. He did fairly well in the contained classroom but had major aggressive outbursts in the school lunchroom that resulted in his expulsion. A long-term residential treatment program was discussed. It was at this point that he was admitted to the day treatment program.

Patient A entered the program and was initially quiet, withdrawn, and cautious in his interaction and communication with peers and staff. He appeared motivated to ''do well and avoid residential placement.'' After a few months in the program, he began to talk more openly about the loss of his father and other emotionally laden issues. Although he has had episodes of frustration and anger, he has managed them more appropriately. He has now attained and maintained level 4 in the program, with plans to return to the public school in the fall.

This patient had experienced the loss of his father at age eleven and subsequently had difficulties with control of anger and resistance to authority figures. He had two brief hospitalizations for suicide gestures, had been in a short-term treatment-oriented group home, and had been in four different school placements before coming to the day treatment program. He was involved with the legal system and was at the point of long-term placement when he entered the program. Although his ability to handle public schools has not yet been assessed, he has been able to be maintained at home for an additional year of his adolescence and has made significant gains that we hope will improve his long-term prognosis.

Clinical Case Example B

Patient B was a fourteen-year-old male who was referred to the day treatment program after he had been hospitalized on an inpatient adolescent unit. Past history revealed that the patient, an only child, had fetal dilantin syndrome characterized by cleft lip and cleft palate at birth. He had surgical repair of the structural anomalies in early childhood. Developmental milestones were delayed. He never crawled, walked at fourteen months, and said his first sentence at age four. Toilet training occurred at age six.

When he entered school, the patient received IQ testing that revealed a full-scale IQ of fifty. He had severe articulation problems, echolalia, and ritualistic behavior. He was placed in a class for severely emotionally disturbed children. He functioned fairly well in this academic setting until age thirteen, when the increase in ritualistic behaviors began.

The patient had no previous psychiatric evaluations until age thirteen, when he was seen by a child psychiatrist. He then had a deterioration in his ability to function, increased ritualistic behavior that resulted in his taking hours before getting a bit of food to his mouth, and staring spells that appeared to be a response to auditory hallucinations. He was placed on low-dose antidepressant and had some improvement.

At age fourteen, an exacerbation of symptoms necessitated hospitalization. He had again been unable to eat, weighed fifty-seven pounds, and was dehydrated. Inpatient treatment consisted of a behavior modification program, antipsychotic medication, and tube feedings. His parents were both employed but had limited hospitalization insurance coverage. In order to expedite discharge from the hospital, the patient was admitted to the day treatment program, where he could be in a structured program and have nursing and medical personnel available. Diagnoses included pervasive developmental disorder, psychosis NOS, fetal dilantin syndrome, and mild mental retardation.

On admission to the day treatment center, patient B initially was noted to engage in ritualistic behaviors, to refuse to perform his academic assignments, and to engage in inappropriate behaviors such as kissing staff and peers. He was placed on an individualized behavior modification program, which placed time limits on his lunch time and interrupted his rituals. The program was also used at home by his parents. His neuroleptic was titrated as tolerated, and his weight was monitored. By the end of his sixth month, he was eating his entire lunch in the lunchroom with peers, was performing his school assignments, and was communicating more with peers. He continued to laugh inappropriately and engage in intermittent rituals. He was discharged after one year to return to public school. He was able to be contained in a public school setting for the next school year.

Day treatment services for this child served as a less restrictive and less expensive alternative to inpatient care. He had cooperative, involved, and concerned parents who enabled the patient to be maintained in a day treatment center setting. Although his illness has not been "cured," he has now returned to baseline and is functioning in an even less restrictive environment.

Clinical Case Example C

Patient C was referred to the day treatment program at age fifteen by a local child psychiatrist and his family. The patient had multiple social and academic problems and had a diagnosis of pervasive developmental disorder and attention deficit hyperactivity disorder. He is the only child of a working, middle-class couple. The patient had no language development until age four and was impulsive and hyperactive. His parents sought psychiatric and speech services for him during his preschool years. They were able to have him placed in a small, private elementary school that could offer individualized academic instruction and one-to-one supervision when necessary. After completion of their eighth grade program, he entered a larger private high school and was dismissed after two days. He had been socially and sexually inappropriate and had been unable to handle changing classes, lockers, and other new situations.

The patient had been followed by a psychiatrist and tried on stimulants, antidepressants, and neuroleptics in an effort to manage his behavior. His difficulties have included impulsivity, hyperactivity, stealing small objects from stores or books from libraries, inappropriate forwardness with strangers, inappropriate talk about his sexual and aggressive fantasies, and poor academic functioning.

At puberty, the patient became virtually obsessed with sexual thoughts and topics. He discussed these, wrote about these, and required constant parental supervision. The parents were considering residential placement but did not have private insurance coverage for residential programs and did not qualify for public assistance owing to their income.

At admission, the patient was initially anxious, very active, and had difficulty adjusting to the newness of the program. He has always had difficulty with change. He engaged in frequently silly, attention-seeking behaviors, tried to monopolize the group and therapeutic community meetings, and asked constant, repetitive questions of staff and anyone else he encountered in the hallways. Interventions have included a time-out program that has been used effectively to decrease stimulation and enable the patient to regain enough control to return to the classroom. He has required close supervision. On one occasion, he called the university police to vividly describe a rape that he falsely reported was happening in a nearby building. He has not been aggressive or actually harmed anyone. The patient is now in his third year in the program. His clinical course is variable. He has marked regression when a new person enters the program or there is a change in his routine. The staff has noted an improvement in his overall behavior, that is, he is now less in time out and his social skills have improved. He responds more quickly to cues and is less attention seeking.

Patient C has been able to remain at home rather than in an inpatient setting or residential treatment program. He remains delayed developmentally, emotionally, socially, and academically, but he has made some progress and has remained at home throughout his adolescence.

Clinical Case Example D

Patient D was a seventeen-year-old male who was referred to the program by his private psychiatrist. He was a young man of bright, normal intelligence, who had been in an accelerated high school program in creative writing. He left that program after his first suicide attempt. He was receiving psychiatric treatment for depression and obsessive-compulsive disorder. He had a history of increasing social withdrawal and ritualistic behavior prior to his first overdose. After an initial hospitalization and treatment with an antidepressant, he returned to school. He was unable to function and subsequently made a second suicide attempt. Because he was unable to handle a public school placement, he was placed on a homebound program until the day treatment center program became available. While in the homebound program he was also begun on chlomipramine.

The patient was admitted to the day treatment center program, where he was initially quiet, somewhat guarded, and only minimally interactive with peers. He was noted to exhibit ritualistic tapping, counting, and an elaborate pattern of hand movements. Intervention included maintaining his academic studies in a regular grade-level curriculum, positive reinforcement and support of verbalization of feelings, physical activities such as basketball and adventure classes, individual and group therapy, and titration of the chlomipramine.

The patient gradually became more confident and appropriately assertive in his interactions with peers and had a marked reduction in his ritualistic behavior. He was an identified leader in group and other activities. He also began to develop peer relations outside the group. The patient was discharged after twenty-one months in the program. He was able to obtain a regular high school diploma, work as a volunteer in a local charitable agency, and now plans to take his college entrance exam.

Discussion

In general, patients are not "cured" of their psychopathology by treatment in a day treatment setting. However, patients like patient A, who have had ongoing problems at home and school, can often experience a sense of competency and mastery, be given an opportunity to develop trusting relationships with authority figures, and develop enhanced coping skills. With the structure of the day treatment program, patient A was maintained at home rather than in a more costly residential or detention program.

Patient B represents one of the most complicated types of patients referred to the day treatment program. His combination of pervasive developmental disorder and medical complication of malnutrition mandated an intensive treatment setting that could attend to his psychiatric and medical needs. Other patients with psychiatric diagnoses and med-

537

ical complications, such as diabetes and burns, have also benefited from the medical care available through the day treatment program. Patient B's parents had very limited inpatient insurance coverage but were able to handle his care at home, at night, and on weekends owing to the support they received from his day treatment program.

The third patient had a pervasive developmental disorder, and the family was considering an expensive residential program owing to lack of other resources. The day treatment program has enabled the patient to remain at home while providing him with structure, social skills, training, and medication management. Yet his long-term prognosis remains poor.

The fourth patient represents a more encouraging prognostic picture. His obsessive-compulsive symptoms and his depression have improved during his twenty-one months in the program. He was able to continue his education and obtain a high school diploma while spending eight hours each weekday in a treatment program geared toward improving his adaptive functioning and working through his intrapsychic conflicts. In all the above cases, day treatment has offered a less costly and less restrictive treatment option for these adolescents.

Most of the studies comparing the efficiency of day hospitalization to inpatient and/or outpatient therapy are based on the treatment of adult populations (Herz, Endicott, Spitzer, and Mesnikoff 1971). These studies consistently show that day hospitalization patients return to full-time life in the community faster, resume their occupational roles sooner, and are less likely to require subsequent readmission to hospitals. Measures of psychopathology also show more striking improvement in comparison to inpatients. Day treatment appears to reduce the regression seen with institutionalization and gives patients greater opportunity to maintain healthy areas of functioning. In a review of a series of psychoeducational day school program outcomes, almost 80 percent of patients showed considerable improvement, based on clinical observations, behavior ratings, and psychological tests (Baenen et al. 1986; Kettlewell, Jones, and Jones 1985).

Conclusions

Day treatment as opposed to residential treatment keeps the adolescent with the family, which is more desirable in terms of the child's natural relationships and dependency needs as well as the parents' self-esteem. It permits simultaneous growth of child and parents so that readjustment is a continuous and not a sudden process. The family also shares the burden of managing the child's behavior. Keeping a child in the community and using community facilities also makes for less sense of adjustment back to the family and community later. La Vietes, Cohen, Reens, and Ronall (1964) have shown that residential treatment offering comparable professional services to day treatment, but needing to provide continuous care, can cost from 45 to 90 percent more per child.

Day treatment is also more cost effective than hospital care. Controlled studies have shown that this use of partial hospitalization can reduce the cost of treatment by up to 80 percent in comparison to inpatient treatment (Fink, Longabough, and Stout 1978; Sharfstein 1985). The results of these controlled studies indicate that inpatient hospitalization should be used for acutely disturbed individuals who need a twenty-four-hour protective environment. However, for patients who need a structured therapeutic environment, who are able to cooperate in their own treatment program, and who have community supports, partial hospitalization is preferable to inpatient care.

NOTE

Our appreciation is due to Professor Jane Dow for her sponsorship and consultation.

REFERENCES

Baenen, R. S.; Stephens, M. A. P.; and Glewick, D. S. 1986. Outcome in psychoeducational day school programs: a review. *American Journal of Orthopsychiatry* 20(2): 263–270.

Casarino, J. P.; Wilner, M.; and Maxey, J. T. 1982. American Association for Partial Hospitalization (AAPH) standards and guidelines for partial hospitalization. *International Journal of Partial Hospitalization* 1(1): 5–21.

Fink, E. B.; Longabough, R.; and Stout, R. 1978. The paradoxical underutilization of partial hospitalization. *American Journal of Psychiatry* 135(6): 713–716.

Herz, M. J.; Endicott, J.; Spitzer, R. L.; and Mesnikoff, A. 1971. Day versus inpatient hospitalization: a controlled study. *American Journal of Psychiatry* 127(10): 1371–1381.

Kettlewell, P. W.; Jones, J. K.; and Jones, R. H. 1985. Adolescent partial hospitalization: some preliminary outcome data. *Journal of Clinical Child Psychology* 14(2): 139–144.

La Vietes, R.; Cohen, R.; Reens, R.; and Ronall, R. 1964. Day treatment center and school: seven years experience. *American Journal of Orthopsychiatry* 34(1): 160–169.

Medicine and behavior definition of partial hospitalization released jointly by NAPPH/AAPH. 1990. *Psychiatric Times* (March), p. 9.

Sharfstein, S. 1985. Financial incentives for alternatives to hospital care. *Psychiatric Clinics of North America* 8(3): 449–460.

31 DAY TREATMENT FOR SERIOUS MENTAL ILLNESS

MARTIN H. STEIN

Day treatment is a genuine treatment setting for the majority of seriously ill psychiatric patients. Although its efficacy and cost saving has been demonstrated in the past, the current crisis in American health economics has set forth the conditions whereby day treatment now appears to be the most practical and cost-effective modality to replace inpatient psychiatric care. My recent experience in this modality has demonstrated that most patients of all ages and diagnoses, including suicidal and self-destructive patients, can be successfully treated in day treatment.

How can day treatment be successful without locked doors, quiet rooms, or restraints? In the inpatient treatment setting, the major elements of patient control are doors, locks, walls, leather, and staff muscle. In day treatment, the agent of control is the moral, ethical, and clinical authority of the staff. Patient stabilization results from fostering the interpersonal relationships between patient and staff, patient and patient, and patient and family or significant others. Without the power to hold and restrain, the cooperation of a seriously ill patient is gained through respect, understanding, and empathy.

The three tasks required to manage an intensive psychiatric case are keeping the patient safe, obtaining a clinical assessment, and developing and implementing a treatment plan. The only task that may require inpatient care is patient safekeeping. However, an important question with a less than obvious answer is, What constitutes an unsafe patient? To what extent do our expectations of a patient's dangerousness to self or others add to the probability of dangerous behavior? In the past, the knowledge base, training, and clinical guidelines for the assessment and treatment of dangerous behaviors were developed in protected inpatient settings. There were also no incentives for treating other than in hospitals. Because of the new economics, outpatient centers are now developing a knowledge base for working with many of those same difficult patients in unprotected settings.

Until day treatment became an alternative, there was never a reason to challenge the assumption that all suicidal patients should be treated in hospitals. Goffman's (1961) *Asylums* documented the deadly effect of total institutional control on the psyche of an inpatient. When a patient resisted the directive of a hospital staff member, he was considered out of control. His protest, however justifiable, was interpreted as a sign of his illness, which then justified the need for more control, that is, continued inpatient care and more limits.

The expectations that people have of each other constitute a matrix of social control. In human relationships, expectations are communicated by language and nonverbal behaviors. In the inpatient setting, the nursing policy manual clearly sets out a system of patient control and staff responsibility based on the assumption that the entering psychiatric patient is unpredictable and liable to go out of control. A further incentive for control is that hospitals have been successfully sued when they failed in this task. To keep this unpredictable, litigious patient safe, there is no latitude for the appropriate risks of a therapeutic relationship. Instead, an authoritarian relationship (the staff controls the patient) is established, with the assumption that, later, a more communicative and therapeutic relationship will develop. In the current mental health care climate, little more than triage occurs behind the locked door. Patients are medicated, cooled off, and sorted out. For most patients, the presenting problem will be defined and stabilized, following which the patient may be sent to outpatient or day treatment. If the patient must remain longer, he will be initiated into the hospital "game," where outbursts are punished "therapeutically" until the patient learns who is in charge and what is allowed. The patient usually learns the hospital game. When he behaves and says the right words, he is discharged. Although the episode is over, little has been learned. Learning how to be a "good patient" in the hospital is not the same as learning how to live a functional life at home. Too much control is antithetical to therapy.

How does day treatment differ? By virtue of having unlocked doors and partial possession of the patient, day treatment centers do not have the tools to maintain physical responsibility for the maintenance of a safe patient. Yet day treatment has a moral, legal, and clinical obligation that its patients remain safe. Instead of locking the door, day treatment transfers the obligation for safekeeping to the patient and the family. How is this done? We tell the truth and confront the patient with our inability to control him.

We tell the adult that we cannot stop her from cutting herself. We understand why she may want to do so. We tell the multiple personality that we understand that splitting into more than one person was the best solution that she could invent to survive. Now that her actual danger has ended, we will help her learn new skills to live in a safer world. We will also help her rid herself of her hidden nightmares. We tell the adolescent that we cannot control him. Yes, he can run away. But, if he stays, he will have a chance to tell his side of the story to staff and peers and go home at night. We do not expect miracles. Slow progress in real life is acceptable.

When we relate to a patient, we do not threaten him with a locked door or a forced overnight stay. We do not break his will. We do not demoralize a vulnerable parent who tearfully leaves her child locked behind the hospital door. We support the parent who wants to remain in full contact with her child while he is in treatment. We invest our clinical energies in that healthy part of the patient who wants help without the trauma or stigma of institutionalization. Our success in avoiding hospitalization may simply be due to the fact that, when a seriously ill psychiatric patient is treated with dignity and allowed to save face, he will remain safe in a day treatment setting. He will choose to stay safe and attend day treatment because his dignity is intact.

When we point out our inability to keep a patient safe, we avoid the bind of who is in control. The patient is always in control. Day treatment offers a noncontrolling therapeutic experience for which a patient is usually willing to trade keeping himself safe. The trade is solace, respect, sympathy, honesty, understanding, and caring in exchange for safety. This is why patients choose to stay safe in day treatment. The interpersonal transaction that is offered in day treatment provides as much safekeeping for the majority of patients as a locked door.

Day treatment accelerates the pace of therapy. When adolescents are placed in locked hospital settings, during the first few weeks of treatment up to 100 percent of all patient-staff and patient-family trans-actions revolve around control issues. The adolescent protest is seen in refusal to conform to unit norms, attempts to run away, bargaining with parents to remove them from the hospital, strikes, trashing of rooms, sneaking of contraband, and continual confrontations with staff over language and behavior. The staff need to maintain control often escalates minor conflict into major power struggles where each side must save face. The outcome is often restraint, seclusion, and ex-tended stays with questionable benefit and great cost. With open doors and the ability to return home nightly, these same patients do not need to prove themselves in the day treatment setting. Free from these issues of ultimate control and the responsibility of full-time safekeep-ing, the day treatment staff is able to put all its energy into treatment interactions.

What Is "Treatment" in a Day Treatment Program?

Empathic responsiveness of staff and peers is treatment. Many patients feel isolated and become depressed, self-destructive, or ag-gressive because of a parental failure, or inability for neuropsychiatric reasons to develop empathic connections to others. The ability em-pathically to relate to others is modeled and taught in groups between peers and staff. The feeling of being connected to another human dra-matically reduces the level of aggression directed toward self and others.

Expectation is treatment. The expectation that a patient is capable of keeping safe and arriving at the center each day is a powerful mes-sage. Similarly powerful is the expectation that the patient can survive at home each night. We say to the patient, "You must find a way to survive in this world, and we will support your attempts to do so." To the family we say, "You are the parents; we respect your difficult job; we will empower you, and we will work with you." We say to both, "Yes, you can call us any time, and we will be there for you."

Interaction is treatment. Day treatment staff encourage interaction in a more radical manner than inpatient settings. We depend on the groups and relationships that develop among patients to contain and sustain each other. Unlike most inpatient settings, which proscribe intense patient-patient relationships, we promote, respect, and work with patient-patient relationships. We respect them as genuine relationships with the potential to sustain the patient at this time in her life. Patients may go to each other's houses, socialize with each other after program hours, and, on occasions, spend nights and weekends with each other. Families of adolescents often get together on their own to support each other in the difficult job of being parents of complex adolescents.

Education is treatment. Adolescent patients have a daily education program to keep up with school. Adult patients spend an hour each day with a psychiatrist, who uses their cases for psychoeducation. The psychiatrist discusses the origin and natural history of each illness. He teaches the connections between a person's biology, chemistry, genetics, and family history and the effects of past events on current symptoms.

Expression and sharing are treatment. Interaction between people is therapeutic when a person becomes aware that he has a meaningful effect on another person. Meaningful interactions occur continually in day treatment owing to the absence of control issues. Group therapy allows patients to share their feelings with each other. Patients may discuss private concerns with staff in a one-to-one meeting. Art therapy allows abused patients to use crayon and paint to draw the unspeakable. Recreational outings are designed to help patients make better use of community resources.

Involvement with family and significant others is treatment. In day treatment, the family and community become the evening, night, and weekend staff. Intensive family work is critical in helping the patient discover how to use, if possible, the most naturally sustaining groups in our culture. Frequent individual family therapy as well as multifamily and family support groups help bolster the family connections of our patients. Families who transport a patient to the center have the opportunity to spend time together in the car and to meet with staff members twice daily.

Psychopharmacology is treatment. Serious mental illness is a brain disease as much as a psychological and social illness. Persons with vulnerable brains are often unable to control or modulate mood, perception, or attention. They are unable to compete in the world of interaction at work, home, or school or with intimates. Skilled psychopharmacology can stabilize or lift mood, clear clouded perceptions, and improve attention with appropriate medication.

Continuity of care is treatment. Day treatment supports the continuation of an established outpatient treatment relationship. A patient is encouraged to continue in treatment with his or her personal therapist while engaging in the intensive experience of day treatment. Day treatment schedules are designed to be flexible to allow patients to engage in their important obligations while in treatment. This flexibility allows a patient to remain or become involved in job and school programs or in parent and family responsibilities.

Staff members must be secure enough in their identity to endure and enjoy the intense contact, and often conflict, that occurs with each patient. They must feel good enough about themselves to be confident when acting both in role and in their person. They must be introspective enough to allows analysis of their countertransference feelings toward patients, staff, and management. They must be mature enough to make changes in their behavior as they understand underlying dynamics. When the staff system is working well, the patient-staff interactions will have a major therapeutic effect and become part of the center's holding environment.

There are few settings in which mental health professionals can learn to do the work of day treatment. There are fewer settings where a philosophy of treatment without control is taught, particularly for the more seriously ill patient. Most mental health staff who apply for positions in day treatment have acquired their experience in hospital or other residential settings. To transform them to work effectively in the day treatment setting, they must be helped accept the following principles: (*a*) There is no absolute control of day treatment patients. (*b*) There is no way to guarantee the safety of patients. (*c*) Very sick patients will be treated in day treatment. (*d*) Most patients will remain ill longer than the course of intense day treatment. (*e*) Day treatment will have increasingly limited and specific objectives (to which staff will object). (*f*) The staff does not always know what is best for a patient. (*g*) Professionals will be held responsible for adverse patient outcomes.

Much of the staff teaching is subtle and modeled by the center leadership. One concept that must be taught is the retailing dictum, "The customer is always right." This idea appears to be heretical to many professionals, but, in day treatment, the patient-customer must make a decision each day whether to come to the center. If her needs are not met as she sees them, she has the option of remaining home. The managed-care customer who wants to purchase a painfully limited outcome is also right if it is chosen to accept her referrals. Treatment plan strategies are not painless to the patient. To make them acceptable, staff must learn the art of negotiation and compromise with patients and their families or risk losing the case. All patients volunteer their energy and cooperation to carry out the objectives of the treatment plan. Obtaining patient cooperation without coercion is the art of day treatment. It is achieved through the subtleties of the interpersonal relationships between staff and patient. Such skills are not taught in most inpatient settings.

Senior staff can convey these skills by becoming very human role models. They must share their feelings and frustrations as they struggle with difficult clinical situations that in the past might instinctively have called for power and muscle. They must guide staff toward the creation of palatable strategies that their "customers" will accept so that they will return the next day.

The following clinical examples were chosen to illustrate how clinicians have learned to operate without getting into a power struggle. In each case, there could have been a confrontation, which might have led to inpatient hospitalization or discharge from the program. In each case, the staff succeeded by the use of the "self" in a more personal way than is usual in treatment settings. The staff joined with the patient, deflected the struggle, and allowed the patient to save face.

Clinical Example 1

A twenty-nine-year-old woman was admitted to an adult day treatment program with chronic suicidal ideation and a sense of hopelessness. She had recently signed herself out of a psychiatric hospital owing to a conflict with her insurance company and out of another day treatment facility because she did not like the doctor. She had been in intensive psychotherapy for three years with a psychologist and had her medication managed by a psychiatrist. In addition to her depression and suicidal thoughts, she had been bulimic for the past two years and was purging every night. The day hospital doctor felt that control of the bulimia with different antidepressant medication was of clinical importance. The patient's shame over her behavior would not allow her to deal with the issue. The program psychiatrist wanted to consult with her doctors about her suicidal feelings and discuss changing her antidepressant. She would not agree to his talking to either of her doctors. The day treatment psychiatrist's control instincts motivated him to want to tell her either to submit to his wishes or to leave treatment. However, he observed that she was heavily invested in the program and seemed to enjoy fighting with him. The psychiatrist held a treatment team meeting in which he shared his dilemma. The team helped him prepare an open letter to the patient's psychiatrist stating his concerns. The patient disagreed with the contents but agreed to deliver it. The next day the patient agreed to communication between her two doctors.

Clinical Example 2

An adolescent patient had cut her leg with a sharp object. The nurse saw the patient, gave her a bandage, and said, "Hurry, clean that mess up, put this bandage on, group therapy is starting."

Clinical Example 3

A provocative, obnoxious, narcissistic adolescent male put his arms about the neck of the well-dressed, demure-appearing, female program director as if to taunt her with his power to strangle her. She looked him in the eye and told him. "Get your ——— hands off my neck, and if you ever do that again, I will beat the hell out of you and kick you in the butt." The patient was able to remain in the program for another month and be discharged to his home.

Clinical Example 4

A depressed, oppositional, and school-avoidant seventeen-year-old girl was being admitted to day treatment. The patient was ambivalent about being in the center. The psychiatrist showed her the open doors and pointed out the best direction for a successful runaway. He told her where the bus stops, where stores were located, and on which route she would be more likely to get a ride. She stayed.

Clinical Example 5

A surly oppositional adolescent refused to speak in school or to any staff. In the past, he had been threatening to the staff. The program director put him in her sports car and drove him to a restaurant. There she fed him and asked him to talk about what was bothering him. He began to talk about how bad he was feeling because he felt he could never live up to his parents' expectations. He also spoke of chronic feelings of depression. When the staff asked her why she took him to lunch in view of his past threats, she replied, "McDonald's is a kid's place; they don't act out in their restaurant."

Clinical Example 6

An angry adolescent stormed out of a family meeting after threatening his mother. He was not seen for two hours until he called the center and asked for help. He did not know where he was but was able to walk back. Following a conference call with his social worker and family, the center director took him to McDonald's and then arranged for him to spend the night at an adolescent runaway house. He returned to the program the next morning.

Clinical Example 7

A boisterous, hyperactive, twelve-year-old was diagnosed with attention-deficit hyperactivity disorder. He was prescribed methylphenidate by the psychiatrist but refused to take his medication. The case was presented to the program director as a need for transfer to a psychiatric hospital. The director was adamant. "Don't you ever talk to me about using a hospital for medication. What have you done to get him to take his medication? Have you taken him to get a toy to use after he takes his medication? Have you discussed what kind of ice cream he could hide the pill in? Have you discovered what special activity he wants to do after he takes the pill?" Suffice it to say, the patient took his medication.

Conclusions

In each of these vignettes, a creative solution was used to overcome a clinical impasse and allow the patient to continue in treatment. The need for physical control is rare—and only for moments. In each of the excerpts, the need for control was finessed into a productive interaction. An open letter to the patient's psychiatrist, a lack of an expected response to a self-destructive act, a verbally aggressive counterattack, a joining with the elopement fantasies, feeding the patient, and, yes, even bribing were mechanisms that were used to continue and foster a relationship rather than a confrontation. In each case, the staff goal was achieved.

The critical clinical task is to invent a way to get beyond the confrontational episode. Following the confrontation, a family meeting and a staff meeting may be held to process the conflict. In this manner, most patients can be successfully managed in day treatment. The patients and the clinical issues are the same in inpatient and day treatment settings. The difference in day treatment is the nature of the clinical response to those difficult situations for which less skilled clinicians may select a hospital setting. The secret to success in day treatment is trading overt control for relationship control with an enlightened and creative staff. If the leadership believes in the model and can teach new ways to relate to patients, most patients with serious psychiatric illness can be treated in day treatment.

NOTE

Many of the ideas presented in this chapter were developed through dialogue with David Wood, Peter Robbins, Patricia Petralia, and the staff at the American Day Treatment Center, Fairfax, Virginia.

REFERENCE

Goffman, E. 1961. *Asylums*. New York: Doubleday.

THE AUTHORS

HERVÉ BENHAMOU is *Psychiatre d'Hospitaux* and Head of the Evening Intensive Care Unit, French National Concourse, Paris.

JONATHAN COHEN is Adjunct Associate Professor in Clinical Psychology, Columbia University, and Faculty Member, Institute for Child, Adolescent, and Family Studies, New York.

ADRIAN D. COPELAND is Clinical Professor of Psychiatry and Chief, Adolescent Psychiatry, Jefferson Medical College of Thomas Jefferson University, Philadelphia.

SUSAN DAILY is Clinical Faculty Member, University of Oklahoma School of Medicine, and Director, Day Treatment Services, Children's Medical Center, Tulsa, Oklahoma.

AARON H. ESMAN is Professor of Clinical Psychiatry, Cornell University Medical College; Director, Adolescent Services, Payne Whitney Clinic, the New York Hospital; and Faculty Member, New York Psychoanalytic Institute.

BARBARA FAJARDO is a Faculty Member, Chicago Institute for Psychoanalysis and the Department of Pediatrics, Humana–Michael Reese Hospital, Chicago.

SHERMAN C. FEINSTEIN is Clinical Professor of Psychiatry, University of Illinois School of Medicine at Chicago; Director of Child and Adolescent Psychiatry Training, Michael Reese Medical Center; and Editor in Chief of this volume.

551

HEINZ VON FOERSTER is Professor Emeritus, Departments of Biophysics, Physiology, and Electrical Engineering, and Director, Biological Computer Laboratory, University of Illinois at Champaign/Urbana.

ROBERT M. GALATZER-LEVY is Training and Supervisory Analyst, Chicago Institute for Psychoanalysis.

ROBERT M. GLUCKMAN is Associate Professor of Clinical Psychiatry, Northwestern University Medical School, and Senior Attending Psychiatrist Emeritus, Evanston Hospital, Evanston, Illinois

GHISLAINE D. GODENNE is Professor of Psychology, Psychiatry, Pediatrics, and Mental Hygiene, the John Hopkins University, Baltimore, and a Past President of this Society.

HAROLD GRAFF was Director, Adolescent Psychiatry, Rockford Center, Newark, Delaware.

LINDA GREENBERG is Lecturer in Psychiatry, Cornell University Medical College, and Supervisor of Inpatient Social Work, Payne Whitney Clinic, New York.

STEVEN HANUS is Associate in the Department of Psychiatry and Behavioral Sciences, Northwestern University Medical School, and Attending Psychiatrist, Evanston Hospital, Evanston, Illinois.

STUART T. HAUSER is Professor of Psychiatry, Harvard Medical School, Cambridge, Massachusetts.

HARVEY A. HOROWITZ is Clinical Associate Professor of Psychiatry, School of Medicine of the University of Pennsylvania; Senior Attending Psychiatrist and Director, Adolescent Research Project, Institute of Pennsylvania Hospital; Medical Director, Westmeade Center, Warwick; and a Senior Editor of this volume.

JUDITH V. JORDAN is Assistant Professor in Psychiatry, Harvard Medical School, and Director of Training in Psychology and Women's Studies, McLean Hospital, Belmont, Massachusetts.

RICHARD P. KLUFT is Clinical Professor of Psychiatry, Temple University School of Medicine, and Director, Dissociative Disorders Program, the Institute of Pennsylvania Hospital, Philadelphia.

R. ROGERS KOBAK is Professor of Psychiatry, University of Delaware, Newark, Delaware.

MARSHALL KORENBLUM is Assistant Professor of Psychiatry, Faculty of Medicine, University of Toronto, and Director, Adolescent Clinical Investigation Unit, C. M. Hicks Treatment Center, Toronto.

JANICE M. KOWALSKI is Clinical Psychologist, Evanston Hospital, Evanston, Illinois.

HILARY A. LEVINE is Research Assistant, Harvard Medical School, Cambridge, Massachusetts, and Community Residence Counselor, McLean Hospital, Belmont, Massachusetts.

JOSEPH D. LICHTENBERG is Faculty Member, Washington Psychoanalytic Institute and the Baltimore–District of Columbia Institute for Psychoanalysis.

RICHARD C. MAROHN is Professor of Psychiatry and the Behavioral Sciences, Northwestern University School of Medicine; Faculty Member, Chicago Institute of Psychoanalysis; Past President of the American Society for Adolescent Psychiatry; and Co-editor of this volume.

DEREK MILLER is Professor of Adolescent Psychiatry, Northwestern University Medical School, Chicago.

MICHAEL D. MILLER is Clinical Associate, Department of Psychiatry, University of Pennsylvania School of Medicine, and Associate Psychiatrist, Institute of Pennsylvania, Philadelphia.

VIVIAN M. RAKOFF is Professor of Psychiatry, University of Toronto, Clarke Institute of Psychiatry, Toronto.

CONSUELO REDDICK is Clinical Instructor in Psychiatry, Harvard Medical School, and Psychiatrist, Harvard Law School Health Services and Harvard Street Neighborhood Health Center, Boston.

DIANA S. ROSENSTEIN is Research Psychologist, the Institute of Pennsylvania Hospital, Philadelphia.

ARTHUR SALZ is Associate Professor, Department of Elementary and Early Childhood Education and Services, School of Education, Queens College, City University of New York.

JACQUELYN SEEVAK SANDERS is Clinical Associate Professor of Psychiatry, Senior Lecturer in Education, and Director, Sonia Shankman Orthogenic School, University of Chicago.

ROSALYN SCHULTZ is Assistant Clinical Professor of Psychiatry, St. Louis University School of Medicine.

ALLAN Z. SCHWARTZBERG is Clinical Professor of Psychiatry, Georgetown University School of Medicine, Washington, D.C.

EITAN D. SCHWARZ is Clinical Assistant Professor of Psychiatry and Behavioral Sciences, Northwestern University Medical School, and Head, Division of Child and Adolescent Psychiatry, Department of Psychiatry, Evanston Hospital, Evanston, Illinois.

STEVEN S. SHARFSTEIN is Clinical Professor of Psychiatry, University of Maryland, and President and Medical Director, Sheppard Pratt Health System, Baltimore.

MARTIN H. STEIN is Medical Director, American Day Treatment Centers, Fairfax, Virginia.

MAX SUGAR is Clinical Professor of Psychiatry, Louisiana State University School of Medicine and Tulane University School of Medicine, New Orleans, and is Past President of this Society.

LYMAN C. WYNNE is Professor of Psychiatry, Rochester University School of Medicine, Rochester, New York.

POLLY YOUNG-EISENDRATH is Senior Research Psychologist, the Institute of Pennsylvania Hospital, Philadelphia.

CHARLES H. ZEANAH is Professor of Psychiatry, Louisiana State University, School of Medicine, New Orleans.

CONTENTS OF VOLUMES 1–18

564

NAME INDEX

591

SUBJECT INDEX